The Book is a Gift of
Ann Hall, Butler Student
February 15, 2010

Organizational Theory, Design, and Change

FIFTH EDITION

Gareth R. Jones

Texas A&M University

Upper Saddle River, New Jersey 07458

Library of Congress Cataloging-in-Publication Data

Jones, Gareth R.
  Organizational theory, design, and change / Gareth R. Jones.—5th ed.
    p. cm.
Includes bibliographical references and index.
ISBN 0-13-186542-0
  1. Organizational behavior. 2. Organizational behavior—Case studies I. Title.

HD58.7.J62 2007
302.3′5—dc22

2006046001

Senior Acquisitions Editor: David Parker
VP/Editorial Director: Jeff Shelstad
Product Development Manager: Ashley Santora
Project Manager: Denise Vaughn
Editorial Assistant: Stephanie Kamens
Marketing Manager: Anke Braun
Marketing Assistant: Susan Osterlitz
Associate Director, Production Editorial: Judy Leale
Managing Editor: Renata Butera
Production Editor: Angela Pica
Permissions Coordinator: Charles Morris
Associate Director, Manufacturing: Vinnie Scelta
Manufacturing Buyer: Michelle Klein
Design/Composition Manager: Christy Mahon
Cover Design: Bruce Kenselaar
Cover Photo: B.S.P.I./Corbis
Composition/Full-Service Project Management: GGS Book Services
Printer/Binder: Courier Westford
Typeface: 10/12 Palatino Bold

Credits and acknowledgments borrowed from other sources and reproduced, with permission, in this textbook appear on appropriate page within text.

Pearson Education LTD.
Pearson Education Singapore, Pte. Ltd
Pearson Education, Canada, Ltd
Pearson Education–Japan
Pearson Education Australia PTY, Limited

Pearson Education North Asia Ltd
Pearson Educación de Mexico, S.A. de C.V.
Pearson Education Malaysia, Pte. Ltd.

For Nicholas and Julia

BRIEF CONTENTS

CONTENTS

PREFACE

Jones' *Organizational Theory, Design, and Change* is the only book that brings together coverage of organizational theory and organizational change.

By bringing a discussion of organizational change and renewal to the center stage of organizational theory and design, this book stands alone. The fifth edition continues this focus with the goal of making the book more useful for students. After all, the vocabulary and concepts of organizational theory are the same ones that management consultants, the chief operations officer, and the increasing number of managers responsible for organizational design and change use as they perform their roles and jobs—analyzing and changing organizations.

NEW TO THE FIFTH EDITION

- A new theme linking the book's chapters is the way *outsourcing* is changing organizational boundaries and the nature of interorganizational relations.
- Several additions have been made to the chapters on organizational change. The importance of linking organizational growth to profitability in the organizational life cycle is discussed in Chapter 11. The nature of persuasive communication and its effect on decision making is taken up in Chapter 12. New in Chapter 12 is a discussion of entrepreneurship and the process of creative destruction in creating new organizational forms.

HALLMARK STRENGTHS

We have continued the *integrating theme* of focusing on one company, Amazon.com, to illustrate organizational design and change issues, particularly those that relate to the theme of new information technology.

- "Practicing Organizational Theory" is an experiential exercise designed to give students hands-on experience in organizational theory. Each exercise takes about 20 minutes of class time. Further details on how to use these exercises, which have been class-tested and work very well, are found in the instructor's manual.
- An "Ethical Dimension" feature allows students, either individually or in groups, to debate the ethical dilemmas that confront managers during the process of organizational design and change.
- The ongoing "Analyzing the Organization" feature asks students to select an organization to study and then to complete chapter assignments; the assignments lead to an organizational theory analysis and a written case study of their organization. The case study is presented to the class at the end of the semester. Complete details concerning the use of this and the other learning features are included in the instructor's manual.
- At the end of the book are numerous cases to be used in conjunction with the book's chapters to enrich students' understanding of organizational theory concepts. The cases are largely unchanged from the last edition. To preserve the teaching value of these cases, they should *not* be used for student write-ups; their value is in the class discussion they generate. Detailed instructor notes for these cases are found in the instructor's manual.

Instructor's Resource Center

Register. Redeem. Login.

www.prenhall.com/irc is where instructors can access a variety of print, media, and presentation resources available with this text in downloadable, digital format. For most texts, resources are also available for course management platforms such as Blackboard, WebCT, and Course Compass.

It Gets Better

Once you register, you will not have additional forms to fill out, or multiple usernames and passwords to remember to access new titles and/or editions. As a registered faculty member, you can login directly to download resource files, and receive immediate access and instructions for installing course management content to your campus server.

Need Help?

Our dedicated technical support team is ready to assist instructors with questions about the media supplements that accompany this text. Visit http://247.prenhall.com for answers to frequently asked questions and toll-free user support phone numbers. The following supplements are available to adopting instructors.

For detailed descriptions of all of the supplements, please visit: www.prenhall.com/irc

Instructor's Resource Center (IRC) on CD-ROM—ISBN: 0-13-186544-7
Printed Instructor's Manual with Test Item File—ISBN: 0-13-186543-9
TestGen test-generating software—Visit the IRC (both online and on CD-Rom) for this text.
PowerPoints—Visit the IRC (both online and on CD-Rom) for this text.
Videos on DVD—ISBN: 0-13-186548-X

ACKNOWLEDGMENTS

Finding a way to coordinate and integrate the rich and diverse organizational theory literature is no easy task. Nor is it easy to present the material in a way that students can easily understand (and hopefully enjoy) given the plethora of concepts and theories that abound in what is the most abstract and analytical subfield of management. Across the last editions of *Organizational Theory*, I have been fortunate to have the assistance of several people who contributed greatly to the book's final form. David Parker, my Prentice Hall editor, provided me with timely feedback and information from professors and reviewers, which has allowed me to shape the book to meet the needs of its intended market. Denise Vaughn ably coordinated the book's progress through production. Their efforts can be seen in the comprehensiveness of the package of materials that constitutes *Organizational Theory*. Patsy Hartmangruber provided me with excellent secretarial support and organization. I am also grateful to the following reviewers and colleagues who provided me with detailed feedback on the chapters previous editions of the book:

I'd like to specifically thank reviewers of the current edition:

Jeffrey Nystrom, University of Colorado at Denver and Health Sciences Center
Linda Fried, University of Colorado at Denver and Health Sciences Center
Dennis Mott, Oklahoma State University
Renata Jaworski, University of Illinois at Chicago
John S. Johnson, Indiana Wesleyan University

In addition, I'd like to acknowledge reviewers of past editions:

Ken Betenhausen, Charles Hill, John Butler, Sara Keck, Tina Dacin, Alan Bluedorn, Pat Feltes, Richard Goodman, Richard Deluca, Gordon Dehler, Janet Barnard, Richard Paulson, Steven Floyd, Marian Clark, John A. Seeger, James Segouis, Arie Lewin, Paul W. Swierez, Bruce H. Johnson, Sonny Ariss, Nate Bennett, Ronald Locke, George Strauss, Ed Conlon, Parthiban David, Lawrence Gales, Mary Jane Saxton, Judi McLean-Parus, Dayle Smith, Janet Near, Tony Buono, John Schaubroeck, Paul Collins, Dave Partridge, Karl Magnusen, Dan Svyantek, Karen Dill Bowerman, Robert Figler, David Loree, Greg Saltzman, Leonidas Doty, Steven Farner, Dane Partridge, Janita Rawls, Kaviraj Parboteeah, Frances Milliken, Nancy Kucinski, Deborah Gibbons, and Pracheta Mukherjee

Chapter 1

Organizations and Organizational Effectiveness

Learning Objectives

Organizations exist in uncertain, changing environments and continually confront new challenges and problems. Managers must find solutions to these challenges and problems if organizations are to survive, prosper, and perform effectively.

After studying this chapter you should be able to:

1. Explain why organizations exist and the purposes they serve.
2. Describe the relationship between organizational theory and organizational design and change, and differentiate between organizational structure and culture.
3. Understand how managers can utilize the principles of organizational theory to design and change their organizations to increase organizational effectiveness.
4. Identify the three principal ways in which managers assess and measure organizational effectiveness.
5. Appreciate the way in which several contingency factors influence the design of organizations.

WHAT IS AN ORGANIZATION?

Few things in today's world are as important or as taken for granted as organizations. Although we routinely enjoy the goods and services that organizations provide, we rarely bother to wonder about how these goods and services are produced. We see news film of production lines churning out automobiles or computers, and we read in newspapers that local schools or hospitals are using new technologies such as the Internet and online learning to improve their productivity. Yet we rarely question how or why these organizations go about their business. Most often, we think about organizations only when they fail us in some way—for example, when we are forced to wait two hours in the emergency room to see a doctor, when our new computer crashes, or when we are at the end of a long line in a bank on a Friday afternoon. When such things happen, we wonder why the bank did not anticipate

1

the rush of people and put on more tellers, why the hospital made us spend 30 minutes filling out paperwork in order to obtain service and then kept us waiting for an hour and a half, or why computer companies don't insist on higher quality hardware and bug-free software from their suppliers.

Most people have a casual attitude toward organizations because organizations are *intangible*. Even though most people in the world today are born, work, and die in organizations, nobody has ever seen or touched an organization. We see the products or services that an organization provides, and sometimes we see the people whom the organization employs as, for example, when we go into a FedExKinko's store or doctor's office. But the reason an organization, such as FedExKinko's, is motivated to provide goods and services, and the way it controls and influences its members so that it can provide them, are not apparent to most people outside the organization. Nevertheless, grouping people and other resources to produce goods and services is the essence of organizing and of what an organization does.[1]

Organization
A tool used by people to coordinate their actions to obtain something they desire or value.

An **organization** is a tool used by people to coordinate their actions to obtain something they desire or value—that is, to achieve their goals. People who value security create an organization called a *police force*, an *army*, or a *bank*. People who value entertainment create organizations such as the Walt Disney Company, CBS, or a local club. People who desire spiritual or emotional support create churches, social service organizations, or charities. An organization is a response to and a means of satisfying some human need. New organizations are spawned when new technologies become available and new needs are discovered, and organizations die or are transformed when the needs they once satisfied are no longer important or have been replaced by other needs. The need to invent improved drugs, for example, led to the creation of Amgen, Icos, and other biotechnology organizations. The need to handle increasing amounts of information and the availability of an emerging new computer technology led to the rise of IBM, Microsoft, and other computer companies and the shrinking and dying of typewriter companies, such as Smith Corona, whose technology had become outdated. Retail stores such as Wal-Mart, Target, and Sears are continually being transformed—not always successfully—as they seek to respond to the changing tastes and needs of consumers.

Who creates the organizations that arise to satisfy people's needs? Sometimes an individual or a few people believe they possess the necessary skills and knowledge and set up an organization to produce goods and services. In this way organizations like sandwich shops, Yahoo!, and design studios are created. Sometimes several people form a group to respond to a perceived need by creating an organization. People with a lot of money may invest jointly to build a vacation resort. A group of people with similar beliefs may form a new church, or a nation's citizens may move to establish a new political party. In general, **entrepreneurship** is the term used to describe the process by which people recognize opportunities to satisfy needs and then gather and use resources to meet those needs.[2]

Entrepreneurship
The process by which people recognize opportunities to satisfy needs and then gather and use resources to meet those needs.

Today, many organizations being founded; those experiencing the fastest growth are producing goods and services related in some way to new information technology. The increasing use of computers and new information technologies such as the Internet is revolutionizing the way all organizations operate. This book examines this crucial issue by focusing on one company that has achieved explosive growth: Amazon.com. The story of this company is used to illustrate how the new information technology revolution is affecting the way organizations operate and create value today. We begin this analysis by examining why and how Amazon.com was founded.[3]

How Does an Organization Create Value?

The way in which an organization creates value is depicted in Figure 1.1. Value creation takes place at three stages: input, conversion, and output. Each stage is affected by the environment in which the organization operates.

In 1994, Jeffrey Bezos, a computer science and electrical engineering graduate from Princeton University, was growing weary of working for a Wall Street investment bank. With his computer science background prompting him, he saw an entrepreneurial opportunity in the fact that usage of the Internet was growing at over 2,300% a year as more and more people were becoming aware of its information advantages.

Searching for an opportunity to exploit his skills in the new electronic, virtual marketplace, he decided that the book-selling market would be a good place to invest his personal resources. Deciding to make a break, he packed his belongings and drove to the West Coast, deciding en route that Seattle, Washington, a new Mecca for high-tech software developers and the hometown of Starbuck's coffee shops, would be an ideal place to begin his venture.

What was his vision for his new venture? To build an online bookstore that would be customer-friendly and easy to navigate, and would offer the broadest possible selection of books. Bezos's mission? "To use the Internet to offer products that would educate, inform, and inspire."[4] Bezos realized that, compared to a real "bricks and mortar" bookstore, an online bookstore would be able to offer a much larger and more diverse selection of books. Moreover, online customers would be able to search easily for any book in print on a computerized, online catalogue, browse different subject areas, read reviews of books, and even ask other shoppers for online recommendations—something most people would hesitate to do in a regular bookstore.

With a handful of employees and operating from his garage in Seattle, Bezos launched his venture online in July 1995 with $7 million in borrowed capital. Word of his venture spread like wildfire across the Internet, and book sales quickly picked up as satisfied customers spread the good word. Within weeks Bezos was forced to relocate to larger premises and to hire more employees as book sales soared. Bezos's new venture seemed to be poised for success.

Figure 1.1
How an Organization Creates Value

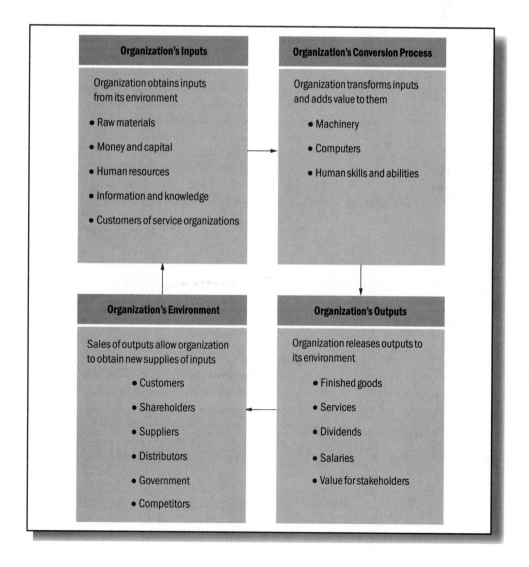

Inputs include human resources, information and knowledge, raw materials, and money and capital. The way an organization chooses and obtains from its environment the inputs it needs to produce goods and services determines how much value the organization creates at the input stage. For example, Jeff Bezos chose to make the design of the Amazon.com website as simple and user-friendly as he possibly could, and he recruited only people who could provide high-quality, customer-friendly service that would most appeal to his Internet customers. If he had made poor choices and customers had not liked Amazon.com's website or customer service, his company would not have been successful.

The way the organization uses human resources and technology to transform inputs into outputs determines how much value is created at the conversion stage. The amount of value the organization creates is a function of the quality of its skills, including its ability to learn from and respond to the environment. For example, Jeff Bezos had to decide how best to sell and market his products to attract customers. His answer was to offer wide choice, low prices, and to ship books quickly to customers. His skill at these activities created the value that customers saw in his concept.

The result of the conversion process is an output of finished goods and services that the organization releases into its environment, where they are purchased and used by customers to satisfy their needs. The organization uses the money earned from the sale of its output to obtain new supplies of inputs, and the cycle begins again. An organization that continues to satisfy people's needs will be able to obtain increasing amounts of resources over time and will be able to create more and more value as it adds to its stock of skills and capabilities.[5] Amazon.com has grown from strength to strength because satisfied customers have provided the revenues it needs to improve its skills and expand its operations.

A value creation model can be used to describe the activities of most kinds of organizations. Manufacturing companies, such as General Motors (GM) and IBM, take from the environment component parts, skilled or semiskilled labor, and technical knowledge and at the conversion stage create value by using their manufacturing skills to organize and assemble those inputs into outputs, such as cars and computers. Service organizations, such as McDonald's, Amazon.com, the Salvation Army, and your family doctor, interact directly with customers or clients, who are the "inputs" to their operations. Hungry people who go to McDonald's for a meal, needy families who go to the Salvation Army for assistance, and sick people who go to a doctor for a cure are all "inputs." In the conversion stage, service organizations create value by applying their skills to yield an output: satisfied hunger, a cared-for family, a cured patient. Figure 1.2 is a simplified model of how McDonald's creates value.

Why Do Organizations Exist?

The production of goods and services most often takes place in an organizational setting because people working together to produce goods and services usually can create more value than people working separately. Figure 1.3 summarizes five reasons for the existence of organizations.

To Increase Specialization and the Division of Labor

People who work in organizations may become more productive and efficient at what they do than people who work alone. For many kinds of productive work, the use of an organization allows the development of specialization and a division of labor. The collective nature of organizations allows individuals to focus on a narrow area of expertise; this allows them to become more skilled or specialized at what they do. For example, engineers working in the engineering design department of a large car manufacturer like GM or Toyota might specialize in improving the design of carburetors or other engine components. An engineer working for a small car manufacturer might be responsible for designing the whole engine. Because the engineer in the small company must do many more things than the engineer in the large company, the degree of specialization in the small company is lower; there is less chance

Figure 1.2
How McDonald's Creates Value

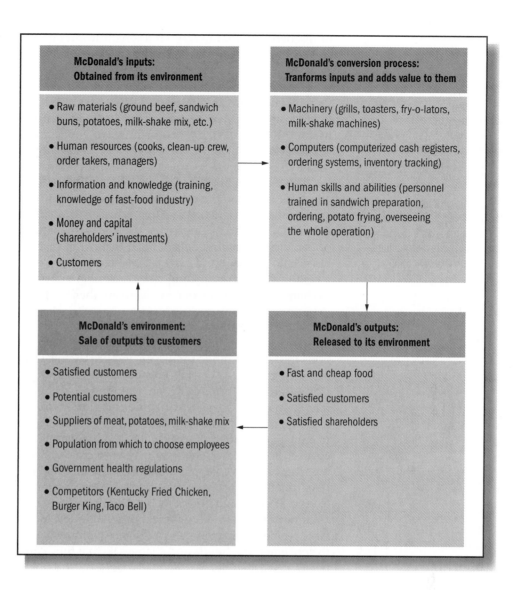

McDonald's inputs:
Obtained from its environment

- Raw materials (ground beef, sandwich buns, potatoes, milk-shake mix, etc.)

- Human resources (cooks, clean-up crew, order takers, managers)

- Information and knowledge (training, knowledge of fast-food industry)

- Money and capital (shareholders' investments)

- Customers

McDonald's conversion process:
Tranforms inputs and adds value to them

- Machinery (grills, toasters, fry-o-lators, milk-shake machines)

- Computers (computerized cash registers, ordering systems, inventory tracking)

- Human skills and abilities (personnel trained in sandwich preparation, ordering, potato frying, overseeing the whole operation)

McDonald's environment:
Sale of outputs to customers

- Satisfied customers

- Potential customers

- Suppliers of meat, potatoes, milk-shake mix

- Population from which to choose employees

- Government health regulations

- Competitors (Kentucky Fried Chicken, Burger King, Taco Bell)

McDonald's outputs:
Released to its environment

- Fast and cheap food

- Satisfied customers

- Satisfied shareholders

Figure 1.3
Why Organizations Exist

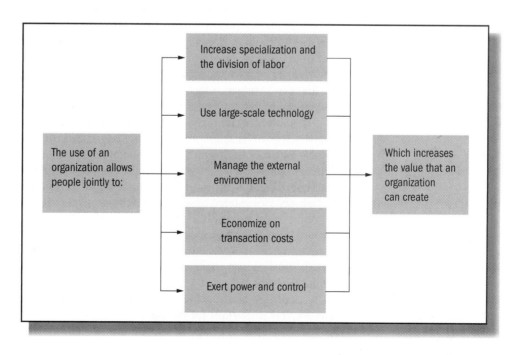

The use of an organization allows people jointly to:

- Increase specialization and the division of labor
- Use large-scale technology
- Manage the external environment
- Economize on transaction costs
- Exert power and control

Which increases the value that an organization can create

of discovering what makes for a great carburetor and thus creating more value for someone who desires high speed.

To Use Large-Scale Technology

Organizations are able to take advantage of the economies of scale and scope that result from the use of modern automated and computerized technology. **Economies of scale** are cost savings that result when goods and services are produced in large volume on automated production lines. **Economies of scope** are cost savings that result when an organization is able to use underutilized resources more effectively because they can be shared across several different products or tasks. Economies of scope (as well as of scale) can be achieved, for example, when it is possible to design an automated production line to produce several different types of products simultaneously. Toyota and Honda were the first carmakers to design assembly lines capable of producing three models of a car instead of just one. Ford and DaimlerChrysler have followed suit and have achieved impressive gains in efficiency. Multimodel assembly lines give car companies lower manufacturing costs and greater flexibility to change quickly from one model to another to meet customer needs.

To Manage the External Environment

Pressures from the environment in which organizations operate also make organizations the favored mode for organizing productive resources. An organization's environment includes not only economic, social, and political factors but the sources from which the organization obtains inputs and the marketplace into which it releases outputs, as well. Managing complex environments is a task beyond the abilities of most individuals, but an organization has the resources to develop specialists to anticipate or attempt to influence the many demands from the environment. This specialization allows the organization to create more value for the organization, its members, and its customers. Huge companies like IBM, AT&T, and Ford have whole departments of corporate executives who are responsible for monitoring, responding to, and attempting to manage the external environment, but those activities are just as important for small organizations. Although local stores and restaurants do not have whole departments to scan the environment, their owners and managers need to spot emerging trends and changes so that they can respond to changing customer needs, just as Jeff Bezos did; otherwise, they will not survive.

To Economize on Transaction Costs

When people cooperate to produce goods and services, certain problems arise. As they learn what to do and how to work with others to perform a task effectively, people jointly have to decide who will do which tasks (the division of labor), who will get paid what amounts, and how to decide if each worker is doing his or her share of the work. The costs associated with negotiating, monitoring, and governing exchanges between people to solve these kinds of transaction difficulties are called **transaction costs**. Organizations' ability to control the exchanges between people reduces the transaction costs associated with these exchanges. Suppose Intel bought the services of its scientists on a daily basis, and thousands of scientists had to spend time every day discussing what to do and who should work with whom. Such a system would be very costly and would waste valuable time and money. The structure and coordination imposed by the Intel organization, however, lets managers hire scientists on a long-term basis, assigns them to specific tasks and work teams, and gives Intel the right to monitor their performance. The resulting stability reduces transaction costs and increases productivity.

To Exert Power and Control

Organizations can exert great pressure on individuals to conform to task and production requirements in order to increase production efficiency.[6] To get a job done efficiently, it is important for people to come to work in a predictable fashion, to behave in the interests of the organization, and to accept the authority of the organization and

Economies of scale
Cost savings that result when goods and services are produced in large volume on automated production lines.

Economies of scope
Cost savings that result when an organization is able to use underutilized resources more effectively because they can be shared across different products or tasks.

Transaction costs
The costs associated with negotiating, monitoring, and governing exchanges between people.

its managers. All these requirements make production less costly and more efficient but put a burden on individuals who must conform to organizational requirements. When individuals work for themselves, they need to address only their own needs. When they work for an organization, however, they must pay attention to the organization's needs as well as their own. Organizations can discipline or fire workers who fail to conform and can reward good performance with promotion and increased rewards. Because employment, promotion, and increased rewards are important and often scarce, organizations can use them to exert power over individuals.

Taken together, these five factors help to explain why often more value can be created when people work together, coordinating their actions in an organized setting, than when they work alone. Over time, the stability created by an organization provides a setting in which the organization and its members can increase their skills and capabilities, and the ability of the organization to create value increases by leaps and bounds. In the past 20 years, for example, Microsoft has grown to become the biggest and most powerful software company in the world because Bill Gates, its founder, created an organizational setting in which people are given freedom to develop their skills and capabilities to create valuable new products. In contrast, in the past 20 years other software companies like WordPerfect, Lotus, and Novell have experienced huge problems because they have not been able to create the software customers want. Why does Microsoft's organization allow Microsoft to create more and more value while these other organizations have actually reduced the value they can create? Before we can answer this question, we need to take a close look at organizational theory, design, and change.

ORGANIZATIONAL THEORY, DESIGN, AND CHANGE

Organizational theory
The study of how organizations function and how they affect and are affected by the environment in which they operate.

Organizational theory is the study of how organizations function and how they affect and are affected by the environment in which they operate. In this book, we examine the principles that underlie the design, operation, change, and redesign of organizations to maintain and increase their effectiveness. Understanding how organizations operate, however, is only the first step in learning how to control and change organizations so that they can effectively create wealth and resources. Thus, the second aim of this book is to equip you with the conceptual tools to influence organizational situations in which you find yourself. The lessons of organizational design and change are as important at the level of first-line supervisor as they are at the level of chief executive officer, in small or large organizations, and in settings as diverse as the not-for-profit organization or the assembly line of a manufacturing company.

People and managers knowledgeable about organizational design and change are able to analyze the structure and culture of the organization for which they work (or which they wish to help, such as a charity or church), diagnose problems, and make adjustments that help the organization to achieve its goals. Figure 1.4 outlines the relationship among organizational theory, structure, culture, design, and change.

Organizational Structure

Organizational structure
The formal system of task and authority relationships that control how people coordinate their actions and use resources to achieve organizational goals.

Once a group of people has established an organization to accomplish collective goals, organizational structure evolves to increase the effectiveness of the organization's control of the activities necessary to achieve its goals. **Organizational structure** is the formal system of task and authority relationships that control how people coordinate their actions and use resources to achieve organizational goals.[7] The principal purpose of organizational structure is one of control: to control the way people coordinate their actions to achieve organizational goals and to control the means used to motivate people to achieve these goals. At Microsoft, for example, the control problems facing Bill Gates were how to coordinate scientists' activities to make the best

Figure 1.4 The Relationship Among Organizational Theory and Organizational Structure, Culture, and Design, and Change

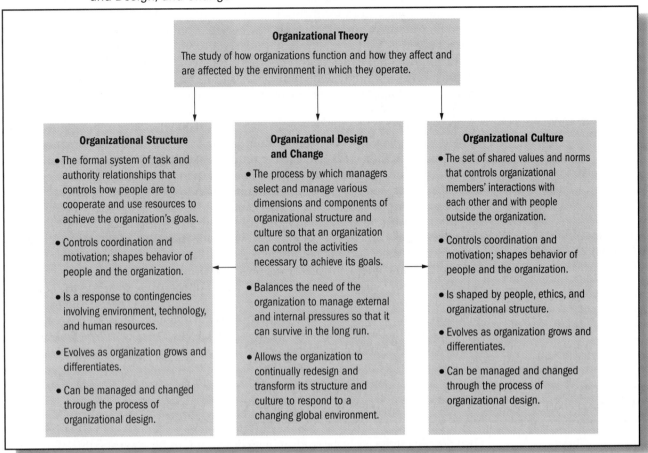

use of their talents, and how to reward scientists when they developed innovative products. Gates's solution was to place scientists in small, self-contained teams and to reward them with stock in Microsoft based on team performance.

For any organization, an appropriate structure is one that facilitates effective responses to problems of coordination and motivation—problems that can arise for any number of environmental, technological, or human reasons.[8] As organizations grow and differentiate, the structure likewise evolves. Organizational structure can be managed through the process of organizational design and change.

Organizational Culture

At the same time that organizational structure is evolving, so is organizational culture. **Organizational culture** is the set of shared values and norms that control organizational members' interactions with each other and with suppliers, customers, and other people outside the organization. An organization's culture is shaped by the people inside the organization, by the ethics of the organization, by the employment rights given to employees, and by the type of structure used by the organization. Like organizational structure, organizational culture shapes and controls behavior within the organization. It influences how people respond to a situation and how they interpret the environment surrounding the organization. At Microsoft, Bill Gates attempted to create values that encouraged entrepreneurship and risk taking in order to build an organizational culture in which innovation was a valued activity. The small-team structure was helpful because scientists were continually meeting face to face to coordinate their activities and to learn from one another, which encouraged them to experiment and to find new ways of solving problems.

The cultures of organizations that provide essentially the same goods and services can be very different. For example, Coca-Cola and PepsiCo are the two largest and most successful companies in the soft-drink industry.[9] Because they sell similar products and face similar environments, we might expect their cultures to be similar, but they are not. Coca-Cola takes pride in its long-term commitment to employees; its loyal managers, many of whom spend their entire careers with the organization; and its cautious and cooperative approach to planning. By contrast, PepsiCo has a highly political and competitive culture in which conflicts over decision making cause frequent disputes, and often turnover, among top managers. Like organizational structure, organizational culture evolves and can be managed through organizational design and change.

Organizational Design and Change

Organizational design is the process by which managers select and manage aspects of structure and culture so that an organization can control the activities necessary to achieve its goals. Organizational structure and culture are the *means* the organization uses to achieve its goals; organizational design is about how and why various means are chosen. An organization's behavior is the result of its design and the principles behind its operation. It is a task that requires managers to strike a balance between external pressures from the organization's environment and internal pressures from, for example, its choice of technology. Looking outward, the design can cause organizational members to view and respond to the environment in different ways. Looking inward, an organization's design puts pressure on work groups and individuals to behave in certain ways.

Achieving the proper balance helps to ensure that the organization will survive in the long run. The theories, concepts, and techniques covered in this book are intended to provide you with working models that you can use to analyze organizational situations and to propose and implement suitable solutions to change an organization and increase its effectiveness.

Organizations like Microsoft and Intel, which operate in the high-tech computer industry, need to be flexible and capable of quick responses to their rivals' competitive moves, and they need to be innovative in developing new technology. At the same time, such organizations must have stable task relationships that allow their members to work together to create value, solve problems, and accomplish organizational objectives. In contrast, organizations like Nucor and Alcoa, which produce sheet steel and aluminum, respectively, face relatively stable environments in which customer needs are more predictable and technology changes more slowly. Consequently, their organizational design choices are likely to reflect the need for a structure and culture that reduces production costs rather than a structure and culture that promotes flexibility. In Chapters 4, 5, 6, and 7 we discuss the organizational structures and cultures that managers can design to help ensure their organizations' survival.

Organizational change is the process by which organizations move from their current state to some desired future state to increase their effectiveness. The goal of organizational change is to find new or improved ways of using resources and capabilities to increase an organization's ability to create value and, hence, its performance.[10] Once again, organizational structure and culture are the principal means or fulcrum managers use to change the organization so it can achieve its future desired state.

Organizational design and change are thus highly interrelated. Indeed, organizational change can be understood as the process of organizational redesign and transformation. As we discuss in later chapters, as organizations grow their structure and culture is constantly evolving, changing and becoming more complex. A large organization faces a different set of design and redesign problems than a small organization because its structure and culture are different from a small organization's.

In 1976, Steven P. Jobs sold his Volkswagen van and his partner Steven Wozniak sold his two programmable calculators, and they invested the $1,350 proceeds to build a computer circuit board in Jobs's garage. So popular was the circuit board, which was eventually developed into the Apple II computer, that in 1977 they incorporated their new business as Apple Computer. By 1985, the company had sales of almost $2 billion.[11] In 1984, Michael Dell took $1,000 of his savings and used it to establish a national mail-order computer company, the Dell Computer Corp. At the beginning Dell worked with three employees around a 6-foot table, assembling low-cost personal computers that were sold by telephone to customers nationwide. By 1993, his company had achieved sales of over $2 billion a year.[12]

In 1985, Steve Jobs was forced out of the company he helped found. Michael Dell, however, never lost control of his company, which today is the largest and most profitable PC maker in the world. Why did Steve Jobs lose control while Michael Dell did not? Jobs's and Dell's different approaches to organizing are a large part of the reason.

When Apple was founded, Steve Jobs announced that he had little interest in being responsible for the day-to-day management of his company, and experienced managers from other companies were recruited to oversee Apple's operations. However, as Apple grew, Jobs desired more power and began to demand more control over the company. In 1981, he became chairman of the board and began to intervene actively in the company's day-to-day operations; for example, Jobs started many new project teams to develop new models of personal computers. As his power and reputation increased, Jobs adopted an arbitrary and overbearing style toward members of the different project teams, often playing favorites. His actions led to a high level of competition between the different teams, many misunderstandings, and much distrust among team members.[13]

His divisive management style brought Jobs into conflict with John Sculley, Apple's CEO and the person formally responsible for managing the company. Increasingly, Jobs began to compete with Sculley for control of the company. This caused major problems. First, employees had no clear picture of who was leading the company—Jobs (the chairman) or Sculley (the CEO). Second, both executives were so busy competing for control of Apple that neither had the time or energy to ensure it was using its resources efficiently. For example, little attention was paid to evaluating the performance of the different project teams. No budget was in place to curb their research and development (R&D) spending. Apple's costs started to soar, its profits fell, and the organization started to disintegrate. Apple's board of directors, realizing that Jobs's management style was leading to poor company performance, demanded that he resign as chairman. He left the company in 1985.

At Dell Computer, Michael Dell adopted a very different approach to managing his company. Like Jobs, Dell assumed the position of chairman and established many project teams to develop new kinds of PCs. Dell, however, developed a participative management approach, involved employees in decision making, and fostered a spirit of comradeship and cooperation among team members to encourage top performance. His management style engendered intense loyalty from his employees, who liked his hands-on approach and his close attention to managing his company.[14] For example, Dell was careful to watch the teams' progress closely. When a project seemed not to be working out or was costing too much, he would quickly end it and transfer engineers to other projects. He was very conscious of the need to control costs.

As his company grew, Dell like Jobs realized the need to recruit expert managers to help him manage his company. He hired experienced executives from companies like EDS and IBM and decentralized control of its functional operations like production and marketing to them. Unlike Jobs, Dell recognized that he could not be personally responsible for managing all of his company's activities, and he never tried to compete with his managers, recognizing their expertise and his limitations. Dell's organizing approach fostered a different kind of company culture, where people cooperate to improve its performance, and as noted earlier it has become the industry leader.[15]

In 1997, after Apple's profits continue to decline, the board of directors suggested to Jobs that he take control of the company again and become its CEO. In control of the company once more, he put the organizing skills he had subsequently developed as the founder of other companies such as NeXT Computer and Pixar to good use. Understanding that what a company needs is a clear hierarchy of authority and task responsibilities, he energized and motivated employees to develop the next generation of Apple computers that would allow the company to survive. He established a clear structure of teams and team leadership to allow programmers to work together to develop the new computer. He delegated considerable authority to these team leaders, but he also established strict timetables and challenging "stretch goals" for these teams to achieve.

Through his new method of organizing, Jobs revitalized Apple and created a new culture that sped product development. One result of this was its entry into the digital music business with its phenomenally successful iPod product line, which is also being continually updated as technology advances.[16] By all accounts, however, Jobs still makes enormous demands of his employees, constantly challenging their ideas and demanding superhuman efforts to keep Apple ahead of agile competitors like Dell, Sony, and Samsung.

Managers need to recognize that their initial design choices will have important ramifications in the future as their organizations grow; indeed, it has been argued that initial choices are an important determinant of differences in long-run performance. For an example of this, consider the difference in the way Steve Jobs and Michael Dell created the structures and cultures of the organizations they founded.

As the example of Steven Jobs and Michael Dell illustrates, people who start new organizations may lack the kinds of skills, knowledge, and ability to manage an organization's structure and culture effectively. However, both these CEOs did develop that ability over time. An understanding of the principles behind organizational design and change speeds this process and deepens appreciation for the many subtle technical and social processes that determine how organizations operate.

The Importance of Organizational Design and Change

Because of increased global competitive pressures and because of the increasing use of advanced information technology (IT), organizational design has become one of management's top priorities. Today, as never before, managers are searching for new and better ways to coordinate and motivate their employees to increase the value their organizations can create. There are several specific reasons why designing an organization's structure and culture, and changing them to increase its effectiveness, are such important tasks. Organizational design and change have important implications for a company's ability to deal with contingencies, achieve a competitive advantage, effectively manage diversity, and increase its efficiency and ability to innovate.

Dealing with Contingencies

Contingency
An event that might occur and must be planned for.

A **contingency** is an event that might occur and must be planned for, such as a changing environment or a competitor like Amazon.com that decides to use new technology in an innovative way. The design of an organization determines how effectively it responds to various factors in its environment and obtains scarce resources. For example, an organization's ability to attract skilled employees, loyal customers, or government contracts is a function of the degree to which it can control those three environmental factors.

An organization can design its structure in many ways to increase control over its environment. An organization might change employee task relationships so that employees are more aware of the environment, or it might change the way the organization relates to other organizations by establishing new contracts or joint ventures. For example, when Microsoft wanted to attract new customers for its Windows XP software in the United States and globally, it recruited large numbers of customer service representatives and created a new department to allow them to better meet customers' needs. The strategy was very successful, and the Windows platform is currently used on over 90% of all PCs globally.

As pressures from competitors, consumers, and the government increase, the environment facing all organizations is becoming increasingly complex and difficult to respond to, and more effective types of structure and culture are continually being developed and tried. We discuss how the changing nature of the environment affects organizations in Chapter 3 and how organizations can influence and control their environments in Chapter 8.

One part of the organizational environment that is becoming more important and more complex is the global environment. Increasingly, U.S. companies like AT&T, IBM, and Dell are under pressure to expand their global presence and produce and sell more of their products in markets overseas to reduce costs, increase efficiency, and survive. Organizational design is important in a global context because, to become a global competitor, a company often needs to create a new structure and culture. Chapter 8 also looks at the structures and cultures that a company can adopt as it engages in different kinds of global activities.

Changing technology is another contingency to which organizations must respond. Today, the Internet and other advanced IT have become the principal methods organizations use to manage relationships with their employees, customers, and suppliers. The growing use of IT is fundamentally changing the design of organizational structure and has led to a huge round of organizational change as organizations have redesigned their structures to make most effective use of IT. We will examine the effects of IT on organizational design and change in almost all the chapters of this book, but particularly in Chapter 12.

In particular, a theme throughout the book is to examine how IT is changing the nature of the boundary of the organization, and the specific ways organizations coordinate people and tasks. The growth of outsourcing and the number of global network organizations whose members are linked primarily through electronic means have changed the way organizations operate in many ways. The pros and cons of this change in organizing, as organizations seek to increase their effectiveness and gain a competitive advantage, are discussed in depth in later chapters.

Gaining Competitive Advantage

Competitive advantage
The ability of one company to outperform another because its managers are able to create more value from the resources at their disposal.

Core competences
Managers' skills and abilities in value-creating activities.

Strategy
The specific pattern of decisions and actions that managers take to use core competencies to achieve a competitive advantage and outperform competitors.

Increasingly, organizations are discovering that organizational design, change, and redesign are sources of sustained competitive advantage. **Competitive advantage** is the ability of one company to outperform another because its managers are able to create more value from the resources at their disposal. Competitive advantage springs from **core competences**, managers' skills and abilities in value-creation activities such as manufacturing, research and development (R&D), managing new technology, or organizational design and change. Core competences allow a company to develop a strategy to outperform competitors and produce better products, or produce the same products but at a lower cost. **Strategy** is the specific pattern of decisions and actions that managers take to use core competences to achieve a competitive advantage and outperform competitors.

The *way* managers design and change organizational structure is an important determinant of how much value the organization creates because this affects how it implements strategy. Many sources of competitive advantage, such as skills in research and development that result in novel product features or state-of-the-art technology, evaporate because they are relatively easy for competitors to imitate. It is much more difficult to imitate good organizational design and carefully managed change that brings into being a successful organizational structure and culture. Such imitation is difficult because structure and culture are embedded in the way people in an organization interact and coordinate their actions to get a job done. Moreover, because successful structures and cultures form early, as at Dell and Apple, and take a long time to establish and develop, companies that possess them can have a long-term competitive advantage.

An organization's strategy is always changing in response to changes in the environment; organizational design must be a continuously evolving managerial activity for a company to stay ahead of the competition. There is never a single optimal or "perfect" design to fit an organization's needs. Managers must constantly evaluate how well their organization's structure and culture work, and they should change and redesign them on an ongoing basis to improve them. In Chapter 8 we consider how organizations create value by means of their strategy.

Managing Diversity

Differences in the race, gender, and national origin of organizational members have important implications for the values of an organization's culture and for organizational effectiveness. The quality of organizational decision making, for example, is a function of the diversity of the viewpoints that get considered and of the kind of analysis that takes place. Similarly, in many organizations, particularly service organizations, a large part of the workforce consists of minority employees, whose needs and preferences must be taken into consideration. Also, changes in the characteristics of the workforce, such as an influx of immigrant workers or the aging of the current workforce, require attention and advance planning. An organization needs to design a structure to make optimal use of the talents of a diverse workforce and to develop cultural values that encourage people to work together. An organization's structure and culture determine how effectively managers are able to coordinate and motivate workers. Today, as companies increasingly operate in countries with widely disparate cultures around the globe, organizational design becomes even more important to harmonize national with organizational culture.

Promoting Efficiency, Speed, and Innovation

Organizations exist to produce goods and services that people value. The better organizations function, the more value, in the form of more or better goods and services, they create. Historically, the capacity of organizations to create value has increased enormously as organizations have introduced better ways of producing and distributing goods and services. Earlier, we discussed the importance of the division of labor and the use of modern technology in reducing costs, speeding work processes, and increasing efficiency. The design and use of new and more efficient organizational structures are equally important. In today's global environment, for example, competition from countries with low labor costs is pressuring companies all over the world to become more efficient in order to reduce costs or increase quality.

The ability of companies to compete successfully in today's competitive environment is increasingly a function of how well they innovate and how quickly they can introduce new technologies. Organizational design plays an important role in innovation. For example, the way an organization's structure links people in different specializations, such as research and marketing, determines how fast the organization can introduce new products. Similarly, an organization's culture can affect people's desire to be innovative. A culture that is based on entrepreneurial norms and values is more likely to encourage innovation than is a culture that is conservative and bureaucratic because entrepreneurial values encourage people to learn how to respond and adapt to a changing situation.

Organizational design involves a constant search for new or better ways of coordinating and motivating employees. Different structures and cultures cause employees to behave in different ways. We consider structures that encourage efficiency and innovation in Chapters 4, 5, and 6 and cultures that do so in Chapter 7.

The Consequences of Poor Organizational Design

Many management teams fail to understand the important effects organizational design and change can have on their company's performance and effectiveness. Although behavior is controlled by organizational structure and culture, managers are often unaware of the many factors that affect this relationship, paying scant attention to the way employees behave and their role in the organization—until something happens.

GM, IBM, Sears, Kodak, and AT&T have all experienced enormous problems in the last decade adjusting to the reality of modern global competition and have seen their sales and profits fall dramatically. In response, they have slashed their workforces, reduced the number of products they make, and even reduced their investment in research and development (R&D). Why did the performance of these blue-chip companies deteriorate to such a degree? A major reason is that managers lost control of their organizational structures and cultures. These companies became so big and bureaucratic that their managers and employees were unable to change and adapt to changing conditions.

The consequence of poor organizational design or lack of attention to organizational design is the decline of the organization. Talented employees leave to take positions in strong, growing companies. Resources become harder and harder to acquire, and the whole process of value creation slows down. Neglecting organizational design until a crisis threatens forces managers to make changes in organizational structure and culture that derail the company's strategy. In the last decade one

Chrysler Cars, now a part of the German DaimlerChrysler Group, has had a turbulent history in the last few decades. Chrysler was rescued from bankruptcy by Lee Iacocca in the late 1980s, when he focused on developing skills in low-cost lean car manufacturing and design. Chrysler's new competitive strengths made it a takeover target for Daimler-Benz, which saw many global advantages if it combined the engineering skills of its prestigious Mercedes-Benz car group with Chrysler's new cost-competencies to fashion innovative cars for the U.S. car market—the most important market in the world.

The merger proved to be a disaster. The new U.S. DaimlerChrysler top management team was unable to fashion a new structure and culture that combined the resources of both companies, and the hoped-for cooperation was slow to emerge. In addition, both a declining U.S. economy and cutthroat competition from Japanese carmakers forced U.S. carmakers to offer large price cuts to get their cars off dealers' lots. In desperation its German parent sent one of their top executives, Dieter Zetsche, to head its U.S.–based operations.

Known as a cost-cutter, Zetsche streamlined Chrysler's operations, closing plants and laying off thousands of employees to stem billions in losses. In addition, he recruited Tom LaSorda, a former GM top manager who had extensive experience in developing flexible low-cost manufacturing operations, to become his COO. They worked together to build new efficient manufacturing facilities and to streamline the new product development process. Zetsche charged Chrysler's design engineers to

take advantage of the German parent's expertise to build the quality cars that would appeal to U.S. customers. He also worked hard to market Chrysler's new cars and prevent U.S. customers from switching to Japanese cars. Zetsche championed new cars like Chrysler's successful 300C, for example. LaSorda also made the product development process so effective that today the company designs 50% more new cars on a budget that has been cut to $6 billion from $8.5 billion in 2000.[17] At the same time the company is increasing production so it can boost sales by 1 million cars by 2010 and make billions more in profits.

By 2005 the success of their efforts became apparent when Chrysler became the highest performing U.S.–based carmaker. Indeed it was the only one making any profit; both GM and Ford were losing billions and there was even rumor of GM declaring bankruptcy. Their reward? Dieter Zetsche was selected to become the CEO of the whole DaimlerChrysler empire. One of his new challenges is to remake Mercedes-Benz, whose prestigious cars have suffered major declines in quality in recent years compared to leader Toyota! As for LaSorda, the COO became the U.S. division's new CEO and his challenge is to strengthen all aspects of its operations. The son of a former Chrysler United Auto Workers (UAW) union representative, he understands the problems ahead as Japanese carmakers continue to increase their lead in the global battle for market share. So too do Chrysler's workers, who now understand that they will keep their jobs only if the company can remain competitive, which today means competing head-to-head with the Japanese—not GM or Ford.

major development at large companies has been the appointment of chief operating officers (COOs), who are made responsible for overseeing organizational structure and culture. COOs create and oversee teams of experienced senior managers who are responsible for organizational design and for orchestrating not only small and incremental but also organization-wide changes in strategy, structure, and culture. An interesting example of the way a new German CEO and American COO took control of Chrysler in the 2000s and made it the most successful U.S.–based carmaker is discussed in the preceding organizational insight.

HOW DO MANAGERS MEASURE ORGANIZATIONAL EFFECTIVENESS?

Because managers are responsible for utilizing organizational resources in a way that maximizes an organization's ability to create value, it is important to understand how they evaluate organizational performance. Researchers analyzing what CEOs and managers do have pointed to control, innovation, and efficiency as the three most important processes managers use to assess and measure how effective they, and their organizations, are at creating value.[18]

Table 1.1

Approaches to Measuring Organizational Effectiveness

Approach	Description	Goals to Set to Measure Effectiveness
External resource approach	Evaluates the organization's ability to secure, manage, and control scarce and valued skills and resources	• Lower costs of inputs • Obtain high-quality inputs of raw materials and employees • Increase market share • Increase stock price • Gain support of stakeholders such as government or environmentalists
Internal systems approach	Evaluates the organization's ability to be innovative and function quickly and responsively	• Cut decision-making time • Increase rate of product innovation • Increase coordination and motivation of employees • Reduce conflict • Reduce time to market
Technical approach	Evaluates the organization's ability to convert skills and resources into goods and services efficiently	• Increase product quality • Reduce number of defects • Reduce production costs • Improve customer service • Reduce delivery time to customer

In this context, *control* means having control over the external environment and having the ability to attract resources and customers. *Innovation* means developing an organization's skills and capabilities so that the organization can discover new products and processes. It also means designing and creating new organizational structures and cultures that enhance a company's ability to change, adapt, and improve the way it functions.[19] *Efficiency* means developing modern production facilities using new information technologies that can produce and distribute a company's products in a timely and cost-effective manner. It also means introducing techniques like Internet-based information systems, total quality management, and just-in-time inventory systems (discussed in Chapter 9) to improve productivity.

To evaluate the effectiveness with which an organization confronts each of these three challenges, managers can take one of three approaches (see Table 1.1). An organization is effective if it can (1) secure scarce and valued skills and resources from outside the organization (external resource approach); (2) creatively coordinate resources with employee skills to innovate products and adapt to changing customer needs (internal systems approach); and (3) efficiently convert skills and resources into finished goods and services (technical approach).

The External Resource Approach: Control

External resource approach
A method managers use to evaluate how effectively an organization manages and controls its external environment.

The **external resource approach** allows managers to evaluate how effectively an organization manages and controls its external environment. For example, the organization's ability to influence stakeholders' perceptions in its favor and to receive a positive evaluation by external stakeholders is very important to managers and the organization's survival.[20] Similarly, an organization's ability to utilize its environment and to secure scarce and valuable resources is another indication of its control over the environment.[21]

To measure the effectiveness of their control over the environment, managers use indicators such as stock price, profitability, and return on investment, which compare the performance of their organization with the performance of other organizations.[22] Top managers watch the price of their company's stock very closely because of the impact it has on shareholder expectations. Similarly, in their attempt to attract customers and gauge the performance of their organization, managers

In the last decade, Mattel Inc., the well-known maker of such classic toys as Barbie dolls and Hot Wheels, realized that customer preferences for toys around the world were changing rapidly. The popularity of electronic toys and computer games was increasing. Sales of computer games had increased dramatically as more and more parents saw the educational opportunities offered by games that children would also enjoy playing. Moreover, many kinds of computer games could be played with other people over the Internet, so it seemed that in the future the magic of electronics and information technology would turn the toy world upside down.

Mattel's managers feared that core products, such as its Barbie dolls, might lose their appeal and become old, given the future possibilities created by chips, computers, and the Internet. Mattel's managers believed that its customers' needs were changing, and that it needed to find new ways to satisfy those needs if it was to remain the biggest toy seller in the United States. Fearing they would lose their customers to the new computer game companies, Mattel's managers decided that the quickest and easiest way to redefine its business and become a major player in the computer game market would be to acquire one of these companies. So, in 1998 Mattel paid $3.5 billion for The Learning Company, the maker of such popular games as "Thinking Things." Its goal was to use this company's expertise and knowledge both to build an array of new computer games and to take Mattel's toys such as Barbie and create new games around them. In this way it hoped to better meet the needs of its existing customers and cater to the needs of the new computer game customers.[23]

In addition, although some classic toys like Barbie have the potential to satisfy customers' needs for generations, the popularity of many toys is fleeting and is often linked to the introduction of a new movie from Disney, Pixar, or DreamWorks. To ensure that it could meet the changing needs of customers for these kinds of toys, Mattel signed contracts with these companies to become the supplier of the toys linked to these movies. For example, in 2001 it agreed to pay Warner Brothers, 15% of the gross revenues, and a guaranteed $20 million, for the rights to produce electronic toys linked to the Harry Potter movie, based upon the books of the same name.[24]

Though Mattel's managers correctly sensed that customers' needs were changing, the way in which it decided to satisfy these customer needs—by buying The Learning Company—was not the right decision. It turned out that the skills to rapidly develop new games linked to Mattel's products were not present in The Learning Company; few popular games were forthcoming. Moreover, it had underestimated the need to promote and update its core toys, and the $3.5 billion could have been much better spent boosting and developing these toys. In 2001, CEO Bob Eckert sold off The Learning Company and decided that henceforth it would hire independent specialist companies to develop new electronic toys and computer games, including many related to its well-known products.

The 2000s have proved challenging to Mattel because of changing customer demands. The market has fragmented as many new kinds of electronic toys, especially those that are computer linked, have emerged. Moreover, the crucial doll market also changed as new lines of contemporary dolls, such as the Bratz doll, emerged to compete with Barbie. To compete, Mattel introduced new kinds of electronic products linked to Barbie, a new Diva Starz doll line to compete with Bratz. However, Bratz dolls continued to make large inroads into Mattel's market. Sales of Barbie dolls declined 30% in 2005, compared to 2004, as Mattel's U.S. sales fell by 13%.[25] In response, in the fall of 2005, Mattel announced it would combine its Mattel Brands and Fisher-Price Brands divisions into just one division to cut costs and streamline the organization. Clearly, Mattel has a major battle ahead to remain the leading U.S. toymaker.

gather information on the quality of their company's products as compared to their competitors' products.

Top management's ability to perceive and respond to changes in the environment or to initiate change and be first to take advantage of a new opportunity is another indicator of an organization's ability to influence and control its environment. For instance, the ability and willingness of the Walt Disney Company to manage its environment by seizing any chance to use its reputation and brand name to develop new products that exploit market opportunities are well known. Similarly, Bill Gates has stated that his goal is to be at the forefront of software development in order to maintain Microsoft's competitive advantage in new product development. By their competitive attitude, these companies signify that they intend to stay in control of their environment so that they can continue to obtain scarce and valued resources such as customers and markets. Managers know that the organization's aggressiveness, entrepreneurial nature, and reputation are all criteria by which stakeholders (especially shareholders) judge how well a company's management is controlling its environment. One company that has had mixed fortunes in managing its environment and understanding the changing needs of its customers is Mattel, profiled in the preceding organizational insight.

In the fast-changing toy market, where customers' needs evolve and where new groups of customers emerge as new technologies result in new kinds of toys, toy companies like Mattel must learn to define and redefine their businesses to satisfy those needs. Companies have to listen closely to their customers and decide how best to meet their changing needs and preferences.

The Internal Systems Approach: Innovation

Internal systems approach
A method that allows managers to evaluate how effectively an organization functions and operates.

The **internal systems approach** allows managers to evaluate how effectively an organization functions and operates. To be effective, an organization needs a structure and a culture that foster adaptability and quick responses to changing conditions in the environment. The organization also needs to be flexible so that it can speed decision making and rapidly create products and services. Measures of an organization's capacity for innovation include the length of time needed to make a decision, the amount of time needed to get new products to market, and the amount of time spent coordinating the activities of different departments.[26] These factors can often be measured objectively. For example, one year after the HP–Compaq merger, the new HP announced that its redesigned decision-making system had allowed it to speed the rate at which it could bring new products to market; it was still unable to match Dell's low costs, however. Mattel also had to change its approach to developing new and exciting toys that would capture customer interest.

Improvements to internal systems that influence employee coordination or motivation have a direct impact on an organization's ability to respond to its environment. The reduction in product development time will allow HP to match Japanese companies like Hitachi, which have always enjoyed short development cycles because of their extensive use of product teams in the development process. In turn, HP's improved ability to get a product to market is likely to make the company attractive to new customers and may bring about an increase in shareholder returns.

The Technical Approach: Efficiency

Technical approach
A method managers use to evaluate how efficiently an organization can convert some fixed amount of organizational resources into finished goods and services.

The **technical approach** allows managers to evaluate how efficiently an organization can convert some fixed amount of organizational skills and resources into finished goods and services. Technical effectiveness is measured in terms of productivity and efficiency (the ratio of outputs to inputs).[27] Thus, for example, an increase in the number of units produced without the use of additional labor indicates a gain in productivity, and so does a reduction in the cost of labor or materials required to produce each unit of output.

Productivity measures are objective indicators of the effectiveness of an organization's production operations. Thus it is common for production line managers to measure productivity at all stages of the production process using indicators such as number of defective products or wasted material. When they find ways to increase productivity, they are then rewarded for reducing costs. In service organizations, where no tangible good is produced, line managers measure productivity using indicators such as amount of sales per employee or the ratio of goods sold to goods returned to judge employee productivity. For most work activities, no matter how complex, there is a way to measure productivity or performance. In many settings the rewards offered to both employees and managers are closely linked to improvements in productivity, and it is important to select the right measures to evaluate effectiveness.[28] Employee attitude and motivation and a desire to cooperate are also important factors influencing productivity and efficiency.[29] The importance of

In 1971, Federal Express (FedEx) turned the package delivery world upside down when it began to offer overnight package delivery by air. Its founder, Fred Smith, had seen the opportunity for next-day delivery because both the U.S. Postal Service and United Parcel Service (UPS) were, at that that time, taking several days to deliver packages. Several companies imitated FedEx's new strategy and introduced their own air overnight service. None, however, could match FedEx's efficiency because of its state-of-the-art information systems, which allowed continuous tracking of all packages while in transit. Several of its competitors went out of business. Then things changed.

Once only a road delivery package service, in 1988 UPS initiated an overnight air delivery service of its own.[30] It began aggressively to imitate FedEx's operating and information systems, especially its tracking systems. Slowly and surely UPS increased its operating efficiency, but it was still way behind FedEx. Even its well-developed, highly efficient road delivery system that could reach every customer in the United States—its major source of costs savings—was not really helping it to catch up. Then, in 1999, UPS introduced a new tracking and shipping information system that matched, and even exceeded, the efficiency of FedEx's system because it could work with *any* IT system used by corporate customers. In contrast, customers had to install and use FedEx's proprietary IT, causing more work and cost for them.

In the 2000s, UPS also developed crucial new IT that allowed it to integrate its overnight air service into this nationwide delivery service. This gave it an enormous competitive advantage over FedEx because UPS can more efficiently deliver short-range and mid-distance packages, those around 500 miles, than FedEx, as well as match FedEx's long-range operations. Moreover, UPS can offer customers lower prices because it has lower costs than FedEx.[31]

To get nearer its customers in 2001, UPS acquired Mail Boxes Etc., which it named "The UPS Store." To compete, in 2003 FedEx acquired Kinko's, and it newly rebranded FedExKinko's chain has 1,200 locations in 10 countries and provides a global storefront to compete with The UPS Store. By 2002, UPS's overnight business was growing at 10% and FedEx's was growing at 3.6%.[32] Then, in 2004, the German company, DHL, entered the battle when it bought U.S Airborne Express. Today, these companies compete head-to-head not only in the United States, but also globally, in the package delivery business, and price competition has hurt their profits. Nevertheless, analysts believe that the efficiency and flexibility of UPS's delivery systems will make it the market leader and that it is poised to become the global leader in the next decade.

continuously improving efficiency is very clear in the ongoing battle between FedEx and UPS, profiled in the preceding organizational insight.

Measuring Effectiveness: Organizational Goals

Official goals
Guiding principles that the organization formally states in its annual report and in other public documents.

Mission
Goals that explain why the organization exists and what it should be doing.

Operative goals
Specific long-term and short-term goals that guide managers and employees as they perform the work of the organization.

Managers create goals that they use to assess how well the organization is performing. Two types of goals used to evaluate organizational effectiveness are official goals and operative goals. **Official goals** are guiding principles that the organization formally states in its annual report and in other public documents. Usually these goals lay out the **mission** of the organization—they explain why the organization exists and what it should be doing. Official goals include being a leading producer of a product, demonstrating an overriding concern for public safety, and so forth. Official goals are meant to legitimize the organization and its activities, to allow it to obtain resources and the support of its stakeholders.[33] Consider the way the mission and goals of Amazon.com have changed during the period 1995–2005 as its managers have changed its business to better manage its environment (see Table 1.2).

Operative goals are specific long- and short-term goals that guide managers and employees as they perform the work of the organization. The goals listed in Table 1.2 are operative goals that managers can use to evaluate organizational effectiveness. Is market share increasing or decreasing? Is the cost of inputs rising or falling? Similarly, they can measure how well the organization is functioning by measuring how long it takes to make a decision or how great conflict is between organizational members. Finally, they can measure how efficient they are by creating operative goals that allow them to "benchmark" themselves against their competitors—that is, compare their competitors' costs and quality achievements with their own.

Table 1.2

Amazon.com's Mission and Goals, 1995–2005

Where We Started

Amazon.com opened its virtual doors in July 1995 with a mission to use the Internet to transform book buying into the fastest, easiest, and most enjoyable shopping experience possible. While our customer base and product offerings have grown considerably since our early days, we still maintain our founding commitment to customer satisfaction and the delivery of an educational and inspiring shopping experience.

Where We Are Today

Today, Amazon.com is the place to find and discover anything you want to buy online. We're very proud that millions of people in more than 220 countries have made us the leading online shopping site. We have Earth's Biggest Selection of products, including free electronic greeting cards, online auctions, and millions of books, CDs, videos, DVDs, toys and games, electronics, kitchenware, computers and more.

GM used Toyota's costs and quality as benchmarks for what it sought to achieve in its Saturn plant.

An organization may be effective in one area but not in others.[34] For example, in 1975 GM was a very efficient producer of full-size cars. Few other companies could produce a full-size car at as low a cost per unit. GM, however, was not an effective organization, because it was not producing cars that people wanted and thus was not managing its external environment. Nobody wanted to buy a full-size gas-guzzler when oil cost $35 a barrel and gasoline prices were soaring. Thus, GM was very ineffective when judged by measures of being innovative or quick in responding to customers' changing needs. Customers did not want GM cars, GM dealers and suppliers were suffering, and the company's performance was declining rapidly. How did GM get into this unfortunate position?

One possibility is that GM was ineffective on the internal systems/innovation dimension of effectiveness. GM was a successful global company at this time. Its European operation, which had an extensive history of innovation in small-car production, was one of Europe's largest automobile companies. Why then did GM not transplant its skills and competences in small-car production to the United States? The answer is that GM failed to coordinate and utilize its internal resources effectively. The company was dominated by a few powerful top managers who had no background or expertise in small-car production and who would not heed the message being sent by U.S. consumers, who were buying large numbers of small foreign cars. The dominant philosophy of GM's management was that small cars meant small profits; thus, no coordination of U.S. and European operations was introduced.

It has taken GM 20 years to recover from these problems, learn from its mistakes, and find the right way to redesign its structure to allow it to coordinate its skills and resources on a global basis. Throughout the 1990s, GM lagged behind Ford and DaimlerChrysler, which had found ways to lower costs and improve the quality of their cars. Finally, in 2002, GM announced that it had matched the efficiency of other U.S. car companies after spending hundreds of billions of dollars in the process.[35] Although it still lags behind the most efficient Japanese auto companies, GM continues to work to increase its effectiveness in all three dimensions. In late 2005, for example, it negotiated a new deal with the United Auto Workers union that will save it one-and-a-half billion dollars a year in health-care costs, which add hundreds of dollars to the cost of making each GM car. Its main problem now is to innovate exciting new car models U.S. customers want to buy.

Managers must be careful to develop goals that measure effectiveness on all three dimensions: control, innovation, and efficiency. Moreover, companies must be careful to align their official and operative goals and eliminate any conflict between them. For example, throughout the 1980s and 1990s, GM's annual reports reiterated the company's determination to reduce its costs, increase product quality, and remain a leading global car company. During this same period, however, management's operative goals never allowed it to achieve these stated goals, often because of infighting between its top managers. Mistaken choices of strategy were harming the company. Managers were not making concerted efforts to lower production costs and raise quality, and they were not making hard decisions about downsizing the organization and laying off managers and employees. By the time it became obvious that GM's operative goals conflicted with its official goals, the organization was in crisis. Subsequent layoffs were much more severe than they would have been if managers had been following the official goals they claimed to believe. When managers create a set of goals to measure organizational effectiveness, they must make sure that official goals and operative goals work together to enhance effectiveness.

The Plan of This Book

To understand how to manage organizational design and change, it is first necessary to understand how organizations affect, and are affected by, their environments. Then the principles of organizational design and change that managers use to improve the match or fit of an organization with its environment can be better understood. To facilitate this learning process, the chapters in this book are organized so that each builds upon the ones that have come earlier. Figure 1.5 shows how the various chapters fit together and provide a model of the components involved in organizational design and change.

After the scandals at Enron, Arthur Andersen, WorldCom, and Adelphia, it is more important than ever that a clear link be made between ethics and organizational effectiveness, because managers are responsible for protecting organizational resources and using them effectively. Chapter 2 examines the roles top managers perform in an organization, the claims and obligations of different organizational stakeholder groups, and the many ethical issues managers face in dealing with the claims of these different groups.

The environment in which an organization operates is a principal source of uncertainty. If customers withdraw their support, if suppliers withhold inputs, if a global recession occurs, then considerable uncertainty is created. Thus the organization must design its structure to manage adequately the contingencies it faces in the external environment. Chapter 3 presents models that reveal why the environment is a source of uncertainty and theories about how and why organizations act to meet uncertainties in the environment. Resource dependence theory examines how organizations attempt to gain control over scarce resources. Transaction cost theory examines how organizations manage environmental relations to reduce transaction costs.

Organizational Design

Organizational design is complicated by the contingencies that must be considered as an organization makes its design choices. Several types of contingency—the organization's environment, its strategy, technology, and internal processes, which develop in an organization over time—cause uncertainty and influence an organization's choice of structure and culture. Throughout this book we analyze the sources of this uncertainty and how organizations manage it. We also discuss how organizations can change and redesign their structures and cultures as contingencies change and lead managers to develop new goals and strategies for their organizations.

Chapters 4 through 7 examine the principles on which organizations operate and the choices available for designing and redesigning their structures and cultures to match the environment. As these chapters show, the same basic organizational problems occur in all work settings, and the purpose of organizational design is to develop an organizational structure and culture that will respond effectively to these challenges.

Chapter 8 discusses organizations' attempts to manage their environments by using their structures and strategies to improve their fit with their environments. We discuss how organizations develop functional, business, and corporate strategies to increase their control over and share of scarce resources. We also discuss the global strategies managers can adopt as they expand and work to increase their presence overseas.

Figure 1.5 Components of Organizational Theory, Design, and Change

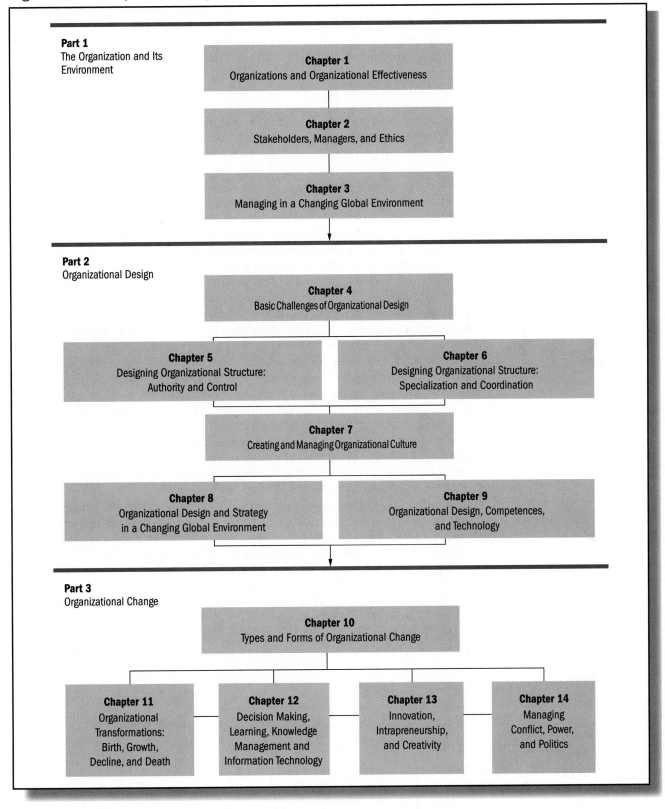

Part 1
The Organization and Its Environment

Chapter 1
Organizations and Organizational Effectiveness

Chapter 2
Stakeholders, Managers, and Ethics

Chapter 3
Managing in a Changing Global Environment

Part 2
Organizational Design

Chapter 4
Basic Challenges of Organizational Design

Chapter 5
Designing Organizational Structure:
Authority and Control

Chapter 6
Designing Organizational Structure:
Specialization and Coordination

Chapter 7
Creating and Managing Organizational Culture

Chapter 8
Organizational Design and Strategy
in a Changing Global Environment

Chapter 9
Organizational Design, Competences,
and Technology

Part 3
Organizational Change

Chapter 10
Types and Forms of Organizational Change

Chapter 11
Organizational
Transformations:
Birth, Growth,
Decline, and Death

Chapter 12
Decision Making,
Learning, Knowledge
Management and
Information Technology

Chapter 13
Innovation,
Intrapreneurship,
and Creativity

Chapter 14
Managing
Conflict, Power,
and Politics

Organizations produce goods and services. The competences they develop to produce goods and services, and the uncertainty associated with different production methods or technologies, are major factors in the design of an organization. In Chapter 9, some theories that describe different competences and technologies, and that explain the way in which they affect organizational structure and culture, are discussed.

Organizational Change

The third part of this book deals with the many different but related issues involved in changing and redesigning organizations to improve their effectiveness. It also highlights how the need to foster innovation, utilize new information technologies effectively and speed the rate at which organizations adjust to their environments has been changing organizations.

Chapter 10 examines the nature of organizational change and outlines several important kinds of organizational change processes, such as restructuring, reengineering, and innovation management. It also provides a model that explains the many different kinds of issues that must be confronted if managers are to succeed in their efforts to achieve a better fit with the environment.

When organizations are created and set in motion, various internal processes occur. As organizations grow and mature, many of them experience a predictable series of organizing crises, and as they attempt to change their strategies and structures, they confront similar problems. Chapter 11 presents a life cycle model of organizations and charts the typical problems they confront as they grow, mature, and decline.

Chapter 12 discusses organizational learning and decision making, and relates these processes to the use of information technologies to show the many ways in which IT is changing organizations. First, the ways in which managers make decisions are examined. Then, the increasingly important question of why managers make mistakes, both strategically and ethically, is discussed. The chapter includes suggestions as to how managers can avoid these mistakes and speed the level of organizational learning to improve the quality of decision making. Finally, we look at how new innovations in information technology, including the Internet, have been affecting organizations and changing organizational structure and culture.

Chapter 13 looks at the related issues of innovation and project management in organizations. Project management focuses on how project managers can utilize various techniques to speed and promote the development of new and improved goods and services. How to foster innovation and manage research and development is a pressing problem, particularly for organizations competing globally.

Finally, Chapter 14 covers problems of politics and conflicts that arise as managers attempt to change and redesign organizational structure and culture. These chapters highlight the complex social and organizational processes that must be managed for the organization to conduct the change process successfully and increase its effectiveness.

SUMMARY

We have examined what organizations are; why they exist; the purpose of organizational theory, design, and change; and the different ways in which they can be evaluated. Organizations play a vital role in increasing the wealth of a society; the purpose of managing organizational design and change is to enhance their ability to create value and thus organizational effectiveness. Chapter 1 has made the following main points:

1. An organization is a tool used by people to coordinate their actions to obtain something they desire or value—to achieve their goals.

2. Organizations are value-creation systems that take inputs from the environment and use skills and knowledge to transform these inputs into finished goods and services.

3. The use of an organization allows people to increase specialization and the division of labor, use large-scale technology, manage the external environment, economize on transaction costs, and exert power and control—all of which increase the value that the organization can create.

4. Organizational theory is the study of how organizations function and how they affect and are affected by the environments in which they operate.
5. Organizational structure is the formal system of task and authority relationships that control how people coordinate their actions and use resources to achieve an organization's goals.
6. Organizational culture is the set of shared values and norms that control organizational members' interactions with each other and with suppliers, customers, and other people outside the organization.
7. Organizational design is the process by which managers select and manage aspects of structure and culture so that an organization can control the activities necessary to achieve its goals. Organizational design has important implications for a company's competitive advantage, its ability to deal with contingencies and manage diversity, its efficiency, its

ability to generate new goods and services, its control of the environment, its coordination and motivation of employees, and its development and implementation of strategy.
8. Organizational change is the process by which organizations redesign and transform their structures and cultures to move from their current state to some desired future state to increase their effectiveness. The goal of organizational change is to find new or improved ways of using resources and capabilities to increase an organization's ability to create value and, hence, performance.
9. Managers can use three approaches to evaluate organizational effectiveness: the external resource approach, the internal systems approach, and the technical approach. Each approach is associated with a set of criteria that can be used to measure effectiveness and a set of organizational goals.

DISCUSSION QUESTIONS

1. How do organizations create value? What is the role of entrepreneurship in this process?
2. What is the relationship among organizational theory, design, change, and organizational structure and culture?
3. What is organizational effectiveness? Discuss three approaches to evaluating effectiveness and the problems associated with each approach.

4. Draw up a list of effectiveness goals that you would use to measure the performance of (a) a fast-food restaurant and (b) a school of business.

ORGANIZATIONAL THEORY IN ACTION

Practicing Organizational Theory: Open Systems Dynamics

Form groups of three to five people and discuss the following scenario:

Think of an organization with which you are all familiar, such as a local restaurant, store, or bank. Once you have chosen an organization, model it from an open systems perspective. For example, identify its input, conversion, and output processes.

1. Identify the specific forces in the environment that have the greatest opportunity to help or hurt this organization's ability to obtain resources and dispose of its goods or services.
2. Using the three views of effectiveness discussed in the chapter, discuss which specific measures are most useful to managers in evaluating this organization's effectiveness.

The Ethical Dimension #1

An ethical exercise is present in every chapter to help you understand the many ways in which organizations can help or harm the people and groups in their environments, especially when they are managed in ways that are unethical. This exercise can be done alone or in a small group.

Think of some examples of ways in which a hospital, and the doctors and nurses who work within it, could act unethi-

cally toward patients. Also, think about behaviors that demonstrate that a hospital has high ethical standards.

1. List examples of these ethical and unethical behaviors.
2. How do these behaviors relate to the attempts of doctors and nurses to increase organizational effectiveness in the ways discussed in the chapter? Or, to attempts to pursue their own self-interest?

Making the Connection #1

At the end of every chapter you, will find an exercise that requires you to search newspapers or magazines for an example of a real company that is dealing with some of the issues, concepts, challenges, questions, and problems discussed in the chapter.

Find a company that is seeking to improve its effectiveness in some way. What dimension of effectiveness (control, innovation, or efficiency) is it seeking to improve? What changes is it making to address the issue?

Analyzing the Organization: Design Module #1

To give you insight into the way real-world organizations work, at the end of every chapter there is an organizational design module for which you must collect and analyze information about an organization that you will select now and study all semester. At the end of the semester, you will write a report on your findings, which will be presented to the class.

Suppose you select General Motors. You will collect the information specified in each organizational design module, present and summarize your findings on GM for your class, and then produce a written report. Your instructor will provide the details of what will be required of you—for example, how long the presentation or report should be and whether you will work in a group or by yourself to complete the assignment. By the end of the semester, by completing each module, you will have a clear picture of how organizations operate and how they deal with problems and contingencies they face.

There are two approaches to selecting an organization. One is to choose a well-known organization about which a lot has been written. Large companies like IBM, Apple Computer, and Procter & Gamble receive extensive coverage in business periodicals such as *Fortune* and *Business Week*. Every year, for example, in one of its April issues, *Fortune* publishes a list of the *Fortune* 500 manufacturing companies; in one of its May issues, it publishes a list of the *Fortune* 500 service companies, the biggest companies in the United States. If you choose a company on the *Fortune* lists, you can be sure that considerable information is published about it.

The best sources of information are business periodicals like *Fortune, Business Week*, and *Forbes*; news magazines like *Time* and *Newsweek*; and *The Wall Street Journal* and other newspapers. *F&S Predicasts, Value Line Investment Survey, Moody's Manuals on Investment*, and many other publications summarize articles written about a particular company. In addition, you should check industry and trade publications.

Finally, you should take advantage of the Internet and explore the World Wide Web to find information on your company. Most large companies have detailed websites that provide a considerable amount of information. You can find these sites by using a search engine such as Google, Yahoo! or Altavista and then downloading the information you need.

If you consult these sources, you will obtain a lot of information that you can use to complete the design modules. You may not get all the specific information you need, but you will have enough to answer many of the design module questions.

The second approach to selecting an organization is to choose one located in your city or town—for example, a large department store, manufacturing company, hotel, or nonprofit organization (such as a hospital or school) where you or somebody you know works. You could contact the owners or managers of the organization and ask whether they would be willing to talk to you about the way they operate and how they design and manage their company.

Each approach to selecting a company has advantages and disadvantages. The advantage of selecting a local company and doing your own information gathering is that in face-to-face interviews you can ask for detailed information that may be unavailable from published sources. You will gain an especially rich picture of the way a company operates by doing your research personally. The problem is that the local organization you choose has to be big enough to offer you insight into the way organizations work. In general, it should employ at least 20 people and have at least three levels in its hierarchy.

If you use written sources to study a very large organization, you will get a lot of interesting information that relates to organizational theory, because the organization is large and complex and is confronting many of the problems discussed in this book. But you may not be able to obtain all the detailed information you want.

Regardless of the selection approach you use, be sure that you have access to enough interesting information to complete the majority of the organizational design modules. One module, for example, asks about the international or global dimension of your organization's strategy and structure. If you pick a local company that does not have an international dimension, you will be unable to complete that assignment. However, to compensate for this lack of information, you might have very detailed information about the company's structure or product lines. The goal is to make sure that you can gain access to enough information to write an interesting report.

Assignment

Choose a company to study, and answer the following questions about it:

1. What is the name of the organization? Give a short account of the history of the company. Describe the way it has grown and developed.
2. What does the organization do? What goods and services does it produce/provide? What kind of value does it create? If the company has an annual report, what does the report describe as the company's organizational mission?
3. Draw a model of the way the organization creates value. Briefly describe its inputs, throughputs, outputs, and environment.
4. Do an initial analysis of the organization's major problems or issues. What challenges confront the organization today—for example, in its efforts to attract customers, to lower costs, to increase operating efficiency? How does its organizational design relate to these problems?
5. Read its annual report and determine which kinds of goals, standards, or targets the organization is using to evaluate performance. How well is the organization doing when judged by the criteria of control, innovation, and efficiency?

CASE FOR ANALYSIS

Change and More Change at AOL–Time Warner

When America Online and Time Warner joined to form the $97 billion global entertainment media and information technology giant, AOL–Time Warner, Bob Pittman was put in charge of managing the organizational design and change process.[36] Pittman's task? To find the best way to combine the people and resources of both companies efficiently and effectively to create more products and services, such as Internet TV and video on demand, for customers and therefore increase profits. Pittman's challenge was to find a way to get all the company's managers not just to focus on their own particular tasks and roles, but to think about ways to better use the company's extensive resources throughout the organization, too. For example, Pittman needed to get the managers of *Time* magazine to think about how they could use AOL's Internet presence to increase the circulation and advertising revenues of their magazine. He also needed AOL managers to think about how best to expand their service into Time Warner's cable networks and get cable customers to sign up for AOL Internet service. Pittman was put in charge of this vital task because of his past successes at managing organization-wide change at AOL at a time when it was buying many small dot.com companies and expanding its range of product offerings. Pittman is renowned for his diplomacy and his ability to get what he wants done by persuasion rather than command and for forging a team among managers from different parts of an organization, making collaboration, rather than competition, the basis value in AOL's culture. At the same time, Pittman's success had been due to concern for the bottom line: managing costs. His rise through the AOL hierarchy was achieved partly because he has great operational skills and recognizes ways to design and change structure to cut costs and speed new products to market. Pittman did this by decentralizing authority to managers and by establishing challenging targets for each manager and for each part of the company. One target was to increase annual revenues by 12% to 15% and realize more than $1 billion in cost savings in the first year. To achieve these ambitious targets, Pittman set revenue and cost saving targets for his top managers to achieve; they in turn set targets for their subordinates to achieve; and so on down the organization.

Pittman also coordinated meetings that involved thousands of managers from different parts and all levels of the company coming together weekly to discuss, decide, and envision how they could create valuable new products or services that customers would want.[37] Countless meetings took place to decide what course of action or goals to set for the new company.[38]

One immediate obstacle he faced was that the previously separate companies had very different structures and cultures. The old Time Warner had been very hierarchical in nature; it was bureaucratic, and decision making was slow. At AOL, on the other hand, managers were used to the fast-changing environment of the Internet and the IT industry. They were used to making decisions in teams and to making them quickly. Pittman, who was from AOL, decided that the AOL organizing model was the one that would be most successful in the new company. He created teams of AOL and Time Warner managers but made AOL managers responsible for taking the lead, developing an organizational culture that would bring new products to market quickly.

As it happened, all of Pittman's huge efforts to change the company were not enough after the huge implosion of dot.com companies' share price and the recession of the early 2000s. The collapsing value of AOL stock led AOL–Time Warner's board to side with old Time Warner executives, and a power struggle took place in which Pittman and most other senior AOL executives lost their leading roles; old Time Warner executives reassumed control of the company.[39] In 2002, a new executive, Jonathan Miller, was put in charge of restructuring AOL to make it an Internet portal that could compete head-to-head with Yahoo! and MSN for the billions in advertising revenues that are at stake in online advertising. In 2005, the success of his efforts was seen when AOL became a potential takeover target for companies like Microsoft and Yahoo!. However, in 2005 Time Warner said it did not want to spin off AOL; instead, it wanted to form a marketing alliance with Google or Microsoft. Whether there would be a split between the two companies was unclear in 2005.

DISCUSSION QUESTIONS

1. What kinds of organizational problems did Bob Pittman face in managing the new, merged company?
2. What steps did he take to solve those problems?

3. In what ways might a split between Time Warner and AOL increase both their effectiveness? Why might it be better to keep them together in one organization?

REFERENCES

1. A. W. Gouldner, "Organizational Analysis," in R. K. Merton, ed., *Sociology Today* (New York: Basic Books, 1959); A. Etzioni, *Comparative Analysis of Complex Organizations* (New York: Free Press, 1961).
2. I. M. Kirzner, *Competition and Entrepreneurship* (Chicago: University of Chicago Press, 1973).
3. www.amazon.com, 2006.
4. www.amazon.com, "About Amazon.com," 2006.
5. P. M. Blau, "A Formal Theory of Differentiation in Organizations,"*American Sociological Review, 35* (1970), 201–218; D. S. Pugh and D. J. Hickson, "The Comparative Study of Organizations," in G. Salaman and K. Thompson, eds., *People and Organizations* (London: Penguin, 1977), pp. 43–55.
6. P. M. Blau, *Exchange and Power in Social Life* (New York: Wiley, 1964); P. M. Blau and W. R. Scott, *Formal Organizations* (San Francisco: Chandler, 1962).
7. C. I. Barnard, *The Functions of the Executive* (Cambridge, MA: Harvard University Press, 1948); A. Etzioni, *Modern Organizations* (Upper Saddle River, NJ: Prentice Hall, 1964).
8. P. R. Lawrence and J. W. Lorsch, *Organization and Environment* (Boston: Graduate School of Business Administration, Harvard University, 1967); W. R. Scott, *Organizations: Rational, Natural, and Open Systems* (Upper Saddle River, NJ: Prentice Hall, 1981).
9. www.cocacola.com, 2006; www.pepsico, 2006.
10. M. Beer, *Organizational Change and Development* (Santa Monica, CA: Goodyear, 1980); J. I. Porras and R. C. Silvers, "Organization Development and Transformation," *Annual Review of Psychology, 42* (1991), 51–78.
11. M. Moritz, *The Little Kingdom: The Private Story of Apple Computer* (New York: W. Morrow, 1984).
12. S. Anderson Forest and C. Arnst, "The Education of Michael Dell," *Business Week*, March 22, 1993, pp. 82–88.
13. R. Cringely, *Accidental Empires* (New York: Harper Business, 1994).
14. D. McGraw, "The Kid Bytes Back," *U.S. News & World Report*, December 12, 1994, pp. 70–71.
15. www.dell.com, 2006.
16. www.apple.com, 2006.
17. K. Naughton, "The Blue-Collar CEO," *Newsweek*, December 5, 2005, pp. 42–44.
18. L. Galambos, "What Have CEO's Been Doing?" *Journal of Economic History, 18* (1988), 243–258.
19. Ibid., p. 253.
20. Campbell, "On the Nature of Organizational Effectiveness." In Goodman, P. S. & Pennings, J. M. (Eds.), *New Perspectives on Organizational Effectiveness* (pp. 13–55). San Francisco: Jossey-Bass.
21. F. Friedlander and H. Pickle, "Components of Effectiveness in Small Organizations," *Administrative Science Quarterly, 13* (1968), 289–304; Miles, *Macro Organizational Behavior*.
22. Campbell, "On the Nature of Organizational Effectiveness."
23. C. Palmeri, "Mattel: Up the Hill Minus Jill," *Business Week*, April 9, 2001, pp. 53–54.
24. www.mattel.com, 2005.
25. www.mattel.com, 2005.
26. Ibid., p. 38.
27. J. D. Thompson, *Organizations in Action* (New York: McGraw-Hill, 1967).
28. R. M. Steers, *Organizational Effectiveness: A Behavioral View* (Santa Monica, CA: Goodyear, 1977).
29. D. E. Bowen and G. R. Jones, "Transaction Cost Analysis of Customer-Service Organization Exchange," *Academy of Management Review, 11* (1986), 428–441.
30. www.ups.com, 2001.
31. C. Haddad and J. Ewing, "Ground Wars," *Business Week*, May 21, 2001, pp. 64–68.
32. www.ups.com, 2006; www.fedex.com, 2006.
33. T. M. Jones, "Instrumental Stakeholder Theory: A Synthesis of Ethics and Economics," *Academy of Management Review, 20* (1995), 404–437.
34. Campbell, "On the Nature of Organizational Effectiveness," pp. 43–53; R. E. Quinn and J. Rohrbaugh, "A Spatial Model of Effectiveness Criteria: Towards a Competing Values Approach to Organizational Analysis," *Management Science, 29* (1983), 33–51.
35. www.gm.com, 2006.
36. www.aoltimewarner.com, 2005.
37. Ibid.
38. S. Prasso, "AOL Time Warner's Power Towers," *Business Week*, June 11, 2001, p. 43.
39. www.timewarneraol.com, 2005.

Chapter 2

Stakeholders, Managers, and Ethics

Learning Objectives

Organizations exist to create valuable goods and services that people desire. But who decides which goods and services an organization should provide, or how to divide the value that an organization creates among different groups of people like employees, customers, or shareholders? If people behave in a self-interested manner, what mechanisms or procedures govern the way an organization uses its resources, and what is to stop the different groups from trying to maximize their share of the value created? At a time when the issue of corporate ethics and top management greed has come under intense scrutiny, these questions must be answered before the issue of designing an organization to increase its effectiveness can be addressed.

After studying this chapter you should be able to:

1. Identify the various stakeholder groups and their interests or claims on an organization.

2. Understand the choices and problems inherent in distributing the value an organization creates.

3. Appreciate who has authority and responsibility at the top of an organization, and distinguish between different levels of management.

4. Describe the agency problem that exists in all authority relationships and the various mechanisms, such as the board of directors and stock options, which can be used to help control illegal and unethical managerial behavior.

5. Discuss the vital role played by ethics in constraining managers and employees to pursue the goals that lead to long-run organizational effectiveness.

Stakeholders
People who have an interest, claim, or stake in an organization, in what it does, and in how well it performs.

Inducements
Rewards such as money, power, and organizational status.

Contributions
The skills, knowledge, and expertise that organizations require of their members during task performance.

Organizations exist because of their ability to create value and acceptable outcomes for various groups of **stakeholders**, people who have an interest, claim, or stake in the organization, in what it does, and in how well it performs.[1] In general, stakeholders are motivated to participate in an organization if they receive inducements that exceed the value of the contributions they are required to make.[2] **Inducements** include rewards such as money, power, and organizational status. **Contributions** include the skills, knowledge, and expertise that organizations require of their members during task performance.

There are two main groups of organizational stakeholders: inside stakeholders and outside stakeholders. The inducements and contributions of each group are summarized in Table 2.1.[3]

Inside Stakeholders

Inside stakeholders are people who are closest to an organization and have the strongest or most direct claim on organizational resources: shareholders, managers, and the workforce.

Shareholders

Shareholders are the owners of the organization, and, as such, their claim on organizational resources is often considered superior to the claims of other inside stakeholders. The shareholders' contribution to the organization is to invest money in it by buying the organization's shares or stock. The shareholders' inducement to invest is the prospective money they can earn on their investment in the form of dividends and increases in the price of stock. Investment in stock is risky, however, because there is no guarantee of a return. Shareholders who do not believe that the inducement (the possible return on their investment) is enough to warrant their contribution (the money they have invested) sell their shares and withdraw their support from the organization. As the following example illustrates, more and more shareholders are relying on large institutional investment companies to protect their interests and to increase their collective power to influence organizations.

Table 2.1
Inducements and Contributions of Organizational Stakeholders

STAKEHOLDER	CONTRIBUTION TO THE ORGANIZATION	INDUCEMENT TO CONTRIBUTE
Inside		
Shareholders	Money and capital	Dividends and stock appreciation
Managers	Skills and expertise	Salaries, bonuses, status, and power
Workforce	Skills and expertise	Wages, bonuses, stable employment, and promotion
Outside		
Customers	Revenue from purchase of goods and services	Quality and price of goods and services
Suppliers	High-quality inputs	Revenue from purchase of inputs
Government	Rules governing good business practice	Fair and free competition
Unions	Free and fair collective bargaining	Equitable share of inducements
Community	Social and economic infrastructure	Revenue, taxes, and employment
General public	Customer loyalty and reputation	National pride

The collapse of the stock market in the early 2000s made large mutual fund companies like Fidelity or TIAA/CREF realize their increasing responsibility to their investors, who lost billions in their pension funds.[4] In particular, the mutual funds realized their increasing responsibility to prevent the kinds of unethical and illegal behaviors that caused the collapse of Enron, WorldCom, Tyco, Arthur Andersen, and many other companies whose dubious accounting practices led to a collapse in their stock price. How can these mutual funds intervene in the running of a company?

Take the California Public Employees Retirement System (CalPERS), the largest public-sector pension fund in the United States, which manages $70 billion for over 1,100,000 of its members.[5] Because the fund is so large, it is a major shareholder in many U.S. companies and therefore has a vital interest in how well they perform. During the last decade, CalPERS realized that it had an ever-increasing duty to protect the interests of its investors by paying more attention to what the top management and boards of directors of these companies were doing. If mutual fund companies are to protect the interests of their shareholders, they need to monitor and influence the behavior of the companies they invest in, to make sure that the top managers pursue actions that do not threaten shareholders' interests while enhancing their own.

As a result of this concern for shareholders, CalPERS and other mutual funds are taking an active interest in controlling the ability of a corporation's managers to create antitakeover provisions. These provisions protect managers from corporate raiders who might like to take a company over, a process that would earn a lot of money for shareholders but might cost top managers their jobs. Mutual funds are also exerting their right as shareholders to intervene in long-run management decisions such as the acquisition of a company that might hurt the value of the acquiring company's stock. The funds have also been showing an interest in controlling the salaries and bonuses that top managers give themselves, which have reached record levels in recent years. They have also reacted to the collapse of Enron and other companies by demanding that companies clarify their accounting procedures and by lobbying for new rules that will make it much more difficult for companies to hide unethical or illegal transactions that might benefit managers but hurt other stakeholders. One result of this was the passage of the Sarbanes–Oxley Act. As the power of mutual funds and other institutional investors increases, so does the power of shareholders as organizational stakeholders. In a way, large mutual fund companies are the shareholders' equivalent of a union for employees. Just as unions increase the bargaining power of individual workers in relation to management, so mutual fund companies increase the power of individual shareholders in dealing with management.

Managers

Managers are the employees who are responsible for coordinating organizational resources and ensuring that an organization's goals are successfully met. Top managers are responsible for investing shareholder money in resources in order to maximize the future output of goods and services. Managers are, in effect, the agents or employees of shareholders; they are appointed indirectly by shareholders through an organization's board of directors, which shareholders elect to oversee managers' performance.

Managers' contributions are the skills they use to direct the organization's response to pressures from within and outside the organization. For example, a manager's skills at opening up global markets, identifying new product markets, or solving transaction cost and technological problems can greatly facilitate the achievement of organizational goals.

Various types of rewards induce managers to perform their activities well: monetary compensation (in the form of salaries, bonuses, and stock options) and the psychological satisfaction they get from controlling the corporation, exercising power, or taking risks with other people's money. Managers who do not believe that the inducements meet or exceed their contributions are likely to withdraw their support by leaving the organization. Thus top managers move from one organization to another to obtain greater rewards for their contributions.

The Workforce

An organization's workforce consists of all nonmanagerial employees. Members of the workforce have responsibilities and duties (usually outlined in a job description) that they are responsible for performing. An employee's contribution to the organization is the performance of his or her duties and responsibilities. How well an employee performs is, in some measure, within the employee's control. An employee's motivation to perform well relates to the rewards and punishments that the organization uses to influence job performance. Employees who do not feel that the inducements meet or exceed their contributions are likely to withdraw their support for the organization by reducing the level of their performance or by leaving the organization.

Outside Stakeholders

Outside stakeholders are people who do not own the organization and are not employed by it, but do have some interest in it. Customers, suppliers, the government, trade unions, local communities, and the general public are all outside stakeholders.

Customers

Customers are usually an organization's largest outside stakeholder group. Customers are induced to select a product (and thus an organization) from alternative products by their estimation of what they are getting relative to what they have to pay. The money they pay for the product is their contribution to the organization and reflects the value they feel they receive from the organization. As long as the organization produces a product whose price is equal to or less than the value customers feel they are getting, they will continue to buy the product and support the organization.[6] If customers refuse to pay the price the organization is asking, they withdraw their support, and the organization loses a vital stakeholder. Southwest Airlines' attention to its customers has resulted in their loyal support.

Suppliers

Suppliers, another important outside stakeholder group, contribute to the organization by providing reliable raw materials and component parts that allow the organization to reduce uncertainty in its technical or production operations and thus reduce production costs. Suppliers have a direct effect on the organization's efficiency and an indirect effect on its ability to attract customers. An organization that has high-quality inputs can make high-quality products and attract customers. In turn, as demand for its products increases, the organization demands greater quantities of high-quality inputs from its suppliers.

ORGANIZATIONAL INSIGHT 2.2
Southwest Airlines Serves Its Customers

Southwest Airlines, based in Phoenix, Arizona, attributes its success to the way it handles customers. At a time when most airlines are losing money, Southwest posts profits.[7] Former CEO Herb Kelleher attributes his airline's effectiveness to its policy of "dignifying the customer."[8] Southwest sends birthday cards to its frequent fliers, responds personally to the thousands of customer letters it receives each week, and regularly obtains feedback from customers on ways to improve service. Such personal attention makes customers feel valued and inclined to fly Southwest. Moreover, Southwest believes that if management fails to treat employees right, employees will not treat customers right. So Southwest's employees, most of whom are

unionized, own 20% of the airline's stock. Ownership of the company increases their motivation to contribute to the organization and improve customer service.[9] One stakeholder group (employees) thus helps another (customers).

Southwest's president, Coleen Barrett, spends a great deal of time managing the complex relationships with Southwest's pilots, mechanics, and cabin crew that are a key factor affecting customer satisfaction. In the 2000s, many airlines such as Northwest, Delta, and United experienced damaging strikes by employees that caused thousands of passengers to miss their flights. While these airlines sought bankruptcy protection to survive, Southwest continues to be the most effective and profitable U.S. airline.

One of the reasons why Japanese cars remain so popular with U.S. consumers is that they still require fewer repairs than the average U.S.–made vehicle. This reliability is a result of the use of component parts that meet stringent quality control standards. In addition, Japanese parts suppliers are constantly improving their efficiency.[10] The close relationship between the large Japanese automakers and their suppliers is a stakeholder relationship that pays long-term dividends for both parties. Realizing this, in the last decade U.S. car manufacturers have also moved to establish strong relationships with their suppliers to increase quality, and the reliability of their vehicles has increased as a result. However, costs remain high and in 2005 GM's biggest parts supplier, Delphi, sought bankruptcy protection and announced plans to cut over 20,000 jobs and reduce pay and benefits to allow it to reduce costs and survive in the increasingly cutthroat global carmaking business.

The Government

The government has several claims on an organization. It wants companies to compete in a fair manner and obey the rules of free competition. It also wants companies to obey agreed-upon rules and laws concerning the payment and treatment of employees, workers' health and workplace safety, nondiscriminatory hiring practices, and other social and economic issues about which Congress has enacted legislation. The government makes a contribution to the organization by standardizing regulations so that they apply to all companies and so that no company can obtain an unfair competitive advantage. The government controls the rules of good business practice and has the power to punish any company that breaks these rules by taking legal action against it. Since the company scandals of the early 2000s, many analysts have argued that more stringent rules are needed to govern many aspects of the way businesses function. They point to the need to control the relationship between a company and the accounting firm that audits its books by, for example, limiting the number of years such a relationship can endure.

Trade Unions

The relationship between a trade union and an organization can be one of conflict or cooperation. The nature of the relationship has a direct effect on the productivity and effectiveness of the organization and the union. Cooperation between managers and the union can lead to positive long-term outcomes if both parties agree on an equitable division of the gains from an improvement in a company's fortunes. Managers and the union might agree, for example, to share the gains from cost savings due to productivity improvements that resulted from a flexible work schedule. Traditionally, however, the management–union relationship has been antagonistic because unions' demands for increased benefits conflict directly with shareholders' demands for greater company profits and thus greater returns on their investments.

Local Communities

Local communities have a stake in the performance of organizations because employment, housing, and the general economic well-being of a community are strongly affected by the success or failure of local businesses. The fortunes of Seattle, for example, are closely tied to the fortunes of the Boeing Corporation, and Austin to those of Dell and other computer companies.

The General Public

The public is happy when organizations do well against overseas competitors. This is hardly surprising, given that the current and future wealth of a nation is closely related to the success of its businesses and economic institutions. The French and Italians, for example, prefer domestically produced cars and other products, even when foreign products are clearly superior. To some degree, they are induced by pride in their country to contribute to their country's organizations by buying their products. Typically, U.S. consumers do not support their companies in the same way. They prefer competition to loyalty as the means to ensure the future health of U.S. businesses.

A nation's public also wants its corporations to act in a socially responsible way, which means that corporations refrain from taking any actions that may injure or impose costs on other stakeholders. In the 1990s, for example, a scandal rocked United Way of America after it was revealed that its president, William Aramony, had misused the agency's funds for lavish personal expenditures. To encourage past contributors, including large donors like Xerox and General Electric, not to withhold contributions, United Way appointed Elaine L. Chao, the former head of the Peace Corps and an experienced investment banker, as the new president of the organization. She quickly introduced strict new financial controls and staved off a serious decline in public contributions. Within a few years the scandal was forgotten and contributions had returned to their former levels.

ORGANIZATIONAL EFFECTIVENESS: SATISFYING STAKEHOLDERS' GOALS AND INTERESTS

An organization is used simultaneously by different groups of stakeholders to accomplish their goals. The contributions of all stakeholders are needed for an organization to be viable and to accomplish its mission of producing goods and services. Each stakeholder group is motivated to contribute to the organization by its own set of goals, and each group evaluates the effectiveness of the organization by judging how well it meets the group's specific goals.[11]

Shareholders evaluate an organization by the return they receive on their investment; customers, by the reliability and value of its products relative to their price; and managers and employees, by their salaries, stock options, conditions of employment, and career prospects. Often these goals conflict, and stakeholder groups must bargain over the appropriate balance between the inducements that they should receive and the contributions that they should make. For this reason, organizations are often regarded as alliances or coalitions of stakeholder groups that directly (and indirectly) bargain with each other and use their power and influence to alter the balance of inducements and contributions in their favor.[12] An organization is viable as long as a dominant coalition of stakeholders has control over sufficient inducements so that it can obtain the contributions it needs from other stakeholder groups. Enron and WorldCom collapsed when their illegal actions became public and their stakeholders refused to contribute: Shareholders sold their stock, banks refused to lend money, and debtors called in their loans.

There is no reason to assume, however, that all stakeholders will be equally satisfied with the balance between inducements and contributions. Indeed, the implication of the coalition view of organizations is that some stakeholder groups have priority over others. To be effective, however, an organization must at least minimally satisfy the interests of all the groups that have a stake in the organization.[13] The claims of each group must be addressed: Otherwise, a group might withdraw its support and injure the future performance of the organization, such as when banks refuse to lend a company money, or a group of employees goes out on strike. When all stakeholder interests are minimally satisfied, the relative power of a stakeholder group to control the distribution of inducements determines how an organization will attempt to satisfy different stakeholder goals and what criteria stakeholders will use to judge its effectiveness.

Problems that an organization faces as it tries to win stakeholders' approval include choosing which stakeholder goals to satisfy, deciding how to allocate organizational rewards to different stakeholder groups, and balancing short-term and long-term goals.

Competing Goals

Organizations exist to satisfy stakeholders' goals, but who decides which goals to strive for and which goals are most important? An organization's choice of goals has political and social implications. In a capitalistic country like the United

States, it is taken for granted that shareholders who are the owners of an organization's accumulated wealth or capital—its machines, buildings, land, and goodwill—have first claim on the value it creates. According to this view, the job of managers is to maximize shareholder wealth, and the best way to do this is to maximize the organization's return on the resources and capital invested in the business (a good measure of an organization's effectiveness relative to other organizations).

Is maximizing shareholder wealth always management's primary goal? According to one argument, it is not. When shareholders delegate to managers the right to coordinate and use organizational skills and resources, a divorce of ownership and control occurs.[14] Although in theory managers are the employees of shareholders, in practice—because managers have control over organizational resources—this gives them real control over the company even though shareholders own it. The result is that managers may follow goals that promote their own interests and not the interests of shareholders.[15]

An attempt to maximize stockholder wealth, for example, may involve taking risks into uncharted territory and making capital investments in R&D that may bear fruit only in the long term, as new inventions and discoveries generate new products and a stream of new revenues. Managers, however, may prefer to maximize short-term profits because that is the goal on which they are evaluated by their peers and by stock market analysts who do not take the long-term view.[16]

Another view is that managers prefer a quiet life in which risks are small, and they have no incentive to be entrepreneurial because they control their own salaries. Moreover, because managers' salaries are closely correlated with organizational size, managers may prefer to pursue low-risk strategies even though these may not maximize return on invested capital. For these reasons the goals of managers and shareholders may be incompatible, but because managers are in the organizational driver's seat shareholder goals are not the ones most likely to be followed.

But even if all stakeholders agreed upon the goals that an organization should follow, selecting goals that will enhance an organization's chances of survival and future prosperity is no easy task. Suppose managers decide to pursue the primary goal of maximizing shareholder wealth. How should they strive to achieve this goal? Should managers try to increase efficiency and reduce costs to improve profitability or improve quality? Should they increase the organization's ability to influence its outside stakeholders and invest billions to become a global company? Should they invest organizational resources in new R&D projects that will increase its competences in innovation, something vital in high-tech industries? An organization's managers could take any of these actions to achieve the goal of maximizing shareholder wealth.

As you can see, there are no easy rules to follow; in many ways, being effective means making more right choices than wrong choices. One thing is certain, however: An organization that does not pay attention to its stakeholders and does not attempt to satisfy their interests at least minimally will lose legitimacy in their eyes and be doomed to failure. The importance of using organizational ethics to avoid this outcome is discussed later in the chapter.

Allocating Rewards

Another major problem that an organization has to face is how to allocate the profits it earns as a result of being effective among the various stakeholder groups. That is, managers must decide which inducements or rewards each group should receive. An organization needs to minimally satisfy the expectations of each group. But when rewards are more than enough to meet each group's minimum need, how should the "extra" rewards be allocated? How much should the workforce or managers receive relative to shareholders? What determines the appropriate reward for managers? Most people answer that managerial rewards should be determined by the organization's effectiveness. But this answer raises another question: What are the best indicators of effectiveness on which to base managerial rewards? Short-term profit? Long-term wealth maximization? Organizational growth? The choice of different criteria leads to different

Since the 1990s, there has been an increasing trend for medical doctors to become stockholders in the hospitals and clinics in which they work. Sometimes teams of doctors in a particular area join to open their own clinic. Other times, large hospital chains give doctors stock in the hospital. Such a trend has the potential to cause a major conflict of interest between doctors and their patients.

Take the case of the Columbia/HCA hospital chain. In 1993, Columbia began offering doctors a financial stake in their chain, a move to encourage doctors to send their patients to a Columbia hospital for treatment.[17] However, when they become owners, doctors then might have the incentive to give their patients minimum standard care in order to cut costs and increase the hospital's bottom line, or more likely to overcharge patients for their services and reap extra profits that way. In addition, the financial link between doctors and hospitals means that other hospitals that may have better records at minimizing postoperative infections, or better history in general patient care, will not be used by these doctors.

Clearly, the potentially competing goals of doctors and patients when doctors are shareholders have important implications for managing stakeholder interests. Indeed, there has been some support for banning doctors from holding a financial stake in their own clinics and hospitals. In 2002, a major HMO owned by its doctors settled charges that it used its power to demand lower prices from its suppliers and high fees from patients. However, doctors claim that they are in the same situation as lawyers or accountants, and there is no more reason to suppose that they will take advantage of their patients than accountants their clients.

answers to the question. Indeed, in the 1980s a CEO's average salary was about 40 times greater than the average worker; by the 2000s, the CEO's salary was *400* times greater and this number is increasing! Can this kind of huge increase be justified? More and more, given the many examples of corporate greed, analysts are saying no, and some have called for an across-the-board decrease in CEO pay or for Congress to pass legislation to regulate CEO salaries in some way.

The same kinds of consideration are true for other organizational members. What are the appropriate rewards for a middle manager who invents a new process that earns the organization millions of dollars a year, or for the workforce as a whole when the company is making record profits? Should they be given company stock or short-term bonuses? Should an organization guarantee long-term or lifetime employment as the ultimate inducement for good performance? Similarly, should shareholders receive regular dividend payments, or should all profits be reinvested in a company to increase its skills and resources? The way in which these goals can come into conflict is illustrated in the preceding organizational insight.

The allocation of rewards, or inducements, is an important component of organizational effectiveness because the inducements offered to stakeholders now determine their motivation—that is, the form and level of their contributions—in the future. Stakeholders' future investment decisions depend on the return they expect from their investments, whether the returns are in the form of dividends, stock options, bonuses, or wages. It is in this context that the roles of top managers and boards of directors become important, because they are the stakeholder groups that possess the power to determine the level of reward or inducements each group—including themselves—will ultimately receive. As the employees and shareholders of Enron, who lost almost all the value of their pensions and shares found out, directors and top managers often do not perform their roles well.

TOP MANAGERS AND ORGANIZATIONAL AUTHORITY

Because top management is the stakeholder group that has the ultimate responsibility for setting company goals and objectives, and for allocating organizational resources to achieve these objectives, it is useful to take a closer look at these top managers. Who are they, what roles and functions do they perform, and how do managers cooperate to run a company's business?

Authority is the power to hold people accountable for their actions and to influence directly what they do and how they do it. The stakeholder group with ultimate authority over the use of a corporation's resources is shareholders. Legally, they own the company and exercise control over it through their representatives, the board of directors. Through the board, shareholders delegate to managers the legal authority and responsibility to use the organization's resources to create value and to meet goals (see Figure 2.1). Accepting this authority and responsibility from shareholders and the board of directors makes corporate managers accountable for the way they use resources and for how much value the organization creates.

The board of directors monitors corporate managers' activities and rewards corporate managers who pursue activities that satisfy stakeholder goals. The board has

Authority
The power to hold people accountable for their actions and to make decisions concerning the use of organizational resources.

Figure 2.1
The Top-Management Hierarchy

This chart shows the ranking of the positions in the hierarchy, not necessarily the typical reporting relationships.

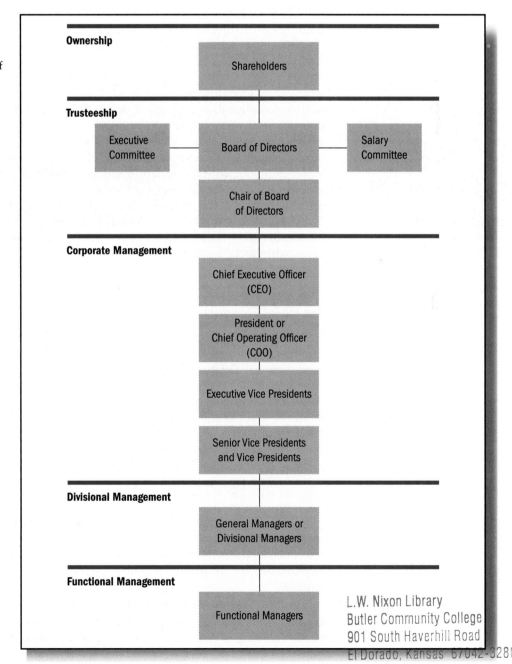

the legal authority to hire, fire, and discipline corporate management. The chair of the board of directors is the principal representative of the shareholders and, as such, has the most authority in an organization. Through the executive committee, which consists of the organization's most important directors and top managers, the chair has the responsibility for monitoring and evaluating the way corporate managers use organizational resources. The position of the chair and the other directors is one of trusteeship: They act as trustees to protect the interests of shareholders and other stakeholders. The salary committee sets the salaries and terms of employment for corporate managers.

There are two kinds of directors: inside directors and outside directors. Inside directors are directors who also hold offices in a company's formal hierarchy; they are full-time employees of the corporation. Outside directors are not employees of the company; many are professional directors who hold positions on the boards of many companies, or are executives of other companies who sit on other companies' boards. The goal of having outside directors is to bring objectivity to a company's decision making and to balance the power of inside directors, who obviously side with an organization's management. In practice, however, boards tend to be dominated by inside directors because these people have access to the most information about the company, and they can use that information to influence decision making in management's favor. Moreover, many outside directors tend to be passive and serve as rubber stamps for management's decisions. It has been claimed that many of the problems that arose in Enron, WorldCom, and other companies were the result of passive or captive directors, appointed by the CEO, who failed to exercise adequate supervision. Directors of some companies have been sued for their failure to do so and have paid millions in fines.[18]

Corporate-level management is the inside stakeholder group that has ultimate responsibility for setting company goals and objectives, for allocating organizational resources to achieve objectives, and for designing the organization's structure. Who are the corporate managers? What exactly do they do, and what roles do they play? Figure 2.1 shows the typical hierarchy of management titles and the **chain of command**, that is, the system of hierarchical reporting relationships of a large corporation. A **hierarchy** is a vertical ordering of organizational roles according to their relative authority.

Chain of command
The system of hierarchical reporting relationships in an organization.

Hierarchy
A classification of people according to authority and rank.

The Chief Executive Officer

The chief executive officer (CEO) is the person ultimately responsible for setting organizational strategy and policy. Even though the CEO reports to the chair of the board (who has the most legal authority), in a real sense the CEO is the most powerful person in the corporation because he or she controls the allocation of resources. The board of directors gives the CEO the power to set the organization's strategy and use its resources to create value. Often the same person is *both* chief executive officer and chair of the board. A person who occupies both positions wields considerable power and directly links the board to corporate management.

How does a CEO actually affect the way an organization operates? A CEO can influence organizational effectiveness and decision making in five principal ways.[19]

1. *The CEO is responsible for setting the organization's goals and designing its structure.* The CEO allocates authority and task responsibilities so that resources are coordinated and motivated to achieve organizational goals. Different organizational structures promote different methods of coordinating and motivating resources.

2. *The CEO selects key executives to occupy the topmost levels of the managerial hierarchy.* This sort of staffing is a vital part of the CEO's job because the quality of decision making is directly affected by the abilities of the organization's top managers. The CEO of General Electric, for example, personally selects and promotes

GE's 100 top managers and approves the promotions of 600 other executives.[20] By choosing key personnel, the CEO determines the values, norms, and culture that emerge in the organization. The culture determines the way organization members approach problems and make decisions: Are they entrepreneurial or are they conservative?

3. *The CEO determines top management's rewards and incentives.* The CEO influences the motivation of top managers to pursue organizational goals effectively. Even though they knew Enron was collapsing, in the days before, its top managers decided to award themselves over $80 million in compensation for their "work." In 2002, a judge in Houston opened the way for representatives of its shareholders to go after this money and other money its top executives had extracted from the company. The same was true at Tyco, where its top three executives were accused of looting hundreds of millions of dollars from the company.

4. *The CEO controls the allocation of scarce resources such as money and decision-making power among the organization's functional areas or business divisions.* This control gives the CEO enormous power to influence the direction of the organization's future value-creation activities—the kinds of products the company will make, the markets in which it will compete, and so on. Henry Ford III won back the CEO's job at Ford after its former CEO, Jacques Nasser, came under criticism after spending tens of billions on countless global projects that had done little to increase the company's profitability. Ford's philosophy is that his managers must prove their projects will make money before he will allow funds to be spent. CEO Ford has not been much more successful than former CEOs, however, and the company's global car sales dropped by 15% in 2005.

5. *The CEO's actions and reputation have a major impact on inside and outside stakeholders' views of the organization and affect the organization's ability to attract resources from its environment.* A CEO's personality and charisma can influence an organization's ability to obtain money from banks and shareholders and influence customers' desire to buy a company's products. So can a reputation for honesty and integrity and a track record of making sound, ethical business decisions.

The ability to influence organizational decision making and managerial behavior gives the CEO enormous power to directly influence organizational effectiveness. This power is also indirect, for CEOs influence decision making through the people they appoint or the organizational structure or culture they create and leave behind them as their legacy. Thus the top management team that the CEO creates is critical not only to the organization's success now, but in the future as well.

The Top Management Team

After the chair and CEO, the chief operating officer (COO), who is next in line for the CEO's job, or president, who may or may not be the CEO's successor, is the next most important executive. The COO or president reports directly to the CEO, and together they share the principal responsibility for managing the business. In most organizations, a division of labor takes place at the top between these two roles. Normally, the CEO has primary responsibility for managing the organization's relationship with external stakeholders and for planning the long-term strategic objectives of the organization as a whole and all its business divisions. The COO or president has primary responsibility for managing the organization's internal operations to make sure that they conform to the organization's strategic objectives. In a large company the COO also oversees the operation of its most important business divisions and units.

At the next level of top management are the executive vice presidents. People with this title have responsibility for overseeing and managing a company's most significant line and staff responsibilities. A **line role** is held by managers who have direct responsibility for the production of goods and services. An executive vice

Line role
Managers who have direct responsibility for the production of goods and services.

president, for example, might have overall responsibility for overseeing the performance of all 200 of a company's chemical divisions or all of a company's international divisions. A **staff role** is held by managers who are in charge of a specific organizational function such as sales or R&D. For example, the executive vice president for finance manages an organization's overall financial activities, and the executive vice president for R&D oversees a company's research operations. Staff roles are advisory only; they have no direct production responsibilities, but their occupants possess enormous influence on decision making.

The CEO, COO, and the executive vice presidents are at the top of an organization's chain of command. Collectively, managers in these positions form a company's **top management team**, the group of managers who report to the CEO and COO and help the CEO set the company's strategy and its long-term goals and objectives.[21] All the members of the top management team are **corporate managers**, whose responsibility is to set strategy for the corporation as a whole.

The way the CEO handles the top management team and appoints people to it is a vital part of the CEO's task. When for example, the CEO appoints the COO, he or she is sending a clear signal to the top management team about the kinds of issues and events that are of most importance to the organization. Often, for example, an organization will pick a new CEO, or appoint a COO who has the functional and managerial background that can deal with the most pressing issues facing a corporation. Many companies carefully select a successor to the CEO to develop a long-term orientation; obviously, appointment to the top management team is the first step in this process of developing the future CEO.[22] More and more, the composition of the top management team is becoming one of the main priorities of the CEO and of a company's board of directors.

Other Managers

At the next level of management are a company's senior vice presidents and vice presidents, senior corporate-level managers in both line and staff functions. A large company like AOL–Time Warner or GM has hundreds or thousands of corporate-level managers. Also, at this level are those managers who head one of a company's many operating companies or divisions and who are known as general managers. In practice, general managers of the divisions commonly have the title of CEO of their divisions because they have direct line responsibility for their division's performance and normally report to the corporate CEO or COO. However, they set policy only for the division they head, not for the whole corporation, and are **divisional managers**, not corporate managers. Inside Ford, for example, are the divisional managers responsible for the operation of each of its carmaking divisions or units.

An organization or a division of an organization also has functional managers with titles such as marketing manager or production manager. **Functional managers** are responsible for developing the functional skills and capabilities that collectively provide the core competencies that give the organization its competitive advantage. Each division, for example, has a set of functional managers who report to the general or divisional manager.

AN AGENCY THEORY PERSPECTIVE

Agency theory offers a useful way of understanding the complex authority relationship between top management and the board of directors. An agency relation arises whenever one person (the principal) delegates decision-making authority or control over resources to another (the agent). Starting at the top of a company's hierarchy of authority, shareholders are the principals; top management are their agents, appointed by shareholders to utilize organizational resources most effectively. The

---

Staff role
Managers who are in charge of a specific organizational function such as sales or R&D.

Top management team
A group of managers who report to the CEO and COO and help the CEO set the company's strategy and its long-term goals and objectives.

Corporate managers
The members of top management teams whose responsibility is to set strategy for the corporation as a whole.

Divisional managers
Managers who set policy only for the division they head.

Functional managers
Managers who are responsible for developing the functional skills and capabilities that collectively provide the core competences that give the organization its competitive advantage.

Agency problem
A problem in determining managerial accountability which arises when delegating authority to managers.

average shareholder, for example, has no in-depth knowledge of a particular industry or how to run a company. They appoint experts in the industry—managers—to perform this work for them. However, in delegating authority to managers an **agency problem**—a problem in determining managerial accountability—arises. This is because if you employ an expert manager, by definition that person must know more than you; how then can you question the decisions of the expert and the way managers are running the company? Moreover, the results of managers' performance can be evaluated only after considerable time has elapsed. Consequently, it is very difficult to hold managers accountable for what they do. Most often shareholders don't until it is too late—when the company suffers billion-dollar losses. In delegating authority, to a large extent shareholders lose their ability to influence managerial decision making in a significant way.

The problem is that shareholders or principals are at an *information disadvantage* as compared to top managers. It is very difficult for them to judge the effectiveness of a top management team's actions when this can often only be judged over several years. Moreover, as noted earlier, there may be a divergence in the goals and interests of managers and shareholders. Managers may prefer to pursue courses of action that lead to short-term profits, or short-term control over the market, while shareholders might prefer actions that lead to long-term profitability such as increased efficiency and long-term innovation.

The Moral Hazard Problem

When these two conditions exist so that (1) the principal finds it very difficult to evaluate how well the agent has performed because the agent possesses an information advantage, and (2) the agent has an incentive to pursue goals and objectives that are different from the principal's, a *moral hazard* problem exists. Here, agents have the opportunity and incentive to pursue their own interests. For example, in 2005 Time Warner, the entertainment giant, came under attack because its top management had made many acquisitions (such as AOL) that had not led to increased innovation, efficiency, and higher profits. Shareholders felt Time Warner's top management team was pursuing the wrong strategies to increase the company's profitability; for example, they wanted the company to divest AOL and its TV cable business quickly. Shareholders felt its top managers were avoiding confronting the hard issues; they began to demand (1) a change in the direction and goals of the company and (2) more financial information to reduce their information disadvantage. In short, they wanted more control over the affairs of the corporation to overcome the agency problem.

Other more specific examples of moral hazard are regularly reported in the press, such as when former newspaper tycoon Conrad Black and other top managers of his Hollinger empire were charged with racketeering, obstruction of justice, money laundering, cheating on taxes, and looting more than $80 million from the company through a series of fraudulent payments linked to the sale of several hundred U.S. and Canadian publishing properties. Prosecutors allege that Black, whose holdings once included *The Daily Telegraph* of London and other major papers, misused company perks such as taking the corporate jet for a vacation in Bora Bora and throwing a lavish birthday party for his wife. Even after his indictment, in May 2005 surveillance cameras at Hollinger Inc.'s Toronto headquarters caught former CEO Conrad Black red-handed, making off with cartons of files through a back door, flouting a court order baring his entry while under criminal and securities investigations.[23] Black faces the prospect of 95 years in prison and a $7 million fine.

Also in 2005 American Express filed suit against Savvis Inc. and its CEO, Robert McCormick, for failing to pay McCormick's $241,000 one-night tab at a Manhattan topless club. Although McCormick claimed he only charged $20,000, the club provided AmEx with signed receipts for the full sum. Savvis placed its CEO on unpaid leave.[24] Clearly, top managers have enormous opportunities to pursue their own interests at the expense of other stakeholders.

Solving the Agency Problem

Governance mechanisms
The forms of control which align the interests of principal and agent so that both parties have the incentive to work together to maximize organizational effectiveness.

In agency theory, the central issue is to overcome the agency problem by using **governance mechanisms**, or forms of control that align the interests of principal and agent so that both parties have the incentive to work together to maximize organizational effectiveness. There are many different kinds of governance mechanisms.

First, the principal role of the board of directors is to monitor top managers' activities, question their decision making and strategies, and intervene, when necessary. Some have argued for a clear separation between the role of CEO and chair to curb the CEO's power, arguing that the huge increase in CEO pay is evidence of the need to prevent abuses of power. Another vital task here is to reinforce and develop the organization's code of ethics.

The next step in solving the agency problem is to find the right set of incentives to align the interests of managers and shareholders. Recall that it is very difficult for shareholders to monitor and evaluate the effectiveness of managers' decisions because the results of these can only be assessed after several years have elapsed. Thus, basing rewards on decisions is often not an effective alignment strategy. The most effective way of aligning interests between management and shareholders is to make managers' rewards contingent on the outcomes of their decisions, that is, contingent on organizational performance. There are several ways of doing this, each of which has advantages and disadvantages.

Stock-Based Compensation Schemes

Stocks-based compensation schemes
Monetary rewards in the form of stocks or stock options that are linked to the company's performance.

Stock-based compensation schemes are one way of achieving this. Here, managers receive a large part of their monetary reward in the form of stocks or stock options that are linked to the company's performance. If the company does well, then the value of their stock options and monetary compensation is much enhanced. Effectively, interests are aligned because managers become stockholders. This strategy has been used in some companies like GM and IBM, where traditionally top managers had very low stock ownership in the corporation. The board of directors insisted that top managers purchase stock in the companies and awarded stock options as a means of increasing top managers' stake in the company's long-term performance.

Promotion Tournaments and Career Paths

Incentives can also take other forms. One way of linking rewards to performance over the long term is by developing organizational career paths that allow managers to rise to the top of the organization. The power of the CEO role is something that many top managers aspire to; a board of directors demoting some top executives and promoting or hiring new ones—often from the outside—can send a clear signal to top managers about what kinds of behaviors will be rewarded in the future. All organizations have "promotion tournaments," where executives compete for limited promotion opportunities by displaying their superior skills and competencies. By directly linking promotion to performance, the board of directors can send a clear signal about managerial behaviors that will lead to promotion—and make managers focus on long-term, not short-term, objectives.

The reward from promotion to the top is not just the long-term monetary package that goes with promotion, but it also includes the opportunity to exercise power over resources, and the prestige, status, and intrinsic satisfaction that accompany the journey to the top of the organization.

The issue of designing corporate governance mechanisms to ensure long-term effectiveness is complex and one that is currently stirring enormous debate.[25] Congress has enacted some new governance mechanisms and more are planned. In 2002, for example, Congress passed the Sarbanes–Oxley Act, which introduced a new requirement that CEOs sign off on company balance statements so they can be held personally and legally liable for accidental or deliberate mistakes found later. This requirement has led organizations to more fully disclose their financial results. Similarly, new rules for governing relations between companies and their accountants are being developed, as are new regulations that will force companies to show shareholders exactly how stock options and top management compensation are affecting the bottom line. In 2005, guidelines for setting CEO compensation were also proposed and issues of regulating CEO pay are on the agenda.

Indeed, stockholders' rights have become increasingly important in the 2000s as company after company has admitted that they broke business laws and regulations. In 2002, for example, Salomon Smith Barney agreed to pay a $5 million fine to settle charges that one of their star brokers was promoting a stock to investors even though internal emails suggested the stock was a dog. Brokers at Merrill Lynch were also found to have done a similar thing, privately laughing about the poor prospects of companies whose stocks they nevertheless continued to recommend to their thousands of investors. In 2004, many major mutual fund companies admitted they had allowed their fund managers and large investors to make stock market trades that earned them millions of dollars but hurt millions of small investors. In 2005, many large insurance companies admitted they had paid "kickbacks" to brokers to obtain their business, something that artificially raised the cost of insurance policies to customers. All these companies have paid hundreds of millions in fines to settle these charges, and their top managers, many of whom possessed enormous influence in their industries, have been fired. The way in which Amazon.com approaches corporate governance issues is summarized in Table 2.2.

Table 2.2   Amazon.Com, Inc., Board of Directors Guidelines on Corporate Governance Issues[26]

I. Responsibility of the Board

The Board of Directors is responsible for the control and direction of the Company. It represents and is accountable only to shareowners. The Board's primary purpose is to build long-term shareowner value.

II. Board Composition

The Board believes that there should at all times be a majority of independent directors on the Board. The Board also believes it is appropriate that the Chief Executive Officer serve as a director. An independent director is a person that meets the definition of independent under applicable NASDAQ requirements and does not have any other relationship with Amazon.com that, in the opinion of the Board, would interfere with the exercise of independent judgment in carrying out director responsibilities.

III. Board Membership

The full Board, on the recommendation of the Nominating and Corporate Governance Committee, nominates candidates for election to the Board. In selecting candidates for recommendation to the Board, the Nominating and Corporate Governance Committee considers all aspects of a candidate's qualifications in the context of the needs of the Company at that point in time with a view to creating a Board with a diversity of experience and perspectives. Among the qualifications, qualities and skills of a candidate considered important by the Nominating and Corporate Governance Committee are a commitment to representing the long-term interests of the shareowners; an inquisitive and objective perspective; the willingness to take appropriate risks; leadership ability; personal and professional ethics, integrity and values; practical wisdom and sound judgment; and business and professional experience in fields such as operations, technology, finance or marketing.

IV. Stock Ownership

Each director is required to make an investment in Amazon.com within one year of election.

V. Code of Business Conduct and Ethics

Directors must abide by the relevant provisions of the Company's Code of Business Conduct and Ethics.

VI. Executive Performance and Succession; Executive and Board Compensation

The Board will review its own performance and the performance of the CEO and will set goals at least annually. The CEO will review succession planning and leadership development with the Board at least annually. The independent directors will consult together privately (without the presence of the CEO or any other employee director) on an informal basis periodically to review the compensation and performance of the CEO and the other executive officers.

TOP MANAGERS AND ORGANIZATIONAL ETHICS

Ethical dilemma
The quandary people find themselves in when they have to decide if they should act in a way that might help another person or group even though doing so might go against their own self-interest.

A very important mechanism of corporate governance, and one that has become increasingly significant for a board of directors to emphasize after the recent corporate scandals, is to insist that managers follow ethical guidelines in their decision making when confronted with an ethical dilemma. An **ethical dilemma** is the quandary people find themselves in when they have to decide if they should act in a way that might help another person or group, and is the "right" thing to do, even though doing so might go against their own self-interest. A dilemma may also arise when a person has to decide between two different courses of action, knowing that whichever course he or she chooses will result in harm to one person or group even while it may benefit another. The ethical dilemma here is to decide which course of action is the "lesser of two evils."

People often know they are confronting an ethical dilemma when their moral scruples come into play and cause them to hesitate, debate, and reflect upon the "rightness" or "goodness" of a course of action. Moral scruples are thoughts and feelings that tell a person what is right or wrong; they are a part of a person's ethics. **Ethics** are the inner-guiding moral principles, values, and beliefs that people use to analyze or interpret a situation and then decide what is the "right" or appropriate way to behave. At the same time, ethics also indicate what inappropriate behavior is and how a person should behave to avoid doing harm to another person.

Ethics
Moral principles or beliefs about what is right or wrong.

The essential problem in dealing with ethical issues, and thus solving moral dilemmas, is that there are no absolute or indisputable rules or principles that can be developed to decide if an action is ethical or unethical. Put simply, different people or groups may dispute which actions are ethical or unethical depending on their own personal self-interests and specific attitudes, beliefs, and values. How, therefore, are we and companies and their managers to decide what is ethical and so act appropriately toward other people and groups?

Ethics and the Law

The first answer to this question is that society as a whole, using the political and legal process, can lobby for and pass laws that specify what people and organizations can and cannot do. For example, there are many different kinds of laws, such as antitrust law and employment law, that exist to govern business. Laws also specify what sanctions or punishments will follow if those laws are broken. Different groups in society lobby for laws to be passed based on their own personal interests and beliefs with regard to what is right or wrong. The group that can summon most support is able to pass the laws that most closely align with its interests and beliefs. Once a law is passed, a decision about what the appropriate behavior is with regard to a person or situation is taken from the personally determined ethical realm to the societally determined legal realm. If you do not conform to the law, you can be prosecuted; if you are found guilty of breaking the law, you can be punished.

In studying the relationship between ethics and law, it is important to understand that *neither laws nor ethics are fixed principles* that remain constant over time. Ethical beliefs alter and change as time passes, and as they do so, laws change to reflect the changing ethical beliefs of a society. There are many types of behavior—such as theft, industrial espionage, the sale of unsafe products, and insider trading—that most, if not all, people currently believe are totally unacceptable and unethical and should therefore be illegal. There are also, however, many other kinds of actions and behaviors whose ethical nature is open to dispute. Some people might believe that a particular behavior—for example, top managers receiving stock options and bonuses worth hundreds of millions or outsourcing millions of jobs to lower cost locations abroad—is unethical and so should be made illegal. Others might argue that it is up to a company's board of directors to decide if such behaviors are ethical or not and thus whether a particular behavior should remain legal.

Although ethical beliefs lead to the development of laws and regulations to prevent certain behaviors or encourage others, laws themselves can and do change and disappear as ethical beliefs change. Thus, both ethical and legal rules are *relative*: No absolute or unvarying standards exist to determine how we should behave, and people are caught up in moral dilemmas all the time. Because of this we have to make ethical choices.

This highlights an important issue in understanding the relationship among ethics, law, and business. In the 2000s, many scandals plagued major companies such as Enron, Arthur Andersen, WorldCom, Tyco, Adelphia, and others. Managers in some of these companies clearly broke the law and used illegal means to defraud investors; in others, they acted unethically. At Enron, former chief financial officer Andrew Fastow and his wife pleaded guilty to falsifying the company's books so that they could siphon off tens of millions of Enron's money for their own use.

In other cases, some managers encouraged members of their company's board of directors to behave unethically and divert millions of dollars of company capital for their own personal use. At WorldCom, for example, former CEO Bernie Ebbers used his position to place six personal, long-time friends on its 13-member board of directors. Though this is not illegal, obviously these people would vote in his favor at board meetings. As a result of their support, Ebbers received huge stock options and a personal loan of over $150 million from WorldCom. In return, his supporters were well rewarded for being directors; for example, Ebbers allowed them to use WorldCom's corporate jets for a minimal cost—something that saved them hundreds of thousands of dollars a year—amongst other perks amounting to millions of dollars.

In the light of these events, some people said, "Well, what these people did was not illegal," implying that because such behavior was not illegal it was also not unethical. However, because behavior may not be illegal does *not* mean it is ethical; such behavior is clearly unethical. In many cases laws are passed *later* to close the loopholes and prevent unethical people, such as Fastow and Ebbers, from behaving in this way. In any event, in March 2005, Ebbers was found guilty of fraud and sentenced to 20 years in jail; many other executives from companies like Tyco and Adelphia have received similar sentences. Like ordinary people, managers must confront the need to decide what is appropriate and inappropriate as they use organizational resources to create products customers want to buy.

Ethics and Organizational Stakeholders

As noted earlier, ethics are moral principles or beliefs about what is right or wrong. These beliefs guide individuals in their dealings with other individuals and groups (stakeholders) and provide a basis for deciding whether a particular decision or behavior is right and proper.[27] Ethics help people determine moral responses to situations in which the best course of action is unclear. Ethics guide managers in their decisions about what to do in various situations. Ethics also help managers decide how best to respond to the interests of various organizational stakeholders.

In guiding a company's business, both its dealings with outside and inside stakeholders, top managers are constantly making choices about what is the right or appropriate way to deal with these stakeholders. For example, a company might wonder whether it should give advance notice to its employees and middle managers about impending layoffs or plant closings; whether it should issue a recall of its cars because of a known defect that may cause harm or injury to passengers; or whether it should allow its managers to pay bribes to government officials in foreign countries where corruption is the accepted way of doing business. In all these situations, managers are in a difficult situation because they have to balance their interests, and the interests of the organization, against the interests of other stakeholder groups. Essentially, they have to decide how to apportion the "helps and harms" that arise from an organization's actions among stakeholder groups. Sometimes, making a decision is easy because some obvious standard, value, or norm of behavior applies. In other cases, managers have trouble deciding what to do and experience an ethical dilemma when weighing or comparing the competing claims or rights of various stakeholder groups.[28]

Table 2.3 Utilitarian, Moral Rights, and Justice Models of Ethics

Utilitarian model
An ethical decision is a decision that produces the greatest good for the greatest number of people.

Managerial implications
Managers should compare and contrast alternative courses of action based on the benefits and costs of these alternatives for different organizational stakeholder groups. They should choose the course of action that provides the most benefits to stakeholders. For example, managers should locate a new manufacturing plant at the place that will most benefit its stakeholders.

Problems for managers
How do managers decide on the relative importance of each stakeholder group? How are managers to measure precisely the benefits and harms to each stakeholder group? For example, how do managers choose between the interests of stockholders, workers, and customers?

Moral rights model
An ethical decision is a decision that best maintains and protects the fundamental rights and privileges of the people affected by it. For example, ethical decisions protect people's rights to freedom, life and safety, privacy, free speech, and freedom of conscience.

Managerial implications
Managers should compare and contrast alternative courses of action based on the effect of these alternatives on stakeholders' rights. They should choose the course of action that best protects stakeholders' rights—for example, decisions that would involve significant harm to the safety or health of employees or customers are unethical.

Problems for managers
If a decision will protect the rights of some stakeholders and hurt the rights of others, how do managers choose which stakeholder rights to protect? For example, in deciding whether it is ethical to snoop on an employee, does an employee's right to privacy outweigh an organization's right to protect its property or the safety of other employees?

Justice model
An ethical decision is a decision that distributes benefits and harms among stakeholders in a fair, equitable, or impartial way.

Managerial implications
Managers should compare and contrast alternative courses of action based on the degree to which the action will promote a fair distribution of outcomes. For example, employees who are similar in their level of skill, performance, or responsibility should receive the same kind of pay. The allocation of outcomes should not be based on arbitrary differences such as gender, race, or religion.

Problems for managers
Managers must learn not to discriminate against people because of observable differences in their appearance or behavior. Managers must also learn how to use fair procedures to determine how to distribute outcomes to organizational members. For example, managers must not give people they like bigger raises than they give to people they do not like or bend the rules to help their favorites.

Philosophers have debated for centuries about the specific criteria that should be used to determine whether decisions are ethical or unethical. Three models for determining whether a decision is ethical—the utilitarian, moral rights, and justice models—are summarized in Table 2.3.[29]

In theory, each model offers a different and complementary way of determining whether a decision or behavior is ethical, and all three models should be used to sort out the ethics of a particular course of action. Ethical issues, however, are seldom clear-cut, and the interests of different stakeholders often conflict, so it is often extremely difficult for a decision maker to use these models to ascertain the most ethical course of action. For this reason many experts on ethics propose this practical guide to determining whether a decision or behavior is ethical.[30] A decision is probably acceptable on ethical grounds if a manager can answer "yes" to each of these questions:

1. Does my decision fall within the accepted values or standards that typically apply in the organizational environment?
2. Am I willing to see the decision communicated to all stakeholders affected by it—for example, by having it reported in newspapers or on television?
3. Would the people with whom I have a significant personal relationship, such as family members, friends, or even managers in other organizations, approve of the decision?

From a management perspective, an ethical decision is a decision that reasonable or typical stakeholders would find acceptable because it aids stakeholders, the organization, or society. By contrast, an unethical decision is a decision a manager

The Use of Animals in Cosmetics Testing

Along with other large cosmetics companies, Gillette, the well-known maker of razors and shaving-related products, has come under increasing attack for its use of animals in product testing to determine the safety and long-term effects of new product formulations. Gillette's managers have received hundreds of letters from angry adults and children who object to the use of animals in cosmetics testing because they regard such testing as cruel and unethical. Managers at several other companies have tried to avoid this ethical issue, but Gillette's managers have approached the problem head on. Gillette's ethical stance is that the health of people is more important than the health of animals, and no other reliable method that would be accepted by a court of law exists to test the properties of new formulations. Thus, if the company is to protect the interests of its stockholders, employees, and customers and develop new, safe products that consumers want to buy, it must conduct animal testing.

Gillette's managers respond to each letter protesting this policy and often even telephone children at home to explain their ethical position.[31] They emphasize that they use animals only when necessary, and they discuss their ethical position with their critics. Other cosmetics companies, such as The Body Shop, do not test their products on animals, however, and their managers are equally willing to explain their ethical stance to the general public: They think animal testing is unethical. However, even though The Body Shop does not directly test its products on animals, some of the ingredients in its products have been tested on animals by Gillette and other companies to ensure their safety.

Clearly, the ethics of animal testing is a difficult issue, as are most other ethical questions. The view of the typical stakeholder at present seems to be that animal testing is an acceptable practice as long as it can be justified in terms of benefits to people. At the same time, most stakeholders believe such testing should minimize the harm done to animals and be used only when necessary.

would prefer to disguise or hide from other people because it enables a company or a particular individual to gain at the expense of society or other stakeholders. How ethical problems arise, and how different companies respond to them, is profiled in the preceding organizational insight.

Ethical rules develop over time through negotiation, compromise, and bargaining among stakeholders. Ethical rules also can evolve from outright conflict and competition between different stakeholder groups where the ability of one group to impose their solution on another group decides which ethical rules will be followed. For example, employees might exert moral pressure on management to improve their working conditions or to give them warning of possible layoffs. Shareholders might demand that top management not invest their capital in countries that practice racism, or that employ children in factories under conditions close to slavery.[32] Over time, many ethical rules and values are codified into the law of a society, and from that point on unethical behavior becomes illegal behavior. Individuals and organizations are required to obey these legal rules and can be punished for not doing so.

Sources of Organizational Ethics

In order to understand the nature of an organization's ethical values, it is useful to discuss the sources of ethics. The three principal sources of ethical values that influence organizational ethics are (1) societal ethics, (2) group or professional ethics, and (3) individual ethics.

Societal Ethics

One important determinant of organizational ethics is societal ethics. Societal ethics are codified in a society's legal system, in its customs and practices, and in the unwritten norms and values that people use to interact with each other. Many ethical norms and values are followed automatically by people in a society because people have internalized society's values and made them part of their own. These internalized norms and values, in turn, reinforce what is taken as custom and practice in a society in people's dealings with one another. For example, ethics concerning the inalienable rights of the individual are the result of decisions made by members of a

In recent years, the number of U.S. companies that buy their inputs from low-cost foreign suppliers has been growing, and concern about the ethics associated with employing young children in factories has been increasing. In Pakistan, children as young as age 6 work long hours in deplorable conditions to make rugs and carpets for export to Western countries. Children in poor countries throughout Africa, Asia, and South America work in similar conditions. Is it ethical to employ children in factories, and should U.S. companies buy and sell products made by these children?

Opinions about the ethics of child labor vary widely. Robert Reich, an economist and secretary of labor in the first Clinton administration, believes that the practice is totally reprehensible and should be outlawed on a global level. Another view, championed by *The Economist* magazine, is that, although nobody wants to see children employed in factories, citizens of rich countries need to recognize that in poor countries children are often a family's only breadwinners. Thus, denying children employment would cause whole families to suffer, and one wrong (child labor) might produce a greater wrong (poverty). Instead, *The Economist* favors regulating the conditions under which children are employed and hopes that over time, as poor countries become richer, the need for child employment will disappear.

Many U.S. retailers typically buy their clothing from low-cost foreign suppliers, and managers in these companies have had to take their own ethical stance on child labor. Managers at Wal-Mart, Target, JC Penney, and K-mart have followed U.S. standards and rules and have policies that dictate that their foreign suppliers not employ child labor; they also vow to sever ties with any foreign supplier found to be in violation of this standard.

Apparently, however, retailers differ widely in the way they choose to enforce this policy. Wal-Mart and some others take a tough stance and immediately sever links with suppliers who break this rule. However, it has been estimated, for example, that more than 300,000 children under age 14 are being employed in garment factories in Guatemala, a popular low-cost location for clothing manufacturers that supply the U.S. market.[33] These children frequently work more than 60 hours a week and often are paid less than $2.80 a day, the minimum wage in Guatemala. Many U.S. retailers do not check up on their foreign suppliers. Clearly, if U.S. retailers are to be true to their ethical stance on this troubling issue, they cannot ignore the fact that they are buying clothing made by children, and they must do more to regulate the conditions under which these children work.

society about how they want to be treated by others. Ethics governing the use of bribery and corruption, or the general standards of doing business in a society, are the result of decisions made and enforced by people deciding what is appropriate in a society. These standards differ by society, and ethical values accepted in the United States are not accepted in other countries. For example, if I buy a pound of rice in India, I can expect that a certain percentage of that rice will be dust; moreover, I know that the more I pay for the rice the less dust I can expect. It is the custom and practice in India. In the United States, on the other hand, there are many complex rules governing the purity of foodstuffs that companies are required to follow by law. Although many U.S. organizations voluntarily provide layoff benefits, many do not. In general, the poorer a country is, the more likely are employees to be treated with little regard. One issue of particular ethical concern on a global level is the use of child labor, which is discussed in the preceding organizational insight.

When societal ethics are codified into law and then judged by the ethical standards of a society, all illegal behavior may be regarded as unethical behavior. An organization and its managers are legally required to follow all the laws of a society and to behave toward individuals and stakeholders according to the law. It is one of top management's main responsibilities to ensure that managers and employees below them in the organizational hierarchy are obeying the law, for top managers can be held accountable in certain situations for the performance of their subordinates. However, not all organizations behave according to the law. The typical kinds of crimes committed by these organizations are not only illegal: They may be also regarded as unethical to the extent they harm other stakeholder groups.

Professional Ethics

Professional ethics are the moral rules and values that a group of people uses to control the way they perform a task or use resources. For example, medical ethics control the way that doctors and nurses are expected to perform their tasks and help patients. Doctors are expected not to perform unnecessary medical procedures, to exercise due diligence, and to act in the patient's interest, not in their own. Scientific and technical researchers are expected to behave ethically in preparing and presenting their results in order to ensure the validity of their conclusions. As with society, most professional groups can enforce the ethics of their profession. For example, doctors and lawyers can be disbarred should they break the rules and put their own interests first.

In an organization, there are many groups of employees whose behavior is governed by professional ethics, such as lawyers, researchers, and accountants. People internalize the rules and values of their profession, just as they do those of society, and they follow these principles automatically in deciding how to behave.

Individual Ethics

Individual ethics are the personal and moral standards used by individuals to structure their interactions with other people. People may or may not perform certain actions or make certain decisions based upon these ethics. Many behaviors that one person may find unethical another person may find ethical. If those behaviors are not illegal, individuals may agree to disagree about their ethical beliefs or they may try to impose those beliefs on other people by attempting to make their ethical beliefs the law. If personal ethics conflict with law, a person may be subject to legal sanction. Many personal ethics follow society's ethics and have their origin in law. Personal ethics are also the result of a person's upbringing and may stem from family, friends, membership in a church, or other significant social institution. Personal ethics influence how a person will act in an organization. For example, managers' behavior toward other managers and toward subordinates will depend on the personal values and beliefs they hold.

These three sources collectively influence the ethics that develop inside an organization (organizational ethics); organizational ethics may be defined as the rules or standards used by an organization and its members in their dealings with other stakeholders groups. Each organization has a set of ethics; some of these are unique to the organization and are an important aspect of its culture, a topic discussed in detail in Chapter 7. However, many ethical rules go beyond the boundaries of any individual company. Companies, collectively, are expected to follow ethical and legal rules because of the advantages that are produced for a society and its members when its organizations and institutions behave ethically.

Why Do Ethical Rules Develop?

Ethical rules often develop to slow or temper the pursuit of self-interest. A good way to understand the self-interest issue is by studying the "tragedy of the commons" problem. When common land, that is, land owned by everyone, exists, it is rational for every person to maximize individual use of it because it is a free resource. So everybody will graze their cattle on the land to promote the individual interests of each. But if everybody does this, what happens to land, the common resource? The answer is that it is destroyed by erosion as overgrazing leaves it defenseless to the effects of wind and rain. Thus, the rational pursuit of individual self-interest results in a collective disaster. The same holds true in many organized situations: Left to their own devices, people will pursue their own goals at the expense of collective goals.

Ethical laws and rules emerge to control self-interested behavior by individuals and organizations that threatens society's collective interests. For example, laws establishing what is good or appropriate business practice develop because they provide benefits to everybody. Free and fair competition among organizations is only possible when rules and standards exist that constrain the actions that people can take in a certain situation. As a businessperson, it is ethical for me to compete with a rival and maybe drive that person out of business if I do so by legal means such as by producing a cheaper, better or more reliable product. However, it is not ethical for me to do so by shooting that person or by blowing up his factory. Competition by quality or price creates value for the consumer; competition by force results in monopoly and hurts the customer and the public interest. This is not to say that no one gets hurt—the rival I force out of business gets hurt—but the harm I do him has to be weighed against the gain to consumers and to myself.

Ethical issues are inherently complex ones where the problem is to distribute the helps and harms between different stakeholders. The issue is to try to act as people of goodwill and to try to follow the moral principles that seem to produce the most good. Ethical rules and moral codes develop to increase the value that can be produced by people when they interact with each other. They protect people. Without these rules, free and fair competition degenerates into conflict and warfare, and everybody loses. Another way of putting this is to say that ethical rules reduce the costs people have to bear to decide what is right or appropriate. Following an ethical rule avoids expending time and effort in deciding the right thing to do. In other words, ethical rules reduce *transaction costs* between people, that is, the costs of monitoring, negotiating, and enforcing agreements with other people. Transaction costs can be enormous when strangers meet to engage in business. For example, how do I trust the other person to behave ethically when I don't know that person? It is here again that the power of ethics is so important. If I can rely on the other person to follow the rules, I do not need to expend effort in monitoring the other person to make sure he performs as we agreed. Monitoring wastes my time and effort and is largely unproductive. When people share common ethics, this helps to reduce transaction costs.

Behavior that follows accepted ethical rules confers a *reputation effect* on an individual or an organization that also reduces transaction costs. If, over time, an organization becomes known for engaging in illegal acts, how will people view that organization? Most likely, with suspicion and hostility. However, suppose an organization always follows the rules and is known for its ethical business practices over and above strict legal requirements. It will have gained a good reputation, which is valuable because people will want to deal with that organization. Unethical organizations will be penalized because people will refuse to deal with them, proving that there are constraints on organizations beyond those of the law.

Reputation effects also help explain why managers and employees who work in organizations also follow ethical rules. Suppose an organization behaves unethically; what will be the position of its employees? To outsiders, employees come to be branded with the same reputation as the unethical organization because they are assumed to have performed according to its code of ethics. Even if the organization's unethical behavior was the product of a few self-seeking individuals, this will affect and harm all employees. For example, in Japan in the stock crash of the 1990s many brokerage firms went bankrupt, with irate clients suing these firms for disguising the real risks associated with investment in the inflated stock market. Employees of these firms found it very difficult to obtain jobs in other organizations because they were branded with the "shame" of having worked for these companies. Thus employees have the incentive for their firm to behave ethically because their fortunes are tied to the organization's fortunes. An organization's bad reputation will hurt their reputation, too. This is true at Arthur Andersen, Enron, and other disgraced companies whose employees suffered because of their former companies' bad reputations.[34]

One intangible reward that comes from behaving ethically is feeling good about one's behavior and enjoying the good conscience that comes with acting within the rules of the game. Success by stealth and deceit does not provide the same intangible reward as success from following the rules simply because it is not a fair test of ability or personal qualities. Personal reputation is the outcome of behaving ethically, and the esteem or respect of one's peers has always been a reward that people desire.

In sum, acting ethically promotes the good of a society and the well-being of its members. More value is created in societies where people follow ethical rules, and where criminal and unethical behavior are prevented by law and by custom and practice from emerging. Nevertheless, individuals and organizations do perform unethical and illegal acts.

Why Does Unethical Behavior Occur?

Although there are good reasons for individuals and organizations to behave ethically, there are also many reasons why unethical behavior takes place.

Personal Ethics

In theory, people learn ethical principles and moral codes as they mature as individuals in a society. Ethics are obtained from such sources as family and friends, churches, education, professional training, and from organizations of all kinds. From these, people learn to differentiate right from wrong in a society or in a social group. However, suppose you are the son or daughter of a mobster, or an enormously wealthy landed family, and your upbringing and education take place in such a context. You may come to believe that it is ethical to do anything and perform any act, up to and including murder, if it benefits your family's interests. These are your ethics. These are obviously not the ethics of the wider society and as such are subject to sanction, but in a similar way managers in an organization may come to believe that any actions that promote or protect the organization are more important than any harm the organization does to others.

Self-Interest

We normally confront ethical issues when we are weighing our personal interests against the effects of our actions on others. Suppose you know that you will get a promotion to vice president of your company if you can secure a $100 million contract, but you know that to get the contract you must bribe the contract-giver with $1 million. What would you do? On one hand, your career and future seem to be assured by performing this act, and what harm would it do? Bribery is common anyway, and if you don't pay the million you can be sure that somebody else will. So what do you do? Research seems to suggest that people who realize they have most at stake in a career sense or a monetary sense are the ones most likely to act unethically. Similarly it has been shown that organizations that are doing badly in an economic sense and are struggling to survive are the ones most likely to commit unethical and illegal acts such as collusion, price fixing, or bribery.

Outside Pressure

Many studies find that the likelihood of a person's engaging in unethical or criminal behavior is much greater when outside pressure exists for that person to do so. In Sears, for example, top managers' desires to increase performance led them to create a reward system that had the intentional or unintentional effect of making employees act unethically and overcharge consumers. Top managers can feel themselves to be under similar pressures from shareholders if company performance is deteriorating; under the threat of losing their jobs, they may engage in unethical behaviors to satisfy shareholders.

If all these pressures work in the same direction, we can easily understand how unethical organizational cultures such as those of Enron, WorldCom, and Arthur Andersen developed as managers bought into unethical acts and a generalized climate of "the end justifies the means" permeated these organizations. The organization becomes more defensive as organization members pull together to disguise their unethical actions and to protect one another from prosecution.

The temptation for organizations collectively to engage in unethical and illegal anticompetitive behavior is very great. Industry competitors can see quite clearly the advantages to acting together to raise prices because of the extra profits they will earn. The harm they inflict is much more difficult to see because their customers may number in the millions, and each is affected in such a small way that from the perspective of the companies they are hardly hurt at all. However, if every company in every industry behaved this way, and they all tried to extract money from their customers, customers would have much less to spend. This would result in a misallocation of society's resources as companies collectively spent less and less on improving their products—why should they? They could make all the money they wanted with the products they already made.

The social costs of unethical behavior are very hard to measure but they can be easily seen over the long run in the form of mismanaged, top heavy, and overbureaucratized organizations that become less innovative, spending less and less on research and development, and more and more on advertising or managerial salaries. When the environment changes or competitors arrive that refuse to play the game, the mismanaged empire starts to crumble—as happened at Tyco and WorldCom.

CREATING AN ETHICAL ORGANIZATION

In what ways can ethical behavior be promoted so that, at the very least, organizational members can resist temptation to engage in illegal acts that promote personal or organizational interests at the expense of society's interests? Ultimately, an organization is ethical if the people inside it are ethical. How can people judge whether they are making ethical decisions and thus acting ethically? They can use the rule discussed earlier concerning a person's willingness to have his or her action or decision shared with other people.

Beyond personal considerations, an organization can encourage people to act ethically by putting in place incentives for ethical behavior and disincentives to punish those who behave unethically. Because the board and top managers have the ultimate responsibility for setting policy, they establish the ethical culture of the organization. There are many ways in which they can influence organizational ethics. For example, a manager or board member outlining a company's position on business ethics acts as a figurehead and personifies the organization's ethical position. As a leader, a manager can promote moral values that result in the specific ethical rules and norms that people use to make decisions. Outside the organization, as a liaison or spokesperson, a manager can inform prospective customers and other stakeholders about the organization's ethical values and demonstrate those values through behavior toward stakeholders—such as by being honest and acknowledging errors. A manager also sets employees' incentives to behave ethically and can develop rules and norms that state the organization's ethical position. Finally, a manager can make decisions to allocate organizational resources and pursue policies based on the organization's ethical position.

Designing an Ethical Structure and Control System

Ethics influence the choice of the structure and culture that coordinate resources and motivate employees.[35] Managers can design an organizational structure that reduces the incentives for people to behave unethically. The creation of authority relationships and rules that promote ethical behavior and punish unethical acts, for example, will encourage members to behave in a socially responsible way. The federal government continually tries to improve the standards of conduct for employees of the executive branch. Standards cover ethical issues such as giving and receiving gifts, impartiality in government work and the assignment of contracts, conflicting financial interests, and outside work activities. These regulations affect approximately 5 million federal workers.[36] Often, an organization uses its mission statement to guide employees in making ethical decisions.[37]

Whistle-blowing occurs when an employee tells an outside person or agency, such as a government agency, a newspaper, or television reporter, about an organization's (its managers') illegal or immoral behavior. Employees typically become whistle-blowers when they feel powerless to prevent an organization from committing an unethical act or when they fear retribution from the company if they voice their concerns. However, an organization can take steps to make whistle-blowing an acceptable and rewarded activity.[38] Procedures that allow subordinates access to upper-level managers to voice concerns about unethical organizational behavior can be established. The position of ethics officer can be created to investigate claims of unethical behavior, and ethics committees can make formal ethical judgments. Ten percent of *Fortune* 500 companies have ethics officers who are responsible for keeping employees informed about organizational ethics, for training employees, and for investigating breaches of ethical conduct. Ethical values flow down from the top of the organization but are strengthened or weakened by the design of the organizational structure.

Creating an Ethical Culture

The values, rules, and norms that define an organization's ethical position are part of culture. The behavior of top managers strongly influences organizational culture. An ethical culture is most likely to emerge if top managers are ethical, and an unethical culture can become an ethical one if the top management team is changed. This transformation occurred at General Dynamics and other defense contracting firms where corruption was common at all levels, and over billing and cheating the government had become a popular managerial sport. But neither culture nor structure can make an organization ethical if its top managers are not ethical. The creation of an ethical corporate culture requires commitment at all levels of an organization, from the top down.[39]

Supporting the Interests of Stakeholder Groups

Shareholders are the owners of an organization. Through the board of directors they have the power to hire and fire top management and thus in theory can discipline managers who engage in unethical behavior. Shareholders want higher profits, but do they want them to be gained by unethical behavior? In general, the answer is no, because unethical behavior will make a company a riskier investment. If an organization loses its reputation, the value of its shares will be lower than the value of shares offered by firms that behave ethically. In addition, many shareholders do not want to hold stock in companies that engage in socially questionable activities. Amazon.com's ethical position, which is shaped by its beliefs about its obligations to its shareholders and, ultimately, to its customers, can be clearly seen in its message to shareholders (see Table 2.4).

Table 2.4
Amazon.com's "Message to Our Shareholders"[40]

A fundamental measure of our success will be the shareholder value we create over the long term. From the very beginning, our emphasis has been on the long term and as a result, we may make decisions and weigh trade-offs differently than some other companies. Accordingly, it is important for you, our shareholders, to understand our fundamental management and decision-making approach so that you may ensure that it is consistent with your own investment philosophy. We will continue to:

I. Focus relentlessly on our customers.
II. Make bold investment decisions in light of long-term leadership considerations rather than short-term profitability considerations. There is more innovation ahead of us than behind us, and to that end, we are committed to extending our leadership in e-commerce in a way that benefits customers and therefore, inherently, investors—you can't do one without the other. Some of these bold investments will pay off, others will not, but we will have learned a valuable lesson in either case.
III. Focus on cash. When forced to choose between optimizing the appearance of our GAAP accounting and maximizing the present value of future cash flows, we'll take the cash flows.
IV. Work hard to spend wisely and maintain our lean culture. We understand the importance of continually reinforcing a cost-conscious culture.
V. Focus on hiring and retaining versatile and talented employees, and weight their compensation to significant stock ownership rather than cash. We know our success will be largely affected by our ability to attract and retain a motivated employee base, each of whom must think like, and therefore must actually be, an owner.

We are firm believers that the long-term interests of shareholders are tightly linked to the interests of our customers. If we do our jobs right, today's customers will buy more tomorrow, we'll add more customers in the process, and it will all add up to more cash flow and more long-term value for our shareholders. As Amazonians, we thank you, our owners, for your support, your encouragement, and for joining us on this adventure. If you're a customer, we thank you again!

Pressure from outside stakeholders has become increasingly important in promoting ethical organizational behavior.[41] The government and its agencies, industry councils and regulatory bodies, and consumer watchdog groups all play a role in establishing the ethical rules that organizations should follow when doing business. Outside regulation sets the rules of the competitive game and, as noted earlier, plays an important part in creating and sustaining ethics in society.

Large organizations possess enormous power to benefit and harm society. But if corporations act to harm society and their own stakeholders, society will move to regulate and control business to minimize its ability to inflict harm. Societies, however, differ in the extent to which they are willing to impose regulations on organizations. In general, poor countries have the least restrictive regulations. In many countries, people pay large bribes to government officials to get permission to start a company; once in business, they operate unfettered by any regulations pertaining to child labor, minimum wages, or employee health and safety. In contrast, Americans take ethical behavior on these fronts for granted because laws as well as custom and practice discourage child labor, slave wages, and unsafe working conditions.

SUMMARY

Organizations are embedded in a complex social context that is driven by the needs and desires of its stakeholders. The interests of all stakeholders have to be considered when designing an organizational structure and culture that promotes effectiveness and curtails the ability of managers and employees to use organizational resources for their own ends or that damages the interests of other stakeholders. Creating an ethical culture, and making sure organizational members use ethical rules in their decision making, is a vital task for all those who have authority over organizational resources. Chapter 2 has made the following main points:

1. Organizations exist because of their ability to create value and acceptable outcomes for stakeholders. The two main groups of stakeholders are inside stakeholders and outside stakeholders. Effective organizations satisfy, at least minimally, the interests of all stakeholder groups.
2. Problems that an organization faces as it tries to win stakeholders' approval include choosing which stakeholder goals to satisfy, deciding how to allocate organizational rewards to different stakeholder groups, and balancing short- and long-term goals.
3. Shareholders delegate authority to managers to use organizational resources effectively. The CEO, COO, and top management team have ultimate responsibility for using those resources effectively.
4. The agency problem and moral hazard arise when shareholders delegate authority to managers, and governance mechanisms must be created to align the interests of shareholders and managers to ensure that managers behave in the interests of all stakeholders.
5. Ethics are the moral values, beliefs, and rules that establish the right or appropriate ways in which one person or stakeholder group should interact and deal with another. Organizational ethics are a product of societal, professional, and individual ethics.
6. The board of directors and top managers can create an ethical organization by designing an ethical structure and control system, creating an ethical culture, and supporting the interests of stakeholder groups.

DISCUSSION QUESTIONS

1. Give some examples of how the interests of different stakeholder groups may conflict.
2. What is the role of the top management team?
3. What is the agency problem? What steps can be taken to solve it?
4. Why is it important for managers and organizations to behave ethically?
5. Ask a manager to describe an instance of ethical behavior that she or he observed, and an instance of unethical behavior. What caused these behaviors, and what were the outcomes?
6. Search business magazines such as *Fortune* or *Business Week* for an example of ethical or unethical behavior, and use the material in this chapter to analyze it.

Practicing Organizational Theory: Creating a Code of Ethics

Form groups of three to five people, and appoint one group member as the spokesperson who will communicate your findings to the class when called on by the instructor. Then discuss the following scenario:

You are the managers of a large chain of supermarkets, and you have been charged with the responsibility for developing a code of ethics to guide the members of your organization in their dealings with stakeholders. To guide you in creating the ethical code, do the following:

1. Discuss the various kinds of ethical dilemmas that supermarket employees—checkers, pharmacists, stockers, butchers—may encounter in their dealings with stakeholders such as customers or suppliers.
2. Identify a specific behavior that the kinds of employees mentioned in item 1 might exhibit, and characterize it as ethical or unethical.
3. Based on this discussion, identify three standards or values that you will incorporate into the supermarket's ethical code to help determine whether a behavior is ethical or unethical.

The Ethical Dimension #2

Think about the last time that a person treated you unethically or you observed someone else being treated unethically; then, answer these questions.

1. What was the issue? Why do you think that person acted unethically?
2. What prompted them to behave in an unethical fashion?
3. Was the decision maker aware that he or she was acting unethically?
4. What was the outcome?

Making the Connection #2

Identify an organization whose managers have been involved in unethical actions toward one or more stakeholder groups or who have pursued their own self-interest at the expense of other stakeholders. What did they do? Who was harmed? What was the outcome of the incident?

Analyzing the Organization: Design Module #2

In this model you will identify your organization's major stakeholders, analyze the top management structure, investigate its code of ethics, and try to uncover its ethical stance.

Assignment

1. Draw a stakeholder map that identifies your organization's major stakeholder groups. What kinds of conflicts between its stakeholder groups would you expect to occur most often?
2. Using information on the company's Web site, draw a picture of its hierarchy of authority. Try to identify the members of the top management team. Is the CEO also the chair of the board of directors?
3. Does the company have divisional managers? What functional managers seem to be most important to the organization in achieving a competitive advantage? What is the functional background of the top management team?
4. Does the organization have a published code of ethics or ethical stance? What kinds of issues does it raise in this statement?
5. Search for information concerning the ethical or unethical behavior of the managers of your organization. What does this tell you about its ethical stance?

CASE FOR ANALYSIS

Ethical Stances at Johnson & Johnson and Dow Corning

In 1982, managers at Johnson & Johnson, the well-known maker of pharmaceutical and medical products, experienced a crisis. Seven people in the Chicago area had died after taking Tylenol capsules that had been laced with cyanide. Johnson & Johnson's top managers needed to decide what to do. The FBI advised them to take no action because the likelihood that supplies of Tylenol outside the Chicago area were contaminated was very low. Moreover, withdrawing the drug from the market would cost the company millions of dollars. Johnson & Johnson's managers were of a different mind, however. They immediately ordered that supplies of all Tylenol capsules in the U.S. market be withdrawn and sent back to the company, a move that eventually cost more than $150 million.

In 1992, managers at Dow Corning, a large pharmaceutical company that had pioneered the development of silicon breast implants, received disturbing news. An increasing number of reports from doctors throughout the United States indicated that many women who had received Dow Corning silicon breast implants were experiencing health problems ranging from fatigue to cancer and arthritis due to ruptured implants.[42] Dow Corning's managers believed that the available evidence did not prove that fluid leaking from the implants was the cause of these health problems. Nevertheless, a few months later, Dow Corning's chairman, Keith McKennon, announced that the company was discontinuing its breast implant business and closing the factories that produced them.

At first glance, it appears that the goal of managers at both companies was to protect their customers and that both companies behaved very responsibly. However, this was not the case. Soon after Dow Corning's withdrawal from the implant business, it became known that a Dow Corning engineer had questioned the safety of silicon breast implants as early as 1976. In 1977, the engineer had sent top managers a memo summarizing the results of a study by four doctors who reported that 52 out of 400 implant procedures had resulted in ruptures. In response to a court order, the company eventually released this memo, along with hundreds of other pages of internal documents. Women filed hundreds of lawsuits against Dow Corning for knowingly selling a product that may have been defective. Lawyers accused Dow Corning of deliberately misleading the public and of giving women whose implants had caused medical problems false information to protect the interests of the company.

The behavior of Dow Corning's managers seemed out of character to many people, for Dow Corning had widely publicized its well-developed ethics system, which monitored the behavior of its scientists and managers. Each of Dow Corning's main divisions was supposed to be visited by six of its top managers every three years. Top managers were charged with the responsibility of questioning employees about wrongdoing at any level and of helping to reveal ethical lapses that could be corrected. The results of this ethics audit were then to be reported to the company's board of directors. Obviously, this ethics system had not prevented Dow Corning's managers from behaving unethically toward customers with regard to its breast implant product.[43]

Johnson & Johnson also had an ethics system in place. At its center was a credo describing in detail Johnson & Johnson's ethical stance toward customers, employees, and other groups. Why did Johnson & Johnson's credo lead its managers to behave ethically while Dow Corning's ethics audit failed?

One reason appears to be that Johnson & Johnson's managers had internalized the company's ethical position. Thus, to them, the credo clearly represented the company's values, and they routinely followed the credo when they needed to make a decision that was likely to affect customers' health. At Dow Corning, in contrast, it appears that managers had been just going through the motions in their efforts to explore ethical issues and had not been taking appropriate steps to ensure that their own behavior was above reproach. Ethics experts agree that talking to large groups of employees every three years without an objective approach (the scientists' bosses were in the room listening to their subordinates' concerns or objections) was a poor way to uncover ethical lapses.[44]

DISCUSSION QUESTIONS

1. Why did the managers at the two organizations have different ethical stances toward their customers? (Hint: Go to Johnson & Johnson's Web site and look at its Code of Ethics).

2. Outline a series of steps Dow Corning's directors and managers should have taken to prevent this problem.

REFERENCES

1. T. Donaldson and L. E. Preston, "The Stakeholder Theory of the Corporation: Concepts, Evidence, and Implications," *Academy of Management Review*, 20 (1995), 65–91.
2. J. G. March and H. Simon, *Organizations* (New York: Wiley, 1958).
3. Ibid.; J. A. Pearce, "The Company Mission as a Strategic Tool," *Sloan Management Review* (Spring 1982), 15–24.
4. www.TIAACREF.com, 2006; www.fidelity.com, 2006.
5. www.calpers.com, 2006.
6. C.W.L. Hill and G. R. Jones, *Strategic Management: An Integrated Approach*, 7e (Boston: Houghton Mifflin, 2006).
7. www.swa.com, 2006.
8. B. O'Reilly, "Where Service Flies Right," *Fortune*, August 24, 1992, pp. 115–116.
9. K. Cleland, "Southwest Tries Online Ticketing," *Advertising Age*, 67 (1996), 39.
10. J. P. Womack, D. T. Jones, D. Roos, and D. Sammons Carpenter, *The Machine That Changed the World* (New York: Macmillan, 1990).
11. R. F. Zammuto, "A Comparison of Multiple Constituency Models of Organizational Effectiveness," *Academy of Management Review*, 9 (1984), 606–616; K. S. Cameron, "Critical Questions in Assessing Organizational Effectiveness," *Organizational Dynamics*, 9 (1989), 66–80.
12. R. M. Cyert and J. G. March, *A Behavioral Theory of the Firm* (Upper Saddle River, NJ: Prentice Hall, 1963).
13. R. H. Miles, *Macro Organizational Behavior* (Santa Monica, CA: Goodyear, 1980), p. 375.
14. A. A. Berle and G. C. Means, *The Modern Corporation and Private Property* (New York: Commerce Clearing House, 1932).
15. Hill and Jones, *Strategic Management*, Chapter 2.
16. G. R. Jones and J. E. Butler, "Managing Internal Corporate Entrepreneurship: An Agency Perspective," *Journal of Management*, 18 (1994), 733–749.
17. C. Yang, "Money and Medicine: Physician Disentangle Thyself," *Academic Universe*, April 21, 1997, p. 34.
18. W. Zeller, "The Fall of Enron," *Business Week*, December 17, 2001, pp. 30–40.
19. A. K. Gupta, "Contingency Perspectives on Strategic Leadership," in D. C. Hambrick, ed., *The Executive Effect: Concepts and Methods for Studying Top Managers* (Greenwich, CT: JAI Press, 1988), pp. 147–178.
20. Ibid., p. 155.
21. D. C. Ancona, "Top-Management Teams: Preparing for the Revolution," in J. S. Carroll, ed., *Applied Social Psychology in Organizational Settings* (Hillsdale, NJ: Lawrence Erlbaum Associates, 1990), pp. 99–128.
22. R. F. Vancil, *Passing the Baton* (Boston: Harvard Business School Press, 1987).
23. www.fortune.com, December 2005.
24. www.yahoo.com, 2005.
25. Hill and Jones, *Strategic Management*, Chapter 11.
26. Adapted from Amazon.com Web site, corporate governance guidelines, 2005.
27. T. L. Beauchamp and N. E. Bowie, eds., *Ethical Theory and Business* (Upper Saddle River, NJ: Prentice Hall, 1979); A. MacIntyre, *After Virtue* (South Bend, IN: University of Notre Dame Press, 1981).
28. R. E. Goodin, "How to Determine Who Should Get What," *Ethics*, July 1975, pp. 310–321.
29. T. M. Jones, "Ethical Decision Making by Individuals in Organizations: An Issue Contingent Model," *Academy of Management Journal*, 16 (1991), 366–395; G. F. Cavanaugh, D. J. Moberg, and M. Velasquez, "The Ethics of Organizational Politics," *Academy of Management Review*, 6 (1981), 363–374.
30. L. K. Trevino, "Ethical Decision Making in Organizations: A Person–Situation Interactionist Model," *Academy of Management Review*, 11 (1986), 601–617; W. H. Shaw and V. Barry, *Moral Issues in Business*, 6e (Belmont, CA: Wadsworth, 1995).
31. B. Carton, "Gillette Faces Wrath of Children in Testing on Rats and Rabbits," *The Wall Street Journal*, September 5, 1995, p. A1.
32. W. H. Shaw and V. Barry, op. cit.
33. B. Ortega, "Broken Rules: Conduct Codes Garner Goodwill for Retailers But Violations Go On," *The Wall Street Journal*, July 3, 1995, pp. A1, A4.
34. "Why Honesty Is the Best Policy," *The Economist*, March 9, 2002, p. 23.
35. P. E. Murphy, "Implementing Business Ethics," *Journal of Business Ethics*, 7 (1988), 907–915.
36. "Ethics Office Approves Executive-Branch Rules," *The Wall Street Journal*, August 7, 1992, p. A14.
37. P. E. Murphy, "Creating Ethical Corporate Structure," *Sloan Management Review* (Winter 1989), 81–87.
38. J. B. Dozier and M. P. Miceli, "Potential Predictors of Whistle-Blowing: A Prosocial Behavior Perspective," *Academy of Management Review*, 10 (1985), 823–836; J. P. Near and M. P. Miceli, "Retaliation Against Whistle-Blowers: Predictors and Effects," *Journal of Applied Psychology*, 71 (1986), 137–145.
39. J. A. Byrne, "The Best Laid Ethics Programs . . . ," *Business Week*, March 9, 1992, pp. 67–69.
40. Adapted from Amazon.com Web site, corporate stakeholder rights, 2005.
41. D. Collins, "Organizational Harm, Legal Consequences and Stakeholder Retaliation," *Journal of Business Ethics*, 8 (1988), 1–13.
42. M. J. Galen, A. Byrne, T. Smart, and D. Woodruff, "Debacle at Dow Corning: How Bad Will It Get?" *Business Week*, March 2, 1992, pp. 36–38.
43. J. A. Byrne, "Here's What to Do Next, Dow Corning," *Business Week*, February 24, 1992, p. 33.
44. J. A. Byrne, "The Best Laid Ethics Programs . . . ," *Business Week*, March 9, 1992, pp. 67–69.

Managing in a Changing Global Environment

Learning Objectives

An organization's environment is the complex network of changing forces that affect the way it operates. The environment is a major contingency for which an organization must plan and to which it must adapt. Furthermore, it is a source of uncertainty that an organization must try to control. This chapter examines the forces that make managing in a global environment an uncertain, complex process.

After studying this chapter you should be able to:

1. List the forces in an organization's specific and general environment that give rise to opportunities and threats.
2. Identify why uncertainty exists in the environment.
3. Describe how and why an organization seeks to adapt to and control these forces to reduce uncertainty.
4. Understand how resource dependence theory and transaction cost explain why organizations choose different kinds of interorganizational strategies to manage their environments to gain the resources they need to achieve their goals and create value for their stakeholders.

WHAT IS THE ORGANIZATIONAL ENVIRONMENT?

Environment

The set of forces surrounding an organization that have the potential to affect the way it operates and its access to scarce resources.

The **environment** is the set of forces surrounding an organization that have the potential to affect the way it operates and its access to scarce resources. Scarce resources include the raw materials and skilled employees an organization needs to produce goods and services; the information it needs to improve its technology or decide on its competitive strategy; and the support of outside stakeholders, such as customers who buy its goods and services, and banks and financial institutions that supply the capital to sustain it. Forces in the environment that affect an organization's ability to secure these scarce resources include competition from rivals for customers; rapid changes in technology that might erode its competitive advantage; and an increase in the price of important inputs that raises operating costs.

In the global environment, U.S. companies have been heavily involved in international trade since colonial days, when they shipped their stocks of tobacco and sugar to Europe in return for manufactured products. Throughout the twentieth century, GM, Heinz, IBM, Campbell's, Procter & Gamble, and thousands of other U.S. companies have established overseas divisions and have transferred their domestic core competencies abroad to produce goods and services valued by overseas consumers. Indeed, U.S. companies have been established in overseas countries for so long that they are often treated as domestic companies by people in those countries. People in Britain, for example, regard Heinz, Hoover, Ford, and Eastman Kodak as British companies, often forgetting their U.S. origins. Similarly, the fact that Britain is the biggest overseas investor in the United States and that British companies own or have owned such "American" institutions as Burger King, Howard Johnson's, and Jacuzzi is not generally known by Americans.

Organizational domain
The particular range of goods and services that the organization produces and the customers and other stakeholders whom it serves.

An organization attempts to manage the forces in its environment to obtain the resources necessary to produce goods and services for customers and clients (see Figure 3.1). The term **organizational domain** refers to the particular range of goods and services that the organization produces, and the customers and other stakeholders whom it serves.[1] An organization establishes its domain by deciding how to manage the forces in its environment to maximize its ability to secure needed resources. To obtain inputs, for example, an organization has to decide which suppliers to deal with from the range of possible suppliers and how to manage its relationships with its chosen suppliers. To obtain money, an organization has to decide which bank to deal with and how to manage its relationship with the bank so that the bank will be inclined to authorize a loan. To obtain customers, a company has to decide which set of customers it is going to serve and then how to satisfy them.

An organization attempts to structure its transactions with the environment to protect and enlarge its domain so that it can increase its ability to create value for customers, shareholders, employees, and other stakeholders. For example, Gerber

Figure 3.1
The Organizational Environment

In the specific environment are forces that directly affect an organization's ability to obtain resources. In the general environment are forces that shape the specific environments of all organizations.

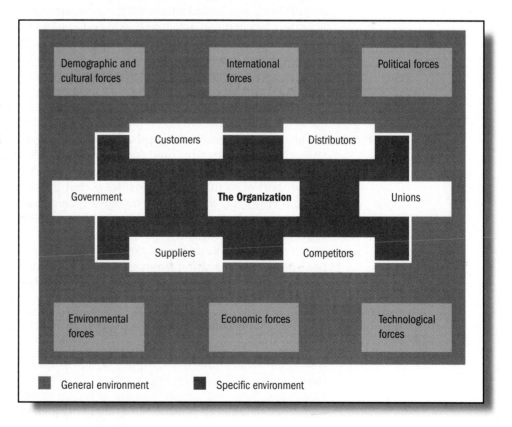

Chapter 3   Managing in a Changing Global Environment   **57**

Products' domain is a wide range of baby foods and other baby-related products (clothing, diapers, pacifiers) that the company makes to satisfy the needs of babies and their families.[2] Gerber structures transactions with its environment—that is, with suppliers, bankers, customers, and other stakeholders—to obtain the resources it needs to protect and enlarge its domain.

An organization can enlarge and protect its domain by expanding internationally. Global expansion allows an organization to seek new opportunities to take advantage of its core competencies to create value for stakeholders. Before discussing the specific ways in which organizations manage their environment to protect and enlarge their domain, we must understand in detail which forces in the environment affect organizations. The concepts of specific environment and general environment provide a useful basis for analysis.[3]

The Specific Environment

Specific environment
The forces from outside stakeholder groups that directly affect an organization's ability to secure resources.

The **specific environment** consists of forces from outside stakeholder groups that directly affect an organization's ability to secure resources.[4] Customers, distributors, unions, competitors, suppliers, and the government are all important outside stakeholders who can influence and pressure organizations to act in certain ways (see Figure 3.1).

For baby-food maker Gerber, competitors, such as Beech-Nut and Heinz, are an important force that affects the organization's ability to attract resources: customer revenue. Competition makes resources scarce and valuable because the greater the competition for resources, the more difficult they are to obtain. Competitors can be domestic or international. Each type has different implications for a company's ability to obtain resources. Overseas competitors have not been as important a force in the baby-food industry as they have been in the U.S. automobile industry, where they have reduced the U.S. car companies' ability to attract resources.

In the United States, Sony, Toyota, Philips, BMW, and other overseas companies compete with American companies for consumers. Abroad, American companies face competition from organizations both inside and outside the countries in which they operate. The European divisions of GM and Ford, for example, compete not only with European car companies such as Fiat, Peugeot, and BMW but also with Japanese companies such as Toyota and Honda. Indeed, in the 2000s Japanese car companies operating in Europe established plants with the capacity to produce 750,000 new cars a year and have threatened the prosperity of Volkswagen, Ford, and Fiat.

Changes in the number and types of customers, and changes in customer tastes, are another force that affects an organization. An organization must have a strategy to manage its relationship with customers and attract their support—and the strategy must change over time as customer needs change. Gerber has a national reputation based on its high standards of purity, quality, and caring, and it has gained the support of so many U.S. consumers that it holds 65 percent of the baby-food market. However, in the 2000s, increasing demands from customers for additive-free, organic baby food led it to change the formulation of some of its food products to keep its customers loyal.

In the global environment satisfying customer needs presents new challenges because customers differ from country to country. For example, customers in Europe—unlike Americans—typically do not like their cereal sweetened, so Kellogg and General Mills modify their products to suit local European tastes. An organization must be willing and able to tailor or customize its products to suit the tastes and preferences of different consumers if it expects to attract their business.

Besides responding to the needs of customers, organizations must decide how to manage relationships with suppliers and distributors to obtain access to the resources they provide. An organization has to make many choices concerning how to manage these exchanges in order to secure most effectively a stable supply of inputs or dispose of its products in a timely manner. For example, should Gerber buy or make its inputs? Should it raise cattle and chickens and vegetables and fruits? Should it make glass jars? Or should it buy all of these inputs from suppliers? The purity of baby foods is a vital issue; can input suppliers be trusted to ensure product quality? What is the best way for Gerber to distribute its products to ensure their quality? Should Gerber own its own fleet of vehicles and sell directly to retail stores, or should it use wholesalers to distribute its products?

In the global environment supplies of inputs can be obtained not just from domestic sources but from any country in the world. If U.S. companies had not used outsourcing as a means to lower the cost of their inputs by buying from overseas suppliers, they would have lost their competitive advantage to overseas competitors that did pursue outsourcing. AT&T, for example, found it impossible to compete with Panasonic and Hitachi for the lucrative telephone-answering-machine market until it started to buy and assemble its inputs abroad. AT&T components are made in Taiwan, China, and Hong Kong, and access to low-cost inputs has allowed AT&T to reduce its prices and recapture market share from its Japanese competitors.

The challenges associated with distributing and marketing products increase in the global environment. Because the tastes of customers vary from country to country, many advertising and marketing campaigns are country specific, and many products are customized to overseas customers' preferences. Moreover, in Japan and some other countries, domestic producers tightly control distribution systems, and that arrangement makes it very hard for companies to enter the market and sell their products. Global distribution also becomes difficult when an organization's products are complex and customers need a lot of information to operate or use them successfully. All of these factors mean that an organization has to consider carefully how to handle the global distribution of its products to attract and retain customer support. Should the organization handle overseas sales and distribution itself? Should it sell to a wholesaler in the overseas market? Should it enter into an alliance with an organization in a particular country and allow that company to market and distribute its products? Organizations operating in many countries must weigh all these options.

Other outside stakeholders include the government, unions, and consumer interest groups. Various government agencies are interested in Gerber's policies concerning equal employment opportunity, food preparation and content, and health and safety standards, and these agencies pressure the organization to make sure it follows legal rules. Unions pressure Gerber to secure favorable wages and benefits, and to protect the jobs of their members who work for Gerber. Consumer interest groups seek to prevent Gerber from reducing the quality of its foods.

An organization that establishes global operations has to forge a working relationship with its new workforce and develop relationships with any unions that represent its new employees. If a Japanese manufacturer opens a new U.S. plant, its Japanese management team has to understand the expectations of their American employees—that is, their attitudes toward pay, seniority, and other conditions of employment. A global organization has to adapt its management style to fit the expectations of the local workforce.

Finally, each country has its own system of government and its own laws and regulations that control the way business is conducted. A U.S. company that enters a new country must learn to conform to the host country's institutional and legal system. Sometimes, as in the European Union (EU), the rules governing business conduct are standardized across many countries. Although this can make it easier for U.S. companies to operate across countries, it also makes it easier for these countries to protect their own home-based companies. Boeing, for example, complains that subsidies from European taxpayers have allowed Airbus Industries to undercut the price of Boeing's airplanes and develop new planes such as Airbus's new super "jumbo" at artificially reduced prices. Similarly, U.S. farmers complain that European tariffs protect inefficient European farmers and close the market to the products of more efficient U.S. producers. Often, domestic competitors lobby their home governments to combat "unfair" global competition.

An organization must engage in transactions with each of the forces in its specific environment if it is to obtain the resources it requires to survive and to protect and enhance its domain. Over time, the size and scope of its domain will change as those transactions change. For example, an organization that decides to expand its domain to satisfy the needs of new sets of customers by producing new kinds of products will encounter new sets of forces and may need to engage in a different set of transactions with the environment to gain resources.

The General Environment

General environment

The forces that shape the specific environment and affect the ability of all organizations in a particular environment to obtain resources.

The **general environment** consists of forces that shape the specific environment and affect the ability of all organizations in a particular environment to obtain resources (see Figure 3.1). *Economic forces*, such as interest rates, the state of the economy, and the unemployment rate, determine the level of demand for products and the price of inputs. National differences in interest rates, exchange rates, wage levels, gross domestic product, and per capita income have a dramatic effect on the way organizations operate internationally. Generally, organizations attempt to obtain their inputs or to manufacture their products in the country with the lowest labor or raw-materials costs. Sony, GE, and GM have closed many of their U.S. manufacturing plants and moved their operations to Mexico because doing so has enabled them to match the low costs of overseas competitors that outsource production to China and Malaysia. Obviously, overseas competitors operating from countries with low wages have a competitive advantage that may be crucial in the battle for the price-conscious U.S. consumer. So, many U.S. companies have been forced to move their operations abroad or outsource production to compete. Levi Strauss, for example, closed the last of its U.S. factories in the 2000s and moved jeans production to Mexico and the Dominican Republic to reduce production costs. (Chapter 8 looks specifically at how an organization manages global expansion).

Technological forces, such as the development of new production techniques and new information-processing equipment, influence many aspects of organizations' operations. The use of computerized manufacturing technology can increase productivity. Similarly, investment in advanced research and development activities influences how organizations interact with each other and how they design their structures. (The role of technology is examined further in Chapter 9).

The international transfer of technology has important implications for an organization's competitive advantage. Organizations must be able to learn about and have access to technological developments abroad that might provide a low-cost or differentiation advantage. Traditionally, the United States has exported its technology and overseas companies have been eager to use it, but in some industries U.S. companies have been slow to take advantage of overseas technological developments. Critics charge that global learning has often been one-way—from the United States to the rest of the world—to the detriment of U.S. competitiveness. It has been estimated that after World War II, Japanese companies paid U.S. companies $100 million for the rights to license certain technologies and in return gained over $100 billion in sales revenue from U.S. consumers. Today, U.S. companies are eager and willing to learn from overseas competitors to close the technological gap. Such technological learning allows an organization to develop its core competencies and apply them around the world to create value, as Amazon.com has done.

Political and environmental forces influence government policy toward organizations and their stakeholders. For example, laws that favor particular business interests, such as a tariff on imported cars, influence organizations' customers and competitors. Pressure from environmentalists, such as pressure to reduce air pollution or a desire to decrease the nation's level of solid waste, affects organizations' production costs. Environmentally friendly product design and packaging may alter organizations' relationships with competitors, customers, and suppliers. New car engines introduced by Toyota and Honda in 2002 created virtually no pollution, and met and exceeded California's stringent clean air requirements. Toyota also pioneered the development of gas-saving hybrid vehicles and licensed this technology to GM and Ford in 2005. Globally, countries that do little to protect the environment see an influx of companies that take advantage of lax regulations to set up low-cost operations there. The result can be increased pollution and mounting environmental problems, which have occurred in many Eastern European and Asian countries.

Demographic, cultural, and social forces—such as the age, education, lifestyle, norms, values, and customs of a nation's people—shape organizations' customers, managers, and employees. The demand for baby products, for example, is linked to national birth rates and age distributions. Demographic, cultural, and social forces are important sources of uncertainty in a global environment because they directly affect the tastes and needs of a nation's customers. Cultural and social values affect a country's attitudes toward both domestic and overseas products and companies. Customers in France and Italy, for example, generally prefer domestically produced cars even though overseas products are superior in quality and value.

A U.S. company establishing operations in a country overseas must be attuned to the host country's business methods and practices. Countries differ in how they do business and in the nature of their business institutions. They also differ in their attitudes toward union–management relationships, in their ethical standards, and in their accounting and financial practices. In some countries bribery and corruption are acceptable business practices. Japanese law, for example, supports home-based companies that seek to protect their market and distribution systems against the entry of more efficient overseas competitors. However, the laws are changing and companies like Wal-Mart now operate in Japan. The story of GE's experiences in Hungary illustrates many of these issues.

As the example of GE and Tungsram illustrates, managers who wish to take advantage of the opportunities created by changing global political, legal, social, and economic forces face a major challenge. If an organization manages the forces in its general and specific environments effectively, so that it obtains the resources it needs, its domain will grow as it produces more goods and services and attracts new

ORGANIZATIONAL INSIGHT 3.1
GE's U.S. Managers Stumble in Hungary

Seeking to expand globally, General Electric (GE) agreed to acquire 51% of Tungsram, a maker of lighting products and widely regarded as one of Hungary's best companies, at a cost of $150 million. GE was attracted to Tungsram because of Hungary's low wage rates and the possibility of using the company as a base from which to export lighting products to western Europe. At the time, many analysts believed that GE would show other Western companies how to turn organizations once run by communist party officials into capitalist moneymakers. GE transferred some of its best managers to Tungsram and waited for the miracle to happen. It took a long time, for several reasons.

One problem resulted from major misunderstandings between the American managers and the Hungarian workers. The Americans complained that the Hungarians were lazy; the Hungarians thought the Americans were pushy. GE's management system depends on extensive communication between workers and managers, a practice uncommon in the previously communist country. Changing behavior at Tungsram proved to be difficult. The Americans wanted strong sales and marketing functions that would pamper customers; in Hungary's former planned economy, these were unnecessary. In addition, Hungarians expected GE to deliver Western-style wages; but GE came to Hungary to take advantage of the country's low-wage structure.[5]

As Tungsram's losses mounted, GE learned what happens when grand expectations collide with the grim reality of inefficiency and indifference toward customers and quality. Looking back, GE managers admit that, because of differences in basic attitudes between countries, they had underestimated the difficulties they would face in turning Tungsram around. To improve performance, GE laid off half of Tungsram's employees, including two out of every three managers. It invested over $1 billion in a new plant and equipment and in retraining the remaining employees and managers to help them learn the work attitudes and behaviors that a company needs to survive in a competitive global environment. In the 2000s, its Hungarian operation has become one of the most efficient in Europe; the plant exports its lightbulbs all over the European Union.

customers. If an organization manages the forces in its general and specific environments poorly, however, stakeholders will withhold their support, the organization will not obtain scarce resources, and its domain will shrink. Eventually, unless it can find a better way to manage its environment the organization may cease to exist.

Sources of Uncertainty in the Organizational Environment

An organization likes to have a steady and abundant supply of resources so that it can easily manage its domain and satisfy stakeholders. All the forces discussed earlier cause uncertainty for organizations, however, and make it more difficult for managers to control the flow of resources they need to protect and enlarge their organizational domains. The forces that cause these problems can be viewed in another way: in terms of how they cause uncertainty because they affect the *complexity*, *dynamism*, and *richness* of the environment. As these forces cause the environment to become more complex, less stable, and poorer, the level of uncertainty increases (see Figure 3.2).

Environmental Complexity

Environmental complexity

The strength, number, and interconnectedness of the specific and general forces that an organization has to manage.

Environmental complexity is a function of the strength, number, and interconnectedness of the specific and general forces that an organization has to manage.[6] The greater the number, and the greater the differences between them, the more complex and uncertain is the environment and the more difficult to predict and control. Ford, for example, used to obtain inputs from over 3,000 different suppliers. To reduce the uncertainty that resulted from dealing with so many suppliers, Ford embarked on a program to reduce their number—and thus the complexity of its environment. Now Ford deals with fewer than 500 suppliers; acquiring the information needed to manage its relationships with them is much easier than acquiring information to manage 10 times that number.

Complexity also increases if, over time, a company produces a wider variety of products for different groups of customers. For example, if a company like McDonald's suddenly decided to enter the insurance and banking businesses, it would need a massive infusion of information to reduce the uncertainty surrounding the new transactions.

Complexity can increase greatly when specific and general forces in the environment become *interconnected*—that is, when forces begin to interact so their effects on the organization become unpredictable.[7] The more interconnected the forces in an

Figure 3.2
Three Factors Causing Uncertainty

As the environment becomes more complex, less stable, and poorer, the level of uncertainty increases.

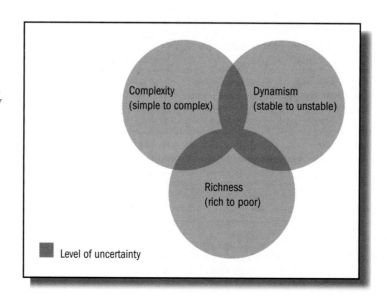

organization's specific and general environments are, the more uncertainty the organization faces. Suppose a major breakthrough in carmaking technology makes existing factories obsolete. This general force will cause the price of a carmaker's stock (like Ford's) to fluctuate wildly and will send financial markets into turmoil. Car manufacturers will be unsure how the breakthrough will affect their business, competition between rivals will increase (a specific force), and both management and the unions will be uncertain of the effect this will have on jobs and the future of the organization. If customers then stop buying cars (another specific force) until new models made with the new technology come out, the result may be layoffs and further decreases in the price of car company stocks.

This happened in 2005 when both GM and Ford began to lose billions of dollars because they could not reduce their costs or innovate vehicles that matched those of their Japanese competitors. To survive, these carmakers and the UAW negotiated large savings in health-care and benefit costs to reduce costs. Now their survival depends on their ability to make innovate new kinds of high-quality vehicles, in flexible factories, that U.S. customers will desire.

The more complex an organization's environment, the greater the uncertainty about that environment. Predicting and controlling the flow of resources becomes extremely difficult, and problems associated with managing transactions with the environment increase. GM and Ford face a highly challenging future.

Environmental Dynamism

Environmental dynamism is a function of how much and how quickly forces in the specific and general environments change over time and thus increase the uncertainty an organization faces.[8] An environment is *stable* if forces affect the supply of resources in a predictable way. An environment is *unstable and dynamic* if an organization cannot predict the way in which the forces will change over time. If technology, for example, changes rapidly as it does in the computer industry, the environment is very dynamic. An organization in a dynamic, unstable environment will seek ways to make it more predictable and so lessen the uncertainty it faces. Later in the chapter, we discuss strategies for managing potentially dynamic parts of the environment, including long-term contracts and vertical integration.

Today, the existence of large new global markets for companies to enter, such as in China and Eastern Europe, and the possibility of gaining access to new global resources and core competencies, provide opportunities for an organization to enlarge its domain and create more value for stakeholders. However, as companies compete both at home and abroad the environment becomes increasingly complex (there are greater numbers of forces to be managed, and the forces are interconnected) and increasingly dynamic (the forces change rapidly). Consequently, global expansion makes the environment more difficult to predict and control.

Environmental Richness

Environmental richness is a function of the amount of resources available to support an organization's domain.[9] In rich environments, uncertainty is low because resources are plentiful and so organizations need not compete for them. Biotechnology companies in Boston, for example, have a large pool of high-quality scientists to choose from because of the presence of so many universities in the area (MIT, Harvard, Boston University, Boston College, Tufts, and Brandeis, among others). In poor environments, uncertainty is high because resources are scarce and organizations do have to compete for them. The supply of high-quality scientists in Alaska, for example, is limited and meeting the demand for them is expensive.

Environments may be poor for two reasons: (1) an organization is located in a poor country or poor region of a country; and (2) there is a high level of competition and organizations are fighting over available resources.[10] In poor environments, the greater the problems organizations face in managing resource transactions. Organizations have to battle to attract customers or to obtain the best inputs or the latest technology. These battles result in uncertainty for an organization.

Environmental dynamism
The degree to which forces in the specific and general environments change quickly over time and, thus, contribute to the uncertainty an organization faces.

Environmental richness
The amount of resources available to support an organization's domain.

In an environment that is poor, unstable, and complex, resources are especially hard to obtain and organizations face the greatest uncertainty. By contrast, in a rich, stable, and simple environment, resources are easy to come by and uncertainty is low. U.S. airlines such as American, United, and Delta are currently experiencing a highly uncertain environment. Low-cost airlines such as Southwest that are expanding nationally have increased the level of industry competition. The environment has become poorer as airlines fight for customers (a resource) and must offer lower prices to attract them. The airline industry environment is complex because competing airlines (part of each airline's specific environment) are very interconnected: If one airline reduces prices, they all must reduce prices to protect their domains, but the effect of this is to further increase uncertainty. Finally, the high price of oil, increasing competition from airlines overseas, and the changing state of the economy are all interconnected in the airlines' environment—and change over time—making it difficult to predict or plan for contingencies.

In contrast, the environment of the pharmaceutical industry is relatively certain. Merck, Bristol-Myers Squibb, Pfizer, and other large companies that invent drugs

FOCUS ON NEW INFORMATION TECHNOLOGY
Amazon.com, Part 2

The book distribution and book-selling industry was changed forever in July 1995 when Jeff Bezos brought virtual bookseller Amazon.com online. His new company's strategy revolutionized the nature of the environment. Previously, book publishers had sold their books either indirectly to book wholesalers who supplied small bookstores, directly to large book chains like Barnes & Noble or Borders, or to book-of-the-month clubs. There were so many book publishers and so many booksellers that the industry was relatively stable, with both large and small bookstores enjoying a comfortable niche in the market. In this relatively stable, simple, rich environment, uncertainty was low and all companies enjoyed good revenues and profits.

Amazon.com's virtual approach to buying and selling books changed all this. First, because it was able to offer customers quick access to all the more than 1.5 million books in print and offer customers discounted book prices, this raised the level of industry competition and made the book-selling environment poorer. Second, because Amazon.com also negotiated directly with large book publishers over price and supply because it wanted to get books quickly to its customers, this led to an increase in the complexity of the environment: all players—book publishers, wholesalers, stores, and customers—became more closely linked. Third, these factors, combined with continuing changes in information technology, made the environment more unstable and resources (customers) became harder to obtain.

How has this increase in uncertainty in the environment changed the book-selling business? First, these changes quickly threatened the prosperity of small bookstores, many of which soon closed their doors and left the business because they were unable to compete with online bookstores. Second, large booksellers like Barnes & Noble

and Borders started their own online stores to compete with Amazon.com. Third, Amazon.com and these new online bookstores engaged in a price war, and the prices of books were further discounted. This resulted in an even more competitive and uncertain environment.

IT is not specialized to any one country or world region. Access to the Internet and the World Wide Web enables any online company to sell to customers around the world—providing of course that its products can be customized to the needs of overseas customers. Jeff Bezos was quick to realize that his U.S.–based Amazon.com IT could be profitably transferred to other countries to sell books. However, his ability to enter new overseas markets was limited by one major factor: Amazon.com offers its customers the biggest selection of books written in the English language; he had to find overseas customers who could read English. Where to locate then?

An obvious first choice would be the United Kingdom, because its population speaks English, then other English-speaking nations such as Canada, Australia, New Zealand, and Germany. Germany? Of probably of any nation in the world, Germany has the highest proportion of English-as-a-second-language speakers because English is taught in all its high schools.

So Bezos decided to replicate Amazon.com's value-creation functions and customize its IT for other nations. First, in the United Kingdom it bought the company Bookpages, installed its proprietary technology, and renamed it Amazon.co.uk in 1996. In Germany, it acquired a small online bookseller and created Amazon.de in 1998.[11] Since then Amazon.com has also established online stores in Japan and China. In addition, customers anywhere in the world can buy its books from one of these online stores and Amazon will ship its books to customers anywhere in the world.

receive patents and are the sole providers of their respective new drugs for 17 years. During this period, the patent-owning company can charge a high price for its drug because it faces no competition and customers have no option but to buy the drug from it. Organizations in the pharmaceutical industry exist in a stable, rich environment: Competition is low and no change occurs until patents expire. Because of a huge increase in the price of drugs during the 2000s, however, health-care providers and the U.S. government have moved to find ways to reduce drug prices. This has increased the complexity of the environment and increased uncertainty for pharmaceutical companies. To manage complexity and slow the pace of change, the industry heavily lobbies the government to safeguard its interests; pharmaceutical companies donate tens of millions to political parties and members of Congress and the Senate. Throughout the rest of this chapter, the strategies that organizations pursue to manage their environments are examined in more detail. First, however, it is useful to examine the nature of the environment that confronted Jeff Bezos after he founded Amazon.com.[12]

MANAGERIAL IMPLICATIONS

ANALYZING THE ENVIRONMENT

1. Managers at all levels and in all functions should periodically analyze the organizational environment and identify sources of uncertainty.
2. To manage transactions with the organizational environment effectively, managers should chart the forces in the organization's specific and general environments, noting (a) the number of forces that will affect the organization, (b) the pattern of interconnectedness or linkages between these forces, (c) how rapidly these forces change, and (d) the extent and nature of competition, which affects how rich or poor the environment is.
3. Taking that analysis, managers should plan how to deal with contingencies. Designing interorganizational strategies to control and secure access to scarce and valuable resources in the environment in which they operate is the first stage in this process.

RESOURCE DEPENDENCE THEORY

Resource dependence theory
A theory that argues that the goal of an organization is to minimize its dependence on other organizations for the supply of scare resources in its environment and to find ways of influencing them to make resources available.

Organizations are dependent on their environment for the resources they need to survive and grow. The supply of resources, however, is dependent on the complexity, dynamism, and richness of the environment. If an environment becomes poorer because important customers are lost or new competitors enter the market, resources become scarce and more valuable and uncertainty increases. Organizations attempt to manage their transactions with the environment to ensure access to the resources they depend on. They want their access to resources to be as predictable as possible because this simplifies managing their domains and promotes survival.

According to **resource dependence theory** the goal of an organization is to minimize its dependence on other organizations for the supply of scarce resources in its environment and to find ways to influence them to secure needed resources.[13] Thus an organization must simultaneously manage two aspects of its resource dependence: (1) It has to exert influence over other organizations so that it can obtain resources, and (2) it must respond to the needs and demands of the other organizations in its environment.[14]

The strength of one organization's dependence on another for a particular resource is a function of two factors. One factor is how vital the resource is to the organization's survival. Scarce and valuable inputs (such as component parts and raw materials) and resources (such as customers and distribution outlets) are very important to an organization's survival.[15] The other factor is the extent to which the resource is controlled by other organizations. Crown Cork & Seal and other can manufacturers, for example, need aluminum to produce cans, but for many years the supply of aluminum was controlled by Alcoa, which had a virtual monopoly and thus could charge high prices for its aluminum.

The PC industry illustrates the operation of both factors. PC makers such as HP, Gateway, and Dell are dependent on organizations such as Samsung and Intel that supply memory chips and microprocessors. Some, like Apple and Sony who do not sell online (Dell and Gateway are the online leaders), are also dependent on chains of computer stores and other retail outlets that stock their products, and on school systems and corporate customers that buy large quantities of their PCs. When there are few suppliers of a resource such as memory chips, or few organizations that distribute and sell a product, companies become highly dependent on the ones that do exist. Intel, for example, makes many of the most advanced microchips and has considerable power over PC makers who need its chips to compete successfully. The greater the dependence of one organization on another, the weaker it is, and the more powerful company can threaten or take advantage of the dependent organization if it chooses to do so.

To manage their resource dependence and control their access to scarce resources, organizations develop various strategies.[16] Just as nations attempt to craft an international policy to increase their ability to influence world affairs, so organizations try to find ways of increasing their influence over the global environment. Avon offers a good example of the management of the environment to control resource dependence.

ORGANIZATIONAL INSIGHT 3.2
Avon's Global Empire

Avon reported record profits in 2005 on booming global sales of its well-known makeup, soaps, hair care, jewelry, and other products.[17] Since its founding over 100 years ago, Avon has used personal home selling by sales reps, its "Avon ladies," to distribute and sell its products. Today it has 4 million sales reps located around the world who generate the majority of its $6 billion revenues and profits.

Avon has recognized the importance of protecting and increasing its share of global resources, in this case, the business of women around the world. Under its hard-driving CEO, Andrea Jung, it is pioneering new ways to promote its products to existing and new customers around the globe. Jung, for example, has been pushing the Avon ladies to make use of the Internet to increase sales. In the late 1990s, she recognized the importance of the Internet as a method of direct distribution to global customers—one that fits perfectly with its personal selling approach. Avon created a sophisticated online global storefront to display its products and inform customers about their high quality and value for money.

At first, this Internet direct-distribution approach caused considerable anxiety for Avon reps because they thought this distribution channel would bypass them and would reduce their personal sales and commissions. Jung worked hard to show reps that once Internet customers had bought and tried Avon's products they would likely buy more of Avon's product and become loyal customers. To convince them of this, she set up a program whereby reps would also gain a commission when their customers purchased directly from Avon's online store, and today 60% of Avon Ladies use the World Wide Web to increase sales of Avon products.

Under Jung's leadership Avon also began to aggressively search out new opportunities to attract global customers. First, Avon is reaching beyond the typical customer it has served in the past, the 30- to 55-year-old woman. Jung decided to target the critical 16- to 24-year-old woman to attract and build brand loyalty among younger customers; after all, these customers will be it main customers in the future. The sales potential is enormous; the 17 million women in this segment spend 20% of their income on personal care products. In 2003, a new Avon division called *Mark* debuted to distribute a new line of hip cosmetics designed specifically to meet the needs of younger women. At the same time, Avon is working to attract increased sales from older women. It intends to increase its U.S. sales force from 500,000 to over 1 million reps in the next five years.

To attract more global customers, Avon also has designed lines of cosmetics and jewelry that appeal to customers in different national markets—recall that 4 million of its sales reps are in countries abroad. Avon does not just distribute its U.S.–made products globally, however; it also designs and makes them abroad. This has also paid off handsomely because many products developed to appeal to customers in a particular overseas market, such as colors of lipstick and jewelry, have then been marketed successfully to U.S. customers. Small wonder then that the innovative sales and distribution methods it is using to promote and sell its products resulted in its record revenues and profits.

INTERORGANIZATIONAL STRATEGIES FOR MANAGING RESOURCE DEPENDENCIES

Symbiotic interdependencies
Interdependencies that exist between an organization and its suppliers and distributors.

Competitive interdependencies
Interdependencies that exist among organizations that compete for scarce inputs and outputs.

As the Avon example suggests, obtaining access to resources is uncertain and problematic. Customers, for example, are notoriously fickle and switch to competitors' products. To reduce uncertainty, an organization needs to devise interorganizational strategies to manage the resource interdependencies in its specific and general environment. Managing these interdependencies allows an organization to protect and enlarge its domain. In the specific environment, an organization needs to manage its relationships with suppliers, unions, and consumer interest groups. If they restrict access to resources, they can increase uncertainty.

In the specific environment, two basic types of interdependencies cause uncertainty: symbiotic and competitive.[18] Interdependencies are symbiotic when the outputs of one organization are inputs for another; thus **symbiotic interdependencies** generally exist between an organization and its suppliers and distributors. Intel and computer makers like HP and Dell have a symbiotic interdependency. **Competitive interdependencies** exist among organizations that compete for scarce inputs and outputs.[19] HP and Dell are in competition for customers for their computers and for inputs such as Intel's latest microchips.

Organizations can use various linkage mechanisms to control symbiotic and competitive interdependencies.[20] The use of these mechanisms, however, requires the actions and decisions of the linked organizations to be coordinated. This need for coordination reduces each organization's freedom to act independently and perhaps in its own best interests. Suppose that HP, to protect its future supply of chips, signs a contract with Intel agreeing to use only Intel chips. But then a new chip manufacturer comes along with a less expensive chip. The contract with Intel obliges HP to pay Intel's higher prices even though doing so is not in HP's best interests.

Whenever an organization involves itself in an interorganizational linkage, it must balance its need to reduce resource dependence against the loss in autonomy or freedom of choice that will result from the linkage.[21] In general, *an organization aims to choose the interorganizational strategy that offers the most reduction in uncertainty for the least loss of control.*[22]

In the next sections we examine the interorganizational strategies that organizations can use to manage symbiotic interdependencies and competitive interdependencies. A linkage is formal when two or more organizations agree to coordinate their interdependencies directly in order to reduce uncertainty. The more *formal* a linkage is, the greater are both the direct coordination and the likelihood that coordination is based on an explicit, written agreement or involves some common ownership between organizations. The more *informal* a linkage is, the more indirect or loose is the method of coordination and the more likely is the coordination to be based on an implicit or unspoken agreement.

STRATEGIES FOR MANAGING SYMBIOTIC RESOURCE INTERDEPENDENCIES

To manage symbiotic interdependencies, organizations have a range of strategies from which to choose. Figure 3.3 indicates the relative degree of formality of four strategies. The more formal a strategy is, the greater the prescribed area of cooperation between organizations.

Reputation
A state in which an organization is held in high regard and trusted by other parties because of its fair and honest business practices.

Developing a Good Reputation

The least formal, least direct way to manage symbiotic interdependencies with suppliers and customers is to develop a **reputation**, a state in which an organization is held in high regard and trusted by other parties because of its fair and honest

Figure 3.3 Interorganizational Strategies for Managing Symbiotic Interdependencies

Symbiotic interdependencies generally exist between an organization and its suppliers and distributors. The more formal a strategy is, the greater the cooperation between organizations.

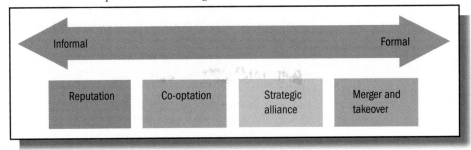

business practices. For example, paying bills on time and providing high-quality goods and services lead to a good reputation and trust on the part of suppliers and customers. If a car repair shop has a reputation for excellent repair work and fair prices for parts and labor, customers will return to the shop whenever their cars need servicing, and the organization will be managing its linkages with customers successfully.

The De Beers diamond cartel uses trust and reputation to manage its linkages with suppliers and customers. De Beers customers are a select group of the world's biggest diamond merchants. When these merchants buy from De Beers, they ask for a certain quantity of diamonds—say, $10 million worth. De Beers then selects an assortment of diamonds that it values at $10 million. Customers have no opportunity to bargain with De Beers over the price or quality of the diamonds. They can buy or not buy, but they always buy because they know that De Beers will not cheat them. The organization's reputation and survival depend on maintaining customers' goodwill.

Reputation and trust are probably the most common linkage mechanisms for managing symbiotic interdependencies. Over the long run, companies that behave dishonestly are likely to be unsuccessful; thus organizations as a group tend to become more honest over time.[23] Acting honestly, however, does not rule out active bargaining and negotiating over the price and quality of inputs and outputs. Every organization wants to strike the deal that best suits it and therefore attempts to negotiate terms in its favor.

Co-Optation

Co-optation is a strategy that manages symbiotic interdependencies by neutralizing problematic forces in the specific environment.[24] An organization that wants to bring opponents over to its side gives them a stake in or claim on what it does and tries to satisfy their interests. Pharmaceutical companies co-opt physicians by sponsoring medical conferences, giving away free samples of drugs, and advertising extensively in medical journals. Physicians become sympathetic to the interests of the pharmaceutical companies, which brings them onto the "team" and tells them that they and the companies have interests in common. Co-optation is an important political tool.

A common way to co-opt problematic forces such as customers, suppliers, or other important outside stakeholders is to bring them within the organization and, in effect, make them inside stakeholders. If some stakeholder group does not like the way things are being done, an organization co-opts the group by giving it a role in changing the way things are. All kinds of organizations use this strategy. Local schools, for example, attempt to co-opt parents by inviting them to become members of school boards or by establishing teacher–parent committees. In such an exchange, the organization gives up some control but usually gains more than it loses.

Outsiders can be brought inside an organization through bribery, a practice widespread in many countries but illegal in the United States. They can also be brought inside through the use of an **interlocking directorate**—a linkage that results

Co-optation
A strategy that manages symbiotic interdependencies by neutralizing problematic forces in the specific environment.

Interlocking directorate
A linkage that results when a director from one company sits on the board of another company.

when a director from one company sits on the board of another company. An organization that uses an interlocking directorate as a linkage mechanism invites members of powerful and significant stakeholder groups in its specific environment to sit on its board of directors.[25] An organization might invite the financial institution from which it borrows most of its money to send someone to sit on the organization's board of directors. Outside directors interact with an organization's top management team, ensuring supplies of scarce capital, exchanging information, and strengthening ties between organizations.

Strategic Alliances

Strategic alliances are becoming an increasingly common mechanism for managing symbiotic (and competitive) interdependencies between companies inside one country or between countries. A strategic alliance is an agreement that commits two or more companies to share their resources to develop joint new business opportunities. In 2005, for example, Microsoft and MTV formed a strategic alliance to integrate MTV's entertainment offerings into its Windows Media platform to compete against Apple's iPod platform. The idea is to make theirs compatible with, and superior too Apple's, something Real Networks is also trying to do. Also in 2005, BMW and Intel announced that they had formed an alliance to integrate Intel's technology into all BMW vehicles. Intel's chips will manage all aspects of the way BMW's vehicles operate, as well devices such as phones and MP3 players installed in them.

There are several types of strategic alliance. Figure 3.4 indicates the relative degree of formality of long-term contracts, networks, minority ownership, and joint ventures. The more formal an arrangement, the stronger and more prescribed the linkage and the tighter the control of the joint activities. In general, as uncertainty increases, organizations choose a more formal alliance to protect their access to resources.

Long-Term Contracts

At the informal end of the continuum shown in Figure 3.4 are alliances spelled out in long-term contracts between two or more organizations. The purpose of these contracts is usually to reduce costs by sharing resources or by sharing the risk of research and development, marketing, construction, and other activities. Contracts are the least formal type of alliance because no ties link the organizations apart from the agreement set forth in the contract. For example, to reduce financial risk, Bechtel Corp. and Willbros Group Inc., two leading multinational construction companies, agreed to pool their resources to construct an $850 million oil pipeline in the Caspian Sea.[26] J. B. Hunt Transport, a trucking company, formed an alliance with Santa Fe Pacific Corporation, a railroad company. Santa Fe agreed to carry Hunt's trailers across the country on railroad cars. At the end of the trip, the trains were met by Hunt's trucks, which transported the trailers to their final destination. This arrangement lowered Hunt's costs while increasing Santa Fe's revenues.

Figure 3.4 Types of Strategic Alliance

Companies linked by a strategic alliance share resources to develop joint new business opportunities. The more formal an alliance, the stronger the link between allied organizations.

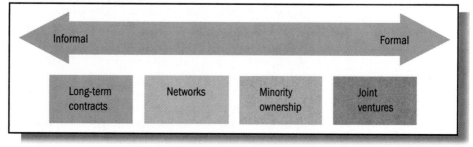

Contracts can be oral or written, casual, shared or implicit. The CEOs or top managers of two companies might agree over lunch to meet regularly to share information and ideas on some business activity, such as standardizing computer systems or changing customer needs. Some organizations, in contrast, develop written contracts to specify procedures for sharing resources or information and for using the benefits that result from such agreements. Kellogg, the breakfast cereal manufacturer, enters into written contracts with the farmers who supply the corn and rice it needs. Kellogg agrees to pay a certain price for their produce regardless of the market rate prevailing when the produce is harvested. Both parties gain because a major source of unpredictability (fluctuations in corn and rice prices) is eliminated from their environments.

Networks

Network
A cluster of different organizations whose actions are coordinated by contracts and agreements rather than through a formal hierarchy of authority.

A **network** or network structure is a cluster of different organizations whose actions are coordinated by contracts and agreements rather than through a formal hierarchy of authority. Members of a network work closely to support and complement one another's activities. The alliance resulting from a network is more formal than the alliance resulting from a contract, because more ties link member organizations and there is greater formal coordination of activities.[27] Nike and other organizations establish networks to build long-term relationships with suppliers, distributors, and customers while keeping the core organization from becoming too large or bureaucratic.

The goal of the organization that created the network is to share its manufacturing, marketing, or R&D skills with its partners to allow them to become more efficient and help it to reduce its costs or increase product quality. For example, AT&T created a network organization and linked its partners so that it could produce digital answering machines at low cost. AT&T electronically sends designs for new component parts and assembly instructions for new products to its network partners, who coordinate their activities to produce the components in the desired quantities and then ship them to the final assembly point.[28]

Minority Ownership

A more formal alliance emerges when organizations buy a minority ownership stake in each other. Ownership is a more formal linkage than contracts and network relationships. Minority ownership makes organizations extremely interdependent, and that interdependence forges strong cooperative bonds.

Keiretsu
A group of organizations, each of which owns shares in the other organizations in the group, that work together to further the group's interests.

The Japanese system of keiretsu shows how minority ownership networks operate. A **keiretsu** is a group of organizations, each of which owns shares in the other organizations in the group, and all of which work together to further the group's interests. Japanese companies employ two basic forms of keiretsu. Capital keiretsu are used to manage input and output linkages. Financial keiretsu are used to manage linkages among many diverse companies and usually have at their center a large bank.[29]

A particularly good example of the way a capital keiretsu network can benefit all the companies in it, but particularly the dominant ones, comes from the Japanese car industry.[30] Toyota is the most profitable car company in the world. Its vehicles are consistently ranked among the most reliable and the company enjoys strong customer loyalty. Interdependencies with its customers are not problematic because Toyota has a good reputation. One of the reasons for this good reputation is the way Toyota controls its input interdependencies.

Because a car's reliability depends on the quality of its inputs, managing this crucial linkage is vital for success today in the global car market. To control its inputs, Toyota owns a minority stake, often as much as 49%, in most of the companies that supply its components. Because of these formal ownership ties, Toyota can exercise strong control over the prices that suppliers charge and over the quality of their products. An even more important result of this formal alliance, however, is that it allows Toyota and its suppliers to work together to improve product quality and reliability.

Toyota is not afraid to share proprietary information with its suppliers because of its ownership stake. As a result, parts suppliers *participate* significantly in the car design process, which often leads to the discovery of new ways to improve the quality and reduce the cost of components. Both Toyota and its suppliers share the benefits that accrue from this close cooperation. Over time these alliances have given Toyota a global competitive advantage, which translates into control over important environmental interdependencies. Note also that Toyota's position as a shareholder in its suppliers' businesses means that there is no reason for Toyota to take advantage of them by demanding lower and lower prices from them. All partners benefit from the sharing of activities. These close linkages paid off once again when Toyota introduced the latest model of the Camry sedan. By taking advantage of the skills in its network, Toyota was able to engineer $1,700 in cost savings in the new model and to introduce it at a price below that of the old model.

A financial keiretsu, which is dominated by a large bank, functions like a giant interlocking directorate. The dominant members of the financial keiretsu, normally drawn from diverse companies, sit on the board of directors of the bank and often on the boards of each other's companies. The companies are linked by substantial long-term stockholdings managed by the bank at the center of the keiretsu. Member companies are able to trade proprietary information and knowledge that benefits them collectively. Indeed, one of the benefits that comes from a financial keiretsu is the way businesses can transfer and exchange managers to strengthen the network.

Figure 3.5 shows the Fuyo keiretsu, which centers on Fuji Bank. Its members include Nissan, NKK, Hitachi, and Canon. The directors of Fuji Bank link all the largest and most significant keiretsu members. Each large member company has its

Figure 3.5
The Fuyo Keiretsu

A financial keiretsu centered around Fuji Bank in which organizations in the keiretsu are linked by minority share ownership in each other.

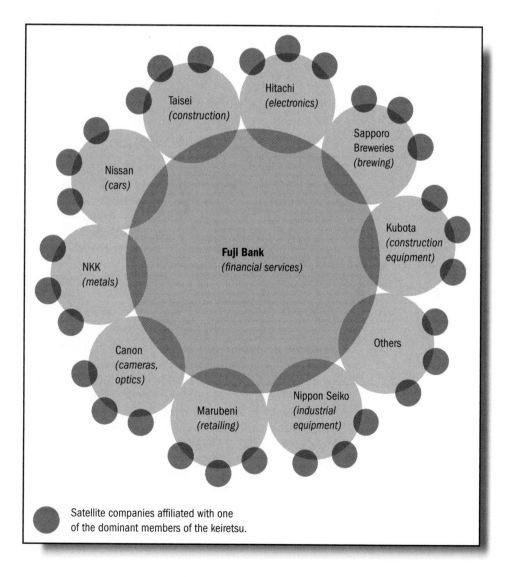

Taisei (construction)

Hitachi (electronics)

Sapporo Breweries (brewing)

Nissan (cars)

Kubota (construction equipment)

Fuji Bank (financial services)

NKK (metals)

Others

Canon (cameras, optics)

Nippon Seiko (industrial equipment)

Marubeni (retailing)

Satellite companies affiliated with one of the dominant members of the keiretsu.

Figure 3.6
Joint Venture Formation

Two separate organizations
pool resources to create a third
organization. A formal legal
document specifies the terms of
this type of strategic alliance.

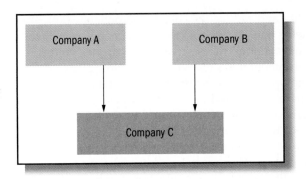

own set of satellite companies. For example, Nissan has a minority ownership stake
in many of the suppliers that provide inputs for its auto operations.

Joint Venture

Joint venture

A strategic alliance among two
or more organizations that agree
to jointly establish and share the
ownership of a new business.

A **joint venture** is a strategic alliance among two or more organizations that agree to
jointly establish and share the ownership of a new business.[31] Joint ventures are the
most formal of the strategic alliances because the participants are bound by a formal
legal agreement that spells out their rights and responsibilities. For example,
Company A and Company B agree to set up a new organization, Company C, and
then jointly design its organizational structure and select its top management team
(see Figure 3.6). Both Company A and Company B send executives to manage
Company C, and they also provide the resources Company C needs to grow and
prosper. Participants in a joint venture often pool their distinctive competences. One,
for example, might contribute expert knowledge on efficient production techniques
and the other its competencies in R&D. The pooling of skills in a new venture
increases the value that can be produced.

The shared ownership of a joint venture reduces the problems of managing complex interorganizational relationships that might arise if the basis of the strategic
alliance were simply a long-term contract. Moreover, the newly created organization
(Company C in Figure 3.6) is free to develop the structure that best suits its needs,
so problems of managing interdependencies with the parent companies are
reduced. Also, a joint venture may allow the founding companies (Company A and
Company B) to remain small and entrepreneurial, as well as new Company C.

In sum, organizations use informal and formal strategic alliances to manage
symbiotic resource interdependencies. The degree of formality increases as environmental uncertainty increases.

Merger and Takeover

The most formal strategy (see Figure 3.4) for managing symbiotic (and competitive)
resource interdependencies is to merge with or take over a supplier or distributor. As
a result of a merger or a takeover, resource exchanges occur *within* one organization
rather than *between* organizations, and an organization can no longer be held hostage
by a powerful supplier (that might demand a high price for its products) or by a powerful customer (that might try to drive down the price it pays for a company's products).[32] For example, Shell, a major producer of chemicals, owns several oil fields and
thus controls the prices of its oil and petroleum products that are vital inputs in chemical manufacturing. Similarly, McDonald's owns vast ranches in Brazil where it rears
low-cost cattle for its hamburgers. Alcoa owns or manages most of the world's supply
of aluminum ore and has dominated the global aluminum industry for decades.

An organization that takes over another company normally incurs great expense
and faces the problems of managing the new business. Thus an organization is likely
to take over a supplier or distributor only when it has a very great need to control a
crucial resource or manage an important interdependency.

STRATEGIES FOR MANAGING COMPETITIVE RESOURCE INTERDEPENDENCIES

Organizations do not like competition. Competition threatens the supply of scarce resources and increases the uncertainty of the specific environment. Intense competition can threaten the very survival of an organization as product prices fall to attract customers and the environment becomes poorer and poorer. For example, AT&T was forced to reduce the price of its long-distance services to just 7 cents a minute to compete with WorldCom, SBC Communications, and Qwest, which had been making large inroads into its market share.[33] The higher the level of competition, the more likely some companies in an industry are to go bankrupt.[34] Ultimately, the organizational environment consists of a handful of the strongest survivors competing head-to-head for resources.

Organizations use a variety of techniques to directly manipulate the environment to reduce the uncertainty of their competitive interdependent activities.[35] Figure 3.7 indicates the relative formality of four strategies. The more formal the strategy selected, the more explicit the attempt to coordinate competitors' activities. Some of these strategies are illegal, but unethical organizations break antitrust laws to gain a competitive edge. For example, in 2005 Samsung and other flash memory chip makers admitted to artificially increasing the price of their chips to consumers; these companies paid hundreds of millions of dollars in fines for their illegal actions.

Collusion and Cartels

Collusion
A secret agreement among competitors to share information for a deceitful or illegal purpose.

Cartel
An association of firms that explicitly agree to coordinate their activities.

A **collusion** is a secret agreement among competitors to share information for a deceitful or illegal purpose, such as keeping prices high as in the flash memory chip industry. Organizations collude in order to reduce the competitive uncertainty they experience. A **cartel** is an association of firms that explicitly agree to coordinate their activities as Samsung and other chip makers did.[36] Cartels and collusion increase the stability and richness of an organization's environment and reduce the complexity of relations among competitors. Both collusions and cartels are illegal in the United States.

Sometimes, competitors in an industry can collude by establishing industry standards.[37] Industry standards function like rules of conduct that tell competitors, for example, what prices they should charge, what their product specifications should be, or what a product's profit markup should be. Industry standards may result from price leadership. The strongest company, like Samsung in memory chips, is likely to be the price leader. It sets the prices for its products and then the weaker organizations charge prices similar to the price leader's. In this way, industry prices are fixed at an artificially high level. Organizations can always make more profit if they collectively coordinate their activities than if they compete; customers lose because they must pay the inflated prices.

Organizations can also collude and form a cartel without formal written agreement by signaling their intentions to each other by public announcements about

Figure 3.7
Interorganizational Strategies for Managing Competitive Interdependencies

Competitive interdependencies exist between an organization and its rivals. The more formal a strategy, the more explicit the attempt to coordinate competitors activities.

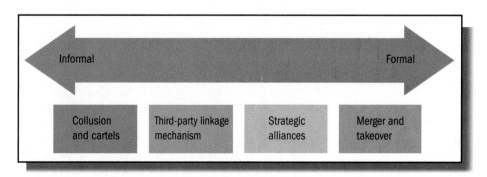

their future strategy. For example, they can announce price increases that they are contemplating and see whether their rivals will match those increases. This is common in the airline industry when one airline announces a price hike and then waits to see how the other airlines respond. Organizations in an industry can try to discipline companies that break informal competitive industry rules. Some large companies have a reputation for ruthlessly going after competitors that break their industry's informal pricing rules. For example, Dell is always ready to match any price decreases announced by HP and Gateway, so these companies come to realize they will gain no advantage by lowering prices.

Third-Party Linkage Mechanisms

A more formal but still indirect way for competing organizations to coordinate their activities is through a **third-party linkage mechanism**—a regulatory body that allows organizations to share information and regulate the way they compete.[38] An example is a trade association, an organization that represents companies in the same industry and enables competitors to meet, share information, and informally allow them to monitor one another's activities.[39] This interaction reduces the fear that one organization may deceive or outwit another. A trade association also has the collective resources (obtained from member organizations) to lobby strongly for government policies that protect the interests of its industry. We saw earlier how the pharmaceutical industry uses its powerful lobby to fend off attempts to reduce the price of drugs. The cable TV industry, defense, farming, and virtually every other industry seek to protect their own interests and increase their access to scarce resources.

Other examples of third-party linkage mechanisms include agencies such as the Chicago Board of Trade, stock markets, the National Collegiate Athletic Association (NCAA), and any other organization that is set up to regulate competitive interdependencies. Third-party linkage mechanisms provide rules and standards that stabilize industry competition and thus increase the richness of the environment. They reduce the complexity of the environment because they regulate the interactions of organizations. Also, by increasing the flow of information they enable organizations to react more easily to change or to the dynamism of the environment. In short, third-party linkage mechanisms provide a way for competitors to manage resource interdependencies and reduce uncertainty.

Organizations that use a third-party linkage mechanism co-opt themselves and jointly receive the benefits of the coordination that they obtain from the third-party linkage mechanism. For example, Microelectronics and Computer Corporation, an applied R&D cooperative funded by industry members such as Intel and Motorola, was set up to improve research in semiconductors. This organization channels the results of its research to its funding members. After three years, the funding members can license the results to other companies in the industry.[40] The number of U.S. research and development cooperatives formed by competitors to fund joint research interests is rapidly increasing as global competition increases. Japan is the model for such third-party linkage mechanisms. Its Ministry of International Trade and Industry (MITI) has a long history of promoting industry cooperation among domestic rivals to foster joint technical developments that help Japanese companies achieve global leadership in some industries.

Strategic Alliances

Strategic alliances can be used to manage not only symbiotic interdependencies, but competitive interdependencies, as well.[41] Competitors can cooperate and form a joint venture to develop common technology that will save them all a lot of money, even though they may be in competition for customers when their final products hit the market. Apple and IBM, for example, formed a long-term joint venture to share the costs of developing a common microchip that will make their machines compatible, even though they will be competitors in the PC market. Both Ford and Mazda have benefited from a strategic alliance (Ford owns a 25% stake in Mazda). Ford gained detailed knowledge of Japanese production techniques, and Mazda and Ford jointly cooperated to produce vehicles in the same U.S. plant.

Although the kinds of joint ventures just described are not anticompetitive, organizations sometimes use joint ventures to deter new entrants or harm existing competitors. Philips and Bang & Olufsen, two leading consumer electronics companies, signed an agreement to share their production and design skills, respectively, to compete with Japanese giants Sony and Panasonic.[42] Organizations can also form a joint venture to develop a new technology that they can then protect from other rivals by obtaining and defending patents. The use of strategic alliances to manage competitive interdependencies is limited only by the imagination of rival companies.

Merger and Takeover

The ultimate weapon in an organization's armory for managing problematic competitive (and symbiotic) interdependencies is to merge with, or take over, a competing organization.[43] Mergers and takeovers can improve a company's competitive position by allowing the company to strengthen and enlarge its domain and increase its ability to produce a wider range of products to better serve more customers. For example, NationsBank bought up smaller banks at a very fast rate, and in 1998 merged with Bank of America to become the biggest bank in the United States. Wells Fargo, Capital one, and Citibank are also pursuing this strategy in the 2000s.

Many organizations might like to use merger to become a monopoly, the sole player in the marketplace. Fortunately for consumers, and for organizations themselves, monopolies are illegal in the United States and in most other developed countries. So, if an organization becomes too strong and dominant, such as Microsoft or GE, they are prevented by antitrust law from taking over other companies to become even more powerful.[44] Nevertheless, cartels, collusion, and other anticompetitive practices can ultimately be bad for organizations themselves. In the long run, as a result of changes in technology, cheap sources of labor, changes in government policy, and so forth, new entrants will be able to enter an industry, and existing companies that have reduced competition among themselves will then find themselves ineffective competitors. Protected from competition in an environment where uncertainty has been low, these monopoly-like organizations have become large top-heavy bureaucracies unable to meet the challenges of a rapidly changing environment. GM, IBM, Kodak, and Xerox are organizations that controlled their competitive environments for a very long time and suffered greatly when it changed, allowing more agile competitors to enter and beat the established companies at their own game.

MANAGERIAL IMPLICATIONS

RESOURCE DEPENDENCE THEORY

1. To maintain an adequate supply of scarce resources, study each resource transaction individually in order to decide how to manage it.
2. Study the benefits and costs associated with an interorganizational strategy before using it.
3. To maximize the organization's freedom of action, always prefer an informal to a formal linkage mechanism. Use a more formal mechanism only when the uncertainty of the situation warrants it.
4. When entering into strategic alliances with other organizations, be careful to identify the purpose of the alliance and future problems that might arise between organizations, in order to decide whether an informal or a formal linkage mechanism is most appropriate. Once again, choose an informal rather than a formal alliance whenever possible.
5. Use transaction cost theory to identify the benefits and costs associated with the use of different linkage mechanisms to manage particular interdependencies.

TRANSACTION COST THEORY

Transaction costs
The costs of negotiating, monitoring, and governing exchanges between people.

Transaction cost theory
A theory that states that the goal of an organization is to minimize the costs of exchanging resources in the environment and the costs of managing exchanges inside the organization.

In Chapter 1, we defined **transaction costs** as the costs of negotiating, monitoring, and governing exchanges between people. Whenever people work together, there are costs—transaction costs—associated with controlling their activities.[45] Transaction costs also arise when organizations exchange resources or information. Organizations interact with other organizations to get the resources they require, and they have to control those symbiotic and competitive interdependencies. According to resource dependence theory, organizations attempt to gain control of resources and minimize their dependence on other organizations. According to **transaction cost theory**, the goal of the organization is to minimize the costs of exchanging resources in the environment and the costs of managing exchanges inside the organization.[46] Every dollar or hour of a manager's time spent in negotiating or monitoring exchanges with other organizations, or with managers inside one organization, is a dollar or hour that is not being used to create value. Organizations try to minimize transaction costs and bureaucratic costs because they siphon off productive capacity. Organizations try to find mechanisms that make interorganizational transactions relatively more efficient.

Health care provides a dramatic example of just how large transaction costs can be and why reducing them is so important. It is estimated that over 40% of the U.S. health-care budget is spent handling exchanges (such as bills and insurance claims) between doctors, hospitals, the government, insurance companies, and other parties.[47] Clearly, any improvements that reduce transaction costs would result in a major saving of resources. The desire to reduce transaction costs was the impetus for the formation of health maintenance organizations (HMOs) and other networks of health-care providers. HMO providers agree to reduce their costs in return for a more certain flow of patients, among other things. This trade-off reduces the uncertainty they experience.

Sources of Transaction Costs

Transaction costs result from a combination of human and environmental factors.[48] (See Figure 3.8.)

Environmental Uncertainty and Bounded Rationality

The environment is characterized by considerable uncertainty and complexity. People, however, have only a limited ability to process information and to understand the environment surrounding them.[49] Because of this limited ability, or bounded rationality, the higher the level of uncertainty in an environment, the greater the difficulty of managing transactions between organizations.

Suppose Organization A wants to license a technology developed by Organization B. The two organizations could sign a contract. Considerable uncertainty, however, would surround this contract. For example, Organization B might want to find new ways of using the technology to make new products for itself. Given bounded

Figure 3.8
Sources of Transaction Costs

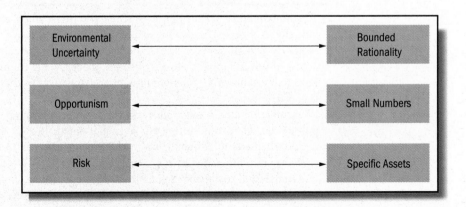

rationality, it would be difficult and prohibitively expensive to try to write a contract that not only protected Organization B, which developed the technology, but also spelled out how the two organizations might jointly share in the future benefits from the technology. In this situation, the developing company (Organization B) might prefer to proceed alone and not exchange resources with Organization A, even though it knows it could create more value by engaging in the exchange. Thus, because of bounded rationality and the high transaction costs of drawing up a contract, potential value that could have been created is lost. Environmental uncertainty may make the cost of negotiating, monitoring, and governing agreements so high that organizations resort to more formal linkage mechanisms—such as strategic alliances, minority ownership, or even mergers—to lower transaction costs.

Opportunism and Small Numbers

Most people and organizations behave honestly and reputably most of the time, but some always behave opportunistically—that is, they cheat or otherwise attempt to exploit other forces or stakeholders in the environment.[50] For example, an organization contracts for component parts of a particular quality. To reduce costs and save money, the supplier deliberately substitutes inferior materials but bills for the more expensive, higher quality parts. Individuals, too, act opportunistically: Managers pad their expense reports or exploit customers by manufacturing inferior products.

When an organization is dependent on one supplier or on a small number of trading partners, the potential for opportunism is great. The organization has no choice but to transact business with the supplier, and the supplier, knowing this, might choose to supply inferior inputs to reduce costs and increase profit.

When the prospect for opportunism is high because of the small number of suppliers to which an organization can go for resources, the organization has to expend resources to negotiate, monitor, and enforce agreements with its suppliers to protect itself. For example, the U.S. government spends billions of dollars a year to protect itself from being exploited by defense contractors such as Hughes Aircraft and General Dynamics, which have been known to take advantage of their ability to exploit the government because they have so few competitors for defense-related work.

Risk and Specific Assets

Specific assets
Investments—in skills, machinery, knowledge, and information—that create value in one particular exchange relationship but have no value in any other exchange relationship.

Specific assets are investments—in skills, machinery, knowledge, and information—that create value in one particular exchange relationship but have no value in any other exchange relationship. A company that invests $100 million in a machine that makes microchips for IBM machines only has made a very specific investment in a very specific asset. An organization's decision to invest money to develop specific assets for a specific relationship with another organization in its environment involves a high level of risk. Once the investment is made, the organization is locked into it. If the other party tries to exploit the relationship by saying, for example, "We will not buy your product unless you sell it to us for $10 less per unit than you're charging now," the organization is in a very difficult situation. This tactic is akin to blackmail.

An organization that sees any prospect of being trapped or blackmailed will judge the investment in specific assets to be too risky. The transaction costs associated with the investment become too high, and value that could have been created is lost.[51]

Transaction Costs and Linkage Mechanisms

Organizations base their choice of interorganizational linkage mechanisms on the level of transaction costs involved in an exchange relationship. Transaction costs are low when these conditions exist:

1. Organizations are exchanging nonspecific goods and services.
2. Uncertainty is low.
3. There are many possible exchange partners.

In these environmental conditions, it is easy for organizations to negotiate and monitor interorganizational behavior. Thus, in a low-transaction-cost environment, organizations can use relatively informal linkage mechanisms, such as reputation and unwritten, word-of-mouth contracts.

Transaction costs increase when these conditions exist:

1. Organizations begin to exchange more specific goods and services.
2. Uncertainty increases.
3. The number of possible exchange partners falls.

In this kind of environment, an organization will begin to feel that it cannot afford to trust other organizations, and it will start to monitor and use more formal linkages, such as long-term contracts, to govern its exchanges. Contracts, however, cannot cover every situation that might arise. If something unexpected happens, what will the other party to the exchange do? It has a perfect right to act in the way that most benefits itself, even though its actions are harmful to the other organization.

How does an organization act in a high-transaction-cost situation? According to transaction cost theory, an organization should choose a more formal linkage mechanism to manage exchanges as transaction costs increase. The more formal the mechanism used, the more control organizations have over each other's behavior. Formal mechanisms include strategic alliances (joint ventures), merger, and takeover, all of which internalize the transaction and its cost. In a joint venture, two organizations establish a third organization to handle their joint transactions. Establishing a new entity that both organizations own equally reduces each organization's incentives to cheat the other and provides incentives for them to do things (for example, invest in specific assets) that will create value for them both. With mergers, the same arguments hold because one organization now owns the other.

From a transaction cost perspective, the movement from less formal to more formal linkage mechanisms (see Figures 3.3, 3.4, and 3.7) occurs because of an organization's need to reduce the transaction costs of its exchanges with other organizations. Formal mechanisms minimize the transaction costs associated with reducing uncertainty, opportunism, and risk.

Bureaucratic Costs

If formal linkage mechanisms are such an efficient way to minimize the transaction costs of exchanges with the environment, why do organizations not use these mechanisms all the time? Why do they ever use an informal linkage mechanism such as a contract if a joint venture or a merger gives them better control of their environment? The answer is that bringing the transactions inside the organization minimizes but does not eliminate the costs of managing transactions.[52] Managers must still negotiate, monitor, and govern exchanges between people inside the organization. Internal transaction costs are called *bureaucratic costs* to distinguish them from the transaction costs of exchanges between organizations in the environment.[53] We saw in Chapter 2 how difficult communication and integration between functions and divisions are. Now we see that integration and communication are not only difficult to achieve but also cost money, because managers have to spend their time in meetings rather than creating value.[54] Thus managing an organization's structure is a complex and expensive problem that becomes much more expensive and complex as the organization grows—as GM, Kodak, and IBM discovered.

Using Transaction Cost Theory to Choose an Interorganizational Strategy

Transaction cost theory can help managers choose an interorganizational strategy by enabling them to weigh the savings in transaction costs achieved from using a particular linkage mechanism against the bureaucratic costs of operating the linkage mechanism.[55]

The Ekco Group of Nashua, New Hampshire, makes a wide range of bakeware products, kitchen tools and equipment, household plastic products (such as laundry baskets), and pest-control devices.[56] It produces thousands of nonelectric consumer and office products that require no assembly and are replaced rather than repaired when they wear out.

Ekco's wide product range reflects the needs of retail customers like Wal-Mart and K-mart, which are continually trying to reduce the transaction costs associated with obtaining products. Obtaining a wide range of products from one supplier reduces the transaction costs associated with building many supplier relationships. By offering a broad range of products that K-mart, Wal-Mart, and others are interested in carrying, Ekco helps the retailers minimize the number of companies they must go to for the products they want to carry. In this way, Ekco is implicitly inviting customers to increase their links with Ekco.

To foster long-term commitment and trust with its customers, Ekco recently installed a state-of-the-art $4 million data-processing system (a specific asset) that allows Ekco to provide just-in-time inventory service to retailers who supply the company with data. This system simplifies retailers' ordering and tracking of their inventory. By managing customers' transactions at no cost to them, the Ekco system further reduces the retailers' transaction costs with Ekco and strengthens their perception that Ekco is a good company to do business with. Ekco's attempt to develop informal linkage mechanisms with its customers paid off and sales to its major customers increase every year.[57]

Because transaction cost theory brings into focus the costs associated with different linkage mechanisms to reduce uncertainty, it is able to make better predictions than is resource dependence theory about why and when a company will choose a certain interorganizational strategy. Managers deciding which strategy to pursue must take the following steps:

1. Locate the sources of transaction costs that may affect an exchange relationship and decide how high the transaction costs are likely to be.
2. Estimate the transaction cost savings from using different linkage mechanisms.
3. Estimate the bureaucratic costs of operating the linkage mechanism.
4. Choose the linkage mechanism that gives the most transaction cost savings at the lowest bureaucratic cost.

The experience of the Ekco Group offers an interesting example of how a supplier can use a linkage mechanism to reduce transaction costs for customers in order to gain their support. Ekco and its customers jointly benefit from close personal ties, and there is no need for formal and expensive mechanisms to coordinate their interorganizational exchanges.

The implication of a transaction cost view is that a formal linkage mechanism should be used only when transaction costs are high enough to warrant it. An organization should take over and merge with its suppliers or distributors, for example, only if the saving in transaction costs outweighs the costs of managing the new acquisition.[58] Otherwise, like Ekco and its customers, the organization should rely on less formal mechanisms, such as strategic alliances and long-term contracts, to handle exchange relationships. The relatively informal linkage mechanisms avoid the need for an organization to incur bureaucratic costs. Three linkage mechanisms that help organizations to avoid bureaucratic costs while still minimizing transaction costs are keiretsu, franchising, and outsourcing.

Keiretsu

The Japanese system of keiretsu can be seen as a mechanism for achieving the benefits of a formal linkage mechanism without incurring its costs.[59] The policy of owning a minority stake in its suppliers' companies gives Toyota substantial control over the exchange relationship and allows it to avoid problems of opportunism and uncertainty with its suppliers. Toyota also avoids the bureaucratic costs of actually owning and managing its suppliers. Indeed, keiretsu was developed to provide the benefits of full ownership without the costs.

In contrast, GM has full ownership of more suppliers than does any other car manufacturer and pays more for its inputs than the other car companies pay for theirs. Critics charge that these high costs arise because GM's internal suppliers are in a protected situation. GM is a captive buyer, so its supplying divisions have no incentive to be efficient and thus behave opportunistically.[60]

What should GM do? One course of action would be to divest its inefficient suppliers and then establish strategic alliances or long-term contracts with them to encourage them to lower their costs and increase their efficiency. If they cannot improve their cost or quality, GM would form new alliances with new suppliers. GM has been trying to do exactly that; in 1999 it spun off its Delco electronic parts subsidiary into an independent operating company.[61] GM is trying to obtain the benefits that Toyota has achieved from its strategy of minority ownership. Conversely, if GM were experiencing problems with obtaining the benefits from a strategic alliance (if, for example, its partner were acting opportunistically), it should move to a more formal linkage mechanism and buy and merge with its suppliers. GM is not in this situation, however. Its problem is finding the combination of ownership, strategic alliances, and long-term contracts that will minimize its input costs, which are still about $1,000 higher per car than the input costs of Japanese car manufacturers.

Franchising

A franchise is a business that is authorized to sell a company's products in a certain area. The franchiser sells the right to use its resources (for example, its name or operating system) to a person or group (the franchisee) in return for a flat fee or a share of the profits. Normally, the franchiser provides the inputs used by the franchisee, who deals directly with the customer. The relationship between franchiser and franchisee is symbiotic. The transaction cost approach offers an interesting insight into why interorganizational strategies such as franchising emerge.[62]

Consider the operational differences between McDonald's and Burger King. A very large proportion of McDonald's restaurants are owned by franchisees, but most Burger King restaurants are owned by the company. Why doesn't McDonald's own its restaurants? Why is McDonald's willing to make its franchisees millionaires instead of enriching its stockholders? From a transaction cost point of view, the answer lies in the bureaucratic costs that McDonald's would incur if it attempted to manage all its own restaurants.

The single biggest challenge for a restaurant is to maintain the quality of its food and customer service. Suppose McDonald's employed managers to run all its company-owned restaurants. Would those managers have the same incentive to maintain as high a quality of customer service as franchisees who own and so directly benefit from a high-performing restaurant? McDonald's believes that if it owned and operated all its restaurants—that is, if it used a formal linkage mechanism—the bureaucratic costs incurred to maintain the quality and consistency of the restaurants would exceed any extra value the organization and its shareholders would obtain from full ownership. Thus McDonald's generally owns only those restaurants that are located in big cities or near highways. In big cities it can spread the costs of employing a management team over many restaurants and reduce bureaucratic costs. On interstate highways, McDonald's believes, franchisees realize that they are unlikely to see the same travelers ever again and have no incentive to maintain standards.

The same issue arises on the output side when an organization is choosing how to distribute its products. Should an organization own its distribution outlets? Should it sell directly to customers? Should it sell only to franchised dealers? Again the answer depends on the transaction cost problems the organization can expect in dealing with the needs of its customers. Generally, the more complex products are and the more information customers need about how they work or how to repair them, the greater the likelihood that organizations have formal hierarchical control over their distributors and franchisees or own their own distribution outlets.[63]

Cars are typically sold through franchised dealers because of the need to provide customers with reliable car repair. Also, because cars are complicated products and customers need a lot of information before they buy one, it is effective for manufacturers to have some control over their distributors. Thus car manufacturers have considerable control over their dealerships and monitor and enforce the service that dealerships give to customers. Toyota, for example, closely monitors the number of customer complaints against a dealership. If the number of complaints gets too high, it punishes the dealership by restricting its supply of new cars. As a result, dealers have strong incentives to give customers good service. In contrast, the transaction costs involved in handling simple products like clothes or food are low. Thus few clothing or food companies choose to use formal linkages to control the distribution of their products. Less formal mechanisms such as contracts with wholesalers or with large retail store chains become the preferred distribution strategy.

Outsourcing

Outsourcing

The process of moving a value creation activity that was performed inside an organization to outside where it is done by another company.

Another strategy for managing interdependencies is outsourcing. **Outsourcing** is moving a value-creation activity that was performed inside an organization to outside, where it is done by another company—for example, hiring a company to manage a company's computer network or to distribute its products instead of performing the activity itself. Increasingly, organizations are turning to specialized companies to manage their information processing needs. Dell, HP, and IBM, for example, have set up divisions that supply this specialized service to companies in their environments.

What prompts an organization to outsource a function is the same calculation that determines whether an organization makes or buys inputs. Does the extra value

ORGANIZATIONAL INSIGHT 3.4
Li & Fung's Global Supply Chain Management

Finding the overseas suppliers that offer the lowest priced and highest quality products is an important task facing the managers of global organizations. Because these suppliers are located in thousands of cities in many countries around the world, finding them is a difficult business. Often, global companies use the services of overseas intermediaries or brokers, located near these suppliers, to find the one that best meets their input requirements. Li & Fung, now run by brothers Victor and William Fung, is one of these brokers that has helped hundreds of global companies to locate suitable overseas suppliers, especially suppliers in mainland China.[64]

In the 2000s, however, managing global companies' supply chains has become a more complicated task. To reduce costs, overseas suppliers are increasingly specializing in just one part of the task of producing a product. For example, in the past, a company such as Target might have negotiated with an overseas supplier to manufacture 1 million units of some particular shirt at a certain cost per unit. But with specialization, Target might find it can reduce the costs of producing the shirt even further by splitting apart the operations involved in producing the shirt and having different overseas suppliers, often in different countries, perform each operation. For example, to get the lowest cost per unit, rather than just negotiate with a overseas supplier over the price of making a particular

shirt, Target might first negotiate with a yarn manufacturer in Vietnam to make the yarn; then ship the yarn to a Chinese supplier to weave it into cloth; and then ship to several different factories in Malaysia and the Philippines to cut the cloth and sew the shirts. Then, another overseas company might take responsibility for packaging and shipping the shirts to wherever in the world they are required. Because a company such as Target has thousands of different clothing products under production, and these change all the time, the problems of managing such a supply chain to get the full cost savings from global expansion are clear.

Li & Fung has capitalized on this opportunity. Realizing that many global companies do not have the time or expertise to find such specialized low-price suppliers, they moved quickly to provide such a service. Li & Fung employs 3,600 agents who travel across 37 countries to find new suppliers and inspect existing suppliers to find new ways to help their global clients get lower prices or higher quality products. Global companies are happy to outsource their supply chain management to Li & Fung because they realize significant cost savings. Even though they pay a hefty fee to Li & Fung, they avoid the costs of employing their own agents. As the complexity of supply chain management continues to increase, more and more companies like Li & Fung are appearing.

that the organization obtains from performing its own marketing or information processing exceed the extra bureaucratic costs of managing such functions? If the answer is yes, the organization develops its own function. If it is no, the organization outsources the activity.[65] This decision is likely to change over time. Perhaps in 1996 it was best to have an information-processing department inside the organization. By 2006, however, specialized organizations may be able to process information more cheaply, and then it will pay to outsource that function. Outsourcing within networks, such as the one established by Nike, is another example of how outsourcing helps hold down the bureaucratic costs of managing exchanges inside an organization. Global supply chain management offers another example of how companies can reduce transaction costs and avoid bureaucratic costs.

The specific method a company adopts to manage the outsourcing process will be the one that most effectively reduces the uncertainty involved in the exchange—to ensure a stable supply of inexpensive components, to improve quality, or to protect valuable proprietary technology. For example, in terms of the different kinds of strategic alliances presented in Figure 3.4, when uncertainty is relatively low companies can choose to create long-term contracts with many low-cost overseas suppliers. As uncertainty increases, a company might develop a network to manage interdependencies between these suppliers and global manufacturers and distributors, or it might take a minority ownership interest in these global companies to gain legal control over the transaction. Finally, when uncertainty is high a company might decide to form a joint venture to control all aspects of the value-creation activity.

A transaction cost approach sheds light on why and how organizations choose different linkage mechanisms to manage their interdependencies. It improves our ability to understand the process that organizations use to manage their environments to enhance their chances for growth and survival. The solutions that exist for managing uncertain resource exchanges and organizational interdependencies range from less formal mechanisms like contracts to more formal mechanisms like ownership. The best mechanism for an organization is one that minimizes transaction and bureaucratic costs.

SUMMARY

Managing the organizational environment is a crucial task for an organization. The first step is identifying sources of uncertainty and examining the sources of complexity, how rapidly it is changing, and how rich or poor it is. An organization then needs to evaluate the benefits and costs of different interorganizational strategies and choose the one that best allows it to secure valuable resources. Resource dependence theory weighs the benefit of securing scarce resources against the cost of a loss of autonomy. Transaction cost theory weighs the benefit of reducing transaction costs against the cost of increasing bureaucratic costs. An organization must examine the whole array of its exchanges with its environment in order to devise the combination of linkage mechanisms that will maximize its ability to create value. Chapter 3 has made the following main points:

1. The organizational environment is the set of forces in the changing global environment that affect the way an organization operates and its ability to gain access to scarce resources.

2. The organizational domain is the range of goods and services that the organization produces and the clients that it serves in the countries in which it operates. An organization devises interorganizational strategies to protect and enlarge its domain.

3. The specific environment consists of forces that most directly affect an organization's ability to secure resources. The general environment consists of forces that shape the specific environments of all organizations.

4. Uncertainty in the environment is a function of the complexity, dynamism, and richness of the environment.

5. Resource dependence theory argues that the goal of an organization is to minimize its dependence on other organizations for the supply of scarce resources and to find ways of influencing them to make resources available.

6. Organizations have to manage two kinds of resource interdependencies: symbiotic interdependencies with suppliers and customers and competitive interdependencies with rivals.

7. The main interorganizational strategies for managing symbiotic relationships are the development of a good reputation, co-optation, strategic alliances, and merger and takeover. The main interorganizational strategies for managing competitive relationships are collusion and cartels, third-party linkage mechanisms, strategic alliances, and merger and takeover.

8. Transaction costs are the costs of negotiating, monitoring, and governing exchanges between people and organizations. There are three sources of transaction costs: (a) the combination of uncertainty and bounded rationality, (b) opportunism and small numbers, and (c) specific assets and risk.

9. Transaction cost theory argues that the goal of organizations is to minimize the costs of exchanging resources in the environment and the costs of managing exchanges inside the organization. Organizations try to choose interorganizational strategies that minimize transaction costs and bureaucratic costs.

10. Interorganizational linkage mechanisms range from informal types such as contracts and reputation to formal types such as strategic alliances and ownership strategies such as merger and takeover.

DISCUSSION QUESTIONS

1. Pick an organization, such as a local travel agency or supermarket. Describe its organizational domain; then draw a map of the forces in its general and specific environments that affect the way it operates.

2. What are the major sources of uncertainty in an environment? Discuss how these sources of uncertainty affect a small biotechnology company and a large carmaker.

3. According to resource dependence theory, what motivates organizations to form interorganizational linkages? What is the advantage of strategic alliances as a way of exchanging resources?

4. According to transaction cost theory, what motivates organizations to form interorganizational linkages? Under what conditions would a company prefer a more formal linkage mechanism to a less formal one?

5. What interorganizational strategies might work most successfully as a company expands globally? Why?

ORGANIZATIONAL THEORY IN ACTION

Practicing Organizational Theory: Protecting Your Domain

Break up into groups of three to five people and discuss the following scenario:

You are entrepreneurs who have recently launched a new kind of root beer, made from exotic herbs and spices, that has quickly obtained a loyal following in a large southwestern city. Inspired by your success, you have decided that you would like to increase production of your root beer to serve a wider geographical area, with the eventual goal of serving all of the United States and Canada.

The problem you have is deciding the best way to secure your domain and manage the environment as you grow. On one hand, both the ingredients in your root beer and your method of making it are secret, so you have to protect it from potential imitators at all costs—large soda companies will quickly copy it if they have a chance. On the other hand, you lack the funds for quick expansion, and finding a partner who can help you grow quickly and establish a brand name reputation would be an enormous advantage.

1. Analyze the pros and cons of each of the types of strategic alliances (long-term contracts, networks, minority ownership, and joint ventures) as your means of managing the environment.

2. Based on this analysis, which one would you choose to maximize your chance of securing a stable niche in the soda market?

The Ethical Dimension #3

In their search to reduce costs, many global companies are buying products from suppliers in overseas countries that are made in sweatshops by women and children who work long hours for a few dollars a day. As we saw in Chapter 2 (Organizational Insight 2.5), there are complex arguments surrounding this issue. However, from an ethical perspective discuss:

1. When and under what conditions it is right for companies to buy their inputs from suppliers that do employ women and children?

2. What kinds of interorganizational strategies could U.S. companies use to enforce any ethical codes they develop?

Making the Connection #3

Find an example of a company that is using a specific interorganizational strategy, such as a joint venture or a long-term contract. What linkage mechanism is it using? Use resource dependence theory or transaction cost theory to explain why the organization might have chosen that type of mechanism.

Analyzing the Organization: Design Module #3

This module and the modules in the next two chapters allow you to analyze the environment of your organization and to understand how the organization tries to manage its environment to control and obtain the resources it needs to protect its domain.

Assignment

1. Draw a chart of your organization's domain. List the organization's products and customers and the forces in the specific and general environments that have an effect on it. Which are the most important forces that the organization has to deal with?

2. Analyze the effect of the forces on the complexity, dynamism, and richness of the environment. From this analysis, how would you characterize the level of uncertainty in your organization's environment?

3. Draw a chart of the main interorganizational linkage mechanisms (for example, long-term contracts, strategic alliances, mergers) that your organization uses to manage its symbiotic resource interdependencies. Using resource dependence theory and transaction cost theory, discuss why the organization chose to manage its interdependencies in this way. Do you think the organization has selected the most appropriate linkage mechanisms? Why or why not?

4. Draw a chart of the main interorganizational linkage mechanisms (for example, collusion, third-party linkage mechanisms, strategic alliances) that your organization uses to manage its competitive resource interdependencies. Using resource dependence theory or transaction cost theory, discuss why the organization chose to manage its interdependencies in this way. Do you think the organization has selected the most appropriate linkage mechanisms? Why or why not?

5. In view of the analysis you have just made, do you think your organization is doing a good or a not-so-good job of managing its environment? What recommendations would you make to improve its ability to obtain resources?

CASE FOR ANALYSIS

How Ford Manages Its Environment

Ford Motor Company has a long history of finding innovative ways to manage its environment (its suppliers, customers, and so on) in order to control the resources it needs. In its early years, Ford relied heavily on independent suppliers for inputs of engines, gearboxes, and wheels. Ford established a series of contracts with suppliers to provide parts, and all Ford did was bolt the parts together into a finished vehicle. Ford, however, soon had trouble maintaining the quality of the parts. Moreover, the parts made by one supplier tended to be incompatible with the parts made by other suppliers, so Ford spent considerable time making adjustments.

To improve the quality of its auto parts, Ford began to produce them itself. The company took control of some of its suppliers and merged them into the Ford organization, but Ford also started its own supply operations. Ford soon became a highly vertically integrated company—that is, it produced most of its own inputs. To ensure access to resources, for example, Ford owned iron mines in northern Michigan and transported iron ore across Lake Superior on its own barges. At its smelting plant outside Detroit, Ford made and then shaped steel into body parts for Ford cars and trucks.

In the 1950s, this vertical strategy became too expensive. Sheet steel and other inputs that Ford made were costing it more than comparable materials purchased from efficient independent suppliers would cost. Consequently, Ford resumed the use of long-term contracts to manage its relationships with suppliers. Ford used its buying power to negotiate favorable prices, and it gained a cost advantage over General Motors, which remained highly vertically integrated.

Prior to the 1980s, dealing with competitors posed few problems for Ford. There were no significant overseas competitors, and the "Big Three" American carmakers—GM, Chrysler, and Ford—were able to coordinate their pricing policies informally to avoid competition over customers. GM, the largest and most powerful company, established the prices that it would charge for different classes of cars; Ford and Chrysler priced their cars accordingly. The three companies competed primarily over quality and features—who had the most chrome or the biggest fins, for example.

In the 1980s, however, the competitive environment facing American car manufacturers became more hostile as Japanese carmakers increasingly competed for a share of the ultimate resource: customers. The development of several new techniques for managing the resource environment gave the Japanese a strong advantage over their counterparts in the United States. For example, Toyota and Nissan each owned a significant stake of their parts suppliers and thus were better able than the American Big Three to control the price and quality of their inputs and obtain the benefits of just-in-time inventory systems. Keiretsu, as these formal linkages between companies are called in Japan, link Japanese car companies not only to parts suppliers but also to large banks and to companies in other industries. Such linkages increase the financial power of Toyota and Nissan and give them the ability to control resources across industries. Also, the government of Japan sanctions the use of industry consortia, associations established by competitors to fund joint research into pollution control, advanced plastics research, and so forth.

The Japanese companies' efforts to control their environment were not unnoticed by Ford, which moved to establish its own keiretsu-type arrangement. Ford bought a minority interest in Cummings U.S., which produces engines; in Excel Industries, which produces windows; and in Decoma International, which produces body parts and wheels. Ford also forged links with rivals: It owns 25% of Mazda, with which it has established many strategic alliances to share technology and design facilities. It bought Aston Martin Lagonda and Jaguar of Britain, as well as KIA Motors of Japan, in order to gain their resources and skills.

In addition to linking up with other car manufacturers and suppliers, Ford owns several business units that handle commercial and consumer credit and that finance dealers' purchases of cars. Ford owns 49% of the Hertz car rental company, which, not surprisingly, uses Ford cars, and Ford has agreements with other rental car companies to use Ford products. Ford also belongs to eight industry consortia, in which it joins with GM, DaimlerChrysler, and other companies to fund joint research on projects such as a $200 million joint venture to develop more efficient and lighter batteries for electric cars.[66] Clearly, Ford has adopted a sophisticated strategy to respond to the need to control its environment and protect the quality and supply of scarce resources.

DISCUSSION QUESTIONS

1. List the various ways in which Ford has attempted to manage its environment over time.

2. Why did Ford change the methods it used to manage its environment?

REFERENCES

1. J. D. Thompson, *Organizations in Action* (New York: McGraw-Hill, 1967).
2. www.gerber.com, 2006.
3. R. H. Hall, *Organizations: Structure and Process* (Upper Saddle River, NJ: Prentice Hall, 1972).
4. R. H. Miles, *Macro Organizational Behavior* (Santa Monica, CA: Goodyear, 1980).
5. J. Perez, "GE Finds Tough Going in Hungary," *The New York Times*, July 25, 1994, pp. C1, C3.
6. J. Child, "Organizational Structure, Environment, and Performance: The Role of Strategic Choice," *Sociology, 6* (1972), 1–22; G. G. Dess and D. W. Beard, "Dimensions of Organizational Task Environments," *Administrative Science Quarterly, 29* (1984), 52–73.
7. F. E. Emery and E. L. Trist, "The Causal Texture of Organizational Environments," *Human Relations, 18* (1965), 21–32.
8. H. Aldrich, *Organizations and Environments* (Upper Saddle River, NJ: Prentice Hall, 1979).
9. W. H. Starbuck, "Organizations and Their Environments," in M. D. Dunnette, ed., *Handbook of Industrial Psychology* (Chicago: Rand McNally, 1976), pp. 1069–1123; Dess and Beard, "Dimensions of Organizational Task Environments."
10. Aldrich, *Organizations and Environments.*
11. www.amazon.com, 2006.
12. www.amazon.com, 2006.
13. J. Pfeffer and G. R. Salancik, *The External Control of Organizations* (New York: Harper and Row, 1978).
14. Pfeffer, *Organizations and Organizational Theory,* (Boston:Pitman, 1982), p. 193.
15. Pfeffer and Salancik, *The External Control of Organizations*, pp. 45–46.
16. D. Miller and J. Shamsie, "The Resource-Based View of the Firm in Two Environments: The Hollywood Film Studios from 1936–1965," *Academy of Management Journal, 39* (1996), 519–543.
17. www.avon.com, 2005.
18. Pfeffer and Salancik, *The External Control of Organizations*, p. 114.
19. H.R. Greve, "Patterns of Competition: The Diffusion of Market Position in Radio Broadcasting," *Administrative Science Quarterly, 41* (1996), 29–60.
20. J. M. Pennings, "Strategically Interdependent Organizations," in J. Nystrom and W. Starbuck, eds., *Handbook of Organizational Design* (New York: Oxford University Press, 1981), pp. 433–455.
21. J. Galaskeiwicz, "Interorganizational Relations," *Annual Review of Sociology, 11* (1985), 281–304.
22. G. R. Jones and M. W. Pustay, "Interorganizational Coordination in the Airline Industry, 1925–1938: A Transaction Cost Approach," *Journal of Management, 14* (1988), 529–546.
23. C.W.L. Hill, "Cooperation, Opportunism, and the Invisible Hand," *Academy of Management Review, 15* (1990), 500–513.
24. P. Selznick, *TVA and the Grassroots* (New York: Harper and Row, 1949).
25. J. Pfeffer, "Size and Composition of Corporate Boards of Directors," *Administrative Science Quarterly, 17* (1972), 218–228; R. D. Burt, "Co-optive Corporate Actor Networks: A Reconsideration of Interlocking Directorates Involving American Manufacturing," *Administrative Science Quarterly, 25* (1980), 557–581.
26. "Bechtel, Willbros to Build Pipeline at Caspian Sea," *The Wall Street Journal*, October 26, 1992, p. A3.
27. W. W. Powell, K. W. Kogut, and L. Smith-Deorr, "Interorganizational Collaboration and the Locus of Innovation: Networks of Learning in Biotechnology," *Administrative Science Quarterly, 41* (1996), 116–145.
28. R. Miles and C. Snow, "Causes of Failure in Network Organizations," *California Management Review, 4* (1992), 13–32.
29. M. Aoki, *Information, Incentives, and Bargaining in the Japanese Economy* (New York: Cambridge University Press, 1988).
30. D. Roos, D. T. Jones, and J. P. Womack, *The Machine That Changed the World* (New York: Macmillan, 1990).
31. B. Kogut, "Joint Ventures: Theoretical and Empirical Perspectives," *Strategic Management Journal, 9* (1988), 319–333.
32. J. Pfeffer, "Merger as a Response to Organizational Interdependence,"*Administrative Science Quarterly, 17* (1972), 382–394.
33. I. Simpson, "AT&T Slashes Calls to 7 Cents a Minute," Reuters, August 30, 1999.
34. F. M. Scherer, *Industrial Market Structure and Economic Performance*, 2e (Boston: Houghton Mifflin, 1980).
35. A. Phillips, "A Theory of Interfirm Competition," *Quarterly Journal of Economics, 74* (1960), 602–613; J. K. Benson, "The Interorganizational Network as a Political Economy," *Administrative Science Quarterly, 20* (1975), 229–250.
36. D. W. Carlton and J. M. Perloff, *Modern Industrial Organization* (Glenview, IL: Scott, Foresman, 1990).
37. K. G. Provan, J. M. Beyer, and C. Kruytbosch, "Environmental Linkages and Power in Resource Dependence Relations Between Organizations," *Administrative Science Quarterly, 25* (1980), 200–225.
38. H. Leblebichi and G. R. Salancik, "Stability in Interorganizational Exchanges: Rule-Making Processes in the Chicago Board of Trade," *Administrative Science Quarterly, 27* (1982), 227–242; A. Phillips, "A Theory of Interfirm Organization."
39. M. Olson, *The Logic of Collective Action* (Cambridge, MA: Harvard University Press, 1965).
40. A. Allison, "Computer Vendors Consolidate Resources," *Mini-Micro Systems* (June 19, 1992), 54–57.
41. B. Kogut, "Joint Ventures: Theoretical and Empirical Perspectives," *Strategic Management Journal, 9* (1988), 319–332.
42. www.phillips.com, 2006.
43. Scherer, *Industrial Market Structure and Economic Performance.*

44. J. Cook, "When 2 + 2 = 5," *Forbes*, June 8, 1992, pp. 128–129.
45. A. Alchian and H. Demsetz, "Production, Information Costs, and Economic Organization," *American Economic Review*, 62 (1972), 777–795.
46. O. E. Williamson, *Markets and Hierarchies* (New York: The Free Press, 1975); O. E. Williamson, "The Governance of Contractual Relationships," *Journal of Law and Economics*, 22 (1979), 232–261.
47. www.msnbc.com, September 1999.
48. Williamson, *Markets and Hierarchies*.
49. H. A. Simon, *Models of Man* (New York: Wiley, 1957).
50. Williamson, *Markets and Hierarchies*.
51. B. Klein, R. Crawford, and A. Alchian, "Vertical Integration: Appropriable Rents and the Competitive Contracting Process," *Journal of Law and Economics*, 21 (1978), 297–326.
52. R. H. Coase, "The Nature of the Firm," *Economica, n.s. 4* (1937), 386–405.
53. G. R. Jones, "Transaction Costs, Property Rights, and Organizational Culture: An Exchange Perspective," *Administrative Science Quarterly*, 28 (1983), 454–467.
54. R. A. D'Aveni and D. J. Ravenscraft, "Economies of Integration Versus Bureaucracy Costs: Does Vertical Integration Improve Performance?" *Academy of Management Journal*, 37 (1994), 1167–1206.
55. G. R. Jones and C.W.L. Hill, "Transaction Cost Analysis of Strategy–Structure Choice," *Strategic Management Journal*, 9 (1988), 159–172.
56. "Ekco Group," *Fortune*, September 21, 1992, p. 87.
57. "CCPC Acquisition Corp. Completes Acquisition of EKCP Group Inc.," company press release, 1999.
58. G. Walker and D. Weber, "A Transaction Cost Approach to Make or Buy Decisions," *Administrative Science Quarterly*, 29 (1984), 373–391.
59. J. F. Hennart, "A Transaction Cost Theory of Equity Joint Ventures," *Strategic Management Journal*, 9 (1988), 361–374.
60. K. G. Provan and S. J. Skinner, "Interorganizational Dependence and Control as Predictors of Opportunism in Dealer–Supplier Relations," *Academy of Management Journal*, 32 (1989), 202–212.
61. www.gm.com, press release, 1998.
62. S. A. Shane, "Hybrid Organizational Arrangements and Their Implications for Firm Growth and Survival: A Study of New Franchisors," *Academy of Management Journal*, 39 (1996), 216–234.
63. D. E. Bowen and G. R. Jones, "Transaction Cost Analysis of Service Organization–Customer Exchange," *Academy of Management Review*, 11 (1986), 428–441.
64. "Business: Link in the Global Chain," *The Economist*, June 2, 2001, pp. 62–63.
65. E. Anderson and D. C. Schmittlein, "Integration of the Sales Force: An Empirical Examination," *Rand Journal of Economics*, 26 (1984), 65–79.
66. K. Kelly, O. Port, G. George, and Z. Schiller, "Learning from Japan," *Business Week*, January 27, 1992, pp. 52–60.

Chapter 4

Basic Challenges of Organizational Design

Learning Objectives

If an organization is to remain effective as it changes and grows with its environment, managers must continuously evaluate the way their organizations are designed: for example, the way work is divided among people and departments, and the way it utilizes its human, financial, and physical resources. Organizational design involves difficult choices about how to control—that is, coordinate organizational tasks and motivate the people who perform them—to maximize an organization's ability to create value. This chapter examines the challenges of designing an organizational structure so that it achieves stakeholder objectives.

After studying this chapter you should be able to:

1. Describe the four basic organizational design challenges confronting managers and consultants.

2. Discuss the way in which these challenges must be addressed simultaneously if a high-performing organizational structure is to be created.

3. Distinguish among the design choices that underlie the creation of either a mechanistic or an organic structure.

4. Recognize how to use contingency theory to design a structure that fits an organization's environment.

DIFFERENTIATION

Differentiation
The process by which an organization allocates people and resources to organizational tasks and establishes the task and authority relationships that allow the organization to achieve its goals.

As organizations grow, managers must decide how to control and coordinate the activities that are required for the organization to create value. The principal design challenge is how to manage differentiation to achieve organizational goals. **Differentiation** is the process by which an organization allocates people and resources to organizational tasks and establishes the task and authority relationships that allow the organization to achieve its goals.[1] In short, it is the process of

Design Challenge 1

People in this organization take on new tasks as the need arises, and it's unclear who is responsible for what, and who is supposed to report to whom. This makes it difficult to know on whom to call when the need arises and makes it difficult to coordinate people's activities so they work together as a team.

Figure 4.1 Design Challenge

Differentiation at the B.A.R. and Grille.

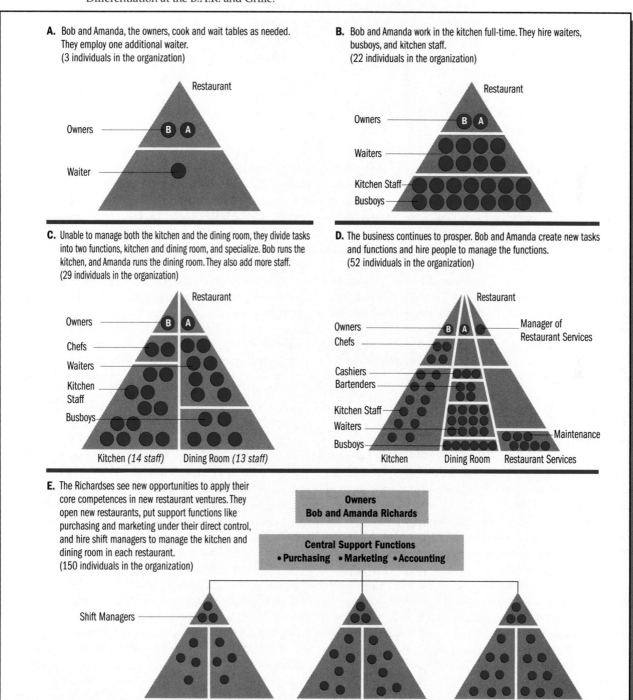

A. Bob and Amanda, the owners, cook and wait tables as needed. They employ one additional waiter.
(3 individuals in the organization)

B. Bob and Amanda work in the kitchen full-time. They hire waiters, busboys, and kitchen staff.
(22 individuals in the organization)

C. Unable to manage both the kitchen and the dining room, they divide tasks into two functions, kitchen and dining room, and specialize. Bob runs the kitchen, and Amanda runs the dining room. They also add more staff.
(29 individuals in the organization)

D. The business continues to prosper. Bob and Amanda create new tasks and functions and hire people to manage the functions.
(52 individuals in the organization)

E. The Richardses see new opportunities to apply their core competences in new restaurant ventures. They open new restaurants, put support functions like purchasing and marketing under their direct control, and hire shift managers to manage the kitchen and dining room in each restaurant.
(150 individuals in the organization)

Division of labor

The process of establishing and controlling the degree of specialization in the organization.

establishing and controlling the **division of labor**, or degree of specialization, in the organization.

An easy way to illustrate why differentiation occurs and why it poses a design challenge is to examine an organization and chart the problems it faces as it attempts to achieve its goals (see Figure 4.1). In a *simple* organization, differentiation is low because the division of labor is low. Typically, one person or a few people perform all organizational tasks, so there are few problems with coordinating who does what, for whom, and when. With growth, however, comes complexity. In a *complex* organization, both the division of labor and differentiation are high. The story of how the B.A.R. and Grille restaurant grew illustrates the problems and challenges that organizational design must address. As the B.A.R. and Grille changed, its owners had to find new ways to control the activities necessary to meet their goal of providing customers with a satisfying dining experience.

ORGANIZATIONAL INSIGHT 4.1
B.A.R. and Grille Restaurant

In 2001, Bob and Amanda Richards (hence B.A.R.) trained as chefs and obtained the capital they needed to open their own restaurant, the B.A.R. and Grille, a 1950s–style restaurant specializing in hamburgers, hot dogs, french fries, fresh fruit pies, and fountain drinks. At the beginning, with the help of one additional person hired to be a waiter, Bob and Amanda took turns cooking and waiting on tables (see Figure 4.1A). The venture was wildly successful. The combination of good food, served in a "Happy Days" atmosphere, appealed to customers, who swamped the restaurant at lunchtime and every night.

Right away Bob and Amanda were overloaded. They worked from dawn to midnight to cope with all the jobs that needed to be done: buying supplies, preparing the food, maintaining the property, taking in money, and figuring the accounts. It was soon clear that both Bob and Amanda were needed in the kitchen and that they needed additional help. They hired waiters, busboys, and kitchen help to wash the mountains of dishes. The staff worked in shifts, and by the end of the third month of operations Bob and Amanda were employing 22 people on a full- or part-time basis (Figure 4.1B).

With 22 staff members to oversee, the Richardses confronted a new problem. Because both of them were working in the kitchen, they had little time to oversee what was happening in the dining room. The waiters, in effect, were running the restaurant. Bob and Amanda had lost contact with the customers and no longer received their comments about the food and service. They realized that to make sure their standards of customer service were being met, one of them needed to take control of the dining room and supervise the waiters and busboys while the other took control of the kitchen. Amanda took over the dining room, and she and Bob hired two chefs to replace her in the kitchen. Bob oversaw the kitchen and continued to cook. The business continued to do

well, so they increased the size of the dining room and hired additional waiters and busboys (Figure 4.1C).

It soon became clear that Bob and Amanda needed to employ additional people to take over specific tasks because they no longer had the time or energy to handle them personally. To control the payment system, they employed full-time cashiers. To cope with customers' demands for alcoholic drinks, they hired a lawyer, got a liquor license, and employed full-time bartenders. To obtain restaurant supplies and manage restaurant services such as cleaning and equipment maintenance, they employed a restaurant manager. The manager was also responsible for overseeing the restaurant on days when the owners took a well-deserved break. By the end of its first year of operation, the B.A.R. and Grille had 50 full- and part-time employees, and the owners were seeking new avenues for expansion (Figure 4.1D).

Eager to use their newly acquired skills to create yet more value, the Richardses began to search for ideas for a new restaurant. Within 18 months they opened a waffle and pancake restaurant, and a year later they opened a pizza restaurant. With this growth, Bob and Amanda left their jobs in the B.A.R. and Grille. They hired shift managers to manage each restaurant, and they spent their time managing central support functions such as purchasing, marketing, and accounting, training new chefs, and developing menu and marketing plans (Figure 4.1E). To ensure that service and quality were uniformly excellent at all three restaurants, they developed written rules and procedures that told chefs, waiters, and other employees what was expected of them—for example, how to prepare and present food and how to behave with customers. After five years of operation, they employed over 150 people full or part-time in their three restaurants, and their sales volume was over $2 million a year.

Figure 4.2
Building Blocks of
Differentiation

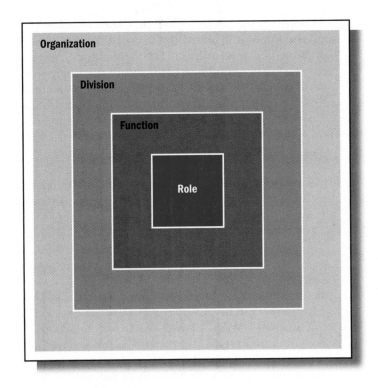

The basic design challenge facing the owners of the B.A.R. and Grille was managing the increasing complexity of the organization's activities. At first, Bob and Amanda performed all the major organizational tasks themselves, and the division of labor was low. As the volume of business grew, the owners needed to increase the division of labor and decide which people would do which jobs. In other words, they had to differentiate the organization and allocate people and resources to organizational tasks.

Organizational Roles

Organizational role
The set of task-related behaviors required of a person by his or her position in an organization.

The basic building blocks of differentiation are organizational roles (see Figure 4.2). An **organizational role** is a set of task-related behaviors required of a person by his or her position in an organization.[2] For example, the organizational role of a B.A.R. and Grille waiter is to provide customers with quick, courteous service to enhance their dining experience. A chef's role is to provide customers with high-quality, appetizing, cooked-to-order meals. A person who is given a role with identifiable tasks and responsibilities can be held accountable for the resources used to accomplish the duties of that position. Bob and Amanda held the waiter responsible for satisfying customers, the restaurant's crucial stakeholder group. The chef was accountable for providing high-quality meals to customers consistently and speedily.

As the division of labor increases in an organization, managers specialize in some roles and hire people to specialize in others. Specialization allows people to develop their individual abilities and knowledge, which are the ultimate source of an organization's core competences. At the B.A.R. and Grille, for example, the owners identified various tasks to be done, such as cooking, bookkeeping, and purchasing, and hired people with the appropriate abilities and knowledge to do them.

Organizational structure is based on a system of interlocking roles, and the relationship of one role to another is defined by task-related behaviors. Some roles require people to oversee the behavior of others: Shift managers at the B.A.R. and Grille oversee the waiters and busboys. A person who can hold another person accountable for his or her performance possesses authority over the other person.

Authority
The power to hold people accountable for their actions and to make decisions concerning the use of organizational resources.

Control
The ability to coordinate and motivate people to work in the organization's interests.

Function
A subunit composed of a group of people, working together, who possess similar skills or use the same kind of knowledge, tools, or techniques to perform their jobs.

Division
A subunit that consists of a collection of functions or departments that share responsibility for producing a particular good or service.

Support functions
A function which facilitate an organization's control of its relations with its environment and its stakeholders.

Production functions
Functions manage and improve the efficiency of an organization's conversion processes so that more value is created.

Maintenance functions
The functions which enable an organization to keep its departments in operation.

Adaptive functions
The functions which allow an organization to adjust to changes in the environment.

Managerial functions
The functions which facilitate the control and coordination of activities within and among departments.

Authority is the power to hold people accountable for their actions and to make decisions about how to invest and use organizational resources.[3] The differentiation of an organization into individual organizational roles results in clear authority and responsibility requirements for each role in the system. When an individual clearly understands the responsibilities of his or her role and what a superior can require of a person in that role, the result within the organization is **control**—the ability to coordinate and motivate people to work in the organization's interests.

Subunits: Functions and Divisions

In most organizations, people with similar and related roles are grouped into a subunit. The main subunits that develop in organizations are functions (or departments) and divisions. A **function** is a subunit composed of a group of people, working together, who possess similar skills or use the same kind of knowledge, tools, or techniques to perform their jobs. For example, in the B.A.R. and Grille, chefs are grouped together as the kitchen function, and waiters are grouped together as the dining room function. A **division** is a subunit that consists of a collection of functions or departments that share responsibility for producing a particular good or service. Take another look at Figure 4.1E. Each restaurant is a division composed of just two functions—dining room and kitchen—which are responsible for the restaurant's activities. Large companies like General Electric and Procter & Gamble have dozens of separate divisions, each one responsible for producing a particular product. In addition, these companies face the problem of how to organize these divisions' activities on a global level so they can create the most value, an issue discussed in detail in Chapter 8.

The number of different functions and divisions that an organization possesses is a measure of the organization's complexity—its degree of differentiation. Differentiation into functions and divisions increases an organization's control over its activities and allows the organization to accomplish its tasks more effectively.

As organizations grow in size, they differentiate into five different kinds of functions.[4] **Support functions** facilitate an organization's control of its relations with its environment and its stakeholders. Support functions include *purchasing*, to handle the acquisition of inputs; *sales and marketing*, to handle the disposal of outputs; and *public relations and legal affairs*, to respond to the needs of outside stakeholders. Bob and Amanda Richards hired a manager to oversee purchasing for all three restaurants and an accountant to manage the books (see Figure 4.1E).

Production functions manage and improve the efficiency of an organization's conversion processes so that more value is created. Production functions include *production operations*, *production control*, and *quality control*. At Ford, the production operations department controls the manufacturing process; production control decides on the most efficient way to produce cars at the lowest cost; and quality control monitors product quality.

Maintenance functions enable an organization to keep its departments in operation. Maintenance functions include *personnel*, to recruit and train employees and improve skills; *engineering*, to repair broken machinery; and *janitorial services*, to keep the work environment safe and healthy—conditions that are very important to a restaurant like the B.A.R. and Grille.

Adaptive functions allow an organization to adjust to changes in the environment. Adaptive functions include *research and development, market research*, and *long-range planning*, which allow an organization to learn from and attempt to manage its environment and thus increase its core competences. At the B.A.R. and Grille, developing new menu choices to keep up with customers' changing tastes is an important adaptive activity.

Managerial functions facilitate the control and coordination of activities within and among departments. Managers at different organizational levels direct the *acquisition of, investment in*, and *control of resources* to improve the organization's ability to create value. Top management, for example, is responsible for formulating strategy and establishing the policies the organization uses to control its environment. Middle managers are responsible for managing the organization's resources to meet its goals. Lower-level managers oversee and direct the activities of the workforce.

Differentiation at the B.A.R. and Grille

In the B.A.R. and Grille, differentiation at first was minimal. The owners, with the help of one other person, did all the work. But with unexpected success came the need to differentiate activities into separate organizational roles and functions, with Bob managing the kitchen and Amanda the dining room. As the restaurant continued to grow, Bob and Amanda were confronted with the need to develop skills and capabilities in the five functional areas. For the support role, they hired a restaurant services manager to take charge of purchasing supplies and local advertising. To handle the production role, they increased the division of labor in the kitchen and dining room. They hired cleaning staff, cashiers, and an external accountant for maintenance tasks. They themselves handled the adaptive role of ensuring that the organization served customer needs. Finally, Bob and Amanda took on the managerial role of establishing the pattern of task and functional relationships that most effectively accomplished the restaurant's overall task of serving customers good food. Collectively, the five functions constituted the B.A.R. and Grille and gave it the ability to create value.

As soon as the owners decided to open new kinds of restaurants and expand the size of their organization, they faced the challenge of differentiating into divisions, to control the operation of three restaurants simultaneously. The organization grew to three divisions, each of which made use of support functions centralized at the top of the organization (see Figure 4.1E). In large organizations each division is likely to have its own set of the five basic functions and is, thus, a *self-contained division*.

As Chapter 1 discusses, functional skills and abilities are the source of an organization's *core competences*, the set of unique skills and capabilities that give it a competitive advantage.[5] An organization's competitive advantage may lie in any or all of an organization's functions. An organization could have superior low-cost production, exceptional managerial talent, or a leading R&D department.[6] A core competence of the B.A.R. and Grille was the way Bob and Amanda took control of the differentiation of their restaurant and increased its ability to attract customers who appreciated the good food and good service they received. In short, they created a core competence that gave their restaurant a competitive advantage over other restaurants. In turn, this competitive advantage gave them access to resources that allowed them to expand by opening new restaurants.

Vertical and Horizontal Differentiation

Figure 4.3 shows the organizational chart that emerged in the B.A.R. and Grille as differentiation unfolded. An organizational chart is a drawing that shows the end result of organizational differentiation. Each box on the chart represents a role or function in the organization. Each role has a vertical and a horizontal dimension.

The organizational chart *vertically* differentiates organizational roles in terms of the amount of authority that goes with each role. A classification of people according to their relative authority and rank is called a **hierarchy**. Roles at the top of an organization's hierarchy possess more authority and responsibility than do roles farther down in the hierarchy; each lower role is under the control or supervision of a higher one. Managers designing an organization have to make decisions about how much vertical differentiation to have in the organization—that is, how many levels should there be from top to bottom. To maintain control over the various functions in the restaurant, for example, Bob and Amanda realized that they needed to create the role of restaurant manager. Because the restaurant manager would report to them and would supervise lower level employees, this new role added a level to the hierarchy. **Vertical differentiation** refers to the way an organization designs its hierarchy of authority and creates

Hierarchy
A classification of people according to authority and rank.

Vertical differentiation
The way an organization designs its hierarchy of authority and creates reporting relationships to link organizational roles and subunits.

Figure 4.3   Organizational Chart of the B.A.R. and Grille

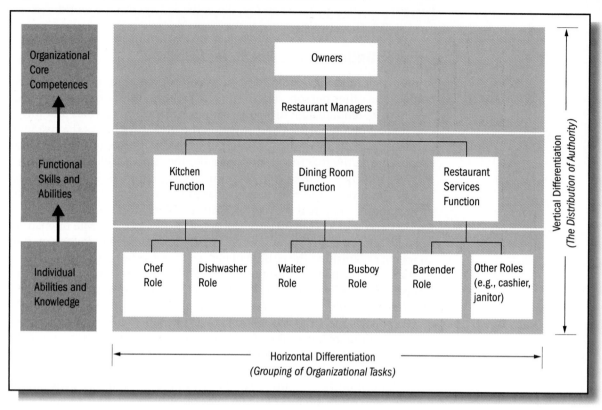

reporting relationships to link organizational roles and subunits.[7] Vertical differentiation establishes the distribution of authority between levels to give the organization more control over its activities and increase its ability to create value.

The organizational chart *horizontally* differentiates roles according to their main task responsibilities. For example, when Bob and Amanda realized that a more complex division of tasks would increase restaurant effectiveness, they created new organizational roles—such as restaurant manager, cashier, bartender, and busboy—and grouped these roles into functions. **Horizontal differentiation** refers to the way an organization groups organizational tasks into roles and roles into subunits (functions and divisions).[8] Horizontal differentiation establishes the division of labor that enables people in an organization to become more specialized and productive and increases its ability to create value.

Horizontal differentiation
The way an organization groups organizational tasks into roles and roles into subunits (functions and divisions).

Organizational Design Challenges

We have seen that the principal design challenge facing an organization is to choose the levels of vertical and horizontal differentiation that allow the organization to control its activities in order to achieve its goals. In Chapters 5 and 6, we examine the major design principles that guide these choices.

In the remainder of this chapter, we look at three more design challenges that confront managers who attempt to create a structure that will maximize their organization's effectiveness (see Figure 4.4). The first of the three is how to link and coordinate organizational activities. The second is to determine who will make decisions. The third is to decide which types of mechanisms are best suited to controlling specific employee tasks and roles. The choices managers make as they grapple with all four challenges determine how effectively their organization works.

Figure 4.4
Organizational Design
Challenges

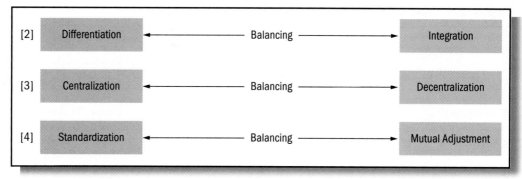

MANAGERIAL IMPLICATIONS

DIFFERENTIATION

1. No matter what your position in an organization is, draw an organizational chart so that you can identify the distribution of authority and the division of labor.
2. No matter how few or how many people you work with or supervise, analyze each person's role and the relationships among roles to make sure that the division of labor is best for the task being performed. If it is not, redefine role relationships and responsibilities.
3. If you supervise more than one function or department, analyze relationships among departments to make sure that the division of labor best suits the organization's mission: the creation of value for stakeholders.

BALANCING DIFFERENTIATION AND INTEGRATION

Subunit orientation
A tendency to view one's role in the organization strictly from the perspective of the time frame, goals, and interpersonal orientations of one's subunit.

Horizontal differentiation is supposed to enable people to specialize and thus become more productive. However, companies have often found that specialization limits communication between subunits and prevents them from learning from one another. As a result of horizontal differentiation, the members of different functions or divisions develop a **subunit orientation**—a tendency to view one's role in the organization strictly from the perspective of the time frame, goals, and interpersonal orientations of one's subunit.[9] For example, the production department is most concerned with reducing costs and increasing quality; thus it tends to have a short-term outlook because cost and quality are production goals that must be met daily. In R&D, on the other hand, innovations to the production process may take years to come to fruition; thus, R&D employees usually have a longer term outlook. When different functions see things differently, communication fails and coordination becomes difficult, if not impossible.

To avoid the communication problems that can arise from horizontal differentiation, organizations try to find new or better ways to integrate functions—that is, to

Design Challenge 2

We can't get people to communicate and coordinate in this organization. Specifying tasks and roles is supposed to help coordinate the work process, but here it builds barriers between people and functions.

Table 4.1 Types and Examples of Integrating Mechanisms

INTEGRATION MECHANISM (IN ORDER OF INCREASING COMPLEXITY)	DESCRIPTION	EXAMPLE (E.G., IN JOHNSON & JOHNSON)
Hierarchy of authority	A ranking of employees integrates by specifying who reports to whom.	Salesperson reports to Diaper Division sales manager.
Direct contact	Managers meet face-to-face to coordinate activities.	Diaper Division sales and manufacturing managers meet to discuss scheduling.
Liaison role	A specific manager is given responsibility for coordinating with managers from other subunits on behalf of his or her subunit.	A person from each of J&J's production, marketing, and research and development departments is given responsibility for coordinating with the other departments.
Task force	Managers meet in temporary committees to coordinate cross-functional activities.	A committee is formed to find new ways to recycle diapers.
Team	Managers meet regularly in permanent committees to coordinate activities.	A permanent J&J committee is established to promote new-product development in the Diaper Division.
Integrating role	A new role is established to coordinate the activities of two or more functions or divisions.	One manager takes responsibility for coordinating Diaper and Baby Soap divisions to enhance their marketing activities.
Integrating department	A new department is created to coordinate the activities of functions or divisions.	A team of managers is created to take responsibility for coordinating J&J's centralization program to allow divisions to share skills and resources.

promote cooperation, coordination, and communication among separate subunits. Most large companies today use advanced forms of IT that allow different functions or divisions to share databases, memos, and reports, often on a real-time basis. Increasingly, companies are using electronic means of communication like email, teleconferencing, and enterprise management systems to bring different functions together. For example, buyers at Wal-Mart's home office use television linkups to show each individual store the appropriate way to display products for sale. Nestle uses advanced enterprise management systems that supply all functions with detailed information about the ongoing activities of other functions.

Integration and Integrating Mechanisms

How to facilitate communication and coordination among subunits is a major challenge for managers. One problem on this front is the development of subunit orientations that make communication difficult and complex. Another reason for lack of coordination and communication is that managers often fail to use the appropriate mechanisms and techniques to integrate organizational subunits. **Integration** is the process of coordinating various tasks, functions, and divisions so that they work together, not at cross-purposes. Table 4.1 lists seven integrating mechanisms or techniques that managers can use as their organization's level of differentiation increases.[10] The simplest mechanism is a hierarchy of authority; the most complex is a department created specifically to coordinate the activities of diverse functions or divisions. The table includes examples of how a company like Johnson & Johnson might use all seven types of integration mechanisms as it goes about managing one major product line—disposable diapers. We will examine each mechanism separately.

Hierarchy of Authority

The simplest integrating technique is the organization's hierarchy of authority, which differentiates people by the amount of authority they possess. Because the hierarchy dictates who reports to whom, it coordinates various organizational roles. Managers must carefully divide and allocate authority within a function and between one

Integration
The process of coordinating various tasks, functions, and divisions so that they work together and not at cross-purposes.

function and others to promote coordination. For example, at Becton Dickinson, a high-tech medical instrument maker, the marketing and engineering departments frequently squabbled over product specifications. Marketing argued that the company's products needed more features to please customers. Engineering wanted to simplify product design to reduce costs.[11] The two departments could not resolve their differences because the head of marketing reported to the head of engineering. To resolve this conflict, Becton Dickinson reorganized its hierarchy so that both marketing and engineering reported to the head of the Instrument Product Division. The head of the division was an impartial third party who had the authority to listen to both managers' cases and make the decision that was best for the organization as a whole.

Direct Contact

Direct contact between people in different subunits is a second integrating mechanism. Using direct contact often involves more problems than using hierarchy of authority. The principal problem with integration across functions is that a manager in one function has *no authority* over a manager in another. Only the CEO or some other top manager above the functional level has power to intervene if two functions come into conflict. Consequently, establishing personal relationships and

Figure 4.5 Integrating Mechanisms

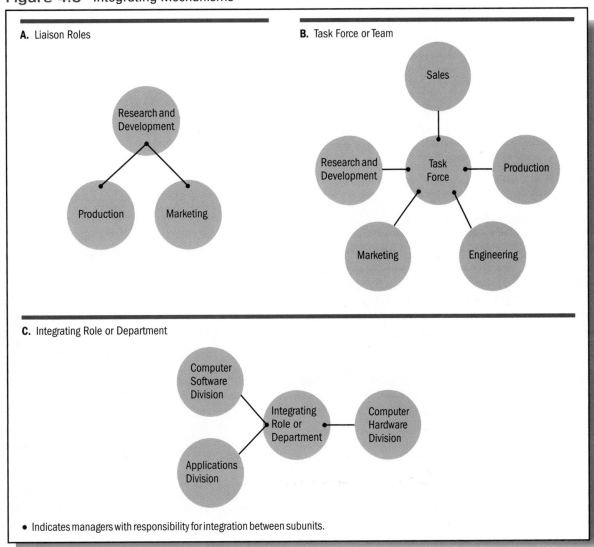

• Indicates managers with responsibility for integration between subunits.

professional contacts among people at all levels in different functions is a crucial step in overcoming the problems that arise because subunit orientations differ. Managers from different functions who have the ability to make direct contact with each other can then work together to solve common problems—and prevent them from arising in the first place. If disputes still occur, however, it is important for both parties to be able to appeal to a common superior who is not far removed from the scene of the problem.

Liaison Roles

As the need for communication between two subunits becomes increasingly important, often because of a rapidly changing environment, one or a few members from each subunit are often given the primary responsibility to work together to coordinate subunit activities. The people who hold these connecting, or liaison, roles are able to develop in-depth relations with people in other subunits. This interaction helps overcome barriers between subunits. Over time, as the people in liaison roles learn to cooperate, they can become increasingly flexible in accommodating other subunits' requests. Figure 4.5A illustrates a liaison role.

Task Forces

Task force
A temporary committee set up to handle a specific problem.

As an organization increases in size and complexity, more than two subunits may need to work together to solve common problems. Increasing an organization's ability to serve its customers effectively, for example, may require input from production, marketing, engineering, and R&D. The solution commonly takes the form of a **task force**, a temporary committee set up to handle a specific problem (Figure 4.5B). One or a few members of each function join a task force that meets regularly until a solution to the problem is found. Task force members are then responsible for taking the solution back to their functions to gain their input and approval. To increase the

ORGANIZATIONAL INSIGHT 4.2
Integration at Amgen

Amgen is experiencing great success with its recombinant DNA drugs Epogen (an anemia drug) and Neupogen (an immune system stimulant). With Amgen's success has come growth, and the company is seeking new ways to integrate its employees so that it can preserve its small-company atmosphere, which is based on personal contact between employees. Amgen is relying on a team system to coordinate its people. It has devised two types of teams. Product development teams organize the whole process of bringing a new drug to market, and task forces handle other needs of the business down to the level of organizing the firm's annual picnic. The product development teams are composed of people from all areas of the company and report directly to top management. They meet daily or weekly, as needed; at other times the team members return to their regular jobs in the organization. Any employee can join any team at any time, and in this way the company hopes to keep its levels of innovation and flexibility high.

Amgen prides itself on searching out new ways of organizing itself to minimize the need to standardize work activities. The company's goals are to maximize employees'

opportunities to be innovative and to find new ways to integrate employees' skills to speed the development of new products to the market.[12] As Amgen continued to grow, however, it sensed some problems with its use of teams. Employees seemed to be more loyal to their teams than to their regular job assignments, and this situation was starting to cause communication problems between the teams and the regular functions. To control team activities and make sure that the teams coordinated effectively with the functions, Amgen started to fully integrate its teams into its hierarchy of authority to facilitate the flow of information.[13] Amgen has had considerable success with its new structure in the 2000s because the company claims, "Our teams work quickly to move scientific breakthroughs from the lab through the clinic to the marketplace and to support other aspects of our business. Diverse teams working together generate the best decisions . . . our team structure provides opportunities for Amgen staff to impact the direction of the organization, to gain broader perspective about other functions within Amgen and to reach their full potential.[14]

effectiveness of task forces, a senior manager who is not a member of any of the functions involved usually chairs the meetings.

Teams

When the issue a task force is dealing with becomes an ongoing strategic or administrative issue, the task force becomes permanent. A *team* is a permanent task force or committee. Most companies today, for example, have formed product development and customer-contact teams to monitor and respond to the ongoing challenges of increased competition in a global market. At Amgen, one of the most successful global biotechnology companies, for example, the team system has proved to be a vital contributor to the company's success.

Approximately 70% of a manager's time is spent in committee meetings.[15] Teams provide the opportunity for the face-to-face contact and continual adjustment that managers need to deal effectively with ongoing complex issues. As they set up a team structure, managers face the ongoing challenge of creating a committee system that gives them effective control over organizational activities. Sometimes teams become ineffective over time because the problems facing the organization change but team membership and structure remain unchanged. People often fight to stay on a committee, or protect their team, because team membership gives a person power in the organization. But this power does not necessarily promote organizational goals. At Whirlpool, the appliance maker, CEO David Whitwam established hundreds of minimanagement teams throughout the company to bring about change, improve quality control, and streamline production. Whitwam's goal? To use teams to change patterns of authority and decision making to increase interaction and promote creativity among managers.[16]

Integrating Roles or Departments

As organizations become large and complex, communication barriers between functions and divisions are likely to increase. Managers in divisions making different products, for example, may never meet one another. Coordinating subunits is especially difficult in organizations that employ many thousands of people. One way to overcome these barriers is to create integrating roles that coordinate subunits. An **integrating role** is a *full-time* managerial position established specifically to improve communication between divisions. (A liaison role, by contrast, is just one of the tasks involved in a person's full-time job.) Figure 4.5C shows an integrating role that might exist in a large computer company like Dell or Apple.

The purpose of an integrating role is to promote the sharing of information and knowledge to better pursue organizational goals such as product innovation, increased flexibility, and improved customer service. People in integrating roles are often senior managers who have decided to give up authority in a specific function and focus on company-wide integration. They often chair important task forces and teams and report directly to top management.

When a company has many employees in integrating roles, it creates an integrating department that coordinates the activities of all subunits. DuPont, the chemical maker, has a department that employs over 200 people in integrating roles; so do Microsoft and IBM. In general, the more complex and highly differentiated an organization, the more complex are the integration mechanisms it needs to overcome communication and coordination barriers between functions and divisions.

Differentiation Versus Integration

The design issue facing managers is to establish a level of integration that matches the organization's level of differentiation. Managers must achieve an appropriate *balance* between differentiation and integration. A complex organization that is highly differentiated needs a high level of integration to effectively coordinate its activities. By contrast, when an organization has a relatively simple, clearly defined

Integrating role
A full-time position established specifically to improve communication between divisions.

role structure it normally needs to use only simple integrating mechanisms. Its managers may find that the hierarchy of authority provides all the control and coordination they need to achieve organizational goals.

At all costs, managers need to be sure they do not differentiate or integrate their organization too much. Differentiation and integration are both expensive in terms of the number of managers employed and the amount of managerial time spent on coordinating organizational activities. For example, every hour that employees spend on committees that are not really needed costs the organization thousands of dollars because these employees are not being put to their most productive use.

Managers facing the challenge of deciding how and how much to differentiate and integrate must do two things: (1) carefully guide the process of differentiation so that an organization builds the core competences that give it a competitive advantage; and (2) carefully integrate the organization by choosing appropriate coordinating mechanisms that allow subunits to cooperate and work together to strengthen its core competences.[17]

BALANCING CENTRALIZATION AND DECENTRALIZATION

In discussing vertical differentiation, we note that establishing a hierarchy of authority is supposed to improve the way an organization functions because people can be held accountable for their actions—the hierarchy defines the area of each person's authority within the organization. Many companies, however, complain that when a hierarchy exists employees are constantly looking to their superiors for direction.[18] When some new or unusual issue arises, they prefer not to deal with it, or they pass it on to their superior, rather than assume responsibility and the risk of dealing with it. As responsibility and risk taking decline, so does organizational performance because its members do not take advantage of new opportunities for using its core competences. When nobody is willing to take responsibility, decision making becomes slow and the organization becomes inflexible—that is, unable to change and adapt to new developments.

At Levi Strauss, for example, employees often told former CEO Roger Sant that they felt they couldn't do something because "*They* wouldn't like it." When asked who "they" were, employees had a hard time saying; nevertheless, the employees felt that they did not have the authority or responsibility to initiate changes. Sant started a "Theybusters" campaign to renegotiate authority and responsibility relationships so that employees could take on new responsibilities.[19] The solution involved decentralizing authority; that is, employees at lower levels in the hierarchy were given the authority to decide how to handle problems and issues that arose while they performed their jobs. The issue of how much to centralize or decentralize the authority to make decisions offers a basic design challenge for all organizations.

Centralization Versus Decentralization of Authority

Authority gives one person the power to hold other people accountable for their actions and the right to make decisions about the use of organizational resources. As we saw in the B.A.R. and Grille example, vertical differentiation involves choices about how to distribute authority. But even when a hierarchy of authority exists, the problem of how much decision-making authority to delegate to each level must be solved.

Design Challenge 3

People in this organization don't take responsibility or risks. They are always looking to the boss for direction and supervision. As a result, decision making is slow and cumbersome, and we miss out on a lot of opportunities to create value.

Centralized
Organizational setup whereby the authority to make important decisions is retained by managers at the top of the hierarchy.

Decentralized
An organizational setup whereby the authority to make important decisions about organizational resources and to initiate new projects is delegated to managers at all levels in the hierarchy.

It is possible to design an organization in which managers at the top of the hierarchy have all power to make important decisions. Subordinates take orders from the top, are accountable for how well they obey those orders, and have no authority to initiate new actions or use resources for purposes that they believe are important. When the authority to make important decisions is retained by managers at the top of the hierarchy, authority is said to be highly **centralized**.[20] By contrast, when the authority to make important decisions about organizational resources and to initiate new projects is delegated to managers at all levels in the hierarchy, authority is highly **decentralized**.

Each alternative has certain advantages and disadvantages. The advantage of centralization is that it lets top managers coordinate organizational activities and keep the organization focused on its goals. Centralization becomes a problem, however, when top managers become overloaded and immersed in operational decision making about day-to-day resource issues (such as hiring people and obtaining inputs). When this happens, they have little time to spend on long-term strategic decision making, and planning crucial future organizational activities, such as deciding on the best strategy to compete globally, is neglected.

The advantage of decentralization is that it promotes flexibility and responsiveness by allowing lower level managers to make on-the-spot decisions. Managers remain accountable for their actions but have the opportunity to assume greater responsibilities and take potentially successful risks. Also, when authority is decentralized managers can make important decisions that allow them to demonstrate their personal skills and competences, and so they may be more motivated to perform well for the organization. The downside of decentralization is that if so much authority is delegated that managers at all levels can make their own decisions, planning and coordination become very difficult. Thus, too much decentralization may lead an organization to lose control of its decision-making process! The following organizational insight reveals many of the issues surrounding this design choice.

As these examples suggest, the design challenge for managers is to decide on the correct balance between centralization and decentralization of decision making in an organization. If authority is too decentralized, managers have so much freedom that they can pursue their own functional goals and objectives at the expense of

ORGANIZATIONAL INSIGHT 4.3
Centralize or Decentralize?

Is it best to centralize or decentralize authority? It depends on the situation, as the following examples illustrate.

In 1998, the United Way was suffering from a public perception that it was spending too much of the donations it received on itself and not enough for the needy people it was set up to serve. The solution? It called in management consultants who recommended that the best way to save money and increase efficiency was to reduce the number of local organizations and centralize many business functions such as data processing, marketing, and wealthy donor programs. However, many local organizations then became concerned that they would receive a smaller share of donations. To date the United Way is still working out the right balance between centralization and decentralization.[21]

Managers at Union Pacific Railroad, in response to complaints from customers and employees about traffic bottlenecks and poor quality service, made a radical decision. They would abandon the company's centralized operating system and decentralize authority to regional managers who could make on-the-spot decisions.[22] The

result? A significant increase in efficiency; the penalties it was forced to pay its customers for late shipments declined sharply once regional managers made the decisions.[23]

To reduce disposal costs and save money, managers at a Waste Management plant decided to deliberately turn off the plant's pollution-monitoring equipment. Soon after this decision was made, a container of chemicals exploded; the company's managers were accused of mislabeling up to a hundred barrels of hazardous waste to avoid disposal costs. Although Waste Management's top managers blamed local management and denied any knowledge of the situation, the decentralized management style of the company was blamed for the problems. According to former company managers, top managers took no interest in the plant's operations and put local management under intense pressure to reduce costs. The combination of decentralized control and bottom-line pressure led to the problems that occurred. The plant's top managers claimed that Waste Management's attitude was "Don't tell us what's going on; just keep turning out the profit."[24]

organizational goals. On the other hand, if authority is too centralized and top management makes all important decisions, managers lower down in the hierarchy become afraid to make new moves and lack the freedom to respond to problems as they arise in their own groups and departments.

The ideal situation is a balance between centralization and decentralization of authority so that middle and lower managers who are at the scene of the action are allowed to make important decisions, and top managers' primary responsibility becomes managing long-term strategic decision making. The result is a good balance between long-term strategy making and short-term flexibility and innovation as lower level managers respond quickly to problems and changes in the environment as they occur.

Why were the Levi Strauss managers so reluctant to take on new responsibilities and assume extra authority? A previous management team had centralized authority so that it could retain day-to-day control over important decision making. The company's performance suffered, however, because in spending all their time on day-to-day operations, top managers lost sight of changing customer needs and evolving trends in the clothing industry. The new top management team that took over in the late 1990s recognized the need to delegate authority for operational decision making to lower level managers so that they could concentrate on long-term strategic decision making. Consequently, top management decentralized authority until they believed they had achieved the correct balance.

As noted earlier, the way managers and employees behave in an organization is a direct result of managers' decisions about how the organization is to operate. Managers who want to discourage risk taking and to maximize control over subordinates' performance centralize authority. Managers who want to encourage risk taking and innovation decentralize authority. In the army, for example, the top brass generally wishes to discourage lower level officers from acting on their own initiative for, if they did, the power of centralized command would be gone and the army would splinter. Consequently, the army has a highly centralized decision-making system that operates by strict rules and with a well-defined hierarchy of authority. By contrast, at Amgen and Becton Dickson, the medical equipment maker, authority is decentralized and employees are provided with a broad framework within which they are free to make their own decisions and take risks—as long as these are consistent with the company's master plan. In general, high-tech companies decentralize authority because this encourages innovation and risk taking.

Decisions about how to distribute decision-making authority in an organization change as an organization changes—that is, as it grows and differentiates. How to balance authority is not a design decision that can be made once and forgotten; it must be made on an ongoing basis and is an essential part of the managerial task. We examine this issue in more detail in Chapters 5 and 6.

BALANCING STANDARDIZATION AND MUTUAL ADJUSTMENT

Written rules and standard operating procedures (SOPs) and unwritten values and norms are important forms of behavior control in organizations. They specify *how* employees are to perform their organizational roles, and they set forth the tasks and responsibilities associated with each role. Many companies, however, complain that employees tend to follow written and unwritten guidelines too rigidly instead of

Design Challenge 4

People in this organization pay too much attention to the rules. Whenever I need somebody to satisfy an unusual customer request or need real quick service from another function, I can't get it because no one is willing to bend or break the rules.

adapting them to the needs of a particular situation. Strictly following rules may stifle innovation; detailed rules specifying how decisions are to be made leave no room for creativity and imaginative responses to unusual circumstances. As a result, decision making becomes inflexible and organizational performance suffers.

IBM, for example, was traditionally a company respected for being close to its customers and responsive to their needs. But as IBM grew, it standardized responses to customers' requests, and its sales force was instructed to sell certain kinds of machines to certain kinds of customers—regardless of what the customer needed.[25] Standardizing operations had become more important than giving customers what they wanted. Moreover, internal communication among IBM's divisions and functions was increasingly conducted in accordance with formal rules rather than by relatively informal direct contact. These rigid patterns of communication slowed product development and ultimately resulted in dissatisfied customers.

The challenge facing all organizations, large and small, is to design a structure that achieves the right balance between standardization and mutual adjustment. **Standardization** is conformity to specific models or examples—defined by sets of rules and norms—that are considered proper in a given situation. Standardized decision-making and coordination procedures make people's actions routine and predictable.[26] **Mutual adjustment** is the process through which people use their judgment rather than standardized rules to address problems, guide decision making, and promote coordination. The right balance makes some actions predictable so that basic organizational tasks and goals are achieved, yet it gives employees the freedom to behave flexibly so that they can respond to new and changing situations creatively.

Formalization: Written Rules

Formalization is the use of written rules and procedures to standardize operations.[27] In an organization in which formalization and standardization are extensive—for example, the military, FedEx, or UPS—everything is done by the book. There is no room for mutual adjustment; rules specify how people are to perform their roles and how decisions are to be made, and employees are accountable for following the rules. Moreover, employees have no authority to break the rules. A high level of formalization typically implies centralization of authority. A low level of formalization implies that coordination is the product of mutual adjustment among people across organizational functions and that decision making is a dynamic process in which employees apply their skills and abilities to respond to change and solve problems. Mutual adjustment typically implies decentralization of authority because employees must have the authority to commit the organization to certain actions when they make decisions.

In the 1990s IBM began fostering mutual adjustment to increase the flexibility of its decision making.[28] In five years, IBM underwent four major structural reorganizations designed to make the organization less formalized and more decentralized. IBM has used IT to promote its new decentralized global strategy and is once again performing at a high level in the 2000s.

Socialization: Understood Norms

Rules are formal, written statements that specify the appropriate means for reaching desired goals. When people follow rules, they behave in accordance with certain specified principles. **Norms** are standards or styles of behavior that are considered typical for a group of people. People follow a norm because it is a generally agreed-upon standard for behavior. Many norms arise informally as people work together over time. In some organizations it is the norm that people take an hour and a quarter for lunch, despite a formally specified one-hour lunch break. Over time, norms become part of peoples' way of viewing and responding to a particular situation.

Standardization
Conformity to specific models or examples—defined by sets of rules and norms—that are considered proper in a given situation.

Mutual adjustment
The compromise that emerges when decision making and coordination are evolutionary processes and people use their judgment rather than standardized rules to address a problem.

Formalization
The use of written rules and procedures to standardize operations.

Rules
Formal, written statements that specify the appropriate means for reaching desired goals.

Norms
Standards or styles of behavior that are considered acceptable or typical for a group of people.

Although many organizational norms—such as always behaving courteously to customers and leaving the work area clean—promote organizational effectiveness, many do not. Studies have shown that groups of employees can develop norms that reduce performance. Several studies have found that work groups can directly control the pace or speed at which work is performed by imposing informal sanctions on employees who break the informal norms governing behavior in a work group. An employee who works too quickly (above group productivity norms) is called a "rate-buster," and an employee who works too slowly (below group norms) is called a "chiseler."[29] Having established a group norm, employees actively enforce it by physically and emotionally punishing violators.

This process occurs at all levels in the organization. Suppose a group of middle managers has adopted the norm of not rocking the organizational boat by changing outdated work rules, even if this will increase efficiency. A new manager who enters the picture will soon learn from the others that rocking the boat doesn't pay as other managers find ways to punish the new person for violating this norm—even if a little shaking up is what the organization really needs. Even a new manager who is high in the hierarchy will have difficulty changing the informal norms of the organization.

The taken-for-granted way in which norms affect behavior has another consequence for organizational effectiveness. We noted in the Levi Strauss example that even when an organization changes formal work rules, the behavior of people does not change quickly. Why is behavior rigid when rules change? The reason is that rules may be internalized and become part of a person's psychological makeup so that *external rules* become *internalized norms*. When this happens, it is very difficult for people to break a familiar rule and follow a new rule; also, they will slip back into the old way of behaving. Consider, for example, how difficult it is to keep new resolutions and break bad habits.[30]

Paradoxically, an organization often wants members to buy into a particular set of corporate norms and values. IBM and Intel, for example, cultivate technical and professional norms and values as a means of controlling and standardizing the behavior of highly skilled organizational members. However, once these norms are established they are very difficult to change. When an organization wants to pursue new goals and foster new norms, people find it difficult to alter their behavior. There is no easy solution to this problem. At Levi Strauss, organizational members had to go through a major period of relearning before they understood that they did not need to apply the old set of internalized norms. IBM underwent major upheavals to unlearn its old, conservative norms; new IT helped it develop new ones that encourage innovation and responsiveness to customers.

The name given to the process by which organizational members learn the norms of an organization and internalize these unwritten rules of conduct is **socialization**.[31] In general, organizations can encourage the development of *standardized* responses or *innovative* ones. These issues are examined in more detail in Chapter 7.

Standardization Versus Mutual Adjustment

The design challenge facing managers is to find a way of using rules and norms to standardize behavior while at the same time allowing for mutual adjustment to provide employees with the opportunity to discover new and better ways of achieving organizational goals. Managers facing the challenge of balancing the need for standardization against the need for mutual adjustment need to keep in mind that, in general, people at higher levels in the hierarchy and in functions that perform complex, uncertain tasks rely more on mutual adjustment than on standardization to coordinate their actions. For example, an organization wants its accountants to follow standard practices in performing their tasks, but in R&D the organization wants to encourage creative behavior that leads to innovation. Many of the integrating mechanisms discussed earlier, such as task forces and teams, can increase mutual adjustment by providing an opportunity for people to meet and work out improved ways of doing things. In addition, an organization

Socialization
The process by which organizational members learn the norms of an organization and internalize these unwritten rules of conduct.

How did Jeff Bezos address these design challenges given his need to create a structure to manage an e-commerce business that operated through the Internet and never saw its customers, but whose mission was to provide customer's great selection at low prices? Since the success of his venture depended upon providing high-quality customer responsiveness, it was vital for customers to find Amazon.com's 1-Click (SM) information system Internet software easy and convenient to use and the service reliable. So his design choices were driven by the need to ensure that his software linked customers to the organization most effectively.

First, he quickly realized that customer support was the most vital link between customer and organization, so to ensure good customer service he decentralized control and empowered his employees to find a way of meeting customers needs quickly. Second, realizing that customers wanted the book quickly he moved quickly to develop an efficient distribution and shipping system. Essentially, his main problem was handling inputs into the system (customer requests) and outputs (delivered books). So, he developed information systems to standardize the work or throughput process to increase efficiency, but also encouraged mutual adjustment at the input or customer end to improve customers' responsiveness—employees were able to manage exceptions such as lost orders or confused customers as the need arose. (Note that Amazon's information systems also play the dominant role in integrating across functions in the organization; they provide the backbone for the company's value-creation activities.) Third, because Amazon.com employs a relatively small number of people—about 2,500 worldwide—Bezos was able to make great use of socialization to coordinate and motivate his employees. All Amazon.com employees are carefully selected and socialized by the other members of their functions so that they quickly learn their organizational roles and—most important—Amazon's important norm of providing excellent customer service. Finally, to ensure that Amazon.com's employees are motivated to provide the best possible customer service, Bezos gives all employees stock in the company. Employees currently own over 10% of their company. Amazon.com's rapid growth suggests that Bezos has designed an effective organizational structure.

can emphasize, as Levi Strauss did, that rules are not set in stone but are just convenient guidelines for getting work done. Managers can also promote norms and values that emphasize change rather than stability. For all organizational roles, however, the appropriate balance between these two variables is one that promotes creative and responsible employee behavior as well as organizational effectiveness.

MANAGERIAL IMPLICATIONS

THE DESIGN CHALLENGES

1. To see whether there is enough integration between your department and the departments that you interact with the most, create a map of the principal integrating mechanisms in use. If there is not enough integration, develop new integrating mechanisms that will provide the extra coordination needed to improve performance.

2. Determine which levels in the managerial hierarchy have responsibility for approving which decisions. Use your findings to decide how centralized or decentralized decision making is in your organization. Discuss your conclusions with your peers, subordinates, and superior to ascertain whether the distribution of authority best suits the needs of your organization.

3. Make a list of your principal tasks and role responsibilities; then, list the rules and SOPs that specify how you are to perform your duties. Using this information, decide how appropriate the rules and SOPs are, and suggest ways of changing them so that you can perform more effectively. If you are a manager, perform this analysis for your department to improve its effectiveness and to make sure the rules are necessary and efficient.

4. Be aware of the informal norms and values that influence the way members of your work group or department behave. Try to account for the origin of these norms and values and the way they affect behavior. Examine whether they fulfill a useful function in your organization. If they do, try to reinforce them. If they do not, develop a plan for creating new norms and values that will enhance effectiveness.

MECHANISTIC AND ORGANIC ORGANIZATIONAL STRUCTURES

Each design challenge has implications for how an organization as a whole and the people in the organization behave and perform. Two useful concepts for understanding how managers manipulate all these challenges collectively to influence the way an organizational structure works are the concepts of mechanistic structure and organic structure.[32] The design choices that produce mechanistic and organic structures are contrasted in Figure 4.6

Mechanistic Structures

Mechanistic structures are designed to induce people to behave in predictable, accountable ways. Decision-making authority is centralized, subordinates are closely supervised, and information flows mainly in a vertical direction down a clearly defined hierarchy. In a mechanistic structure the tasks associated with a role are also clearly defined. There is usually a one-to-one correspondence between a person and a task. Figure 4.7A depicts this situation. Each person is individually specialized and knows exactly what he or she is responsible for, and behavior inappropriate to the role is discouraged or prohibited.

At the functional level, each function is separate, and communication and cooperation among functions are the responsibility of someone at the top of the hierarchy. Thus, in a mechanistic structure, the hierarchy is the principal integrating mechanism both within and between functions. Because tasks are organized to prevent miscommunication, the organization does not need to use complex integrating mechanisms. Tasks and roles are coordinated primarily through standardization, and formal written rules and procedures specify role responsibilities. Standardization, together with the hierarchy, is the main means of organizational control.

Given this emphasis on the vertical command structure, the organization is very status conscious, and norms of "protecting one's turf" are common. Promotion is normally slow, steady, and tied to performance, and each employee's progress in the

Mechanistic structures
Structures which are designed to induce people to behave in predictable, accountable ways.

Figure 4.6 How the Design Challenges Result in Mechanistic or Organic Structures

Mechanistic structures result when an organization makes these choices.	Organic structures result when an organization makes these choices.
• Individual Specialization Employees work separately and specialize in one clearly defined task.	• Joint Specialization Employees work together and coordinate their actions to find the best way of performing a task.
• Simple Integrating Mechanisms Hierarchy of authority is clearly defined and is the major integrating mechanism.	• Complex Integrating Mechanisms Task forces and teams are the major integrating mechanisms.
• Centralization Authority to control tasks is kept at the top of the organization. Most communication is vertical.	• Decentralization Authority to control tasks is delegated to people at all levels in the organization. Most communication is lateral.
• Standardization Extensive use is made of rules and SOPs to coordinate tasks, and work process is predictable.	• Mutual Adjustment Extensive use is made of face-to-face contact to coordinate tasks, and work process is relatively unpredictable.

Figure 4.7
Task and Role
Relationships

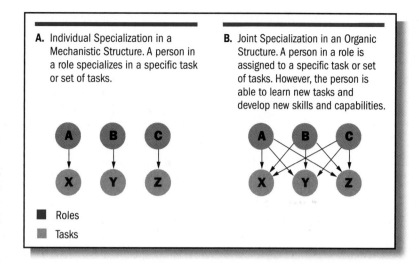

A. **Individual Specialization in a Mechanistic Structure.** A person in a role specializes in a specific task or set of tasks.

B. **Joint Specialization in an Organic Structure.** A person in a role is assigned to a specific task or set of tasks. However, the person is able to learn new tasks and develop new skills and capabilities.

■ Roles

■ Tasks

organization can be charted for years to come. Because of its rigidity, a mechanistic structure is best suited to organizations that face stable, unchanging environments.

Organic Structures

Organic structures
Structures which promote flexibility, so people initiate change and can adapt quickly to changing conditions.

Organic structures are at the opposite end of the organizational design spectrum from mechanistic structures. **Organic structures** promote flexibility, so people initiate change and can adapt quickly to changing conditions.

Organic structures are decentralized so that decision-making authority is distributed throughout the hierarchy; people assume the authority to make decisions as organizational needs dictate. Roles are loosely defined and people continually develop new kinds of job skills to perform continually changing tasks. Figure 4.7B depicts this situation. Each person performs all three tasks, and the result is joint specialization and increased productivity. As employees from different functions work together to solve problems, they become involved in each other's activities. As a result, a high level of integration is needed so that employees can share information and overcome problems caused by differences in subunit orientation. The integration of functions is achieved by means of complex mechanisms like task forces and teams (see Figure 4.6). Coordination is achieved through mutual adjustment as people and functions negotiate role definitions and responsibilities, and informal rules and norms emerge from the ongoing interaction of organizational members. This organic approach to decision making is very different from the mechanistic one used by the old IBM, which was discussed earlier. In IBM's vertical, centralized product development system, getting a decision made was, according to one engineer, "like wading through a tub of peanut butter."

Over time, in an organic structure, specific norms and values develop that emphasize personal competence, expertise, and the ability to act in innovative ways. Status is conferred by the ability to provide creative leadership, and not by any formal position in the hierarchy. Once again, this was the case in the old IBM, whose mechanistic structure made grade, seniority, and loyalty the foundation of its norms and values. The result was slow and ponderous decision making and managers who were afraid to rock the boat.

Clearly, organic and mechanistic structures have very different implications for the way people behave. Is an organic structure better than a mechanistic structure? It seems to encourage the kinds of innovative behaviors that are in vogue at present: teamwork and self-management to improve quality and customer service, and to reduce the time needed to get new products to market. However, would you want to use an organic structure to coordinate the armed forces? Probably not, because of the many authority and status problems that would arise in getting the army, air force, marines, and navy to cooperate. Would you want an organic structure in a nuclear power plant? Probably not: If employees adopt a creative, novel response in an emergency situation, this might result in a catastrophe. Would you even want an organic structure in a restaurant, in which chefs take the roles of waiters and waiters take the roles of chefs, and authority and power relationships are worked out on an ongoing basis? Probably not, because the one-to-one correspondence of person and role allows each restaurant employee to perform their role in the most effective manner. Conversely, would you want to use a mechanistic structure in a high-tech company like Apple or Microsoft, where innovation is a function of the skills and abilities of teams of creative programmers working jointly on a project?

The Contingency Approach to Organizational Design

The decision about whether to design an organic or a mechanistic structure depends on the *particular situation an organization faces*: the environment it confronts, its technology and the nature of the tasks it performs, and the type of people it employs. In general, the contingencies or sources of uncertainty facing an organization shape the organization's design. The **contingency approach** to organizational design tailors organizational structure to the sources of uncertainty facing an organization.[33] The structure is designed to respond to various contingencies—things that might happen and therefore must be planned for. One of the most important of these is the nature of the environment.

According to contingency theory, in order to manage its environment effectively, an organization should design its structure to fit with the environment in which the organization operates.[34] In other words, an organization must design its internal structure to control the external environment (see Figure 4.8). A poor fit between structure and environment leads to failure; a close fit leads to success. Support for contingency theory comes from two studies of the relationship between structure and the environment. These studies, conducted by Paul Lawrence and Jay Lorsch, and by Tom Burns and G. M. Stalker, are examined next.

Lawrence and Lorsch on Differentiation, Integration, and the Environment

The strength and complexity of the forces in the general and specific environments have a direct effect on the extent of differentiation inside an organization.[35] The number and size of an organization's functions mirror the organization's needs to manage exchanges with forces in its environment (see Figure 4.9). Which function

Contingency approach
A management approach in which the design of an organization's structure is tailored to the sources of uncertainty facing an organization.

Figure 4.8
The Fit between the Organization and Its Environment

A poor fit leads to failure; a close fit leads to success.

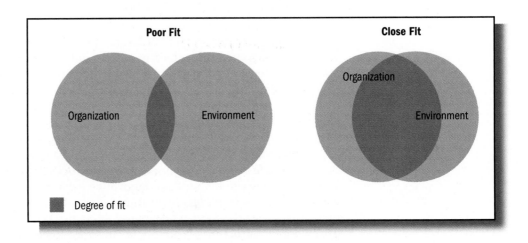

Figure 4.9
Functional Differentiation and Environmental Demands

A functional structure emerges in part to deal with the complexity of demands from the environment.

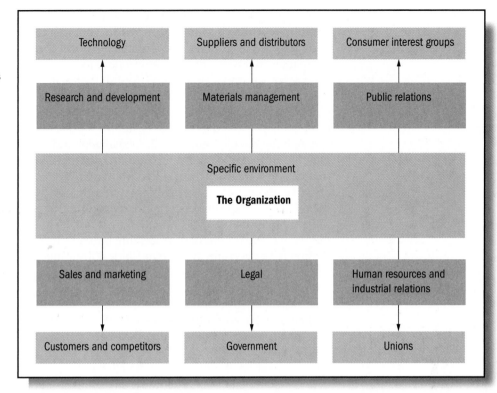

handles exchanges with suppliers and distributors? Materials management does. Which function handles exchanges with customers? Sales and marketing. With the government and consumer organizations? Legal and public relations. A functional structure emerges, in part, to deal with the complexity of environmental demands.

Paul Lawrence and Jay Lorsch investigated how companies in different industries differentiate and integrate their structures to fit the characteristics of the industry environment in which they compete.[36] They selected three industries that, they argued, experienced different levels of uncertainty as measured by variables such as rate of change (dynamism) of the environment. The three industries were (1) the plastics industry, which they said experienced the greatest level of uncertainty; (2) the food-processing industry; and (3) the container or can-manufacturing industry, which they said experienced the least uncertainty. Uncertainty was highest in plastics because of the rapid pace of technological and product change. It was lowest in containers, where organizations produce a standard array of products that change little from year to year. Food-processing companies were in between because, although they introduce new products frequently, production technology is quite stable.

Lawrence and Lorsch measured the degree of differentiation in the production, research and development, and sales departments of a set of companies in each industry. They were interested in the degree to which each department adopted a different internal structure of rules and procedures to coordinate its activities. They also measured differences in subunit or functional orientations (differences in time, goal, and interpersonal orientations). They were interested in the differences between each department's attitude toward the importance of different organizational goals, such as sales or production goals or short- and long-term goals. They also measured how companies in different industries integrated their functional activities.

They found that when the environment was perceived by each of the three departments as very complex and unstable, the attitudes and orientation of each department diverged significantly. Each department developed a different set of values, perspectives, and way of doing things that suited the part of the specific environment that it was dealing with. Thus the extent of differentiation between departments was greater in companies that faced an uncertain environment than in companies that were in stable environments.

Lawrence and Lorsch also found that when the environment is perceived as unstable and uncertain, organizations are more effective if they are less formalized, more decentralized, and more reliant on mutual adjustment. When the environment is perceived as relatively stable and certain, organizations are more effective if they have a more centralized, formalized, and standardized structure. Moreover, they found that effective companies in different industries had levels of integration that matched their levels of differentiation. In the uncertain plastics industry, highly effective organizations were highly differentiated but were also highly integrated. In the relatively stable container industry, highly effective companies had a low level of differentiation, which was matched by a low level of integration. Companies in the moderately uncertain food-processing industry had levels of differentiation and integration in between the other two. Table 4.2 summarizes these relationships.

As Table 4.2 shows, a complex, uncertain environment (such as the plastics industry) requires that different departments develop different orientations toward their tasks (a high level of differentiation) so that they can deal with the complexity of their specific environment. As a result of this high degree of differentiation, such organizations require more coordination (a high level of integration). They make greater use of integrating roles between departments to transfer information so that the organization as a w hole can develop a coordinated response to the environment. In contrast, no complex integrating mechanisms such as integrating roles are found in companies in stable environments because the hierarchy, rules, and SOPs provide sufficient coordination.

The message of Lawrence and Lorsch's study was that organizations must adapt their structures to match the environment in which they operate if they are to be effective. This conclusion reinforced that of a study by Burns and Stalker.

Burns and Stalker on Organic Versus Mechanistic Structures and the Environment

Tom Burns and G. M. Stalker also found that organizations need different kinds of structure to control activities when they need to adapt and respond to change in the environment.[37] Specifically, they found that companies with an organic structure were more effective in unstable, changing environments than were companies with a mechanistic structure. The reverse was true in a stable environment: There, the

Table 4.2 The Effect of Uncertainty on Differentiation and Integration in Three Industries

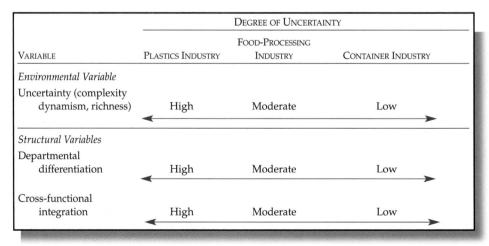

VARIABLE	DEGREE OF UNCERTAINTY		
	PLASTICS INDUSTRY	FOOD-PROCESSING INDUSTRY	CONTAINER INDUSTRY
Environmental Variable			
Uncertainty (complexity dynamism, richness)	High	Moderate	Low
Structural Variables			
Departmental differentiation	High	Moderate	Low
Cross-functional integration	High	Moderate	Low

centralized, formalized, and standardized way of coordinating and motivating people that is characteristic of a mechanistic structure worked better than the decentralized, team approach that is characteristic of an organic structure.

What is the reason for those results? When the environment is rapidly changing and on-the-spot decisions have to be made, lower-level employees need to have the authority to make important decisions—in other words, they need to be empowered. Moreover, in complex environments, rapid communication and information sharing are often necessary to respond to customer needs and develop new products.[38] When the environment is stable, in contrast, there is no need for complex decision-making systems. Managing resource transactions is easy, and better performance can be obtained by keeping authority centralized in the top management team and using top-down decision making. Burns and Stalker's conclusion was that organizations should design their structure to match the dynamism and uncertainty of their environment. Figure 4.10 summarizes the conclusions from Burns and Stalker's and Lawrence and Lorsch's contingency studies. McDonald's offers an interesting insight into the way a change in an organization's environment can bring about a change in its structure.

Later chapters examine in detail how to choose the appropriate organizational structure to meet different strategic and technological contingencies. For now, it is important to realize that mechanistic and organic structures are ideals: They are useful for examining how organizational structure affects behavior, but they probably do not exist in a pure form in any real-life organization. Most organizations are a mixture of the two types. Indeed, according to one increasingly influential view of organizational design, the most successful organizations are those that have achieved a balance between the two, so that they are simultaneously mechanistic and organic—something McDonald's is seeking to achieve.

An organization may tend more in one direction than in the other, but it needs to be able to act in both ways to be effective. The army, for example, is well known for having a mechanistic structure in which hierarchical reporting relationships are clearly specified. However, in wartime, this mechanistic command structure allows the army to become organic and flexible as it responds to the uncertainties of the quickly changing battlefield. Similarly, an organization may design its structure so that some functions (such as manufacturing and accounting) act in a mechanistic

Figure 4.10
The Relationship Between Environmental Uncertainty and Organizational Structure

Studies by Lawrence and Lorsch and by Burns and Stalker indicate that organizations should adapt their structure to reflect the degree of uncertainty in their environment. Companies with a mechanistic structure tend to fare best in a stable environment. Those with an organic structure tend to fare best in an unstable, changing environment.

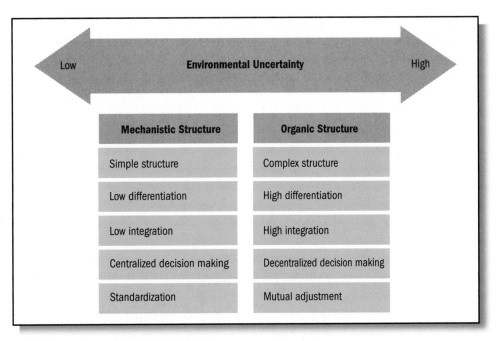

McDonald's environment is changing rapidly and becoming increasingly difficult to manage. The company has been experiencing increasing problems since the early 2000s.[39] Consumer tastes are shifting as a health-conscious public is eating less beef and less fat. Environmentalists are attacking the packaging that McDonald's uses. Competitors are becoming more numerous and are seizing McDonald's customers. Chili's and the Olive Garden are luring upscale customers, and Rally's, Taco Bell, and Wendy's are challenging McDonald's for patrons who want a quick, cheap meal. McDonald's has been searching for ways to increase its control of an environment that is becoming poorer, more complex, and less predictable.

At the center of its new approach is a dramatic change in McDonald's view of its domain. In the past, at the heart of McDonald's were its standardized production operation and its mechanistic structure based on formalization, which together ensured that burgers and fries served in London and Moscow tasted and looked the same as burgers and fries served in New York. The operations manual for the kitchen alone was 600 pages long!

New customers, however, demanded new kinds of food, so McDonald's new approach to production is based on flexibility. It has experimented with over 200 kinds of food—from barbecue to pizza to lobster—and is allowing franchisees to design a menu that appeals to local customers. For example, McDonald's restaurants on the Eastern Shore of Maryland serve crab cake sandwiches; in Mexico, McDonald's has introduced a guacamole burger.[40] McDonald's is also allowing franchisees to design a décor to suit their location: For instance, the McDonald's on Wall Street has a grand piano.[41] Also, McDonald's has opened many different types of restaurants, for example, at Wal-Mart stores and air-conditioned playhouse restaurants. In addition, McDonald's experimented with owning different kinds of restaurants—it bought a small pizza chain in 1999 and bought and expanded Chipotle, a Mexican restaurant, and Boston Market, in the late 1990s.[42]

All this flexibility placed a severe strain on McDonald's mechanistic structure. The organization was forced to develop a more organic structure to allow its 8,800 restaurants to customize the food they served and restaurant design to their specific situation. McDonald's decentralized authority to managers in different U.S. regions and allowed them to make the important decisions that most affected them. In this new competitive environment the name of the game became flexibility; the goal was a quick response to customers' needs and competitors' moves and the need to squeeze out costs to keep prices low.

By 2003 McDonald's new approach to design proved to be a disaster. Although decentralization had allowed franchises to better respond to local needs, McDonald's core operations, and the thousands of managers who controlled the way its empire operated, had not been affected by these changes. They were still working to perfect its current operating strategy and were not responding to the major changes in taste taking place. Customers were turning to chicken to reduce fat in their diets, salads were becoming increasingly popular, "healthy" fast food was their goal. McDonald's stock plunged over 200% in value as its sales dropped; its managers strove to find a better way to operate.

The answer was to decentralize control at McDonald's core operations and create teams of food specialists that were given the authority to experiment with new kinds of food offerings and test them with customers. McDonald's old top management team, one used to a centralized approach to control, was replaced with managers who had long advocated the need to be proactive and responsive to customers' changing demands. At the same time, McDonald's also had been experiencing increasing complaints of falling standards of quality and cleanliness in its restaurants, which were among its claims to fame. Its decision to decentralize control to franchisees had led them to cut their restaurant's operating costs, but this had also reduced restaurant quality. So, McDonald's moved to recentralize control over quality and take back control in this area.

Managing a more complex environment requires a more complex structure. After a few years of struggling, by 2004 McDonald's overall organic approach to operating paid off. Its stock price more than doubled by 2005 as its new menu offerings attracted customers, while its restaurants were all redesigned to suit contemporary tastes—and more attention was paid to cleanliness. Clearly, even the most successful organizations continually need to overhaul their structures and modify their design to suit changing conditions.

way and others (marketing or R&D) develop a more organic approach to their tasks. To achieve the difficult balancing act of being simultaneously mechanistic and organic, organizations need to make appropriate choices (see Figure 4.6). In the next three chapters we look in more detail at the issues involved in designing organizational structure and culture to improve organizational effectiveness.

SUMMARY

This chapter has analyzed how managers' responses to several organizational design challenges affect the way employees behave and interact and how they respond to the organization. We have analyzed how differentiation occurs and examined three other challenges that managers confront as they try to structure their organization to achieve organizational goals. Chapter 4 has made the following main points:

1. Differentiation is the process by which organizations evolve into complex systems as they allocate people and resources to organizational tasks and assign people different levels of authority.
2. Organizations develop five functions to accomplish their goals and objectives: support, production, maintenance, adaptive, and managerial.
3. An organizational role is a set of task-related behaviors required of an employee. An organization is composed of interlocking roles that are differentiated by task responsibilities and task authority.
4. Differentiation has a vertical and a horizontal dimension. Vertical differentiation refers to the way an organization designs its hierarchy of authority. Horizontal differentiation refers to the way an organization groups roles into subunits (functions and divisions).
5. Managers confront four design challenges as they coordinate organizational activities. The choices they make are interrelated and collectively determine how effectively an organization operates.
6. The first challenge is to choose the right extent of vertical and horizontal differentiation.
7. The second challenge is to strike an appropriate balance between differentiation and integration and use appropriate integrating mechanisms.
8. The third challenge is to strike an appropriate balance between the centralization and decentralization of decision-making authority.
9. The fourth challenge is to strike an appropriate balance between standardization and mutual adjustment by using the right amounts of formalization and socialization.
10. Different organizational structures cause individuals to behave in different ways. Mechanistic structures are designed to cause people to behave in predictable ways. Organic structures promote flexibility and quick responses to changing conditions. Successful organizations strike an appropriate balance between mechanistic and organic structures.
11. Contingency theory argues that in order to manage its environment effectively, an organization should design its structure and control systems to fit with the environment in which the organization operates.

DISCUSSION QUESTIONS

1. Why does differentiation occur in an organization? Distinguish between vertical and horizontal differentiation.
2. Draw an organizational chart of the business school or college that you attend. Outline its major roles and functions. How differentiated is it? Do you think the distribution of authority and division of labor are appropriate?
3. When does an organization need to use complex integrating mechanisms? Why?
4. What factors determine the balance between centralization and decentralization, and between standardization and mutual adjustment?
5. Under what conditions is an organization likely to prefer (a) a mechanistic structure, (b) an organic structure, or (c) elements of both?

ORGANIZATIONAL THEORY IN ACTION

Practicing Organizational Theory: Growing Pains

Form groups of three to five people and discuss the following scenario:

You are the founding entrepreneurs of Zylon Corporation, a fast-growing Internet software company that specializes in electronic banking. Customer demand to license your software has boomed so much that in just two years you have added over 50 new software programmers to help develop a new range of software products. The growth of your company has been so swift that you still operate informally with a loose and flexible arrangement of roles, and programmers are encouraged to find solutions to problems as they go along. Although this structure has worked well, there are signs that problems are arising.

There have been increasing complaints from employees that good performance is not being recognized in the organization and that they do not feel equitably treated. Moreover, there have been complaints about getting managers to listen to their new ideas and to act on them. A bad atmosphere seems to be developing in the company, and recently several talented employees left. You are meeting to discuss these problems.

1. Examine your organizational structure to see what might be causing these problems.
2. What kinds of design choices do you need to make to solve them?

Making the Connection #4

Find an example of a company that has been facing one of the design challenges discussed in this chapter. What problem has the company been experiencing? How has it attempted to deal with the problem?

The Ethical Dimension #4

The way an organizational structure is designed affects the way its members behave. Rules can be applied so strictly and punitively that they harm employees by, for example, increasing the stress of the job. Inappropriate norms can develop that might reduce employee incentive to work or cause employees to abuse their peers. Similarly, in some organizations, superiors use their authority to abuse and harangue employees. Think about the ethical implications of the design challenges discussed in this chapter.

1. Using the design challenges, design an organization that you think would result in highly ethical decision making; then design one that would lead to the opposite. Why the difference?
2. Do you think ethical behavior is more likely in a mechanistic or an organic structure?

Analyzing the Organization: Design Module #4

This module attempts to get at some of the basic operating principles that your organization uses to perform its tasks. From the information you have been able to obtain, describe the aspects of your organization's structure in the following assignment.

Assignment

1. How differentiated is your organization? Is it simple or complex? List the major roles, functions, or departments in your organization. Does your organization have many divisions? If your organization engages in many businesses, list the major divisions in the company.
2. What core competences make your organization unique or different from other organizations? What are the sources of the core competences? How difficult do you think it would be for other organizations to imitate these distinctive competences?
3. How has your organization responded to the design challenges? (a) Is it centralized or decentralized? How do you know? (b) Is it highly differentiated? Can you identify any integrating mechanisms used by your organization? What is the match between the complexity of differentiation and the complexity of the integrating mechanisms that are used? (c) Is behavior in the organization very standardized, or does mutual adjustment play an important role in coordinating people and activities? What can you tell about the level of formalization by looking at the number and kinds of rules the organization uses? How important is socialization in your organization?
4. Does your analysis in item 3 lead you to think that your organization conforms more to the organic or to the mechanistic model of organizational structure? Briefly explain why you think it is organic or mechanistic.
5. From your analysis so far, what do you think could be done to improve the way your organization operates?

CASE FOR ANALYSIS

Where Should Decisions Be Made?

In 1995, Procter & Gamble's top managers took a long, hard look at the giant company's global operations and decided that they could make much better use of organizational resources if they changed the level at which decisions were made in their organization. Until 1995, managers in each of Procter & Gamble's divisions, in each country in the world in which it operated, were more or less free to make their own decisions, and decision making was decentralized. Thus managers in charge of the British soap and detergent division operated quite independently from managers in French and German divisions. Moreover, even within Britain, the soap and detergent division operated quite independently from other Procter & Gamble divisions such as its health-care and beauty products divisions. Top managers believed that this highly decentralized global decision making resulted in the loss of possible gains to be obtained from cooperation both among managers of the same kind of division in the different countries (soap and detergent divisions throughout Europe) and among managers in the different kinds of divisions operating in the same country or world regions.

Therefore, Procter & Gamble's top management team pioneered a new kind of organizational structure. First, they divided P&G's global operations into four main areas—North America, Europe, the Middle East and Africa, and Asia—and in each area they created the new role of global executive vice president, responsible for overseeing the operation of all the different kinds of divisions inside that world region. This approach was something Procter & Gamble had never attempted.[43] It is the global vice president's responsibility to get the different kinds of divisions inside each area to cooperate and to share information and knowledge so that authority is centralized at the world area level. Each of these new top managers then reports directly to the president of Procter & Gamble, further centralizing authority.

In another change to further centralize authority, P&G's managers grouped divisions operating in the same area and put them under the control of one manager. For example, the manager of the U.K. soap and detergent division took control over soap and detergent operations in the United Kingdom, Ireland, Spain, and Portugal and became responsible for getting them to cooperate so the company could reduce costs and innovate more quickly across Europe.

Procter & Gamble has been delighted with its new balance between centralized and decentralized authority because its top managers feel they are making much better use of organizational resources to meet customers' needs. They believe Procter & Gamble is poised to become the dominant consumer goods company in the world, not merely in the United States, and in 1996 the company earned record operating profits on record global sales.

DISCUSSION QUESTIONS

1. Why did Procter & Gamble move to centralize control?
2. When might managers realize that they have gone too far and "centralized" control too much?

REFERENCES

1. T. Parsons, *Structure and Process in Modern Societies* (Glencoe, IL: Free Press, 1960); J. Child, *Organization: A Guide for Managers and Administrators* (New York: Harper and Row, 1977).

2. R. K. Merton, *Social Theory and Social Structure*, 2e (Glencoe, IL: Free Press, 1957).

3. D. Katz and R. L. Kahn, *The Social Psychology of Organizing* (New York: Wiley, 1966).

4. Ibid., pp. 39–47.

5. P. Selznick, "An Approach to a Theory of Bureaucracy," *American Sociological Review, VIII* (1943), 47–54.

6. M. E. Porter, *Competitive Strategy* (New York: Free Press, 1980).

7. R. H. Miles, *Macro Organizational Behavior* (Santa Monica, CA: Goodyear, 1980), pp. 19–20.

8. Child, *Organization*.

9. P. R. Lawrence and J. W. Lorsch, *Organization and Environment* (Boston: Graduate School of Business Administration, Harvard University, 1967).

10. J. R. Galbraith, *Designing Complex Organizations* (Reading, MA: Addison-Wesley, 1973).

11. B. Dumaine, "The Bureaucracy Busters," *Fortune*, June 7, 1991, p. 42.

12. B. P. Sunoo, "Amgen's Latest Secrets," *Personnel Journal*, February 1996, pp. 38–45.

13. A. Erdman, "How to Keep That Family Feeling," *Fortune*, April 6, 1992, pp. 95–96.

14. www.amgen.com, "Mission and Values," 2006.

15. H. Mintzberg, *The Nature of Managerial Work* (Upper Saddle River, NJ: Prentice Hall, 1973).

16. www.whirlpool, 2006.

17. P. P. Gupta, M. D. Dirsmith, and T. J. Fogarty, "Coordination and Control in a Government Agency: Contingency and Institutional Theory Perspectives on GAO Audits," *Administrative Science Quarterly, 39* (1994), 264–284.

18. A detailed critique of the workings of bureaucracy in practice is offered in P. M. Blau, *The Dynamics of Bureaucracy* (Chicago: University of Chicago Press, 1955).

19. Dumaine, "The Bureaucracy Busters," pp. 36–50.

20. D. S. Pugh, D. J. Hickson, C. R. Hinings, and C. Turner, "Dimensions of Organizational Structure," *Administrative Science Quarterly, 13* (1968), 65–91; D. S. Pugh and D. J. Hickson, "The Comparative Study of Organizations," in G. Salaman and K. Thompson, eds., *People and Organizations* (London: Longman, 1973), pp. 50–66.

21. M. Vevrka, "United Way Weighs Pros and Cons of Centralizing," *The Wall Street Journal*, January 7, 1998, p. 2.

22. C. Wian, "Union Pacific to Reorganize," www.cnnfn.com, August 20, 1998.

23. www.up.com, 2002.

24. J. Flynn, "The Ugly Mess at Waste Management," *Business Week*, April 13, 1992, pp. 76–77.

25. C. L. Loomis, "Can John Akers Save IBM?" *Fortune*, April 22, 1992, pp. 41–56.

26. See H. Mintzberg, *The Structuring of Organizational Structures* (Upper Saddle River, NJ: Prentice Hall, 1979), for an in-depth treatment of standardization and mutual adjustment.

27. Pugh and Hickson, "The Comparative Study of Organizations."

28. Loomis, "Can John Akers Save IBM?" p. 54.

29. M. Dalton, "The Industrial Ratebuster: A Characterization," *Applied Anthropology, 7* (1948), 5–18.

30. J. Van Maanen and E. H. Schein, "Towards a Theory of Organizational Socialization," in B. M. Staw, ed., *Research in Organizational Behavior*, vol. 1 (Greenwich, CT: JAI Press, 1979), pp. 209–264.

31. G. R. Jones, "Socialization Tactics, Self-Efficacy, and Newcomers' Adjustments to Organizations," *Academy of Management Journal, 29* (1986), 262–279; Van Maanen and Schein, "Towards a Theory of Organizational Socialization."

32. T. Burns and G. M. Stalker, *The Management of Innovation* (London: Tavistock, 1966).

33. J. Pfeffer, *Organizations and Organizational Theory* (Boston: Pitman, 1982), pp. 147–162; J. Child, "Organizational Structure, Environment, and Performance: The Role of Strategic Choice," *Sociology, 6* (1972), 1–22.

34. J. Pfeffer, *Organizations and Organizational Theory* (Boston: Pitman, 1982).

35. P. R. Lawrence and J. W. Lorsch, *Organization and Environment* (Boston: Graduate School of Business Administration, Harvard University, 1967).

36. Ibid.

37. T. Burns and G. M. Stalker, *The Management of Innovation*.

38. J. A. Courtright, G. T. Fairhurst, and L. E. Rogers, "Interaction Patterns in Organic and Mechanistic Systems," *Academy of Management Journal, 32* (1989), 773–802.

39. J. Forster, "Thinking Outside the Burger Box," *Business Week*, September 16, 2002, pp. 20–22.

40. "McDonald's Goes Local with a Guacamole Burger," *Daily World Wire*, March 16, 1999, p.1.

41. L. Therrien, "McRisky," *Business Week*, October 21, 1991, pp. 114–122.

42. A. Edgecliffe-Johnson, "McDonald's Buys Pizza Restaurant Chain in Midwest," *Financial Times*, May 7, 1999, p. 19.

43. "P&G Divides to Rule," *Marketing*, March 23, 1995, p. 15.

Chapter 5

Designing Organizational Structure: Authority and Control

Learning Objectives

To protect stakeholders' goals and interests, managers must continually analyze and redesign an organization's structure so that it most effectively controls people and other resources. In this chapter the many crucial design choices involving the vertical dimension of organizational structure—the hierarchy of authority that an organization creates to control its members—is examined.

After studying this chapter you should be able to:

1. Explain why a hierarchy of authority emerges in an organization and the process of vertical differentiation.

2. Discuss the issues involved in designing a hierarchy to coordinate and motivate organizational behavior most effectively.

3. Understand the way in which the design challenges discussed in Chapter 4—such as centralization and standardization—provide methods of control that substitute for the direct, personal control that managers provide and affect the design of the organizational hierarchy.

4. Appreciate the principles of bureaucratic structure and explain their implications for the design of effective organizational hierarchies.

5. Explain why organizations are flattening their hierarchies and making more use of empowered teams of employees, both inside and across different functions.

AUTHORITY: HOW AND WHY VERTICAL DIFFERENTIATION OCCURS

A basic design challenge, identified in Chapter 4, is deciding how much authority to centralize at the top of the organizational hierarchy and how much authority to decentralize to middle and lower levels. (Recall from Chapter 2 that *authority* is the power to hold people accountable for their actions and to directly influence what they do and how they do it.) But what determines the shape of an organization's hierarchy, that is, the number of levels of authority within an organization? This question is important because the shape of an organization (evident in its organizational chart) determines how effectively the organization's decision-making and communication systems work. The decisions managers make about the shape of the hierarchy, and the balance between centralized and decentralized decision making, establish the level of vertical differentiation in an organization.

The Emergence of the Hierarchy

An organization's hierarchy begins to emerge when managers find it more and more difficult to coordinate and motivate employees effectively.[1] As an organization grows, employees increase in number and begin to specialize, performing widely different kinds of tasks; the level of differentiation increases and this makes coordinating employees' activities more difficult.[2] Similarly, the division of labor and specialization produce motivational problems. When each employee performs only a small part of a total task, it is often difficult to determine how much he or she actually contributes to the task, and thus it is often difficult to evaluate each individual's performance. Moreover, if employees cooperate to achieve a goal it is often impossible to measure, evaluate, and reward them based on their individual performance level. For example, if two waiters cooperate to serve tables, how does their boss know how much each contributed? If two chefs work together to cook a meal, how is each person's individual impact on food quality to be measured and rewarded?[3]

An organization does two things to improve its ability to control—that is, coordinate and motivate—its members: (1) It increases the number of managers it uses to monitor, evaluate, and reward employees; and (2) it increases the number of levels in its managerial hierarchy, thereby making the hierarchy of authority taller.[4] Increasing both the number of managers and the levels of management increases vertical differentiation and gives the organization direct, face-to-face control over its members—managers *personally* control their subordinates.

Direct supervision allows managers to shape and influence the behavior of subordinates as they work face-to-face in the pursuit of a company's goals. Direct supervision is a vital method of control because managers can continually question, probe, and consult with subordinates about problems or new issues they are facing to get a better understanding of the situation. It also ensures that subordinates are performing their work effectively and not hiding any information that could cause problems down the line. Personal control also creates greater opportunity for on-the-job task learning to occur and competencies to develop, as well as greater opportunities to prevent free-riding or shirking.

Moreover, when managers personally supervise subordinates, they lead by example and in this way can help subordinates develop and increase their personal management skills. At GE, for example, considerable importance is given to each manager's responsibility to develop their subordinates and improve their chances of being promoted. The continual improvement of management skills at all levels inside GE is one of its core competencies. Any manager who fails in this task is quickly rooted out and fired, while those who best succeed are rapidly promoted up the hierarchy. Thus personal supervision can be a very effective way of motivating employees and promoting behaviors that increase effectiveness. The personal authority relationship in an organization is perhaps the most significant or tangible one that creates and bonds people into an organization and determines how well they perform.

Size and Height Limitations

Tall organization
An organization in which the hierarchy has many levels relative to the size of the organization.

Figure 5.1 shows two organizations that have the same number of employees, but one has three levels in its hierarchy and the other has seven. An organization in which the hierarchy has many levels relative to the size of the organization is a **tall organization**.

Figure 5.1
Flat and Tall Organizations
A tall organization has more hierarchical levels and more managers to direct and control employees activities than does a flat organization with the same number of employees.

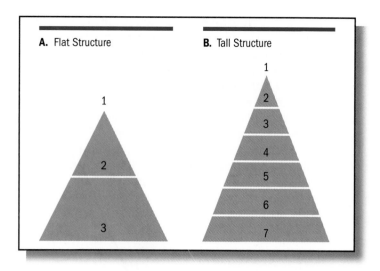

A. Flat Structure

B. Tall Structure

Figure 5.2
The Relationship Between Organizational Size and Number of Hierarchical Levels

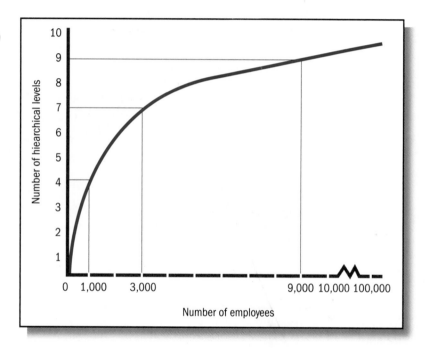

Flat organization

An organization that has few levels in its hierarchy relative to its size.

An organization that has few levels in its hierarchy is a **flat organization**. The tall organization in Figure 5.1 has four more levels than the flat organization, and uses many more managers to direct and control employee' activities. Research evidence suggests that an organization with 3,000 employees is most likely to have seven levels in its hierarchy. Thus a 3,000-employee organization with only four levels in its hierarchy is considered flat, while one with nine levels is considered tall.

Figure 5.2 illustrates an interesting research finding concerning the relationship between organizational size (measured by number of employees) and the height of the vertical hierarchy. By the time an organization has grown to 1,000 members, it is likely to have about four levels in its hierarchy: CEO, function or department heads, department supervisors, and employees. An organization that grows to 3,000 members is likely to have seven levels. After that size is reached, however, something striking happens: Organizations that employ 10,000 or even 100,000 employees typically do not have more than nine or ten levels in their hierarchy. Moreover, large organizations do not increase the numbers of managers at each level to compensate for this restriction in the number of levels in the hierarchy.[5] Thus most organizations have a pyramid-like structure and fewer and fewer managers at each level (see Figure 5.3A), rather than a bloated structure (Figure 5.3B) in which proportionally more managers at all levels control the activities of increasing numbers of members.

In fact, research suggests that the increase in the size of the managerial component in an organization is *less than proportional* to the increase in size of the organization as it grows.[6] This phenomenon is illustrated in Figure 5.4. An increase from 2,000 to 3,000 employees (a 50% increase in organizational size) results in an increase from 300 to 400 managers (a 33% increase). However, an increase from 6,000 to 10,000 employees (a 66% increase) increases the size of the managerial component by only 100 managers (from 700 to 800, a 14% increase).

Why do organizations seem to actively restrain the increase in the number of managers and hierarchical levels as they grow and differentiate? The answer is that many significant problems arise as the organizational hierarchy becomes taller and taller.[7]

Figure 5.3
Types of Managerial Hierarchies

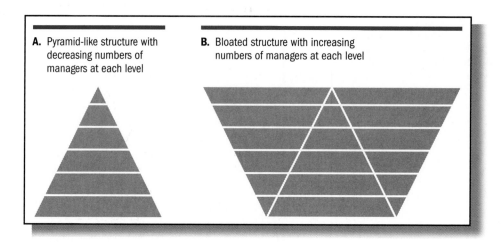

Figure 5.4
The Relationship Between Organizational Size and the Size of the Managerial Component

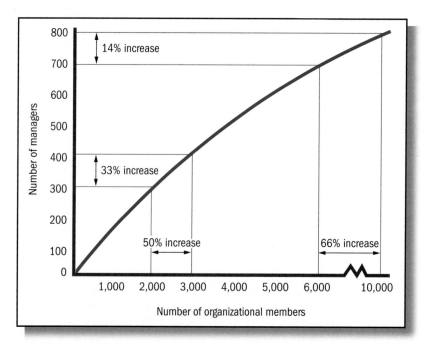

Problems with Tall Hierarchies

Choosing the right number of managers and hierarchical levels is important because this decision impacts organizational effectiveness. Specifically, this choice can increase or reduce communication, motivation, and bottom-line profitability.[8]

Communication Problems

Having too many hierarchical levels may hinder communication. As the chain of command lengthens, communication between managers at the top and bottom of the hierarchy takes longer. Decision making slows, and the slowdown hurts the performance of organizations that need to respond quickly to customers' needs or the actions of competitors.[9] At FedEx, fast decision making is a prerequisite for success, so the company has only five hierarchical levels; it believes that with any more levels the speed of communication and decision making would suffer.[10] Similarly, when Liz Claiborne was designing the structure of her organization, she was careful to keep the hierarchy flat—four levels for 4,000 employees—to maximize the organization's ability to respond to quickly changing fashion trends.

Another significant communication problem is distortion. Information becomes distorted as it flows up and down the hierarchy through many levels of management.[11] Experiments have shown that a message that starts at one end of a chain of people can become something quite different by the time it reaches the other end of the chain.

In addition, managers up and down the hierarchy may manipulate information to serve their own interests. It has been demonstrated that managers can lead others to make certain kinds of decisions by restricting the flow of information or by selectively feeding information to them.[12] When this happens, the top of the hierarchy may lose control over the bottom. Managers at low levels may also selectively transmit up the hierarchy only the information that serves their interests. A rational subordinate, for example, may decide to give a superior only information that makes him or her or the superior look good. Again, if this happens often, the top of the hierarchy may have little idea about or control over what is happening below, and the quality of decision making at all levels suffers.

Studies show that communication problems get progressively worse as the number of hierarchical levels increases. Thus managers are wise to try to limit and restrict the growth of the organizational hierarchy. When the number of levels surpasses seven or eight, communication problems can cause a breakdown in control and slow and unresponsive decision making, as DuPont's experience suggests.

ORGANIZATIONAL INSIGHT 5.1
The Shake-Up at DuPont

DuPont, one of America's largest chemical companies, is well known for developing such products as Nylon and Teflon.[13] Recently, DuPont ran into problems in developing new products, managing its diverse businesses, and responding to customer needs. Sales of its products were slowing and its earnings were dropping. Its CEO attributed these problems to an increase in the number of top levels of management that had occurred gradually over time. Believing too many managers were slowing down recognition of, and reaction to, problems, he decided to shake up top management.

First, the topmost level of management—the executive committee, a group of former and current top executives who had been guiding DuPont for decades—was eliminated! Then began the elimination of levels of top management within the individual operating divisions. For example, in the huge Polymer Division, where nylon is made, one out of every four management jobs was cut. Where 11 levels of management were used to separate the top management team from a salesperson in the field, the number is now five.

The name of the game has been to flatten the structure so that the organization can be more responsive to customer needs. If field personnel can quickly inform company scientists about new customer needs as they develop, both innovation and sales will be boosted.[14] At the same time, the costs of operating DuPont's management hierarchy have been greatly reduced, and the company achieved $1 billion in salary savings from the changes.

Motivation Problems

As the number of levels in the hierarchy *increases*, the relative difference in the authority possessed by managers at each level *decreases*, as does their area of responsibility. A flat organization (see Figure 5.1) has fewer managers and hierarchical levels than a tall organization, so managers of a flat organization possess relatively more authority and responsibility than those of a tall organization. Many studies have shown that when more authority and responsibility are given to managers and employees, they are more motivated to perform their organizational roles, other things being equal. Thus motivation in an organization with a flat structure may be stronger than motivation in a tall organization. Also, when a hierarchy has many levels, it is easy for managers to pass the buck and evade responsibility by shifting this responsibility to the manager above them—actions that worsen the problem of slow decision making and poor communication.

Bureaucratic Costs

Managers cost money. The greater the number of managers and hierarchical levels, the greater the bureaucratic costs—that is, the costs associated with running and operating an organization. It has been estimated that the average middle manager costs over $300,000 per year in salary, bonuses, benefits, and an office. Employing a thousand excess managers, therefore, costs an organization $300 million a year—an enormous sum that companies often belatedly recognize they do not need to pay. Because of the cost of a tall and bloated hierarchy, it is common, especially during a recession, for a company to announce that it will reduce the number of levels in its hierarchy and lay off excess employees to reduce bureaucratic costs. In 2005, for example, Ford announced that it would eliminate two levels in its hierarchy and lay off 600 managers, for a savings of $500 million. HP, GM, Xerox, Kodak, and DuPont are some of the many large companies that have saved billions of dollars from streamlining their managerial hierarchies in the 2000s.

Why do companies suddenly perceive the need to reduce their workforce drastically, thus subjecting employees to the uncertainty and misery of the unemployment line with a minimum of notice? Why do companies not have more foresight and restrict the growth of managers and hierarchical levels to avoid large layoffs? Sometimes layoffs are unavoidable, as when a totally unexpected situation arises in the organization's environment. For example, innovation may render technology obsolete or uncompetitive, or a general economic crisis may abruptly reduce demand for an organization's product. Much of the time, however, dramatic changes in employment and structure are simply the result of bad management.

Managers of an organization that is doing well often do not recognize the need to control, prune, and manage the organization's hierarchy as the organization confronts new or changing situations. Or they may see the need but prefer to do little or nothing. As organizations grow, managers usually pay little attention to the hierarchy; their most pressing concern is to satisfy customer needs by bringing products or services to the market as quickly as possible. As a result, hierarchical levels multiply as new people are added without much thought about long-term consequences. When an organization matures, its structure is likely to be streamlined; for example, two or more managerial positions may be combined into one, and levels in the hierarchy are eliminated to improve decision making and reduce costs. The terms *restructuring* and *downsizing* are used to describe the process by which managers streamline hierarchies and lay off managers and workers to reduce bureaucratic costs. This is discussed in detail in Chapter 10, where the focus of analysis is organizational change and redesign.

The Parkinson's Law Problem

While studying administrative processes in the British Navy, C. Northcote Parkinson, a former British civil servant, came upon some interesting statistics.[15] He discovered that from 1914 to 1928, the number of ships in operation decreased by

68%; however, the number of dockyard officials responsible for maintaining the fleet had increased by 40% and the number of top brass in London responsible for managing the fleet had increased by 79%. Why had this situation occurred? Parkinson argued that growth in the number of managers and hierarchical levels is controlled by two principles: (1) "An official wants to multiply subordinates, not rivals," and (2) "Officials make work for one another."[16]

Managers value their rank, grade, or status in the hierarchy. The fewer managers at their hierarchical level and the greater the number of managers below them, the larger is their "empire" and the higher their status. Not surprisingly then, managers seek to increase the number of their subordinates. In turn, these subordinates realize the status advantages of having subordinates, so they try to increase the number of their subordinates, causing the hierarchy to become taller and taller. As the number of levels increases, managers must spend more of their time monitoring and controlling the actions and behaviors of their subordinates and thus create unnecessary work for themselves. More managers lead to more work—hence, the British Navy results. Parkinson further contended that his principles apply to all hierarchies if they are not controlled. Because managers in hierarchies make work for each other, "Work expands so as to fill the time available." That is Parkinson's Law.

The Ideal Number of Hierarchical Levels: The Minimum Chain of Command

Managers should base the decision to employ an extra manager on the difference between the value added by the last manager employed and the cost of the last manager employed. However, as Parkinson noted, a person may have no second thoughts about spending the organization's money to improve his or her own position, status, and power. Well-managed organizations control this problem by simple rules—for example, "Any new recruitment has to be approved by the CEO"—that prompt upper-level managers to evaluate whether another lower-level manager or another hierarchical level is really necessary. An even more general principle for designing a hierarchy is the principle of minimum chain of command.

Principle of minimum chain of command
An organization should choose the minimum number of hierarchical levels consistent with its goals and the environment in which it operates.

According to the **principle of minimum chain of command**, an organization should choose the minimum number of hierarchical levels consistent with its goals and the environment in which it exists.[17] In other words, an organization should be kept as flat as possible, and top managers should be evaluated for their ability to monitor and control its activities with the fewest managers possible.

An organization with a flat structure will also experience fewer communication, motivation, and cost problems than a tall organization. The only reason for an organization to choose a tall structure over a flat structure is when it needs a high level of direct control or personal supervision over subordinates. Nuclear power plants, for example, typically have extremely tall hierarchies so that managers at all levels can maintain effective supervision of operations. Because any error could produce a disaster, managers continually oversee and cross-check the work of managers below them to ensure that rules and SOPs are followed accurately and consistently.

In Chapter 9 we examine factors such as technology and task characteristics that make tall structures the preferred choice. Here, organizations should strive to keep hierarchical levels to the minimum necessary to accomplish their mission. Organizational problems produced by factors such as Parkinson's Law do not satisfy any stakeholder interest, for sooner or later they will be discovered by a new management team, which will purge the hierarchy to reduce excess managers. In the 2000s, this has happened at many companies, such as IBM, AOL–Time Warner, Lucent, and EMI, which is profiled in the following organizational insight.

EMI is the British record company that launched the careers of the Beatles, Rolling Stones, and Garth Brooks.[18] The 105-year-old company used to be the most profitable in the industry, but during the 1990s its performance collapsed. The reason, believes Alain Levy, its French-born CEO, is that EMI came to be managed by a top-heavy team of overpaid executives who lacked the entrepreneurial ability either to recognize and promote new talent or to help their subordinates acquire that ability.

So Levy set out to shake up EMI's hierarchy and change the motivation of his top managers. Given the years of problems, he adopted a radical approach. First, he fired almost 2,000 entrenched executives and eliminated three levels in the management hierarchy. Then, giving his remaining managers a greater area of responsibility, he abolished the old reward system of guaranteed bonuses based upon signing new talent. Henceforth, EMI managers were put on contracts and their performance bonuses were based on the future performance of the artists they signed and promoted. Executives whose performance slips are put on shorter contracts; managers who can demonstrate a track record of success receive longer contracts.[19]

After these changes no manager had a guaranteed lifetime position in EMI's hierarchy, as was true in the old system. A manager's ability to hold a high office is a function of continuing high performance. Levy includes developing subordinates—so they acquire the entrepreneurial skills needed to run a company that depends on recognizing and promoting creative talent—as one of his managers' main responsibilities. So far, his approach has worked; the music groups' performance improved sharply by 2005 in the very challenging world of digital music and digital piracy.

Span of Control

Span of control
The number of subordinates a manager directly manages.

Organizations that become too tall inevitably experience problems. Nevertheless, a growing organization must be able to monitor and control the activities of newly hired employees. How can an organization avoid becoming too tall yet maintain effective control of its workforce? One way is to increase its managers' **span of control**—the number of subordinates each manager directly manages.[20] If the span of control of each manager increases as the number of employees increases, then the number of managers or hierarchical levels does *not* increase in proportion to increases in the number of employees. Instead, each manager coordinates the work of more subordinates, and the organization substitutes an increase in the span of control for an increase in hierarchical levels.

Figure 5.5 depicts two different spans of control. Figure 5.5A shows an organization with a CEO, five managers, and 10 employees; each manager supervises two people. Figure 5.5B shows an organization with a CEO, two managers, and 10 employees, but Manager A supervises two people, and Manager B supervises eight people. Why does Manager A's span of control extend over only two people and

Figure 5.5 Spans of Control

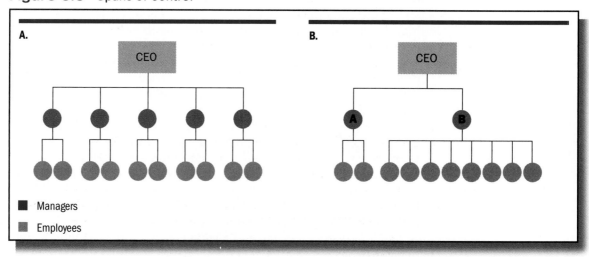

Figure 5.6
The Increasing Complexity of a Manager's Job as the Span of Control Increases

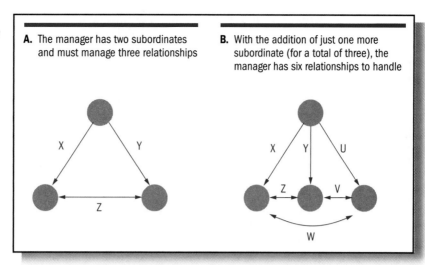

A. The manager has two subordinates and must manage three relationships

B. With the addition of just one more subordinate (for a total of three), the manager has six relationships to handle

Manager B's extend over eight? Or, more generally, what determines the size and limit of a manager's span of control?

Perhaps the single most important factor limiting the managerial span of control is the inability to exercise adequate supervision over the activities of subordinates as they grow in number. It has been demonstrated that an arithmetic increase in the number of subordinates is accompanied by an exponential increase in the number of subordinate relationships that a manager has to supervise.[21] Figure 5.6 illustrates this point.

The manager in Figure 5.6A has two subordinates and must manage three relationships: X, Y, and Z. The manager in Figure 5.6B has only one more subordinate than the manager in Figure 5.6A but must manage six relationships: X, Y, and Z, as well as U, V, and W. (The number of relationships is determined by the formula n (n minus 1)/2.) Thus a manager with eight subordinates, as in Figure 5.6B, has 28 relationships to manage. If managers lose control of their subordinates and the relationships among them, subordinates will have the opportunity to follow their own goals, to coast along on the performance of other group members, or to shirk their responsibilities.

Given these problems, there is a limit to how wide a manager's span of control should be.[22] If the span is too wide, the manager loses control over subordinates and cannot hold them accountable for their actions. In general, a manager's ability to directly supervise and control subordinates' behavior is limited by two factors: the complexity and the interrelatedness of subordinates' tasks.

When subordinates' tasks are complex and dissimilar, a manager's span of control needs to be small. If tasks are routine and similar so that all subordinates perform the same task, the span of control can be widened. In mass production settings, for example, it is common for a supervisor's span of control to extend over 30 or 40 people. But in the research laboratory of a biotechnology company, supervising employees is more difficult, and the span of control is much narrower. It is sometimes argued that the span of control of a CEO should not exceed six top executives because of the complexity of the tasks a CEO's subordinates perform.

When subordinates' tasks are closely interrelated, so that what one person does has a direct effect on what another person does, coordination and control are greater challenges for a manager. In Figure 5.6B, the interrelatedness of tasks means that the manager has to manage relationships V, W, and Z. When subordinates' tasks are not closely interrelated, the horizontal relationships between subordinates become relatively unimportant (in Figure 5.6B, relationships V, W, and Z would be eliminated) and the manager's span of control can be dramatically increased.

Managers supervising subordinates who perform highly complex, interrelated tasks have a much narrower span of control than managers supervising workers who perform separate, relatively routine tasks. Indeed, organizations are often pictured as a pyramid because at higher levels in the hierarchy tasks are more complex and interrelated, and so the span of control narrows.

Design choices concerning the number of hierarchical levels and the span of control are major determinants of the shape of the organizational hierarchy. There are limits to how much an organization can increase the number of levels in the hierarchy, the number of managers, or the span of control, however. Even though a hierarchy of authority emerges to provide an organization with control over its activities, if the structure becomes too tall or too top-heavy with managers, or if managers become overloaded because they are supervising too many employees, the organization can lose control of its activities. How can an organization maintain adequate control over its activities as it grows but avoid problems associated with a hierarchy that is too tall or a span of control that is too wide?

CONTROL: FACTORS AFFECTING THE SHAPE OF THE HIERARCHY

When there are limits on the usefulness of direct personal supervision by managers, organizations have to find other ways to control their activities. Typically, organizations first increase the level of horizontal differentiation and then decide on their responses to the other design challenges discussed in Chapter 4. Keep in mind that successful organizational design requires managers to meet all of those challenges (see Figure 5.7).

Horizontal Differentiation

Horizontal differentiation leads to the emergence of specialized subunits—functions or divisions. Figure 5.8 shows the horizontal differentiation of an organization into five functions. Each of the five smaller triangles represents a specific function in which people perform the same kind of task; together, they make up the pyramid that depicts the whole organization.

An organization that is divided into subunits has many different hierarchies, not just one. Each distinct function, department, or division has its own hierarchy. Horizontal differentiation is the principal way in which an organization retains control over employees when it cannot increase the number of levels in the organizational hierarchy without encountering the sorts of problems discussed earlier in the chapter.

Figure 5.7 Factors Affecting the Shape of the Hierarchy

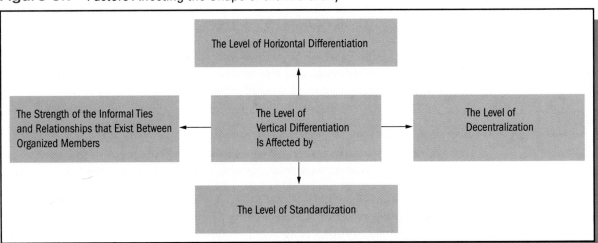

Figure 5.8
Horizontal Differentiation into Functional Hierarchies

The sales and R&D departments have three levels in their hierarchies, manufacturing has seven.

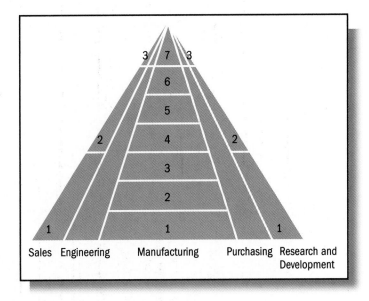

In Figure 5.8, the hierarchy of the manufacturing department has seven levels. The production manager, at level 7, reports to the CEO. In contrast, both the research and development and the sales functions have only three levels in their hierarchies. Why? Like the organization as a whole, each function follows the principle of minimum chain of command when designing its hierarchy. Each function chooses the lowest number of hierarchical levels it can operate with effectively and achieve its goals.[23] The manufacturing function traditionally has many levels because managers need to exert tight control over subordinates and reign in production costs. The sales department has fewer levels because standardization by means of written reporting requirements and output controls that measure the amount salespeople sell are used to monitor and control salespeople. Extensive personal supervision is not required. The R&D function also usually has few levels, but for a different reason. Personal supervision on a continuing basis is superfluous: R&D tasks are complex, and even if managers continually monitor researchers they cannot evaluate how well they are performing because years may pass before significant research projects come to fruition. In an R&D context, control is generally achieved by scientists working in small teams, where they can monitor and learn from each other. As a result, there can be yet another level of horizontal differentiation within an organization: that within a function or department.

Figure 5.9 shows the horizontal differentiation of the R&D function into project teams. Each team focuses on a specific task, but the teams' tasks are likely to be related. The use of teams is also a way to keep the span of control small, something necessary when tasks are complex and interrelated, as they are in R&D. Moreover, in an R&D setting informal norms and values develop to standardize behavior, and the "informal" organization becomes an important means of linking R&D to other functions.

Increasing horizontal differentiation thus increases vertical differentiation within an organization because many subunit hierarchies come into being. But horizontal differentiation avoids many of the problems of tall hierarchies because the development of many subunit hierarchies allows the organization to remain flat. Nevertheless, the problems associated with horizontal differentiation such as the development of divergent subunit orientations (see Chapter 4) can lead to additional coordination and motivation problems. Managers can control these problems by making wise choices concerning centralization, standardization, and the influence of the informal organization. (In Chapter 6 we discuss the coordination of activities between subunits.[24])

Figure 5.9
Horizontal Differentiation
Within the R&D Functions

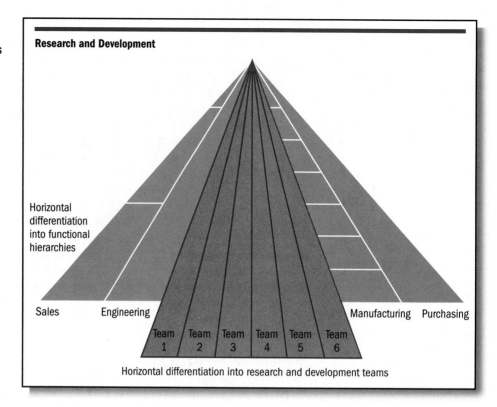

Research and Development

Horizontal differentiation into functional hierarchies

Sales   Engineering   Manufacturing   Purchasing

Team 1   Team 2   Team 3   Team 4   Team 5   Team 6

Horizontal differentiation into research and development teams

Centralization

As the hierarchy becomes taller and the number of managers increases, communication and coordination problems grow. Managers begin to spend more and more time monitoring and supervising their subordinates and less time planning and goal setting, and organizational effectiveness suffers. One solution this problem is to decentralize authority because now less direct managerial supervision is needed. When authority is decentralized, the authority to make significant decisions is delegated to people throughout the hierarchy, not concentrated at the top. The delegation of authority to lower-level managers reduces the monitoring burden on top managers and reduces the need for "managers to monitor managers."

One organization that took steps to decentralize authority and flatten its structure because it was experiencing a crisis was Union Pacific, one of the biggest U.S. railroad freight carriers. An economic boom was causing a record increase in the amount of freight that it needed to transport but, at the same time, Union Pacific was experiencing record delays in moving the freight. Its customers were irate and complained bitterly about late shipments, and the delays were also costing the company millions of dollars in penalty payments—$150 million![25]

Why the problem? Union Pacific, in its attempt to cut costs, had adopted a highly centralized management approach. All scheduling and route planning was handled centrally at its headquarters in the belief that this would promote operating efficiency. The job of regional managers became mainly to ensure the smooth flow of freight through their regions. Recognizing that efficiency had to be balanced by the need to be responsive to customers, its CEO Dick Davidson announced a sweeping reorganization to the company's customers. Henceforth, regional managers were to be given the authority to make operational decisions at the level at which it was most important—field operations. Regional managers could now alter scheduling and routing to accommodate customer requests even if this raised costs.[26] In making this decision, the company was following the lead of its competitors—most of whom had recognized that, far from increasing efficiency, centralization actually reduced it— who had already moved to decentralize their operations.

Almost all organizations confront similar problems sooner or later. For example, in the 1990s managers at Quaker Oats made many poor acquisitions, and competitors like Kraft and Heinz forged ahead with many innovative product ideas. Quaker Oats CEO, Robert Morrison, decided that the problem was that the organization's structure put authority in the wrong place—with top executives above the level of the heads of the different food divisions, rather than with the heads of the food divisions themselves. So he took action. First, he eliminated the entire upper level of management—even though it contained many competent executives. Then he promoted the next level of managers, the division heads, who now reported directly to him, and made them totally responsible for the food products under their control. In this way he flattened and decentralized control at the same time.

Coca-Cola Enterprises, the bottling arm of the soft-drink giant, faced a similar problem. Its CEO, Summerfield Johnston, noted his company's inability to respond quickly to the changing needs of the different regions in which Coke is bottled. Johnston decided that centralized control (regional operations were controlled from the Atlanta head office) was hurting the bottling operations. Because of the long chain of command, many problems that the regions were experiencing were being dealt with slowly, and managers at the head office were often unaware of the problems faced by people on the front line. Moreover, the hierarchy was very expensive to operate, and Johnston believed that bureaucratic costs could be reduced at the regional level if there was more local control over marketing and production.

Johnston redesigned the management hierarchy. He fired 100 middle and top managers at company headquarters, eliminating several levels in the hierarchy. He then decentralized operations to 10 regional units, one for each region, and put a strong vice president in charge of each unit. Each regional vice president was given the responsibility of streamlining regional operations and cutting costs.[27]

Decentralization does not eliminate the need for many hierarchical levels in a large and complex organization that has to control work activities among many subunits. However, it can assist even a relatively tall structure to be more flexible in its responses to changes in the external environment and reduce the amount of direct supervision needed *within* a subunit.

Standardization

Managers can also gain control over employees by standardizing their behavior and making their actions predictable. The use of standardization reduces the need for personal control by managers, and extra levels in the hierarchy, because rules and SOPs *substitute* for direct supervision; they reduce the need for face-to-face contact. Recall from Chapter 4 that managers standardize activities not only by creating detailed work rules but also by socializing employees into organizational norms and values. As subordinates' tasks become increasingly standardized and controlled by means of rules and norms, the amount of supervision required lessens, and a manager's span of control can be increased. Salespeople, for instance, are typically controlled by a combination of sales quotas that they are expected to achieve and written reports that they are required to submit after calling on their clients. Managers do not need to monitor salespeople directly because they can evaluate their performance through those two standardized output controls. Standardization also allows upper level managers to delegate responsibility more confidently when subordinates have clearly specified procedures to follow.

We have seen that an organization can control its members and their activities in different ways, ranging from personal control by managers in the hierarchy to control through formalization and standardization, to informal control by means of norms and values. Structuring an organization to solve control problems requires decisions about all the different methods of control. The structure of every organization reflects the particular contingencies it faces, so every organization has a structure that is somewhat different. Nevertheless, some generalizations can be made about how organizations fashion a structure to control people and resources effectively.

First, managers increase the level of vertical differentiation, paying particular attention to keeping the organization as flat as possible and to maintaining an appropriate balance between centralization and decentralization. Second, they increase horizontal differentiation and thereby also increase vertical differentiation. Third, they decide how much they can use rules, SOPs, and norms to control activities. The more they can use them, the less they will need to rely on direct supervision from the managerial hierarchy, and the need for managers and for additional levels in the hierarchy will be reduced.

Organizational design is difficult because all these decisions affect one another and must be made simultaneously. For example, managers very often start out by designing an organic structure (see Chapter 4) with a flat hierarchy and rely on norms and values rather than on rules to control organizational activities. Very quickly, however, as the organization grows, they are forced to add levels to the hierarchy and to develop rules and SOPs to maintain control. Before managers realize it, their organization has a mechanistic structure, and they face a new set of control problems. Organizational structure evolves and has to be managed constantly if an organization is to maintain its competitive advantage.

MANAGERIAL IMPLICATIONS

AUTHORITY AND CONTROL

1. Managers must control the organizational hierarchy and make sure that it matches the current needs of the organization. Periodically, managers should draw a new organizational chart of their organization or department and measure (a) the number of current employees, (b) the number of levels in the hierarchy, and (c) the size of the span of control of managers at different levels.

2. Using that information, managers should consider whether the hierarchy has grown too tall or too centralized. If they find that the hierarchy has grown too tall, they should combine managerial positions and eliminate levels by reassigning the responsibilities of the eliminated positions to managers in the level above or, preferably, by decentralizing the responsibilities to managers or employees in the levels below.

3. If managers find the hierarchy does not provide the control they need to maintain adequate supervision over people and resources, they should consider how to increase organizational control. They may need to add a level to the organizational hierarchy or, preferably, use an alternative means of control, such as increasing standardization or decentralization or making better use of the norms and values of the informal organization.

4. Managers should periodically meet in teams to consider how best to design and redesign the hierarchy so that it allows the organization to create the most value at the lowest operating cost.

THE PRINCIPLES OF BUREAUCRACY

Bureaucracy
A form of organizational structure in which people can be held accountable for their actions because they are required to act in accordance with rules and standard operating procedures.

Around 1900 Max Weber (1864–1920), a German sociologist, developed principles for designing a hierarchy so that it effectively allocates decision-making authority and control over resources.[28] Weber's interest was in identifying a system of organization or an organizational structure that could improve the way organizations operated—that is, increase the value they created and make them more effective.

A **bureaucracy** is a form of organizational structure in which people can be held accountable for their actions because they are required to act in accordance with well-specified and agreed-upon rules and standard operating procedures. Weber's bureaucratic organizing principles offer clear prescriptions for how to create and

Table 5.1 The Principles of Bureaucratic Structure

Principle One: A bureaucracy is founded on the concept of rational-legal authority.

Principle Two: Organizational roles are held on the basis of technical competence.

Principle Three: A role's task responsibility and decision-making authority and its relationship to other roles should be clearly specified.

Principle Four: The organization of roles in a bureaucracy is such that each lower office in the hierarchy is under the control and supervision of a higher office.

Principle Five: Rules, standard operating procedures, and norms should be used to control the behavior and the relationship between roles in an organization.

Principle Six: Administrative acts, decisions, and rules should be formulated and put in writing.

differentiate organizational structure so that task responsibility and decision-making authority are distributed in a way that maximizes organizational effectiveness. Because his work has been so influential in organizational design, it is useful to examine the six bureaucratic principles that, Weber argued, underlie effective organizational structure. Together these principles define what a bureaucracy or bureaucratic structure is (see Table 5.1).

Principle One: A bureaucracy is founded on the concept of rational-legal authority.

Rational-legal authority
The authority a person possesses because of his or her position in an organization.

Rational-legal authority is the authority a person possesses because of his or her position in an organization. In a bureaucracy, obedience is owed to a person not because of any personal qualities that he or she might possess (such as charisma, wealth, or social status) but because of the level of authority and responsibility that is associated with the organizational position the person occupies. Thus, we obey a police officer not because he or she wears an impressive uniform and carries a gun but because that person holds the position of police officer, which brings with it certain powers, rights, and responsibilities that compel obedience. In theory, a bureaucracy is impersonal. People's attitudes and beliefs play no part in determining the way a bureaucracy operates. If people base decisions and orders on their personal preferences instead of on organizational goals, effectiveness suffers.

Weber's first principle indicates that choices that affect the design of an organization's hierarchy should be based on the needs of the task, not on the needs of the person performing the task.[29] Thus, subordinates obey the CEO because of the authority and power vested in the position, not because of the individual currently filling it. For a bureaucracy to be effective, however, the distinction between positions and the people who hold them must be clear: People are appointed to positions; they do not own them.

Principle Two: Organizational roles are held on the basis of technical competence, not because of social status, kinship, or heredity.

In a well-designed hierarchy, roles are occupied by people who can do the job, not because of who they are or whom they know. Although this principle seems self-evident and the logical way to run an organization, it has often been ignored. Until 1850, for example, an officer's commission in the British Army could be bought by anybody who could afford the price. The higher the rank, the more the commission cost. As a result, most officers were rich aristocrats who had little or no formal army training, and many military disasters resulted from this system. Today, in many organizations and industries, "old-boy" networks—personal contacts and relations—and not job-related skills influence the decision about who gets a job. The use of such criteria to fill organizational roles can be harmful to an organization because talented people get overlooked.

Picking the best person for the job seems an obvious principle to follow. In practice, however, following this principle is a difficult process that requires managers to view all potential candidates objectively. It is important for people always to remember that holding a role in an organization in a legal sense means that their job is to use the organization's resources wisely for the benefit of all stakeholders, not just for personal gain.

Weber's first two principles establish the organizational role (and not the person in that role) as the basic component of bureaucratic structure. The next three principles specify how the process of differentiation should be controlled.

Principle Three: A role's task responsibility and decision-making authority and its relationship to other roles in the organization should be clearly specified.

According to Weber's third principle, a clear and consistent pattern of vertical differentiation (decision-making authority) and horizontal differentiation (task responsibility) is the foundation for organizational effectiveness. When the limits of authority and control are specified for the various roles in an organization, the people in those roles know how much power they have to influence the behavior of others. Similarly, when the tasks associated with various roles are clearly specified, people in those roles clearly know what is expected of them. Thus, with those two aspects of a person's role in an organization clearly defined, a stable system emerges in which each person has a clear expectation and understanding of the rights and responsibilities attached to other organizational roles. In such a stable system, all individuals know how much their supervisor can require of them and how much they can require of their subordinates. People also know how to deal with their peers—people who are at the same level in the organization as they are and over whom they have no authority, and vice versa.

Clear specification of roles avoids many problems that can arise when people interact. If, for example, some task responsibilities are assigned to more than one role, the people in those roles may have to fight over the same set of resources or claim responsibility for the same tasks. Is sales or marketing responsible for handling customer requests for information? Is the head of the army or the head of the air force responsible for invasive operations in enemy territory? The military is a vast bureaucracy in which the division of labor among the armed services is continually being negotiated to prevent such problems from emerging.

A clear pattern of vertical (authority) and horizontal (task) differentiation also cuts down on role conflict and role ambiguity.[30] **Role conflict** occurs when two or more people have different views of what another person should do and, as a result, make conflicting demands on the person. The person may be caught in the crossfire between two supervisors or the needs of two functional groups. **Role ambiguity** occurs when a person's tasks or authority are not clearly defined and the person becomes afraid to act on or take responsibility for anything. Clear descriptions of task and authority relationships solve conflict and ambiguity problems: When people know the dimensions of their position in the organization, they find it easier to take responsibility for their actions and to interact with one another.

Principle Four: The organization of roles in a bureaucracy is such that each lower office in the hierarchy is under the control and supervision of a higher office.

To control vertical authority relationships, the organization should be arranged hierarchically so that people can recognize the chain of command.[31] The organization should delegate to each person holding a role the authority needed to make certain decisions and to use certain organizational resources. The organization can then hold the person in the role accountable for the use of those resources. The hierarchical pattern of vertical differentiation also makes clear that a person at a low level in the hierarchy can go to someone at a higher level to solve conflicts at the low level. In the U.S. court system, for example, participants in a court case can ask a higher court to review the decision of a lower court if they feel a bad decision has been made. The right to appeal to a higher organizational level also needs to be specified in case a subordinate feels that his or her immediate superior has made a bad or unfair decision.

Principle Five: Rules, standard operating procedures, and norms should be used to control the behavior and the relationship among roles in an organization.

Rules and SOPs are formal, written instructions that specify a series of actions to be taken to achieve a given end; for example, if A happens, then do B. Norms are

Role conflict
The state of opposition that occurs when two or more people have different views of what another person should do and, as a result, make conflicting demands on the person.

Role ambiguity
The uncertainty that occurs for a person whose tasks or authority are not clearly defined.

unwritten standards or styles of behavior that govern how people act and lead people to behave in predictable ways. Rules, SOPs, and norms provide behavioral guidelines that can increase efficiency because they specify the best way to accomplish a task. Over time, these guidelines should change; as improved ways of doing things are discovered, the goal is constant progress to meeting organizational goals.

Rules, SOPs, and norms clarify people's expectations about one another and prevent misunderstandings over responsibility or the use of power. Such guidelines can prevent a supervisor from arbitrarily increasing a subordinate's workload and prevent a subordinate from ignoring tasks that are a legitimate part of the job. A simple set of rules established by the supervisor of some custodial workers (Crew G) at a Texas A&M University building clearly established task responsibilities and clarified expectations (see Table 5.2).

Rules and norms enhance the integration and coordination of organizational roles at different levels and between different functions. Vertical and horizontal differentiation break the organization up into distinct roles that must be coordinated and integrated to accomplish organizational goals.[32] Rules and norms are important aspects of integration. They specify how roles interact, and they provide procedures that people should follow to jointly perform a task.[33] For example, a rule could stipulate that "Sales must give production five days' notice of any changes in customer requirements." Or an informal norm could require underutilized waiters to help waiters who have fallen behind in serving their customers. It is important never to underestimate the power of rules, as the following organizational insight makes clear.

Alas, these moves came too late to save the chain; nothing kills a restaurant as much as a reputation for poor food quality. Customers tell their friends; the news spreads. The China Coast episode illustrates an important lesson in organizational design: Managers must have a structure planned, worked out, and tested before they embark on ambitious attempts at expansion. This is why today, before starting a chain of restaurants or any other kind of business, a prototype is created and tested at some typical location. All the bugs involved in operating the business are worked

Table 5.2 Crew G's Rules of Conduct

1. All employees must call their supervisor or leader before 5:55 A.M. to notify of absence or tardiness.
2. Disciplinary action will be issued to any employee who abuses sick leave policy.
3. Disciplinary action will be issued to any employee whose assigned area is not up to custodial standards.
4. If a door is locked when you go in to clean an office, it's your responsibility to lock it back up.
5. Name tags and uniforms must be worn daily.
6. Each employee is responsible for buffing hallways and offices. Hallways must be buffed weekly, offices periodically.
7. All equipment must be put in closets during 9:00 A.M. and 11 A.M. breaks.
8. Do not use the elevator to move trash or equipment from 8:50 to 9:05, 9:50 to 10:05, 11:50 to 12:05, or 1:50 to 2:05, to avoid breaks between classes.
9. Try to mop hallways when students are in classrooms, or mop floors as you go down to each office.
10. Closets must be kept clean, and all equipment must be clean and operative.
11. Each employee is expected to greet building occupants with "Good morning."
12. Always knock before entering offices and conference rooms.
13. Loud talking, profanity, and horseplay will not be tolerated inside buildings.
14. All custodial carts must be kept uniform and cleaned daily.
15. You must have excellent "public relations" with occupants at all times.

Your supervisor stands behind workers at all times when the employee is in the right and you are doing what you are supposed to. But when you are wrong, you are wrong. Let's try to work together to better Crew G, because there are many outstanding employees in this crew.

General Mills, the cereal maker best known for Cheerios cereal and Yoplait yogurt, created two of the best-known restaurant chains in the United States—Red Lobster and the Olive Garden. Inspired by this success, its managers decided that they could use the skills and experience they had gained from operating their growing restaurant chains to start a new chain specializing in Chinese food. Called *China Coast*, a prototype restaurant was opened in Orlando, Florida; customers were favorably impressed by the decor and by the food.

General Mills managers were excited by customers' positive response to the new restaurant and decided that they would rapidly expand the chain. Operating at break-neck speed, managers opened 38 restaurants in nine states. With the restaurant chain in full swing, however, problems began to arise. Customers were no longer so enthusiastic about the quality of the food or the customer service, and sales volume fell. What had gone wrong?

Apparently, in the attempt to open so many restaurants so quickly, managers lost control of quality. Chinese food is difficult to prepare properly, and employees require extensive training if they are to keep quality consistently high. Top managers had created a set of company-wide food-quality standards for restaurant managers to follow, but the restaurant managers failed to ensure that these output standards were met consistently. Moreover, there were customer complaints about the quality of service that had

not been reported to managers at the Orlando prototype. While searching for reasons for the failure of the new restaurants to meet company standards, top managers discovered that the primary problem was that they had not put the right set of bureaucratic rules in place.

Restaurant managers had not received enough restaurant operations training. Top managers had not created enough rules and SOPs for restaurant managers either to follow or to teach to their employees—the cooks who actually prepared the food and the waiters who served it. Top managers decided that in the future each restaurant manager would attend a four-month intensive training course during which he or she would be taught the rules to be followed when preparing and serving the food. The rules would be written down and formalized in an operations manual that managers would take back to their restaurants for reference when training employees.

To make sure that restaurant managers did indeed follow the rules to ensure high-quality food and customer service, General Mills managers created a new layer of managers—regional managers, whose responsibility was to supervise restaurant managers. Regional managers also were responsible for giving restaurant managers additional training as new dishes were introduced on the menu and for informing them of any changes in operating procedures that top managers had developed to improve the performance of individual restaurants.

out, and rules and SOPs are developed and codified in operations manuals before the concept is rolled out.

Principle Six: Administrative acts, decisions, and rules should be formulated and put in writing.

When rules and decisions are written down, they become official guides to the way the organization works. Thus, even when an employee leaves an organization, an indication of what that person did is part of the organization's written records. A bureaucratic structure provides an organization with memory, and it is the responsibility of its members to train their successors and ensure that there is continuity in the organizational hierarchy. Written records also ensure that organizational history cannot be altered and that people can be held accountable for their decisions.

The Advantages of Bureaucracy

Almost every organization possesses some features of bureaucracy.[34] The primary advantage of a bureaucracy is that it lays out the ground rules for designing an organizational hierarchy that efficiently controls interactions between organizational levels.[35] Bureaucracy's clear specification of vertical authority and horizontal task relationships means that there is no question about each person's role in the organization. Individuals can be held accountable for what they do, and such accountability reduces the transaction costs that arise when people must continually negotiate and define their organizational roles. Similarly, the specification of roles and the use of rules, SOPs, and norms to regulate how tasks are performed reduce the costs associated with monitoring the work of subordinates and increase integration within the organization. Finally, written rules regarding the reward and punishment of employees, such as rules for promotion and termination, reduce the costs of enforcement and evaluating employee performance.

Another advantage of bureaucracy is that it separates the position from the person. The fairness and equity of bureaucratic selection, evaluation, and reward systems encourage organizational members to advance the interests of all organizational stakeholders and meet organizational expectations.[36] Bureaucracy provides people with the opportunity to develop their skills and pass them on to their successors. In this way, a bureaucracy fosters differentiation, increases the organization's core competences, and improves its ability to compete in the marketplace against other organizations for scarce resources.[37] Bureaucracies provide the stability necessary for organizational members to take a long-term view of the organization and its relationship to its environment.

If a bureaucracy is based on such clear guidelines for allocating authority and control in an organization, why is "bureaucracy" considered a dirty word by some people, and why are terms like "bureaucrats" and "bureaucratic red tape" meant as insults? Why do bureaucratic structures generate such ill feeling?

One problem that emerges within a bureaucracy over time is that managers fail to properly control the development of the organizational hierarchy in the manner advocated by Weber. As a result, these organizations often become very tall, centralized, and inflexible. Decision making slows down, the organization begins to stagnate, and bureaucratic costs increase because managers start to make work for each other.

Another problem with bureaucracy is that organizational members come to rely too much on rules and SOPs to make decisions, and this over-reliance makes them unresponsive to the needs of customers and other stakeholders. Organizational members lose sight of the fact that their job is to create value for stakeholders. Instead, to protect their personal positions and interests, their chief goals become following rules and procedures and obeying authority.

Organizations that suffer from those problems are accused of being bureaucratic or of being run by bureaucrats. However, whenever we hear this claim, we must be careful to distinguish between the principles of bureaucracy and the people who manage bureaucratic organizations. Remember: There is nothing intrinsically bad or inefficient about a bureaucracy. When organizations become overly bureaucratic, the fault lies with the people who run them—with managers who prefer the pursuit of power and status to the pursuit of operating efficiency, who prefer to protect their careers rather than their organizations, and who prefer to use resources to benefit themselves rather than stakeholders. Indeed, one technique that can be used to mitigate these problems is management by objectives (MBO), although care has to be taken to ensure that an MBO system is based on Weber's principles.

Management by Objectives

Management by objectives
A system of evaluating subordinates on their ability to achieve specific organizational goals or performance standards and to meet operating budgets.

To provide a framework within which to evaluate subordinates' behavior and, in particular, to allow managers to monitor progress toward achieving goals, many organizations implement some version of management by objectives. **Management by objectives (MBO)** is a system of evaluating subordinates for their ability to achieve specific organizational goals or performance standards and to meet operating budgets. Most organizations make some use of management by objectives because it is pointless to establish goals and then fail to evaluate whether or not they are being achieved. Management by objectives involves three specific steps:

Step 1: *Specific goals and objectives are established at each level of the organization.*
Management by objective starts when top managers establish overall organizational objectives, such as specific financial performance targets.

Then objective setting cascades down throughout the organization as managers at the divisional and functional levels set their objectives to achieve corporate objectives. Finally, first-level managers and workers jointly set objectives that will contribute to achieving functional goals.

Step 2: *Managers and their subordinates together determine the subordinates' goals.*

An important characteristic of management by objectives is its participatory nature. Managers at every level sit down with the subordinate managers who report directly to them and together they determine appropriate and feasible goals for the subordinate and bargain over the budget that the subordinate will need so as to achieve these goals. The participation of subordinates in the objective-setting process is a way of strengthening their commitment to achieving their goals and meeting their budgets. Another important reason for subordinates (both individuals and teams) to participate in goal setting is so they can tell managers what they think they can realistically achieve.

Step 3: *Managers and their subordinates periodically review the subordinates' progress toward meeting goals.*

Once specific objectives have been agreed upon for managers at each level, managers are accountable for meeting those objectives. Periodically, they sit down with their subordinates to evaluate their progress. Normally, salary raises and promotions are linked to the goal-setting process, and managers who achieve their goals receive greater rewards than those who fall short. (The issue of how to design reward systems to motivate managers and other organizational employees is discussed in Chapter 10.)

In companies that have decentralized responsibility for the production of goods and services to teams, particularly cross-functional teams, management by objectives works somewhat differently. Managers ask each team to develop a set of goals and performance targets that the team hopes to achieve—goals that are consistent with organizational objectives. Managers then negotiate with each team to establish its final goals and the budget the team will need to achieve them. The reward system is linked to team performance, not to the performance of any one team member.

One company that has spent considerable time developing a formal MBO system is Zytec Corporation, a leading manufacturer of power supplies for computers and other electronic equipment. Each of Zytec's managers and workers participates in goal setting. Top managers first establish cross-functional teams to create a five-year plan for the company and to set broad goals for each function. This plan is then reviewed by employees from all areas of the company. They evaluate the plan's feasibility and make suggestions about how to modify or improve it. Each function then uses the broad goals in the plan to set more specific goals for each manager and each team in the organization; these goals are reviewed with top managers. The MBO system at Zytec is organization-wide and fully participatory, and performance is reviewed both from an annual and a five-year time horizon. Zytec's MBO system has been very effective. Not only have organizational costs dropped dramatically, but the company also won the Baldridge Award for quality.

MANAGERIAL IMPLICATIONS

USING BUREAUCRACY TO BENEFIT THE ORGANIZATION

1. If organizational hierarchies are to function effectively and the problems of overly bureaucratized organizations are to be avoided, both managers and employees must follow bureaucratic principles.
2. Both employees and managers should realize that they do not own their positions in an organization and that it is their responsibility to use their authority and control over resources to benefit stakeholders and not themselves.

3. Managers should strive to make human resource decisions such as hiring, promoting, or rewarding employees as fair and equitable as possible. Managers should not let personal ties or relationships influence their decisions, and employees should complain to managers when they feel that their decisions are inappropriate.

4. Periodically, the members of a work group or function should meet to ensure that reporting relationships are clear and unambiguous and that the rules members are using to make decisions meet current needs.

5. Both managers and employees should adopt a questioning attitude toward the way the organization works in order to uncover the taken-for-granted assumptions and beliefs on which it operates. For example, to make sure that they are not wasting organizational resources by performing unnecessary actions, they should always ask questions such as "Is that rule or SOP really necessary?" and "Who will read the report that I am writing?" An MBO system can also help managers evaluate the working of their hierarchy.

THE INFLUENCE OF THE INFORMAL ORGANIZATION

The hierarchy of authority designed by management that allocates people and resources to organizational tasks and roles is a blueprint for how things are supposed to happen. However, at all levels in the organization, decision making and coordination frequently take place outside the formally designed channels as people interact informally on the job. Moreover, many of the rules and norms that employees use to perform their tasks emerge out of informal interactions between people and not from the formal blueprint and rules established by managers. Thus, while establishing a formal structure of interrelated roles, managers are also creating an informal social structure that affects behavior in ways that may be unintended. The importance of understanding the way in which the network of personal relationships that develop over time in an organization, the informal organization, affects the way the formal hierarchy works is illustrated in the following organizational insight.[38]

By reintroducing the plant's formal hierarchy of authority, the new management team totally changed the informal organization that had been governing the way workers thought they should act. The changes destroyed the norms that had made the plant work smoothly (though not from top management's perspective). The result of changing the informal organization, however, was lower productivity because of the strikes.

This case shows that managers need to consider the effects of the informal organization on individual and group behavior when they make any organizational changes. Altering the formal structure often disrupts the informal norms that make the organization work. Because an organization is a network of informal social relations, as well as a hierarchy of formal task and authority relations, managers must harness the power of the informal organization to help achieve organizational goals.

People in organizations go to enormous lengths to increase their status and prestige and always want others to know about and recognize their status. Every organization has an established informal organization that does not appear on any formal chart but is familiar to all employees. Much of what gets done in an organization gets done through the informal organization, in ways not revealed by the organizational chart. Managers need to consider carefully the implications of the interactions between the formal and informal hierarchies when changing the ways they motivate and coordinate employees.

The informal organization can actually enhance organizational performance. New approaches to organization design argue that managers need to tap into the power of the informal organization to increase motivation and provide informal avenues for employees to use to improve organizational performance. The formal hierarchical structure is the main mechanism of control, but managers should use the informal structure along with the formal one to allow people to work out solutions to their problems.

Gypsum is a mineral that is extracted from the ground, then crushed, refined, and compacted into wallboard. A gypsum mine and processing plant owned by the General Gypsum Company[39] was located in a rural community, and farmers and laborers frequently supplemented their farm income by working in the plant. The situation in the mine was stable, the management team had been in place for many years, and workers knew exactly what they had to do. Coordination in the plant took place through long-established informal routines that were taken for granted by management and workers alike. Workers did a fair day's work for a fair day's pay. For its part, management was very liberal. It allowed workers to take the inexpensive wallboard for their own personal use and overlooked absences from work, which were especially common during the harvest season.

The situation changed when the corporate office sent a new plant manager to take over the plant's operations and improve its productivity. When the new man arrived, he was amazed by the situation. He could not understand how the previous manager had allowed workers to take wallboard, break work rules (such as those concerning absenteeism), and otherwise take advantage of the company. He decided that these practices had to stop, and he took steps to change the way the company was operated.

He began by reactivating the formal rules and procedures, which, though they had always existed, had never been enforced by the previous management team. He reinstituted rules concerning absenteeism and punished workers who were excessively absent. He stopped the informal practice of allowing employees to take wallboard even though it cost only pennies, and he took formal steps to reestablish management's authority in the plant. In short, he reestablished the formal organizational structure—one that worked through the rigid hierarchy of authority and strictly enforced rules that no longer indulged the employees.

The results were immediate. The workforce walked out and, in a series of wildcat strikes, refused to return until the old system was restored. It made no difference to the workers that the formal rules and procedures had always been on the books. They were used to the old, informal routines and they wanted them back. Eventually, after prolonged negotiation about new work practices, the union and company reached an agreement that defined the relative spheres of authority of management and the union, and established a bureaucratic system for managing future disputes. When the new work routines were in place, the wildcat strikes ended.

IT, EMPOWERMENT, AND SELF-MANAGED TEAMS

An important trend, which is accelerating as the result of advances in IT, is the increasing use of empowered workers, self-managed teams, cross-functional teams, and contingent or temporary workers. IT is making it much easier for managers to cost-effectively design a structure and control system that gives them much more and much better information about subordinates' activities, and allows managers to assess functional performance and intervene as necessary to better achieve organizational goals. IT, providing as it does a way of standardizing behavior through the use of a consistent, and often cross-functional, software platform, is an important means of controlling behavior. When all employees or functions use the same software platform to provide up-to-date information on their activities, this codifies and standardizes organizational knowledge and makes it easier to monitor progress toward goals. IT provides people at all levels in the hierarchy with more of the information and knowledge they need to perform their roles effectively. For example, employees are able to access information from other employees easily via cross-functional software systems that keep them all informed about changes in product design, engineering, manufacturing schedules, and marketing plans. In this way, IT overlays and supports the structure of tasks and roles that is normally regarded as the "real" organizational structure.

Thus, the increasing use of IT has led to a decentralization of authority in organizations and an increasing use of teams. As discussed earlier, decentralizing authority to lower-level employees and placing them in teams reduces the need for direct, personal supervision by managers, and organizations become flatter. **Empowerment** is the process of giving employees at all levels in an organization's hierarchy the authority to make important decisions and to be responsible for their outcomes.

Empowerment
The process of giving employees throughout an organization the authority to make important decisions and to be responsible for their outcomes.

Self-managed teams
Work groups consisting of people who are jointly responsible for ensuring that the team accomplishes its goals and who lead themselves.

Cross-functional teams
Formal work groups of employees from across an organization's different functions who are empowered to direct and coordinate the value creation activities necessary to complete different programs or projects.

Contingent workers
Workers who are employed for temporary periods by an organization and who receive no indirect benefits such as health insurance or pensions.

Self-managed teams are formal work groups consisting of people who are jointly responsible for ensuring that the team accomplishes its goals and who are empowered to lead themselves. **Cross-functional teams** are formal work groups of employees from across an organization's different functions that are empowered to direct and coordinate the value-creation activities necessary to complete different programs or projects.

The movement to flatten organizations by empowering workers in this way has increased steadily since the 1990s and has met with great success, according to many stories in the popular press. However, although some commentators have forecasted the "end of hierarchy" and the emergence of new organizational forms based purely on lateral relations both inside and between functions, other commentators are not so sure. They argue that even a flat, team-based organization composed of empowered workers must have a hierarchy and some minimum set of rules and SOPs if the organization is to have sufficient control over its activities. Organizations sacrifice the advantages of bureaucratic structure only at their peril.[40] The challenge for managers is to combine the best aspects of both systems—of bureaucratic structure and empowered work groups. Essentially, what this comes down to is that managers must be sure they have the right blend of mechanistic and organic structure to meet the contingencies they face. Managers should use bureaucratic principles to build a mechanistic structure, and they should enhance the organization's ability to act in an organic way by empowering employees and making teams a principal way of increasing the level of integration in an organization.

Finally, as organizations have flattened their structures, there has been an increasing trend for companies to employ contingent workers to lower operating costs. **Contingent workers** are those who are employed for temporary periods by an organization and who receive no indirect benefits such as health insurance or pensions. Contingent workers may work by the day, week, or month performing some functional task, or may contract with the organization for some fee to perform a specific service to the organization. Thus, for example, an organization may employ 10 temporary accountants to "do the books" when it is time or it may contract with a software programmer to write some specialized software for a fixed fee.

The advantages an organization obtains from contingent workers are that they cost less to employ because they receive no indirect benefits and they can be let go easily when their services are no longer needed. However, there are also some disadvantages associated with contingent workers. First, coordination and motivation problems may arise because temporary workers may have less incentive to perform at a high level, given that there is no prospect for promotion or job security. Second, organizations must develop core competences in their functions to gain a competitive advantage, and it is unlikely that contingent workers will help them develop such competences. Contingent workers do not remain with the organization very long and are not committed to it.

Nevertheless, it has been estimated that 20% of the U.S. workforce today consists of contingent workers, and this figure is expected to increase as managers work to find new ways to reduce bureaucratic costs. Indeed, one method that managers are already employing to keep their structures flat is the use of outsourcing and network structures, which are discussed in detail in the next chapter.

SUMMARY

Stakeholder goals and objectives can be achieved only when organizational skills and capabilities are controlled through organizational structure. The activities of organizational members would be chaotic without a structure that assigns people to roles and directs the activities of people and functions.[41] This chapter has examined how organizations should design their hierarchy of authority and choose control systems that create an effective organizational structure. The shape of the hierarchy determines how decision making takes place. It also determines how motivated people will be to pursue organizational goals. Designing the hierarchy should be one of management's major tasks, but, as we have seen, it is a task that many organizations do not do well or fail to consider at all. Chapter 5 has made the following main points:

1. The height of an organization's structure is a function of the number of levels in the hierarchy, the span of control at each level, and the balance between centralization and decentralization of authority.
2. As an organization grows, the increase in the size of the managerial component is less than proportional to the increase in the size of the organization.
3. Problems with tall hierarchies include communication, motivation, and bureaucratic costs.
4. According to the principle of minimum chain of command, an organization should choose the minimum number of hierarchical levels consistent with the contingencies it faces.
5. The span of control is the number of subordinates a manager directly manages. The two main factors that affect the span of control are task complexity and task interrelatedness.
6. The shape of the hierarchy and the way it works are also affected by choices concerning horizontal differentiation, centralization versus decentralization, differentiation versus integration, standardization versus mutual adjustment, and the influence of the informal organization.
7. The six principles of bureaucratic theory specify the most effective way to design the hierarchy of authority in an organization.
8. Bureaucracy has several advantages. It is fair and equitable, and it can promote organizational effectiveness by improving organizational design. However, problems can arise if bureaucratic principles are not followed and if managers allow the organization to become too tall and centralized.
9. Managers need to recognize how the informal organization affects the way the formal hierarchy of authority works and make sure the two fit to enhance organizational performance.
10. To keep their organizations as flat as possible, managers are increasingly making use of IT and creating self-managed work teams of empowered workers and/or turning to contingent workers.

DISCUSSION QUESTIONS

1. Choose a small organization in your city, such as a restaurant or school, and draw a chart showing its structure. Do you think the number of levels in its hierarchy and the span of control at each level are appropriate? Why or why not?
2. In what ways can the informal organization and the norms and values of its culture affect the shape of an organization?
3. What factors determine the appropriate authority and control structure in (a) a research and development laboratory, (b) a large department store, and (c) a small manufacturing company?
4. How can the principles of bureaucracy help managers to design the organizational hierarchy?
5. When does bureaucracy become a problem in an organization? What can managers do to prevent bureaucratic problems from arising?

ORGANIZATIONAL THEORY IN ACTION

Organizational Theory: How to Design a Hierarchy

Form groups of three to five people and discuss the following scenario:

You are the managers charged with reducing high operating costs. You have been instructed by the CEO to eliminate 25% of the company's managerial positions and then to reorganize the remaining positions so that the organization still exercises adequate supervision over its employees.

1. How would you go about analyzing the organizational hierarchy to decide which managerial positions should be cut first?
2. How will you be able to ensure adequate supervision with fewer managers?
3. What can you do to help make the downsizing process less painful for those who leave and for those who remain?

The Ethical Dimension #5

Suppose an organization is purging its top and middle managers. Some managers charged with deciding who to terminate might decide to keep the subordinates they like, and who are obedient to them, rather than the ones who are difficult or the best performers. They might decide to lay off the most highly paid subordinates even if they are high performers. Think of the ethics issues involved in designing a hierarchy and its effect on stakeholders.

1. What ethical rules should managers use when deciding who to terminate and when redesigning their hierarchy?
2. Some people argue that employees who have worked for an organization for many years have a claim on the organization at least as strong as its shareholders. What do you think of the ethics of this position: Can employees claim to "own" their jobs if they have contributed significantly to past success?

Making the Connection #5

Find an example of a company that recently changed its hierarchy of authority or its top management team. What changes did it make? Why did it make them? What does it hope to accomplish as a result of them? What happened as a result of the changes?

Analyzing the Organization: Design Module #5

This module focuses on vertical differentiation and understanding the managerial hierarchy in your organization and the way the organization allocates decision-making authority.

Assignment

1. How many people does the organization employ?
2. How many levels are there in the organization's hierarchy?
3. Is the organization tall or flat? Does the organization experience any of the problems associated with tall hierarchies? Which ones?
4. What is the span of control of the CEO? Is this span appropriate, or is it too wide or too narrow?
5. How do centralization, standardization, and horizontal differentiation affect the shape of the organization?
6. Do you think your organization does a good or a poor job in managing its hierarchy of authority? Give reasons for your answer.

CASE FOR ANALYSIS

Sony's Magic Touch

Product engineers at Sony turn out an average of four ideas for new products every day. Despite the fact that Sony is a huge, diversified organization employing over 100,000 employees worldwide, the company continues to lead the way in innovation in the consumer electronics industry. Why? A large part of the answer lies in the way the company uses its structure to motivate and coordinate employees. First, a policy of "self-promotion" allows Sony engineers, without notifying their supervisors, to seek out projects anywhere in the company where they feel they can make a contribution. If they find a new project to which they can make a contribution, their current boss is expected to let them join the new team. Sony has over 20 business groups composed of hundreds of development teams, and this movement of people cross-pollinates ideas throughout the organization.

Sony deliberately emphasizes the lateral movement of people and ideas between design and engineering groups. The "Sony Way" emphasizes communication between groups to foster innovation and change. Sony has a corporate research department full of people in integrating roles who coordinate the efforts of the business groups and product development teams. It is their responsibility to make sure that each team knows what the others are doing, not only to share knowledge but also to avoid overlap or duplication of effort. Once a year, the corporate research department organizes an in-house three-day "special event," open only to Sony employees, where each product development team can display its work to its peers. Moreover, Sony rewards its engineers with promotion and more control of resources if they are successful.

Sony is hard-headed, however, when it comes to making the best use of its resources. Top management takes pains to distance itself from decision making inside a team or even a business group, so that the magic of decentralized decision making can work. But it does intervene when it sees different groups duplicating one another's efforts. For example, when Sony made a big push into computers it reorganized the relationships among its audio, video, and computer groups so that they improved the way they coordinated new product developments. Once again, however, Sony takes a lateral view of the way the organization works, and its vertical chain of command is oriented toward finding ways to decentralize authority and still make the best use of resources.

DISCUSSION QUESTIONS

1. How does Sony design its structure to help increase the speed of product innovation?
2. How could Sony make use of new kinds of information technologies to help its hierarchy of authority work better?

REFERENCES

1. J. R. Galbraith, *Designing Complex Organizations* (Reading, MA: Addison-Wesley, 1973).
2. P. R. Lawrence and J. W. Lorsch, *Organization and Environment* (Boston: Graduate School of Business Administration, Harvard University, 1967).
3. G. R. Jones, "Task Visibility, Free Riding, and Shirking: Explaining the Effect of Organization Structure on Employee Behavior," *Academy of Management Review, 4* (1984), 684–695.
4. P. M. Blau, "A Formal Theory of Differentiation in Organizations," *American Sociological Review*, 35 (1970), 201–218.
5. J. Child, *Organization: A Guide for Managers and Administrators* (New York: Harper and Row, 1977), pp. 10–15; P. Blau, "A Formal Theory of Differentiation."
6. P. Blau, "A Formal Theory of Differentiation"; W. R. Scott, *Organizations: Rational, Natural, and Open Systems* (Upper Saddle River, NJ: Prentice Hall, 1981), pp. 235–240.
7. D. D. Baker and J. C. Cullen, "Administrative Reorganization and the Configurational Context: The Contingent Effects of Age, Size, and Changes in Size," *Academy of Management Journal, 36* (1993), 1251–1277.
8. P. M. Blau and R. A. Schoenherr, *The Structure of Organizations* (New York: Basic Books, 1971).
9. R. Carzo and J. N. Zanousas, "Effects of Flat and Tall Structure," *Administrative Science Quarterly, 14* (1969), 178–191; A. Gupta and V. Govindarajan, "Business Unit Strategy, Managerial Characteristics, and Business Unit Effectiveness at Strategy Implementation," *Academy of Management Journal, 27* (1984), 25–41.
10. W. H. Wagel, "Keeping the Organization Lean at Federal Express," *Personnel, 4* (1984), 4.
11. D. Katz and R. L. Kahn, *The Social Psychology of Organizing* (New York: Wiley, 1966), p. 255.
12. A. M. Pettigrew, *The Politics of Organizational Decision Making* (London: Tavistock, 1973).
13. www.dupont.com, 2006.
14. "DuPont R&D to Boost Polyester Recycling Efforts," *Machine Design*, March 7, 1996, p. 60.
15. C. N. Parkinson, *Parkinson's Law* (New York: Ballantine Books, 1964).
16. Ibid., p. 17.
17. See, for example, "Preparing the Company Organization Manual," *Studies in Personnel Policy*, no. 157 (New York: National Industrial Conference Board, 1957), p. 28.
18. www.emi.com, 2006.
19. C. Goldsmith and J. Ordonez, "Levy Jolts EMI: Can He Reform the Music Industry?" *The Wall Street Journal*, September 6, 2002, pp. B1, B4.
20. V. A. Graicunas, "Relationships in Organizations," in L. Gulick and L. Urwick, eds., *Papers in the Science of Administration* (New York: Institute of Public Administration, 1937), pp. 181–185.
21. Ibid.
22. D. D. Van Fleet, "Span of Management Research and Issues," *Academy of Management Journal, 4* (1983), 546–552.
23. J. W. Lorsch and J. J. Morse, *Organizations and Their Members: A Contingency Approach* (New York: Harper and Row, 1974).
24. Lawrence and Lorsch, *Organization and Environment*.
25. C. Wian, "Union Pacific to Reorganize," cnnfn.com, August 20, 1998, p.20.
26. www.unionpacific.com, press release, 1998.
27. W. Konrad, "The Bottleneck at Coca-Cola Enterprises," *Business Week*, September 14, 1992, pp. 28–30.
28. M. Weber, *From Max Weber: Essays in Sociology*, in H. H. Gerth and C. W. Mills, eds. (New York: Oxford University Press, 1946); M. Weber, *Economy and Society*, in G. Roth and C. Wittich, eds. (Berkeley: University of California Press, 1978).
29. C. Perrow, *Complex Organizations*, 2e (Glenview, IL: Scott, Foresman, 1979).
30. R. L. Kahn, D. M. Wolfe, R. P. Quinn, J. D. Snoek, and R. A. Rosenthal, *Organizational Stress: Studies in Role Conflict and Ambiguity* (New York: Wiley, 1964).
31. Weber, *From Max Weber*, p. 331.
32. Lawrence and Lorsch, *Organization and Environment*; J. R. Galbraith, *Organization Design* (Reading, MA: Addison-Wesley, 1977).
33. Lawrence and Lorsch, *Organization and Environment*.
34. Perrow, *Complex Organizations*.
35. G. R. Jones and C.W.L. Hill, "Transaction Cost Analysis of Strategy-Structure Choice," *Strategic Management Journal, 9* (1989), 159–172.
36. See Perrow, *Complex Organizations*, Chapter 1, for a detailed discussion of these issues.
37. P. S. Adler and B. Borys, "Two Types of Bureaucracy," *Administrative Science Quarterly, 41* (1996), 61–89.
38. A. W. Gouldner, *Wildcat Strike: A Study of Worker—Management Relationships* (New York: Harper and Row, 1954).
39. This is a pseudonym used by Gouldner, ibid.
40. L. Donaldson, *Redeeming the Organization* (New York: The Free Press, 1996).
41. Child, *Organization: A Guide for Managers and Administrators*, pp. 50–72.

Designing Organizational Structure: Specialization and Coordination

Learning Objectives

In this chapter the second principal issue in organizational design is addressed: how to group and coordinate tasks to create a division of labor that gives an organization a competitive advantage. The design challenge is to create the optimal pattern of vertical and horizontal relationships among roles, functions, teams, and divisions that will enable an organization to best coordinate and motivate people and other resources to achieve its goals.

After studying this chapter you should be able to:

1. Explain why most organizations initially have a functional structure and why, over time, problems arise that require a change to a more complex structure.

2. Distinguish between three kinds of divisional structures (product, geographic, and market), describe how a divisional structure works, and explain why many organizations use this structure to coordinate organizational activities and increase their effectiveness.

3. Discuss how the matrix and product-team structures differ, and why and when they are chosen to coordinate organizational activities.

4. Identify the unique properties of network structures and the conditions under which they are most likely to be selected as the design of choice.

FUNCTIONAL STRUCTURE

In Chapter 4 we noted that the tasks involved in running the B.A.R. and Grille became more numerous and more complex as the number of customers increased and the organization needed to serve more meals. At first, the owners, Bob and

Amanda Richards, performed multiple roles, but as the business grew, they became overloaded and were forced to develop specialized roles and institute a division of labor. As Chapter 4 discusses, the assignment of one person to a role is the start of specialization and horizontal differentiation. As this process continues, the result is a **functional structure**, a design that groups people on the basis of their common skills and expertise or because they use the same resources. At the B.A.R. and Grille, waiters and busboys were grouped into the dining-room function, and chefs and kitchen staff were grouped into the kitchen function (see Figure 4.1). Similarly, research scientists at companies like Amazon.com and Johnson & Johnson are grouped in specialized laboratories because they use the same skills and resources, and accountants are grouped in an accounting function.

Functional structure is the bedrock of horizontal differentiation. An organization groups tasks into functions to increase the effectiveness with which it achieves its principal goal: providing customers with high-quality products at competitive prices.[1] As functions specialize, skills and abilities improve, and the core competences that give an organization a competitive advantage emerge. Different functions emerge as an organization responds to increasingly complex task requirements. The owner of a very small business, for example, might hire outside specialists to handle accounting and marketing. As an organization grows in size and complexity, however, it normally develops those functions internally because handling accounting and marketing itself becomes more efficient than hiring outside contractors. This is how organizations become more complex as they grow: They develop not only more functions, but also more specialization within each function. (They also become vertically differentiated and develop a hierarchy of authority, as we saw in Chapter 5.) Amazon.com provides a good example of horizontal differentiation leading to the development of a functional structure.

Advantages of a Functional Structure

Functional structure develops first and foremost because it provides people with the opportunity to learn from one another and become more specialized and productive. When people with skills in common are assembled into a functional group, they can

FOCUS ON NEW INFORMATION TECHNOLOGY
Amazon.com, Part 4

As we saw in Chapter 1, Jeff Bezos, the founder of Amazon.com, achieved phenomenal success with his concept for an online bookstore. In large part, his success has been due to the functional structure that he created for his company, which has allowed Amazon.com's proprietary Internet software to be used so effectively to link employees to customers (see Figure 6.1).

First, Bezos created Amazon.com's R&D department to continue to develop and improve the in-house software that he had initially developed for Internet-based retailing. Then, he established the information systems department to handle the day-to-day implementation of these systems and to manage the interface between the customer and the organization. Third, he created the materials management/logistics department to devise the most cost-efficient ways to obtain books from book publishers and distributors and to ship them quickly to customers. For example, the department developed new IT to ensure one-day shipping to customers. Next, as Amazon.com grew, he created a separate financial department and a strategic planning department to help chart the company's future. As we will see in later chapters, these departments have helped Amazon to expand into providing many other kinds of products, such as music CDs, electronics, and gifts.

By focusing on the best way to divide the total task facing the organization (the creation of valuable products for customers) into functions, and recruiting experienced functional managers from other organizations like Wal-Mart to run them, Bezos created core competences that allowed his online bookstore to compete effectively with bricks-and-mortar bookstores. Many bookstores have disappeared because their small size did not allow them to differentiate and provide customers with the sheer range of books and convenient service that Amazon.com can. Amazon.com is able to do this because of the way it has developed a structure to effectively manage its new information technology.

(continued)

Figure 6.1
Functional Structure

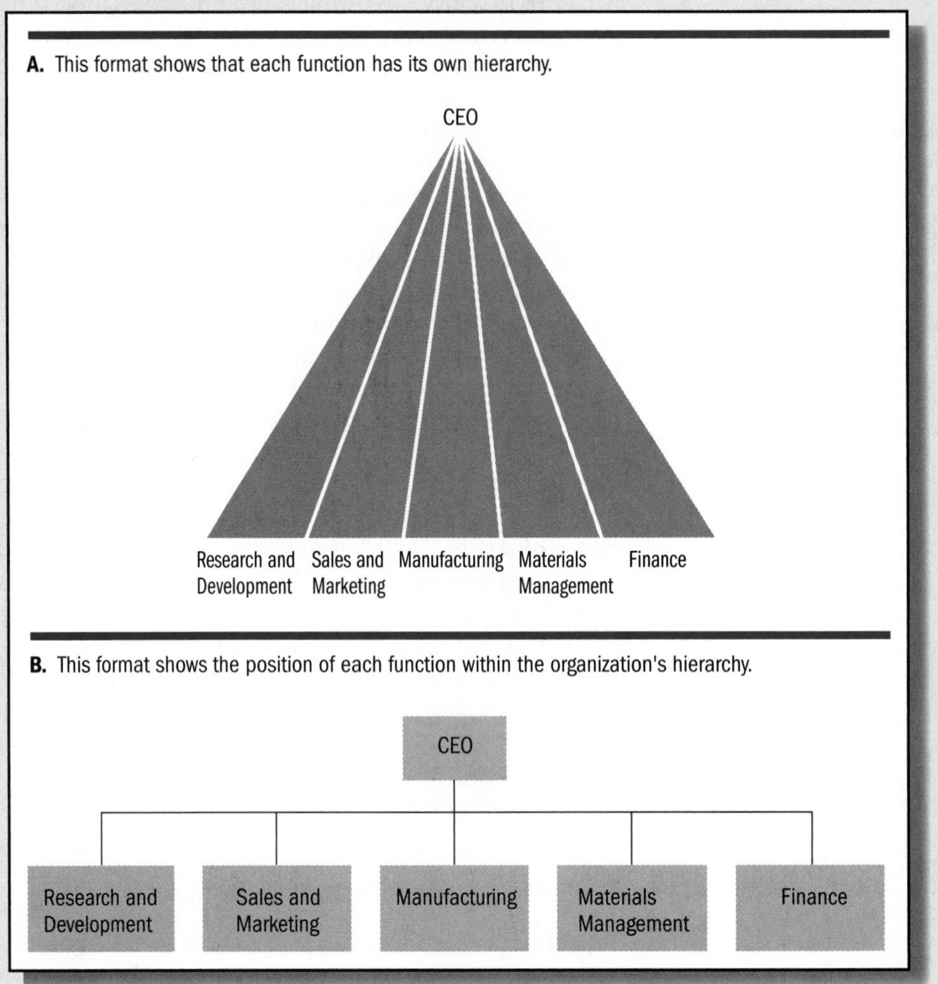

A. This format shows that each function has its own hierarchy.

CEO

Research and Development   Sales and Marketing   Manufacturing   Materials Management   Finance

B. This format shows the position of each function within the organization's hierarchy.

CEO

Research and Development   Sales and Marketing   Manufacturing   Materials Management   Finance

learn the most efficient techniques for performing a task, or the best way to solve problems, from one another. The most skilled employees are given the responsibility to train new recruits, and they are the people who are promoted to become supervisors and managers. In this way an organization can increase its store of skills and abilities. For example, Microsoft has revenues of more than $10 billion per year, but only 40,000 employees. Microsoft's value-creation ability is embedded in the skills of its employees and in the way the organization groups and organizes them to promote and develop their skills.

Another advantage of the functional structure is that people who are grouped together by common skills can supervise one another and control each other's behavior. We discussed in Chapter 5 how a hierarchy develops within each function to help the organization control its activities (see Figure 5.8). In addition to functional managers, peers in the same function can monitor and supervise one another and keep work activities on track. Peer supervision is especially important when work is complex and relies on cooperation; in such situations, supervision from above is very difficult.

Finally, people in a function who work closely with each other over extended time periods develop norms and values that allow them to become more effective at what they do. They become team members who are committed to organizational activities. This commitment may develop into a core competence for an organization.

Control Problems in a Functional Structure

All organizations initially are organized by function because the development of separate functions allows organizations to manage an increase in specialization and the division of labor most efficiently. As in Amazon.com, functional structure breeds core competences and increases an organization's ability to control its people and resources. However, as an organization continues to grow and differentiate, functional structure creates new problems. Often the problems arise from the organization's success: As an organization's skills and abilities increase and the organization is able to produce a better or wider variety of goods or services, its ability to service the needs of its growing product line becomes strained. For example, it becomes increasingly difficult for sales and marketing to provide the in-depth attention that the launch of new products requires, so new products tend not to do well. Similarly, as more customers perceive value in the products an organization creates, customer demand goes up. Increasing demand may strain the ability of manufacturing to produce products fast enough or of a uniformly high quality. Moreover, costs may start to rise as manufacturing is forced to increase production. In turn, the pressure of staying ahead of the competition puts more pressure on R&D or engineering to improve product quality and increase the range or sophistication of products, such as Apple's quest to offer a continuous flow of new kinds of iPods.

The problem facing a successful organization is how to keep control of increasingly complex activities as it grows and differentiates. As it produces more and more products, becomes geographically diverse, or faces increasing competition for customers, control problems impede managers' ability to coordinate organizational activities.[2]

Communication Problems

As more organizational functions develop, each with its own hierarchy, they become increasingly distant from one another. They develop different subunit orientations that cause communication problems.[3] For example, sales thinks the organization's main problem is the need to satisfy customer demands quickly to increase revenues; manufacturing thinks the main problem is to simplify products to reduce costs; and R&D thinks the biggest problem is to increase a product's technical sophistication. As a result of such differences in perception, communication problems develop that reduce the level of coordination and mutual adjustment among functions and make it more difficult for the organization to respond to customer and market demands. Thus differentiation produces communication problems that companies try to solve, in part, by using more complex integrating mechanisms.

Measurement Problems

To exercise control over a task or activity, there has to be a way to measure it; otherwise, there is no benchmark to use to evaluate how task performance changes over time. However, as organizations grow and the number and complexity of their functions and products increases, the information needed to measure the contribution of any one function or product to overall profitability is often difficult to obtain because the cost of *each* function's contribution to the development of *each* product becomes increasingly difficult to measure. For example, one or more products might actually be losing the company money, but managers are unaware of this because they cannot allocate functional costs to each individual product. Thus, the organization is not making the most effective use of its resources.

Location Problems

As a company grows, it may need to set up shop and establish manufacturing or sales facilities in different geographical regions to better serve customers. Geographical spread can pose a control problem within a functional structure when centralized control from one geographical location prevents this from happening: Manufacturing, sales, and other support activities are not allowed to become responsive to the needs of each region. An organization with more than one location must develop a control and information system that can balance the need to centralize decision-making authority with the need to decentralize authority to regional operations. In fact, as Amazon.com expanded it established five main U.S. distribution centers, located in Delaware, Nevada, Georgia, Kansas, and Kentucky.

Customer Problems

As the range and quality of an organization's products increase, more and more customers are attracted to the organization, and these customers have different kinds of needs. Servicing the needs of new kinds of customer groups and tailoring products to suit them are relatively difficult in a functional structure. Functions like production, marketing, and sales have little opportunity to specialize in the needs of a particular customer group; instead, they are responsible for servicing the complete product range. Thus, in an organization with a functional structure, the ability to identify and satisfy customer needs may fall short and sales opportunities may be lost.

Strategic Problems

As an organization becomes more complex, top managers may be forced to spend so much time finding solutions to everyday coordination problems that they have no time to address the longer-term strategic problems facing the company. For example, they are likely to be so involved in solving communication and integration problems between functions that they have no time to plan for future product development. As a result, the organization loses direction.

Solving Control Problems in a Functional Structure

Sometimes managers can solve the control problems associated with a functional structure, such as poor communication between functions, by redesigning the functional structure to increase integration between functions (see Figure 6.2). For example, one ongoing organizational challenge is how to manage the relationship between sales and marketing. Figure 6.2A shows the traditional relationship between them: Each is a separate function with its own hierarchy. Many organizations have recognized the need to alter this design and have combined those activities into one function. Figure 6.2B shows that modification. Such changes to the functional structure increase control by increasing integration between functions.

Figure 6.2 Improving Integration in a Functional Structure by Combining Sales and Marketing

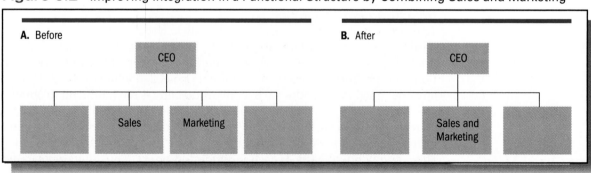

1. For an entrepreneur starting a small business, or for a manager of a work group or department, creating the correct division of labor within a function and between functions is a vital design task.
2. To ensure that the division of labor is correct, list the various functions that currently exist in your organization, and itemize the tasks they perform.
3. Draw a diagram of task relationships both within and between functions, and evaluate to what degree your organization is obtaining the advantages of the functional structure (such as the development of new or improved skills) or experiencing the disadvantages of the functional structure (such as lack of integration between functions).
4. Experiment with different ways of altering the design of the functional structure to increase effectiveness—for example, by transferring task responsibilities from one function to another or by eliminating unnecessary roles.

FROM FUNCTIONAL STRUCTURE TO DIVISIONAL STRUCTURE

If an organization (1) limits itself to producing a small number of similar products, (2) produces those products in one or a few locations, and (3) sells them to only one major type of customer, managers will be able to solve many of the control problems associated with a functional structure. As organizations grow over time, however, they begin to produce more and more products that are often very different from one another. For example, GE produces hundreds of different models of refrigerators, ranges, and washing machines; its NBC television studio produces hundreds of different kinds of television shows; and its financial services unit is involved in many different kinds of lending activities, from providing loans to providing insurance. Moreover, when an organization increases its production of goods and services, it usually does so at an increasing number of locations and for many different types of customers.

When organizations grow in these ways, what is needed is a structure that will simultaneously (1) increase managers' control of its different individual subunits so that subunits can better meet product and customer needs, and (2) allow managers to control and integrate the operation of the whole company to ensure all its subunits are meeting organizational goals. Managers regain control of their organizations when they decide to adopt a more complex structure, which is the result of three design choices:

1. *An increase in vertical differentiation.* To regain control, managers need to increase vertical differentiation. This typically involves (a) increasing the number of levels in the hierarchy; (b) deciding how much decision-making authority to centralize at the top of the organization; and (c) deciding how much to use rules, SOPs, and norms to standardize the behavior of low-level employees.

2. *An increase in horizontal differentiation.* To regain control, managers need to increase horizontal differentiation. This involves overlaying a functional grouping of activities with some other kind of subunit grouping—most often, self-contained product teams or product divisions that contain the functional resources needed to meet their goals.

3. *An increase in integration.* To regain control, managers need to increase integration between subunits. The higher the level of differentiation, the more complex the integrating mechanisms that managers need to use to control organizational activities. Recall from Chapter 4 that complex integrating mechanisms include task forces,

teams, and integrating roles. Organizations need to increase integration between subunits to increase their ability to coordinate activities and motivate employees.

The way those three design choices increase differentiation and integration is shown in Figure 6.3. The organization illustrated in Figure 6.3A has two levels in its hierarchy and three subunits, and the only integrating mechanism that it uses is the hierarchy of authority. Figure 6.3B shows the effects of growth and differentiation. To manage its more complex activities, the organization has developed three levels in its hierarchy and has eight subunits. Because of the increase in differentiation, it needed a greater degree of integration and thus created a series of task forces to control activities among subunits.

All of the more complex organizational structures discussed in the remainder of this chapter come into being as a result of managers' design decisions about vertical differentiation, horizontal differentiation, and integration. The move to a complex structure normally involves changes in all three characteristics.

Moving to a Divisional Structure

Divisional structure
A structure in which functions are grouped together according to the specific demands of products, markets, or customers.

The structure that organizations most commonly adopt to solve the control problems that result from producing many different kinds of products in many different locations for many different types of customers is the divisional structure. A **divisional structure** groups functions according to the specific demands of *products*, *markets*, or *customers*. The purpose behind the change to a divisional structure is to create smaller, more manageable subunits within an organization. The type of divisional structure managers select depends on the specific control problems (discussed earlier) that need to be solved.

Figure 6.3
Differentiation and Integration: How Organizations Increase Control over Their Activities

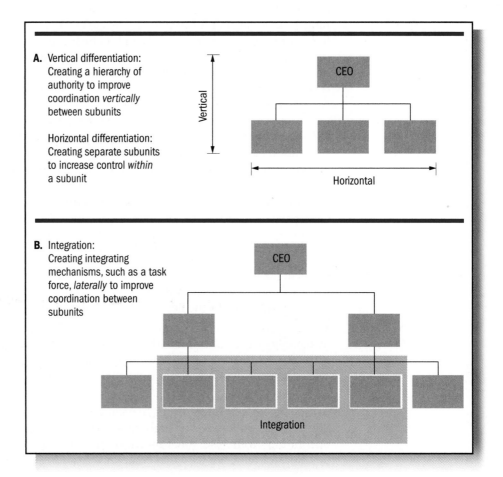

A. Vertical differentiation: Creating a hierarchy of authority to improve coordination *vertically* between subunits

Horizontal differentiation: Creating separate subunits to increase control *within* a subunit

B. Integration: Creating integrating mechanisms, such as a task force, *laterally* to improve coordination between subunits

If the control problem is due to the number and complexity of products, the organization will divide its activities by product and use a *product structure*. If the control problem is due to the number of locations in which the organization produces and sells its products, the organization will divide its activities by region and use a *geographic structure*. If the control problem is due to the need to service a large number of different customer groups, the organization will divide its activities by customer group and use a *market structure*.

In the following sections, we discuss these types of divisional structure, which are designed to solve specific control problems. Each type of divisional structure has greater vertical and horizontal differentiation than a functional structure and employs more complex integrating mechanisms.

DIVISIONAL STRUCTURE I: THREE KINDS OF PRODUCT STRUCTURE

Product structure
A divisional structure in which products (goods or services) are grouped into separate divisions, according to their similarities or differences.

As an organization increases the kinds of goods it manufactures or the services it provides, a functional structure becomes less effective at coordinating task activities. Imagine the coordination problems a furniture maker like Drexel Heritage would experience if it were to produce 100 styles of sofas, 150 styles of tables, and 200 styles of chairs in the same manufacturing unit. Adequately controlling value-creation activities would be impossible. To maintain effectiveness and simplify control problems as the range of its products increases, an organization groups its activities not only by function but also by type of product. To simplify control problems, a furniture maker might create three product groups or divisions: one for sofas, one for tables, and one for chairs. A **product structure** is a divisional structure in which products (goods or services) are grouped into separate divisions, according to their similarities or differences, to increase control.

An organization that decides to group activities by product must also decide how to coordinate its product divisions with support functions like R&D, marketing and sales, and accounting. In general, there are two choices that an organization can make: (1) centralize the support functions at the top of the organization so that one set of support functions services all the different product divisions; or (2) create multiple sets of support functions, one for each product division. In general, the decision that an organization makes reflects the degree of complexity of and difference between its products. An organization whose products are broadly similar and aimed at the same market will choose to centralize support services and use a *product division* structure. An organization whose products are very different and that operates in several different markets or industries will choose a *multidivisional structure*. An organization whose products are very complex technologically or whose characteristics change rapidly to suit changing customer needs will choose a *product team structure*.

Product Division Structure

Product division structure
A divisional structure in which a centralized set of support functions services the needs of a number of different product lines.

A **product division structure** is characterized by the splitting of the manufacturing function into several different product lines or divisions; a centralized set of support functions then services the needs of *all* these product divisions. A product division structure is commonly used by food processors, furniture makers, and companies that make personal care products, paper products, or other products that are broadly similar and use the same set of support functions. Figure 6.4 shows a product division structure for a large food processor such as Heinz.

Because controlling the production of many different foods within the same manufacturing unit proved to be difficult and resulted in increasing costs, Heinz created separate product divisions that make frozen vegetables, frozen entrees, canned soups, and baked goods. This design decision increased horizontal differentiation

Figure 6.4
Product Division Structure

Each product division manager (PDM) has responsibility for coordinating with each support function.

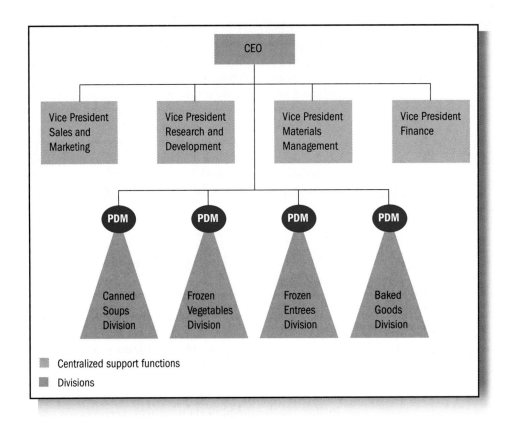

within the organization, for each division is a separate manufacturing unit that has its own hierarchy headed by a product division manager. Each product division manager (PDM, in Figure 6.4) is responsible for his or her division's product (manufacturing or service) activities. The product division manager is also responsible for coordinating with the central support functions like marketing and materials management and for making effective use of their skills to enhance product development. The role of product division manager adds a level to the hierarchy or authority and so also increases vertical differentiation in an organization.

Figure 6.4 shows that in a product division structure, support functions such as sales and marketing, R&D, materials management, and finance are centralized at the top of the organization. Each product division uses the services of the central support functions and does not have its own support functions. Creating separate support functions for each product division would be expensive and the cost could be justified only if the needs of the different divisions were so *diverse* and *dissimilar* that different functional specialists were required for each type of product.

Each support function is divided into product-oriented teams of functional specialists who focus on the needs of one particular product division. Figure 6.5 shows the grouping of the R&D function into four teams, each of which focuses on a separate product division. This arrangement allows each team to specialize and become expert in managing the needs of "its" product group. However, because all of the R&D teams belong to the same centralized function, they can share knowledge and information. The R&D team that focuses on frozen vegetables can share discoveries about new methods for quick-freezing vegetables with the R&D team for frozen entrees. Such sharing of skills and resources increases a function's ability to create value across product divisions.

Multidivisional Structure

As an organization begins to produce a wide range of complex products, such as many car or truck models, or to enter new industries and produce completely different products, such as cars and fast food, the product division structure cannot

Figure 6.5
The Assignment of
Product-Oriented
Functional Teams to
Individual Divisions

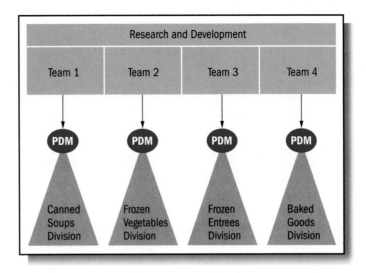

Multidivisional structure

A structure in which support functions are placed in self-contained divisions.

provide the control the organization needs. Managing complex and diverse value-creation activities requires a **multidivisional structure**, a structure in which each product division is given its own set of support functions so they become *self-contained* divisions. Figure 6.6 depicts the multidivisional structure used by a large consumer products company. Four divisions are illustrated, although a company such as GE, IBM, Johnson & Johnson, or Matsushita might have 150 different operating divisions.

Compare the multidivisional structure shown in Figure 6.6 with the product division structure shown in Figure 6.4. A multidivisional structure has two innovations that overcome the control problems a company experiences with the product division structure when managers decide to produce a wider and wider range of different products in different industries.[4] The first innovation is the independence of each division. In a multidivisional structure, each division is independent and

Figure 6.6
Multidivisional Structure

Each division is independent and has its own set of support functions. The corporate headquarters staff oversees the activities of the divisional managers, and there are three levels of management: corporate, divisional, and functional.

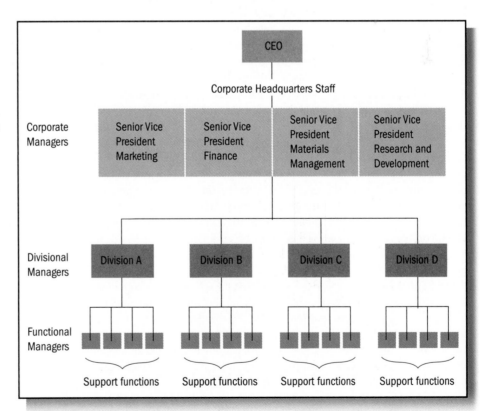

Self-contained division
A division that has its own set of support functions and controls its own value creation activities.

Corporate headquarters staff
Corporate managers who are responsible for overseeing the activities of the divisional managers heading up the different divisions.

self-contained (in a product division structure, the divisions share the services of a set of centralized functions). When divisions are **self-contained**, each division has its own set of support functions and controls its own value-creation activities. Each division needs its own set of support functions because it is impossible for one centralized set of support functions to service the needs of totally different products—such as automobiles, computers, and consumer electronics. As a result, horizontal differentiation increases.

The second innovation in a multidivisional structure is a new level of management, a **corporate headquarters staff**, composed of corporate managers who are responsible for overseeing the activities of the divisional managers heading up the different divisions.[5] The corporate headquarters staff is functionally organized, and one of the tasks of corporate managers is to coordinate the activities of the divisions. For example, managers at corporate headquarters can help the divisions share information and learn from one another so that divisional innovations can be quickly communicated throughout the organization. Recall from Chapter 4 that managers acting in that way are performing an *integrating role*.

Because corporate managers constitute another level in the hierarchy, there is an increase in vertical differentiation, which provides more control. The heads of the divisions (divisional managers) link corporate headquarters and the divisions. Compared to a functional or a product division structure, a multidivisional structure

ORGANIZATIONAL INSIGHT 6.1
Creating GM's Multidivisional Structure

William C. Durant formed the General Motors Company on September 16, 1908. Into it he brought about 25 different companies. Originally, each company retained its own operating identity, and the GM organization was simply a holding company, a central office surrounded by 25 satellites. When Alfred P. Sloan took over as president of GM in 1923, he inherited this collection of independently managed car companies, which made their own decisions, did their own R&D, and produced their own range of cars.

GM's main competitor, Ford, was organized very differently. From the beginning, Henry Ford had pursued the advantages of economies of scale and mass production and designed a mechanistic structure to achieve them. He created a highly-centralized organization in which he had complete personal control over important decision making. To reduce costs, Ford at first produced only one vehicle, the Model T, and focused on finding ways to make the car more efficiently. Because of its organizational design, Ford's company was initially much more profitable than GM. The problem facing Sloan was to compete with Ford, not only in terms of making a successful product but also to improve GM's financial performance.

Confronted with Ford's success, Sloan must have been tempted to close several of GM's small operations and concentrate production in a few locations where the company could enjoy the benefits of cost savings from making fewer models and from economies of scale. For example, he could have chosen a product division structure, created three product divisions to manufacture three kinds of car, and centralized support functions such as marketing, R&D, and engineering to reduce costs. Sloan, however, recognized the advantages of developing the diverse sets of research, design, and marketing skills and competencies present in the small car companies. He realized that there was a great risk of losing this diversity of talent if he combined all these skills into one centrally located research and design department. Moreover, if the same set of support functions, such as engineering and design, worked for all of GM's divisions, there was a danger that all GM cars would begin to look alike. Nevertheless, Sloan also recognized the advantages of centralized control in achieving economies of scale, controlling costs, and providing for the development of a strategic plan for the company as a whole, rather than for each company separately.

So Sloan searched for an organizational structure that would allow him to achieve all these objectives simultaneously, and he found his answer in the multidivisional structure, which had been used successfully by DuPont Chemicals. In 1920, he instituted this change, noting that GM "needs to find a principle for coordination without losing the advantages of decentralization."[6]

Each different GM car company was placed in one of five self-contained operating divisions (Chevrolet, Pontiac, Oldsmobile, Buick, and Cadillac) with support services like sales, production, engineering, and finance. Each division became a profit center and was evaluated on its return on investment. Sloan was quite clear about the main advantage of linking decentralization to return on investment: It raised the visibility of each division's performance. And, Sloan

(continued)

observed, it (1) "increases the morale of the organization by placing each operation on its own foundation, . . . assuming its own responsibility and contributing its share to the final result"; (2) "develops statistics correctly reflecting . . . the true measure of efficiency"; and (3) "enables the corporation to direct the placing of additional capital where it will result in the greatest benefit to the corporation as a whole."[7]

Sloan recommended that transactions between divisions be set by a transfer pricing scheme based on cost plus some predetermined rate of return. However, to avoid protecting a high-cost internal supplier, he also recommended a number of steps involving analysis of the operations of outside competitors to determine the fair price. Sloan established a strong, professional, centralized headquarters management staff to perform such calculations. Corporate management's primary role was to audit divisional performance and to plan strategy for the total organization. Divisional managers were to be responsible for all product-related decisions.

In the 1980s, after fierce competition from the Japanese, GM took a hard look at its multidivisional structure. The duplication of R&D and engineering and the purchasing of inputs by each division independently were costing the company billions of extra dollars. In 1984, GM's five autonomous car divisions were combined into two groups: Chevrolet and Pontiac would concentrate on small cars; Buick, Oldsmobile, and Cadillac would focus on large cars.[8]

GM hoped that the reorganization would reduce costs and speed product development, but it was a disaster. With control of design and engineering more centralized at the group level, the cars of the different divisions started to look the same. Nobody could tell a Buick from a Cadillac or an Oldsmobile. Sales plummeted. Moreover, the reorganization did not speed decision making. It increased the number of levels in the hierarchy by introducing the group level into the organization. As a result, GM had 13 levels in its hierarchy as compared with Toyota, for example, which had just five. Once again the company was in trouble: Before the reorganization, it had been too decentralized; now it was too centralized. What to do?

Realizing its mistake, GM moved to return control over product design to the divisions while continuing to centralize high-cost functions like engineering and purchasing. This restructuring has had some success. Cadillac's management moved quickly to establish a new product identity and design new models. Throughout the 1990s, GM reduced the number of different models it produced, and in 2004 it closed down its Oldsmobile division. GM has also increased its efficiency in the 2000s and is still working to reduce overhead costs.[9] However, in 2005, it was still struggling to make the innovative cars U.S. customers want to buy and its sales dropped sharply.[10]

provides additional differentiation and integration, which facilitate the control of complex activities.

A corporate staff and self-contained divisions are two factors that distinguish a multidivisional structure from a product division structure. But there are other important differences between them. A product division structure can only be used to control the activities of a company that is operating in *one* business or industry. In contrast, a multidivisional structure is designed to allow a company to operate in many different businesses. Each division in a multidivisional structure is essentially a different business. Moreover, it is the responsibility of each divisional manager to design the divisional structure that best meets the needs of the products and customers of that division. Thus, one or more of the independent divisions within a multidivisional structure could use a product division structure or any other structure to coordinate its activities. This diversity is illustrated in Figure 6.7.

The multidivisional organization depicted in Figure 6.7 has three divisions, each with a different structure. The car-making division has a functional structure because it produces a small range of simple components. The PC division has a product division structure; each of its divisions develops a different kind of computer. The consumer electronics division has a matrix structure (which we discuss later in the chapter) because it has to respond quickly to customer needs. At its peak, Beatrice, a food and consumer products company, had over 100 different divisions. Both its Samsonite Division, which produced luggage, and its Hunt and Wesson Division, best known for tomato-based products, operated with product division structures; but the whole Beatrice empire was operated through a multidivisional structure.

Most *Fortune* 500 companies use a multidivisional structure because it allows them to grow and expand their operations while maintaining control over their activities. Only when an organization has a multidivisional structure does the management hierarchy expand to include the three most powerful levels of management: corporate managers who oversee the operations of *all* the divisions; divisional

Functional Structure
Automotive Products Division

Product Division Structure
Personal Computers Division

Matrix Structure
Consumer Electronics Division

managers who run the individual divisions; and functional managers who are responsible for developing the organization's core competences. The story of GM's decision to move to a multidivisional structure illustrates many of the issues involved in operating a multidivisional structure and the difference between it and a product division structure.

As the GM story suggests, operating a multidivisional structure is no easy task. It is perhaps the biggest challenge that top managers face. Because the multidivisional structure is so widely used, we need to look closely at its advantages and disadvantages.

Advantages of a Multidivisional Structure

When the multidivisional structure is managed effectively, it provides a large, complex organization with several advantages.[11]

Increased Organizational Effectiveness. A division of labor generally increases organizational effectiveness. In a multidivisional structure there is a clear division of labor between corporate and divisional managers. Divisional managers are responsible for the day-to-day operations of their respective divisions and for tailoring divisional activities to the needs of customers. Corporate managers are responsible for long-term planning for the corporation as a whole and for tailoring the mission of the divisions to suit the goals of the whole organization.

Increased Control. Corporate managers monitor the performance of divisional managers. The extra control provided by the corporate office encourages the stronger pursuit of internal organizational efficiency by divisional managers. Knowing that they have to answer to corporate managers, divisional managers may curb their inclination to increase the size of their personal staffs and thus increase their status and reign in costs. They may also think twice before investing in products that increase their status but do little to promote corporate performance.

More generally, as the GM example suggests, the creation of self-contained divisions means that corporate managers can develop control systems to compare the performance of one division with the performance of another by measuring profitability or product development time. Consequently, corporate managers are in a good position to intervene and take selective action to correct inefficiencies when they arise.

Profitable Growth. When each division is its own profit center—that is, when its individual profitability can be clearly evaluated—corporate headquarters can identify the divisions in which an investment of capital will yield the highest returns.[12] Thus, corporate executives can make better capital resource allocation decisions to promote corporate growth. At the same time, their role as monitor rather than as administrator means that they can oversee a greater number of different businesses and activities. The multidivisional structure allows a company to grow without suffering from the problems of communication or information overload that can occur when the two roles are mixed, as they are in the functional structure.

Internal Labor Market. The most able divisional managers are promoted to become corporate managers. Thus, divisional managers have an incentive to perform well because superior performance results in promotion to high office. A large divisional company possesses an internal labor market, which increases managers' motivation to work to increase organizational effectiveness.

Disadvantages of a Multidivisional Structure

Like other structures, certain problems can develop with multidivisional structures over time. Although good management can control most of the problems, it cannot eliminate them.

Managing the Corporate–Divisional Relationship. The central management problem posed by a multidivisional structure is how much authority to centralize at the corporate level and how much authority to decentralize to the operating divisions. On one hand, each division is closest to its particular operating environment and is in the best position to develop plans to increase its own effectiveness, so decentralization is a logical choice. On the other hand, headquarters' role is to adopt the long-term view and to tailor divisional activities to the needs of the whole organization, so centralization has advantages too.

The balance between the two has to be managed all the time. Too much centralization of authority can straitjacket divisional managers; they lose control of decision making to headquarters managers who are far from the firing line, and the result can be poor performance. GM's attempt to centralize decision making to reduce costs was a disaster because all GM cars started to look the same. Too much decentralization, however, can result in giving divisional managers so much freedom that they slack off and fail to control their division's costs. The corporate–divisional relationship needs to be managed continually. Over time as the operating environment changes the decision about which managerial activities to centralize and which to decentralize will change.

Coordination Problems Between Divisions. When a multidivisional structure is created, measures of effectiveness such as return on investment can be used to compare divisions' performance, and corporate headquarters can allocate capital to the divisions on the basis of their performance. One problem with this approach is that divisions may begin to compete for resources, and rivalry between them may prevent them from cooperating. Such rivalry can lower organizational performance when a company's effectiveness depends on the divisions' sharing of knowledge and information about innovations to enhance the performance of all divisions. It would be counterproductive, for example, if one of GM's divisions invented a new super-efficient engine and refused to share the information with other divisions.

Transfer price
The price at which one division sells a product or information about innovations to another division.

Transfer Pricing. Problems between divisions often revolve around the **transfer price**—the price at which one division sells a product or information about innovations to another division. To maximize its own return on investment, one division will want a high transfer price, but that will penalize the other division, which is, after all, part of the same organization. Thus, as each division pursues its own goals, coordination problems inside the organization can emerge. The role of the corporate center is to manage such problems, as Sloan of GM noted. It is very important that a multidivisional organization establish integrating mechanisms that enable managers from different divisions to cooperate. Mechanisms like integrating roles and departments are important in promoting cooperation. The corporate office itself is a type of integrating department.

Bureaucratic Costs. Multidivisional structures are very expensive to operate. Each division has a full complement of support functions, including R&D. Thus, there is extensive duplication of activities within the organization—and there are the costs of corporate headquarters managers. The high costs of operating a multidivisional structure must continually be evaluated against the benefits the company obtains. If the benefits relative to the costs fall, the company should move to reduce the size of corporate headquarters, the number of divisions, or find a way to reduce the costs of its support functions. It might be possible, for example, for an organization to change to a product division structure or to a product team structure (discussion follows) and service the needs of its different products through one set of centralized support functions.

Communication Problems. Communication problems—particularly the distortion of information—arise in tall hierarchies. These problems are common in multidivisional structures because they tend to be the tallest of all organizational structures. The gap between the corporate center and the divisions is especially large. The head of a division may deliberately disguise falling divisional performance in order to receive larger capital allocations; when a company has 200 divisions, such deception can be hard to detect. In addition, it may take so long for headquarters to make decisions and transmit them to divisions that responses to competitors are too slow. The more centralized an organization is, the more of a problem communication will be.

Product Team Structure

In a product division structure, members of support functions such as marketing and R&D coordinate with the different divisions as their services are needed, but their main loyalty is to their function, not to the division. Increasingly, organizations are finding that the functional orientation of specialists is not in an organization's best interests because industry competition has become focused on the product. Today, it is especially important to customize products to suit customer needs while containing product development costs. Moreover, increased competition has made it important to reduce the time needed to bring a new product to market by speeding the product development process. One solution to this problem might be a multidivisional structure in which each division has its own set of support functions. But, as we just discussed, this structure is very expensive to operate, and communication problems between divisions can slow innovation and product development. Many companies, in their search for a new structure to solve these problems, have reengineered their divisional structures into a product team structure.

Product team structure
A divisional structure in which specialists from the support functions are combined into product development teams that specialize in the needs of a particular kind of product.

A product team structure is a cross between the product division structure, in which the support functions are centralized, and the multidivisional structure, in which each division has its own support functions. In a **product team structure**, specialists from the support functions are combined into product development teams that specialize in the needs of a particular kind of product (see Figure 6.8). Each team is, in effect, a self-contained division headed by a product team manager (PTM, in Figure 6.8), who supervises the operational activities associated with developing and

Figure 6.8
Product Team Structure

Each product team manager (PTM) supervises the activities associated with developing and manufacturing a product.

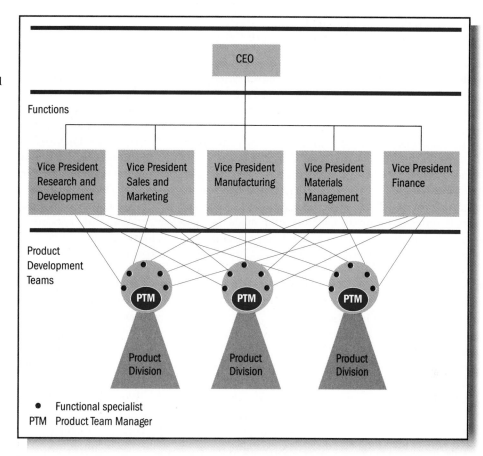

- Functional specialist
- PTM Product Team Manager

manufacturing the product. The product teams focus on the needs of one product (or client) or a few related products, and they owe their allegiance not to their functions, but to the product team they join. The vice presidents of the functions, at the top of the organization, retain overall functional control, but decision-making authority for each product is decentralized to the team, and each team becomes responsible for the success of a project. Hallmark Cards has found this approach to coordinating functions and products to be an effective way to develop new products quickly.

In the past, Hallmark used a functional structure to coordinate its activities. A large number of artists, writers, lithographers, and designers working in different functional departments produced a huge array of greeting cards. The problems of coordinating the activities of 700 writers and artists across functional boundaries became so complex and difficult that it was taking Hallmark two years to develop a new card. To solve its product development problems, Hallmark reengineered to a product team structure. Artists and writers were formed into product teams around particular categories of greeting cards, such as Mother's Day cards, Christmas cards, and so on. With no differences in subunit orientation to impede the flow of information, mutual adjustment became much easier, and work was performed much more quickly. Product development time shrank from years to weeks.

A product team structure is more decentralized than a functional structure or a product division structure, and specialists in the various product teams are permitted to make on-the-spot decisions—something particularly important in service organizations. The grouping into self-contained product teams increases integration because each team becomes responsible for all aspects of its operations. Through close collaboration, team members become intensely involved in all aspects of product development and in tailoring the product to its market. Moreover, the high level of integration produced by teams makes it possible to make decisions quickly and

After Lee Iacocca took control of troubled Chrysler in the 1980s, he restructured its approach to product development. Before Iacocca, the company had come up with an idea for a new model of car, then formed a product division to take control of the idea and made the division managers responsible for obtaining the inputs of the various functions located at corporate headquarters. The functions made their contributions sequentially; so, for example, design had the idea, engineering designed the prototype, purchasing and supply ordered the inputs, manufacturing made the vehicle, and marketing and sales sold it. Iacocca decided that this approach was ineffective because it took Chrysler seven or eight years to bring a new car to market—more than twice as long as Toyota or Nissan. Moreover, this system resulted in vehicles that were more expensive to make and of lower quality than Japanese vehicles.

According to Iacocca, getting different functional support groups to cooperate and coordinate their activities to arrive at the final product design is a nightmare. One function's activities often conflict with another function's, and no learning takes place because they each approach the development process with their own respective subunit orientations. The engineering department says, "Our aim is to develop an aerodynamic, lightweight car that gets good mileage, and we are not really interested in how difficult it is to assemble or how costly it is to build." The marketing department says,

"You engineers and production folks had better control your costs so that we can price this car competitively."

Iacocca was determined to change this situation. As an experiment he used what he called a "platform team" to develop the Dodge Viper, a new luxury sports car. In a platform team, which is the same as a product development team, the functions are organized around the product. A team consists of product and manufacturing engineers, planners and buyers, designers, financial analysts, and marketing and salespeople, and each team has sole responsibility for designing and getting its car to customers. Iacocca's goal? Using teams to encourage different specialists to interact, speed communication, facilitate rapid problem solving, and increase efficiency. Moreover, when specialists start to learn from one another product quality improves and the pace of innovation quickens. The concept was wildly successful at Chrysler. "Team Viper" got the product to market in three years—a record time for the organization. Moreover, the car was a hit and customers lined up to buy it.

With the success of the platform team concept established, Iacocca then restructured the rest of Chrysler's functionally organized product development operations into product-oriented platform teams including large-car, small-car, minivan and Jeep/truck.

respond to fast-changing customer requirements. DaimlerChrysler (then just Chrysler) was one of the first large companies to experiment with moving to a product team structure. The preceding organizational insight illustrates how Chrysler's choice of this structure saved the company from bankruptcy.

In the mid 1990s, Chrysler's turnaround led to its acquisition by Daimler Benz, which wanted to obtain Chrysler's new competencies in low-cost production and rapid product development and implant them in its own organization. The new DaimlerChrysler has been attempting to combine these competences with Daimler's engineering and design competencies to produce world-class cars in all price ranges. The company ran into new problems in the early 2000s when managers had a hard time combining two very different structures and cultures into a cohesive whole. Costs shot up and sales fell, but then a new German manager took control of its U.S. operations and restructured the company once again. In 2005, DaimlerChrysler's new line of redesigned cars made it the most successful U.S.–based car company.[13] We discuss these restructuring issues in Chapter 10, when organizational change and redesign is examined in detail.

The division of activities by product is the second most common method organizations use to group activities, after grouping them by function. Product structure increases horizontal differentiation and vertical differentiation and leads to the differentiation of managers into corporate-level, division-level, and function-level managers. In recent years, many large companies have moved from one type of product structure to another in an attempt to save money or make better use of their functional resources. It is important for managers continually to evaluate how well their product structure is working because it has a direct impact on the effectiveness of their organization.

DIVISIONAL STRUCTURE II: GEOGRAPHIC STRUCTURE

Geographic divisional structure

A divisional structure in which divisions are organized according to the requirements of the different locations in which an organization operates.

Of the three types of product structure discussed earlier, the multidivisional structure is the one most often used by large organizations. It provides the extra control that is important when a company produces a wide array of complex products or services or enters new industries and needs to deal with different sets of stakeholders and competitive forces. However, when the control problems that companies experience are a function of geography, a **geographic divisional structure**, in which divisions are organized according to the requirements of the different locations in which an organization operates, is available.

As an organization grows, it often develops a national customer base. As it spreads into different regions of a country, it needs to adjust its structure to align its core competencies with the needs of customers in different geographic regions. A geographic structure allows some functions to be centralized at one headquarters location and others to be decentralized to a regional level. For example, the can manufacturer Crown Cork and Seal produces many of the cans used in canning soft drinks, vegetables, and fruits. Because cans are bulky objects that are expensive to transport, it makes sense to establish manufacturing plants in the different parts of the country where cans are most in demand. Also, there is a limit to how many cans it is possible for the company to produce efficiently at just one plant location; when economies of scale become exhausted at one location, it makes sense to establish another plant in a new location. Recognizing these limiting factors, Crown Cork and Seal operates several manufacturing plants throughout the United States and Canada. Each plant has its own purchasing, quality control, and sales departments. R&D and engineering, however, are centralized at its headquarters location.

Figure 6.9
Geographic Structure

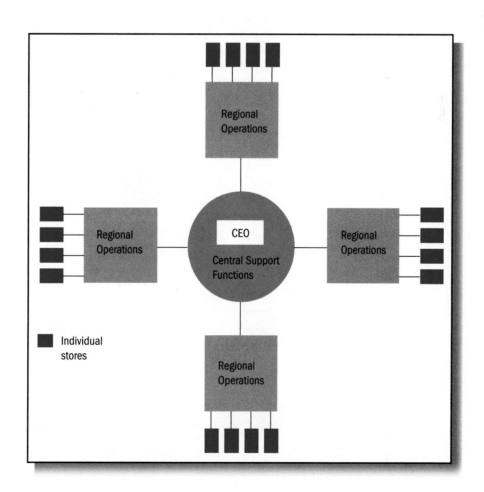

Neiman-Marcus, the specialty department store, also has a geographic structure, but for a different reason. When Neiman-Marcus operated only in Texas, it used a functional structure to coordinate activities. But as it opened stores at selected sites across the United States, it confronted a dilemma: how to respond to the needs of well-heeled customers that differ region by region while achieving the cost advantages of central purchasing. Neiman-Marcus's solution was to establish a geographic structure that groups stores by region (see Figure 6.9). Individual stores are under the direction of a regional office, which is responsible for coordinating the specific product needs of the stores in its region—for example, swimwear and sportswear in Los Angeles and hats, gloves, and down parkas in Chicago. The regional office feeds customer-specific requirements back to headquarters in Dallas, where centralized purchasing functions make decisions for the company as a whole.

Both Crown Cork and Seal and Neiman-Marcus superimposed a geographic grouping over their basic functional grouping, thereby increasing horizontal differentiation. The creation of a new level in the hierarchy—regional managers—and the decentralization of control to regional hierarchies also increased vertical differentiation. The regional hierarchies provide more control than is possible with one centralized hierarchy and, in the cases of Crown Cork and Seal and Neiman-Marcus, have increased effectiveness. The following organizational insight profiles Wal-Mart's geographic structure.

ORGANIZATIONAL INSIGHT 6.3
Wal-Mart Goes National, Then Global

Wal-Mart is one company that has found the right balance between a mechanistic and organic style of operating and has prospered. Its explosive growth has continued unabated; in the 2000s, the company has opened over 300 new supercenters, 60 discount stores, and 12 Sam's Clubs, and has taken over scores of supermarket chains in Mexico, Europe, Japan, and South America. In 2005, for example, it bought 140 Brazilian supermarkets and wholesale outlets for over $750 million, to speed its expansion into Latin America.[14] These new openings will add another $100 billion in sales over the next five years.[15] The problem facing Wal-Mart is choosing a structure complex enough to

Figure 6.10 Wal-Mart's Corporate Structure

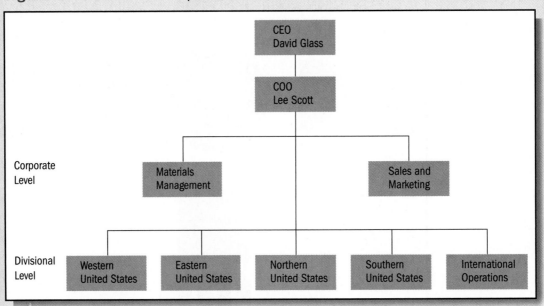

(continued)

operate its growing global empire while allowing it to maintain its mechanistic/organic balance for low prices and responsiveness to customers, the keys to its success. The structure it has chosen is a geographic structure (see Figure 6.10).

Under the control of CEO Lee Scott, Wal-Mart centralizes its materials management and sales and marketing activities at corporate headquarters. Then it divides its store operations into regions, including international operations, and gives its regional managers input into what mix of products should be sold in their regions to maximize sales. At the moment, Wal-Mart is working on replicating its materials management and marketing activities in other regions of the world. Wal-Mart intends to become a large—if not the largest—retailer in Europe in the decade ahead, and it also plans to open operations in Japan, where its entry into the market is causing turmoil among slow-moving Japanese store chains that have not experienced the effects of an efficient global competitor. As it expands the global scope of its operations, no doubt it will further subdivide its international division to meet customer needs. This is especially true in Mexico and Central America, which are rapidly becoming major suppliers of many of its food and home products such as cookies, hot sauce, and pottery products.[16]

DIVISIONAL STRUCTURE III: MARKET STRUCTURE

The grouping of activities by product or geography makes the product or region the center of attention. In contrast, a market structure aligns functional skills and competencies with the product needs of different customer groups. Marketing, not manufacturing, determines how managers decide to group organizational activities into divisions. Figure 6.11 shows a market structure with divisions created to meet the needs of commercial, consumer, corporate, and government customers.

Each customer division has a different marketing focus, and the job of each division is to develop products to suit the needs of its specific customers. Each division makes use of centralized support functions. Engineering tailors products to suit the various needs of each division, and manufacturing follows each division's specifications. Because the market structure focuses the activities of the whole organization on the needs of the customer, the organization can quickly sense changes in its market and transfer skills and resources to satisfy the changing needs of this vital stakeholder group. As described in the following organizational insight, Mellon Bank had great success when it moved from a product structure to a market structure.

Figure 6.11
Market Structure

Each division focuses on the needs of a distinct customer group.

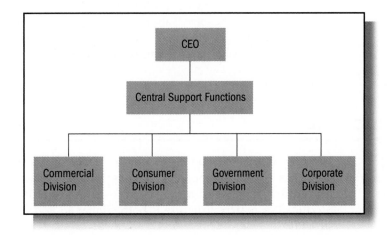

Mellon Bank used to group activities around its principal products: certificates of deposit (CDs), insurance, mortgages, credit cards, and customer deposits. Each product division had its own manager and set of support services, and this arrangement created a lot of problems. Each product manager ignored the effect of his or her actions on the products of the other managers, and potential customer-attracting linkages between product divisions were ignored because the product, not the customer, was the organization's focus. Although the product divisions were maximizing the sale of their own products, sales across product divisions were small compared to what they could have been if there had been cooperation between divisions. The company was missing out on an important opportunity to increase sales by offering each customer a wide array of banking services.[17]

To provide customers with a full line of banking services, Mellon decided to reorganize to a market-based structure based on divisions that would offer a complete range of Mellon's financial products to different customer groups—for example, affluent customers (those with a portfolio of over $1 million) and corporate clients. The new structure enhanced communication among the customer-specific divisions and encouraged them to share information because they were not competing for each other's customers.

To provide a centralized support service for the customer divisions, Mellon decided to centralize the support functions of advertising, market research, and computers. This change produced major benefits, saving $2 million from economies of scale. With the old financial product focus, these support functions had often been in conflict with the product managers over the best use of the bank's resources. With the market focus, those conflicts disappeared, and the customer divisions were able to take much more advantage of their expertise and offer customers more effective financial services. The result was that Mellon's customer base increased rapidly, and the company has grown from strength to strength.[18]

MANAGERIAL IMPLICATIONS

CHANGING ORGANIZATIONAL STRUCTURE

1. As an organization grows, be sensitive to the need to change a functional structure to improve the control of organizational activities.
2. When the control problem is to manage the production of a wide range of products, consider using a form of divisional structure.
3. Use a product division structure if the organization's products are generally similar.
4. Move to a multidivisional structure if the organization produces a wide range of different or complex goods and services or operates in more than one business or industry.
5. When the control problem is to reduce product development time by increasing the integration between support functions, consider using a product team structure.
6. When the control problem is to customize products to the needs of customers in different geographic areas, consider using a geographic structure.
7. When the control problem is to coordinate the marketing of all of a company's products to several distinct groups of customers, use a market structure.
8. Always weigh the benefits that will arise from moving to a new structure (that is, the control problems that will be solved) against the costs that will arise from moving to the new structure (that is, the higher operating costs associated with managing a more complex structure) to see whether changing organizational structure will increase organizational effectiveness.

MATRIX STRUCTURE

Matrix structure
A structure in which people and resources are grouped in two ways simultaneously: by function and by project or product.

The search for better and faster ways to develop products and respond to customer needs has led some companies to choose a **matrix structure**, an organizational design that groups people and resources in two ways simultaneously: by function and by product.[19] A matrix structure is both similar to and different from a product team structure.

Figure 6.12 Matrix Structure

Team members are two-boss employees because they report to both the product team manager and the functional manager.

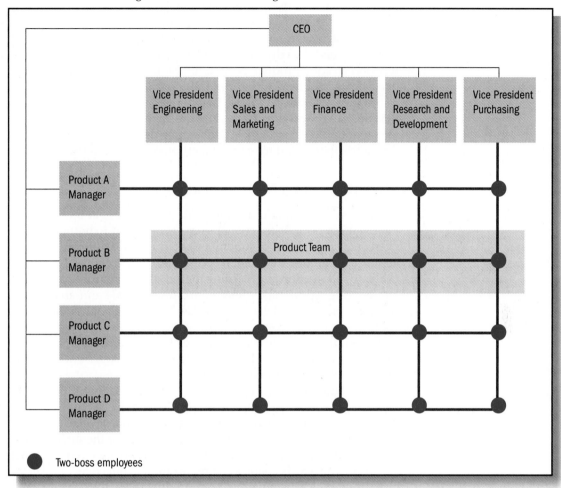

Before examining those differences, it is necessary to examine how a matrix structure works (see Figure 6.12). In the context of organizational design, a matrix is a rectangular grid that shows a *vertical* flow of *functional* responsibility and a *horizontal* flow of *product* responsibility. In Figure 6.12 the lines pointing down represent the grouping of tasks by function, and the lines pointing from left to right represent the grouping of tasks by product. An organization with a matrix structure is differentiated into whatever functions the organization needs to achieve its goals. The organization itself is very flat, having minimal hierarchical levels within each function and decentralized authority. Functional employees report to the heads of their respective functions (usually, functional vice presidents) but do not work under their direct supervision. Instead, the work of functional personnel is determined primarily by membership in one of several cross-functional product teams under the leadership of a product manager. The members of the team are called **two-boss employees** because they report to two superiors: the product team manager and the functional manager. The defining feature of a matrix structure is the fact that team members have two superiors.

The team is both the basic building block of the matrix and the principal mechanism for coordination and integration. Role and authority relationships are deliberately left vague because the underlying assumption of matrix structure is that when team members are given more responsibility than they have formal authority, they are forced to cooperate to get the job done. The matrix thus relies on minimal vertical control from the formal hierarchy and maximal horizontal control from the use of

Two-boss employees
Employees who report to two superiors: the product team manager and the functional manager.

integrating mechanisms—teams—which promote mutual adjustment. Matrix structures are a principal form of organic structure (see Chapter 4).

Both matrix structure and product team structure make use of teams to coordinate activities, but they differ in two major respects. First, team members in a product team structure have only one boss: the product team manager. Team members in a matrix structure have two bosses—the product manager and the functional manager—and thus divided loyalty. They must juggle the conflicting demands of the function and the product. Second, in the matrix structure, team membership is not fixed. Team members move from team to team, to where their skills are most needed.

In theory, because of those two differences, the matrix structure should be more flexible than the product team structure, in which lines of authority and coordination are more stable. The matrix is deliberately designed to overcome differences in functional orientation and to force integration on its members. Does it work?

Advantages of a Matrix Structure

A matrix structure has four significant advantages over more traditional structures.[20] First, the use of cross-functional teams is designed to reduce functional barriers and overcome the problem of subunit orientation. With differentiation between functions kept to a minimum, integration becomes easier to achieve. In turn, the team structure facilitates adaptation and learning for the whole organization. The matrix's team system is designed to make the organization flexible and able to respond quickly to changing product and customer needs. Not surprisingly, matrix structures were first used in high-tech companies for which the ability to develop technologically advanced products quickly was the key to success. TRW Systems, a U.S. defense contractor, developed the matrix system to make the Atlas and Titan rockets that formed the U.S. space program in the 1960s.

A second advantage of the matrix structure is that it opens up communication between functional specialists and provides an opportunity for team members from different functions to learn from one another and develop their skills. Thus, matrix structure facilitates technological progress because the interactions of different specialists produce the innovations that give a company its core competences.

Third, the matrix enables an organization to effectively utilize the skills of its specialized employees who move from product to product as needed. At the beginning of a project, for example, basic skills in R&D are needed, but after early innovation, the skills of engineers are needed to design and make the product. People move around the matrix to wherever they are most needed; team membership is constantly changing to suit the needs of the product.

Fourth, the dual functional and product focus promotes concern for both cost and quality. The primary goal of functional specialists is likely to be technical: producing the highest quality, most innovative product possible (regardless of cost). In contrast, the primary goals of product managers are likely to concern cost and speed of development—doing whatever can be done given the amount of time and money available. This built-in focus on quality *and* cost keeps the team on track and keeps technical possibilities in line with commercial realities.

Disadvantages of a Matrix Structure

In theory, the principles underlying matrix structures seem logical. In practice, however, many problems arise.[21] To identify the sources of these problems, consider what is missing in a matrix.

A matrix lacks the advantages of bureaucratic structure (discussed in Chapter 5). With a flat hierarchy and few rules and SOPs, the matrix lacks a control structure that allows employees to develop stable expectations of each another. In theory, team members continually negotiate with one another about role responsibilities, and the resulting give-and-take makes the organization flexible. In practice, many people do not like the role ambiguity and role conflict that matrix structures can produce. For example, the functional boss, focused on quality, and the product boss, focused on cost, often have different expectations of the team members. The result is role conflict. Team members become unsure of what to do, and a structure designed to promote flexibility may actually reduce it if team members become afraid to assume responsibility.

The lack of a clearly defined hierarchy of authority can also lead to conflict between functions and product teams over the use of resources. In theory, product managers are supposed to buy the services of the functional specialists on the team (say, for example, the services of 10 engineers at $2,000 per day). In practice, however, cost and resource allocation becomes fuzzy as products exceed their budgets and specialists cannot overcome technical obstacles. Power struggles emerge between product and functional managers, and politicking takes place to gain the support of top management.

As this suggests, matrix structures have to be carefully managed to retain their flexibility. They do not automatically produce the high level of coordination that is claimed of them, and people who work in a matrix often complain about high levels of stress and uncertainty. Over time, people in a matrix structure are likely to experience a vacuum of authority and responsibility and move to create their own informal organization to provide them with some sense of structure and stability. Informal leaders emerge within teams. These people become increasingly recognized as experts or as great "team leaders." A status hierarchy emerges within teams. Team members often resist transfer to other teams in order to remain with their colleagues.

When top managers do not get the results they expect, they sometimes try to increase their control over the matrix and to increase their power over decision making. Slowly but surely, as people jockey for power and authority, a system that started out very flat and decentralized turns into a centralized, less flexible structure.

Matrix structures need to be managed carefully if their advantages are to outweigh their disadvantages. Matrix structures are not designed for use in normal, everyday, organizational situations, however. They are mainly appropriate when a high level of coordination between functional experts is needed because an organization must respond quickly to a changing environment. Given the problems associated with managing a complex matrix structure, many growing companies have chosen to overlay a functional structure or a product division structure with product teams rather than attempt to manage a full-fledged matrix. The use of IT greatly facilitates this process for it provides the extra integration needed to coordinate complex value-creation activities.

The Multidivisional Matrix Structure

Multidivisional structures allow an organization to coordinate activities effectively but are difficult to manage. Communication and coordination problems arise because of the high degree of differentiation within a multidivisional structure. Consequently, a company with several divisions needs to be sure that it has sufficient integration mechanisms in place to handle its control needs. Sometimes the corporate center becomes very remote from divisional activities and is unable to play this important integrating role. When this happens, organizations sometimes introduce the matrix structure at the top of the organization and create a **multidivisional matrix structure**, a structure that provides for more integration between corporate and divisional managers and between divisional managers. Figure 6.13 depicts this structure.

Multidivisional matrix structure
A structure that provides for more integration between corporate and divisional managers and between divisional managers.

As the figure shows, this structure allows senior vice presidents at the corporate center to send corporate-level specialists to each division, perform an in-depth evaluation of their performance, and to devise a functional action plan for each division. Divisional managers meet with corporate managers to exchange knowledge and information and to coordinate divisional activities. The multidivisional matrix structure makes it much easier for top managers from the divisions and corporate headquarters to cooperate and jointly coordinate organizational activities. Many large

Figure 6.13
Multidivisional Matrix
Structure

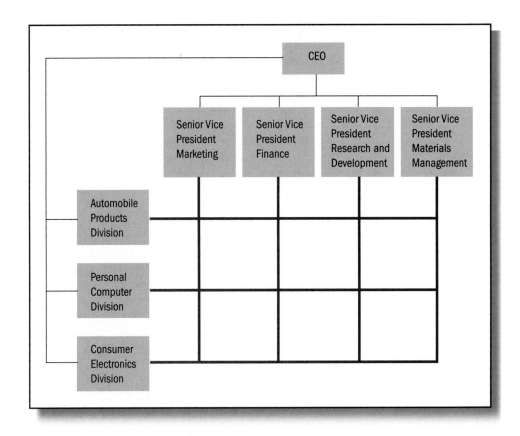

Figure 6.14
Target's Hybrid Structure

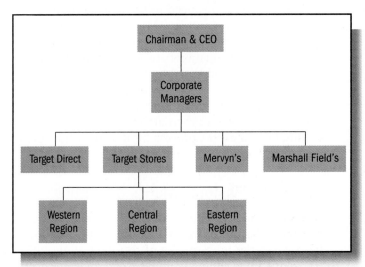

international companies that operate globally use this structure. However, a discussion of how to design an international organizational structure is left until Chapter 8.

Hybrid Structure

As the previous discussion suggests, large, complex organizations that have many divisions often simultaneously make use of many different structures, that is, they operate with a **hybrid structure**. As we discussed earlier, many large organizations operating in several industries use a multidivisional structure and create self-contained divisions; then each product division's managers select the structure that best meets the needs of the particular environment, strategy, and so on (see Figure 6.14). Thus, one product division may choose to operate with a functional structure, a second may choose a geographic structure, and a third may choose a product team structure because of the nature of the division's products or the desire to be more responsive to customers' needs.

Companies that operate in only one industry, but choose to compete in different market segments of the industry, also may use a hybrid structure. For example, Target uses a hybrid structure in the retail industry and groups its activities by type of market/customer segment and by geography.

As shown in Figure 6.14, Target operates its different store chains as four independent divisions in a market division structure. Its four market divisions are Mervyns and Marshall Field's, which cater to the needs of affluent customers; Target Stores, which competes in the low-price segment; and target.direct, Target's Internet division, which manages online sales.[22]

Beneath this organizational layer is another layer of structure because both Target Stores and Marshall Field's operate with a geographic structure that groups stores by region. Individual stores are under the direction of a regional office, which is responsible for coordinating the market needs of the stores in its region and for responding to regional customer needs. The regional office feeds information back to divisional headquarters, where centralized merchandising functions make decisions for all Target or Marshall Field's stores.

Organizational structure may thus be likened to the layers of an onion. The outer layer provides the overarching organizational framework—most commonly some form of product or market division structure—and each inner layer is the structure that each division selects for itself in response to the contingencies it faces—such as a geographic or product team structure. The ability to break a large organization into smaller units or divisions makes it much easier for managers to change structure when the need arises—for example, when a change in technology or an increase in competition in the environment necessitates a change from a functional to a product team structure.

NETWORK STRUCTURE AND THE BOUNDARYLESS ORGANIZATION

Another innovation in organizational design has been sweeping across the United States: the use of network structures. Recall from Chapter 3, that a *network structure* is a cluster of different organizations whose actions are coordinated by contracts and agreements, rather than by a formal hierarchy of authority.[23] Very often one organization takes the lead in creating the network as it searches for a way to increase effectiveness; for example, a clothing manufacturer may search for ways to produce and market clothes more cheaply. Rather than manufacturing the clothes in its own factories, the company decides to outsource its manufacturing to a low-cost Asian company; it also forms an agreement with a large Madison Avenue advertising agency to design and implement its sales campaign. Recall also how *outsourcing* is moving a value-creation activity that was done *inside* an organization to the *outside*, where it is performed by another company.

Often, network structures become very complex as a company forms agreements with a whole range of suppliers, manufacturers, and distributors to outsource many of the value-creation activities necessary to produce and market goods and services.[24] For example, Nike, the largest and most profitable sports shoe manufacturer in the world, has developed a very complex network structure to produce its shoes. At the center of the network is Nike's product design and research function located in Beaverton, Oregon, where Nike's designers pioneer innovations in sports shoe design. Almost all the other functional specialisms that Nike needs to produce and market its shoes have been outsourced to companies around the world![25]

How does Nike manage the relationships between all the companies in its network? Principally by using modern IT (discussed in depth in Chapter 12). Nike's designers use computer-aided design (CAD) to design shoes, and all new product information, including manufacturing instructions, is stored electronically. When the designers have done their work, they relay all the blueprints for the new products electronically to Nike's network of suppliers and manufacturers in Southeast Asia.[26] For example, instructions for the design of a new sole may be sent to a supplier in Taiwan, and instructions for the leather uppers to a supplier in Malaysia. These suppliers then produce the shoe parts, which are then sent for final assembly to a manufacturer in China with whom Nike has established an alliance. From China these shoes are shipped to distributors throughout the world and are marketed in each country by an organization with which Nike has formed some form of alliance, such as a long-term contract.

Advantages of Network Structures

Why does Nike use a network structure to control the value-creation process rather than perform all the functional activities itself? There are several advantages that Nike, and other organizations, can realize by using a network structure.

First, to the degree that an organization can find a network partner that can perform a specific functional activity reliably, and at a lower cost, production costs are reduced.[27] Almost all of Nike's manufacturing is done in Asia, for example, because wages in Southeast Asia are a fraction of what they are in the United States. Second, to the degree that an organization contracts with other organizations to perform specific value-creation activities, it avoids the high bureaucratic costs of operating a complex organizational structure. For example, the hierarchy can be kept as flat as possible and fewer managers are needed. Also, because Nike outsources many functional activities it is able to stay small and flexible. Control of the design process is decentralized to teams that are assigned to develop each of the new kinds of sports and leisure shoes for which Nike is well-known.

Third, a network structure allows an organization to act in an organic way. If the environment changes, for example, and new opportunities become apparent, an organization can quickly alter its network in response. For example, it can sever the links to companies whose services it no longer needs and develop new linkages with companies that do have the skills it needs. An organization that performs all of its own functional activities would take a longer time to respond to the changes taking place. Fourth, if any of its network partners fail to perform up to Nike's standards they can be replaced with new partners. Finally, a very important reason for the development of networks has been that organizations gain access to low-cost overseas sources of inputs and functional expertise, something crucial in today's changing global environment.

Disadvantages of Network Structures

Although network structure has several advantages, it also has drawbacks in certain situations. To see what these are, imagine a high-tech company racing to bring to market proprietary hardware and software faster than its competitors. How easy would it be to outsource the functional activities necessary to ensure that the hardware and software are compatible and work with other companies' software? Not easy at all. Close interaction is needed between the hardware and software divisions, and between the different groups of hardware and software programmers responsible for designing the different parts of the system. A considerable level of mutual adjustment is needed to permit the groups to interact so that they can learn from one another and constantly improve the final product. Also, managers must be there to integrate the activities of the groups to make sure their activities mesh well. The coordination problems arising from having different companies perform different parts of the work process would be enormous. Moreover, there has to be considerable trust between the different groups so that they are willing to share their ideas, something necessary for successful new product development.

It is unlikely that a network structure would provide an organization with the ability to control such a complex value-creation process because managers lack the means to effectively coordinate and motivate the various network partners. First, it would be difficult to obtain the ongoing learning that builds core competences over time inside a company because separate companies have less incentive to make such an investment.[28] As a result, many opportunities to cut costs and increase quality would be lost. Second, if one of Nike's suppliers failed to perform well, Nike could easily replace it by forming a contract with another. But how easy is it to find reliable software companies who can both do the job and be trusted not to take proprietary information and use it themselves or give it to a company's competitors?

In general, the more complex the value-creation activities necessary to produce and market goods and services, the more problems there are associated with using a network structure.[29] Like the other structures discussed in this chapter, network structures are appropriate in some situations and not in others.

The Boundaryless Organization

The ability of managers to develop a network structure to produce or provide the goods and services their customers want, rather than create a complex organizational structure to do so, has led many researchers and consultants to popularize the idea of the "boundaryless organization." The boundaryless organization is composed of people who are linked by computers, faxes, computer-aided design systems, and video teleconferencing, and who may rarely or ever see one another face to face.[30] People come and go as their services are needed, much as in a matrix structure, but they are not formal members of an organization. They are independent functional experts who form an alliance with an organization, fulfill their contractual obligations, and then move on to the next project.

The use of outsourcing and the development of network organization are increasing rapidly as organizations recognize the many opportunities they offer to reduce costs and increase flexibility. Clearly, managers have to assess carefully the relative benefits of having their own organization perform a functional activity or make a particular input, versus forming an alliance with another organization to do so to increase organizational effectiveness. Designing organizational structure is becoming an increasingly complex management activity in today's changing world.

E-Commerce

E-commerce
Trade that takes place between organizations, and between organizations and customers using IT and the Internet.

E-commerce is trade that takes place between companies, and between companies and individual customers, using IT and the Internet. *Business-to-business (B2B) commerce* is trade that takes place between companies using IT and the Internet to link and coordinate the value chains of *different* companies (see Figure 6.15). Companies use B2B commerce because it allows them to reduce their operating costs and may improve product quality. A main B2B network application is the B2B marketplace an industry-specific trading network set up to connect buyers and sellers using the Internet. To participate in a B2B marketplace companies agree to use the network software standard that allows them to search for and share information with each other. Then, companies can work together over time to find ways to reduce costs or improve quality.

Business-to-customer (B2C) commerce is trade that takes place between a company and its network of *individual customers* using IT and the Internet. When a company uses IT to connect directly to customers, they have increased control of their network; for example, they can handle their own marketing and distribution and do not need to use intermediaries like wholesalers and retailers. Dell computer, for example, was one of the first companies to create a B2C network that allowed it to sell directly to the customer and to customize its PCs to their needs. The use of online storefronts allows companies to provide customers with a much wider range of products and to give them much more information about these products in a very

Figure 6.15
Types of E-Commerce

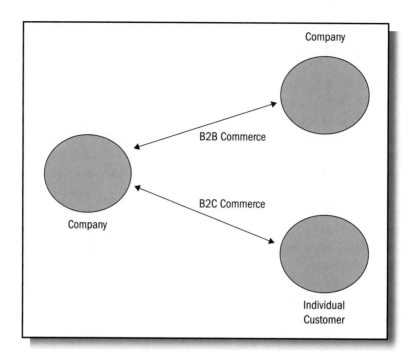

cost-effective way. This often allows them to attract more customers, and so a company's network strengthens over time. This is the goal of Dell and of course Amazon.com, which has opened over 40 different kinds of storefronts to be able to sell its millions of loyal customers a wider and wider range of products. Amazon has also created a network structure that links it to bricks-and-mortar outlets such as Circuit City and Toys "Я" Us, where customers who buy online can go to physically pick up their products. Thus, all these different types of networks work together to benefit an organization.

SUMMARY

Designing organizational structure is a difficult and challenging task. Managers have to manage the vertical and horizontal dimensions of the structure continually and choose an appropriate allocation of authority and task responsibilities. As an organization grows and becomes more complex, changing its structure to respond to changing needs or contingencies becomes important.

Designing a structure that fits a company's needs is a major challenge. Each structure has advantages and disadvantages, and managers have to be ready and willing to redesign their organization to obtain the advantages and anticipate and minimize the problems of whichever structure they choose. An organization that is in control of its structure has an important competitive advantage over one that is not.

Many organizations ignore the coordination problems inherent in the organizing process. Too often, an organization waits until it is already in trouble (in decline) before attempting to deal with coordination and motivation problems. The characteristics of the top management team are very important in this regard because they determine how decisions get made and how top managers perceive the problems the organization is experiencing. Chapter 6 has made the following main points:

1. A functional structure is a design that groups people because they have similar skills or use the same resources. Functional groups include finance, R&D, marketing, and engineering. All organizations begin as functional structures.
2. An organization needs to adopt a more complex structure when it starts to produce many products or when it confronts special needs, such as the need to produce new products quickly, to deal with different customer groups, or to handle growth into new regions.
3. The move to a more complex structure is based on three design choices: increasing vertical differentiation, increasing horizontal differentiation, and increasing integration.

4. Most organizations move from a functional structure to some kind of divisional structure: a product structure, a geographic structure, or a market structure.

5. There are three kinds of product structure: product division structure, multidivisional structure, and product team structure.

6. Product division structure is used when an organization produces broadly similar products that use the same set of support functions.

7. Multidivisional structures are available to organizations that are growing rapidly and producing a wide variety of products or are entering totally different kinds of industries. In a multidivisional structure, each product division is a self-contained division with the operating structure that best suits its needs. A central headquarters staff is responsible for coordinating the activities of the divisions in the organization. When a lot of coordination between divisions is required, a company can use a multidivisional matrix structure.

8. Product team structures put the focus on the product being produced. Teams of functional specialists are organized around the product to speed product development.

9. Geographic structures are used when organizations expand into new areas or begin to manufacture in many different locations.

10. Market structures are used when organizations wish to group activities to focus on the needs of distinct customer groups.

11. Matrix structures group activities by function and product. They are a special kind of structure that is available when an organization needs to deal with new or technically sophisticated products in rapidly changing markets.

12. Network structures are formed when an organization forms agreements or contracts with other organizations to perform specific functional value-creation activities.

DISCUSSION QUESTIONS

1. As organizations grow and differentiate, what problems can arise with a functional structure?

2. How do the product division structure and the multidivisional structure differ?

3. Why might an organization prefer to use a product team structure rather than a matrix structure?

4. What are the principal differences between a functional structure and a multidivisional structure? Why does a company change from a functional to a multidivisional structure?

5. What are the advantages and disadvantages associated with network structures?

ORGANIZATIONAL THEORY IN ACTION

Practicing Organizational Theory: Which New Organizational Structure?

Form groups of three to five people, and discuss the following scenario:

You are a group of managers of a major soft-drinks company that is going head-to-head with Coca-Cola to increase market share. Your strategy is to increase your product range to offer bottled water in every segment of the market to attract customers, and to begin offering soft drinks and other beverage products tailored to the needs of customers in different regions of the country.

Currently you have a functional structure. What you are trying to work out now is how best to implement your strategy in order to launch your new products. To what kind of structure should you move?

1. Debate the pros and cons of the different possible organizational structures.

2. Which structure will allow you to best achieve your goal at (a) lowest cost; (b) give you most responsiveness to customers; or (c) both?

The Ethical Dimension #6

When an organization outsources its functional activities, it typically lays off many, if not most, of the employees who used to perform the functional task within the organization's boundary. Levi Strauss, for example, closed down its last U.S. plant in 2001; Dell Computer outsourced hundreds of its call center customer service jobs to India.

1. Does it make good business sense to outsource? What are the potential advantages and disadvantages?

2. Given these advantages and disadvantages, when and under what conditions is it ethical to outsource organizational activities, lay off workers, and send those jobs abroad?

Making the Connection #6

Find an example of a company that has changed its form of horizontal differentiation in some way. What did the company do? Why did it make the change? What does it hope to accomplish as a result of the change? What structure has it changed to?

Analyzing the Organization: Design Module #6

This module focuses on horizontal differentiation in your organization and on the structure the organization uses to coordinate its tasks and roles.

Assignment

1. What kind of structure (for example, functional, product division, multidivisional) does your organization have? Draw a diagram showing its structure, and identify the major subunits or divisions in the organization.
2. Why does the company use this kind of structure? Provide a brief account of the advantages and disadvantages associated with this structure for your organization.
3. Is your organization experiencing any particular problems in managing its activities? Can you suggest a more appropriate structure that your company might adopt to solve these problems?

CASE FOR ANALYSIS

A New Caterpillar Emerges

A reputation for low-cost manufacturing combined with excellent distribution and after-sales service made Caterpillar one of the largest and most prosperous of all construction equipment companies. Like U.S. car companies, however, Caterpillar found itself under intense competition from Komatsu, Kubota, and Hitachi, Japan's biggest construction equipment manufacturers. By adopting the latest techniques in robotics, just-in-time inventory systems, and flexible manufacturing technology, these Japanese companies had obtained a large cost advantage over Caterpillar and could easily undercut its prices. As a result, Caterpillar's low-cost reputation was slipping, its market share was eroding, and the company was in trouble.

Recognizing the crisis, Caterpillar quickly moved to change its organizational structure. The prime mover of this restructuring was Donald V. Fites, Caterpillar's chairman. During his rise through Caterpillar's managerial hierarchy, Fites had spent much time in Japan. While there, he had noticed two characteristics of Japanese companies' organizational structures that did not exist in his company. First, Japanese companies relied heavily on teams of people from different functions for product development. Each team focused on only one product and paid exclusive attention to improving the quality and reducing the costs of that product. Second, Japanese companies were very decentralized in their approach to decision making; decisions about a product were made by the people most familiar with the product and its market, not by executives far removed in corporate headquarters. Fites saw that the combination of up-to-the-minute technology, cross-functional teams of workers empowered to make decisions about their product, and decentralized control was the ultimate source of the Japanese companies' competitive advantage. Once in control at Caterpillar, he quickly moved to institute Japanese-style organizational practices.

Fites introduced cross-functional teams into Caterpillar's product development process. Each product development team was given its own marketing staff, product designers, and manufacturing engineers, all of whom worked together to integrate their functional specialties. This structural change cut product development time in half. Next, he decentralized control over marketing from corporate headquarters to the regional level—in North America and globally—in order to speed Caterpillar's response to its customers. Manufacturing, too, experienced far-reaching changes. The company embarked on a billion-dollar plant-modernization program based on the use of computer-integrated flexible manufacturing systems by groups of employees in product teams. This new system helped boost productivity by 30%.[31]

The full extent of Fites's push simultaneously toward exploiting the advantages of product teams, decentralizing decision making, and plant modernization was seen in 1990. Fites orchestrated a major structural reorganization of Caterpillar, changing it from a company organized on a functional basis to one organized by product divisions. Although Caterpillar continued to centralize R&D, purchasing, and some support services in four "service divisions," Fites created 14 product divisions, each of which is a profit center and each of which is required to satisfy a 15% return-on-assets target. Each product division has a Japanese-like product team structure in which cross-functional teams are responsible for all aspects of product performance.

Caterpillar's new decentralized structure contrasts sharply with the old structure, in which decisions were made at the top of the various functions and then fed down throughout the organization.[32] With its new structure in place, Caterpillar is poised to reap the fruits of its long and difficult reorganization and compete effectively in the global marketplace.

DISCUSSION QUESTIONS

1. What were the problems with Caterpillar's old organizational structure?
2. How did Fites change Caterpillar's structure to improve its effectiveness?

REFERENCES

1. J. Child, *Organization: A Guide for Managers and Administrators* (New York: Harper and Row, 1977); R. Duncan, "What Is the Right Organization Structure?" *Organization Dynamics* (Winter 1979), 59–80; J. R. Galbraith and R. K. Kazanjian, *Strategy Implementation: Structure, System, and Process*, 2e (St. Paul, MN: West, 1986).

2. O. E. Williamson, *Markets and Hierarchies: Analysis and Antitrust Implications* (New York: Free Press, 1975).

3. P. R. Lawrence and J. W. Lorsch, *Organization and Environment* (Boston: Graduate School of Business Administration, Harvard University, 1967).

4. A. D. Chandler, *Strategy and Structure* (Cambridge, MA: MIT Press, 1962); Williamson, *Markets and Hierarchies*.

5. Chandler, *Strategy and Structure*; B. R. Scott, *Stages of Development* (Cambridge, MA: Harvard Business School, 1971).

6. A. P. Sloan, *My Years at General Motors* (Garden City, NY: Doubleday, 1946), p. 46.

7. Ibid., p. 50.

8. A. Taylor, III, "Can GM Remodel Itself?" *Fortune*, January 13, 1992, pp. 26–34; W. Hampton and J. Norman, "General Motors: What Went Wrong?" *Business Week*, March 16, 1987, pp. 102–110.

9. www.yahoo.com, "GM Will Match Japan Quality in 2–3 Years," September 17, 2002.

10. www.gm.com, 2005.

11. C.W.L. Hill and G. R. Jones, *Strategic Management*, 4e (Boston: Houghton Mifflin, 1998); G. R. Jones and C.W.L. Hill, "Transaction Cost Analysis of Strategy–Structure Choice," *Strategic Management Journal*, 9 (1988), 159–172.

12. Sloan, *My Years at General Motors*.

13. www.daimlerchrysler.com, 2005.

14. yahoo.com, "Wal-Mart Increases Latin America Hold," December 15, 2005.

15. www.walmart.com, 2006.

16. www.walmart.com, 2006.

17. "Mellon: A Sweeter Mix." *Financial World*, August 1, 1995, p. 24.

18. www.mellon.com, 2005.

19. S. M. Davis and P. R. Lawrence, *Matrix* (Reading, MA: Addison-Wesley, 1977); J. R. Galbraith, "Matrix Organization Designs: How to Combine Functional and Project Forms," *Business Horizons*, 14 (1971), 29–40.

20. L. R. Burns, "Matrix Management in Hospitals: Testing Theories of Matrix Structure and Development," *Administrative Science Quarterly*, 34 (1989), 349–368; Duncan, "What Is the Right Organization Structure?"

21. S. M. Davis and P. R. Lawrence, "Problems of Matrix Organization," *Harvard Business Review* (May–June 1978), 131–142; E. W. Larson and D. H. Gobelli, "Matrix Management: Contradictions and Insight," *California Management Review* (Summer 1987), 126–138.

22. www.target.com, 2005.

23. R. E. Miles and C. C. Snow, "Causes of Failure in Network Organizations," *California Management Review* (July 1992), 53–72.

24. W. Baker, "The Network Organization in Theory and Practice," in N. Nohria and R. Eccles, eds., *Networks and Organizations* (Boston, Harvard Business School 1992), pp. 397–429.

25. www.nike.com, 2006.

26. G. S. Capowski, "Designing a Corporate Identity," *Management Review* (June 1993), 37–38.

27. J. Marcia, "Just Doing It," *Distribution* (January 1995), 36–40.

28. R. A. Bettis, S. P. Bradley, and G. Hamel, "Outsourcing and Industrial Decline," *Academy of Management Executive* (February 1992), 7–22.

29. C. C. Snow, R. E. Miles, H. J. Coleman, Jr. "Managing 21st Century Network Organizations," *Organizational Dynamics* (Winter 1992), 5–20.

30. J. Fulk and G. Desanctis, "Electronic Communication and Changing Organizational Forms," *Organizational Science*, 6 (1995), 337–349.

31. T. E. Benson, "Caterpillar Wakes Up," *Industry Week*, May 20, 1991, pp. 33–37; K. Kelly, A. Bernstein, and R. Neff, "Caterpillar's Don Fites: Why He Didn't Blink," *Business Week*, August 10, 1992, pp. 56–57.

32. "Upgrade for Caterpillar," *Fleet Equipment*, 22 (1996), 71.

Chapter

Creating and Managing Organizational Culture

Learning Objectives

In this chapter, the hard-to-define concept of organizational culture is examined. Culture is discussed in terms of the values and norms that influence its members' behavior, determine how its members interpret the environment, bond its members to the organization, and give it a competitive advantage. The global dimension of culture is also examined, and the problems companies encounter when they expand globally are addressed.

After studying this chapter you should be able to:

1. Differentiate between values and norms, and understand the way culture is shared by an organization's members.

2. Describe how individuals learn culture both formally (that is, the way an organization intends them to learn it) and informally (that is, by seeing what goes on in the organization).

3. Identify the four building blocks or foundations of an organization's culture that account for cultural differences among organizations.

4. Understand how an organization's culture, like its structure, can be designed or managed.

5. Discuss an important outcome of an organization's culture: its stance on corporate social responsibility.

WHAT IS ORGANIZATIONAL CULTURE?

Organizational culture
The set of shared values and norms that controls organizational members' interactions with each other and with people outside the organization.

Previous chapters have discussed how the most important function of organizational structure is to control—that is, coordinate and motivate—people within an organization. In Chapter 1, we defined **organizational culture** as the set of shared values and norms that control organizational members' interactions with each other and with suppliers, customers, and other people outside the organization. Just as an organization's structure can be used to achieve competitive advantage and promote stakeholder interests, an organization's culture can also be used to increase organizational effectiveness.[1] This is because organizational culture controls the way members make decisions, the way they interpret and manage the organization's environment,

177

what they do with information, and how they behave.[2] Culture thus affects an organization's competitive position.

What are organizational values, and how do they affect behavior? **Values** are general criteria, standards, or guiding principles that people use to determine which types of behaviors, events, situations, and outcomes are desirable or undesirable. There are two kinds of values: terminal and instrumental (see Figure 7.1).[3] A **terminal value** is a desired end state or outcome that people seek to achieve. Organizations might adopt any of the following as terminal values, that is, as guiding principles: excellence, responsibility, reliability, profitability, innovativeness, economy, morality, quality. Large insurance companies, for example, may value excellence, but their terminal values are often stability and predictability because the company must be there to pay off policyholders' claims.

An **instrumental value** is a desired mode of behavior. Modes of behavior that organizations advocate include working hard, respecting traditions and authority, being conservative and cautious, being frugal, being creative and courageous, being honest, taking risks, and maintaining high standards.

An organization's culture thus consists of the end states that the organization seeks to achieve (its *terminal values*) and the modes of behavior the organization encourages (its *instrumental values*). Ideally, instrumental values help the organization to achieve its terminal goals. For example, a computer software company like Google whose culture emphasizes the terminal value of innovativeness may attain this outcome through the instrumental values of working hard, being creative, and taking risks. That combination of terminal and instrumental values leads to an entrepreneurial culture. On the other hand, a computer hardware company like Gateway that desires stability and predictability to reduce costs may emphasize caution, attention to detail, and conformity to work rules and standard operating procedures (SOPs). The result will be a conservative culture.

Terminal values are reflected in an organization's mission statement and official goals, which tell organization members and other stakeholders what kinds of values and ethical standards it wishes its members to use in their decision making. So that members understand instrumental values—that is, the modes of behavior that they are expected to follow as they pursue desired end states—an organization develops specific norms, rules, and SOPs that embody its instrumental values. In Chapter 4, we defined **norms** as standards or styles of behavior that are considered acceptable or typical for a group of people. The specific norms of being courteous and keeping the work area clean and safe, for example, will develop in an organization whose instrumental values include being helpful and working hard.

Figure 7.1
Terminal and Instrumental Values in an Organization's Culture

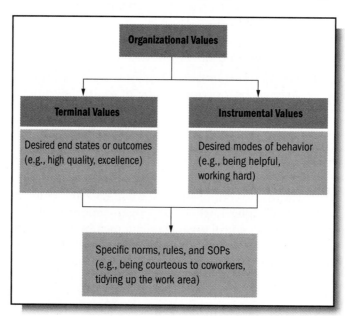

Many of the most powerful and crucial values of an organization are not written down. They exist only in the shared norms, beliefs, assumptions, and ways of thinking and acting that people within an organization use to relate to each other and to outsiders. Members learn from each other how to interpret and respond to various situations in ways that are consistent with the organization's accepted values. Eventually, members choose and follow appropriate values without even realizing that they are making a choice. Over time, they internalize the organization's values and the specific rules, norms, and SOPs that govern behavior; that is, organizational values become part of members' mind-sets—peoples' own values systems—and affect their interpretation of a situation.[4]

The values and norms of different countries also affect an organization's culture. Indeed, differences between the cultures of different countries because of differences in their national values and norms help reveal the powerful effect organizational culture has on behavior.[5] To get a feel for the effect of culture on behavior, consider what happened when a U.S. company and a Mexican company attempted to cooperate in a joint venture, as highlighted in the following organizational insight.

ORGANIZATIONAL INSIGHT 7.1
How Global Culture Affects Organizational Culture

After much negotiation, Pittsburgh-based Corning Glass Works and Vitro, a Mexican glass-making company, formed a joint venture to share technology and market one another's glass products throughout the United States and Mexico. They formed their alliance to take advantage of the opportunities presented by the North American Free Trade Agreement (NAFTA), which opened up the markets of both countries to one another's products. At the signing of the joint venture, both companies were enthusiastic about the prospects for their alliance. Managers in both companies claimed that they had similar organizational cultures. Both companies had a top management team that was still dominated by members of the founding families; both were global companies with broad product lines; and both had been successful in managing alliances with other companies in the past.

Nevertheless, two years later Corning Glass terminated the joint venture and gave Vitro back the $150 million it had given Corning for access to Corning's technology.[6] Why had the venture failed? The cultures and values of the two companies were so different that Corning managers and Vitro managers could not work together.

Vitro, the Mexican company, did business the Mexican way, in accordance with values prevailing in Mexican culture. In Mexico, business is conducted at a slower pace than in the United States. Used to a protected market, Mexican companies are inclined to sit back and make their decisions in a "very genteel," consensual kind of way. Managers typically come to work at 9 A.M.; spend two or more hours at lunch, often at home with their families; and then work late, often until 9 P.M. Mexican managers and their subordinates are intensely loyal and respectful to their superiors; the corporate culture is based on paternalistic, hierarchical values; and most important decision making is centralized in a small team of top managers. This centralization slows decision making because middle managers may come up with a solution to a problem but will not take action without top management approval. In Mexico, building relationships with new companies takes time and effort because trust develops slowly. Thus, personal contacts that develop slowly between managers in different companies are an important prerequisite for doing business in Mexico.

Corning, the American company, did business the American way, in accordance with values prevailing in American culture. Managers in the United States take short lunch breaks or work through lunch so they can leave early in the evening. In many U.S. companies, decision-making authority is decentralized to lower-level managers, who make important decisions and commit their organization to certain courses of action. U.S. managers like to make decisions quickly and worry about the consequences later.

Aware of the differences in their approaches to doing business, managers from Corning and from Vitro tried to compromise and find a mutually acceptable working style. Managers from both companies agreed to take long working lunches together. Mexican managers agreed to forgo going home at lunchtime, and U.S. managers agreed to work a bit later at night so that they could talk to Vitro's top managers and thus speed decision making. Over time, however, the differences in management style and approach to work became a source of frustration for managers from both companies. The slow pace of decision making was frustrating for Corning's managers. The pressure by Corning's managers to get everything done quickly was frustrating for Vitro's managers. Corning's managers working in Mexico discovered that the organizational cultures of Vitro and Corning were not so similar after all, and they decided to go home. Vitro's managers also realized that it was pointless to prolong the venture when the differences were so great.

When BankAmerica merged with Security Pacific, the merger was supposed to be a merger of equals, with the top management of both banks jointly running the new company. Richard Rosenberg, the chairman of BankAmerica, agreed to form an office of the chairman with Security Pacific's chairman Robert Smith; it was also agreed that Smith would succeed Rosenberg as the chairman of the new bank when Rosenberg retired. Similarly, there was supposed to be a 50–50 board split between the directors of both companies, and BankAmerica agreed to name four of Security Pacific's top managers to the new top management team.

After the merger, however, things did not work out as had been expected. BankAmerica had planned the merger hurriedly, without thoroughly investigating the details of Security Pacific's financial condition. After the merger, BankAmerica's managers began to find major flaws in the way Security Pacific's managers made loans, which had resulted in more than $300 million of write-offs for the company, with equally large sums to follow. BankAmerica's top management team came to despise and ridicule the way Security Pacific's managers did business. They blamed a large part of the problem on Security Pacific's culture, which was decentralized and freewheeling, and which allowed top managers to loan large sums of money to clients on the basis of personal ties. Its values had been developed in the savings and loan crisis when unrestrained risk taking, uncurbed by any values of responsibility to stakeholders, had been the norm.

BankAmerica's managers, by contrast, had cultivated a conservative, centralized decision-making style in their organization. Teams of managers made decisions to reduce the possibility of mistakes and fraud, and they curbed the autonomy of lower-level managers to act alone. All loans were made according to company-wide criteria scrutinized by top management. Its traditional, moderate values were based on following the rules of the legal system and acting ethically toward its stakeholders. Its norms emphasized conformity to its operating system and caution in decision making.[7]

Believing that their culture was the one that had to be developed in the new, merged organization, BankAmerica's managers began to use their power as the dominant party in the merger (Rosenberg as chairman of the bigger company had more legitimate power than Smith) to strip authority from Security Pacific's managers and to take control of the reins of the new organization. Less than two weeks after the merger, Smith found himself relieved of all important decision-making authority, which was transferred to Rosenberg and his top management team. Similarly, whenever BankAmerica's top managers were negotiating with Security Pacific's managers over future task and authority relationships, they used their power to cut the authority of Security Pacific's managers and to drive them from the organization. After a few months almost all of Security Pacific's top managers had left the new organization, followed by thousands of middle-level managers, who, BankAmerica managers felt, could not be trusted to maintain the company's new cultural standards and way of doing business. After all, Security Pacific's managers had not developed the right kind of values to be trusted to work ethically on the part of all the bank's stakeholders.

Corning and many other U.S. companies that have entered into global agreements have found that doing business in Mexico or in any other country is different from doing business at home. U.S. managers living abroad should not expect to do business the U.S. way. Because values, norms, customs, and etiquette differ from one country to another, managers working abroad must learn to appreciate and respond to those differences.

The terminal and instrumental values in Corning and Vitro produced very different responses in their employees. Although this example is between companies in different countries, the same holds true between different companies in the same country. Many mergers between companies have failed because of differences in their organizational cultures. Recognizing this, some organizations today that consistently take over companies as they grow, like Microsoft and United Technologies, use seasoned teams of "merger culture" experts who move in after a merger and take the steps necessary to blend the cultures of the merged companies. Before we look in detail at this, consider some problems that occurred during a merger because of differences in organizational culture.

Organizational culture is based on relatively enduring values embodied in organizational norms, rules, SOPs, and goals. People in the organization draw on these cultural values in their actions and decisions; they also draw on these values when dealing with ambiguity or uncertainty both inside and outside the organization.[8] The values in an organization's culture are important shapers of members' behavior and responses to situations, and they increase the reliability of members' behavior.[9] In this context, *reliability* does not necessarily mean consistently obedient or passive behavior; it may also mean consistently innovative or creative behavior.[10] It can also mean totally unethical behaviors.

Arthur Andersen, the disgraced accounting firm, was well known for its insistence that its employees abide by its rigid, constraining rules of behavior and deportment. Employees had to wear dark blue suits and black shoes; in some branches, the managers insisted that those shoes be lace-ups or employees were called to task. It also had in place an extensive and thorough MBO system, and its employees were constantly being evaluated and checked on their performance. Its values were based on obedience to company rules and norms, respect for partners and tradition, and the importance of following rules and SOPs. On the surface, the company demand for its employees to follow its values and norms would seem sound practice for a company whose business it is to accurately measure and account for client resources. Accounting is a precise science; the last thing an accounting company needs is for its employees to practice "creative accounting."

Small wonder, then, that the business world was astounded in 2001 when it became clear that some of Arthur Andersen's most senior partners, its top managers, had apparently been systematically instructing their subordinates, sometimes directly and sometimes indirectly, to overlook or ignore anomalies in client books in order to obtain large consulting fees and maintain the client business. The fact that Arthur Andersen had shredded documents that revealed its dealings with Enron before government regulators could examine them also became well known.

The paradox is that Arthur Andersen's values were so strong that they led subordinates to forget the "real" ethics of what they were doing, and Arthur Andersen's "distorted" ethics became the ones they followed. Apparently, Arthur Andersen's culture was so strong it had an almost cult-like effect on its members, who were afraid to question what was going on because of the enormous status and power the partners wielded, and the threat of sanction if anybody disobeyed or questioned the rules.

A strong organizational culture can be a dangerous thing in the hands of owners or managers who do not behave ethically or legally. On the other hand, a strong organizational culture can be the factor that sends an organization to greatness as its members are inspired to do their utmost to work hard to conceive and make goods and services that improve the welfare of their customers, and thus themselves. There are many ways in which culture can inspire and facilitate the intense kind of personal and team interactions that are necessary to develop organizational competences and obtain a competitive advantage.

First, cultural values are important facilitators of mutual adjustment in an organization. When shared cultural values provide a common reference point, employees do not need to spend much time establishing rapport and overcoming differences in their perceptions of events. Cultural values can smooth interactions among organizational members. People who share an organization's values may come to identify strongly with the organization, and feelings of self-worth may flow from their membership in it.[11] Employees of companies like Google, Southwest Airlines, and Dell Computer, for example, seem to value greatly their membership in the organization and are committed to it.

Second, organizational culture is a form of informal organization that facilitates the workings of the organizational structure. It is an important determinant of the way employees view their tasks and roles. It tells them, for example, if they should stay within established rules and procedures and simply obey orders or whether they are allowed to make suggestions to their superiors, find better or more creative ways of performing their roles, and feel free to demonstrate their competency without fear of reprisal from their peers or superiors.

This is not trivial. One of the most common complaints of employees and junior managers in organizations is that although they know certain tasks or roles could be accomplished better and should be performed in different ways, their organization's values and norms do not permit them to advise or question their superiors up the organizational hierarchy. They feel trapped, become unhappy, and often leave an organization, which causes high turnover. To mitigate this problem, some companies like GE and Microsoft have open lines of communication to the CEO, bypassing the superior. They also go out of their way to develop values of equity and fairness, demonstrating their commitment to reward employees who work toward organizational goals, rather than behaving in their own self-interest. GE even has a name for the managers who are out for themselves—"Type 4" managers. Based on feedback from subordinates, these managers are routinely asked to leave to make room for those who can develop empowered, motivated subordinates. The values expressed in GE's practices demonstrate its values to its members.

HOW IS AN ORGANIZATION'S CULTURE TRANSMITTED TO ITS MEMBERS?

An organization's ability to motivate employees and increase organizational effectiveness is directly related to the way in which members learn the organization's values. Organizational members learn pivotal values from an organization's formal socialization practices and from the stories, ceremonies, and organizational language that develop informally as an organization's culture matures.

Socialization and Socialization Tactics

Newcomers to an organization must learn the values and norms that guide existing members' behavior and decision making.[12] Can they work from 10:00 A.M. to 7:00 P.M. instead of from 8:00 A.M. to 5:00 P.M.? Can they challenge their peers' and superiors' views of a situation or should they simply stand and listen? Newcomers are outsiders, and only when they have learned and internalized the organization's values and act in accordance with its rules and norms will longtime members accept them as insiders.

To learn an organization's culture, newcomers must obtain information about cultural values. They can learn values indirectly, by observing how existing members behave and inferring what behaviors are appropriate and inappropriate. From the organization's perspective, however, the indirect method is risky because newcomers might observe and learn habits that are *not* acceptable to the organization. From the organization's perspective, the most effective way for newcomers to learn appropriate values is through **socialization**, which, as we saw in Chapter 4, is the process by which members learn and internalize the norms of an organization's culture.

Van Maanen and Schein developed a model of socialization that suggests how organizations can structure the socialization experience so that newcomers learn the values that the organization wants them to learn. In turn, these values influence the role orientation that the newcomers adopt.[13] **Role orientation** is the characteristic way in which newcomers respond to a situation: Do they react passively and obediently to commands and orders? Are they creative and innovative in searching for solutions to problems?

Van Maanen and Schein identified 12 socialization tactics that influence a newcomer's role orientation (see Table 7.1). The use of different sets of these tactics leads to two different role orientations: institutionalized and individualized. An *institutionalized role orientation* results when individuals are taught to respond to a new context in the same way that existing organizational members respond to it. An institutionalized orientation encourages obedience and conformity to rules and norms. An *individualized role orientation* results when individuals are allowed and

Socialization
The process by which members learn and internalize the values and norms of an organization's culture.

Role orientation
The characteristic way in which newcomers respond to a situation.

Table 7.1 How Socialization Tactics Shape Employees' Role Orientation

Tactics That Lead to an Institutionalized Orientation	Tactics That Lead to an Individualized Orientation
Collective	Individual
Formal	Informal
Sequential	Random
Fixed	Variable
Serial	Disjunctive
Diverstiture	Investiture

encouraged to be creative and to experiment with changing norms and values so that an organization can better achieve its values.[14] The following list contrasts the tactics used to socialize newcomers to an institutionalized orientation with those tactics used to develop an individualized orientation.

1. *Collective vs. individual.* Collective tactics provide newcomers with common learning experiences designed to produce a standardized response to a situation. With individual tactics, each newcomer's learning experiences are unique, and newcomers can learn new, appropriate responses for each situation.

2. *Formal vs. informal.* Formal tactics segregate newcomers from existing organizational members during the learning process. With informal tactics, newcomers learn on the job, as members of a team.

3. *Sequential vs. random.* Sequential tactics provide newcomers with explicit information about the sequence in which they will perform new activities or occupy new roles as they advance in an organization. With random tactics, training is based on the interests and needs of individual newcomers because there is no set sequence to the newcomer's progress in the organization.

4. *Fixed vs. variable.* Fixed tactics give newcomers precise knowledge of the timetable associated with completing each stage in the learning process. Variable tactics provide no information about when newcomers will reach a certain stage in the learning process; once again, training depends on the needs and interests of the individual.

5. *Serial vs. disjunctive.* When serial tactics are employed, existing organizational members act as role models and mentors for newcomers. Disjunctive processes require newcomers to figure out and develop their own way of behaving; they are not told what to do.

6. *Divestiture vs. investiture.* With divestiture, newcomers receive negative social support—that is, they are ignored or taunted—and existing organizational members withhold support until newcomers learn the ropes and conform to established norms. With investiture, newcomers immediately receive positive social support from other organizational members and are encouraged to be themselves.

When organizations combine the tactics listed in Table 7.1, there is some evidence that they can influence an individual's role orientation.[15] Military-style socialization, for example, leads to an extremely institutionalized orientation. New soldiers are placed in platoons with other new recruits (*collective*); are segregated from existing organizational members (*formal*); go through preestablished drills and learning experiences (*sequential*); know exactly how long this will take them and what they have to do (*fixed*); have superior officers who are their role models (*serial*); and are treated with zero respect and tolerance until they have learned their duties and "gotten with the program" (*divestiture*). As a result, new recruits develop an institutionalized role orientation in which obedience and conformity to organizational norms and values are the signs of success. New members who cannot or will not perform according to these norms and values leave (or are asked to leave), so that by the end of the socialization process the people who stay are clones of existing organizational members.

No organization controls its members to the extent that the military does, but other organizations do use similar practices to socialize their members. Arthur Andersen, discussed earlier, had a very institutionalized program. Recruits were carefully selected for employment because they seemed to possess the values that Arthur Andersen wanted—for example, hard-working, cautious, obedient, thorough. After they were hired, all new recruits attended a six-week course at its training center outside Chicago, where they were indoctrinated as a group into Arthur Andersen's way of doing business. In formal eight-hour-a-day classes, existing organizational members served as role models and told newcomers what was expected of them. Newcomers also learned informally over meals and during recreation what it meant to be working for Arthur Andersen. By the end of this socialization process, they had learned the values of the organization and the rules and norms that governed the way they were expected to behave when they represented Andersen's clients.

This effort to create an institutionalized role orientation worked well until the 1990s, when unethical, greedy partners, seeking to maximize their returns at the expense of other stakeholders, took advantage of its strong culture to lead its employees astray. Andersen's training center was closed down in 2002 after the company's collapse, further hurting its stakeholders.

Should an organization encourage an institutionalized role orientation in which newcomers accept the status quo and perform their jobs in keeping with the commands and orders they are given? Or should an organization encourage an individualized role orientation in which newcomers are allowed to develop creative and innovative responses to the jobs that the organization requires of them? The answer to this question depends on the organization's mission. Arthur Andersen initially developed its strong culture to standardize the way its employees performed auditing activities in order to develop a good reputation for honesty and reliability. A financial institution's credibility and reputation with clients depend on its integrity, so it wants to have control over what its employees do. It needs to adopt a strong socialization program that will reinforce its cultural values, and as in the BankAmerica case earlier, in most cases such an institutionalized orientation is in the best interests of the organization.

One danger of institutionalized socialization lies in the power it gives to those at the top of the organization to manipulate the situation, as in the case of Arthur Andersen, which lost its license to practice accounting in Texas in 2002. A second danger can lie in the sameness it may produce among members of an organization. If all employees have been socialized to share the same way of looking at the world, how will the organization be able to change and adapt when that world changes? When confronted with changes in the organizational environment (for example, a new product, a new competitor, or a change in customer demands), employees indoctrinated into old values will be unable to develop new values that might allow them to innovate. As a result, they—and thus the organization—cannot adapt and respond to the new conditions.

An organization whose mission is to provide innovative products for customers should encourage informal, random experiences from which individuals working on the job gain information as they need it. By all accounts, many of the Internet companies such as Yahoo!, Amazon.com, and eBay rely on individualized socialization tactics and allow members to develop skills in areas that capitalize on their abilities and interests.[16] These companies take this approach because their effectiveness depends not on standardizing individual behavior but on innovation and the ability of members to come up with new and improved solutions to Internet-related problems—such as Amazon.com's push to seek new ways to generate revenues to offset its high operating costs. In 2001, it announced it would start a consultancy arm and sell its IT skills to any interested organizations—something suggested by lower-level employees. In the 2000s, it has used its strong values and norms to support its rapid entry into many new kinds of markets to sell an increasing range of products. In every market, employees know how they should work to meet its goals because they are "Amazonian's." Thus an organization's socialization practices not only help members learn the organization's cultural values and the rules and norms that govern behavior, but also support the organization's mission.

Stories, Ceremonies, and Organizational Language

The cultural values of an organization are often evident in the stories, ceremonies, and language found in the organization.[17] At Southwest Airlines, for example, employees' wearing costumes on Halloween, Friday cookouts with top managers, and managers' periodically working with employees to perform the basic organizational jobs all reinforce and communicate the company's culture to its members.

Organizations use several types of ceremonial rites to communicate cultural norms and values (see Table 7.2).[18] *Rites of passage* mark an individual's entry to, promotion in, and departure from the organization. The socialization programs used by the army, in colleges, and in companies like 3M and Microsoft, which recognize their most creative people with special job titles, plaques, and so on, are rites of passage; so too are the ways in which an organization grooms people for promotion or retirement. *Rites of integration*, such as shared announcements of organizational success, office parties, and company cookouts, build and reinforce common bonds between organizational members. *Rites of enhancement*, such as awards dinners, newspaper releases, and employee promotions, publicly recognize and reward employees' contributions.

Triad Systems, a computer company based in Livermore, California, makes good use of ceremonies to integrate and enhance its organizational culture. Each year it holds a trade show at which all its major divisions and many of its suppliers are represented. At the annual show, managers give out awards to recognize employees for excellent service. With much hoopla the Grindstone Award is given to "individuals who most consistently demonstrate initiative, focus, dedication, and persistence"; the Innovator Award, to those who "conceive and carry out innovative ideas"; and the Busting the Boundaries Award, to "those who work most effectively across departmental and divisional boundaries to accomplish their work."[19] Each year, more than 700 of Triad's 1,500 employees win awards. The goal of Triad's trade show and awards ceremony is to develop organizational folklore to support its work teams and build a productive culture. Triad believes that giving praise and recognition builds a community of employees who share similar values and will jointly strive for organizational success. Also, providing members with organizational experiences in common promotes the development, across functional groups, of a common corporate language that bonds people together and allows them to better coordinate their activities.

Organizational stories and the language of an organization are important media for communicating culture. Stories (whether fact or fiction) about organizational heroes, such as Herb Kelleher of Southwest Airlines, provide important clues about cultural values and norms. Such stories can reveal the kinds of behaviors that the organization values and the kinds of practices that the organization frowns on. Studying stories and language can reveal the values that guide behavior.[20] Because language is the principal medium of communication in organizations, the characteristic phrases that frame and describe events provide important clues about norms and values. For example, if any manager in IBM's old laptop-computer division used

Table 7.2
Organizational Rites

TYPE OF RITE	EXAMPLE OF RITE	PURPOSE OF RITE
Rite of passage	Induction and basic training	Learn and internalize norms and values
Rite of integration	Office Christmas party	Build common norms and values
Rite of enhancement	Presentation of annual award	Motivate commitment to norms and values

the phrase "I non-concur" to disagree with a proposed plan of action, the plan was abandoned because achieving consensus used to be an important instrumental value at IBM. After divisions were given the authority to control their own activities, however, the language changed. A manager who tried to "non-concur" was told by other managers, "We no longer recognize that phrase," indicating that the division had adopted new terminal values that made old instrumental values obsolete.

The concept of organizational language encompasses not only spoken language but also how people dress, the offices they occupy, the company cars they drive, and how they formally address one another. In Microsoft and some other organizations, casual dress is the norm, but in investment banks like Goldman Sachs, and luxury department stores like Neiman Marcus and Saks, expensive, well-tailored clothing is the order of the day.

Many organizations have technical languages that facilitate mutual adjustment between organizational members.[21] At 3M, inside entrepreneurs have to emphasize the relationship between their product and 3M's terminal values in order to push ideas through the product development committee. Because many 3M products are flat—such as compact discs, Post-it notepads, floppy disks, paper, and transparencies—the quality of flatness embodies 3M's terminal values, and flatness is often a winning theme in 3M's corporate language—it increases a new product's chance of getting funded. At Microsoft, employees have developed a shorthand language of technical software phrases to describe communication problems. Technical languages are used by the military, by sports teams, in hospitals, and in many other specialized work contexts. Like socialization practices, organizational language, ceremonies, stories, and even detailed books of organization-specific rules help people learn the ropes and the organization's cultural values. Take the example of siteROCK, profiled in the following organizational insight.

ORGANIZATIONAL INSIGHT 7.3
siteROCK's Military Management Culture

The high-tech, dot.com culture is not usually associated with the values and norms that characterize the military. However, managers of the thousands of dot.coms that went belly-up in the early 2000s might have benefited from some military-style disciplined values and norms. Indeed, a few dot.coms that survived the shakeout did so because their managers used military-style rules and SOPs to control their employees and ensure high performance. One of these companies is siteROCK, based in Emeryville, California, whose COO, Dave Lilly, is an exnuclear submarine commander.

siteROCK is in the business of hosting and managing other companies' Web sites and keeping them up and running and error free. A customer's site that goes down or runs haywire is the major enemy. To maximize the performance of his employees and to increase their ability to respond to unexpected online events, Lilly decided that he needed to develop an institutionalized role orientation and develop a comprehensive set of rules and standard operating procedures to cover all the major known problems.[22] Lilly insisted that every problem-solving procedure be written down and codified. siteROCK now has over 30 thick binders listing all the processes and checklists that employees need to follow when an unexpected event happens. Their job is to try to solve the problem by using these procedures.

Moreover, again drawing from his military experience, Lilly instituted a "two-man" norm: Whenever the unexpected happens, each employee must immediately tell a coworker and the two should attempt to solve the problem together. The goal is simple: Develop strong norms of cooperation to achieve the quick resolution of a complex issue. If the existing rules don't work, then employees must experiment, and when they find a solution, the solution is turned into a new rule to be included in the procedures book to aid the future decision making of all employees in the organization.

At siteROCK, these written rules and SOPs have resulted in values that lead employees to achieve high levels of customer service. Because the goal is 100% reliability, detailed blueprints guide planning and decision making, not seat-of-the-pants problem solving, which might be brilliant 80% of the time but result in disaster the rest. Before siteROCK employees are allowed in the control room each day, they must reread the most important rules and SOPs. At the end of a shift, they spend 90 minutes doing paperwork that logs what they have done and states any new or improved rules that they have come up with. Clearly, siteROCK has developed a company-specific testament that symbolizes to employees the need for sustained, cooperative effort.

Finally, organizational symbols often convey an organization's cultural values to its members and to others outside the organization. In some organizations, for example, the size of peoples' offices, their location on the third floor or the thirty-third floor, or the luxury with which they are equipped are symbols that convey images about the values in an organization's culture. Is the organization hierarchical and status-conscious, for example, or are informal, participative work relationships encouraged? In GM, the executive suite on the top floor of their Detroit headquarters is isolated from the rest of the building and open only to top GM executives. A private corridor and stairway link top managers' offices, and a private elevator connects to their heated parking garage.

Sometimes, the very design of the building itself is a symbol of an organization's values. For example, Walt Disney hired famed Japanese architect Arata Isozaki to design the Team Disney Building, which houses Disney's "imagineering unit," in Orlando, Florida. This building's contemporary and unusual design featuring unusual shapes and bright colors conveys the importance of imagination and creativity to the Walt Disney Company and to the people who work in it.

MANAGERIAL IMPLICATIONS

ANALYZING ORGANIZATIONAL CULTURE

1. Study the culture of your organization, and identify the terminal and instrumental values on which it is based in order to assess how they affect organizational behavior.
2. Assess whether the goals, norms, and rules of your organization are effectively transmitting the values of the organizational culture to members. Identify areas for improvement.
3. Examine the methods your organization uses to socialize new members. Assess whether these socialization practices are effective in helping newcomers learn the organization's culture. Recommend ways to improve the process.
4. Try to develop organizational ceremonies to help employees learn cultural values, to enhance employee commitment, and to bond employees to the organization.

WHERE DOES ORGANIZATIONAL CULTURE COME FROM?

Now that you have seen what organizational culture is and how members learn and become part of an organization's culture, some difficult questions can be addressed: Where does organizational culture come from? Why do different companies have different cultures? Why might a culture that for many years helped an organization pursue its corporate mission suddenly harm the organization? Can culture be managed?

Organizational culture develops from the interaction of four factors: the personal and professional characteristics of people within the organization, organizational ethics, the property rights that the organization gives to employees, and the structure of the organization (see Figure 7.2). The interaction of these factors produces different cultures in different organizations and causes changes in culture over time. The way in which people's personal characteristics shape culture is discussed first.

Characteristics of People Within the Organization

The ultimate source of organizational culture is the people who make up the organization. If you want to know why cultures differ, look at their members. Organizations A, B, and C develop distinctly different cultures because they attract, select, and retain people who have different values, personalities, and ethics.[23] People may be attracted to an organization whose values match theirs; similarly, an organization selects people who share its values. Over time, people who do not fit in leave. The result is that people inside the organization become more and more

Figure 7.2
Where an Organization's
Culture Comes From

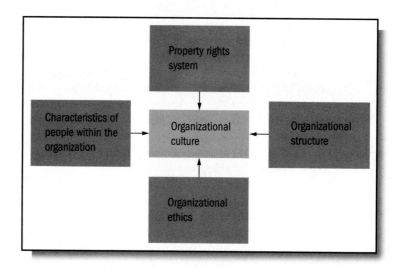

similar, the values of the organization become more and more parochial, and the culture becomes more and more distinct from that of similar organizations.

The founder of an organization has a substantial influence on the organization's initial culture because of his or her personal values and beliefs.[24] Founders set the scene for the later development of a culture because they not only establish the new organization's values, but also hire its first members. Presumably, the people selected by the founder have values and interests similar to the founder's.[25] Over time, members buy into the founder's vision and perpetuate the founder's values in the organization.[26] An important implication of this "people make the place" view of organizational culture is that the culture of an organization can be strengthened and changed over time by the people who control and lead it.[27] The growth of Google provides a good illustration of the important role a company's founders play in developing shared cultural values that establish a strong organizational culture.

Organizational Ethics

Many cultural values derive from the personality and beliefs of the founder and the top management team and are in a sense out of the control of the organization. These values are what they are because of who the founder and top managers are. Microsoft founder Bill Gates is a workaholic who still often works 18 hours a day. His terminal values for Microsoft are excellence, innovation, and high quality, and the instrumental values he advocates are hard work, creativity, and high standards. Gates expects his employees to put in long workdays because he requires this level of commitment from himself, and he expects them to do everything they can to promote innovation and quality because this is what he does. Employees who do not buy into these values leave Microsoft, and those who remain are pressured by organizational norms to stay on the job after the normal workday is over and to go out of their way to help others and take on new tasks that will help the organization. Cultural values at Microsoft are out of the organization's control because they are based on who Gates is.

An organization can, however, consciously and purposefully develop some cultural values to control members' behavior. Ethical values fall into this category. As discussed in Chapter 2, organizational ethics are the moral values, beliefs, and rules that establish the appropriate way for organizational members to deal with one another and with the organization's stakeholders (see Figure 7.3).

In developing cultural values, top managers must constantly make choices about the right or appropriate thing to do. IBM or Sears, for example, might wonder whether it should develop procedural guidelines for giving advance notice to employees and middle managers about impending layoffs or store closings. Traditionally, companies have been reluctant to do so because they fear employee

The history of Google, the Internet search engine company, began in 1995 when two Stanford graduate computer science students collaborated to develop a new kind of search engine technology. They understood the limitations of existing search engines, and by 1998 they had developed a superior engine that they felt was ready to go online. They raised $1 million from family, friends, and risk-taking "angel" investors to buy the hardware necessary to connect Google to the Internet.

At first, Google answered 10,000 inquires a day, but in a few months it was answering 500,000; by the fall of 1999, 3 million; the fall of 2000, 60 million, and in the spring of 2001 it reached 100 million inquiries per day. In the 2000s, Google has become the leading search engine, and is one of the top five most-used Internet companies; rivals like Yahoo! and Microsoft are working hard to catch up and beat Google at its own game.

Google's explosive growth is largely due to the culture or entrepreneurship and innovation its founders cultivated from the start. Although by 2005 Google had grown to more than 2,000 employees worldwide, its founders claim that it still maintains a small-company feel because its culture empowers its employees, which it calls "staffers" or "Googlers," to create the best software possible. Brin and Page created Google's entrepreneurial culture in several ways.

From the beginning, lacking space and seeking to keep operating costs low, Google staffers worked in "high-density clusters." Three or four employees—each equipped with a high-powered Linux workstation, but sharing a desk, couch, and chairs that were large rubber balls—worked together to improve its technology. Even when Google moved into more spacious surroundings at its "Googleplex" headquarters building, staffers continued to work in shared spaces. Google also designed its building so that staffers are constantly meeting each other in Google's funky lobby, in the Google Café where everyone eats together, in its state-of-the-art recreational facilities, and in its "snack rooms" equipped with bins packed with cereals, gummy bears, yogurt, carrots, and, of course, make-your-own cappuccino. They also created many social gatherings for employees, such as a TGIF open meeting and a twice-weekly outdoor roller hockey game, where staffers are encouraged to bring down the founders.

All this attention to creating what just might be the "grooviest" company headquarters in the world did not come about by chance. Brin and Page knew that Google's most important strength would be its ability to attract the best software engineers in the world and then to motivate them to perform well. Common offices, lobbies, cafes, and so on bring staffers into close contact with each other, which develops collegiality and encourages them to share their new ideas with their colleagues in order to constantly improve search engine technology and find new ways to grow the company. The freedom Google gives its staffers to pursue new ideas is a clear signal of its founders' desire to empower them to be innovative and to look off the beaten path for new ideas. Finally, recognizing that staffers who innovate important new software applications should be rewarded for their achievements, Google's founders also gave them stock in the company, which effectively makes the staffers its owners, as well.

Google's founders' understanding that successful innovation requires the need to build a strong organizational culture has paid off. In August 2004, Google went public and its shares, which were sold at $85 a share, were worth more than $100 by the end of the first day of trading. By December 2005, its shares were over $440! This made Brin and Page's stake in the company worth billions, and many of its employees are now multimillionaires.

Figure 7.3
Factors Influencing the Development of Organizational Ethics

hostility and apathy. In 2001 Ford and Firestone had to decide whether to recall Explorers because burst tires were causing many rollovers, resulting in serious harm or injury to passengers. Similarly, a company has to decide whether to allow its managers to pay bribes to government officials in foreign countries where such payoffs are an illegal yet accepted way of doing business. In such situations, managers deciding on a course of action have to balance the interests of the organization against the interests of other stakeholder groups.[28]

To make these decisions, managers rely on ethical instrumental values embodied in the organization's culture.[29] Such values outline the right and wrong ways to behave in a situation in which an action may help one person or stakeholder group, but hurt another.[30] Ethical values, and the rules and norms that they embody, are an inseparable part of an organization's culture because they help shape the values that members use to manage situations and make decisions.

One of top management's main responsibilities is to ensure that organizational members obey the law. Indeed, in certain situations top managers can be held accountable for the conduct of their subordinates. One of the main ways in which top managers can ensure the legality of organizational behavior is to create an organizational culture that instills ethical instrumental values so that members reflexively deal with stakeholders in an ethical manner. Although some companies, such as Johnson & Johnson and Merck, are well known for their ethical cultures, many organizations do act illegally, immorally, and unethically and take few steps to develop ethical values for their employees to follow. The management team that used to be in control at Beech-Nut put personal interests before customers' health and above the law.

Personal and professional ethics (See Chapter 2) also influence how a person will act in an organization, so an organization's culture is strongly affected by the people who are in a position to establish its ethical values. As we saw earlier, the founder of an organization plays a particularly important role in establishing ethical norms and values.

ORGANIZATIONAL INSIGHT 7.5
Apple Juice or Sugar Water

In the early 1980s Beech-Nut, a maker of baby foods, was in financial trouble as it strove to compete with Gerber Products, the market leader. Threatened with the failure of the company if costs could not be lowered, Beech-Nut entered into an agreement with a low-cost supplier of apple juice concentrate. The agreement was suppose to save the company over $250,000 annually at a time when every dollar counted. Soon, one of Beech-Nut's research and development specialists became concerned about the quality of the concentrate. He believed that it was not made from apples alone but contained large quantities of corn syrup, cane sugar, and malic acid. He brought this information to the attention of top managers at Beech-Nut, but they were obsessed with the need to keep costs down and chose to ignore it. The company continued to produce and sell its product as pure apple juice.

Eventually, investigators from the U.S. Food and Drug Administration (FDA), acting on other information, confronted Beech-Nut with evidence that the concentrate was adulterated. The top managers issued denials and quickly shipped the remaining stock of apple juice to the market before their inventory could be seized.

The research and development specialist who had questioned the purity of the apple juice had resigned from Beech-Nut, but he decided to blow the whistle on the company. He told the FDA that Beech-Nut's top management had known of the problem with the concentrate and had acted to maximize company profits rather than to inform customers about the additives in the apple juice. In 1987, the company pleaded guilty to charges that it had deliberately sold adulterated juice and was fined over $2 million. Its top managers were also found guilty and were sentenced to prison terms (which were eventually overturned on a technicality). Consumer trust in Beech-Nut products plummeted, as did the value of Beech-Nut stock. The company was eventually sold to Ralston Purina, which completely revamped it and its management and promoted strict new ethical values to establish a new culture in the organization.[31]

Property Rights

The values in an organization's culture reflect the ethics of individuals in the organization, of professional groups, and of the society in which the organization exists. The values in an organization's culture also stem from how the organization distributes **property rights**—the rights that an organization gives to its members to receive and use organizational resources.[32] Property rights define the rights and responsibilities of each inside stakeholder group and cause the development of different norms, values, and attitudes toward the organization. Table 7.3 identifies some of the property rights commonly given to managers and the workforce.

Shareholders have the strongest property rights of all stakeholder groups because they own the resources of the company and share in its profits. Top managers often have strong property rights because they are given large amounts of organizational resources, such as high salaries, the rights to large stock options, or golden parachutes, which guarantee them large sums of money if they are fired when their company is taken over. Top managers' rights to use organizational resources are reflected in their authority to make decisions and control organizational resources. Managers are usually given strong rights because if they do not share in the value that the organization creates, they are unlikely to be motivated to work hard on behalf of the organization and its other stakeholders.

An organization's workforce may be given strong property rights, such as a guarantee of lifetime employment and involvement in an employee stock-ownership plan (ESOP) or in a profit-sharing plan. Most workers, however, are not given very strong property rights. Few are given lifetime employment or involved in ESOPs, though they may be guaranteed long-term employment or be eligible for bonuses. Often workers' property rights are simply the wages they earn and the health and pension benefits they receive. Workers' rights to use organizational resources are reflected in their responsibilities in the level of control they have over their tasks.

The distribution of property rights has a direct effect on the instrumental values that shape employee behavior and motivate organizational members.[33] Attempts, to limit employees' benefits and reduce their rights to receive and use resources can often result in hostility and high turnover. However, establishing a company-wide stock option plan, as Google did, and encouraging employees to use organizational resources to find better ways of serving customers can foster commitment and loyalty, as at companies like Southwest Airlines, Microsoft, and Wal-Mart.

The distribution of property rights to different stakeholders determines (1) how effective an organization is and (2) the culture that emerges in the organization. Different property rights systems promote the development of different cultures because they influence people's expectations about how they should behave and what they can expect from their actions. The power of property rights over people's expectations is apparent in a situation that occurred at Apple Computer. For its first 10 years in operation, Apple had never had a layoff, and employees had come to take job security for granted. Although no written document promised job security,

Table 7.3 Common Property Rights Given to Managers and the Workforce

Managers' Rights	Workforce Rights
Golden parachutes	Notification of layoffs
Stock options	Severance payments
Large salaries	Lifetime employment
Control over organizational resources	Long-term employment
Decision making	Pension and benefits
	Employee stock ownership plans
	Participation in decision making.

employees believed they were appreciated and possessed an implicit property right to their jobs. Imagine, then, what happened in 1991 when Apple announced the first layoffs in its history, and several thousand middle- and lower-level personnel were terminated to reduce costs. Employees were dumbfounded: This was not how Apple treated its employees. They demonstrated outside Apple headquarters for several weeks. What effect did the layoff have on Apple's culture? It destroyed the belief that Apple valued its employees, and it destroyed an organizational culture in which employees had been motivated to put forth effort above and beyond their formal job descriptions. At Apple, employee loyalty turned into hostility.

Lucent, WorldCom, Kodak, and other large companies that have recently laid off large numbers of employees are in the peculiar position of needing increased commitment from those who remain in order to turn their businesses around. Can they reasonably expect this? How can they encourage it? Perhaps they can give remaining employees property rights that will engender commitment to the organization. That task is the responsibility of top managers.

Top Management and Property Rights

Top managers are in a strong position to establish the terms of their own employment, their salary and benefits packages, and their termination and pension benefits. Top managers also determine the property rights received by others and thus determine what kind of culture will develop in an organization. The core competences of Apple Computer and Microsoft, for example, depend on the skills and capabilities of their personnel. To gain employee commitment, these organizations reward their top programmers and functional experts highly and give them very strong property rights. Apple has a position called "Apple Fellow," which gives top programmers the right to work on any project in the corporation or start any new project that they find promising. Both corporations reward important employees with large stock options. Thousands of people who joined Microsoft in the 1970s and 1980s, for example, are now multimillionaires as a result of stock options that they received in the past. It is not difficult to imagine how committed they are to the organization. Microsoft founder Bill Gates does not hand out stock options because he is generous, however; he does so because he wants to encourage terminal values of excellence and innovation and instrumental values of creativity and hard work. He also wants to prevent his best people from leaving to found their own firms (which would most likely compete with Microsoft) or going to work for Microsoft's competitors!

Does giving stronger property rights to production line or staff workers produce a culture in which they are committed to the organization and motivated to perform highly? The introduction of an employee stock option plan at Bimba Manufacturing had dramatic effects on employee behavior and the culture of the organization.

As the Bimba story illustrates, changing the property rights system changes the corporate culture by changing the instrumental values that motivate and coordinate employees. At Bimba, gone is the need for close supervision and the use of rigid rules and procedures to control behavior. Instead, coordination is achieved by teams of employees who value cooperation and are motivated by the prospect of sharing in the value created by the new work system.

Can Property Rights Be Too Strong?

As the Bimba story suggests, the worth of a person's behavior and the level of his or her performance are, in part, consequences of the rights the person is given. Sometimes, however, employees can be given property rights that are so strong that the organization and its employees are actually harmed over time.

For example, over the years IBM developed a very conservative culture in which employees had strong rights, such as the implicit promise of lifetime employment. As a result, according to one of its CEOs, Lou Gerstner, IBM employees had become cautious and unwilling to make changes. Gerstner claimed that the organization protected IBM employees so well that they had no motivation to perform, to take risks,

The Bimba Manufacturing Company, based in Monee, Illinois, manufactures aluminum cylinders. Its owner, Charles Bimba, decided to sell the company to its employees by establishing an employee stock-ownership plan. He kept 10% of the shares; the other 90% was sold to employees. Some of the employees' money came from an already existing profit-sharing plan; the rest was borrowed from a bank.

Changes in the company since the ESOP was introduced have been dramatic, and the orientation of the workforce to the organization has totally changed. Previously, the company had two groups of employees: managers who made the rules and workers who carried them out. Workers rarely made suggestions and generally just obeyed orders. Now, cross-functional teams composed of managers and workers meet regularly to discuss problems and find new ways to improve quality. These teams also meet regularly with customers to better meet their needs.

Because of the incentives provided by the new ESOP, management and workers have developed new working relationships based on teamwork to achieve excellence and high quality. Each team hires its own members and spends considerable time socializing new employees in the new culture of the organization. The new cooperative spirit in the plant has forced managers to relearn their roles. They now listen to workers and act as advisers rather than superiors.

So far, changing the company's property rights system has paid off. Sales have increased by 70% and the workforce has grown by 59%. Bimba has expanded to a new, large facility and has opened a facility in England. Furthermore, workers have repaid over 60% of the loan they took out to finance the employee stock purchase. The ESOP has totally changed Bimba's corporate culture and altered the commitment of its workforce. In the words of one worker, it has led to "an intense change in the way we look at our jobs."[34]

or to rock the boat. He suggested that the property rights of IBM employees were too strong.

It is easy to understand how property rights can become too strong. Chapter 5 discussed how people in bureaucracies can come to believe that they own their positions and the rights that go with them. When this happens, people take steps to protect their rights and resist attempts by others to wrest their rights away. The result is conflict, internal power struggles, and a loss of flexibility and innovation as the organization loses sight of its mission because its members are preoccupied with their own—not the organization's—interests. Property rights, therefore, must be assigned on the basis of performance and in a discriminating way. Managers must continually evaluate and address this difficult challenge.

Gerstner took steps to change IBM's property rights system and create an entrepreneurial culture by distributing more rewards based on performance and by eliminating employees' expectations of lifetime employment. To create a certain kind of culture, an organization needs to create a certain kind of property rights system. In part, organizational culture reflects the values that emerge as a result of an organization's property rights system.

Organizational Structure

We have seen how the values that coordinate and motivate employees result from the organization's people, its ethics, and the distribution of property rights among various stakeholders. The fourth source of cultural values is organizational structure. Recall from Chapter 1 that *organizational structure* is the formal system of task and authority relationships that an organization establishes to control its activities. Because different structures give rise to different cultures, managers need to design a certain kind of organizational structure to create a certain kind of organizational culture. Mechanistic structures and organic structures, for example, give rise to totally different sets of cultural values. The values, rules, and norms in a mechanistic structure are different from those in an organic structure.

Recall from Chapter 4 that *mechanistic structures* are tall, highly centralized, and standardized, and *organic structures* are flat and decentralized and rely on mutual adjustment. In a tall, centralized organization, people have relatively little personal autonomy, and desirable behaviors include being cautious, obeying superior authority, and respecting traditions. Thus mechanistic structure is likely to give rise to a culture in which predictability and stability are desired end states. In a flat, decentralized structure, people have more freedom to choose and control their own activities, and desirable behaviors include being creative or courageous and taking risks. Thus an organic structure is likely to give rise to a culture in which innovation and flexibility are desired end states.

An organization's structure can promote cultural values that foster integration and coordination. Out of stable task and role relationships, for example, emerge shared norms and rules that help reduce communications problems, prevent the distortion of information, and speed the flow of information. Moreover, norms, values, and a common organizational language can improve the performance of teams and task forces. It is relatively easy for different functions to share information and trust one another when they share similar cultural values. One reason why product development time is short and the organization is flexible in product team structures and matrix structures is that the reliance on face-to-face contact between functional specialists in teams forces those teams quickly to develop shared values and common responses to problems.

Whether a company is centralized or decentralized also leads to the development of different kinds of cultural values. By decentralizing authority, an organization can establish values that encourage and reward creativity or innovation. The founders of Hewlett-Packard established the "Hewlett-Packard Way," an organizational philosophy that gives employees access to equipment and resources so that they can be creative and conduct their own research informally, outside of their normal job responsibilities. At 3M, employees are informally encouraged to spend 15% of their time working on personal projects. In both these companies, the organizational structure produces cultural values that tell members that it is all right to be innovative and to do things in their own way, as long as their actions are consistent with the good of the organization.

Conversely, in some organizations, it is important that employees not make decisions on their own and that their actions be open to the scrutiny of superiors. In such cases, centralization can be used to create cultural values that reinforce obedience and accountability. For example, in nuclear power plants, values that promote stability, predictability, and obedience to superior authority are deliberately fostered to prevent disasters.[35] Through norms and rules, employees are taught the importance of behaving consistently and honestly, and they learn that sharing information with supervisors, especially information about mistakes or errors, is the only acceptable form of behavior.[36]

In sum, organizational structure affects the cultural values that guide organizational members as they perform their activities. In turn, culture improves the way structure coordinates and motivates organizational resources to help an organization achieve its goals. One source of a company's competitive advantage is its ability to design its structure and manage its culture so that there is a good fit between the two. This gives rise to a core competence that is hard for other organizations to imitate. However, when companies fail to achieve a good fit, or when structural changes produce changes in cultural values, problems start to occur.

CAN ORGANIZATIONAL CULTURE BE MANAGED?

Managers interested in understanding the interplay between an organization's culture and the organization's effectiveness at creating value for stakeholders must take a hard look at all four of the factors that produce culture: the characteristics of organizational members (particularly the founder and top managers), organizational ethics, the property rights system, and organizational structure. Changing a culture can be very difficult because those factors interact and because major alterations are often needed to change an organization's values.[37] To change its culture, an organization might need to redesign its structure and revise the property rights it uses to motivate and reward employees. The organization might also need to change its people, especially its top management team. Keeping in mind the difficulty of managing organizational culture, let's look at how Microsoft's culture evolved as a result of the interaction of the four factors.

As we discussed earlier, Bill Gates's personal values and beliefs and his vision of what Microsoft could achieve form the core of Microsoft's culture, with its terminal values of excellence and innovation. With its initial success established by its MS-DOS and Microsoft Word systems, Microsoft began to attract the best software engineers in the world. Gates was therefore in a position to select those people who bought into his values and who could perform at the level that he and his managers required. Over time, norms based on the need for individual initiative (to enhance the instrumental values of creativity and risk taking) and for teamwork (to enhance cooperation) emerged, and Microsoft built a campus-like headquarters complex to promote the development of an informal atmosphere in which people could develop strong working bonds.

Gates designed an organic structure for Microsoft and kept it as flat and decentralized as possible by using small teams to coordinate work activities. This design encourages risk taking and creativity. He also used a product team structure to reinforce the team atmosphere and norms of "team spirit." Gates also established a culture for innovation by rewarding successful risk taking and creativity with strong property rights. Many key employees receive stock options based on company performance, and all employees are eligible to receive bonuses. Furthermore, Microsoft offers high-quality pensions and benefits and has never had to lay off any employees. Finally, the company has a history of behaving ethically toward its employees and customers. Microsoft's people, its structure, its property rights, and its ethics interact and fit together to make up Microsoft's culture.

Compare Microsoft's culture to the one Louis Gerstner, IBM's former CEO, had to change to turn around the failing company: IBM had a conservative, stable culture produced by (1) property rights tied not to performance but to employee longevity in the organization and (2) a tall, centralized structure that promoted obedience and conformity. The people attracted to and retained by this IBM culture were those who liked working in a stable environment where they knew their place, who accepted the status quo, and who did not mind that the culture limited their opportunities to innovate or be creative. Although there was a match among the factors producing IBM's culture, the culture did not serve the company well. Because its cultural values emphasized stability, IBM was unable to adapt to changes in the environment, such as changes in technology and customer needs.

Can a company maintain a creative, entrepreneurial culture as it grows? Analysts wonder whether Gates has been able to maintain Microsoft's dynamic and freewheeling culture as the company has grown. They believe he has missed many opportunities that have been taken by companies like Google and SAP. For his part, Gates argues that Microsoft's policy of using small product development teams and spinning off into a separate product team any unit that reaches 200 people helps Microsoft preserve its entrepreneurial values and prevents the development of inertia and complacency.

To prevent an organization's culture from changing in ways that reduce effectiveness as the organization grows, top managers must design its structure to offset the control problems that occur with large size and complexity.[38] IBM, for example, is continuously being reorganized into new autonomous business units to keep employees focused on its current problems and to give each unit the opportunity to develop a new culture supportive of values such as customer responsiveness and excellence. IBM also made changes in its property rights system to try to change the cultural values guiding employee behavior; now performance, not seniority, determines the distribution of property rights. Furthermore, IBM operates with a campus-style headquarters building to encourage its members to take a flexible, team-based cross-divisional perspective. By changing the foundations on which a company's old culture was built, top managers can build new, more entrepreneurial cultures, something vital in a highly competitive global environment.

MANAGERIAL IMPLICATIONS

DESIGNING ORGANIZATIONAL CULTURE

1. Try to identify the source of the values and norms of your organization's culture and analyze the relative effects of people, ethics, property rights, and structure on influencing organizational culture.
2. Use this analysis to produce an action plan for redesigning the culture of the organization to improve effectiveness.
3. Be sure that the action plan takes all four factors into consideration, for each one affects the others. Changing one factor alone may not be sufficient to change organizational culture.
4. Make the development of ethical organizational values one of your major priorities.

SOCIAL RESPONSIBILITY

One very important consequence of the values and norms of its culture is an organization's stance with regard to social responsibility. The term *social responsibility* refers to a manager's duty or obligation to make decisions that nurture, protect, enhance, and promote the welfare and well-being of stakeholders and society as a whole. Many kinds of decisions signal an organization's interest in being socially responsible (see Table 7.4).

Approaches to Social Responsibility

Obstructionist approach
The low end of the organizations' commitment to social responsibility.

The strength of an organization's commitment to social responsibility ranges from low to high (see Figure 7.4).[39] At the low end of the range is an **obstructionist approach**. Obstructionist managers choose not to behave in a socially responsible way. Instead, they behave unethically and illegally and do all they can to prevent knowledge of their behavior from reaching other organizational stakeholders and society at large. Managers at the Mansville Corporation adopted this approach when evidence that asbestos causes lung damage was uncovered. Managers at Beech-Nut

Table 7.4 Forms of Socially Responsible Behavior

Managers are being socially responsible and showing their support for their stakeholders when they:

- Provide severance payments to help laid-off workers makes ends meet until they can find another job.
- Provide workers with opportunities to enhance their skills and acquire additional education so they can remain productive and do not become obsolete because of changes in technology.
- Allow employees to take time off when they need to and provide health-care and pension benefits for employees.
- Contribute to charities or support various civic-minded activities in the cities or towns in which they are located. (Target and Levi Strauss both contribute 5% of their profits to support schools, charities, the arts, and other good works.)
- Decide to keep open a factory whose closure would devastate the local community.
- Decide to keep a company' operations in the United States to protect the jobs of American workers rather than move abroad.
- Decide to spend money to improve a new factory so that it will not pollute the environment.
- Decline to invest in countries that have poor human rights records.
- Choose to help poor countries develop an economic base to improve living standards.

Figure 7.4
Approaches to Social Responsibility

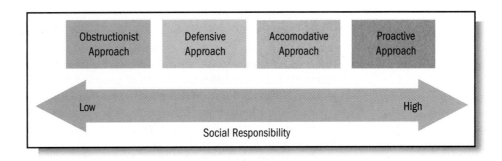

Defensive approach
An approach indicating a commitment to ethical behavior.

Accommodative approach
The acknowledgment of the need to support social responsibility.

Proactive approach
Managers who actively embrace the need to behave in socially responsible ways, go out of their way to learn about the needs of different stakeholder groups, and are willing to utilize organizational resources to promote the interests not only of stockholders but of the other stakeholders.

who sought to hide evidence about the use of corn syrup in their apple juice also adopted this approach. The managers of all these organizations chose an obstructionist approach. The result was not only a loss of reputation but also devastation for their organizations and for all stakeholders involved.

A **defensive approach** indicates at least a commitment to ethical behavior. Defensive managers stay within the law and abide strictly within legal requirements, but make no attempt to exercise social responsibility beyond what the law dictates. Managers adopting this approach do all they can to ensure that their employees behave legally and do not harm others. But when making ethical choices, these managers put the claims and interests of their shareholders first, at the expense of other stakeholders.

The very nature of a capitalist society—in which managers' primary responsibility is to the owners of the corporation, its shareholders—probably encourages the defensive response. Some economists believe that managers in a capitalistic society should always put stockholders' claims first, and that if these choices are not acceptable to other members of society and are considered unethical, then society must pass laws and create rules and regulations to govern the choices managers make.[40] From a defensive perspective, it is not managers' responsibility to make socially responsible choices; their job is to abide by the rules that have been legally established. Thus, defensive managers have little active interest in social responsibility.

An **accommodative approach** is an acknowledgment of the need to support social responsibility. Accommodative managers agree that organizational members ought to behave legally and ethically, and they try to balance the interests of different stakeholders against one another so that the claims of stockholders are seen in relation to the claims of other stakeholders. Managers adopting this approach want to make choices that are reasonable in the eyes of society and want to do the right thing when called on to do so.

Managers taking a **proactive approach** actively embrace the need to behave in socially responsible ways, go out of their way to learn about the needs of different stakeholder groups, and are willing to utilize organizational resources to promote the interests not only of stockholders, but of the other stakeholders as well. Such companies—HP, The Body Shop, McDonald's, Johnson & Johnson—are at the forefront of campaigns for causes such as a pollution-free environment, recycling and conservation of resources, minimizing or avoiding the use of animals in drug and cosmetic testing, and reducing crime, illiteracy, and poverty.

Why Be Socially Responsible?

Several advantages are argued to result when managers and organizations behave in a socially responsible manner. First, workers and society benefit directly, because organizations (rather than the government) bear some of the costs of helping workers. Second, it has been said that if all organizations in a society were socially responsible, the quality of life as a whole would be higher. Indeed, several management experts have argued that the way organizations behave toward their employees determines many of a society's values and norms and the ethics of its citizens. It has been suggested that if all organizations adopted a caring approach and agreed that their responsibility is to promote the interests of their employees, a climate of caring would pervade the wider society.[41] Experts point to Japan, Sweden, Germany, the Netherlands, and Switzerland as countries where organizations are very socially responsible and where, as a result, crime and unemployment rates are relatively low, the literacy rate is relatively high, and sociocultural values promote harmony between different groups of people. Other reasons for being socially responsible are that it is the right thing to do and that companies that act responsibly toward their stakeholders benefit from increasing business and see their profits rise.[42]

Given these advantages, why would anyone quarrel over the pursuit of social responsibility by organizations and their managers? One issue that comes up is that although some stakeholders benefit from managers' commitment to social responsibility, other stakeholders, particularly shareholders, may think they are being harmed when organizational resources are used for socially responsible courses of action. Some people argue that business has only one kind of responsibility: to use its resources for activities that increase its profits and thus reward its stockholders.[43]

How should managers decide which social issues they will respond to and to what extent their organizations should trade profits for social gain? Obviously, illegal behavior should not be tolerated; all managers and workers should be alert to its occurrence and report it promptly. The term **whistle-blower** is used to refer to a person who reports illegal or unethical behavior and takes a stand against unscrupulous managers or other stakeholders who are pursuing their own ends.[44] Laws now exist to protect the interests of whistle-blowers, who risk their jobs and careers to reveal unethical behavior. In part, these laws were enacted because of the experiences of two engineers at Morton Thiokol, who warned that the Challenger space shuttle's O-ring gaskets would be adversely affected by cold weather at launch.[45] Their warnings were ignored by everyone involved in the headlong rush to launch the shuttle. As a result, seven astronauts died when the Challenger exploded shortly after launch in January 1986. Although the actions of the engineers were applauded by the committee of inquiry, their subsequent careers suffered because managers at Morton Thiokol blamed them for damaging the company's reputation and harming its interests.

Another way in which managers can ascertain whether they are acting socially responsibly is to apply ethical standards and values. Managers' own ethics influence their behavior and their own values strongly influence whether they will take a proactive approach to social responsibility. An organization's code of ethics, usually printed in its annual reports and mission statements, also influences how conscientiously managers seek to support the interests of all their stakeholders. Some organizations, like Johnson & Johnson, view the company's code of ethics as the only policy to follow when an ethical dilemma is evident, and they allow this code to govern their choices. Other organizations pay lip service to the organization's ethical code and, as a result, managers facing a moral dilemma seek to protect their own interests first and worry later about how other stakeholders will be affected.[46] When such managers talk about protecting the organization, what they are really talking about is protecting their own interests: their jobs, bonuses, careers, and abilities to use organizational resources for their own ends.

Evidence suggests that managers who behave socially responsibly will, in the long run, most benefit all organizational stakeholders (including stockholders). It appears that socially responsible companies, in comparison with less responsible competitors, are less risky investments, tend to be somewhat more profitable, have a more loyal and committed workforce, and have better reputations, which encourage stakeholders (including customers and suppliers) to establish long-term business relationships with them.[47] Socially responsible companies are also sought out by communities, which encourage such organizations to locate in their cities and offer them incentives such as property-tax reductions and the construction of new roads and free utilities for their plants. Thus, there are many reasons to believe that, over time, strong support of social responsibility confers the most benefits on organizational stakeholders (including stockholders) and on society at large.

Whistle-blowing
Informing (by an employee) an outside person or agency, such as a government agency or a newspaper or television reporter, about an organization's (its managers') illegal or immoral behavior.

SUMMARY

Organizational culture exercises a potent form of control over the interactions of organizational members with each other and with outsiders. By supplying people with a toolbox of values, norms, and rules that tell them how to behave, organizational culture is instrumental in determining how they interpret and react to a situation. Thus an organization's culture can be a source of competitive advantage. Chapter 7 has made the following main points:

1. Organizational culture is a set of shared values that provide organizational members with a common understanding of how they should act in a situation.
2. There are two kinds of organizational values: terminal (a desired end state or outcome) and instrumental (a desired mode of behavior). Ideally, instrumental values help the organization to achieve its terminal goals.
3. Organizational culture affects organizational effectiveness because it can (a) provide an organization with a competitive advantage, (b) improve the way an organizational structure works, and (c) increase the motivation of employees to pursue organizational interests.
4. Culture is transmitted to an organization's members by means of (a) socialization and training programs and (b) stories, ceremonies, and language used by members of the organization.
5. Organizational culture develops from the interaction of (a) the characteristics of organization members, (b) organizational ethics, (c) the property rights distributed among the people in the organization, and (d) organizational structure.
6. Different organizational structures give rise to different patterns of interaction among people. These different patterns lead to the formation of different organizational cultures.
7. Social responsibility is an organization's moral responsibility to stakeholder groups affected by the organization's actions. There are four stances on social responsibility and they have very different implications for organizational behavior.

DISCUSSION QUESTIONS

1. What is the origin of organizational culture? Why do different organizations have different cultures?
2. How do newcomers learn the culture of an organization? How can an organization encourage newcomers to develop (a) an institutionalized role orientation and (b) an individualized role orientation?
3. In what ways can organizational culture increase organizational effectiveness? Why is it important to obtain the right fit between organizational structure and culture?
4. "An organization should always adopt a broad stance on social responsibility." Explain why you agree or disagree with this statement.

ORGANIZATIONAL THEORY IN ACTION

Practicing Organizational Theory: Developing a Service Culture

Form groups of three to five people and discuss the following scenario:

You are the owner/managers of a new five-star resort hotel opening up on the white sand beaches of the western coast of Florida. For your venture to succeed, you need to make sure that hotel employees focus on providing customers with the highest quality customer service possible. You are meeting to discuss how to create a culture that will promote high-quality service, that will encourage employees to be committed to the hotel, and that will reduce the level of employee turnover and absenteeism, which are typically high in the hotel business.

1. What kinds of organizational values and norms encourage employees to behave in ways that lead to high-quality customer service?
2. Using the concepts discussed in this chapter (for example, people, property rights, socialization), discuss how you will create a culture that promotes the learning of these customer service values and norms.

3. Which factor is the most important determinant of the kind of culture you expect to find in a five-star hotel?

The Ethical Dimension #7

The chapter discussed how Arthur Andersen's organizational culture became so strong that some of its partners and their subordinates began to act unethically and pursue their own short-run interests at the expense of other stakeholders. Many employees knew they were doing wrong, but were afraid to refuse to follow orders. At Beech-Nut, the company's ethical values completely broke down: Managers joked about harming stakeholders.

1. Why is it that an organization's values and norms can become too strong and lead to unethical behavior?
2. What steps can a company take to prevent this problem, to stop its values and norms from becoming so inwardly focused that managers and employees lose sight of their obligations to their stakeholders?

Making the Connection #7

Identify an organization that has been trying to change its culture. Describe the culture that it is trying to alter. Why is this culture no longer effective? How has the organization tried to bring about change? How successful has it been?

Analyzing the Organization: Design Module #7

In this module you will analyze the culture of your organization, discuss the characteristic ways in which members act, and its stance on social responsibility.

Assignment

1. Do managers and employees use certain words and phrases to describe the behavior of people in the organization? Are any stories about events or people typically used to describe the way the organization works? (*Hint*: Look at the company's Web page.)
2. How does the organization socialize employees? Does it put them through formal training programs? What kinds of programs are used, and what is their goal?
3. What beliefs and values seem to characterize the way people behave in the organization? How do they affect people's behavior?
4. Given the answers to the first three questions, how would you characterize the organization's culture and the way it benefits or harms the organization? How could the culture be improved?
5. Can you find a written statement of the organization's stance on social responsibility? Are there stories in the press about the company? If there are, what do they say?

CASE FOR ANALYSIS

A Tale of Two Cultures

In an attempt to give Southwest Airlines a competitive advantage based on low-cost, high-quality service, CEO Herbert Kelleher has developed terminal and instrumental values that make Southwest's culture the envy of its competitors. Southwest managers and employees alike are committed to the success of the organization and do all they can to help one another and to provide customers with excellent service (a terminal value). Four times a year, Southwest managers work as baggage handlers, ticket agents, and flight attendants so that they get a feel for the problems facing other employees. An informal norm makes it possible for employees to gather with Kelleher every Friday at noon in the company's Dallas parking lot for a company cookout.

Kelleher keeps the organization as flat and informal as possible, and managers encourage employees to be creative and to develop rules and norms to solve their own problems. To please customers, for example, employees dress up on special days like Halloween and Valentine's Day and wear "fun uniforms" every Friday. In addition, they try to develop innovative ways to improve customer service and satisfaction. All employees participate in a bonus system that bases rewards on company performance, and employees own over 18% of the airline's stock. The entrance hall at company headquarters at Love Field in Dallas is full of plaques earned by employees for their outstanding performance. Everybody in the organization cooperates to achieve Southwest's goal of providing low-cost, high-quality service. The culture of excellence that Southwest has created seems to be working to its advantage. Southwest increased its operating routes and profits every year in the 1990s and is one of the most profitable airlines flying today.

Contrast Southwest's CEO and culture with that of Value Line, Inc. Jean Buttner, publisher of the *Value Line Investment Survey*, has fashioned a culture that the company's employees apparently hate and that no one envies. In her attempt to reduce costs and improve efficiency, she has created instrumental values of frugality and economy that are poisoning employees' attitudes toward the organization. Employees must sign in by 9:00 A.M. every day and sign out when leaving. If they fake their arrival or departure time, they face dismissal. Because at Value Line messy desks are considered signs of being unproductive, Buttner requires department managers to file a "clean surfaces report" every day, certifying that employees have tidied their desks.[48] She keeps salary increases as small as possible and has kept the company's bonus plan and health plan under tight rein.

How have these values paid off? Many highly trained, professional workers have left Value Line because of the hostile atmosphere produced by these "economical" values and by work rules that devalue employees. This turnover has generated discontent among the company's customers. So bad have feelings between employees and Buttner become that employees reportedly put up a notice on their bulletin board criticizing Buttner's management style and suggesting that the company could use some new leadership. Buttner's response to this message from a significant stakeholder group was to remove the bulletin board. Clearly, at Value Line there is no culture of cooperation between managers and employees.

DISCUSSION QUESTIONS

1. List the reasons why Southwest's and Value Line's cultures differ so sharply.
2. Could Value line's next CEO copy Southwest's culture?

REFERENCES

1. L. Smircich, "Concepts of Culture and Organizational Analysis," *Administrative Science Quarterly 28*, (1983), 339–358.
2. S.D.N. Cook and D. Yanow, "Culture and Organizational Learning," *Journal of Management Inquiry*, 2 (1993), 373–390.
3. M. Rokeach, *The Nature of Human Values* (New York: The Free Press, 1973).
4. P. L. Berger and T. Luckman, *The Social Construction of Reality* (Garden City, NY: Anchor Books, 1967).
5. E. H. Schein, "Culture: The Missing Concept in Organization Studies," *Administrative Science Quarterly*, 41 (1996), 229–240.
6. www.corning.com, 2002.
7. www.bankofamerica.com, 2002.
8. J. P. Walsh and G. R. Ungson, "Organizational Memory," *Academy of Management Review*, 1 (1991), 57–91.
9. K. E. Weick, "Organizational Culture as a Source of High Reliability," *California Management Review*, 9 (1984), 653–669.
10. J. A. Chatman and S. G. Barsade, "Personality, Organizational Culture, and Cooperation: Evidence from a Business Simulation," *Administrative Science Theory*, 40 (1995), 423–443.
11. A. Etzioni, *A Comparative Analysis of Organizations* (New York: The Free Press, 1975).
12. G. R. Jones, "Psychological Orientation and the Process of Organizational Socialization: An Interactionist Perspective," *Academy of Management Review*, 8 (1983), 464–474.
13. J. Van Maanen and E. H. Schein, "Towards a Theory of Organizational Socialization," in B. M. Staw, ed., *Research in Organizational Behavior*, vol. 1 (Greenwich, CT: JAI Press, 1979), pp. 209–264.
14. G. R. Jones, "Socialization Tactics, Self-Efficacy, and Newcomers' Adjustments to Organizations," *Academy of Management Review*, 29 (1986), 262–279.
15. Ibid.
16. M. A. Cusumano and R. W. Selby, *Microsoft's Secrets* (New York: The Free Press, 1995).
17. H. M. Trice and J. M. Beyer, "Studying Organizational Culture Through Rites and Ceremonials," *Academy of Management Review*, 9 (1984), 653–669.
18. H. M. Trice and J. M. Beyer, *The Cultures of Work Organizations* (Upper Saddle River, NJ: Prentice Hall, 1993).
19. M. Ramundo, "Service Awards Build Culture of Success," *Human Resources Magazine*, August 1992, pp. 61–63.
20. Trice and Beyer, "Studying Organizational Culture Through Rites and Ceremonials."
21. A. M. Pettigrew, "On Studying Organizational Cultures," *Administrative Science Quarterly*, 24 (1979), 570–582.
22. B. Elgin, "Running the Tightest Ships on the Net," *Business Week*, January 29, 2001, pp. 125–26.
23. B. Schneider, "The People Make the Place," *Personnel Psychology*, 40 (1987), 437–453.
24. E. H. Schein, "The Role of the Founder in Creating Organizational Culture," *Organizational Dynamics*, 12 (1983), 13–28.
25. J. M. George, "Personality, Affect, and Behavior in Groups," *Journal of Applied Psychology*, 75 (1990), 107–116.
26. E. Schein, *Organizational Culture and Leadership*, 2e (San Francisco: Jossey-Bass, 1992).
27. George, "Personality, Affect, and Behavior in Groups"; D. Miller and J. M. Toulouse, "Chief Executive Personality and Corporate Strategy and Structure in Small Firms," *Management Science*, 32 (1986), 1389–1409.
28. R. E. Goodin, "How to Determine Who Should Get What," *Ethics*, July 1975, pp. 310–321.
29. T. M. Jones, "Ethical Decision Making by Individuals in Organizations: An Issue Contingent Model," *Academy of Management Review*, 2 (1991), 366–395.
30. T. L. Beauchamp and N. E. Bowie, eds., *Ethical Theory and Business* (Upper Saddle River, NJ: Prentice Hall, 1979); A. MacIntyre, *After Virtue* (South Bend, IN: University of Notre Dame Press, 1981).
31. "What Led Beech-Nut down the Road to Disgrace," *Business Week*, February 22, 1988, pp. 124–128; "Bad Apples in the Executive Suite," *Consumer Reports*, May 1989, p. 296; R. Johnson, "Ralston to Buy Beech-Nut, Gambling It Can Overcome Apple Juice Scandal," *The Wall Street Journal*, September 18, 1989, p. B11.
32. H. Demsetz, "Towards a Theory of Property Rights," *American Economic Review*, 57 (1967), 347–359.
33. G. R. Jones, "Transaction Costs, Property Rights, and Organizational Culture: An Exchange Perspective," *Administrative Science Quarterly*, 28 (1983), 454–467.
34. "ESOP Brings Change in Corporate Culture," *Employee Benefit Plan Review*, July 1992, pp. 25–26.
35. C. Perrow, *Normal Accidents* (New York: Basic Books, 1984).
36. H. Mintzberg, *The Structuring of Organizational Structures* (Upper Saddle River, NJ: Prentice Hall, 1979).
37. G. Kunda, *Engineering Culture* (Philadelphia: Temple University Press, 1992).
38. J. P. Kotter and J. L. Heskett, *Corporate Culture and Performance* (New York: The Free Press, 1992).
39. E. Gatewood and A. B. Carroll, "The Anatomy of Corporate Social Response," *Business Horizons* (September–October 1981), 9–16.
40. M. Friedman, "A Friedman Doctrine: The Social Responsibility of Business Is to Increase Its Profits," *The New York Times Magazine*, September 13, 1970, p. 33.
41. W. G. Ouchi, *Theory Z: How American Business Can Meet the Japanese Challenge* (Reading, MA: Addison-Wesley, 1981).
42. J. B. McGuire, A. Sundgren, and T. Schneewis, "Corporate Social Responsibility and Firm Financial Performance," *Academy of Management Review, 31* (1988), 854–872.
43. Friedman, "A Friedman Doctrine," pp. 32, 33, 122, 124, 126.
44. J. B. Dozier and M. P. Miceli, "Potential Predictors of Whistleblowing: A Prosocial Perspective," *Academy of Management Review*, 10 (1985), 823–836; J. P. Near and

M. P. Miceli, "Retaliation Against Whistleblowers: Predictors and Effects," *Journal of Applied Psychology, 71* (1986), 137–145.

45. "The Uncommon Good," *The Economist*, August 19, 1995, p. 55.

46. T. L. Beauchamp and N. E. Bowie, eds., *Ethical Theory and Business* (Upper Saddle River, NJ: Prentice Hall, 1979).

47. E. D. Bowman, "Corporate Social Responsibility and the Investor," *Journal of Contemporary Business* (Winter 1973), 49–58.

48. A. Bianco, "Value Line: Too Lean, Too Mean," *Business Week*, March 16, 1992, pp. 104–106.

Chapter 8

Organizational Design and Strategy in a Changing Global Environment

Learning Objectives

Finding the right strategy to respond to changes taking place in the environment (such as changes in the needs of customers or actions of competitors overseas) is a complex issue facing managers. In a changing global environment, it is easy to make mistakes, and managers must constantly monitor their strategies and structures to make sure that they are working effectively both at home and abroad.

After studying this chapter you should be able to:

1. Identify the ways managers can use functional-level strategy to develop core competences that allow an organization to create value and give it a competitive advantage.

2. Explain how managers can combine their organization's distinctive competences to create a successful business-level strategy that allows them to compete for scarce resources.

3. Differentiate among the corporate-level strategies companies can use to enter new domains where they can continue to grow and create value.

4. Appreciate the importance of linking strategy to structure and culture at each level—functional, business, and corporate—to increase the ability to create value.

5. Understand how global expansion strategies allow an organization to seek new opportunities to exploit its core competences to create value for stakeholders.

Strategy
The specific pattern of decisions and actions that managers take to sue core competences to achieve a competitive advantage and outperform competitors.

Core competences
The skills and abilities in value creation activities that allow a company to achieve superior efficiency, quality, innovation, or customer responsiveness.

As discussed in Chapter 1, an organization's **strategy** is a specific pattern of decisions and actions that managers take to use core competences to achieve a competitive advantage and outperform competitors.[1] An organization develops a strategy to increase the value it can create for its stakeholders. In this context, value is anything that satisfies the needs and desires of organizational stakeholders. Stockholders want a company to set goals and develop an action plan that maximizes the long-run profitability of the company and the value of their stock. Customers are likely to respond to a strategy that is based on the goal of offering high-quality products and services at appropriate prices.

Through its strategy, an organization seeks to use and develop core competences to gain a competitive advantage so that it can increase its share of scarce resources in its environment. Recall that **core competences** are skills and abilities in value-creation activities, such as manufacturing, marketing, or R&D, that allow a company to achieve superior efficiency, quality, innovation, or customer responsiveness. An organization that possesses superior core competences can outperform its rivals. Organizational strategy allows an organization to shape and manage its domain to exploit its existing core competences and develop new competences that make it a better competitor for resources.

McDonald's, for example, used its existing core competences in the production of fast food such as burgers and fries to provide fast food for the breakfast segment of the fast-food domain. By investing in food-testing facilities, McDonald's developed R&D competences that led to the development of breakfast items (such as the Egg McMuffin) that could be produced quickly. By using its existing core competences in new ways, and by developing new competences, McDonald's created a new line of breakfast food, which contributes 35% to its revenues. Similarly, Gillette applied its skills in marketing razor blades to selling men's toiletries and expanded its domain into toiletries.

The more resources an organization can obtain from the environment, the better able it is to set ambitious long-term goals and then develop a strategy and invest resources to create core competences to allow it to achieve those goals. In turn, improved competences give an organization a competitive advantage, which allows the organization to attract new resources—for example, new customers, highly qualified employees, or new sources of financial support. Figure 8.1 shows this cyclical value creation process.

Sources of Core Competences

The ability to develop a strategy that allows an organization to create value and outperform competitors is a function of the organization's core competences. The strength of its core competences is a product of the specialized resources and coordination abilities that it possesses and other organizations lack.[2]

Specialized Resources

Functional resources
The skills possessed by an organization's functional personnel.

Two kinds of resources give an organization a competitive advantage: functional resources and organizational resources. **Functional resources** are the skills possessed by an organization's functional personnel. The skills of Microsoft's software design groups constitute Microsoft's single biggest functional resource. The quality of 3M's R&D department is the source of 3M's continued growth. Procter & Gamble's skill in new product development is P&G's greatest functional resource. High-quality functional resources, however, are not enough to give an organization a competitive advantage. To be a source of competitive advantage, a function's core competence must be unique or special and difficult to imitate.[3] Microsoft's claim to uniqueness rests in the breadth and depth of the software talent that it possesses. In theory, a rich competitor like IBM could come along and buy up Microsoft's best people, or

Figure 8.1
The Value Creation Cycle

Ample resources, a well-thought-out strategy, and distinctive competences give an organization a competitive advantage, which facilitates the acquisition of still more resources.

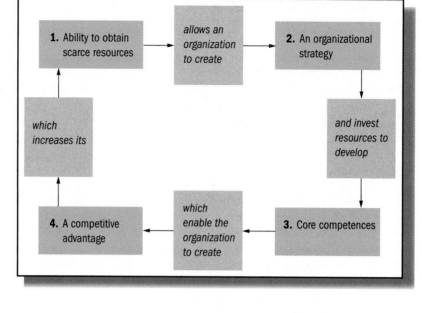

DuPont could lure away 3M's scientists. If that were to happen, those companies' claims to uniqueness would disappear. To maintain its long-term competitive advantage, an organization needs to protect the source of its functional competences. That is why Microsoft gives its best people strong property rights, including making them owners in the company, and why 3M is well known for its long-term employment policies.

Organizational resources
The attributes that give an organization a competitive advantage such as the skills of the top-management team or possession of valuable and scare resources.

Organizational resources are the attributes that give an organization a competitive advantage. They include the skills of a company's top management team, the vision of its founder or CEO, and the possession of valuable and scarce resources such as land, capital reserves, and plant equipment. They also include intangibles such as a company's brand name and its corporate reputation.[4] Like functional resources, to provide a competitive advantage, organizational resources must be unique or difficult to imitate. When organizations can hire away one another's managers, or when any organization can buy the most advanced computer-controlled manufacturing technology from Hitachi or Caterpillar, organizational resources are not unique and do not give an organization a competitive advantage. However, brand names like Coca-Cola and Levi Strauss and reputations such as Toyota's and Microsoft's are organizational resources that are unique and difficult to imitate. Obtaining those resources would entail buying the whole company, not just hiring away individual managers.

Coordination Abilities

Coordination ability
An organization's ability to coordinate its functional and organizational resources to create maximal value.

Another source of core competences is **coordination ability**, an organization's ability to coordinate its functional and organizational resources to create maximal value. Effective coordination of resources (achieved through the control provided by organizational structure and culture) leads to a competitive advantage.[5] The control systems that an organization uses to coordinate and motivate people at the functional and organizational levels can be a core competence that contributes to the organization's overall competitive advantage. Similarly, the way an organization decides to centralize or decentralize authority or the way it develops and promotes shared cultural values increases its effectiveness and allows the organization to manage and protect its domain better than its competitors can protect theirs. Microsoft designs its structure and culture around small teams in order to coordinate activities in a way that facilitates the rapid development and launch of new products.

An organization's ability to use its structure and culture to coordinate its activities is also important at the functional and organizational levels.[6] The way an organization coordinates people and resources within functions determines the strength of its core competences. For example, several organizations have access to fast-food production technology (a functional resource) similar to the technology that McDonald's uses, but none has been able to imitate the rules, standard operating procedures, and norms that make McDonald's production operations so efficient. Competitors have been unable to duplicate the way McDonalds' coordinates people and resources that enables it to produce hamburgers so efficiently and reliably.

Similarly, at the organizational level, the ability to use structure and culture to coordinate and integrate activities between departments or divisions gives some organizations a core competence and thus a competitive advantage. For example, the success of 3M and Procter & Gamble can be explained in part by their ability to develop integrating mechanisms that allow their marketing, product development, and manufacturing departments to combine their skills to develop innovative products. Similarly, PepsiCo's success stems in part from its sharing of resources among its different divisions (Pepsi-Cola, Frito-Lay, and so on).

Although many functional and organizational resources are not unique and can be imitated, an organization's ability to coordinate and motivate its functions and departments is difficult to imitate. It might be possible to buy the functional expertise or technical knowledge of 3M or Microsoft, but the purchase would not include access to the practices and methods that either organization uses to coordinate its resources. These intangible practices are embedded in the way people interact in an organization—in the way organizational structure controls behavior—and they make these companies successful competitors.

Global Expansion and Core Competences

Expanding globally into overseas markets can be an important facilitator of the development of an organization's core competences. Figure 8.2 summarizes four ways in which global expansion allows an organization to create value for its stakeholders.

Transferring Core Competences Abroad
Value creation at the global level begins when an organization transfers a core competence in one or more of its functions to an overseas market to produce cheaper or improved products that will give the organization a low-cost or differentiation advantage over its competitors in that market. For example, Microsoft, with its competence in the production of technologically advanced software, takes this differentiation advantage and produces software tailored to the needs of consumers in different countries. As a result of the transfer of its core competences abroad, over 50% of Microsoft's revenue comes from overseas sales.

Establishing a Global Network
Generally, when an organization decides to transfer its competences abroad, it locates its value-creation activities in countries where economic, political, and cultural conditions are likely to enhance its low-cost or differentiation advantage. It then

Figure 8.2
The Creation of Value Through Global Expansion

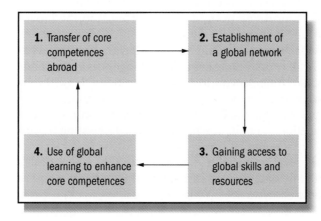

establishes a global network—sets of task and reporting relationships among managers, functions, and divisions that link an organization's value-creation activities around the world. To lower costs, an organization may locate its value-creation functions in the countries in which factor costs—the costs of raw materials, unskilled or skilled labor, land, and taxes—are lowest. To lower costs, a video game company like Nintendo may perform its assembly operations in one country and its design operations in another, have its headquarters in a third country, and buy its inputs and raw materials from still other countries. To link these far-flung activities, the organization creates a global network.

Gaining Access to Global Resources and Skills

An organization with a global network has access to resources and skills throughout the world. Because each country has unique economic, political, and cultural conditions, different countries have different resources and skills that give them a competitive advantage. So, for example, a U.S. organization is likely to benefit from establishing itself in countries with low-cost or differentiation core competences so that it can gain access to and learn how to develop these competences. If organizations in one country have an R&D competence, it would pay a U.S. company to establish operations in that country to gain access to the competence. Japan, for example, has skills in "lean" production and total quality manufacturing, and Kodak, IBM, Ford, and other companies established divisions in Japan to learn these skills.

Toys"Я"Us, the world's largest toy retailer, is one U.S. company that has benefited from a global network. The company established a network of stores throughout Europe to take advantage of its core competence in the distribution and retailing of toys. While establishing a network of suppliers in Europe, Toys"Я"Us found many new, high-quality toys, produced by German and Swiss companies, that it believed would appeal to American consumers; arranged to sell these toys in its American stores; and thus enhanced its differentiation advantage, creating more value.

Using Global Learning to Enhance Core Competences

Organizations set up their global activities to gain access to knowledge that will allow them to improve their core competences. The access to global resources and skills that a global network provides exposes an organization to new ways of improving itself. After an organization masters these new skills, it can transfer them to its domestic base to enhance its core competences and then transfer its enhanced competences back to its overseas operations to increase its competitive advantage abroad. For example, after World War II, the founders of Toyota, Panasonic, and other Japanese companies came to the United States to learn American production and marketing methods, which they then took back to Japan. They were not content just to learn the new techniques, however: They spent considerable time and effort trying to improve them. The engineers who founded Toyota studied GM's and Ford's production techniques and took what they had learned back to Japan, where they improved upon it and adapted it to the Japanese environment. As a result, Japanese companies obtained a competitive advantage over U.S. companies, which made no attempt to improve the techniques they were using.

Of course, there are certain dangers associated with outsourcing important functional competencies to companies abroad. First, a company risks losing control of its technology by sharing it, and its partner might try to improve upon it, and even compete with the company in the future. Second, and related, if a company outsources a functional activity it will no longer be investing resources to improve it, so it is giving away a potential source of competitive advantage in this future. For these reasons organizations need to consider carefully which skills and competencies they should nurture and protect and which they should allow other companies to perform to reduce their costs.

Four Levels of Strategy

An organization should match its strategy and structure so that it can create value from its functional and organizational resources. But where is an organization's strategy created, and by whom? Strategy is formulated at four organizational levels: the functional, business, corporate, and global levels. An organization's ability to create value at one level is an indication of its ability to manage the value-creation process at the other levels.

Functional-level strategy is a plan of action to strengthen an organization's functional and organizational resources, as well as its coordination abilities, in order to create core competences.[7] DaimlerChrysler, for example, invests heavily to improve its skills in R&D and product design, and Coca-Cola invests heavily to devise innovative approaches to marketing.

To strengthen their technical and human resources, functional managers train and develop subordinates to ensure that the organization has skills that match or exceed the skills of its competitors. Another part of the functional manager's job is to scan and manage the functional environment to ensure that the organization knows what is going on both inside and outside its domain.

R&D functional managers, for example, need to understand the techniques and products of their rivals. R&D functional managers at car companies routinely buy competitors' cars and strip them down to their component parts to study the technology and design that went into their manufacture. Taking this information, they can imitate the best aspects of competitors' products. It is also the job of R&D experts to scan other industries to find innovations that may help their company. Innovations in the computer software and microchip industries, for example, are important in product development in the car industry. If all of the functional managers in an organization monitor their respective functional environments and develop their functional resources and abilities, the organization will be better able to manage the uncertainty of its environment.[8]

Business-level strategy is a plan to combine functional core competences in order to position the organization so that it has a competitive advantage in its domain.[9] Mercedes-Benz takes its skills in R&D and positions itself in the luxury segment of the car market. Coca-Cola uses its marketing skills to defend its niche against Pepsi-Cola.

Business-level strategy is the responsibility of the top management team (the CEO and vice presidents in charge of various functions). Their job is to decide how to position the organization to compete for resources in its environment. CBS, NBC, and ABC, for example, compete with each other and with Fox, CNN, and Turner Broadcasting to attract viewers (customers). Programming is the key variable that these companies can manipulate. They rely on functional experts in their news, documentary, comedy, and soap opera departments (among others) to scan the environment and identify future viewing trends so that they can commission programs that will give them a competitive advantage. Because all of the networks are doing this and are trying to outguess their rivals, programming is a complex and uncertain process.

Corporate-level strategy is a plan to use and develop core competences so that the organization not only can protect and enlarge its existing domain but can also expand into new domains.[10] Mercedes-Benz used its competences in R&D and product development to enter the household products and aerospace industries. Coca-Cola took its marketing skills and applied them globally in the soft-drink industry.

Corporate-level strategy is the responsibility of corporate-level managers—the top management team of a multibusiness organization. Their responsibility is to take the value-creation skills present in the divisions and in corporate headquarters and combine them to improve the competitive position of each division and of the organization as a whole. Corporate strategists use the combined resources of the organization to create more value than could be obtained if each division operated alone

---

Functional-level strategy
A plan of action to strengthen an organization's functional and organizational resources, as well as its coordination abilities, in order to create core competences.

Business-level strategy
A plan to combine functional core competences in order to position the organization so that it has a competitive advantage in its domain.

Corporate-level strategy
A plan to use and develop core competences so that the organization can not only protect and enlarge its existing domain but can also expand into new domains.

---

and independently. For example, Honda takes its strengths in engine production and uses them to produce many different kinds of products such as cars, motorbikes, jet skis, and lawnmowers, creating value in many different markets.

Finally, **global expansion strategy** involves choosing the best strategy to expand into overseas markets to obtain scarce resources and develop core competences, as discussed earlier. How does strategy at each level advance the goal of creating value?

FUNCTIONAL-LEVEL STRATEGY

The strategic goal of each function is to create a core competence that gives the organization a competitive advantage. As we have seen, McDonald's production and marketing functions have given the organization important core competences. No competitor can match the efficiency of McDonald's production process, and no competitor has developed the brand-name reputation that McDonald's enjoys.

An organization creates value by applying its functional skills and knowledge to inputs and transforming them into outputs of finished goods and services. To gain a competitive advantage, an organization must be able to do at least one of the following: (1) perform functional activities at a cost lower than that of its rivals or (2) perform functional activities in a way that clearly differentiates its goods and services from those of its rivals—by giving its products unique qualities that customers greatly desire.[11]

Strategies to Lower Costs or Differentiate Products

Any function that can lower the cost at which a product is produced or that can differentiate a product adds value to the product and to the organization. Table 8.1 summarizes the ways in which different organizational functions can advance the goal of value creation.

The manufacturing function can lower the costs of production by pioneering the adoption of the most efficient production methods, such as computer-controlled flexible manufacturing systems. Because manufacturing skills and competence can improve product quality and reliability, manufacturing can also contribute to product differentiation.[12] Sony and Toyota, for example, lead the world in lean manufacturing techniques, which both reduce production costs and increase quality by lowering the number of defects. Manufacturing thus gives Sony and Toyota products a low-cost advantage and a differentiation advantage.

Table 8.1 Low-Cost and Differentiation Advantages Resulting from Functional-Level Strategy

VALUE-CREATING FUNCTION	SOURCE OF LOW-COST ADVANTAGE	SOURCE OF DIFFERENTIATION ADVANTAGE
Manufacturing	• Development of skills in flexible manufacturing technology	• Increase in product quality and reliability
Human resource management	• Reduction of turnover and absenteeism	• Hiring of highly skilled personnel • Development of innovative training programs
Materials management	• Use of just-in-time inventory system/computerized warehousing • Development of long-term relationships with suppliers and customers	• Use of company reputation and long-term relationships with suppliers and customers to provide high-quality inputs and efficient distribution and disposal of outputs
Sales and marketing	• Increased demand and lower production costs	• Targeting of customer groups • Tailoring products to customers • Promoting brand names
Research and development	• Improved efficiency of manufacturing technology	• Creation of new products • Improvement of existing products

On the input side, the human resource management (HRM) function can lower costs by designing appropriate control and reward systems to increase employee motivation and reduce absenteeism and turnover.[13] HRM can contribute to differentiation by selecting and hiring high-quality employees and managers and by running innovative training programs. The use of employee stock-ownership plans, the linking of pay to performance for different job categories, and the development of flexible work hours to allow employees to dovetail work activities with nonwork obligations are all ways in which the HRM function can advance the cause of value creation. Google, IBM, Xerox, and other companies have developed sophisticated HRM systems for selecting and training their employees.

The role of materials management on both the input and the output sides is also crucial. Just-in-time inventory systems and computerized warehousing reduce the costs of carrying and shipping inventory. Purchasing managers' skills in developing long-term links with suppliers and distributors and in fostering an organization's reputation can lead to a low-cost or differentiation advantage.[14] Suppliers who trust an organization may offer more favorable payment terms or be more responsive to the organization when it needs more or different types of inputs in a hurry. The quality of a company–supplier relationship can also affect the quality of inputs. A supplier has more incentive to invest in specialized equipment to produce higher quality inputs if it trusts the organization.[15] Highly skilled purchasing negotiators may be able to strike good contract terms with suppliers, too.

VF Company, the clothes manufacturer that makes Lee and Wrangler jeans, has developed a low-cost core competence on the output side of the value-creation process. VF Company has a state-of-the-art inventory control system. A computer network links its manufacturing and distribution plants directly to its retail customers. When a K-mart customer buys a pair of VF jeans, for example, a record of the sale is transmitted electronically from K-mart to a VF warehouse, which restocks the retailer within five days. When a specified number of garments have been shipped from the VF warehouse, a reorder is automatically placed with the manufacturing plant. This system allows the VF organization to maintain a 97% in-stock rate (the industry average is 70%) and reduce lost sales for both the retailer and the manufacturer.

At the output end of the value-creation process, the skills and expertise of sales and marketing can contribute directly to a low-cost or differentiation advantage. A core competence in marketing can lower the cost of value-creation activities. Suppose a marketing department devises a campaign that significantly increases the sales of a product and, as a result, the organization's market share steadily rises. As the organization expands its output to satisfy the increased demand, it is likely to obtain manufacturing economies of scale, and its costs are likely to fall. Sony and Panasonic have a low-cost advantage because their marketing and sales efforts have developed global markets whose enormous size enables the companies to produce huge volumes of a product at lower and lower unit costs.

Marketing and sales help differentiate products because they tell customers about why one company's products are better than another's. They target customer groups and discover, analyze, and transmit to the product development and R&D departments the needs of customers so that those functions can design new products to attract more customers.[16] A core competence in marketing can allow an organization to discover and respond quickly to customer needs. This speed gives the organization's products a differentiated appeal. Coca-Cola, Philip Morris, and Campbell's Soup are all known for innovative marketing that constantly promotes their brand names and protects their domains from competitors.

Research and development can also contribute significantly to an organization's value-creation activities.[17] R&D can reduce costs by developing cheaper ways of making a product. Skills in R&D have allowed Japanese companies to develop low-cost, flexible manufacturing techniques that are being copied by Xerox, HP DaimlerChrysler, and other U.S. manufacturers. A core competence in R&D that results in the improvement of existing products or the creation of new products gives an organization a strong competitive advantage through differentiation. Intel's

Google, the search engine company, has a bold mission: "to organize the world's information and make it universally accessible and useful." To accomplish this, Google has taken its core competences in developing superior online search engines, which can collect much more customer-relevant information from the billions of pages on the World Wide Web (WWW), and begun to apply these skills to collecting other types of information. Google plans to use its expertise to make digital copies of media such as books and written documents, pictures and videos, and music and other audio content such as plays and musicals; store them on its Web site; and then make them accessible to the 80 million people who use its website each month.[18]

To achieve this, Google has organized its IT specialists into project teams to manage the collection and digital codification of these different kinds of media content. In the process, it is rapidly developing its functional skills in this crucial software domain, a domain that has now been entered by companies like Yahoo! and Microsoft. These companies want to develop digital search and recording capabilities to obtain the billions of dollars in online advertising revenues that are a function of the number of people who visit a company's website. Google will provide this digital information free to customers, but its reward for creating all this value for customers will be billions in advertising revenues.

So far, Google's strategy has worked and its stock price has soared, although it has encountered resistance from copyright holders. Even so, its competitors are rushing to develop their own competencies in this area. Some analysts believe that these competencies might lead Google to overtake Microsoft as the dominant software company in the years ahead when all kinds of information, even information that is now stored on PCs, becomes stored on the WWW. Indeed, in 2006 Google purchased the online word processing company Upstartle so that it can provide its users with word processing capabilities over the WWW and the ability to store documents on Google's servers. Will we need a PC in the years ahead or just a wireless PDA to connect to the WWW?

creation of faster and improved microchips is an example of incremental product improvement. CD-ROM technology developed by Microsoft and other companies has led to the birth of a new generation of computer products. All makers of personal computers rush to modify their products to use a new chip; otherwise, they fear, their products are likely to lose their differentiated appeal. One company that has developed functional-level strategies to take advantage of, and to strengthen, its core competencies is Google, profiled in the preceding organizational insight.

Functional-Level Strategy and Structure

Every function in an organization can develop a core competence that allows an organization to perform value-creation activities at a cost lower than its rivals or that allows it to create clearly differentiated products, such as Google's. One goal of an organization is to provide its functions with the resources and the setting they need to develop superior skills and expertise. Thus organizational structure and culture are very important to the development of functional-level strategy. We first consider structure.

The strength of a function's core competence depends not only on the function's resources, but also on its ability to coordinate the use of its resources. An organization's coordination abilities are, in turn, a product of its structure.[19] In Chapter 4, we discussed Lawrence and Lorsch's findings about how the degree of functional differentiation in the production, sales, and research and development departments within an organization and the extent of integration among those functions directly affect organizational performance. In the most effective organizations, each of the three departments develops an orientation specific to its functional tasks and develops its own ways of responding to its particular functional environment.

According to contingency theory, an organization's design should permit each function to develop a structure that suits its human and technical resources. We will continue to follow the contingency theory approach as we examine how to design a structure that allows the R&D, manufacturing, and sales functions to develop core competences.[20] Figure 8.3 summarizes the characteristics of structures that support the development of core competences by those three functions.

Figure 8.3
Structural Characteristics Associated with the Development of Core Competences in Production, Sales, and Research and Development

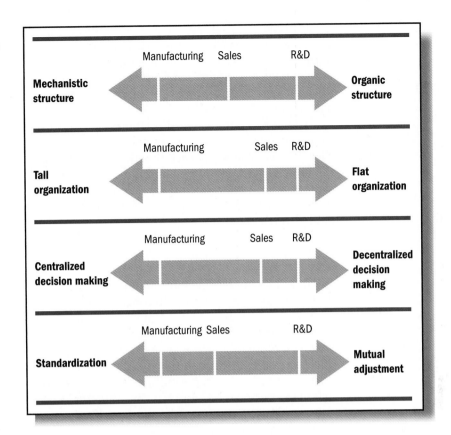

Successful research and development reflects the ability of R&D experts to apply their skills and knowledge in innovative ways and to combine their activities with technical resources to produce new products. The structure most conducive to the development of functional abilities in R&D is a flat, decentralized structure in which mutual adjustment among teams is the main means of coordinating human and technical resources. This is the kind of setting that Google has developed. In such an organic structure, functional norms and values based on self-control and team control are likely to emerge, and a core competence in R&D is likely to emerge and strengthen over time.

What sort of structure supports the development of a core competence in production? Traditionally, the manufacturing function has used a tall hierarchy in which decision making is centralized and the speed of the production line controls the pace of work.[21] Standardization is achieved through the use of extensive rules and procedures, and the result of these design choices is a mechanistic structure. Has such a structure led to a core competence in manufacturing for U.S. companies? If we compare U.S. and Japanese manufacturing companies' competencies today, we see that U.S. companies still lag behind, although they have made major advances in the last decade. What do the Japanese do differently? The manufacturing function in Japanese companies has always had a more organic structure than the manufacturing function in U.S. companies: It is flatter, more decentralized, and relies more on mutual adjustment.

A core competence based on coordination abilities in sales is another important source of competitive advantage that should be planned for in an organization's strategy. Typically, the sales function uses a flat, decentralized structure to coordinate its activities, because incentive pay systems, rather than direct supervision by managers, are the primary control mechanism in sales settings.[22] Salespeople are generally paid on the basis of how much they sell, and information about customer needs and changing customer requirements is relayed to the salespeople's superiors through a standardized reporting system. Because salespeople often work alone, mutual adjustment is relatively unimportant. Thus, the structure of the sales function is likely to be relatively mechanistic, compared to that used by the R&D function, but not as mechanistic as that used by manufacturing.

In some sales settings, however, a differentiated appeal to customers is necessary. Luxury department stores such as Nordstrom and Neiman-Marcus do not use incentive compensation. In such settings, the last thing the organization wants to do is encourage a standardized hard sell to customers. Instead, it wants salespeople to develop competence in a sales technique based on a courteous, personalized, customer-oriented approach.

The same strategic considerations shape the structure of other organizational functions—accounting, human resources, materials management, and so on. The coordination abilities of each function reflect the skill with which managers design the functional structure to suit the resources the function uses in its value-creation activities. The greater the organization's skills at coordinating functional resources, the stronger the core competences the organization develops and the greater its competitive advantage.

Functional-Level Strategy and Culture

The development of functional abilities that lead to core competences is also a result of the culture that emerges in a function or department. Recall from Chapter 7 that organizational culture is a set of shared values that organizational members use when they interact with one another and with other stakeholders. What is the importance of culture for functional-level strategy? A competitor can easily imitate another organization's structure, but it is very difficult for a competitor to imitate another organization's culture, for culture is embedded in the day-to-day interactions of functional personnel. Culture is very difficult to control and manage, let alone imitate or copy, so a company that has an effective culture has an important source of competitive advantage.[23]

Many organizations imitated GM and DuPont and moved to a multidivisional structure to improve their ability to control their operations. Organizations can also imitate one another's incentive pay systems. GM has moved to give its managers stock options like those offered by its competitors, and retail stores have copied Wal-Mart's policy of establishing an employee stock-ownership plan. K-mart, however, despite changes to its structure, found it impossible to imitate Wal-Mart's cultural values of thrift and economy, and GM (except for its Saturn plant) does not operate like Toyota, even though it has imitated many of Toyota's operating systems. The reason for such differences (despite structural similarities) is that the coordination abilities that stem from an organization's culture emerge gradually and are a product of many factors: an organization's property rights system, its structure, its ethics, and the characteristics of its top management team. Because these factors can be combined in many different ways, reproducing another organization's culture is difficult.

To develop functional abilities and produce a core competence, it is necessary to choose the property rights, functional structure, and functional managers that seem most likely to enhance a function's coordination ability. We just saw that R&D uses a flat, decentralized structure and small teams to create norms and values that emphasize teamwork and cooperation. There are other ways in which an organization can build a culture to reinforce those norms and values. Employees can be given strong property rights, including job tenure and a share in the organizational profits; and an organization can recruit people who share its terminal values and socialize them to its functional instrumental values.[24] Microsoft and Google deliberately create an entrepreneurial culture by using small teams to socialize IT specialists to their instrumental values of hard work and cooperation. The same is true in biotech companies like Amgen and Genentech, and consumer products companies like Sony and Samsung.

The coordination abilities of the manufacturing function are also affected by its culture. In some manufacturing cultures (as in the United States, traditionally), the focus is on reducing the level of skill required to perform a task, transferring control to managers, and creating a mechanistic hierarchy in which workers have minimal control over tasks. In such settings, management develops a culture based on values of economy to reduce production costs. As we saw earlier, however, empowering workers and developing cultural values and norms that encourage participation, cooperation, and commitment may be the source of the increased product quality traditionally enjoyed by Japanese automakers. Honda claims that its American manufacturing plant can produce cars more cheaply than its Japanese plants. Honda empowers its workers, involves them in decision making, and uses a pay system based on performance. When demand for a particular Honda model, such as the Accord, falls because the company will soon introduce a new model, Honda shows its commitment to its U.S. workforce by using the downtime in production to train the workers to make a different car model, or repair broken machinery, rather than laying them off until demand for the new model increases. Similarly, at GM's Saturn plant, values and norms based on employee involvement have dramatically increased product quality. The kinds of abilities that a function develops are a product of organizational design decisions about structure and culture.

In sum, to create value at the functional level, the organizational strategy must allow and encourage each function to develop a core competence in lowering costs or differentiating its products from those of competitors. Ultimately, the sources of core competences lie in the resources that the organization assigns to each function and in the abilities of functional experts to coordinate those resources. To gain a competitive advantage, an organization needs to design its functional structure and culture to provide a setting in which core competences develop. The more a function's core competence is based on coordination abilities embedded in the way people in the organization interact, the more difficult it is for competing organizations to duplicate the core competence and the greater is the organization's competitive advantage.

MANAGERIAL IMPLICATIONS

FUNCTIONAL-LEVEL STRATEGY

1. As a member or manager of a function, identify the functional resources or coordination abilities that give your function a core competence. Having identified the sources of your function's core competence, establish a plan to improve or strengthen them, and create a set of goals to measure your progress.
2. Study your competitors and the methods and practices they use to control their functional activities. Pick your most effective competitor, study its methods, and use them as a benchmark for what you wish to achieve in your function.
3. Analyze the way your functional structure and culture affect functional resources and abilities. Experiment to see whether changing a component of structure or culture can enhance your function's core competence.

BUSINESS-LEVEL STRATEGY

At the business level, the task facing the organization is to take the core competences created by the functions and combine them to take advantage of opportunities in the environment. Strategists at the business level select and manage the domain in which the organization uses its value-creation resources and coordination abilities to obtain a competitive advantage.[25] For example, core competences in three functions—manufacturing, marketing, and materials management—jointly give McDonald's a competitive advantage over rivals such as Burger King and Wendy's. Obtaining a competitive advantage is important because, as we noted in Chapter 3, organizations in the same environment (for example, fast food) are in competition for scarce resources. Any organization that fails to devise a business-level strategy to attract resources is at a disadvantage vis-à-vis its rivals and in the long run is likely to fail. Thus the organization needs a business-level strategy that does both of the following: (1) selects the domain the organization will compete in and (2) positions the organization so that it can use its resources and abilities to manage its specific and general environments in order to protect and enlarge that domain.

Strategies to Lower Costs or Differentiate Products

We have seen that the two basic ways in which an organization can create value are by reducing the cost of its value-creation activities and by performing those activities in a way that gives its products a differentiated appeal. Business-level strategy focuses on selecting the domain in which an organization can exploit its functional-level core competences.

Low-cost business-level strategy
A plan whereby an organization produces low-priced goods and services for all customer groups.

Differentiation business-level strategy
A plan whereby an organization produces high-priced, quality products aimed at particular market segments.

Recall from Chapter 3 that the organizational domain is the range of goods and services that the organization produces to attract customers and other stakeholders. Once an organization has chosen its domain, it has two bases on which it can position itself to compete with its rivals. It can use its skills in low-cost value creation to produce for a customer group that wants low-priced goods and services. This plan is called a **low-cost business-level strategy**. Or it can use its skills at differentiation to produce for a customer group that wants and can afford differentiated products that command a high or premium price. This plan is called a **differentiation business-level strategy**.[26] Wal-Mart and Target, for example, specialize in selling low-price clothing to customers who want or can afford to pay only a modest amount for their attire. Neiman-Marcus and Saks Fifth Avenue specialize in selling high-priced clothing made by exclusive designers to wealthy customers.

Both Wal-Mart and Neiman-Marcus are in the retail clothing industry but have chosen different domains in which to compete. They have decided to sell different products to different groups of customers. In essence, Neiman-Marcus and Saks have chosen a business-level strategy based on core competences in differentiation in order to charge a premium price, and Wal-Mart and Target have chosen a business-level strategy based on core competences in low-cost value creation activities in order to charge a low price.

To compete successfully, an organization must develop a low-cost or differentiation strategy to protect and enlarge its domain. An organization can also attempt to pursue both strategies simultaneously and produce differentiated products at low cost.[27] Doing so is extremely difficult and requires an exceptionally strong set of core competences. McDonald's is an organization that has successfully pursued both strategies simultaneously. McDonald's has developed a unique brand-name reputation by means of sophisticated advertising and marketing and has developed low-cost skills in its manufacturing and distribution functions. Moreover, McDonald's has used many of the interorganizational strategies discussed in Chapter 3 to pursue both strategies simultaneously. It has formed strategic alliances with suppliers and obtains bread, rolls, and restaurant fittings (tables, chairs, lights, and so on) from companies with which it has long-term contracts or in which it has a minority ownership interest. McDonald's uses franchising to maintain the reliability and efficiency of its retail outlets and owns many of the sources of its inputs, such as herds of cattle in Brazil.

Over time, an organization has to change its business-level strategy to match changes in its environment. New technological developments, foreign competitors, and changes in customer needs and tastes may all affect the way an organization tries to compete for resources. Amazon.com offers an interesting example of the way changes in information technology affect a company's choice of business-level strategy.

As Amazon.com's strategy suggests, organizations have to defend, protect, and sometimes alter the sources of their competitive advantage if they are to successfully control their environment in the long run. Industry leaders, such as Amazon.com, Google, Toyota, and McDonald's, have so far sustained their competitive advantage by maintaining, improving, or rebuilding their functional-level resources and abilities. Amazon.com, for example, is constantly updating its information systems to take advantage of any new developments, such as streaming audio and video. McDonald's was forced to find new ways to differentiate its fast-food offerings to compete against sandwich chains and salad bars.

Before the advent of online bookstores, competition among bookstores was limited at best. The market was essentially divided between two kinds of competitors: (1) large bookstore chains such as Barnes & Noble and Borders, whose stores, often located in malls or large shopping strips, offered customers the latest lines of best-selling books and (2) independent bookstores, both those that were large and offered a huge selection of books to customers in major cities, and the small, specialized bookstores found in most cities in the United States. The large bookstore chains used their huge purchasing power to negotiate low prices with book publishers, and they pursued a low-cost strategy, often offering price discounts. Bookstores that offered a large selection of books (compared to the chains) or that specialized in some way pursued a differentiation strategy. Thus, the different kinds of bookstores were not in competition and all were able to make comfortable profits.

Jeff Bezos's idea of using the Internet to sell books online made it possible to develop a *simultaneous* low-cost and differentiation strategy, and thus outperform existing bookstore competitors. First, on the differentiation side, the ability of a computerized online catalogue to both describe and make available to customers every book in the English language offered customers a selection that could not be rivaled even by the largest bookstores in cities like New York and San Francisco. Second, on the low-cost side, his use of IT technology to interface inexpensively with book publishers, distributors, and customers allowed him to offer these customers books at discounted prices, and to get them quickly to customers as well.

Small wonder then, that this new low-cost/differentiation strategy gave Amazon.com a competitive advantage over its rivals. Many small and large stand-alone bookstores have exited the market; the large chains responded by opening up book superstores and by going online themselves. However, they have not repeated Amazon.com's success story; Amazon.com has over 25 million customers in its database and claims that over 40% of its business is from repeat customers.[28] In the 2000s its share price has once again soared because investors believe it has the core competencies and business-level strategy that will allow it to become the dominant online storefront in the years ahead.

Focus Strategy

Another business-level strategy is the focus strategy—specialization in one segment of a market, and focusing all of the organization's resources on that segment.[29] KFC specializes in the chicken segment of the fast-food market; Tiffany specializes in the high-price, luxury segment of the jewelry market; Rolls Royce focuses on the highest price segment of the car market—a Rolls Royce Silver Sprite costs $265,000.

Business-Level Strategy and Structure

The value that an organization creates at the business level depends on its ability to use its core competences to gain a competitive advantage. This ability is a product of the way the organization designs its structure.[30] An organization pursuing a differentiation business-level strategy generally confronts design choices different from those faced by organizations pursuing a low-cost strategy. Figure 8.4 summarizes the differences.

Figure 8.4
Types of Business-Level Strategy

Strategy	Number of Market Segments Served	
	Many	Few
Low cost	●	
Focused low cost		●
Differentiation	●	
Focused differentiation		●

The competitive strengths of an organization with a differentiation strategy come from functional skills that give the organization's products unique or state-of-the-art features that distinguish them from the products of competitors. An organization pursuing a differentiation strategy has to be able to develop products quickly, because only if it gets its products to customers ahead of its competitors can it exploit its differentiation advantage. Close cooperation between functions is likely to be required to bring new products to market quickly. For example, R&D, marketing, manufacturing, and product development must be able to communicate easily and adjust their activities to one another smoothly to speed the development process. All these factors make it likely that an organization pursuing a differentiation strategy has an organic structure. An organic structure permits the development of a decentralized, cross-functional team approach to decision making, which is the key to speedy new product development.

A low-cost strategy is associated with the need for close control of functional activities to monitor and lower the costs of product development.[31] Manufacturing and materials management become the central functions for an organization pursuing a low-cost strategy. The other functions (R&D, marketing, and so on) tailor their skills to achieve the goal of producing a low-cost product. A speedy response to market changes is not vital to the competitive success of a low-cost organization. Often, because product development is so expensive, such an organization waits to develop a new or improved product until customers clearly demand it. The low-cost organization generally imitates the differentiator's product and always remains one step behind to keep costs low. Consequently, a mechanistic structure is often the most appropriate choice for an organization pursuing a low-cost strategy (see Figure 8.5). Centralized decision making allows the organization to maintain close control over functional activities and thus over costs. Also, because there is no pressing need to respond quickly or innovatively, a mechanistic structure provides sufficient coordination to meet the demands of the competitive domain.

Further evidence for the match between differentiation strategy and organic structure, and the match between low-cost strategy and mechanistic structure, comes from contingency theory. Recall from Chapter 4 that contingency theory suggests that organizations in uncertain, rapidly changing environments require a greater degree of differentiation and integration than do organizations in more stable environments.[32] Because differentiators generally compete in a complex, uncertain environment where they need to react quickly to rivals' actions, and because low-cost companies usually compete in slow-moving environments, contingency theory suggests that effective differentiators

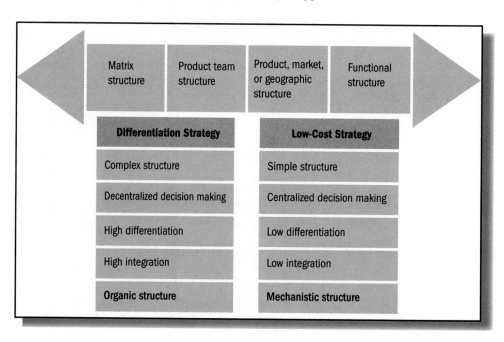

Figure 8.5
Characteristics of Organizational Structure Associated with Business-Level Differentiation and Low-Cost Strategies

will have greater differentiation and integration than low-cost companies have. Given that organizational structures with extensive differentiation and integration are costly to operate, contingency theory implies that low-cost companies should use the simplest structure possible because it will help to keep down the cost of value creation.[33]

In addition to examining the relationship between business-level strategy and organic and mechanistic structures, we can look at the relationship between strategy and the types of organizational structure discussed in Chapter 6: functional, divisional, and matrix structures. From a strategy perspective, three factors affect an organization's choice of a structure to create a competitive advantage for itself:

1. As an organization produces a wider range of products, it will need greater control over the development, marketing, and production of these products.
2. As an organization seeks to find new customer groups for its products, it will need a structure that allows it to serve the needs of its customers.
3. As the pace of new product development in an industry increases, an organization will need a structure that increases coordination among its functions.

Organizations following a low-cost strategy typically focus on producing one product or a few products in order to reduce costs. BIC Corporation, for example, produces one disposable razor for both men and women. A low-cost company does not face the problems of dealing with a wide range of products or with many customer groups. Moreover, low-cost companies are not leaders in product development. Because they are imitators, they do not have the problems of coordinating the activities of different functional groups. For all these reasons, low-cost companies generally adopt the simplest structure that is consistent with their strategy. Normally, a functional structure (one in which people are grouped by common skills or use of similar resources) is sufficient to coordinate the core competences of a low-cost organization.

By contrast, differentiators typically produce a wide range of products to suit the needs of different groups of customers. Also, to the degree that competition between differentiators is based on the development of new and innovative products (a situation found in the car and personal computer industries), differentiators need a structure that allows functional experts to cooperate so that they can quickly develop and introduce new products. For these reasons, differentiators are likely to adopt a more complex structure. If the pressing need is to handle a wide range of products, a product structure (in which products are grouped into separate divisions that are served by the same set of support functions) is the appropriate choice. If handling different groups of customers is the key to success, a market structure or a geographic structure (in which functional activities are grouped to best meet the needs of different types of customers) will best fit the differentiator's needs. A product team structure or a matrix structure (in which product development is coordinated by teams of cross-functional specialists) can be adopted when rapid product development and speedy response to competitors are the keys to competitive advantage.

All of those structures can provide an organization with the ability to coordinate functional and organizational resources to create a core competence. Intel, the microchip manufacturer, has decided that the only way to maintain its lead in the industry is to produce several generations of microchips at the same time. So it has established a product team structure in which teams of research and development specialists work side by side to plan the chips of the future.[34]

To summarize, an organization must match its business-level strategy to the organizational structure that allows the organization to use its functional and organizational resources to create a competitive advantage. A top-quality R&D department is useless unless an organization has a structure that coordinates R&D activities with a marketing department that can correctly forecast changes in customer needs and a product development department that can translate research and marketing findings into commercial products. Choosing the right structure has major payoffs by giving an organization a low-cost or differentiation advantage at the business level, as the following organizational insight demonstrates.

Kodak, long the global leader in the photographic products industry, has fallen on hard times in recent years because the digital revolution is transforming so many markets and industries. Kodak's photographic products division, which makes the film and paper that is the heart of traditional photography, has suffered rapidly declining sales due to the inroads that digital photography has made. Although Kodak sold a line of digital cameras and accessories, its structure was preventing it from capitalizing on its growing skills in digital photography. Its new CEO Antonio Perez decided that far-reaching changes were necessary if Kodak was both to reduce its costs and turn out new kinds of innovative digital products that customers were expecting.[35]

Perez split Kodak's consumer photography division into two groups. One handles the production and sale of digital cameras, home printers, and accessories; the other handles film, paper, and related chemical-imaging products. This change is radical, for it effectively separates the activities of these two groups and creates two hierarchies of managers responsible for developing the right strategies for their business. In the past, the managers of the film group had essentially managed digital decision making. Now, this control has been decentralized to a new management team that reports to CEO Perez, not the head of consumer products. The digital imaging group's goal is to produce a range of differentiated products customers want; the task of the new managers in control of film products is to find ways to lower costs.

Thus, Kodak's structure has been changed to allow it to deal with the harsh realities of the changing photographic industry. If the new structure is not successful, and Kodak fails to either turn out popular new products or reduce its costs, its future looks bleak as it battles against companies like HP, Xerox, Samsung, Canon, Fuji, and Hitachi, who are all fighting for customers moving into the digital age.

Business-Level Strategy and Culture

Organizational culture is another major determinant of the ability to use functional and organizational resources effectively. The challenge at the business level is to develop organization-wide values, and specific norms and rules, all of which allow the organization to combine and use its functional resources to the best advantage. Over time, different functions may develop different subunit orientations, which impede communication and coordination. But if the various functions share values and norms, communication and coordination problems can be overcome. If managers in different functions can develop common ways of dealing with problems, an organization's competitive advantage will be enhanced.

How does the culture of a low-cost organization differ from that of a differentiator? Organizations pursuing a low-cost strategy must develop values of economy and frugality.[36] Frequently, specific norms and rules develop that reflect the organization's terminal and instrumental values. For example, when Ken Iverson was CEO of Nucor, a leading low-cost steel manufacturer, he operated the company in a frugal, careful way. Top managers at Nucor worked in small, unpretentious corporate offices with few of the trappings of luxury. They drove their own cars to work, flew economy class, and on business trips shared rooms in hotels to reduce costs.

The functions within a low-cost organization are likely to develop goals that reflect the organization's values of economy. Marketing views its job as finding the most efficient ways of attracting customers. R&D sees its role as developing new products that offer the greatest potential return for the smallest investment of organizational resources.

In low-cost organizations, a common "language" and a code of behavior based on low-cost values develop. In a differentiator, by contrast, the need to be different from competitors and to develop innovative products puts product development or marketing at center stage. Values that promote innovation and responsiveness to customers, stories of products that became winners or of winning products that were not developed, and boosting the status of employees who create new products all make organizational members aware of the need to be the first or the best.[37] Cultural values of innovation, quality, excellence, and uniqueness help a differentiator implement its chosen strategy, and they become a source of competitive strength. The

After considerable negotiation, American Home Products (AHP), the giant pharmaceutical maker, announced that it would buy Monsanto, another large pharmaceutical and chemical company, for $33 billion. Analysts applauded the merger, believing that it would provide important differentiation and low-cost advantages for the combined firm. Specifically, the merged companies would have a much broader product range, and the merger would eliminate expensive duplication of production facilities, leading to major cost savings.

Analysts were therefore shocked when the two companies later announced that the merger was off because it was not in the best interests of shareholders. Why were the companies forced to give up these potential sources of competitive advantage? AHP has a culture characterized by a short-term focus on bottom-line profits. Its managers are cost conscious and only want to invest in products that have a short-term payoff. Monsanto, on the other hand, has a long-term orientation. It is driven by a desire to produce innovative new products, many of which may not pay off except in the long run. Thus it has strong values of innovation and excellence.

Managers at these companies came to realize that it was impossible to harmonize these different cultures and driving values. They foresaw that the potential low-cost and differentiation gains might be wiped out by politics and infighting between managers of these two companies and it was just not worth the risk to go ahead with the merger.

preceding insight offers a glimpse at the way culture can influence a company's business-level strategy.

An organizational culture that promotes norms and rules that increase effectiveness can be a major source of competitive advantage. In Chapter 7, we saw how organizations deliberately shape their culture to achieve their goals. Sony and Microsoft, for example, promote innovation by establishing norms and rules that enable employees to move to positions where their talents are most valuable to the organization.

Recall, too, that organizational structures are chosen because of their effect on culture. Organic structures foster the development of cultural values of innovation and quality. In contrast, mechanistic structures foster economical values that focus attention on improving existing rules and SOPs, not finding new ones. Low-cost companies that seek to develop Japanese-style lean production systems will find a mechanistic structure useful because it focuses all efforts on improving existing work procedures.

In sum, organizational culture is another important factor shaping an organization's business-level strategy for improving its value-creation skills. As technology changes, as new products and markets come into being, and as the environment changes, an organization's culture likewise will change. Like organizational structure, the way in which organizational culture supports an organization's strategy for value creation can also be a source of competitive advantage. That is one reason why there has been continuing interest in culture as an explanation for differences in organizational effectiveness.

MANAGERIAL IMPLICATIONS

BUSINESS-LEVEL STRATEGY

1. Managers in each function should understand their function's contribution to the organization's low-cost advantage or differentiated appeal. Members of a function should examine their interactions with members of other functions to see if they can devise new ways to reduce costs or develop a differentiated appeal.
2. Managers should act like entrepreneurs and always be on the lookout for new opportunities to protect and enlarge the domain of their organization. They must continually experiment to see whether they can enlarge the existing organizational domain, find new uses for existing products, or develop new products to satisfy customer needs.
3. Managers must always evaluate whether the current organizational structure and culture are congruent with the organization's business-level strategy. If they are not, managers should move quickly to make changes that can improve their competitive position.

Often, an organization that cannot create more value in its current domain tries to find a new domain in which to compete for resources. Corporate-level strategy involves a search for new domains in which to exploit and defend an organization's ability to create value from the use of its low-cost or differentiation core competences.[38] Corporate-level strategy is a continuation of business-level strategy because the organization takes its existing core competences and applies them in new domains. If an organization takes marketing skills developed in one domain and applies them in a new domain, for example, it can create value in that new domain. When Philip Morris took marketing skills developed in the tobacco industry, applied them to Miller Brewing, and made Miller Light the market leader, it created value for Miller's customers and for Philip Morris's shareholders. Now we look in detail at how vertical integration and diversification, two important corporate-level strategies, can help an organization create value. In the next chapter we examine global expansion, the other main kind of corporate strategy.

Vertical Integration

Vertical integration
A strategy in which an organization takes over and owns its suppliers (backward vertical integration) or its distributors (forward vertical integration).

An organization pursuing a strategy of **vertical integration** establishes—or takes over and buys—its suppliers (backward vertical integration) or its distributors (forward vertical integration).[39] In this way, it controls the production of its inputs or the disposal of its outputs (see Figure 8.6). For example, Figure 8.7 shows a soft-drink

Figure 8.6
Corporate-Level Strategies for Entering New Domains

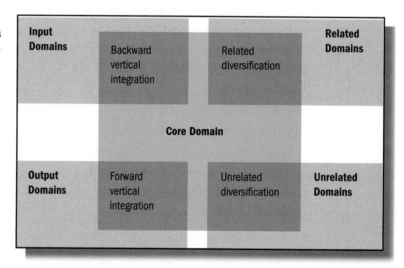

Figure 8.7
Soft-Drink Company's Corporate-Level Strategies for Entering New Domains

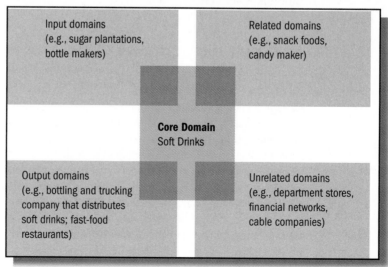

company that enters new domains that overlap its core domain so that it can use, enhance, or protect its low-cost or differentiation value creation skills.

How does vertical integration allow an organization to use or enhance its core competence in value creation? An organization that supplies its own inputs or disposes of its own outputs may be able to keep for itself the profits previously earned by its suppliers. Moreover, production cost savings can sometimes be obtained when an organization owns its input suppliers. Inputs can be designed so that they can be assembled at a lower cost, and control of the reliability and quality of inputs can save an organization a great deal of money if products eventually have to be repaired under guarantee.

An organization can call attention to its uniqueness by making its products different from its rivals'. One way to do this is by controlling the inputs that make a product unique. Coca-Cola, for example, has sole control over the Coke formula, so Coca-Cola tastes like no other cola drink. Controlling inputs also helps the organization control quality, which confers uniqueness on a product. Rolls Royce carefully tends the flocks of sheep from which it obtains the leather for its car upholstery: The sheep are kept in enclosures without barbed wire and are protected so that the leather has no flaws and blemishes. Finally, taking over a supplier by vertical integration avoids the problem that results when there are only a few suppliers in an industry and they act opportunistically and try to cheat an organization by, for example, inflating the costs or reducing the quality of its inputs.

Controlling the way a product is distributed can also result in a low-cost or differentiation advantage. Tandy Corporation, for example, owns Radio Shack, so Tandy obtains all the profit from sales of Radio Shack consumer electronic products and accessories, profit that otherwise would have been made by other retail stores. Tandy can also control the quality of the sales and repair service that Radio Shack customers receive and thus build customer loyalty—a differentiation advantage.

Control of overlapping input and output domains enhances an organization's competitive advantage in its core domain and creates new opportunities for value creation. But an organization also needs to look at the bureaucratic costs associated with full ownership of suppliers and distributors.[40] The organization needs to evaluate whether minority ownership, strategic alliances, and other interorganizational strategies are viable alternatives to vertical integration.[41] The value-creation advantages of vertical integration can sometimes be obtained at much lower bureaucratic costs by means of strategic alliances with already existing businesses, because an organization avoids the costs associated with having to operate the business. The more an organization pursues vertical integration, the larger the organization becomes; the bureaucratic costs associated with managing the strategy are likely to rise sharply because of communication and coordination problems and the simple fact that managers are expensive to employ. Too much vertical integration can be a strategic mistake. Thus managers must be careful to make design choices about organizational structure and culture that will enhance and support such a strategy.

Related Diversification

Related diversification occurs when an organization enters a new domain in which it can exploit one or more of its existing core competences to create a low-cost or differentiated competitive advantage in that new domain. When Honda entered the small-car and lawn-mower markets, for example, it entered a domain in which it could exploit functional skills in engine design and manufacture that it had developed in its core domain, motorbikes, to achieve a low-cost advantage. Whenever an organization enters a new domain to exploit an opportunity to use any of its core competences in a way that can lower costs or create uniqueness, it creates value through related diversification.

Unrelated Diversification

Unrelated diversification
The entry into a new domain that is not related in any way to an organization's core domain.

The value created by related diversification comes from exploiting any of an organization's core competences in a new domain: When a company pursues unrelated diversification, it enters new domains that have nothing in common with its core domain. The value created by **unrelated diversification** comes from exploiting one particular core competence: a top management team's ability to control a set of organizations better than the organizations' existing top management teams.[42]

Suppose a retail organization's top management team has developed unique skills in economizing on bureaucratic costs by designing and managing organizational structure. If the team sees an organization in some new domain—for example, fast food—that is being managed inefficiently and is not making the best use of its resources, team members may see an opportunity for their organization to expand into this new domain and create value there. If the top management team takes over the inefficient organization, restructures its operations, reduces bureaucratic costs, and increases its profitability, it has created value that did not previously exist in the fast-food organization.

An organization that takes over inefficient companies and restructures them to create value is pursuing a strategy of unrelated diversification. If it continues to manage these organizations from a pure profitability standpoint and buys and sells them on the basis of their return on investment, it is also pursuing a strategy of unrelated diversification. For example, Hanson Trust, an organization that is a collection of unrelated British and American divisions, seeks out underperforming organizations, sells off the divisions it does not want, and keeps the divisions it feels it can restructure and operate profitably. Designing an efficient organizational structure is an important part of the strategy of unrelated diversification because companies that perform poorly often do so because they have high bureaucratic costs.

Corporate-Level Strategy and Structure

The appropriate organizational structure must be chosen at the corporate level in order to realize the value associated with vertical integration and related and unrelated diversification. In general, as we discussed in Chapter 6, for organizations that are operating in more than one domain a multidivisional structure is the appropriate choice (see Figure 6.6). The use of self-contained operating divisions supported by a corporate headquarters staff provides the control the organization needs to coordinate resource transfers between divisions so that core competences can be shared across the organization. There are a few variants of the multidivisional structure. Each is suited to realizing the benefits associated with either unrelated or related diversification.

Conglomerate Structure and Unrelated Diversification

Conglomerate structure
A structure in which each business is placed in a self-contained division and there is no contact between divisions.

Organizations pursuing a strategy of unrelated diversification attempt to create value by purchasing underperforming businesses, restructuring them, and then managing them more efficiently. This strategy frees the managers of the parent organization from involvement in the day-to-day running of the various companies that the organization owns. After the restructuring, corporate management's only role is to monitor each company's performance and intervene to take selective action when necessary. Organizations with a strategy of unrelated diversification are likely to use a conglomerate structure.

As Figure 8.8 shows, in a **conglomerate structure**, each unrelated business is a self-contained division. Because there is no need to coordinate activities between divisions, only a small corporate headquarters staff is needed. Communication is from the top down and occurs most often on issues that concern bureaucratic costs, such as decisions about the level of financial expenditure necessary to pursue new value creation opportunities. The conglomerate Hanson Trust, for example, operated with a corporate staff of only 120 people to oversee more than 50 companies; it operated primarily through rules that controlled bureaucratic costs. Hanson Trust had a rule that

Figure 8.8
Conglomerate Structure

A structure in which each business is placed in a self-contained division and there is no contact between divisions.

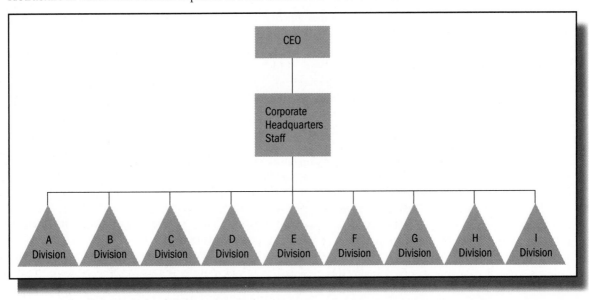

required a corporate executive to approve any expenditure over $3,000.[43] Beyond this, it made little attempt to intervene in the affairs of the operating divisions.

Structures for Related Diversification

An organization pursuing a strategy of related diversification tries to obtain value by sharing resources or by transferring functional skills from one division to another—processes that require a great amount of coordination and integration. Related diversification requires lateral communication between divisions as well as vertical communication between divisions and corporate headquarters. As a result, integrating roles and teams of functional experts are needed to coordinate skill and resource transfers. Coordination is complicated because divisions may fight for resources and may not wish to share information and knowledge unless they are equitably rewarded for doing so. To obtain from related diversification a set of gains comparable to those obtained from unrelated diversification, a much larger corporate headquarters staff is required to coordinate interdivisional activities, and much more managerial time and effort is needed. Hitachi's corporate structure offers an interesting insight into the management of a strategy of related diversification.

Because Hitachi has 28 operating divisions, its coordination problem is intense. Imagine the coordination problem that arises when an organization has over 150 divisions, as do GE and Textron. Often, the coordination problem becomes so severe that a multidivisional matrix structure is used to increase integration (see Figure 6.13). As we saw in Chapter 6, this structure provides the coordination between the divisions and corporate headquarters that allows for the transfer of skills and the sharing of resources around the organization. It gives top-level functional, divisional, and corporate managers the opportunity to meet in teams to plan the organization's future strategy.

The bureaucratic costs associated with managing related diversification (whether in a multidivisional structure or a matrix multidivisional structure) are much greater than those associated with vertical integration or unrelated diversification.[44] Considerably more communication and coordination are needed to create value from related diversification than from the other corporate-level strategies. Bureaucratic costs increase as the size of the corporate staff and the amount of time that both divisional and corporate managers spend in coordinating with other divisions increase. In contrast, the bureaucratic costs associated with unrelated diversification are likely to be low, because there is no need to coordinate resource transfers between divisions—the divisions do not exchange anything.

Hitachi Ltd. is one of Japan's biggest and most innovative companies.[45] Every year the $62 billion giant accounts for 6% of Japan's expenditures on R&D and over 2% of Japan's gross domestic product. Like its biggest competitors, IBM and Fujitsu, Hitachi is a major computer organization. Unlike them, however, it is also engaged in noncomputer businesses that rely heavily on computer technology: consumer electronics, power plants, transportation, medical equipment, and telecommunications.[46] It is pursuing a strategy of related diversification on a grand scale, and research and development forms the bedrock of the organization and its value-creation activities.

Hitachi has 28 divisions. Each has its own R&D laboratory and is responsible for product development from the initial conception to design and final marketing. Control is decentralized to each division, and each division has the ultimate responsibility for choosing its domain. This decentralized approach puts a heavy burden on Hitachi to find ways to integrate and coordinate its divisions so that they can share skills and resources and increase their level of innovation.

Hitachi has responded to the need for interdivisional coordination by adopting various integrating mechanisms:

1. Hitachi employs a large number of corporate executives in integrating roles to oversee each division's activities and control information flows from one division to another.

2. Hitachi has a corporate R&D laboratory that has the responsibility for coordinating the flow of new knowledge among the divisions' R&D laboratories and for disseminating the knowledge it creates to the divisions.

3. Hitachi uses a sophisticated telecommunications and teleconferencing network to link its laboratories, so that scientists and engineers in different labs can effectively work face-to-face to trade knowledge and cooperate on joint research.

4. Hitachi has developed a strong corporate culture based on values of cooperation and teamwork between scientists, and norms that support innovation flourish.

Through all those means, Hitachi has enhanced its ability to transfer its R&D skills around the organization and secure the gains from its strategy of related diversification.

In Hitachi, there are enormous opportunities for finding new ways to create value because the divisions are related to one another through their reliance on computer and electronic technology. The bureaucratic costs of pursuing this strategy, however, are very high because so much time and money is spent on integrating the 28 R&D laboratories in order to keep them aware of each other's activities. The enormous costs of operating so many R&D units also eat into profits. Hitachi has chosen to bear these costs in order to obtain the benefits of its strategy of related diversification. Because it has a time horizon for product development that extends well into the future, it is not concerned with the bottom-line results of any single division in the short run. What matters to Hitachi is maintaining its long-term ability to create value.

Corporate-Level Strategy and Culture

Just as a move to a more appropriate organizational structure can reduce bureaucratic costs, so can a move to a more appropriate organizational culture. Cultural values and the common norms, rules, and goals that reflect those values can greatly facilitate the management of a corporate strategy. For example, Hanson Trust, which pursued a strategy of unrelated diversification, put most value on economy, cost cutting, and the efficient use of organizational resources. Divisional managers at Hanson Trust could not spend large amounts of money without the approval of corporate executives. Knowing that their performance was scrutinized closely, their actions were shaped by corporate values tied to bottom-line results.

By contrast, suppose an organization is pursuing a strategy of related diversification. What kinds of values, norms, and rules are most useful in managing the strategy? Because the creation of value from related diversification requires a large amount of coordination and integration, norms and values that emphasize cooperation between divisions are important. This type of culture lowers the costs of exchanging resources and is likely to feature a common corporate language that the various divisions can use in their dealings with one another. Each division will have its own culture, but the corporate culture can overcome differences in divisional orientation, just as at the business level an organization's culture can overcome differences in functional orientation.

At Sony, for example, corporate values of innovation and entrepreneurship are passed on in the stories that organizational members use to frame significant corporate events. New employees are socialized to the innovative culture and learn the corporate language from their interactions with other people. In its promotions to the corporate headquarters staff, Sony also sends a message about the kinds of values and behaviors that are associated with success in the organization—actions that lead to innovative new products. Similarly, an organization that rewards managers who successfully manage interdivisional attempts to share skills and trade resources has a culture that supports a strategy of related diversification.

Thus different cultures help organizations pursue different corporate-level strategies. An organization needs to create a culture that reinforces and builds on the strategy it pursues and the structure it adopts. In an organization that has a conglomerate structure, in which there is no connection between divisions, it would be pointless to develop a common corporate culture across divisions because the managers in the different divisions would not know one another. A multidivisional matrix structure, in contrast, does support the development of a cohesive corporate culture because it permits the rapid interchange of ideas and the transfer of norms and values around the organization. In sum, as we saw in Chapter 7, corporate culture is an important tool that organizations can use to coordinate and motivate employees.

As at the business level, the interorganizational strategies discussed in Chapter 3 are an important means of increasing the value an organization can create through its corporate strategy. Interorganizational strategies increase value by allowing the organization to avoid the bureaucratic costs often associated with managing a new organization in a new domain. As the number of an organization's divisions increases, for example, the bureaucratic costs associated with managing interdivisional activities increase. Interorganizational strategies such as strategic alliances may allow an organization to obtain the gains from cooperation between divisions without experiencing the costs. Suppose two organizations establish a joint venture to produce a range of products in a domain that is new to both of them. Each organization contributes a different skill or resource to the venture. One provides low-cost manufacturing skills; the other, differentiated R&D and marketing skills. By establishing the joint venture, they have avoided the bureaucratic costs that would be incurred if one organization took over the other or if either organization had to internally coordinate the new resource transfers necessary to make the new venture work. Similarly, the gains from vertical integration can often be realized through minority ownership or long-term contracts, which avoid the need to own the supplier or distributor. An organization that can use an interorganizational strategy to enter and compete in a new domain can often secure the benefits of the diversification and integration strategies without incurring bureaucratic costs.

MANAGERIAL IMPLICATIONS

CORPORATE-LEVEL STRATEGY

1. To protect the organization's existing domains and to exploit the organization's core competences to create value for stakeholders, managers should carefully analyze the environment.
2. To distinguish between a value-creation opportunity and a value-losing opportunity, managers should carefully evaluate the benefits and costs associated with entering a new domain.
3. As part of this analysis, managers should weigh the benefits and costs of various strategies for entering the domain—for example, takeover of an existing company versus establishing a new organization, versus using a strategic alliance such as a joint venture.
4. No matter which corporate strategy managers pursue, as the organization grows, managers must be careful to match their organization's structure and culture to the strategy they are pursuing.

Global strategy can play a crucial role in strengthening a company's control over its environment. There are four principal strategies that companies can use as they begin to market their products and establish production facilities abroad: (1) a *multidomestic strategy*, oriented toward local responsiveness—a company decentralizes control to subsidiaries and divisions in each country in which it operates to produce and customize products to local markets; (2) an *international strategy*, based on R&D and marketing being centralized at home and all the other value-creation functions being decentralized to national units; (3) a *global strategy*, oriented toward cost reduction, with all the principal value-creation functions centralized at the lowest cost global location; and (4) a *transnational strategy*, focused so that it can achieve both local responsiveness *and* cost reduction—some functions are centralized while others are decentralized at the global location best suited to achieving these objectives.

The need to coordinate and integrate global activities increases as a company moves from a multidomestic to an international to a global and then to a transnational strategy. For example, to obtain the benefits of pursuing a transnational strategy, a company must transfer its distinctive competences to the global location where they can create the most value and establish a global network to coordinate its divisions both at home and abroad. The objective of such coordination is to obtain the benefits from transferring or leveraging competencies across a company's global divisions. Thus the bureaucratic costs associated with solving communications and measurement problems that arise in managing transfers across countries to pursue a transnational strategy are much higher than those of pursuing the other strategies. The multidomestic strategy does not require coordination of activities on a global level because value-creation activities are handled locally, by country or world region. The international and global strategies fit between the other two strategies: Although products have to be sold and marketed globally, and hence global product transfers must be managed, there is less need to coordinate skill and resource transfers than for a transnational strategy.

The implication is that as companies change from a multidomestic to an international, global, or transnational strategy, they require a more complex structure, control system, and culture to coordinate the value-creation activities associated with implementing that strategy. In general, the choice of structure and control systems for managing a global business is a function of three factors:

1. The decision how to distribute and allocate responsibility and authority between managers at home and abroad so that effective control over a company's global operations is maintained
2. The selection of the organizational structure that groups divisions both at home and abroad in a way that allows the best use of resources and serves the needs of foreign customers most effectively
3. The selection of the right kinds of integration and control mechanisms and organizational culture to make the overall global structure function effectively

Table 8.2 summarizes the appropriate design choices for companies pursuing each of these strategies.

Implementing a Multidomestic Strategy

When a company pursues a multidomestic strategy, it generally operates with a global geographic structure (see Figure 8.9). When using this structure, a company duplicates all value-creation activities and establishes an overseas division in every country or world area in which it operates. Authority is then decentralized to managers in each overseas division, and they devise the appropriate strategy for responding to the needs of the local environment. Managers at global headquarters use market and output controls, such as ROI, growth in market share, and operation

Table 8.2 Strategy-Structure Relationships in the International Environment

	MULTIDOMESTIC STRATEGY	INTERNATIONAL STRATEGY	GLOBAL STRATEGY	TRANSNATIONAL STRATEGY
	Low ←————— Need for Coordination ————→ High			
Vertical Differentiation Choices				
Levels in the hierarchy	Relatively flat	Relatively tall	Relatively tall	Relatively flat
Centralization of authority	Decentralized	Core competences centralized, others decentralized	Centralized	Simultaneously centralized and decentralized
Horizontal Differentiation	Global geographic structure	Global product group structure	Global product group structure	Global matrix or "matrix in the mind"
Integration				
Need for integrating mechanisms such as task forces and integrating roles	Low	Medium	Medium	High
Need for electronic integration and management networks	Medium	High	High	Very High
Need for integration by international organizational culture	Low	Medium	High	Very High
	Low ←————— Bureaucratic Costs ————→ High			

Figure 8.9
Global Geographic Structure

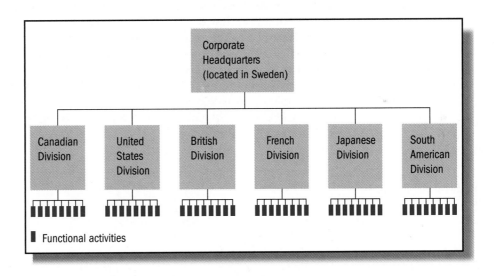

costs, to evaluate the performance of overseas divisions. On the basis of such global comparisons, they can make decisions about capital allocation and orchestrate the transfer of new knowledge among divisions.

A company that makes and sells the same products in many different countries often groups its overseas divisions into world regions to simplify the coordination of products across countries. Europe might be one region; the Pacific Rim, another; and the Middle East, a third. Such grouping allows the same set of output and behavior controls to be applied across all divisions inside a region. Thus, global companies can reduce communications and transfer problems because information can be transmitted more easily across countries with broadly similar cultures. For example, consumers' preferences regarding product design and marketing are likely to be more similar among countries in one world region than among countries in different world regions.

Because the overseas divisions themselves have little or no contact with others in different regions, no integrating mechanisms are needed. Nor does a global organizational culture develop because there are no transfers of skills or resources or transfers of personnel among managers from the various world regions. Historically, car companies such as DaimlerChrysler, GM, and Ford used global-area structures to manage their overseas operations. Ford of Europe, for example, had little or no contact with its U.S. parent, and capital was the principal resource exchanged.

One problem with a global geographic structure and a multidomestic strategy is that the duplication of specialist activities across countries raises a company's overall cost structure. Moreover, the company is not taking advantage of opportunities to transfer, share, or leverage its competences and capabilities on a global basis: For example, it cannot apply the low-cost manufacturing expertise that has developed in one world region in another. Thus, multidomestic companies lose the many benefits of operating globally.

Implementing International Strategy

A company pursuing an international strategy adopts a different route to global expansion. A company with many different products or businesses has the challenging problem of coordinating the flow of different products across different countries. To manage these transfers, many companies use a global product group structure and create product group headquarters to coordinate the activities of domestic and foreign divisions within each product group. Product managers are responsible for organizing all aspects of value creation on a global level (see Figure 8.10).

This arrangement of tasks and roles reduces the transaction costs involved in managing handoffs across countries and world regions. However, managers abroad are essentially under the control of managers in the international division, and if domestic and overseas managers compete for control of making strategy, conflict and lack of cooperation may result. Many companies such as IBM, Citibank, and DaimlerChrysler have experienced this problem. Very often, significant strategic control has been decentralized to overseas divisions. When cost pressures force corporate managers to reassess their strategy, and they decide to intervene, this frequently provokes resistance, much of it due to differences in culture—not just corporate, but country differences.

Figure 8.10
Global Product Group Structure

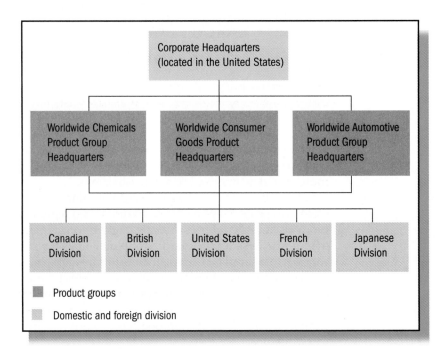

Implementing Global Strategy

When a company embarks on a global strategy today, it locates its manufacturing and other value-chain activities at the global location that will allow it to increase efficiency and quality. In so doing, it has to solve the problems of coordinating and integrating its global activities. It has to find a structure that lowers the bureaucratic costs associated with resource transfers between corporate headquarters and its global divisions and that provides the centralized control that a global strategy requires. The answer for many companies is also a global product group structure (see Figure 8.10).

Once again, the product groups coordinate the activities of home and overseas operations. Then, within each division headquarters managers decide where to locate the different functions at the optimal global location for performing that activity. For example, Philips has one division responsible for global R&D, manufacturing, marketing and sales of its lightbulbs; another for medical equipment; and so on. The headquarters of the medical division and its R&D is located in Bothell, Washington; manufacturing, on the other hand, is done in Taiwan; and the products are sold by sales subsidiaries in each local market.

The product-group structure allows managers to decide how best to pursue a global strategy—for example, to decide which value-chain activities, such as manufacturing or product design, should be performed in which country to increase efficiency. Increasingly, U.S. and Japanese companies are moving manufacturing to low-cost countries such as China but establishing product-design centers in Europe or the United States to take advantage of foreign skills and capabilities to obtain the benefits from this strategy.

Implementing Transnational Strategy

The main failing of the global product-group structure is that although it allows a company to achieve superior efficiency and quality, it is weak when it comes to responsiveness to customers because the focus is still on centralized control. Moreover, this structure makes it difficult for the different product groups to trade information and knowledge and to obtain the benefits from transferring, sharing, and leveraging their competences. Sometimes the potential gains from sharing product, marketing, or R&D knowledge between product groups are high, but so too are the bureaucratic costs associated with achieving these gains. Is there a structure that can simultaneously economize on these costs and provide the coordination necessary to obtain these benefits?

In the 1990s many companies implemented a global matrix structure to simultaneously lower their global cost structures and differentiate their activities through superior innovation and responsiveness to customers globally. In Figure 8.11, the company's overseas divisions are shown on the vertical axis. Managers at the regional or country level control local operations. The company's corporate product groups, which provide specialist services such as R&D, product design, and marketing information to its overseas divisions, are grouped by region and shown on the horizontal axis. These might be the chemicals, consumer goods, and automobile product groups. Through a system of output and behavior controls, they then report to corporate product-group personnel back in the United States and ultimately to the CEO or president. The heads of the world regions or country managers are also responsible for working with U.S. product-group managers to develop the control and reward systems that will promote the transfer, sharing, or leveraging of competences that will result in superior performance.

Implementing a matrix structure thus decentralizes control to overseas managers and provides them with considerable flexibility for managing local issues, but can still give product and corporate managers in the United States the centralized control they need to coordinate company activities on a global level. The matrix structure can allow knowledge and experience to be transferred among geographic

Figure 8.11
Global Matrix Structure

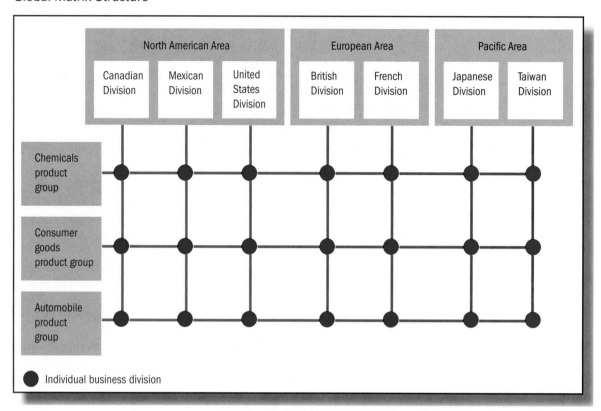

regions, among product groups, and among product groups and regions. Because it offers many opportunities for face-to-face contact between managers at home and abroad, the matrix facilitates the transmission of a company's norms and values and, hence, the development of a global corporate culture. This is especially important for a company with far-flung global operations for which lines of communication are longer. Club Med, for instance, uses a matrix to standardize high-quality customer service across its global vacation villages.

SUMMARY

Organizational strategy is a plan of action that an organization undertakes to create value. Organizations that do not constantly set ambitious new goals and try to find effective means of reaching those goals are likely to be threatened by younger, more agile competitors in search of ways to seize resources for themselves. Consequently, organizational members at all levels in the organization—functional, business, corporate, and global—must develop their value-creation skills and abilities. Managers must manage the interrelationship of strategy (at all levels), structure, and culture to maximize the organization's ability to manage, enhance, and protect its domain so that it can create value to satisfy stakeholders. Chapter 8 has made the following main points:

1. The value that an organization creates by means of its strategy is a function of how the organization positions itself in its environment so that it can use its core competences to compete for resources.

2. An organization's core competences are products of its functional and organizational resources and its coordination ability.

3. An organization must formulate strategy at four levels: functional, business, corporate, and global.

4. The goal of functional-level strategy is to create in each function a low-cost or differentiation competence that gives the organization a competitive advantage.

5. Functional structure and culture produce functional abilities that support the development of functional resources.

6. The goal of business-level strategy is to combine functional low-cost and differentiation competences in order to exploit opportunities in the organizational environment. Business-level

strategy selects and manages the domain in which an organization uses its value-creation resources and coordination abilities.

7. The two main business-level strategies are low-cost business-level strategy and differentiation business-level strategy.

8. An organization chooses a structure and culture to develop coordination abilities that support its business-level strategy.

9. The goal of corporate-level strategy is to use and develop low-cost and differentiation competences so that the organization can protect and enlarge its existing domain and expand into new ones.

10. Three main types of corporate-level strategy are vertical integration, related diversification, and unrelated diversification.

11. An appropriate corporate-level structure and culture can help reduce the bureaucratic costs of managing a strategy.

12. The four strategies that companies use to manage global expansion are a multidomestic strategy, an international strategy, a global strategy, and a transnational strategy. Each is associated with a different approach to value creation and a different set of organizational design problems.

DISCUSSION QUESTIONS

1. How should an organization design its structure and culture to obtain a core competence in manufacturing and in research and development?

2. Pick an organization like a restaurant or a department store, and analyze how it might pursue a low-cost or a differentiation strategy.

3. What is the difference between a low-cost strategy and a differentiation strategy? How should a differentiated biotechnology organization and a low-cost fast-food organization design their structures and cultures to promote their respective competitive advantages?

4. Compare the competitive advantages enjoyed by a large restaurant chain, such as Steak and Ale or Red Lobster, and the sources of competitive advantages enjoyed by a small, local restaurant.

5. Why would an organization choose a corporate-level strategy to expand its value-creation activities beyond its core domain? Discuss how an organization's structure and culture might change as the organization begins to enter new domains.

6. How and why do bureaucratic costs increase as a company goes from a multidomestic to an international to a global to a transnational strategy?

ORGANIZATIONAL THEORY IN ACTION

Practicing Organizational Theory: What Kind of Supermarket?

Form groups of three to five people and discuss the following scenario:

You are a group of investors who are contemplating opening a new supermarket in your city. You are trying to decide what business-level strategy would provide your supermarket with a competitive advantage that would allow you to attract customers and outperform your prospective rivals.

1. List the supermarket chains in your city and identify their business-level strategies (for example, low-cost, differentiation, or focus). Also, list any particular kinds of functional strengths or weaknesses that they might have (such as a great bakery or a lousy fish counter).

2. On the basis of this analysis, what type of business-level strategy do you think will best succeed in the local market? What will the specific elements of this strategy be (for example: What kind of supermarket will it be? What kind of functional strengths will you try to develop? What kinds of customers will you aim for? What will you do to attract them?)?

The Ethical Dimension #8

Bribery and corruption are common in some countries, and for people in those countries, they are a normal part of doing business. U.S. law bans any U.S. company from paying bribes to foreign officials, or taking any steps to use illegal means to secure valuable foreign contracts or resources.

1. Why does the United States adopt this ethical and legal stance if people in the country accept bribery as the norm?

2. What could U.S. companies do to help reduce the incidence of bribery in these countries and promote ethical business practices?

Making the Connection #8

Find an example of an organization pursuing a business, corporate, or global expansion strategy. What kind of strategy is it pursuing? Why did it choose this strategy? How does the strategy create value? How does the strategy affect the organization's structure or culture?

Analyzing the Organization: Design Module #8

This module focuses on the kinds of goods and services that your organization produces, the markets that it competes in, and the kinds of strategies that it uses to create value for its stakeholders.

Assignment

This assignment asks you to explore how your company creates value through its strategy and structure for managing the environment.

1. Briefly describe your organization's domain—that is, the goods and services that it produces and the customer groups that it serves.
2. What core competences give the organization a competitive advantage? What are the organization's functional-level strategies?
3. What is your organization's principal business-level strategy: low cost or differentiation? How successfully is the organization pursuing this strategy? In what ways does it need to improve its core competences to improve its competitive position?
4. In what ways do your organization's structure and culture match its strategy? Is there a good match? In what ways could the match be improved? Is the organization experiencing any problems with its structure?
5. Is your organization operating in more than one domain? If it is, what corporate-level strategies is it pursuing? How is it creating value from these strategies? Is it successful?
6. What kind of strategy is your organization pursuing in the international environment? What kind of structure does your organization use to manage this strategy?

CASE FOR ANALYSIS

Levi Strauss Goes Global

Levi Strauss and Company, the U.S. company that produces the blue jeans that are famous throughout the world, has a strong incentive to increase its global presence: The jeans that retail in the United States for $30 sell in places like London, Paris, and Tokyo for $80 or more! The wholesale price of Levi's jeans in Europe and Japan is $31.99, more than their retail price in the United States.[47] Outside the United States, Levi's jeans are a status symbol and command a premium price from young European and Asian consumers, even though in the United States the status of Levi's has been eroded by competition from manufacturers like Calvin Klein and Ralph Lauren.

To take advantage of its popularity in foreign markets, and at the same time increase profit margins at home, Levi Strauss has increasingly pursued a transnational strategy that requires it to locate its global production operations around the world and to customize its products to suit the needs of customers in different countries and world regions. For example, Levi Strauss has located its raw materials, intermediate manufacturing, and assembly operations at locations where costs are lowest. It buys much of its cotton from Texas, where at El Paso cotton is turned into denim, dyed, and stone washed. The denim fabric is then sent to be tailored into jeans at locations in the Dominican Republic, the Philippines, and elsewhere. Levi Strauss currently has no U.S. assembly operations for its jeans—it closed them all down to take advantage of low-cost labor abroad.

In order to pursue its transnational strategy, Levi Strauss created a number of foreign subsidiaries to handle its marketing throughout the world and to allow it to customize its jeans to the needs of different countries or world regions. Asian customers have a somewhat smaller stature, for example, so it is important for a greater variety of smaller sized jeans to be available in order to increase sales in Asian countries. Popular colors for jeans also differ from country to country. Levi Strauss's European division handles distribution and marketing throughout Europe and is responsible for determining the demands of customers in different European countries. This information is then transmitted to Levi's input suppliers and assembly plants, to ensure that they will produce and tailor jeans to suit the demands of European consumers.

Levi Strauss is also taking advantage of its transnational strategy to transfer abroad the marketing skills it has developed in the United States. For example, it recently introduced Dockers, its very successful line of casual clothes, into Europe and Asia using the experience it had gained in introducing Dockers to the U.S. market. Also recently, it has made a big push to popularize wrinkle-free cotton slacks to U.S. consumers, a concept first developed in Europe. Companies, like Levi Strauss, that pursue transnational strategies are constantly on the lookout for ways to exploit their organizational strengths to better serve the needs of their global customers and increase their profits.

To pursue its strategy effectively, Levi Strauss has created a network structure. Levi keeps its core competences in design centralized in the United States. It has created a series of strategic alliances with foreign companies to produce and distribute its products. Each foreign manufacturer is required to meet Levi's strict production standards and its strict ethical standards concerning the conditions under which foreign labor is employed. If its alliance partners do not meet the standards, they are dropped; Levi's terminated its relationship with 13 suppliers because they were employing child labor and paying employees far below the prevailing wage rate. Levi's ability to form and disband global relationships gives it great flexibility in responding to the changing demands of customers in different parts of the world. Levi's can keep its structure closely aligned with its strategy.

DISCUSSION QUESTIONS

1. How does Levi Strauss take advantage of the global environment?
2. What global expansion strategy is the company pursuing?

REFERENCES

1. A. D. Chandler, *Strategy and Structure: Chapters in the History of the Industrial Enterprise* (Cambridge, MA: MIT Press, 1962).
2. C.W.L. Hill and G. R. Jones, *Strategic Management: An Integrated Approach*, 4e (Boston: Houghton Mifflin, 1998).
3. M. E. Porter, *Competitive Strategy* (New York: The Free Press, 1980).
4. K. Weigelt and C. Camerer, "Reputation and Corporate Strategy." *Strategic Management Journal, 9* (1988), 443–454.
5. Hill and Jones, *Strategic Management*, Chapter 10.
6. R. R. Nelson and S. Winter, *An Evolutionary Theory of Economic Change* (Cambridge, MA: Harvard University Press, 1982).
7. M. E. Porter, *Competitive Advantage: Creating and Sustaining Superior Performance* (New York: The Free Press, 1985).
8. R. W. Ruekert and O. C. Walker, "Interactions Between Marketing and R&D Departments in Implementing Different Business Strategies," *Strategic Management Journal, 8* (1987), pp. 233–248.
9. Porter, *Competitive Strategy*.
10. K.N.M. Dundas and P. R. Richardson, "Corporate Strategy and the Concept of Market Failure," *Strategic Management Journal, 1* (1980), 177–188.
11. Porter, *Competitive Advantage*.
12. S. C. Wheelright, "Manufacturing Strategy: Defining the Missing Link," *Strategic Management Journal, 5* (1984), 77–91.
13. D. Ulrich, "Linking Strategic Planning and Human Resource Planning," in L. Fahey, ed., *The Strategic Planning Management Reader* (Upper Saddle River, NJ: Prentice Hall, 1989), pp. 421–426.
14. E. S. Buffa, "Positioning the Production System—A Key Element in Manufacturing Strategy," in Fahey, *The Strategic Planning Management Reader*, pp. 387–395.
15. O. E. Williamson, *Markets and Hierarchies* (New York: The Free Press, 1975).
16. R. M. Johnson, "Market Segmentation: A Strategic Management Tool," *Journal of Marketing Research, 8* (1971), 15–23.
17. V. Scarpello, W. R. Boulton, and C. W. Hofer, "Reintegrating R&D into Business Strategy," *Journal of Business Strategy, 6* (1986), 49–56.
18. www.google.com, 2005.
19. D. Miller, "Strategy Making and Structure: Analysis and Implications for Performance," *Academy of Management Journal, 30* (1987), 7–32.
20. P. R. Lawrence and J. W. Lorsch, *Organization and Environment* (Boston: Graduate School of Business Administration, Harvard University, 1967).
21. J. Woodward, *Industrial Organization: Theory and Practice* (London: Oxford University Press, 1965).
22. K. M. Eisenhardt, "Control: Organizational and Economic Approaches," *Management Science, 16* (1985), 134–138.
23. J. B. Barney, "Organization Culture: Can It Be a Source of Sustained Competitive Advantage?" *Academy of Management Review, 11* (1986), 791–800.
24. S. M. Oster, *Modern Competitive Analysis* (New York: Oxford University Press, 1990).
25. Porter, *Competitive Strategy*, Chapter 2.
26. Ibid.
27. R. E. White, "Generic Business Strategies, Organizational Context and Performance: An Empirical Investigation," *Strategic Management Journal, 7* (1986), 217–231; G. R. Jones and J. E. Butler, "Costs, Revenue, and Business-Level Strategy," *Academy of Management Review, 13* (1988), 202–213.
28. www.amazon.com, 2006.
29. Porter, *Competitive Strategy*.
30. White, "Generic Business Strategies, Organizational Context and Performance"; D. Miller, "Configurations of Strategy and Structure," *Strategic Management Journal, 7* (1986), 223–249.
31. S. Kotha and D. Orne, "Generic Manufacturing Strategies: A Conceptual Synthesis," *Strategic Management Journal, 10* (1989), 211–231.
32. P. R. Lawrence and J. W. Lorsch, *Organization and Environment* (Cambridge, MA: Harvard University Press, 1967).
33. D. Miller, "Strategy Making and Structure: Analysis and Implications for Performance," *Academy of Management Journal, 30* (1987), 7–32.
34. A. Deutschman, "If They're Gaining on You, Innovate," *Fortune*, November 2, 1992, p. 86.
35. www.kodak.com, 2005.
36. T. J. Peters and R. H. Waterman, Jr., *In Search of Excellence* (New York: Harper and Row, 1982).
37. E. Deal and A. A. Kennedy, *Corporate Cultures* (Reading, MA: Addison-Wesley, 1985).
38. M. E. Porter, "From Competitive Advantage to Competitive Strategy," *Harvard Business Review* (May–June 1987), 43–59.
39. Based on Chandler, *Strategy and Structure*.
40. Chandler, *Strategy and Structure*; J. Pfeffer and G. R. Salancik, *The External Control of Organizations* (New York: Harper and Row, 1978).
41. Williamson, *Markets and Hierarchies*; K. R. Harrigan, *Strategic Flexibility* (Lexington, MA: Lexington Books, 1985).
42. Porter, "From Competitive Advantage to Competitive Strategy."
43. C.W.L. Hill, "Hanson PLC," in C.W.L. Hill and G. R. Jones, *Strategic Management: An Integrated Approach*, 4e (Boston: Houghton Mifflin, 1998), pp. 764–783.
44. G. R. Jones and C.W.L. Hill, "Transaction Cost Analysis of Strategy-Structure Choice," *Strategic Management Journal, 9* (1988), 159–172.
45. www.hitachi.com, 2006.
46. "New In-Flight Adapter Adds to Hitachi's Mobilized Computing Vision and Extends Flexibility and Mobility," *Business Wire*, October 20, 1997.
47. N. Munk, "The Levi Straddle," *Forbes*, January 17, 1994, pp. 44–45.

9

Organizational Design, Competences, and Technology

Learning Objectives

This chapter focuses on technology and examines how organizations use it to build competences and create value. Then, it discusses why certain kinds of organizational structures are likely to be used with certain kinds of technology (just as earlier chapters used a similar contingency approach to examine why certain environments or strategies typically require the use of certain kinds of structure).

After studying this chapter you should be able to:

1. Identify what technology is and how it relates to organizational effectiveness.
2. Differentiate among three different kinds of technology that create different competences.
3. Understand how each type of technology needs to be matched to a certain kind of organizational structure if an organization is to be effective.
4. Understand how technology affects organizational culture.
5. Appreciate how advances in technology, and new techniques for managing technology, are helping to increase organizational effectiveness.

WHAT IS TECHNOLOGY?

When we think of an organization, we are likely to think of it in terms of what it does. We think of manufacturing organizations like Whirlpool or Ford as places where people use their skills in combination with machinery and equipment to assemble inputs into appliances, cars, and other finished products. We view service organizations like hospitals and banks as places where people apply their skills in combination with machinery or equipment to make sick people well or to facilitate customers' financial transactions. In all manufacturing and service organizations, actions are taken to create value—that is, inputs are converted into goods and services that satisfy people's needs.

Progressive Manufacture at Ford

In 1913, Henry Ford opened the Highland Park plant to produce the Model T car. In doing so, he changed forever the way complex products like cars are made, and the new technology of "progressive manufacture" (Ford's term), or mass production, was born. Before Ford introduced mass production, most cars were manufactured by craftswork. A team of workers—a skilled mechanic and a few helpers—performed all the operations necessary to make the product. Individual craftsworkers in the automobile and other industries have the skills to deal with unexpected situations as they arise during the manufacturing process. They can modify misaligned parts so that they fit together snugly, and they can follow specifications and create small batches of a range of products. Because craftswork relies on workers' skills and expertise, it is a costly and slow method of manufacturing. In searching for new ways to improve the efficiency of manufacturing, Ford developed the process of progressive manufacture.

Ford outlined three principles of progressive manufacture:

1. Work should be delivered to the worker; the worker should not have to find the work.[1] At the Highland Park plant, a mechanized, moving conveyor belt brought cars to the workers. Workers did not move past a stationary line of cars under assembly.

2. Work should proceed in an orderly and specific sequence so that each task builds on the task that precedes it. At Highland Park, the implementation of this idea fell to managers, who worked out the most efficient sequence of tasks and coordinated them with the speed of the conveyor belt.

3. Individual tasks should be broken down into their simplest components in order to increase specialization and create an efficient division of labor. The assembly of a taillight, for example, might be broken into two separate tasks to be performed all day long by two different workers. One person puts lightbulbs into a reflective panel; the other person screws a red lens onto the reflective panel.

By following those three principles, Ford made the conversion of inputs (component parts) into outputs (finished cars) much more controllable and predictable than it had been with craftswork. The speed of the conveyor belt relieved supervisors of the need to monitor and direct each employee. In the new work system, a supervisor's job was to evaluate performance and discipline workers for poor performance. Ford's three principles reduced the level of skill and competence needed by production workers: A new worker needed only two days to learn the skills necessary to perform a typical assembly-line job.

As a result of this new work system, by 1914 Ford plants employed 15,000 workers, but only 255 supervisors (not including top management) to oversee them. The ratio of workers to supervisors was 58 to 1. This very wide span of control was possible because the sequence and pacing of the work were not directed by the supervisors but were controlled by work programming and the speed of the production line.[2] The mass production system helped Ford control many workers with a relatively small number of supervisors, but it also created a tall hierarchy. The hierarchy at a typical Ford plant had six levels, reflecting the fact that management's major preoccupation was the vertical communication of information to top management, which controlled decision making for the whole plant.

The introduction of mass production technology to auto making was only one of Henry Ford's technological manufacturing innovations. Another was the use of interchangeable parts. When parts are interchangeable, the components from various suppliers fit together; they do not need to be altered to fit during the assembly process. With the old craftswork method of production, a high level of worker competence was needed to fit together the components provided by different manufacturers, which often differed in size or quality. Ford insisted that component manufacturers follow detailed specifications so that parts needed no remachining, and so that his relatively unskilled workforce would be able to assemble them easily. Eventually, the desire to control the quality of inputs led Ford to embark on a massive program of vertical integration. Ford mined iron ore in its mines in Upper Michigan and transported the ore in a fleet of Ford-owned barges to Ford's steel plants in Detroit, where it was smelted, rolled, and stamped into standard body parts.

As a result of these technological innovations in manufacturing, by the early 1920s Henry Ford's organization was making over two million cars a year. Because of his efficient manufacturing methods, Ford reduced the price of a car by two-thirds. This low-price advantage, in turn, created a mass market for his product.[3] Clearly, as measured by standards of technical efficiency and the ability to satisfy external stakeholders such as customers, Ford Motor Company was a very effective organization. Inside the factories, however, the picture was not so rosy.

Workers hated their work. Ford managers responded to their discontent with repressive supervision. Workers were watched constantly. They were not allowed to talk on the production line, and their behavior both in the plant and outside was closely monitored (for example, they were not allowed to drink alcohol, even when they were not working). Supervisors could instantly fire workers who disobeyed any rules. So repressive were conditions that by 1914 so many workers had been fired or had quit that 500 new workers had to be hired each day to keep the workforce at 15,000.[4] Clearly, the new technology of mass production was imposing severe demands on individual workers.

Technology
The combination of skills, knowledge, abilities, techniques, materials, machines, computers, tools, and other equipment that people use to covert or change raw materials into valuable goods and services.

Mass production
The organizational technology that uses conveyor belts and a standardized, progressive assembly process to manufacture goods.

Craftwork
The technology that involves groups of skilled workers who interact closely to produce custom-designed products.

Technology is the combination of skills, knowledge, abilities, techniques, materials, machines, computers, tools, and other equipment that people use to convert or change raw materials into valuable goods and services. When people at Ford, the Mayo Clinic, and H&R Block use their skills, knowledge, materials, machines, and so forth to produce a finished car, a cured patient, or a completed tax return, they are using technology to bring about change to something to add value to it.

Inside an organization, technology exists at three levels: individual, functional or departmental, and organizational. At the *individual* level, technology is the personal skills, knowledge, and competences that individual women and men possess. At the *functional* or *departmental* level, the procedures and techniques that groups work out to perform their work create competences that constitute technology. The interactions of the members of a surgical operating team, the cooperative efforts of scientists in a research and development laboratory, and techniques developed by assembly-line workers are all examples of competences and technology at the functional or departmental level.

The way an organization converts inputs into outputs is often used to characterize technology at the *organizational* level. **Mass production** is the organizational technology based on competences in using a standardized, progressive assembly process to manufacture goods. **Craftswork** is the technology that involves groups of skilled workers, interacting closely and blending their competences to produce custom-designed products. The difference between these two forms of technology is clearly illustrated by the way Henry Ford revolutionized car production.

TECHNOLOGY AND ORGANIZATIONAL EFFECTIVENESS

Recall from Chapter 1 that organizations take inputs from the environment and create value from the inputs by transforming them into outputs through conversion processes (see Figure 9.1). Although we usually think of technology only at the conversion stage, technology is present in all organizational activities: input, conversion, and output.[5]

At the *input* stage, technology—skills, procedures, techniques, and competences—allows each organizational function to handle relationships with outside stakeholders so that the organization can effectively manage its specific environment. The human resource function, for example, has techniques such as interviewing procedures and psychological testing that it uses to recruit and select qualified employees. The materials management function has developed competences in dealing with input suppliers, for negotiating favorable contract terms, and for obtaining low-cost, high-quality component parts. The finance department has techniques for obtaining capital at a cost favorable to the company.

At the *conversion* stage, technology—a combination of machines, techniques, and work procedures—transforms inputs into outputs. The best technology allows an organization to add the most value to its inputs at the least cost of organizational resources. Organizations often try to improve the efficiency of their conversion processes, and they can improve it by training employees in new time-management techniques and by allowing employees to devise better ways of performing their jobs.

At the *output* stage, technology allows an organization to effectively dispose of finished goods and services to external stakeholders. To be effective, an organization must possess competences in testing the quality of the finished product, in selling and marketing the product, and in managing after-sales service to customers.

The technology of an organization's input, conversion, and output processes is an important source of a company's competitive advantage. Why is Microsoft the most successful software company? Why is Toyota the most efficient car manufacturer? Why is McDonald's the most efficient fast-food company? Why does Wal-Mart consistently outperform K-mart and Sears? Each of these organizations excels

Figure 9.1
Input, Conversion, and
Output Processes

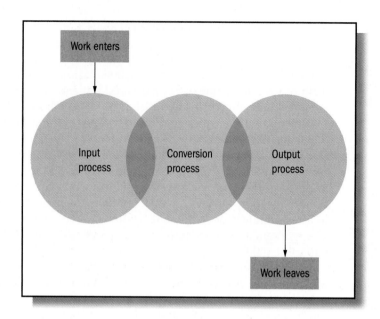

in the development, management, and use of technology to create competences that lead to higher value for stakeholders.

Recall from Chapter 1 three principal approaches to measuring and increasing organizational effectiveness (see Table 1.1). An organization taking the *external resource approach* uses technology to increase its ability to manage and control external stakeholders. Any new technological developments that allow an organization to improve its service to customers, such as the ability to customize products or to increase products' quality and reliability, increases the organization's effectiveness.

An organization taking the *internal systems approach* uses technology to increase the success of its attempts to innovate, to develop new products, services, and processes, and to reduce the time needed to bring new products to market. As we saw earlier, the introduction of mass production at the Highland Park plant allowed Henry Ford to make a new kind of product—a car for the mass market.

An organization taking the *technical approach* uses technology to improve efficiency and reduce costs while simultaneously enhancing the quality and reliability of its products. Ford increased his organization's effectiveness by organizing its functional resources to create better quality cars at lower costs to both manufacturer and consumer.

Organizations use technology to become more efficient, more innovative, and better able to meet the needs and desires of stakeholders. Each department or function in an organization is responsible for building competences and developing technology that allows it to make a positive contribution to organizational performance. When an organization has technology that enables it to create value, it needs a structure that maximizes the effectiveness of the technology. Just as environmental characteristics require organizations to make certain organizational design choices, so do the characteristics of different technologies affect an organization's choice of structure.

In the next three sections we examine three theories of technology that are attempts to capture the way different departmental and organizational technologies work and affect organizational design. Note that these three theories are *complementary* in that each illuminates some aspects of technology that the others don't. All three theories are needed to understand the characteristics of different kinds of technologies. Managers, at all levels and in all functions, can use these theories to (1) choose the technology that will most effectively transform inputs into outputs and (2) design a structure that allows the organization to operate the technology effectively. Thus it is important for these managers to understand the concept of technical complexity, the underlying differences between routine and complex tasks, and the concept of task interdependence.

TECHNICAL COMPLEXITY: THE THEORY OF JOAN WOODWARD

Programmed technology
A technology in which the procedures for converting inputs into outputs can be specified in advance so that tasks can be standardized and the work process can be made predictable.

Technical complexity
A measure of the extent to which a production process can be programmed so that it can be controlled and made predictable.

Some kinds of technology are more complex and difficult to control than others because some are more difficult to program than others. Technology is said to be **programmed** when procedures for converting inputs into outputs can be specified in advance so that tasks can be standardized and the work process be made predictable. McDonald's uses a highly programmed technology to produce hamburgers, and Ford uses a highly programmed technology to produce cars. They do so to control the quality of their outputs—hamburgers or cars. The more difficult it is to specify the process for converting inputs into outputs, the more difficult it is to control the production process and make it predictable.

According to one researcher, Joan Woodward, the **technical complexity** of a production process—that is, the extent to which it can be programmed so that it can be controlled and made predictable—is the important dimension that differentiates technologies.[6] *High technical complexity* exists when conversion processes can be programmed in advance and fully automated. With full automation, work activities and the outputs that result from them are standardized and can be predicted accurately. *Low technical complexity* exists when conversion processes depend primarily on people and their skills and knowledge and not on machines. With increased human involvement and less reliance on machines, work activities cannot be programmed in advance, and results depend on the skills of the people involved.

The production of services, for example, typically relies much more on the knowledge and experience of employees who interact directly with customers to produce the final output than it relies on machines and other equipment. The labor-intensive nature of the production of services makes standardizing and programming work activities and controlling the work process especially difficult. When conversion processes depend primarily on the performance of people, rather than on machines, technical complexity is low, and the difficulty of maintaining high quality and consistency of production is great.

Joan Woodward identified 10 levels of technical complexity, which she associated with three types of production technology: (1) small-batch and unit technology, (2) large-batch and mass production technology, and (3) continuous-process technology (see Figure 9.2).[7]

Small-Batch and Unit Technology

Organizations that employ small-batch and unit technology make one-of-a-kind, customized products or small quantities of products. Examples of such organizations include a furniture maker that constructs furniture designed to suit the tastes of a few individuals; a printer that supplies engraved wedding invitations for specific couples; and teams of surgeons and hospitals, which provide a great variety of services customized to the needs of individual patients. Small-batch and unit technology score lowest on the dimension of technical complexity (see Figure 9.2) because any machines used during the conversion process are less important than people's skills and knowledge. People decide how and when machines will be used, and the production process reflects their decisions about how to apply their knowledge. A custom furniture maker, for example, uses an array of tools—including lathes, hammers, planes, and saws—to transform boards into a cabinet. However, which tools are used and the order in which they are used depends on how the furniture maker chooses to build the cabinet. With small-batch and unit technology, the conversion process is flexible because the worker adapts techniques to suit the orders of individual customers.

The flexibility of small-batch technology gives an organization the capacity to produce a wide range of products that can be customized for individual customers. For example, high-fashion designers and makers of products like fine perfume, custom-built cars, and specialized furniture use small-batch technology. Small-batch

Figure 9.2
Technical Complexity and Three Types of Technology

Joan Woodward identified 10 levels of technical complexity, which she associated with three types of production. *Source*: Adapted from Joan Woodward, "*Management and Technology*," London: Her Majesty's Stationery Office, 1958, p. 11. Reproduced with permission of the Controller of Her Britannic Majesty's Stationery Office.

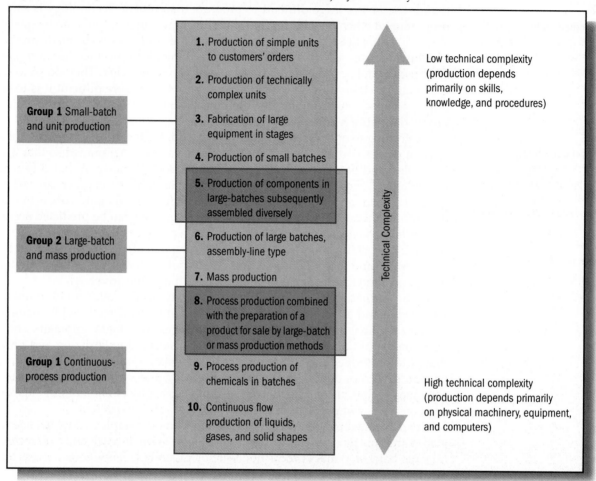

technology allows a custom furniture maker, for example, to satisfy the customer's request for a certain style of table made from a certain kind of wood.

Small-batch technology is relatively expensive to operate because the work process is unpredictable and the production of customized, made-to-order products makes advance programming of work activities difficult. However, flexibility and the ability to respond to a wide range of customer requests make this technology ideally suited to producing new or complex products. Microsoft uses small-batch technology when it assigns a team of programmers to work together to develop new software applications.

Large-Batch and Mass Production Technology

To increase control over the work process and make it predictable, organizations try to increase their use of machines and equipment—that is, they try to increase the level of technical complexity and to increase their efficiency. Organizations that employ large-batch or mass production technology produce large volumes of standardized products such as cars, razor blades, aluminum cans, and soft drinks. Examples of such organizations include Ford, Gillette, Crown Cork and Seal, and Coca-Cola. With large-batch and mass production technology, machines control the work process. Their use allows tasks to be specified and programmed in advance.

Founded in 1937 in Newington, Connecticut, Krispy Kreme is a leading specialty retailer of premium quality, yeast-raised doughnuts. Krispy Kreme's doughnuts have a broad customer following and command a premium price because of their unique taste and quality. Although it has experienced problems in recent years because of its rapid expansion across the United States, the way Krispy Kreme uses small-batch production to increase the efficiency and responsiveness to customers of its store operations is instructive. Krispy Kreme calls its production operations "doughnut theatre" because the physical layout of its stores is designed so that customers can see and smell the doughnuts being made by its impressive, company-built doughnut-making machines.

What are elements of its small-batch production methods? The story starts with the 65-year-old company's secret doughnut recipe that is kept locked in a vault. None of its franchisees know the recipe for making its dough, and Krispy Kreme sells the ready-made dough and other ingredients to its stores. Even the machines used to make the doughnuts are company-designed and produced so no doughnut maker can imitate its unique cooking methods and thus create a similar, competing product.

The doughnut-making machines are designed to produce a wide variety of different kinds of doughnuts in small quantities, and each store makes and sells between 4,000 and 10,000 dozen doughnuts per day.

Krispy Kreme constantly refines its production system to improve the efficiency of its small-batch operations. For example, it redesigned its doughnut machine to include a high-tech extruder that uses air pressure to force doughnut dough into row after row of rings or shells. Employees used to have to manually adjust air pressure as the dough load lightened; now, this is all done automatically. A new doughnut icer tips finished pastries into a puddle of chocolate frosting; employees had to dunk the doughnuts two at a time by hand before the machine was invented. Although these innovations may seem "small," across hundreds of stores and millions of doughnuts they add up to significant gains in productivity—and more satisfied customers.

As a result, work activities are standardized, and the production process is highly controllable.[8] Instead of a team of craftsworkers making custom furniture piece by piece, for example, high-speed saws and lathes cut and shape boards into standardized components that are assembled into thousands of identical tables or chairs by unskilled workers on a production line.

The control provided by large-batch and mass production technology allows an organization to save money on production and charge a lower price for its products. As we saw in the opening case, Henry Ford changed manufacturing history when he replaced small-batch production (the assembly of cars one-by-one by skilled craftsmen) with mass production to manufacture the Model T. The use of a conveyor belt, standardized and interchangeable parts, and specialized, progressive tasks made conversion processes at the Highland Park plant more efficient and productive. Production costs plummeted, and Ford was able to lower the cost of a Model T and create a mass market for his product.

Continuous-Process Technology

With continuous-process technology, technical complexity reaches its height (see Figure 9.2). Organizations that employ continuous-process technology include companies that make oil-based products and chemicals, such as Exxon, DuPont, and Conoco, and brewing companies such as Anheuser-Busch and Miller Brewing. In continuous-process production, the conversion process is almost entirely automated and mechanized; employees generally are not directly involved. Their role in production is to monitor the plant and its machinery and ensure its efficient operation.[9] The task of employees engaged in continuous-process production is primarily to manage exceptions in the work process, such as a machine breakdown or malfunctioning equipment.

The hallmark of continuous-process technology is the smoothness of its operation. Production continues with little variation in output and rarely stops. In an oil refinery, for example, crude oil brought continuously to the refinery by tankers flows through pipes to cracking towers, where its individual component chemicals are extracted and sent to other parts of the refinery for further refinement. Final products such as gasoline, fuel oil, benzene, and tar leave the plant in tankers to be shipped to customers. Workers in a refinery or in a chemical plant rarely see what they are producing. Production takes place through pipes and machines. Employees in a centralized control room monitor gauges and dials to ensure that the process functions smoothly, safely, and efficiently.

Continuous-process production tends to be more technically efficient than mass production because it is more mechanized and automated and thus is more predictable and easier to control. It is more cost efficient than both unit and mass production because labor costs are such a small proportion of its overall cost. When operated at full capacity, continuous-process technology has the lowest production costs.

Woodward noted that an organization usually seeks to increase its use of machines (if it is practical to do so) and move from small-batch to mass production to continuous-process production in order to reduce costs. There are, however, exceptions to this progression. For many organizational activities, the move to automate production is not possible or practical. Prototype development, basic research into new drugs or computers, and the operation of hospitals and schools, for example, are intrinsically unpredictable and thus would be difficult to program in advance with an automated machine. A pharmaceutical company cannot say, "Our research department will invent three new drugs—one for diabetes and two for high blood pressure—every six months." Such inventions are the result of trial and error and depend on the skills and knowledge of the researchers. Moreover, many customers are willing to pay high prices for custom-designed products that suit their individual tastes, such as custom-made suits, jewelry, or even cars. Thus there is a market for the products of small-batch companies even though production costs are high.

Technical Complexity and Organizational Structure

One of Woodward's goals in classifying technologies according to their technical complexity was to discover whether an organization's technology affected the design of its structure. Specifically, Woodward wanted to see whether effective organizations had structures that matched the needs of their technologies. When she compared the structural characteristics of organizations pursuing each of the three types of technology, she found systematic differences in the technology–structure relationship. Figure 9.3 shows some of her findings, together with a simplified model of the organizational structure associated with each type of technology.

On the basis of her findings, Woodward argued that each technology is associated with a different structure because each technology presents different control and coordination problems. Organizations with small-batch technology typically have three levels in their hierarchy; organizations with mass production technology, four levels; and organizations with continuous-process technology, six levels. As technical complexity increases, organizations become taller, and the span of control of the CEO widens. The span of control of first-line supervisors first expands and then narrows. It is relatively small with small-batch technology, widens greatly with mass production technology, and contracts dramatically with continuous-process technology. These findings result in the very differently shaped structures shown at the bottom of Figure 9.3. Why does the nature of an organization's technology produce these results?

The main coordination problem associated with *small-batch technology* is the impossibility of programming conversion activities because production depends on the skills and experience of people working together. An organization that uses small-batch technology has to give people the freedom to make their own decisions so that they can respond quickly and flexibly to the customer's requests and produce the exact product the customer wants. For this reason, such an organization has a relatively flat structure (three levels in the hierarchy), and decision making is decentralized

Figure 9.3
Technical Complexity and Organizational Structure

Woodward's research indicated that each technology presents different control and coordination problems and is, thus, associated with a different organizational structure. *Source*: Adapted from J. Woodward, *"Industrial Organization: Theory and Practice,"* London: Oxford University Press, 1965. Reprinted by permission of Oxford University Press.

	Low ← Technical Complexity → High		
Structural Characteristics	**Small-Batch Technology**	**Mass Production Technology**	**Continuous-Process Technology**
Level in the hierarchy	3	4	6
Span of control of CEO	4	7	10
Span of control of first-line supervisor	23	48	15
Ratio of managers to nonmanagers	1 to 23	1 to 16	1 to 8
Approximate shape of organization	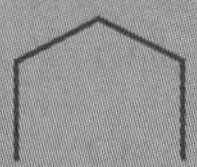 *Relatively flat, with narrow span of control*	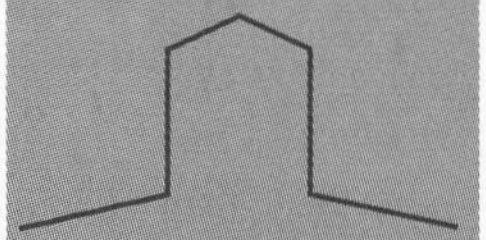 *Relatively tall, with wide span of control*	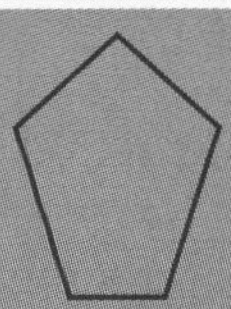 *Very tall, with very narrow span of control*
Type of structure	Organic	Mechanistic	Organic
Cost of operation	High	Medium	Low

to small teams where first-line supervisors have a relatively small span of control (23 employees). With small-batch technology, each supervisor and work group decides how to manage each decision as it occurs at each step of the input-conversion-output process. This type of decision making requires mutual adjustment—face-to-face communication with coworkers and often with customers. The most appropriate structure for unit and small-batch technology is an organic structure in which managers and employees work closely to coordinate their activities to meet changing work demands—hence the relatively flat structure shown in Figure 9.3.[10]

In an organization that uses *mass production technology*, the ability to program tasks in advance allows the organization to standardize the manufacturing process and make it predictable. The first-line supervisor's span of control increases to 48 because formalization through rules and procedures becomes the principal method of coordination. Decision making becomes centralized, and the hierarchy of authority becomes taller (four levels) as managers rely on vertical communication to control the work process. A *mechanistic structure* becomes the appropriate structure to control work activities in a mass production setting, and the organizational structure becomes taller and wider, as shown in Figure 9.3.

In an organization that uses *continuous-process technology*, tasks can be programmed in advance, and the work process is predictable and controllable in a technical sense, but there is still the potential for a major systems breakdown. The principal control problem facing the organization is monitoring the production process to control and correct unforeseen events before they lead to disaster. The consequences of a faulty pipeline in an oil refinery or chemical plant, for example, are potentially disastrous. Accidents at a nuclear power plant, another user of continuous-process technology, can also have catastrophic effects, as accidents at Chernobyl and Three Mile Island showed.

The need to constantly monitor the operating system, and to make sure that each employee conforms to accepted operating procedures, is the reason why continuous-process technology is associated with the tallest hierarchy of authority (six levels). Managers at all levels closely monitor their subordinates' actions. The diamond-shaped hierarchy shown in Figure 9.3 reflects the fact that first-line supervisors have a narrow span of control. Many supervisors are needed to supervise lower-level employees and to monitor and control sophisticated equipment. Because employees also work together as a team and jointly work out procedures for managing and reacting to unexpected situations, mutual adjustment becomes the primary means of coordination. Thus an *organic structure* is the appropriate structure for managing continuous-process technology, because the potential for unpredictable events requires the capability to provide quick, flexible responses.

One researcher, Charles Perrow, argues that complex continuous-process technology such as the technology used in nuclear power plants is so complicated that it is uncontrollable.[11] Perrow acknowledges that control systems are designed with backup systems to handle problems as they arise and that backup systems exist to compensate for failed backup systems. He believes nevertheless that the number of unexpected events that can occur when technical complexity is very high (as it is in nuclear power plants) is so great that managers cannot react quickly enough to solve all the problems that might arise. Perrow argues that some continuous-process technology is so complex that no organizational structure can allow managers to safely operate it, no standard operating procedures can be devised to manage problems in advance, and no use of mutual adjustments will be able to solve problems as they arise. One implication of Perrow's view is that nuclear power stations should be closed because they are too complex to operate safely. Other researchers, however, disagree, arguing that when the right balance of centralized and decentralized control is achieved, the technology can be operated safely.

The Technological Imperative

Woodward's results, which have been replicated by several researchers, strongly suggest that technology is a main factor determining the design of organizational structure.[12] Her results imply that if a company operates with a certain technology, then it needs to adopt a certain kind of structure to be effective. If a company uses mass production technology, for example, then it should have a mechanistic structure with six levels in the hierarchy, a span of control of one to 48, and so forth, to be effective. The argument that technology determines structure is known as the **technological imperative**.

Other researchers also interested in the technology–structure relationship became concerned that Woodward's results may have been a consequence of the sample of companies she studied and may have overstated the importance of technology.[13] They pointed out that most of the companies that Woodward studied were relatively small (82% had fewer than 500 employees) and suggested that her sample may have biased her results. They acknowledged that technology may have a major impact on structure in a small manufacturing company, because improving the efficiency of manufacturing may be management's major priority. But they suggested that the structure of an organization that has 5,000 or 500,000 employees (such as

Technological imperative
The argument that technology determines structure.

Exxon, GM, or IBM) is less likely to be determined primarily by the technology used to manufacture its various products.

In a series of studies known as the Aston Studies, researchers agreed that technology has some effect on organizational structure: The more an organization's technology is mechanized and automated, the more likely is the organization to have a highly centralized and standardized mechanistic structure. But, the Aston Studies concluded, organizational size is more important than technology in determining an organization's choice of structure.[14] We have seen in earlier chapters that as an organization grows and differentiates, control and coordination problems emerge that must be addressed by changes in the organization's structure. The Aston researchers argued that although technology may strongly affect the structure of small organizations, the structure adopted by large organizations may be a product of other factors that cause an organization to grow and differentiate.

We saw in Chapter 8 that organizational strategy and the decision to produce a wider range of products and enter new markets can cause an organization to grow and adopt a more complex structure. Thus the strategic choices that an organization—especially a large organization—makes about what outputs to produce for which markets are at least as important to the design of the organization's structure as the technology the organization uses to produce the outputs. For small organizations or for functions or departments within large organizations, the importance of technology as a predictor of structure may be more important than it is for large organizations.[15]

ROUTINE TASKS AND COMPLEX TASKS: THE THEORY OF CHARLES PERROW

To understand why some technologies are more complex (more unpredictable and difficult to control) than others, it is necessary to understand why the tasks associated with some technologies are more complex than the tasks associated with other technologies. What causes one task to be more difficult than another? Why, for example, do we normally think that the task of serving hamburgers in a fast-food restaurant is more routine—that is, more predictable and controllable—than the task of programming a computer or performing brain surgery? If we think of the range of tasks that people perform, what characteristics of these tasks cause us to believe that some are more complex than others? According to Charles Perrow, two dimensions underlie the difference between routine and nonroutine or complex tasks and technologies: task variability and task analyzability.[16]

Task Variability and Task Analyzability

Task variability
The number of exceptions-new or unexpected situations-that a person encounters while performing a task.

Task variability is the number of exceptions—new or unexpected situations—that a person encounters while performing a task. Exceptions may occur at the input, conversion, or output stage. Task variability is high when a person can expect to encounter many new situations or problems when performing his or her task. In a hospital operating room during the course of surgery, for example, there is much opportunity for unexpected problems to develop. The patient's condition may be more serious than the doctors thought it was, or the surgeon may make a mistake. No matter what happens, the surgeon and the operating team must have the capacity to adjust quickly to new situations as they occur. Similarly, great variability in the quality of the raw materials makes it especially difficult to manage and maintain consistent quality during the conversion stage.

Task variability is low when a task is highly standardized or repetitive so that a worker encounters the same situation time and time again.[17] In a fast-food restaurant, for example, the number of exceptions to a given task is limited. Each customer places a different order, but all customers must choose from the same limited menu, so employees rarely confront unexpected situations. In fact, the menu in a fast-food restaurant is designed for low task variability, which keeps costs down and efficiency up.

Task analyzability is the degree to which search activity is needed to solve a problem. The more analyzable a task is, the more routine it is because the procedures for completing it have been worked out or programmed in advance. For example, although a customer may select thousands of combinations of food from a menu at a fast-food restaurant, the order taker's task of fulfilling each customer's order is relatively easy. The problem of combining foods in a bag is easily analyzable: The order taker picks up the drink and puts it in the bag; then adds the fries, burger, and so on; folds down the top of the bag; and hands the bag to the customer. Little thought or judgment is needed to complete an order.

Tasks are hard to analyze when they cannot be programmed—that is, when procedures for carrying them out and dealing with exceptions cannot be worked out in advance. If a person encounters an exception, procedures for dealing with it must be sought. For example, a scientist trying to develop a new cancer-preventing drug that has no side effects, or a software programmer working on a program to enable computers to understand the spoken word, has to spend considerable time and effort working out the procedures for solving problems, and may fail because he or she cannot find a solution. People working on tasks with low analyzability have to draw on their knowledge and judgment to search for new procedures to solve problems. When a great deal of search activity is needed to find a solution to a problem and procedures cannot be programmed in advance, tasks are complex and nonroutine.

Together, task analyzability and task variability explain why some tasks are more routine than others. The greater the number of exceptions that workers encounter in the work process, and the greater the amount of search behavior that is required to find a solution to each exception, the more complex and less routine are tasks. For tasks that are routine, there are, in Perrow's words, "well-established techniques which are sure to work and these are applied to essentially similar raw materials. That is, there is little uncertainty about methods and little variety or change in the task that must be performed."[18] For tasks that are complex, "there are few established techniques; there is little certainty about methods, or whether or not they will work. But it also means that there may be a great variety of different tasks to perform."[19]

Four Types of Technology

Perrow used task variability and task analyzability to differentiate among four types of technology: routine manufacturing, craftswork, engineering production, and nonroutine research (see Figure 9.4).[20] Perrow's model can be used to categorize the technology of an organization and the technology of departments and functions inside an organization.

Routine Manufacturing

Routine manufacturing is characterized by low task variability and high task analyzability. Few exceptions are encountered in the work process, and when an exception does occur, little search behavior is required to deal with it. Mass production is representative of routine technology.

In mass production settings, tasks are broken down into simple steps to minimize the possibility that exceptions will occur, and inputs are standardized to minimize disruptions to the production process. There are standard procedures to follow if an exception or a problem presents itself. The low-cost advantages of mass production are obtained by making tasks low in variability and high in analyzability. One reason why McDonald's costs are lower than its competitors' costs is that McDonald's constantly streamlines its menu choices and standardizes its work activities to reduce task variability and increase task analyzability.

Figure 9.4
Task Variability, Task
Analyzability, and Four
Types of Technology

Charles Perrow defined two
factors—task variability and
task analyzability—that
account for differences between
tasks and technologies. *Source*:
Adapted from Charles Perrow,
*Organizational Analysis: A
Sociological View* (Belmont, CA:
Wadsworth, 1970), p. 78.

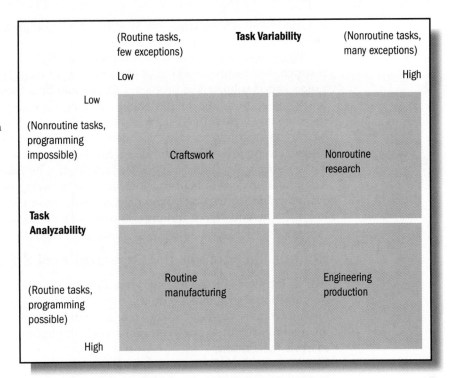

Craftswork

With craft technology, task variability is low (only a narrow range of exceptions is encountered), and task analyzability is also low (a high level of search activity is needed to find a solution to problems). Employees in an organization using this kind of technology need to adapt existing procedures to new situations and find new techniques to handle existing problems more effectively. This technology was used to build early automobiles, as we saw in the opening case. Other examples of craftswork are the manufacture of specialized or customized products like furniture, clothing, and machinery, and trades such as carpentry and plumbing. The tasks that a plumber, for example, is called on to perform center on installing or repairing bathroom or kitchen plumbing. But because every house is different, a plumber needs to adapt the techniques of the craft to each situation and find a unique solution for each house.

Engineering Production

With engineering production technology, task variability is high and task analyzability is high. The number or variety of exceptions that workers may encounter in the task is high, but finding a solution is relatively easy because well understood standard procedures have been established to handle the exceptions. Because these procedures are often codified in technical formulas, tables, or manuals, solving a problem is often a matter of identifying and applying the right technique. Thus, in organizations that use engineering production technology, existing procedures are used to make many kinds of products. A manufacturing company may specialize in custom building machines such as drill presses or electric motors. A firm of architects may specialize in customizing apartment buildings to the needs of different builders. A civil engineering group may use its skills in constructing airports, dams, and hydroelectric projects to service the needs of clients throughout the world. Like craftswork, engineering production is a form of small-batch technology because people are primarily responsible for developing techniques to solve particular problems.

Nonroutine Research

Nonroutine research technology is characterized by high task variability and low task analyzability and is the most complex and least routine of the four technologies in Perrow's classification. Tasks are complex because not only is the number of unexpected situations large, but search activity is high also. Each new situation creates a need to expend resources to deal with it.

High-tech research and development activities are examples of nonroutine research. For people working at the forefront of technical knowledge, there are no prepackaged solutions to problems. There may be a thousand well-defined steps to follow when building the perfect bridge (engineering production technology), but there are few well-defined steps to take to discover a cure for AIDS.

An organization's top management team is another example of a group that uses research technology. The team's job is to chart the future path of the organization and make resource decisions that are likely to ensure its success. They make these decisions in an uncertain context, however, not knowing how successful they will be. Planning and forecasting by top management, and other nonroutine research activities, are inherently risky and uncertain because the technology is difficult to manage.

Routine Technology and Organizational Structure

Just as the types of technology identified by Woodward have implications for an organization's structure, so do the types of technology in Perrow's model. Perrow and others have suggested that an organization should move from a mechanistic to an organic structure as tasks become more complex and less routine.[21] Table 9.1 summarizes this finding.

When technology is routine, employees perform clearly defined tasks according to well-established rules and procedures. The work process is programmed in advance and standardized. Because the work process is standardized in routine technology, employees need only learn the procedures for performing the task effectively. For example, McDonald's uses written rules and procedures to train new personnel so that the behavior of all McDonald's employees is consistent and predictable. Each new employee learns the right way to greet customers, the appropriate way to fulfill customer orders, and the correct way to make Big Macs.

Because employee tasks can be standardized with routine technology, the organizational hierarchy is relatively tall and decision making is centralized. Management's responsibility is to supervise employees and to manage the few exceptions that may occur, such as a breakdown of the production line. Because tasks are routine, all important production decisions are made at the top of the production hierarchy and are transmitted down the chain of command as orders to lower-level managers and workers. It has been suggested that organizations with routine technology, such as that found in mass production settings, deliberately "de-skill" tasks, meaning that they simplify jobs by using machines to perform complex tasks and by designing the work process to minimize the degree to which workers' initiative or judgment is required.[22]

The result of all these design choices is a mechanistic structure for organizations operating a routine technology. However, as we will see in the next chapter, this

Table 9.1 Routine and Nonroutine Tasks and Organizational Design

STRUCTURAL CHARACTERISTIC	NATURE OF TECHNOLOGY	
	ROUTINE TASKS	NONROUTINE TASKS
Standardization	High	Low
Mutual adjustment	Low	High
Specialization	Individual	Joint
Formalization	High	Low
Hierarchy of authority	Tall	Flat
Decision-making authority	Centralized	Decentralized
Overall structure	Mechanistic	Organic

choice may no longer be appropriate for an organization seeking to maintain a competitive advantage in the global environment.

Nonroutine Technology and Organizational Structure

Organizations operating a nonroutine technology face a different set of factors that affect the design of the organization.[23] As tasks become less routine and more complex, an organization has to develop a structure that allows employees to respond quickly to and manage an increase in the number and variety of exceptions and to develop new procedures to handle new problems.[24] As we saw in Chapter 4, an organic structure allows an organization to adapt rapidly to changing conditions. Organic structures are based on mutual adjustment between employees who work together, face-to-face, to develop procedures to find solutions to problems. Mutual adjustment through task forces and teams becomes especially important in facilitating communication and increasing integration between team members. Employees often perform closely related activities in which it is difficult to separate out each individual's contribution.[25]

The more complex an organization's work processes are, the more likely the organization is to have a relatively flat and decentralized structure that allows employees the authority and autonomy to cooperate to make decisions quickly and effectively.[26] The use of work groups and product teams to facilitate rapid adjustment and feedback among employees performing complex tasks is a key feature of such an organization.

The same design considerations are applicable at the departmental or functional level: To be effective, departments employing different technologies need different structures.[27] In general, departments performing nonroutine tasks are likely to have organic structures, and those performing routine tasks are likely to have mechanistic structures. An R&D department, for example, is typically organic, and decision making in it is usually decentralized; but the manufacturing and sales functions are usually mechanistic, and decision making within them tends to be centralized. The kind of technology employed at the departmental level determines the choice of structure.[28]

TASK INTERDEPENDENCE: THE THEORY OF JAMES D. THOMPSON

Task interdependence
The manner in which different organizational tasks are related to one another.

Woodward focused on how an organization's technology affects its choice of structure. Perrow's model of technology focuses on the way in which the complexity of tasks affects organizational structure. Another view of technology, developed by James D. Thompson, focuses on the way in which **task interdependence**, the manner in which different organizational tasks are related to one another, affects an organization's technology and structure.[29] When task interdependence is low, people and departments are individually specialized—that is, they work separately and independently to achieve organizational goals. When task interdependence is high, people and departments are jointly specialized—that is, they depend on one another for supplying the inputs and resources they need to get the work done. Thompson identified three types of technology: mediating, long-linked, and intensive (see Figure 9.5). Each of them is associated with a different form of task interdependence.

Mediating technology
A technology characterized by a work process in which input, conversion, and output activities can be performed independently of one another.

Mediating Technology and Pooled Interdependence

Mediating technology is characterized by a work process where input, conversion, and output activities can be performed independently of one another. Mediating technology is based on *pooled task interdependence*, which means that each part of the organization—whether a person, team, or department—contributes separately to the

Figure 9.5
Task Interdependence and
Three Types of Technology

James D. Thompson's model of
technology focuses on how the
relationship among different
organizational tasks affects an
organization's technology and
structure.

Type of technology	Form of task interdependence	Main type of coordination	Strategy for reducing uncertainty	Cost of coordination
Mediating	Pooled (X) (Y) (Z) (e.g., piecework or franchise)	Standardization	Increase in the number of customers served	Low
Long-linked	Sequential (X)→(Y)→(Z) (e.g., assembly-line or continuous-process plant)	Planning and scheduling	Slack resources Vertical integration	Medium
Intensive	Reciprocal (X)↔(Y)↔(Z) (e.g., general hospital or research and development laboratory)	Mutual adjustment	Specialism of task activities	High

performance of the whole organization. With mediating technology, task interdependence is low because people do not directly rely on others to help them perform their tasks. As illustrated in Figure 9.5, each person or department—X, Y, and Z—performs a separate task. In a management-consulting firm or hair salon, each consultant or hairdresser works independently to solve a client's problems. The success of the organization as a whole, however, depends on the collective efforts of everyone employed. The activities of a gymnastic team also illustrate pooled task interdependence. Each team member performs independently and can win or lose a particular event, but the collective score of the team members determines which team wins. The implications of mediating technology for organizational structure can be examined at both the departmental and the organizational level.

At the departmental level, piecework systems best characterize the way this technology operates. In a piecework system, each employee performs a task independently from other employees. In a machine shop, each employee might operate a lathe to produce bolts, and each is evaluated and rewarded on the basis of how many bolts he or she produces. The performance of the manufacturing department as a whole depends on how well each employee individually performs, but employees themselves are not interdependent because one employee's actions have no effect on the actions of others. Similarly, the performance of the sales department depends on the performance of each salesperson, but the performance of one salesperson is not affected by the performance of others in the department.

The use of a mediating technology to accomplish departmental or organizational activities makes it easy to monitor, control, and evaluate the performance of each individual because the output of each person is observable and the same standards can be used to evaluate each employee.[30]

At the organizational level, mediating technology is found in organizations where the activities of different departments are performed separately and there is little need for integration between departments to accomplish organizational goals. In a bank, for example, the activities of the loan department and the checking account department are essentially independent. The routines involved in lending money have no relation to the routines involved in receiving money, but the performance of the bank as a whole depends on how well each department does its job.[31]

Mediating technology at the organizational level is also found in organizations that use franchise arrangements to organize their businesses or that operate a chain of stores. For example, each McDonald's franchise or Wal-Mart store operates essentially independently. The performance of one store does not affect another store, but together all stores determine the performance of the whole organization. Indeed, one strategy for improving organizational performance for an organization operating a mediating technology is to try to attract new sets of customers by increasing the number of operating units or the number of products it offers. A fast-food chain can open a new restaurant. A retail organization can open a new store. A bank can increase the number of financial services it offers customers to attract new business. Indeed, one major goal of banks is to be given the right to sell stocks or mutual funds to increase their population of potential customers.

Over the past decades the use of mediating technology has been increasing because it is relatively inexpensive to operate and manage. Costs are low because organizational activities can be controlled by standardization. Bureaucratic rules and procedures can be used to specify how the activities of different departments are to be coordinated and to outline the procedures that a department needs to follow to ensure that its activities are compatible with those of other departments. Standard operating procedures and electronic media such as email provide the coordination necessary to manage the business. Wal-Mart, for example, coordinates its stores through a nationwide satellite system that informs managers about new product introductions or changes in rules and procedures.

As computers become more important in coordinating the activities of independent employees or departments, it becomes possible to use a mediating technology to coordinate more types of production activities. Network organizations, discussed in Chapter 6, are developing as computer technologies allow the different departments of an organization to operate separately and at different locations. Similarly, the growth of outsourcing—companies' contracting with other companies to perform their value-creation activities (like production or marketing) for them—shows the increasing use of mediating technology as a way of doing business.

Recall from Chapter 3 how Nike contracts with manufacturers throughout the world to produce and distribute products to its customers on a global basis. Nike designs a shoe but then contracts manufacturing, marketing, and other functional activities out to other organizations. Coordination is achieved by standardization of the product range. Nike has rules and procedures specifying the required quality of input materials, the nature of the manufacturing process, and the required quality of the finished product. Nike constantly monitors production and sales information from its network by means of a sophisticated global computer system.

Long-Linked Technology and Sequential Interdependence

Long-linked technology
A technology characterized by a work process in which input, conversion, and output activities must be performed in series.

Long-linked technology, the second type of technology that Thompson identified, is based on a work process where input, conversion, and output activities must be performed in series. Long-linked technology is based on *sequential task interdependence*, which means that the actions of one person or department directly affect the actions of another, so work cannot be successfully completed by allowing each person or department to operate independently. Figure 9.5 illustrates the dynamics of sequential interdependence. X's activities directly affect Y's ability to perform her task, and in turn the activities of Y directly affect Z's ability to perform.

Mass production technology is based on sequential task interdependence. The actions of the employee at the beginning of the production line determine how successfully the next employee can perform his task, and so forth on down the line.

Because sequential interactions have to be carefully coordinated, long-linked technology requires more coordination than mediating technology. One result of sequential interdependence is that any error that occurs at the beginning of the production process becomes magnified at later stages. Sports activities like relay races or football, in which the performance of one person or group determines how well the next can perform, are based on sequential interdependence. In football, for example, the performance of the defensive line determines how well the offense can perform. If the defense is unable to secure the ball, the offense cannot perform its task: scoring touchdowns.

An organization with long-linked technology can respond in a variety of ways to the need to coordinate sequentially interdependent activities. The organization can program the conversion process to standardize the procedures used to transform inputs into outputs. The organization can also use planning and scheduling to manage linkages among input, conversion, and output processes. To reduce the need to coordinate these stages of production, an organization often creates **slack resources**—extra or surplus resources that enhance its organization's ability to deal with unexpected situations. For example, a mass production organization stockpiles inputs and holds inventories of component parts so that the conversion process is not disrupted if there is a problem with suppliers. Similarly, an organization may stockpile finished products so that it can respond quickly to an increase in customer demand without changing its established conversion processes. Another strategy to control the supply of inputs or distribution of outputs is *vertical integration*, which, as we saw in Chapter 8, involves a company taking over its suppliers or distributors.

The need to manage the increased level of interdependence increases the coordination costs associated with long-linked technology. However, this type of technology provides the organization with enormous benefits, stemming primarily from specialization and the division of labor associated with sequential interdependence. Changing the method of production in a pin factory from a system where each worker produces a whole pin to a system where each worker is responsible for only one aspect of pin production, such as sharpening the pin, for example, can result in a major gain in productivity. Essentially, the factory moves from using a *mediating* technology, in which each worker performs all production tasks, to a *long-linked* technology, in which tasks become sequentially interdependent.

Tasks are routine in long-linked technology because sequential interdependence allows managers to simplify tasks so that the variability of each worker's task is reduced and the analyzability of each task is increased. On mass production assembly lines, for example, the coordination of tasks is achieved principally by the speed of the line and the way tasks are ordered. Programming and the constant repetition of simple tasks increase production efficiency. As we saw in the opening case, Henry Ford was the innovator of long-linked technology. Capitalizing on the gains from specialization and the division of labor, he recognized the cost savings that could result from organizing tasks sequentially and controlling the pace of work by the speed of the production line. This system, however, has two major disadvantages. Employees do not become highly skilled (they learn only a narrow range of simple tasks), and they do not develop the ability to improve their skills because they must follow specified procedures.

At the organizational level, sequential interdependence means that the outputs of one department become the inputs for another and one department's performance determines how well another department performs. The performance of the manufacturing department depends on the ability of the materials management department to obtain adequate amounts of high-quality inputs in a timely manner. The ability of the sales function to sell finished products depends on the quality of the products coming out of the manufacturing department. Failure or poor performance at one stage has serious consequences for performance at the next stage and for the organization as a whole. In the 1970s, for example, U.S. car manufacturers' ability to sell their products was seriously hampered by the poor quality of the cars they were making in their outdated factories, and their inefficient manufacturing was in part the result of outdated materials management practices.

Slack resources
Extra or surplus resources that enhance an organization's ability to deal with unexpected situations.

The pressures of competition in today's global markets are increasing the need for interdependence between departments and thus are increasing organizations' need to coordinate departmental activities. As we saw in Chapter 6, many organizations in all industries (Xerox and Hallmark Cards are two we looked at) are moving toward the product team structure to increase interdepartmental coordination. This type of coordination encourages different departments to develop procedures that lead to greater production innovation and efficiency.

Intensive Technology and Reciprocal Interdependence

Intensive technology A technology characterized by a work process in which input, conversion, and output activities are inseparable.

Intensive technology, the third type of technology identified by Thompson, is characterized by a work process where input, conversion, and output activities are inseparable. Intensive technology is based on *reciprocal task interdependence*, which means that the activities of all people and all departments are fully dependent on one another. Not only do X's actions affect what Y and Z can do, but the actions of Z also affect Y's and X's performance. The task relationships of X, Y, and Z are reciprocally interdependent (see Figure 9.5). Reciprocal interdependence makes it impossible to program in advance a sequence of tasks or procedures to solve a problem because, in Thompson's words, "the selection, combination, and order of [the tasks'] application are determined by *feedback from the object [problem] itself.*"[32] Thus the move to reciprocal interdependence and intensive technology has two effects: Technical complexity declines as the ability of managers to control and predict the work process lessens, and tasks become more complex and nonroutine.

Hospitals are organizations that operate an intensive technology. A hospital's greatest source of uncertainty is the impossibility of predicting the types of problems for which patients (clients) will seek treatment. At any time, a general hospital has to have on hand the knowledge, machines, and services of specialist departments capable of solving a huge number and great variety of medical problems. The hospital requires, for example, an emergency room, X-ray facilities, a testing laboratory, an operating room and staff, skilled nursing staff, doctors, and hospital wards. What is wrong with each patient determines the selection and combination of activities and technology to convert a hospital's inputs (sick people) into outputs (well people). The uncertainty of the input (patient) means that tasks cannot be programmed in advance, as they can be when interdependence is sequential.

Basketball, soccer, and rugby are other activities that depend on reciprocal interdependence. The current state of play determines the sequence of moves from one player to the next. The fast-moving action of these sports requires players to make judgments quickly and obtain feedback from the state of play before deciding what moves to make.

On a departmental level, research and development departments operate with an intensive technology. The sequence and content of an R&D department's activities are determined by the problems the department is trying to solve—for example, a cure for cancer. R&D is so expensive because the unpredictability of the input-conversion-output process makes it impossible to specify in advance the skills and resources that will be needed to solve the problem at hand. A pharmaceutical company like Merck, for example, creates many different research and development teams. Every team is equipped with whatever functional resources it needs in the hope that at least one team will stumble onto a wonder drug that will justify the immense resource expenditures (each new drug costs about $400 million to develop).

The difficulty of specifying the sequencing of tasks that is characteristic of intensive technology makes necessary a high degree of coordination and makes intensive technology more expensive to manage than either mediating or long-linked technology. Mutual adjustment replaces programming and standardization as the principal method of coordination. Product team and matrix structures are suited to operating intensive technologies because they provide the coordination and the decentralized control that allow departments to cooperate to solve problems. At Microsoft, for example, the whole company is organized into product teams so that it can quickly shift resources to the projects that seem most promising. Also, mutual adjustment

Microsoft, like other PC software makers, has been shocked by the increasing number of applications that are available on the Internet and not on the PC, many of which have been pioneered by Google and developed by Yahoo!. These include better and faster versions of Internet applications such as email, advanced specialized search engines, Internet phone services, imaging searching, and mapping such as Google's Earth. Rapid innovation is taking place in these and other areas; the danger for Microsoft is that these online applications will make its vital Windows PC platform less useful and perhaps obsolete. If, in the future, people begin to utilize new kinds of online word-processing and storage applications, then the only important PC software application will become operating system software. This would cause Microsoft's revenues and profits to plummet. So, a major push is on at Microsoft to find ways to make its new software offerings work seamlessly with developing Internet-based service applications and its Windows platform so customers will remain loyal to its PC software.

To achieve this, in the fall of 2005 Microsoft announced that it is redesigning its organizational structure to focus on three major software and service products areas: platform products and services, business, and entertainment and services, each of which will be managed by its own new top management team. In doing this, Microsoft has created a new level in its hierarchy and has decentralized major decision-making responsibility to these managers. Inside each division, IT specialists will continue to work in small project teams.

Microsoft claims that the new structure will not only speed innovation in each division, but it will also create many synergies between the product divisions and foster collaboration, which will improve product development across the organization. In essence, Microsoft is trying to make its structure more organic so that it can better compete with small, nimble companies like Google. As Microsoft's CEO Steve Ballmer commented, "Our goal in making these changes is to enable Microsoft to achieve greater agility in managing the incredible growth ahead and executing our software-based services strategy."[33] Some analysts wonder, however, if adding a new level to the hierarchy will only create a new layer of bureaucracy that will further slow down decision making and allow Google and Yahoo! to take an even greater lead in Internet services in the decade ahead.

and a flat structure allow an organization to quickly exploit new developments and areas for research that arise during the research process itself. In 2005, Microsoft designed a new organizational structure to operate its new intensive approach to Internet software product development.

Organizations do not voluntarily use an intensive technology to achieve their goals because it is so expensive to operate. Like Microsoft, they are forced to use it by the nature of the output they choose to produce. Whenever possible, organizations attempt to reduce the task interdependence necessary to coordinate their activities and revert to a long-linked technology, which is more controllable and predictable. In recent years, for example, hospitals have attempted to control escalating management costs by using forecasting techniques to determine how many resources they need to have on hand to meet customer (patient) demands. If, over a specified period, a hospital knows on average how many broken bones or cardiac arrests it can expect, it knows how many operating theaters it will need to have in readiness and how many doctors, nurses, and technicians to have on call to meet patient demand. This knowledge allows the hospital to control costs. Similarly, in R&D, an organization like Microsoft needs to develop decision-making rules that allow it to decide when to stop investing in a line of research that is showing little promise of success, and how to best allocate resources among projects to try to maximize potential returns from the investment—especially when aggressive competitors like Google exist.

Specialism

Producing only a narrow range of outputs.

Another strategy that organizations can pursue to reduce the costs associated with intensive technology is **specialism**—producing only a narrow range of outputs. A hospital that specializes in the treatment of cancer or heart disease narrows the range of problems to which it is exposed and can target all its resources to solving those problems. It is the general hospital that faces the most uncertainty. Similarly, a pharmaceutical company typically restricts the areas in which it does research. A company may decide to focus on drugs that combat high blood pressure or diabetes or depression. This specialist strategy allows the organization to use its resources efficiently and reduces problems of coordination.[34]

ANALYZING TECHNOLOGY

1. Analyze an organization's or a department's input-conversion-output processes to identify the skills, knowledge, tools, and machinery that are central to the production of goods and services.

2. Analyze the level of technical complexity associated with the production of goods and services. Evaluate whether technical complexity can be increased to improve efficiency and reduce costs. For example, is an advanced computer system available? Are employees using up-to-date techniques and procedures?

3. Analyze the level of task variety and task analyzability associated with organizational and departmental tasks. Are there ways to reduce task variability or increase task analyzability to increase effectiveness? For example, can procedures be developed to make the work process more predictable and controllable?

4. Analyze the form of task interdependence inside a department and between departments. Evaluate whether the task interdependence being used results in the most effective way of producing goods or servicing the needs of customers. For example, would raising the level of coordination between departments improve efficiency?

5. After analyzing an organization's or a department's technology, analyze its structure, and evaluate the fit between technology and structure. Can the fit be improved? What costs and benefits are associated with changing the technology–structure relationship?

FROM MASS PRODUCTION TO ADVANCED MANUFACTURING TECHNOLOGY

As discussed earlier, one of the most influential advances in technology in this century was the introduction of mass production technology by Henry Ford. To reduce costs, a mass production company must maximize the gains from economies of scale and from the division of labor associated with large scale production. There are two ways to do this. One is by using dedicated machines and standardized work procedures. The other is by protecting the conversion process against production slowdowns or stoppages.

Dedicated machines
Machines that can perform only one operation at a time, such as repeatedly cutting or drilling or stamping out a car body part.

Traditional mass production is based on the use of **dedicated machines**—machines that can perform only one operation at a time, such as repeatedly cutting or drilling or stamping out a car body part.[35] To maximize volume and efficiency, a dedicated machine produces a narrow range of products but does so cheaply. Thus this method of production has traditionally resulted in low production costs.

When the component being manufactured needs to be changed, a dedicated machine must be retooled—that is, fitted with new dies or jigs—before it can handle the change. When Ford retooled one of his plants to switch from the Model T to the Model A, he had to close the plant for over six months. Because retooling a dedicated machine can take days, during which no production is possible, long production runs are required for maximum efficiency and lowest costs. Thus, for example, Ford might make 50,000 right-side door panels in a single production run and stockpile them until they are needed, because the money saved by using dedicated machines outweighs the combined costs of lost production and carrying the doors in inventory. In a similar way, both the use of a production line to assemble the final product and the employment of **fixed workers**—workers who perform standardized work procedures—increase an organization's control over the conversion process.

Fixed workers
Workers who perform standardized work procedures increase an organization's control over the conversion process.

A mass production organization also attempts to reduce costs by protecting its conversion processes from the uncertainty that results from disruptions in the external environment.[36] Threats to the conversion process come from both the input and the output stages, but an organization can stockpile inputs and outputs to reduce these threats (see Figure 9.6A).

At the input stage, an organization tries to control its access to inputs by keeping raw materials and semifinished components on hand to prevent shortages that would lead to a slowdown or break in production. The role of purchasing, for example, is to

Figure 9.6

A. The Work Flow in Mass Production
Inventory is used to protect the conversion process and to prevent slowdowns or stoppages in production.

B. The Work Flow with Advanced Manufacturing Technology
No inventory buffers are used between workstations.

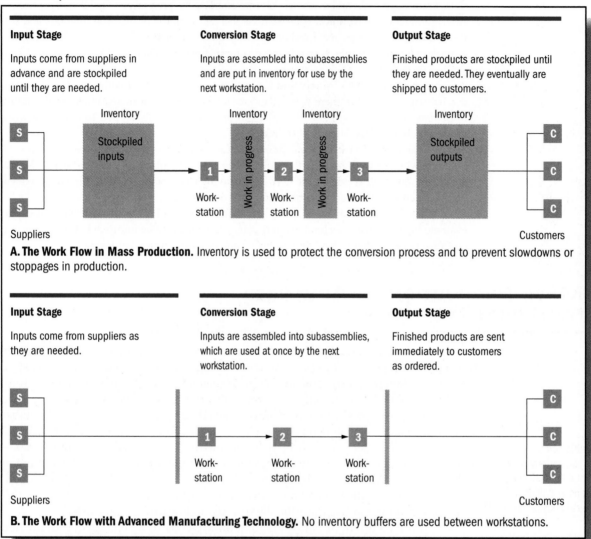

A. The Work Flow in Mass Production. Inventory is used to protect the conversion process and to prevent slowdowns or stoppages in production.

B. The Work Flow with Advanced Manufacturing Technology. No inventory buffers are used between workstations.

negotiate with suppliers contracts that guarantee the organization an adequate supply of inputs. At the output stage, an organization tries to control its ability to dispose of its outputs. It does so by stockpiling finished products so that it can respond quickly to customer demands. An organization can also advertise heavily to maintain customer demand. In that case, the role of the sales department is to maintain demand for an organization's products so that production does not need to slow down or stop because no one wants the organization's outputs. The high technical complexity, the routine nature of production tasks, and the sequential task interdependence characteristic of mass production all make an organization very inflexible. The term *fixed automation* is sometimes used to describe the traditional way of organizing production. The combination of dedicated machines (which perform only a narrow range of operations), fixed workers (who perform a narrow range of fixed tasks), and large stocks of inventory (which can be used to produce only one product or a few related products) makes it very expensive and difficult for an organization to begin to manufacture different kinds of products when customer preferences change.

Suppose an organization had a new technology that allowed it to make a wide range of products—products that could be customized to the needs of individual customers. This ability would increase demand for its products. If the new technology also allowed the organization to rapidly introduce new products that incorporated new features or the latest design trends, demand would increase even more. Finally, suppose the cost of producing this wide range of new, customized products with the new technology was the same as, or only slightly more than, the cost of producing a narrow, standardized product line. Clearly, the new technology would greatly increase organizational effectiveness and allow the organization to pursue both a low-cost and a differentiation strategy, to attract customers by giving them advanced, high-quality, reliable products at low prices.[37]

What changes would an organization need to make to its technology to make it flexible enough to respond to customers while controlling costs? In the last 20 years, many new technological developments have allowed organizations to achieve these two goals. The new developments are sometimes called *flexible production, lean production, or computer-aided production.* Here we will consider them to be components of advanced manufacturing technology.[38] **Advanced manufacturing technology (AMT)** consists of innovations in *materials technology* and in *knowledge technology* that change the work process of traditional mass production organizations.

Advanced manufacturing technology
Technology which consists of innovations in materials technology and in knowledge technology that change the work process of traditional mass production organizations.

ADVANCED MANUFACTURING TECHNOLOGY: INNOVATIONS IN MATERIALS TECHNOLOGY

Materials technology
Technology comprises machinery, other equipment, and computers.

Materials technology comprises machinery, other equipment, and computers. Innovations in materials technology are based on a new view of the linkages between input, conversion, and output activities. Traditional mass production tries to protect the conversion process from disruptions at the input and output stages by using stockpiles of inventory as buffers to increase control and reduce uncertainty. With AMT, however, the organization actively seeks ways to increase its ability to integrate or coordinate the flow of resources between input, conversion, and output activities. AMT allows an organization to reduce uncertainty not by using inventory stockpiles but by developing the capacity to adjust and control its procedures quickly to eliminate the need for inventory at both the input and the output stages (see Figure 9.6B).[39] Several innovations in materials technology allow organizations to reduce the costs and speed the process of producing goods and services. Computer-aided design, computer-aided materials management, just-in-time inventory systems, and computer-integrated manufacturing affect one another and jointly improve organizational effectiveness. The first three are techniques for coordinating the input and conversion stages of production. The last one increases the technical complexity of the conversion stage.

Computer-Aided Design

Mass production systems are set up to produce a large quantity of a few products. To some degree, this arrangement reflects the fact that a large part of the cost associated with mass production is incurred at the design stage.[40] In general, the more complex a product, the higher the design costs. The costs of designing a new car, for example, are enormous. Ford's first world car, the Mondeo, cost over $6 billion to develop.

Traditionally, the design of new parts involved the laborious construction of prototypes and scale models, a process akin to unit or small-batch production. **Computer-aided design (CAD)** is an advanced manufacturing technique that greatly simplifies the design process. CAD makes it possible to design a new component or microcircuit on a computer screen and then press a button, not to print out the plans for the part but to physically produce the part itself. Also, "printers" exist that squirt a stream of liquid metal or plastic droplets to create three-dimensional objects. Detailed prototypes can be sculpted according to the computer program and can be redesigned quickly if necessary. Thus, for example, an engineer at Ford who

Computer-aided design (CAD)
An advanced manufacturing technique that greatly simplifies the design process.

wants to see how a new gear will work in a transmission assembly can experiment quickly and cheaply to fine-tune the design of these inputs.[41]

Cutting the costs of product design by using CAD can contribute to both a low-cost and a differentiation advantage. Design advances that CAD makes possible can improve the efficiency of manufacturing. Well-designed components are easily fitted together into a subassembly, and well-designed subassemblies are easily fitted to other subassemblies. Improvements at the input design stage also make selling and servicing products easier at the output stage. The risk of later failure or of breakdown is reduced if potential problems have been eliminated at the design stage. Designing quality into a product up front improves competitive advantage and reduces costs. Toyota's core competence in product design, for example, evidenced by its relatively low recall rates, gives its cars a competitive advantage. Finally, CAD enhances flexibility because it reduces the difficulty and lowers the cost of customizing a product to satisfy particular customers. In essence, computer-aided design brings to large-scale manufacturing one of the benefits of small-batch production-customized product design—but at far less cost. It also enhances an organization's ability to respond quickly to changes in its environment.[42]

Computer-Aided Materials Management

Materials management, the management of the flow of resources into and out of the conversion process, is one of the most complex functional areas of an organization.[43] Computers are now the principal tool for processing the information that materials managers use for sound decision making, and computer-aided materials management is crucial to organizational effectiveness. **Computer-aided materials management (CAMM)** is an advanced manufacturing technique that is used to manage the flow of raw materials and component parts into the conversion process, to develop master production schedules for manufacturing, and to control inventory.[44] The difference between traditional materials management and the new computer-aided techniques is the difference between the so-called push and pull approaches to materials management.[45]

Traditional mass production uses the push approach. Materials are released from the input to the conversion stage when the production control system indicates that the conversion stage is ready to receive them. The inputs are pushed into the conversion process in accordance with a previously determined plan.

Computer-aided materials management makes possible the *pull* approach. The flow of input materials is governed by customer requests for supplies of the finished products, so the inputs are pulled into the conversion process in response to a pull from the output stage rather than a push from the input stage. Consider how VF Corporation, the manufacturer of Lee jeans, meets customer demand. As jeans sell out in stores, the stores issue requests by computer to Lee to manufacture different styles or sizes. Lee's manufacturing department then pulls in raw materials, such as cloth and thread, from suppliers as it needs them. If Lee were using the push approach, Lee would have a master plan that might say, "Make 30,000 pairs of style XYZ in May"; at the end of the summer, 25,000 pairs might remain unsold in the warehouse because of lack of demand.

CAMM technology allows an organization to increase integration of its input, conversion, and output activities. The use of input and output inventories (see Figure 9.6) allows the activities of each stage of the mass production process to go on relatively independently. CAMM, however, tightly couples these activities. CAMM increases *task interdependence* because each stage must be ready to react quickly to demands from the other stages. CAMM increases technical complexity because it makes input, conversion, and output activities a continuous process, in effect creating a pipeline connecting raw materials to the customer. Because the high levels of task interdependence and technical complexity associated with CAMM require greater coordination, an organization may need to move toward an organic structure, which will provide the extra integration that is needed.

Computer-aided materials management (CAMM)
An advanced manufacturing technique that is used to manage the flow of raw materials and component parts into the conversation process, to develop master production schedules for manufacturing, and to control inventory.

CAMM also helps an organization pursue a low-cost or differentiation strategy. The ability to control the flow of materials in the production process allows an organization to avoid the costs of carrying excess inventory and to be flexible enough to adjust to product or demand changes quickly and easily.

Just-in-Time Inventory Systems

Just-in-time inventory (JIT) system
A system that requires inputs and components needed for production to be delivered to the conversion process just as they are needed, neither earlier nor later, so that input inventories can be kept to a minimum.

Another advanced manufacturing technique for managing the flow of inputs into the organization is the just-in-time inventory system. Developed from the Japanese kanban system (a *kanban* is a card), a **just-in-time inventory (JIT) system** requires inputs and components needed for production to be delivered to the conversion process just as they are needed, neither earlier nor later, so that input inventories can be kept to a minimum.[46] Components are kept in bins, and as they are used up, the empty bins are sent back to the supplier with a request on the bin's card (kanban) for more components. Computer-aided materials management is necessary for a JIT system to work effectively because CAMM provides computerized linkages with suppliers—linkages that facilitate the rapid transfer of information and coordination between an organization and its suppliers.

In theory, a JIT system can extend beyond components to raw materials. A company may supply Ford or Toyota with taillight assemblies. The supplier itself, however, may assemble the taillights from individual parts (screws, plastic lenses, bulbs) provided by other manufacturers. Thus the supplier of the taillight assembly could also operate a JIT system with its suppliers, who in turn could operate JIT systems with their suppliers. Figure 9.7 illustrates a just-in-time inventory system that goes from the customer, to the store, and then back through the manufacturer to the original suppliers.

A JIT system increases task interdependence between stages in the production chain. Traditional mass production draws a boundary between the conversion stage and the input and output stages and sequences conversion activities only. JIT systems break down these barriers and make the whole value-creation process a single chain of sequential activities. Because organizational activities become a continuous process, technical complexity increases, in turn increasing the efficiency of the system.

At the same time, JIT systems bring flexibility to manufacturing. The ability to order components as they are needed allows an organization to widen the range of products it makes and to customize products.[47] JIT systems thus allow a modern mass production organization, because it is not tied to one product by large inventories to obtain the benefits of small-batch technology (flexibility and customization) with little loss of technical efficiency.

Like CAMM, JIT systems require an extra measure of coordination, and an organization may need to adopt new methods to manage this new technology. One of these, as we saw in Chapter 3, is to implement new strategies for managing relations with suppliers. Toyota, which owns a minority stake in its suppliers, periodically meets with its suppliers to keep them informed about new product developments.

Figure 9.7
Just-in-Time Inventory System

The system is activated by customers making purchases.

Toyota also works closely with its suppliers to reduce the costs and raise the quality of input components, and it shares the cost savings with them.[48] Because owning a supplier can increase costs, many organizations try to avoid the need to integrate vertically. Long-term contracts with suppliers can create cooperative working relationships that have long-term benefits for both parties.

In sum, just-in-time inventory systems, computer-aided materials management, and computer-aided design increase technical complexity and task interdependence and thus increase the degree to which a traditional mass production system operates like a continuous-process technology; they also increase efficiency and reduce production costs. The three advanced manufacturing techniques also give modern mass production the benefits of small-batch production: heightened flexibility and the ability to respond to customer needs and increased product quality. Together these techniques confer a low-cost and a differentiation advantage on an organization.

Now that we have looked at advanced techniques for coordinating the input and conversion stages, we can look at new developments inside the conversion stage. At the center of AMTs innovations of conversion processes is the creation of a system based on flexible workers and flexible machines.

Flexible Manufacturing Technology and Computer-Integrated Manufacturing

Traditional mass-manufacturing technology utilizes dedicated machines, which perform only one operation at a time. **Flexible manufacturing technology**, by contrast, allows the production of many kinds of components at little or no extra cost on the same machine. Each machine in a flexible manufacturing system is able to perform a range of different operations, and the machines in sequence are able to vary their operations so that a wide variety of different components can be produced. Flexible manufacturing technology combines the variety advantages of small-batch production with the low-cost advantages of continuous-process production. How is this achieved?

In flexible manufacturing systems, the key factor that prevents the cost increases associated with changing operations is the use of a computer-controlled system to manage operations. **Computer-integrated manufacturing (CIM)** is an advanced manufacturing technique that controls the changeover from one operation to another by means of the commands given to the machines through computer software. A CIM system eliminates the need to retool machines physically. Within the system are a number of computer-controlled machines, each capable of automatically producing a range of components. They are controlled by a master computer, which schedules the movement of parts between machines in order to assemble different products from the various components that each machine makes.[49] Computer-integrated manufacturing depends on computers programmed to (1) feed the machines with components, (2) assemble the product from components and move it from one machine to another, and (3) unload the final product from the machine to the shipping area.

The use of robots is integral to CIM. A group of robots working in sequence is the AMT equivalent of a dedicated transfer machine. Each robot can be quickly programmed by software to perform different operations, and the costs of reprogramming robots are much lower than the costs associated with retooling dedicated transfer machines. Motorola's cellular phone factory illustrates many of the advantages of robots and advanced manufacturing technology.

In sum, computer-integrated manufacturing, just-in-time inventory systems, computer-aided materials management, and computer-aided design give organizations the flexibility to make a variety of products, as well as different models of the same product, rapidly and cost-effectively. They break down the traditional barriers separating the input, conversion, and output stages of production; as a result, input,

---

Flexible manufacturing technology
Technology that allows the production of many kinds of components at little or no extra cost on the same machine.

Computer-integrated manufacturing (CIM)
An advanced manufacturing technique that controls the changeover from one operation to another by means of the commands given to the machines through computer software.

Motorola is one of America's oldest consumer electronics organizations. It developed the world's first car radio in 1930 and quickly entered the home audio and television market. In the 1970s, however, under pressure from the Japanese, it abandoned the home electronics market and entered the high-tech electronics sector. Today, it is a world leader in communications technology, and the organization generates over $8 billion in revenue from the sales of cellular telephones, pagers, information networking systems, and automotive and industrial electronics.

Once again, however, Motorola is experiencing intense competitive pressure from both domestic and foreign competitors for control of the rapidly growing information technology sector. Hitachi, Panasonic, and Samsung already operate state-of-the art factories based on advanced manufacturing technology, and their low production costs make them fierce competitors. Motorola has had to figure out how to use AMT to its advantage.

Motorola decided to use AMT not only to increase technical efficiency, but also to better meet the needs of customers. Using advanced manufacturing technology, Motorola has focused both product design and manufacturing on the customer. At Motorola, salespeople, not engineers, are empowered to direct the company's activities. The sales function is at the top of the organizational hierarchy; the other functions serve its needs. What does this mean for the way the organization utilizes AMT?

Motorola created a "factory of the future" that is able to customize products to individual customer needs within hours. At this futuristic factory at Boynton Beach, Florida, Motorola can respond to a customer order for even one unit of a custom-designed pager within two hours. A salesperson in the field takes the customer's order for a pager that will operate on a specific frequency, be of a certain size, and contain one of a number of customized features. The salesperson electronically relays this information as a bar code to the factory. A computer scans the specifications and through software creates the circuit board design for the pager. The conversion process is handled by a series of computer-controlled robots. As the pager passes down the production line, each robot reads the bar code and performs the necessary operations. Each pager in the line can be different, because CIM adapts the conversion process to the specific needs of each item. Finished products are electronically scanned and tested and are shipped to the customer.

Using AMT in this way is expensive. However, the ability to produce hundreds of different models customized to individual customers gave Motorola a strong competitive advantage and allowed the company to charge a premium price for its products. Unfortunately for Motorola, its competitors began creating such factories of their own and locating them globally where costs were low. As a result, they have been able to outperform Motorola, which has seen its share of the pager market plunge.

Sequential task interdependence is the basis for manufacturing any kind of product. However, the combination of flexible machines and computerization allows any given set of machines to perform many different sequences. In effect, a CIM system has the potential to act reciprocally and to produce a wide range of customized products.[50] It increases technical complexity. It allows an organization's resources to be used more efficiently because it quickens the pace of work and the speed of production. With computer-integrated manufacturing, the conversion of inputs becomes more like a continuous process instead of a mass production process.

conversion, and output activities merge into one another. These four innovations in materials technology decrease the need for costly inventory buffers to protect conversion processes from disruptions in the environment. In addition, they increase product reliability because they increase automation and technical complexity.

SUMMARY

Technical complexity, the differences between routine and nonroutine tasks, and task interdependence jointly explain why some technologies are more complex and difficult to control than others and why organizations adopt different structures to operate their technology. In general, input, conversion, and output processes that depend primarily on people and departments cooperating and trading knowledge that is difficult to program into standard operating routines require the most coordination.

An organization that needs extensive coordination and control to operate its technology also needs an organic structure to organize its tasks. Chapter 9 has made the following main points:

1. Technology is the combination of skills, knowledge, abilities, techniques, materials, machines, computers, tools, and other equipment that people use to convert raw materials into valuable goods and services.

2. Technology is involved in an organization's input, conversion, and output processes. An effective organization manages its technology to meet the needs of stakeholders, foster innovation, and increase operating efficiency.

3. Technical complexity is the extent to which a production process is controllable and predictable. According to Joan Woodward, technical complexity differentiates small-batch and unit production, large-batch and mass production, and continuous-process production.

4. Woodward argued that each technology is associated with a different organizational structure because each technology presents different control and coordination problems. In general, small-batch and continuous-process technologies are associated with an organic structure, and mass production is associated with a mechanistic structure.

5. The argument that technology determines structure is known as the technological imperative. According to the Aston Studies, however, organizational size is more important than technology in determining an organization's choice of structure.

6. According to Charles Perrow, two dimensions underlie the difference between routine and non-routine tasks and technologies: task variability and task analyzability. The higher the level of task variability and the lower the level of task analyzability, the more complex and nonroutine are organizational tasks.

7. Using task variability and analyzability, Perrow described four types of technology: craftswork, nonroutine research, engineering production, and routine manufacturing.

8. The more routine tasks are, the more likely an organization is to use a mechanistic structure. The more complex tasks are, the more likely an organization is to use an organic structure.

9. James D. Thompson focused on the way in which task interdependence affects an organization's technology and structure. Task interdependence is the manner in which different organizational tasks are related to one another and the degree to which the performance of one person or department depends on and affects the performance of another.

10. Thompson identified three types of technology, which he associated with three forms of task interdependence: mediating technology and pooled interdependence; long-linked technology and sequential interdependence; and intensive technology and reciprocal interdependence.

11. The higher the level of task interdependence, the more likely an organization is to use mutual adjustment rather than standardization to coordinate work activities.

12. Advanced manufacturing technology consists of innovations in materials technology that change the work process of traditional mass production organizations. Innovations in materials technology include computer-aided design, computer-aided materials management, just-in-time inventory systems, flexible manufacturing technology, and computer-integrated manufacturing.

DISCUSSION QUESTIONS

1. How can technology increase organizational effectiveness?

2. How does small-batch technology differ from mass production technology?

3. Why is technical complexity greatest with continuous-process technology? How does technical complexity affect organizational structure?

4. What makes some tasks more complex than others? Give an example of an organization that uses each of the four types of technology identified by Perrow.

5. What level of task interdependence is associated with the activities of (a) a large accounting firm, (b) a fast-food restaurant, and (c) a biotechnology company? What different kinds of structure are you likely to find in these organizations? Why?

6. Find an organization in your city, and analyze how its technology works. Use the concepts discussed in this chapter: technical complexity, nonroutine tasks, and task interdependence.

7. Discuss how AMT and innovations in materials technology and in knowledge technology have increased task interdependence and the technical complexity of the work process. How have these innovations changed the structure of organizations operating a mass production technology?

ORGANIZATIONAL THEORY IN ACTION

Practicing Organizational Theory: Choosing a Technology

Form groups of three to five people and discuss the following scenario:

You are investors who are planning to open a large computer store in a big city on the western seaboard. You plan to offer a complete range of computer hardware, ranging from UNIX-based workstations, to powerful PCs and laptop computers, to a full range of printers and scanners. In addition, you propose to offer a full range of software products, from office management systems to personal financial software and children's computer games. Your strategy is to be a one-stop shopping place where all kind of customers—from large companies to private individuals—can get everything they want from salespeople who can design a complete system to meet each customer's unique needs.

You are meeting to decide which kind of technology—which combination of skills, knowledge, techniques, and task relationships—will best allow you to achieve your goal.

1. Analyze the level of (a) technical complexity and (b) task variability and task analyzability associated with the kinds of tasks needed to achieve your strategy.
2. Given your answer to item 1, what kind of task interdependence between employees/departments will best allow you to pursue your strategy?
3. Based on this analysis, what kind of technology will you choose in your store, and what kind of structure and culture will you create to manage your technology most effectively?

The Ethical Dimension #9

The chapter discussed some of Henry Ford's strict labor practices that caused such high turnover. Workers were not allowed to talk on the production line, for example, and he employed detectives to spy on them when they were at home.

1. What limits should be placed on a company's right to monitor and control its employees from an ethical perspective?
2. What moral rules would you create to help managers decide when, and which actions and behaviors, they have a right to influence and control?

Making the Connection #9

Find an example of a company operating with one of the technologies identified in this chapter. Which technology is the company using? Why is the company using it? How does this technology affect the organization's structure?

Analyzing the Organization: Design Module #9

This module focuses on the technology your company uses to produce goods and services and the problems and issues associated with the use of this technology.

Assignment

Using the information at your disposal, and drawing inferences about your company's technology from the activities that your organization engages in, answer the following questions.

1. What kinds of goods or services does your organization produce? Are input, conversion, or output activities the source of greatest uncertainty for your organization?
2. What role does technology in the form of knowledge play in the production of the organization's goods or services?
3. What role does materials technology play in the production of the organization's goods and services?
4. What is the organization's level of technical complexity? Does the organization use a small-batch, mass production, or continuous-process technology?
5. Use the concepts of task variability and task analyzability to describe the complexity of your organization's activities. Which of the four types of technology identified by Perrow does your organization use?
6. What forms of task interdependence between people and between departments characterize your organization's work process? Which of the three types of technology identified by Thompson does your organization use?
7. The analysis you have done so far might lead you to expect your company to operate with a particular kind of structure. What kind? To what extent does your organization's structure seem to fit with the characteristics of the organization's technology? For example, is the structure organic or mechanistic?
8. Do you think that your organization is operating its technology effectively? Do you see any ways in which it could improve its technical efficiency, innovativeness, or ability to respond to customers?

CASE FOR ANALYSIS

The Shape of Things to Come

Intense global competition in the 1990s caused many companies to take another look at the way they manufactured products. In Japan, in particular, the soaring price of the yen in the 1990s put particular pressure on large car and electronics manufacturers to look at ways to cut production costs. To find ways to cut costs, Japanese companies scrutinized the technology they were using, and the mass production system was the subject of most of this attention.

Traditionally, Japanese companies have used the conveyor belt system pioneered by Ford to mass-produce large volumes of identical products. In this system, workers are positioned along a straight or linear production line that can be hundreds of feet long. In examining how this system works, Japanese production managers have come to realize that a considerable amount of handling time is wasted as the product being assembled is passed from worker to worker, and that a line can only move as fast as the least capable worker. Moreover, this system is only efficient when large quantities of the same product are being produced. If customized products are what is needed, the production line is typically down while it is being retooled for the next product.

Recognizing these problems, production engineers began to search for assembly-line layouts that could alleviate these problems, and experimented with layouts of various shapes, such as spirals, Ys, 6s, or even insects. At a Sony camcorder plant in Kohda, Japan, for example, Sony dismantled its previous mass production system in which 50 workers worked sequentially to build a camcorder, and replaced it with a spiral arrangement only 40 feet long in which four workers perform all the operations necessary to assemble the camcorder. Sony says this new arrangement is 10% more efficient than the old system. Why? Because it allows the most efficient assemblers to perform at a higher level: It reduces handling time and work is not being passed from one worker to another.[51]

In the United States, too, these new production layouts, normally referred to as cell layouts, are becoming increasingly common. It has been estimated that 40% of small companies and 70% of large companies have experimented with the new designs. Bayside Controls Inc., for example, a small gearhead manufacturer in Queens, New York, converted its 35-person assembly line into a four-cell design where seven to nine workers form a cell. The members of each cell perform all the operations involved in making the gearheads, such as measuring, cutting, and assembling the new gearheads. Bayside's managers say that the average production time it takes to make a gear has dropped to two days from six weeks, and it now makes 75 gearheads a day (up from 50 before the change) so costs have also gone down.[52] Once again, there has been a large saving in handling costs, inventory costs are lower because production is faster, and employees are more motivated to produce high-quality products with the new system. An additional advantage is that cell designs allow companies to be very responsive to the needs of individual customers, as this system permits the quick manufacture of small quantities of customized products.

DISCUSSION QUESTIONS

1. How do the new "cell" designs change the level of technical complexity, task variability and task analyzability, and task interdependence?
2. Based on this analysis, of what type of technology discussed in the chapter does the new system remind you?
3. What are the advantages associated with the use of the new technology?

REFERENCES

1. H. Ford, "Progressive Manufacturing," *Encyclopedia Britannica* 13e (New York: The Encyclopedia Co., 1926).

2. R. Edwards, *Contested Terrain: The Transformation of the Workplace in the Twentieth Century* (New York: Basic Books, 1979).

3. "Survey: The Endless Road," *The Economist*, October 17, 1992, p. 4.

4. Edwards, *Contested Terrain*, p. 119.

5. D. M. Rousseau, "Assessment of Technology in Organizations: Closed Versus Open Systems Approaches," *Academy of Management Review, 4* (1979), 531–542; W. R. Scott, *Organizations: Rational, Natural, and Open Systems* (Upper Saddle River, NJ: Prentice Hall, 1981).

6. J. Woodward, *Management and Technology* (London: Her Majesty's Stationery Office, 1958), p. 12.

7. Woodward, *Management and Technology*, p. 11.

8. J. Woodward, *Industrial Organization: Theory and Practice* (London: Oxford University Press, 1965).

9. Woodward, *Industrial Organization*.

10. Woodward, *Management and Technology*.

11. C. Perrow, *Normal Accidents: Living with High-Risk Technologies* (New York: Basic Books, 1984).

12. E. Harvey, "Technology and the Structure of Organizations," *American Sociological Review, 33* (1968), 241–259; W. L. Zwerman, *New Perspectives on Organizational Effectiveness* (Westport, CT: Greenwood, 1970).

13. D. J. Hickson, D. S. Pugh, and D. C. Pheysey, "Operations Technology and Organizational Structure: An Empirical Reappraisal," *Administrative Science Quarterly, 14* (1969), 378–397; D. S. Pugh, "The Aston Program of Research: Retrospect and Prospect," in A. H. Van de Ven and W. F. Joyce, eds., *Perspectives on Organizational Design and Behavior* (New York: Wiley, 1981), pp. 135–166; H. E. Aldrich, "Technology and Organizational Structure: A Reexamination of the Findings of the Aston Group," *Administrative Science Quarterly, 17* (1972), 26–43.

14. J. Child and R. Mansfield, "Technology, Size and Organization Structure," *Sociology, 6* (1972), 369–393.

15. Hickson, Pugh, Pheysey, "Operations Technology and Organizational Structure."

16. C. Perrow, *Organizational Analysis: A Sociological View* (Belmont, CA: Wadsworth, 1970).

17. Ibid.

18. Ibid., p. 21.

19. Ibid.

20. This section draws heavily on C. Perrow, "A Framework for the Comparative Analysis of Organizations," *American Sociological Review, 32* (1967), 194–208.

21. Perrow, *Organizational Analysis*; C. Gresov, "Exploring Fit and Misfit with Multiple Contingencies," *Administrative Science Quarterly, 34* (1989), 431–453.

22. Edwards, *Contested Terrain*.

23. J. Beyer and H. Trice, "A Re-Examination of the Relations Between Size and Various Components of Organizational Complexity," *Administrative Science Quarterly, 30* (1985), 462–481.

24. L. Argote, "Input Uncertainty and Organizational Coordination of Subunits," *Administrative Science Quarterly, 27* (1982), 420–434.

25. G. R. Jones, "Task Visibility, Free Riding, and Shirking: Explaining the Effect of Structure and Technology on Employee Behavior," *Academy of Management Review, 9* (1984), 684–696.

26. R. T. Keller, "Technology-Information Processing Fit and the Performance of R&D Project Groups: A Test of Contingency Theory," *Academy of Management Review, 37* (1994), 167–179.

27. C. Perrow, "Hospitals: Technology, Structure, and Goals," in J. March, ed., *The Handbook of Organizations* (Chicago: Rand McNally, 1965), pp. 910–971.

28. D. E. Comstock and W. R. Scott, "Technology and the Structure of Subunits," *Administrative Science Quarterly, 22* (1977), 177–202; A. H. Van de Ven and A. L. Delbecq, "A Task Contingent Model of Work Unit Structure," *Administrative Science Quarterly, 19* (1974), 183–197.

29. J. D. Thompson, *Organizations in Action* (New York: McGraw-Hill, 1967).

30. W. G. Ouchi, "The Relationship Between Organizational Structure and Organizational Control," *Administrative Science Quarterly, 22* (1977), 95–113.

31. Thompson, *Organizations in Action*.

32. Thompson, *Organizations in Action*, p. 17.

33. www.microsoft.com, press release, September 2005.

34. Thompson, *Organizations in Action*; G. R. Jones, "Organization–Client Transactions and Organizational Governance Structures," *Academy of Management Journal, 30* (1987), 197–218.

35. C. Edquist and S. Jacobson, *Flexible Automation: The Global Diffusion of New Technology in the Engineering Industry* (London: Basil Blackwell, 1988).

36. Ibid.

37. M. Jelinek and J. D. Goldhar, "The Strategic Implications of the Factory of the Future," *Sloan Management Review, 25* (1984), 29–37; G. I. Susman and J. W. Dean, "Strategic Use of Computer Integrated Manufacturing in the Emerging Competitive Environment," *Computer Integrated Manufacturing Systems, 2* (1989), 133–138.

38. C. A. Voss, *Managing Advanced Manufacturing Technology* (Bedford, England: IFS [Publications] Ltd., 1986).

39. Ibid.; M. T. Sweeney, "Flexible Manufacturing Systems—Managing Their Integration," in Voss, *Managing Advanced Manufacturing Technology*, pp. 69–81.

40. D. E. Whitney, "Manufacturing by Design," *Harvard Business Review* (July–August 1988), 210–216.

41. "Microtechnology, Dropping Out," *The Economist*, January 9, 1993, p. 75.

42. F. M. Hull and P. D. Collins, "High Technology Batch Production Systems: Woodward's Missing Types," *Academy of Management Journal, 30* (1987), 786–797.

43. R. H. Hayes and S. C. Wheelright, *Restoring Our Competitive Edge: Competing Through Manufacturing* (New York: Wiley, 1984).

44. C. A. Voss, "Managing Manufacturing Technology," in R. Wild, ed., *International Handbook of Production and Operations Management* (London: Cassel, 1989), pp. 112–121.

45. C. C. New and G. R. Clark, "Just-in-Time Manufacturing," ibid., pp. 402–417.

46. S. M. Young, "A Framework for the Successful Adoption and Performance of Japanese Manufacturing Practices in the United States," *Academy of Management Review*, 17 (1992), 677–700.

47. A. Ansari and B. Modarress, *Just-in-Time Purchasing* (New York: The Free Press, 1990).

48. J. P. Womack, D. T. Jones, D. Roos, and D. Sammons, *The Machine That Changed the World* (New York: Macmillan, 1990).

49. H. J. Warnecke and R. Steinhilper, "CIM, FMS, and Robots," in Wild, *International Handbook of Production and Operations Management*, pp. 146–173.

50. P. L. Nemetz and L. W. Fry, "Flexible Manufacturing Organizations: Implications for Strategy Formulation and Organizational Design," *Academy of Management Review*, 13 (1988), 627–638.

51. M. Williams, "Back to the Past," *The Wall Street Journal*, October 24, 1994, p. A1.

52. S. N. Mehta, "Cell Manufacturing Gains Acceptance at Smaller Plants," *The Wall Street Journal*, September 15, 1994, p. B2.

Chapter 10

Types and Forms of Organizational Change

Learning Objectives

Today, as never before, organizations are facing an environment that is changing rapidly, and the task facing managers is to help organizations respond and adjust to the changes taking place. This chapter discusses the various types of change that organizations must undergo, and how organizations can manage the process of change to stay ahead in today's competitive environments.

After studying this chapter you should be able to:

1. Understand the relationship among organizational change, redesign, and organizational effectiveness.

2. Distinguish among the major forms or types of evolutionary and revolutionary change organizations must manage.

3. Recognize the problems inherent in managing change and the obstacles that must be overcome.

4. Describe the change process and understand the techniques that can be used to help an organization achieve its desired future state.

WHAT IS ORGANIZATIONAL CHANGE?

Organizational change
The process by which organizations move from their present state to some desired future state to increase their effectiveness.

Organizational change is the process by which organizations move from their current state to some desired future state to increase their effectiveness. The goal of planned organizational change is to find new or improved ways of using resources and capabilities in order to increase an organization's ability to create value and improve returns to its stakeholders.[1] An organization in decline may need to restructure its resources to improve its fit with the environment. IBM and General Motors, for example, experienced falling demand for their products in the 1990s and have been searching for new ways to use their resources to improve their performance and attract customers. On the other hand, even a thriving organization may need to change the way it uses its resources so that it can develop new products or find new markets for its existing products. Wal-Mart, Target, Blockbuster Video, and

Toys"Я"Us, for example, have been moving aggressively to expand their scale of operations and open new stores to take advantage of the popularity of their products. In the last decade, over half of all *Fortune* 500 companies have undergone major organizational changes to allow them to increase their ability to create value.

Targets of Change

Planned organizational change is normally targeted at improving effectiveness at one or more of four different levels: human resources, functional resources, technological capabilities, and organizational capabilities.

Human Resources

Human resources are an organization's most important asset. Ultimately, an organization's distinctive competences lie in the skills and abilities of its employees. Because these skills and abilities give an organization a competitive advantage, organizations must continually monitor their structures to find the most effective way of motivating and organizing human resources to acquire and use their skills. Typical kinds of change efforts directed at human resources include (1) new investment in training and development activities so that employees acquire new skills and abilities; (2) socializing employees into the organizational culture so that they learn the new routines on which organizational performance depends; (3) changing organizational norms and values to motivate a multicultural and diverse workforce; (4) ongoing examination of the way in which promotion and reward systems operate in a diverse workforce; and (5) changing the composition of the top management team to improve organizational learning and decision making.

Functional Resources

As discussed in previous chapters, each organizational function needs to develop procedures that allow it to manage the particular environment it faces. As the environment changes, organizations often transfer resources to the functions where the most value can be created. Crucial functions grow in importance, while those whose usefulness is declining shrink.

An organization can improve the value that its functions create by changing its structure, culture, and technology. The change from a functional to a product team structure, for example, may speed the new product development process. Alterations in functional structure can help provide a setting in which people are motivated to perform. The change from traditional mass production to a manufacturing operation based on self-managed work teams often allows companies to increase product quality and productivity if employees can share in the gains from the new work system.

Technological Capabilities

Technological capabilities give an organization an enormous capacity to change itself in order to exploit market opportunities. The ability to develop a constant stream of new products or to modify existing products so that they continue to attract customers is one of an organization's core competences. Similarly, the ability to improve the way goods and services are produced in order to increase their quality and reliability is a crucial organizational capability. At the organizational level, an organization has to provide the context that allows it to translate its technological competences into value for its stakeholders. This task often involves the redesign of organizational activities. IBM, for example, has recently moved to change its organizational structure to better capitalize on its strengths in providing IT consulting. Previously, it had been unable to translate its technical capabilities into commercial opportunities because its structure was not focused on consulting, but on making and selling computer hardware and software rather than providing advice.

Organizational Capabilities

Through the design of organizational structure and culture, an organization can harness its human and functional resources to take advantage of technological opportunities. Organizational change often involves changing the relationships between people and functions to increase their ability to create value. Changes in structure and culture take place at all levels of the organization and include changing the routines an individual uses to greet customers, changing work group relationships, improving integration between divisions, and changing corporate culture by changing the top management team.

These four levels at which change can take place are obviously interdependent; it is often impossible to change one without changing another. Suppose an organization invests resources and recruits a team of scientists who are experts in a new technology—for example, biotechnology. If successful, this human resource change will lead to the emergence of a new functional resource and a new technological capability. Top management will be forced to reevaluate its organizational structure and the way it integrates and coordinates its other functions to ensure that they support its new functional resources. Effectively utilizing the new resources may require a move to a product team structure. It may even require downsizing and the elimination of functions that are no longer central to the organization's mission.

FORCES FOR AND RESISTANCE TO ORGANIZATIONAL CHANGE

The organizational environment is constantly changing, and an organization must adapt to these changes in order to survive.[2] Figure 10.1 lists the most important forces for and impediments to change that confront an organization and its managers.

Figure 10.1
Forces for and Resistances
to Change

Forces for Change	Resistances to Change
Competitive Forces	**Organizational Level**
	• Structure
Economic Forces	• Culture
	• Strategy
Political Forces	
	Functional Level
Global Forces	• Differences in Subunit Orientation
	• Power and Conflict
Demographic Forces	
	Group Level
Social Forces	• Norms
	• Cohesiveness
Ethical Forces	• Groupthink
	Individual Level
	• Cognitive Biases
	• Uncertainty and Insecurity
	• Selective Perception and Retention
	• Habit

Forces for Change

Recall from Chapter 3 that many forces in the environment have an impact on an organization and that recognizing the nature of these forces is one of a manager's most important tasks.[3] If managers are slow to respond to competitive, economic, political, global, and other forces, the organization will lag behind its competitors and its effectiveness will be compromised (see Figure 10.1).

Competitive Forces

Organizations are constantly striving to achieve a competitive advantage.[4] Competition is a force for change because unless an organization matches or surpasses its competitors in efficiency, quality, or its capability to innovate new or improved goods or services it will not survive.[5]

To lead on the dimensions of efficiency or quality, an organization must constantly adopt the latest technology as it becomes available. The adoption of new technology usually brings a change to task relationships as workers learn new skills or techniques to operate the new technology.[6] Later in this chapter we discuss total quality management and reengineering, two change strategies that organizations can use to achieve superior efficiency or quality.

To lead on the dimension of innovation and obtain a technological advantage over competitors, a company must possess skills in managing the process of innovation, another source of change that we discuss later.

Economic, Political, and Global Forces

Economic, political, and global forces continually affect organizations and compel them to change how and where they produce goods and services. Economic and political unions among countries are becoming an increasingly important force for change.[7] The North American Free Trade Agreement (NAFTA) paved the way for cooperation among Canada, the United States, and Mexico. The European Union (EU) includes over 20 members eager to exploit the advantages of a large protected market. Japan and other fast-growing Asian countries such as Malaysia, Thailand, and China, recognizing that economic unions protect member nations and create barriers against foreign competitors, have moved to increase their presence in foreign countries. Many Japanese companies, for example, have opened new manufacturing plants in the United States and Mexico, and in European countries such as Spain and the United Kingdom, so that they can share in the advantages offered by NAFTA and the European Union. Toyota, Honda, and Nissan have all opened large car plants in England to supply cars to EU member countries. No organization can afford to ignore the effects of global economic and political forces on its activities.[8]

Other global challenges facing organizations include the need to change an organizational structure to allow expansion into foreign markets, the need to adapt to a variety of national cultures, and the need to help expatriate managers adapt to the economic, political, and cultural values of the countries in which they are located.[9] DaimlerChrysler's German parent, for example, sent 30 managers already experienced in both U.S.– and Japanese-style manufacturing methods to head its new operations in the United States.

Demographic and Social Forces

Managing a diverse workforce is one of the biggest challenges to confront organizations in 2000 and beyond.[10] Changes in the composition of the workforce and the increasing diversity of employees have presented organizations with many challenges and opportunities. Increasingly, changes in the demographic characteristics of the workforce have led managers to change their styles of managing all employees and to learn how to understand, supervise, and motivate diverse members effectively. Managers have had to abandon the stereotypes they unwittingly may have used in making promotion decisions; they have had to accept the importance of equity in the recruitment and promotion of new hires; and they have come to recognize employees' desire for a lifestyle that strikes an acceptable balance between work and leisure. Many companies have helped their workers keep up with changing technology by providing support for advanced education and training. Increasingly, organizations are coming to realize that the ultimate source of competitive advantage and organizational effectiveness lies in fully utilizing the skills of their members, by, for example, empowering employees to make important and significant decisions.[11]

Ethical Forces

Just as it is important for an organization to take steps to change in response to changing demographic and social forces, it is also important for an organization to take steps to promote ethical behavior in the face of increasing government, political, and social demands for more responsible and honest corporate behavior.[12] Many companies have created the position of ethics officer, a person to whom employees can report ethical lapses by an organization's managers or workers and can consult for advice on difficult ethical questions. Organizations are also trying to promote ethical behavior by giving employees more direct access to important decision makers and by protecting whistle-blowers who turn the organization in when they perceive ethical problems with the way certain managers behave.

Many organizations need to make changes to allow managers and workers at all levels to report unethical behavior so that an organization can move quickly to eliminate such behavior and protect the general interests of its members and customers.[13] Similarly, if organizations operate in countries that pay little attention to human rights or to the well-being of organizational members, they have to learn how to change these standards and to protect their foreign employees. The following organizational insight illustrates this issue by highlighting the story of sports shoemakers

ORGANIZATIONAL INSIGHT 10.1
Nike, Reebok, Adidas, and the Sweatshops

Because more and more products are being manufactured in poor third-world countries, the behavior of companies that outsource production to subcontractors in these countries has come under increased scrutiny. Nike, the giant sports shoemaker with sales of more than $9 billion a year, was one of the first to experience a backlash when it became known how workers in these countries were being treated. Indonesian workers were stitching together shoes in hot, noisy factories for only 80 cents a day, or about $18 a month.[14] Workers in Vietnam and China fared better; they could earn $1.60 a day. In all cases, however, critics charged that at least $3 a day was needed to maintain an adequate living standard.

These facts generated an outcry in the United States, where Nike was roundly attacked for its labor practices. There was a backlash against sales of Nike products, and Phil Knight, Nike's billionaire owner, was asked to defend how, when his net worth was over $3 billion, he could defend paying a worker 80 cents a day. As criticism mounted, Knight was forced to reevaluate Nike's labor practices. Nike announced that, henceforth, all the factories producing its shoes and clothes would be independently monitored and inspected. Then after Reebok, a competitor criticized for similar labor practices, announced that it was raising wages in Indonesia by 20%, Nike raised them by

25% to $23 a month.[15] Small though this may seem, it was a huge increase to workers in these countries.

In Europe, Adidas, another sportswear company, had largely escaped such criticism. But in 1999 it was reported that in El Salvador, a Taiwan-based Adidas subcontractor was employing girls as young as 14 in its factories and making them work for over 70 hours a week. They were only allowed to go to the restroom twice a day and, if they stayed longer than three minutes, they lost a day's wages.[16] Adidas moved swiftly to avoid the public relations nightmare that Nike had experienced. Adidas announced that, henceforth, its subcontractors would also be required to abide by more strict labor standards.[17]

Thus, throughout the industry companies were forced to reevaluate the ethics of their labor practices and promise to keep a constant watch on subcontractors in the future. What has happened in the sports shoe industry has happened throughout the clothing industry and other industries like electronics and toys in the 2000s. Companies such as Wal-Mart, Target, The Gap, Sony, and Mattel have all been forced to reevaluate the ethics of their labor practices and to promise to keep a constant watch on subcontractors in the future. A statement to this effect can be found on many of these companies' Web pages, for example, Nike's (www.nikebiz.com) and The Gap's (www.thegap.com).[18]

who are battling with accusations that their shoes are produced in sweatshops in third-world countries.

From customer design preferences to the issue of where clothes should be produced, to the question of whether economic or political unrest will affect the availability of raw materials, the forces of change bombard organizations from all sides. Effective organizations are agile enough to adjust to these forces. But many forces internal to an organization make the organization resistant to change and thus threaten its effectiveness and survival.

Resistances to Change

In the last decade many of best-known (and formerly strongest and most successful) U.S. companies—GM, Kodak, IBM, Sun Microsystems, TWA, and Macy's—have seen their fortunes decline. Some, such as Macy's and TWA, have gone bankrupt; others, such as Kodak and Sun, are still in trouble; and some, such as GM and IBM, have reversed their decline and recovered. How did such former powerhouses lose their effectiveness? The main explanation for such decline is almost always an organization's inability to change in response to changes (such as an increase in competition) in its environment. Research suggests that one of the main reasons for some organizations' inability to change is organizational inertia, the tendency of an organization to maintain the status quo. Resistance to change lowers an organization's effectiveness and reduces its chances of survival.[19] Resistances or impediments to change that cause inertia are found at the organization, group, and individual levels[20] (see Figure 10.1).

Organization-Level Resistance to Change

Many forces inside an organization make it difficult for the organization to change in response to changing conditions in its environment.[21] The most powerful organization-level impediments to change include power and conflict, differences in functional orientation, mechanistic structure, and organizational culture.

Power and Conflict

Change usually benefits some people, functions, or divisions at the expense of others. When change causes power struggles and organizational conflict, an organization is likely to resist it.[22] Suppose that a change in purchasing practices will help materials management to achieve its goal of reducing input costs but will harm manufacturing's ability to reduce manufacturing costs. Materials management will push for the change, but manufacturing will resist it. The conflict between the two functions will slow the process of change and perhaps prevent change from occurring at all. If powerful functions can prevent change, an organization will not change. At IBM, for example, managers in the mainframe computer division were the most powerful in the corporation. To preserve their established prestige and power in the organization, they fought off attempts to redirect IBM's resources to produce the personal computers or minicomputers that customers wanted. This failure to change in response to customer demands severely reduced IBM's speed of response to its competitors. Chapter 14 is devoted to discussing this important obstacle to change.

Differences in Functional Orientation

Differences in functional orientation are another major impediment to change and a source of organizational inertia. Different functions and divisions often see the source of a problem differently because they see an issue or problem primarily from their own viewpoint. This "tunnel vision" increases organizational inertia because the organization must spend time and effort to secure agreement about the source of a problem before it can even consider how the organization needs to change to respond to the problem.

Mechanistic Structure

Recall from Chapter 4 that a mechanistic structure is characterized by a tall hierarchy, centralized decision making, and the standardization of behavior through rules and procedures. By contrast, organic structures are flat and decentralized and rely on mutual adjustment between people to get the job done.[23] Which structure is likely to be more resistant to change?

Mechanistic structures are more resistant to change. People who work within a mechanistic structure are expected to act in certain ways and do not develop the capacity to adjust their behavior to changing conditions. The extensive use of mutual adjustment and decentralized authority in an organic structure fosters the development of skills that allow workers to be creative, responsive, and able to find solutions for new problems. A mechanistic structure typically develops as an organization grows and is a principal source of inertia, especially in large organizations.

Organizational Culture

The values and norms in an organization's culture can be another source of resistance to change. Just as role relationships result in a series of stable expectations between people, so values and norms cause people to behave in predictable ways. If organizational change disrupts taken-for-granted values and norms and forces people to change what they do and how they do it, an organization's culture will cause resistance to change. For example, many organizations develop conservative values that support the status quo and make managers reluctant to search for new ways to compete. As a result, if the environment changes and a company's products become obsolete, the company has nothing to fall back on, and failure is likely.[24] Sometimes, values and norms are so strong that even when the environment is changing and it is clear that a new strategy needs to be adopted, managers cannot change because they are committed to the way they currently do business.

Group-Level Resistance to Change

Much of an organization's work is performed by groups, and several group characteristics can produce resistance to change. First, many groups develop strong informal norms that specify appropriate and inappropriate behaviors and govern the interactions between group members. Often, change alters task and role relationships in a group; when it does, it disrupts group norms and the informal expectations that group members have of one another. As a result, members of a group may resist change because a whole new set of norms may have to be developed to meet the needs of the new situation.

Group cohesiveness, the attractiveness of a group to its members, also affects group performance. Although some level of cohesiveness promotes group performance, too much cohesiveness may actually reduce performance because it stifles opportunities for the group to change and adapt. A highly cohesive group may resist attempts by management to change what it does or even who is a member of the group. Group members may unite to preserve the status quo and to protect their interests at the expense of other groups.

Groupthink is a pattern of faulty decision making that occurs in cohesive groups when members discount negative information in order to arrive at a unanimous agreement. Escalation of commitment worsens this situation because even when group members realize that their decision is wrong, they continue to pursue it because they are committed to it. These group processes make changing a group's behavior very difficult. The more important the group's activities are to the organization, the greater the impact of these processes on organizational performance.

Individual-Level Resistance to Change

There are also several reasons why individuals within an organization may be inclined to resist change.[25] First, people tend to resist change because they feel uncertain and insecure about what its outcome will be.[26] Workers might be given new tasks. Role relationships may be reorganized. Some workers might lose their jobs. Some people might benefit at the expense of others. Workers' resistance to the uncertainty and insecurity surrounding change can cause organizational inertia. Absenteeism and turnover may increase as change takes place, and workers may become uncooperative, attempt to delay or slow the change process, and otherwise passively resist the change in an attempt to quash it.

Moreover, there is a general tendency for people to selectively perceive information that is consistent with their existing views of their organizations. Thus, when change takes place, workers tend to focus only on how it will affect them or their function or division personally. If they perceive few benefits, they may reject the purpose behind the change. Not surprisingly, it can be difficult for an organization to develop a common platform to promote change across an organization and get people to see the need for change in the same way.

Habit, people's preference for familiar actions and events, is a further impediment to change. The difficulty of breaking bad habits and adopting new styles of behavior indicates how resistant habits are to change. Why are habits hard to break? Some researchers have suggested that people have a built-in tendency to return to their original behaviors, a tendency that stymies change.

Lewin's Force-Field Theory of Change

Force-field theory
A theory of organizational change which argues that two sets of opposing forces within an organization determine how change will take place.

A wide variety of forces make organizations resistant to change, and a wide variety of forces push organizations toward change. Researcher Kurt Lewin developed a theory about organizational change. According to his **force-field theory**, these two sets of forces are always in opposition in an organization.[27] When the forces are evenly balanced, the organization is in a state of inertia and does not change. To get an organization to change, managers must find a way to *increase* the forces for change, *reduce* resistance to change, or do *both* simultaneously. Any of these strategies will overcome inertia and cause an organization to change.

Figure 10.2 illustrates Lewin's theory. An organization at performance level P1 is in balance: Forces for change and resistance to change are equal. Management, however, decides that the organization should strive to achieve performance level P2. To get to level P2, managers must increase the forces for change (the increase is represented by the lengthening of the up arrows), reduce resistance to change

Figure 10.2
Lewin's Force-Field
Theory of Change

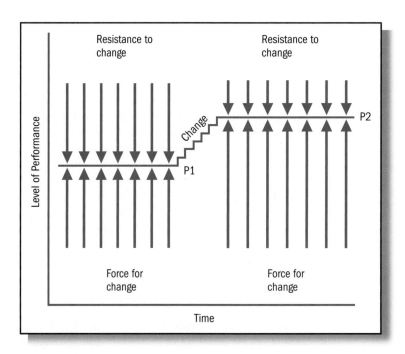

(the reduction is represented by the shortening of the down arrows), or do both. If they pursue any of the three strategies successfully, the organization will change and reach performance level P2.

Before we look in more detail at the techniques that managers can use to overcome resistance and facilitate change, we need to look at the types of change they can implement to increase organizational effectiveness.

MANAGERIAL IMPLICATIONS

FORCES FOR AND RESISTANCES TO CHANGE

1. Periodically analyze the organizational environment and identify forces for change.
2. Analyze how the change in response to these forces will affect people, functions, and divisions inside the organization.
3. Using this analysis, decide what type of change to pursue, and develop a plan to overcome possible resistance to change and to increase the forces for change.

EVOLUTIONARY AND REVOLUTIONARY CHANGE IN ORGANIZATIONS

Evolutionary change
Change that is gradual, incremental, and specifically focused.

Managers continually face choices about how best to respond to the forces for change. There are several types of change that managers can adopt to help their organizations achieve desired future states. In general, types of change fall into two broad categories: evolutionary change and revolutionary change.[28]

Evolutionary change is gradual, incremental, and narrowly focused. Evolutionary change involves not a drastic or sudden altering of the basic nature of an organization's strategy and structure but a constant attempt to improve, adapt, and adjust strategy and structure incrementally to accommodate to changes taking place in the environment.[29] Sociotechnical systems theory, total quality management, and the creation of empowered, flexible work groups are three instruments of evolutionary change that organizations use in their attempt to make incremental improvements in the way work gets done. Such improvements might be a better way to operate a technology or to organize the work process.

Evolutionary change is accomplished gradually, incrementally. Some organizations, however, need to make major changes quickly. They do not want to take the time to set up and implement programs that foster evolutionary change or wait for the performance results that such programs can bring about. Faced with drastic, unexpected changes in the environment (for example, a new technological breakthrough) or with impending disaster resulting from years of inaction and neglect, an organization needs to act quickly and decisively. Revolutionary change is called for.

Revolutionary change
Change that is sudden, drastic, and organization-wide.

Revolutionary change is rapid, dramatic, and broadly focused. Revolutionary change involves a bold attempt to quickly find new ways to be effective. It is likely to result in a radical shift in ways of doing things, new goals, and a new structure. It has repercussions at all levels in the organization—corporate, divisional, functional, group, and individual. Reengineering, restructuring, and innovation are three important instruments of revolutionary change.

Socio-technical systems theory
A theory that proposes the importance of changing role and task or technical relationships to increase organizational effectiveness.

Developments in Evolutionary Change: Sociotechnical Systems Theory

Sociotechnical systems theory was one of the first theories that proposed the importance of changing role and task or technical relationships to increase organizational effectiveness.[30] It emerged from a study of changing work practices in the British coal-mining industry.[31]

After World War II, new technology that changed work relationships between miners was introduced into the British mining industry. Before the war, coal mining was a small-batch or craft process. Teams of skilled miners dug coal from the coal face underground and performed all the other activities necessary to transport the coal to the surface. Work took place in a confined space where productivity depended on close cooperation between team members. Workers developed their own routines and norms to get the job done and provided each other with social support to help combat the stress of their dangerous and confining working conditions.

This method of coal mining, called the "hand got method," approximated small-batch technology (see Chapter 9). To increase efficiency, managers decided to replace it with the "long wall method." This method utilized a mechanized, mass production technology. Coal was now cut by miners using powered drills, and it was transported to the surface on conveyor belts. Tasks became more routine as the work process was programmed and standardized. On paper, the new technology promised impressive increases in mining efficiency. But after its introduction at the mines, however, efficiency rose only slowly, and absenteeism among miners, which had always been high, increased dramatically. Consultants were called to the mines to figure out why the expected gains in efficiency had not occurred.

The researchers pointed out that, to operate the new technology efficiently, management had changed the task and role relationships among the miners. The new task and role relationships had destroyed informal norms and social support, disrupted long-established informal working relationships, and reduced group cohesiveness. To solve the problem, the researchers recommended linking the new technology with the old social system by recreating the old system of tasks and roles and decentralizing authority to work groups. When management redesigned the production process, productivity improved and absenteeism fell.

This study led to the development of sociotechnical systems theory, which argues that managers need to fit or "jointly optimize" the workings of an organization's technical and social systems—or, in terms of the current discussion, culture—to promote effectiveness.[32] A poor fit between an organization's technology and social system leads to failure, but a close fit leads to success. The lesson to take from sociotechnical systems theory is that when managers change task and role relationships, they must recognize the need to adjust the technical and social systems gradually so that group norms and cohesiveness are not disrupted. By taking this gradual approach, an organization can avoid the group-level resistance to change that we discussed earlier in this chapter.

This pioneering study has been followed by many other studies that show the importance of the link between type of technology and cultural values and norms.[33] Managers need to be sensitive to the fact that the way they structure the work process affects the way people and groups behave. Compare the following two mass production settings, for example. In the first, managers routinize the technology, standardize the work process, and require workers to perform repetitive tasks as quickly as possible; workers are assigned to a place on the production line and are not allowed to move or switch jobs; and managers monitor workers closely and make all the decisions involving control of the work process. In the second, managers standardize the work process but encourage workers to find better ways to perform tasks; workers are allowed to switch jobs; and workers are formed into teams that are empowered to monitor and control important aspects of their own performance.

What differences in values and norms will emerge between these two types of sociotechnical systems? What will be their effect on performance? Many researchers have argued that the more team-based system will promote the development of values and norms that will boost efficiency and product quality. Indeed, the goal of total quality management, the continuous improvement in product quality, draws heavily on the principles embedded in sociotechnical systems theory; so does the development of flexible workers and work groups, both discussed next.

Total Quality Management

Total quality management (TQM)

A technique developed by W. Edwards Deming to continuously improve the effectiveness of flexible work teams.

Total quality management (TQM) is an ongoing and constant effort by all of an organization's functions to find new ways to improve the quality of the organization's goods and services.[34] In many companies, the initial decision to adopt a TQM approach signals a radical change in the way activities are organized. Once TQM is adopted by an organization, however, it leads to continuous, incremental change, and all functions are expected to cooperate with each other to improve quality.

First developed by a number of American business consultants such as W. Edwards Deming and Joseph Juran, total quality management was eagerly embraced by Japanese companies after World War II. For Japanese companies, with their tradition of long-term working relationships and cooperation between functions, the implementation of the new TQM system was an incremental step. Shop-floor workers in Japan, for example, had long been organized into **quality circles**, groups of workers who met regularly to discuss the way work was performed in order to find new ways to increase performance.[35] Changes frequently inspired by TQM include altering the design or type of machines used to assemble products and reorganizing the sequence of activities—either within or between functions—necessary to provide a service to a customer. As in sociotechnical systems theory, the emphasis in TQM is on the fit between technical and social systems.

Quality circles

Groups of workers who met regularly to discuss the way work is performed in order to find new ways to increase performance.

Changing cross-functional relationships to help improve quality is very important in TQM. Poor quality often originates at crossover points or after handoffs when people turn over the work they are doing to people in different functions. The job of intermediate manufacturing, for example, is to assemble inputs that are assembled into a final product. Coordinating the design of the various inputs so that they fit together smoothly and operate effectively together is one area of TQM. Members of the different functions work together to find new ways to reduce the number of inputs needed or to suggest design improvements that will enable inputs to be assembled more easily and reliably. Such changes increase quality and lower costs. Note that the changes associated with TQM (as with sociotechnical systems theory) are changes in task, role, and group relationships. The results of TQM activities can be dramatic, as Citibank, a leading global financial institution, discovered when it began to use TQM to increase its responsiveness to customers.

Recognizing that customer loyalty determined the bank's future success, as the first step in its TQM effort Citibank focused upon identifying the factors that dissatisfied its customers. When it analyzed customer complaints, managers found that most of them concerned the time it took to complete a customer's request, such as responding to an account problem or getting a loan. So Citibank's managers began to examine how they handled each kind of customer request. For each distinct kind of request, they formed a cross-functional team of people whose job was to break down a specific request into the steps between people and departments that were needed to complete the request and analyze them. These teams found that often many steps in the process were unnecessary and could be done away with by the use of the right information systems. They also found that very often delays occurred because employees simply did not know how to handle the request. They were not being given the right kind of training and when they couldn't handle a request they simply put it aside until a supervisor could deal it.

So Citibank decided to implement an organization-wide TQM program. Managers and supervisors were charged with reducing the complexity of the work process and finding the most effective way to process a particular request, such as for a loan. They were also charged with training employees on how to answer each specific request. The results were remarkable. For example, in the loan department the TQM program reduced the number of handoffs necessary to process a request by 75%; average time taken to respond to a customer dropped from several hours to 30 minutes. Within one year, over 92,000 employees had been trained worldwide in the new TQM processes, and Citibank could easily measure TQM's effectiveness by the increased speed with which it was handling an increased volume of customer requests.

United Technologies Corp. (UTC), based in Hartford, Connecticut, owns a wide variety of companies that operate in different businesses and industries. Some of the companies it owns are more well known than UTC itself, such as Sikorsky helicopters, Pratt & Whitney (the aircraft engine and component maker), Otis elevators, Carrier air conditioning, and Chubb, the security and lock maker. In the 2000s, UTC has been one of the most profitable companies in the world and the reason, so its CEO George David claims, is its total quality management program.

UTC's TQM program began when it had a major problem in its Otis Elevator division, and David assigned one of its leading total quality management experts, Yuzuru Ito, to head a team of Otis engineers to find out why it performed so poorly. Under Ito's direction, they created a set of "process" techniques, which involved all the employees—managers, designers, production workers—who had produced the elevator to analyze why the elevators were malfunctioning. This intensive study led to a total redesign of the elevator, and when their new and improved elevator was launched worldwide it met with great success.

After this success David decided the best way to increase UTC's profitability was to find ways to use TQM techniques in all its diverse businesses. He convinced Ito to take responsibility for championing the development of UTC's TQM system, which is known as *Achieving Competitive Excellence* or ACE. ACE is a set of tasks and procedures that are used by employees from the shop floor to top managers to analyze all aspects of the way a product is made to find ways to improve quality and reliability, to lower the costs of making the products, and especially to find ways to make the next generation of a particular product perform better: in other words, to encourage technological innovation.

David makes every employee in every function and at every level take responsibility for achieving the incremental, step-by-step gains that can result in innovative products, built with ever increasing quality and efficiency, that can put a company on the path to dominating its industry. David calls these techniques "process disciplines," and he has used them to improve the performance of *all* UTC's companies. In the decade since he took control, he has quadrupled UTC's earnings per share, and its stock price has boomed in the 2000s.

More and more companies are embracing the continuous, incremental type of change that results from the implementation of TQM programs. Many companies have found, however, that implementing a TQM program is not always easy, because it requires workers and managers to adopt new ways of viewing their roles in an organization. Managers must be willing to decentralize control of decision making, empower workers, and assume the role of facilitator rather than supervisor. The "command and control" model gives way to an "advise and support" model. It is important that workers, as well as managers, share in the increased profits that successful TQM programs can provide. In Japan, for example, performance bonuses frequently account for 30% or more of workers' and managers' salaries, and salaries can fluctuate widely from year to year as a result of changes in organizational performance.

Resistance to the changes a TQM program requires can be serious unless management explicitly recognizes the many ways that TQM affects relationships between functions and even divisions. We discuss ways to deal with resistance to change at length later in this chapter.

Despite the success that organizations like Citibank, Harley-Davidson, and Ford have had with TQM, many other organizations have not obtained the increases in quality and reductions in cost that are often associated with TQM and have abandoned their TQM programs. Two reasons for a lack of success with TQM are underestimates of the degree of commitment from people at all levels in the organization that is necessary to implement a TQM program and the long time frame that is necessary for TQM efforts to succeed and show results. TQM is not a quick fix that can turn an organization around overnight. It is an evolutionary process that bears fruit only when it becomes a way of life in an organization.[36]

Flexible Workers and Flexible Work Teams

In many modern manufacturing settings, attention to the goals behind sociotechnical systems theory and TQM has led many organizations to embrace the concept of flexible workers and work teams as a way of changing employee attitudes and behaviors.

First, employees need to acquire and develop the skills to perform any of the tasks necessary for assembling a range of finished products.[37] A worker first develops the skills needed to accomplish one work task and over time is trained to perform other tasks. Compensation is frequently tied to the number of different tasks that a person can perform. Each worker can substitute for any other worker. As the demand for components or finished products rises or falls, flexible workers can be transferred to the task most needed by the organization. As a result, the organization is able to respond quickly to changes in its environment. Performing more than one task also cuts down on repetition, boredom, and fatigue and raises workers' incentives to improve product quality. When workers learn one another's tasks, they also learn how the different tasks relate to each other. This understanding often leads to new ways of combining tasks or to the redesign of a product to make its manufacture more efficient and less costly.

Flexible work team
A group of workers who assume responsibility for performing all the operations necessary for completing a specified stage in the manufacturing process.

To further speed the development of functional capabilities, flexible workers are then grouped into flexible work teams.[38] A **flexible work team** is a group of workers who assume responsibility for performing all the operations necessary for completing a specified stage in the manufacturing process. Production line workers who were previously responsible for only their own tasks are placed in groups and are jointly assigned responsibility for one stage of the manufacturing process. At Ford plants, for example, one work team is responsible for assembling the car transmission and sending it to the body assembly area, where the body assembly team is responsible for fitting it to the car body. A flexible work team is self-managed: The team members jointly assign tasks and transfer workers from one task to another as necessary.

Figure 10.3 illustrates the way in which flexible work teams perform their activities. Separate teams assemble different components and turn those components over to the final-product work team, which assembles the final product. Each team's activities are driven by demands that have their origins in customer demands for the final product. Thus each team has to adjust its activities to the pull coming from the output side of the production process. The experience of Globe Metallurgical, Inc., illustrates many of the factors associated with the use of flexible work teams.

Flexible work teams are involved in more than just conversion or assembly activities: They also assume responsibility for controlling TQM efforts. Because a large, separate quality control function is no longer needed at the end of the production line, the use of work teams reduces costs. Flexible work teams are also responsible for devising ways to improve the efficiency of the manufacturing process. New ideas often originate in quality control circles, team meetings that bring members together specifically to discuss ways of improving productivity. Moreover, the most experienced members of a team assume responsibility for training new members. All team members are often responsible for selecting new recruits who they think will fit in with the team. In this way, a work-team culture emerges.

The managers' role in this system is not to monitor and supervise the work teams' activities but to facilitate team activities and do all they can to allow the teams to develop improved procedures. Since 1983, GM and Toyota have been cooperating in a joint venture that uses flexible work teams. The story of this venture is instructive.

In 1963, General Motors opened a car plant in Fremont, California, 35 miles east of San Francisco. From the outset, the plant was a loser. Productivity and quality were poor. Drug and alcohol abuse were widespread. Absenteeism was so high that hundreds of extra workers were employed to ensure that enough workers were on hand to operate the plant. Managers at the Fremont plant, as at all GM plants, constantly analyzed the worker–task relationship in order to design jobs to raise productivity. Workers strongly resisted these moves, and finally, seeing no chance of improvement, GM closed the plant in 1981.

In 1983, GM and Toyota announced a joint venture: They would cooperate to reopen the Fremont plant. GM wanted to learn how Toyota operated its production system, and Toyota wanted to see whether it could achieve its customary high level

Figure 10.3
The Use of Flexible Work Teams to Assemble Cars

Self-managed teams assemble brake systems, exhaust systems, and other components in accordance with the demands of the final-product team. Driven by customers demands, the final-product team assembles components to produce a car.

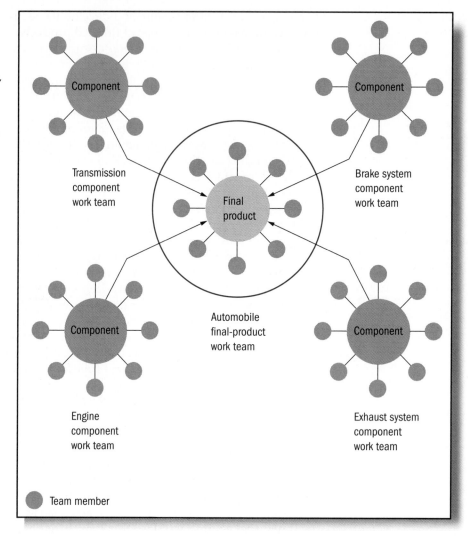

Transmission component work team

Brake system component work team

Final product

Automobile final-product work team

Engine component work team

Exhaust system component work team

Team member

of productivity by using Japanese techniques with American workers. In 1984, the new organization, New United Motors Manufacturing Inc. (NUMMI), opened under the control of Japanese management. By 1986, productivity at NUMMI was higher than productivity at any other GM factory, and the plant was operating at twice the level it had operated at under GM management. Moreover, alcohol and drug abuse had virtually disappeared, and absenteeism had almost stopped. How had this miracle been achieved?

At the NUMMI factory, Toyota divided the workforce into 350 flexible work teams consisting of five to seven people plus a team leader. Each worker could do the jobs of the other workers, and the workers regularly rotated jobs. In addition, all workers were taught procedures for analyzing jobs to improve the employee–task relationship. Team members designed each team's jobs, timed each other with stopwatches, and continually attempted to find better ways of performing the tasks. In the past, GM had employed 80 managers to perform this analysis. Now, flexible work teams not only perform the analysis but also monitor product quality. What is the role of managers in the NUMMI factory? The manager's job is defined explicitly as providing shop-floor workers with support, not monitoring or supervising their activities.

Why do employees buy into this new system? NUMMI has a no-layoff policy; workers are given extensive training; and the use of flexible work teams gives workers, not managers, control over the production line. Apparently, most workers still consider assembly-line work a "lousy job"—but the best job they can expect to get. In the new work system they at least have some control over what they do.[39]

Globe Metallurgical, Inc., of Beverly, Ohio, and Selma, Alabama, was the first small company to win the Malcolm Baldridge National Quality Award. Globe makes specialty steel products and is one of the most successful organizations in its industry, surpassing its competitors in product quality, sales, and profit growth.

Globe's emergence as a leader in quality and particularly in its use of self-managed work teams came in an unusual way. In 1986, Globe wanted to introduce new, flexible work systems in order to raise profitability. When the unions refused to relax rigid work rules so that the new technology could be introduced, the company experienced a yearlong strike. To continue operation, 10 managers and 35 salaried workers took control of two of Globe's furnaces (they closed three others). Lack of manpower forced these 45 people to find new, more efficient ways to produce Globe's output.

With both managers and workers directly involved in production, many possibilities for improving the way the work was performed emerged. In the absence of work rules and job classifications specifying how the furnaces were to be operated, managers experimented with new ways to

run them and within two weeks increased productivity by 20%. Every day brought new suggestions. It soon became obvious that productivity could be increased if welders, crane operators, furnace operators, forklift operators, stokers, furnace tappers, and tapper assistants worked cooperatively in teams. By trial and error, management discovered that a flexible work team of seven employees (one from each function), each of whom could do the others' jobs, could efficiently operate one furnace. Each team was put under the supervision of a team leader, who took responsibility for coordinating his team's work and schedules with those of other teams and with top management.

After the strike was over, Globe found that by using self-managed work teams it could operate all five furnaces with 120 employees (down from the 350 needed before the strike). The unions' fears about the shift to the new technology were justified: Flexible workers and flexible work teams resulted in a loss of jobs. For the employees who remained, however, Globe instituted a profit-sharing plan that allows workers to reap some of the benefits created by the new work system. Today, Globe is the largest supplier of specialty metals in the United States.

Developments in Revolutionary Change Reengineering

The term "reengineering" has been used to refer to the process by which managers redesign how tasks are bundled into roles and functions to improve organizational effectiveness. In the words of Michael Hammer and J. Champy, who popularized the term, reengineering involves the "fundamental rethinking and radical redesign of business processes to achieve dramatic improvements in critical, contemporary measures of performance such as cost, quality, service, and speed."[40] Change resulting from reengineering requires managers to go back to the basics and pull apart each step in the work process to identify a better way to coordinate and integrate the activities necessary to provide customers with goods and services. Instead of focusing on an organization's *functions*, the managers of a reengineered organization focus on business *processes*. Processes, not organizations, are the object of reengineering. Companies don't reengineer their sales or manufacturing departments; they reengineer the work the people in those departments do.

As this definition suggests, an organization that undertakes reengineering must completely rethink how it goes about its business. Instead of focusing on an organization's functions in isolation from one another, managers make business processes the focus of attention. A **business process** is any activity (such as order processing, inventory control, or product design) that cuts across functional boundaries; it is the ability of people and groups to act in a cross-functional way that is the vital factor in determining how quickly goods and services are delivered to customers or that promotes high quality or low costs. Business processes involve activities across functions. Because reengineering focuses on business processes and not functions, an organization must rethink the way it approaches organizing its activities.

Organizations that take up reengineering deliberately ignore the existing arrangement of tasks, roles, and work activities. They start the reengineering process with the customer (not the product or service) and ask the question "How can I reorganize the way we do our work, our business processes, to provide the best quality,

Business process
An activity which cuts across functional boundaries and which is vital to the quick delivery of goods and services or that promotes high quality or low costs.

lowest cost goods and services to the customer?" Frequently when companies ask this question, they realize that there are more effective ways of organizing their activities. For example, a business process that currently involves members of 10 different functions working sequentially to provide goods and services might be performed by one or a few people at a fraction of the original cost, after reengineering.

A good example of how to use reengineering to increase functional integration to increase control of activities comes from attempts to redesign the materials management function to improve its effectiveness (see Figure 10.4). In the past, the three main components of materials management—purchasing (responsible for obtaining inputs), production control (responsible for using inputs most efficiently), and distribution (responsible for disposing of the finished product)—were typically in separate functions and had little to do with one another. Figure 10.4A shows the traditional functional design. The problem with the traditional design is that when all aspects of materials management are separate functions, coordinating their activities is difficult. Each function has its own hierarchy, and there are problems in both vertical and horizontal communication. The structure shown in Figure 10.4A makes it difficult to process information quickly in order to secure cost savings. Computerized production and warehousing, for example, require the careful coordination of activities, but the traditional design of materials management activities does not provide enough control for this to be achieved.

Realizing that this separation of activities has often slowed down production and raised costs, many organizations have moved to reengineer the materials management process. Today, most organizations put all three of the functional activities involved in the materials management process inside one function, as shown in Figure 10.4B. Now, one hierarchy of managers is responsible for all three aspects of materials management, and communication among those managers is easy because they are within the same function. Three guidelines for performing reengineering successfully are:[41]

1. *Organize around outcomes, not tasks.* Where possible, organize work so that one person or one function can perform all the activities necessary to complete the process, thus avoiding the need for transfers (and integration) between functions.

Figure 10.4
Improving Integration in Functional Structure in Creating a Materials Management Function

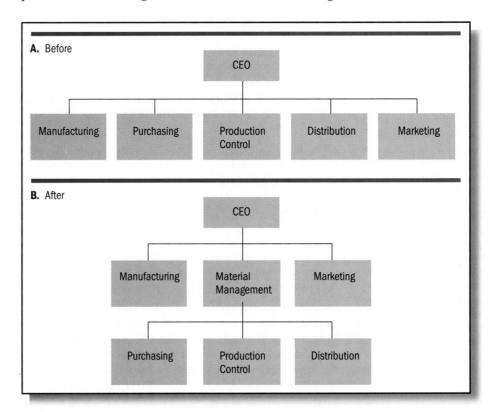

2. *Have those who use the output of the process perform the process.* Since the people who use the output of the process know best what they want, establish a system of rules and SOPs that will allow them to take control over it.

3. *Decentralize decision making to the point where the decision is made.* Allow the people on the spot to decide how best to respond to specific problems that arise.

Take the case of Hallmark Cards, profiled in the following organizational insight.

Reengineering and TQM are highly interrelated and complementary. After revolutionary reengineering has taken place and the question "What is the best way to provide customers with the goods or service they require?" has been answered, evolutionary TQM takes over with its focus on "How can we now continue to improve and refine the new process and find better ways of managing task and role relationships?" Successful organizations examine both questions simultaneously, and they

ORGANIZATIONAL INSIGHT 10.4
How to Stay on Top in the Greeting Card Business

Hallmark Cards, based in Kansas City, Missouri, sells 55% of the 8 billion birthday, Christmas, and other kinds of cards sold each year in the United States.[42] However, in the 1990s, it came under increasing attack from smaller and more agile competitors who pioneered new kinds of specialty greeting cards and sold them, often at discount prices, in supermarkets and discount stores. So, to keep Hallmark on top of its market it was decided to examine how things were currently being done at Hallmark, in order to determine what changes needed to be made.

Top management began this evaluation by placing 100 managers into teams to analyze Hallmark's competitors, the changing nature of customer needs, the organizational structure the company was using to coordinate its activities, and the ways the company was developing, distributing and marketing its cards—its basic business processes. What the teams found startled managers from the top down and showed that there was a need for change.

Managers discovered that although Hallmark had the world's largest creative staff—more than 700 artists and writers who design more than 24,000 new cards each year—it was taking over three years to get a new card to market. Once an artist designed a new card and a writer came up with an appropriate rhyme or message, it took an average of three years for the card to be produced, packaged, and shipped to retailers. Information on changing customer needs, a vital input into decisions about what cards should be designed, took many months to reach artists. That delay made it difficult for Hallmark to respond quickly to its competitors.

Armed with this information, the 100 team managers presented top management with 100 recommendations for changes that would allow the company to do its work more quickly and effectively. The recommendations called for a complete change in the way the company organized its basic business processes. Hallmark began by completely restructuring its activities. The organization had been using a functional structure. Artists worked separately from writers, and both artists and writers worked separately from materials management, printing, and manufacturing personnel. From the time a card went from the creative staff to the printing department, 25 handoffs (work exchanges between functions) were needed to produce the final product, and 90% of the time work was simply sitting in somebody's in- or out-basket. Taking the advice of the teams, Hallmark changed to a cross-functional team structure. People from different functions—artists, writers, editors, and so on—were grouped into teams responsible for producing a specific kind of card, such as Christmas cards, get-well cards, or new lines of specialty cards.

To eliminate the need for handoffs between departments, each team is responsible for all aspects of the design process. To reduce the need for handoffs within a team, all team members work together from the beginning to plan the steps in the design process, and all are responsible for reviewing the success of their efforts. To help each team evaluate its efforts and to give each team the information it needs about customer desires, Hallmark introduced a computerized point-of-sales merchandising system in each of its Hallmark Card stores, so each team has instant feedback on what and how many kinds of cards are selling. Each team can now continuously experiment with new card designs to attract more customers.

The effects of these changes have been dramatic. Cards are introduced in less than one year, and some reach the market in a matter of months. Quality has increased as each team focuses on improving its cards, and costs have fallen because the new work system is so efficient. Increased competition from the Internet, in particular the increasing use of free online greetings from Yahoo! and other companies, is putting pressure on Hallmark in the 2000s, however. Its managers are currently seeking to increase its online presence in order to fight back, and are once again reengineering its processes to make the company a leader in the e-card business.

continuously attempt to identify new and better processes for meeting the goals of increased efficiency, quality, and responsiveness to customers.

E-Engineering

The term "e-engineering" refers to companies' attempts to use all kinds of information systems to improve their performance. In previous chapters, there have been many examples of how the use of Internet-based software systems can change the way a company's strategy and structure operate. New information systems can be employed in all aspects of an organization's business and for all kinds of reasons. For example, Cypress Semiconductor's CEO, T. J. Rodgers, uses the company's online management information system to monitor his managers' activities continually and help him keep the organizational hierarchy flat. Rodgers claims that he can review the goals of all his 1,500 managers in about four hours, and he does so each week. The importance of e-engineering is increasing as it changes the way a company organizes its value-creation functions and links them to improve its performance. We discuss this important issue at length in Chapters 12 and 13.

Restructuring

Restructuring and reengineering are also closely linked, for in practice the move to a more efficient organizational structure generally results in the layoff of employees, unless the organization is growing rapidly so employees can be transferred or absorbed elsewhere in the organization. It is for this reason that reengineering efforts are unpopular both among workers—who fear they will be reengineered out of a job—and among managers—who fear the loss of their authority and empires as new and more efficient ways of structuring task and role relationships are found.

Restructuring
A process by which managers change task and authority relationships and redesign organizational structure and culture to improve organizational effectiveness.

Nevertheless, **restructuring** refers to the process by which managers change task and authority relationships and redesign organizational structure and culture to improve organizational effectiveness. The move from a functional to some form of divisional structure, and the move from one divisional structure to another, represents one of the most common kinds of restructuring effort. As the environment changes, and as the organization's strategy changes, managers must analyze how well their structure now fits them. Frequently, they find that there is a better way of grouping the products they now make to serve customer needs and move, for example, from one kind of product structure to another, for reasons outlined in Chapter 6.

Downsizing
The process by which managers streamline the organizational hierarchy and lay off managers and workers to reduce bureaucratic costs.

Another type of organizational restructuring that has become very common in recent years is **downsizing**, the process by which managers streamline the organizational hierarchy and lay off managers and workers to reduce bureaucratic costs. The size and scope of these recent restructuring and downsizing efforts have been enormous. It is estimated that in the last 10 years, *Fortune* 500 companies have downsized so much that they now employ about 10% fewer managers than they used to. Moreover, in 1998, despite the fact that the economy was booming, companies laid off record numbers of employees as they restructured to reduce costs and improve efficiency.

The drive to reduce bureaucratic costs is often a response to increasing competitive pressures in the environment as companies fight to increase their performance and introduce new information technology.[43] For example, the wave of mergers and acquisitions that has occurred in the 1990s in many industries such as telecommunications, banking, and defense has also resulted in downsizing because merged companies typically require fewer managers.

Often, after one industry company downsizes, other industry companies are forced to examine their own structures to search out inefficiencies; thus, downsizing waves take place across companies in an industry. For example, Molson Breweries, the largest Canadian brewing company, announced that it was slashing the size of its headquarters staff to reduce costs. Apparently, Molson's top managers had watched its main competitor, Labatt Breweries, reduce its headquarters staff to 110 and decided that Molson did not need the 200 headquarters staff it employed.[44]

Although there is no doubt that companies have realized considerable cost savings by downsizing and streamlining their hierarchies, some analysts are now wondering whether this process has gone far enough, or even too far.[45] There are increasing reports that the remaining managers in downsized organizations are working under severe stress, both because they fear they might be the next employees to be let go and because they are forced to do the work that was previously performed by the lost employees—work that often they cannot cope with.

Moreover, there are concerns that in pushing their downsizing efforts too far, organizations may be trading off short-term gains from cost savings for long-term losses because of lost opportunities. The argument is that organizations always need some level of "surplus" managers who have the time and energy to improve current operating methods and search the environment to find new opportunities for growth and expansion.[46] Downsized organizations lack the middle managers who perform this vital task, and this may hurt them in the future. Hence, the terms "anorexic" or "hollow" have been used to refer to organizations that have downsized too much and have too few managers.

Though clearly there are disadvantages associated with excessive downsizing, it remains true that many organizations became too tall and bloated because their past top management teams failed to control the growth of their hierarchies and design their organizational structures appropriately. In such cases, managers are forced to restructure their organizations to remain competitive and even to survive. Organizations experiencing a rapid deterioration in performance frequently resort to eliminating divisions, departments, or levels in the hierarchy to lower operating costs. Change in the relationships between divisions or functions is a common outcome of restructuring. IBM, in an effort to cut development costs and speed cooperation between engineers, created a new division to take control of the production of microprocessors and memory systems. This restructuring move pulled engineers from IBM's 13 divisions and grouped them in brand-new headquarters in Austin, Texas, to increase their effectiveness.

Why does restructuring become necessary, and why may an organization need to downsize its operations? Sometimes, an unforeseen change in the environment occurs: Perhaps a shift in technology makes the company's products obsolete, or a worldwide recession reduces demand for its products. Sometimes an organization has excess capacity because customers no longer want the goods and services it provides if they are outdated or offer poor value for money. Sometimes organizations downsize because they have grown too tall and bureaucratic and their operating costs have become much too high.

All too often, companies are forced to downsize and lay off employees because they have not continually monitored the way they operate—their basic business processes—and have not made the incremental changes to their strategies and structures that would have allowed them to contain costs and adjust to changing conditions. Paradoxically, because they have not paid attention to the need to reengineer themselves, they are forced into a position where restructuring becomes the only way they can survive and compete in an increasingly competitive environment.

Restructuring, like reengineering, TQM, and other change strategies, generates resistance to change. Often, the decision to downsize will require the establishment of new task and role relationships. Because this change may threaten the jobs of some workers, they resist the changes taking place. Many plans to introduce change, including restructuring, take a long time to implement and fail because of the high level of resistance that they encounter at all levels of the organization.

Innovation

Restructuring is often necessary because changes in technology make the technology an organization uses to produce goods and services, or the goods and services themselves, obsolete. For example, changes in technology have made computers much cheaper to manufacture and more powerful and have changed the type of computer that customers want. If organizations are to avoid being left behind in the competitive race to produce new goods and services, they must take steps to introduce new products or develop new technologies to produce those products reliably and at low cost.

Innovation
The process by which organizations use their skills and resources to develop new goods and services or to develop new production and operating systems so that they can better respond to the needs of their customers.

Innovation is the successful use of skills and resources to create new technologies or new goods and services so that an organization can change and better respond to the needs of customers.[47] Innovation is one of the most difficult instruments of change to manage. Chapter 13 describes issues involved in managing innovation and in increasing the level of creativity and entrepreneurship inside an organization.

MANAGING CHANGE: ACTION RESEARCH

No matter what type of evolutionary or revolutionary change an organization adopts, managers face the problem of getting the organization to change. Kurt Lewin, whose force-field theory argues that organizations are balanced between forces for change and resistance to change, has a related perspective on how managers can bring change to their organization (see Figure 10.5).

In Lewin's view, implementing change is a three-step process: (1) unfreezing the organization from its current state, (2) making the change, and (3) refreezing the organization in the new, desired state so that its members do not revert to their previous work attitudes and role behaviors.[48] Lewin warns that resistance to change will quickly cause an organization and its members to revert to their old ways of doing things unless the organization actively takes steps to refreeze the organization with the changes in place. It is not enough to make some changes in task and role relationships and expect the changes to be successful and to endure. To get an organization to remain in its new state, managers must actively manage the change process.

Action research
A Strategy for generating and acquiring knowledge that managers can use to define an organization's desired future state and to plan a change program that allows the organization to reach that state.

Action research is a strategy for generating and acquiring knowledge that managers can use to define an organization's desired future state and to plan a change program that allows the organization to reach that state.[49] The techniques and practices of action research, developed by experts, help managers to unfreeze an organization, move it to its new, desired position, and refreeze it so that the benefits of the change are retained. Figure 10.6 identifies the main steps in action research.

Diagnosing the Organization

The first step in action research requires managers to recognize the existence of a problem that needs to be solved and acknowledge that some type of change is needed to solve it. In general, recognition of the need for change arises because somebody in the organization perceives a gap between desired performance and actual performance. Perhaps customer complaints about the quality of goods or services have increased. Perhaps profits have recently fallen, or operating costs have been escalating. Perhaps turnover among managers or workers has been excessive. In the first stage of action research, managers need to analyze what is going on and

Figure 10.5
Lewin's Three-Step
Change Process

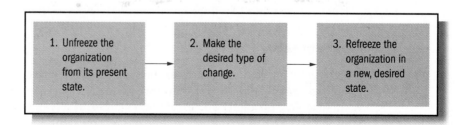

1. Unfreeze the organization from its present state. → 2. Make the desired type of change. → 3. Refreeze the organization in a new, desired state.

Figure 10.6
Steps in Action Research

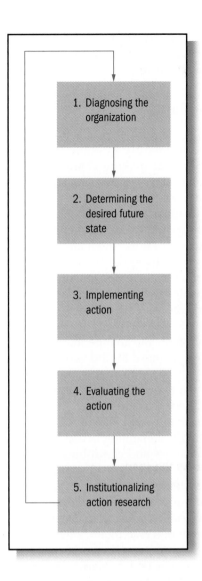

why problems are occurring. For example, the increase in competition from Wal-Mart caused managers at Sears to reevaluate the organization's present state.

Diagnosing the organization can be a complex process. Like a doctor, managers have to distinguish between symptoms and causes. For example, there is little point in introducing new technology to reduce production costs if the problem is that demand is falling because customers do not like the design of the product. Managers have to carefully collect information about the organization to diagnose the problem correctly and get employees committed to the change process. At this early stage of action research, it is important for managers to collect information from people at all levels in the organization and from outsiders such as customers and suppliers. Questionnaire surveys given to employees, customers, and suppliers, and interviews with workers and managers at all levels, can provide information that is essential to a correct diagnosis of the organization's current state.

Determining the Desired Future State

After identification of the current state, the next step is to identify where the organization needs to be—its desired future state. This step also involves a difficult planning process, as managers work out various alternative courses of action that could move the organization to where they would like it to be and determine what type of change to implement. Identifying the desired future state involves deciding what the organization's strategy and structure should be. Should the organization focus on reducing costs and increasing efficiency? Or are raising quality and responsiveness to customers the keys to future success? What is the best kind of organizational structure to adopt to realize organizational goals—a product structure or perhaps a cross-functional team structure?

Implementing Action

Implementing action is the third step of action research.[50] It is a three-step process. First, managers need to identify possible impediments to change that they will encounter as they go about making changes—impediments at the organization, group, and individual levels.[51] Suppose managers choose to reengineer the company from a functional to a cross-functional team structure to speed product development and reduce costs. They must anticipate the obstacles they will encounter when they unfreeze the organization and make the changes. Functional managers, for example, are likely to strongly resist efforts to change the company because the change will reduce their power and prestige in the organization. Similarly, members of each function who have grown accustomed to working with the same people and to stable task and role relationships will resist being assigned to a new team where tasks and roles have to be worked out again and new interpersonal relationships have to be learned.

The more revolutionary the change that is adopted, the greater the problem of implementing it. Managers need to find ways to minimize, control, and co-opt resistance to change. They also need to devise strategies to bring organizational members on board and foster their commitment to the change process. Managers must also look to the future and seek ways to refreeze the changes that they have made so that people cannot slide back into old behaviors.

The second step in implementing action is deciding who will be responsible for actually making the changes and controlling the change process. The choices are to employ **external change agents**, outside consultants who are experts in managing change; **internal change agents**, managers from within the organization who are knowledgeable about the situation; or some combination of both.[52]

The principal problem with using internal change agents is that other members of the organization may perceive them as being politically involved in the changes and biased toward certain groups. External change agents, in contrast, are likely to be perceived as less influenced by internal politics. Another reason for employing external change agents is that as outsiders they have a detached view of the organization's problems and can distinguish between the "forest and the trees." Insiders can be so involved in what is going on that they cannot see the true source of the problems. Management consultants from McKinsey & Co. are frequently brought in by large organizations to help the top management team diagnose an organization's problems and suggest solutions. Many consultants specialize in certain types of organizational change, such as restructuring, reengineering, or implementing total quality management.

The third step in implementing action is deciding which specific change strategy will most effectively unfreeze, change, and refreeze the organization. Specific techniques for implementing change are discussed later in this chapter. The types of change that these techniques give rise to fall into two categories: top-down and bottom-up.[53]

Top-down change is change that is implemented by managers at a high level in the organization. Top-down change is the result of radical organizational restructuring and reengineering. Managers high up in the organization decide to make a change, realizing full well that it will reverberate at all organizational levels. The managers choose to manage and solve problems as they arise at the divisional, functional, or individual levels.

Bottom-up change is change that is implemented by employees at low levels in the organization and gradually rises until it is felt throughout the organization. When an organization wants to engage in bottom-up change, the first step in the action research process—diagnosing the organization—becomes pivotal in determining the

External change agents
People who are outside consultants who are experts in managing change.

Internal change agents
Managers from within the organization who are knowledgeable about the situation to be changed.

Top-down change
Change that is implemented by managers at a high level in the organization.

Bottom-up change
Change that is implemented by employees at low levels in the organization and gradually rises until it is felt throughout the organization.

success of the change. Managers involve employees at all levels in the change process to obtain their input and to lessen their resistance. By reducing the uncertainty that employees experience, bottom-up change facilitates unfreezing and increases the likelihood that employees will retain the new behaviors that they learn during the change process. Top-down change proceeds rapidly and forces employees to keep up with the pace of change, troubleshooting to solve problems as they arise.

In general, bottom-up change is easier to implement than top-down change because it provokes less resistance. Organizations that have the time to engage in bottom-up change are generally well-run organizations that pay attention to change, are used to change, and change often. Poorly run organizations, those that rarely change or postpone change until it is too late, are forced to engage in top-down restructuring simply to survive. This is happening to all the major airline companies in the 2000s; to avoid bankruptcy, they have moved to restructure and downsize and find ways to lower costs in order to compete with low-cost airlines.

Organizations that change the most are able to exploit the advantages of evolutionary bottom-up change because their managers are always open to the need for change and constantly use action research to find new and better ways to operate and increase effectiveness. Organizations in which change happens rarely are likely candidates for revolutionary top-down change. Because their managers do not use action research on a continuing basis, they attempt change so late that their only option is some massive restructuring or downsizing to turn their organization around.

Evaluating the Action

The fourth step in action research is evaluating the action that has been taken and assessing the degree to which the changes have accomplished the desired objectives. Armed with this evaluation, management decides whether more change is needed to reach the organization's desired future state or whether more effort is needed to refreeze the organization in its new state.[54]

The best way to evaluate the change process is to develop measures or criteria that allow managers to assess whether the organization has reached its desired objectives. When criteria developed at the beginning of action research are used consistently over time to evaluate the effects of the change process, managers have ample information to assess the impact of the changes they have made. They can compare costs before and after the change to see whether efficiency has increased. They can survey workers to see whether they are more satisfied with their jobs. They can survey customers to see whether they are more satisfied with the quality of the organization's products. As part of its TQM effort, managers at Citibank carefully surveyed their customers to make sure that service had improved, for example. That information helped them to evaluate the success of their change effort.

Assessing the impact of change is especially difficult because the effects of change may emerge slowly. The action research process that we have been describing may take several years to complete. Typically, reengineering and restructuring take months or years, and total quality management, once under way, never stops. Consequently, managers need valid and reliable measures that they can use to evaluate performance. All too often poorly performing organizations fail to develop and consistently apply criteria that allow them to evaluate their performance. For those organizations, the pressure for change often comes from the outside, as shareholders complain about poor profits, parents complain about their children's poor grades, or state inspectors find high rates of postsurgery infection in hospitals.

Institutionalizing Action Research

The need to manage change is so vital in today's quickly changing environment that organizations must institutionalize action research—that is, make it a required habit or a norm adopted by every member of an organization. The institutionalization of action research is as necessary at the top of the organization (where the top management team plans the organization's future strategy) as it is on the shop floor (where workers meet in quality circles to find new ways to increase efficiency and quality). Because change is so difficult and requires so much thought and effort to implement, members at all levels of the organization must be rewarded for being part of successful change efforts. Top managers can be rewarded with stock options and bonus plans linked to organizational performance. Lower-level members can be rewarded through an employee stock ownership plan and by performance bonuses and pay linked to individual or group performance. Indeed, tangible, performance-related rewards help refreeze an organization in its new state because they help people learn and sustain desired behaviors.

MANAGERIAL IMPLICATIONS

DESIGNING A PLAN FOR CHANGE

1. Develop criteria to evaluate whether change is necessary, and use these criteria systematically throughout the change process to assess progress toward the ideal future state.
2. After analyzing resistances to change, carefully design a plan that both reduces resistance to and facilitates change.
3. Recognize that change is easiest to manage when an organization and its members are used to change, and consider using a total quality management program as a way of keeping the organization attuned to the need for change.

ORGANIZATIONAL DEVELOPMENT

Organizational development (OD)
A series of techniques and methods that managers can use in their action research program to increase the adaptability of their organization.

Organizational development (OD) is a series of techniques and methods that managers can use in their action research program to increase the adaptability of their organization.[55] In the words of organizational theorist Warren Bennis, OD refers to a "complex educational strategy intended to change beliefs, attitudes, values, and structure of organizations so that they can better adapt to new technologies, markets, and challenges and the dizzying rate of change itself."[56] The goal of OD is to improve organizational effectiveness and to help people in organizations reach their potential and realize their goals and objectives. As action research proceeds, managers need to continually unfreeze, change, and refreeze managers' and workers' attitudes and behaviors. Many OD techniques have been developed to help managers do this. We first look at OD techniques to help managers unfreeze an organization and overcome resistances to change. We then look at OD techniques to help managers change and refreeze an organization in its new, desired state.

OD Techniques to Deal with Resistance to Change

Resistance to change occurs at all levels of an organization. It manifests itself as organizational politics and power struggles between individuals and groups, differing perceptions of the need for change, and so on. Tactics that managers can use to reduce resistance to change include education and communication, participation and empowerment, facilitation, bargaining and negotiation, manipulation, and coercion.[57]

Education and Communication
One of the most important impediments to change is uncertainty about what is going to happen. Through education and communication, internal and external agents of change can provide organizational members with information about the change and how it will affect them. Change agents can communicate this information in formal group meetings, by memo, in one-on-one meetings, and, increasingly, through electronic means such as email and videoconferencing. Wal-Mart, for example, has a

state-of-the-art videoconferencing system. Managers at corporate headquarters put on presentations that are beamed to all Wal-Mart stores so that both managers and workers are aware of the changes that will be taking place.

Even when plant closures or massive layoffs are planned, it is still best—from both an ethical and a change standpoint—to inform employees about what will happen to them as downsizing occurs. Many organizations fear that disgruntled employees may try to hurt the organization as it closes or sabotage the closing process. Most often, however, employees are cooperative until the end. As organizations become more and more aware of the benefits offered by incremental change, they are increasing communication with the workforce to gain workers' cooperation and to overcome their resistance to change.

Participation and Empowerment

Inviting workers to participate in the change process is becoming a popular method of reducing resistance to change. Participation complements empowerment, increases workers' involvement in decision making, and gives them greater autonomy to change work procedures to improve organizational performance. In addition, to encourage workers to share their skills and talents, organizations are opening up their books to inform workers about the organization's financial condition. Some organizations use employee stock-ownership plans (ESOPs) to motivate and reward employees and to harness their commitment to change. Wal-Mart, for example, has an ESOP for its ordinary store employees and encourages their continual input into decision making. Participation and empowerment are two key elements of most TQM programs.

When work-group members are empowered, workers often make many of the decisions and have a lot of the responsibility that used to be part of middle managers' jobs. As a result, one major change that has taken place in many organizations is the reduction in the number of middle managers. What do the remaining middle managers do when empowered work groups take on many of their former responsibilities? Essentially they serve as coaches, facilitators, teachers, and sponsors of the empowered groups. They are, in a sense, what some people call the "new nonmanager managers."[58]

One of these new nonmanager managers is 37-year-old Cindy Ransom, a middle manager in charge of a Clorox manufacturing plant in Fairfield, California, that employs around 100 workers. In the attempt to improve plant performance, Ransom decided to empower her subordinates by asking them to reorganize the entire plant. Teams of workers earning hourly wages were suddenly setting up training programs, drafting rules governing absenteeism, and redesigning the plant into five customer-focused business groups. Ransom intentionally did little to interfere with what the workers were doing; her input consisted mainly of answering questions. Middle managers traditionally may have told workers what to do and how and when to do it, but managers of empowered work groups see it as their responsibility to ask the right questions and allow their work groups to decide on the answers.

Two years later, Ransom's plant showed the most improvement in performance in its division. What did Ransom do as workers started taking over many of the responsibilities and tasks she used to perform? She focused on identifying and satisfying the needs of Clorox's customers and suppliers, activities on which she had not spent much time in the past. All in all, empowerment has changed the nature of middle managers' jobs. They have lost some of their old responsibilities, but have gained new ones.

Facilitation

Both managers and workers find change stressful because established task and role relationships alter as it takes place. There are several ways in which organizations can help their members to manage stress: providing them with training to help them learn how to perform new tasks; providing them with time off from work to recuperate from the stressful effects of change; or even giving senior members sabbaticals to allow them to recuperate and plan their future work activities. Companies such as Microsoft and Apple Computer, for example, give their most talented programmers time off from ordinary job assignments to think about ways to create new kinds of products.

Many companies employ psychologists and consultants who specialize in helping employees to handle the stress associated with change. During organizational restructuring, when large layoffs are common, many organizations employ consultants to help laid-off workers deal with the stress and uncertainty of being laid off and having to find new jobs. Some companies pay consultants to help their CEOs manage the responsibilities associated with their own jobs, including the act of laying off workers, which CEOs find particularly stressful, for they understand the impact that layoffs have on employees and their families.

Bargaining and Negotiation

Bargaining and negotiation are important tools that help managers manage conflict. Because change causes conflict, bargaining is an important tool in overcoming resistance to change. By using action research, managers can anticipate the effects of change on interpersonal and intergroup relationships. Managers can use this knowledge to help different people and groups negotiate their future tasks and roles and reach compromises that will lead them to accept change. Negotiation also helps individuals and groups understand how change will affect others so that the organization as a whole can develop a common perspective on why change is taking place and why it is important.

Manipulation

When it is clear that change will help some individuals and groups at the expense of others, senior managers need to intervene in the bargaining process and manipulate the situation to secure the agreement, or at least the acceptance, of various people or groups to the results of the change process. As we discuss in Chapter 14, powerful managers have considerable ability to resist change, and in large organizations infighting among divisions can slow or halt the change process unless it is carefully managed. Politics and political tactics like cooptation and building alliances become important as ways of overcoming the opposition of powerful functions and divisions that feel threatened by the changes taking place.

Coercion

The ultimate way to eliminate resistance to change is to coerce the key players into accepting change and threaten dire consequences if they choose to resist. Workers and managers at all levels can be threatened with reassignment, demotion, or even termination if they resist or threaten the change process. Top managers attempt to use the legitimate power at their disposal to quash resistance to change and to eliminate it. The advantage of coercion can be the speed at which change takes place. The disadvantage is that it can leave people angry and disenchanted and can make the refreezing process difficult.

Managers should not underestimate the level of resistance to change. Organizations work because they reduce uncertainty by means of predictable rules and routines that people can use to accomplish their tasks. Change wipes out the predictability of rules and routines and perhaps spells the end of the status and prestige that accompany some positions. It is not surprising that people resist change and that organizations themselves, as collections of people, are so difficult to change.

OD Techniques to Promote Change

Many OD techniques are designed to make changes and to refreeze them. These techniques can be used at the individual, group, and organization levels. The choice of techniques is determined by the type of change. In general, the more revolutionary a change is, the more likely is an organization to use OD techniques at all three levels. Counseling, sensitivity training, and process consultation are OD techniques directed at changing the attitudes and behavior of individuals. Different techniques are effective at the group and organization levels.

Counseling, Sensitivity Training, and Process Consultation

The personalities of individuals differ and these differences lead individuals to interpret and react to other people and events in a variety of ways. Even though personality cannot be changed significantly in the short run, people can be helped to understand that their own perceptions of a situation are not necessarily the correct or the only possible ones. People can also be helped to understand that they should learn to tolerate differences in perception and to embrace and accept human diversity. Counseling and sensitivity training are techniques that organizations can use to help individuals to understand the nature of their own and other people's personalities and to use that knowledge to improve their interactions with others.[59] The highly motivated, driven boss, for example, must learn that his or her subordinates are not disloyal, lazy, or afflicted with personality problems because they are content to go home at 5 o'clock and want unchallenging job assignments. Instead, they have their own set of work values, and they value their leisure time. Traditionally, one of OD's main efforts has been to improve the quality of the work life of organizational members and increase their well-being and satisfaction with the organization.

Organizational members who are perceived by their superiors or peers as having certain problems in appreciating the viewpoints of others or in dealing with certain types of organizational members are counseled by trained professionals such as psychologists. Through counseling they learn how to more effectively manage their interactions with other people in the organization.

Sensitivity training is an intense type of counseling.[60] Organizational members who are perceived as having problems in dealing with others meet in a group with a trained facilitator to learn more about how they and the other group members view the world. Group members are encouraged to be forthright about how they view themselves and other group members, and through discussion they learn the degree to which others perceive them in similar or different ways. Through examining the source of differences in perception, members of the group may reach a better understanding of the way others perceive them and may learn how to deal more sensitively with others.

Participation in sensitivity training is a very intense experience because a person's innermost thoughts and feelings are brought to light and dissected in public. This process makes many people very uncomfortable, so certain ethical issues may be raised by an organization's decision to send "difficult" members for sensitivity training in the hope that they will learn more about themselves.

Is a manager too directive, too demanding, or too suspicious of subordinates? Does a manager deliberately deprive subordinates of information in order to keep them dependent? **Process consultation** provides answers to such questions. Process consultation bears a resemblance to both counseling and sensitivity training.[61] A trained process consultant, or facilitator, works closely with a manager on the job to help the manager improve his or her interaction with other group members. The outside consultant acts as a sounding board so that the manager can gain a better idea about what is going on in the group setting and can discover the interpersonal dynamics that are determining the quality of work relationships within the group.

Process consultation, sensitivity training, and counseling are just three of the many OD techniques that have been developed to help individuals learn to change their attitudes and behavior so that they can function effectively both as individuals and as organizational members. It is common for many large organizations to provide their higher-level managers with a yearly budget to be spent on individual development efforts such as these, or on more conventional knowledge-gaining events such as executive education programs.

Sensitivity training
An OD technique that consists of intense counseling in which group members, aided by a facilitator, learn how others perceive them and may learn how to deal more sensitively with others.

Process consultation
An OD technique in which a facilitator works closely with a manager on the job to help the manager improve his or her interactions with other group members.

Team Building and Intergroup Training

Team building
An OD technique in which a facilitator first observes the interactions of group members and then helps them become aware of ways to improve their work interactions.

To manage change within a group or between groups, change agents can employ three different kinds of OD techniques. **Team building**, a common method of improving relationships within a group, is similar to process consultation except that all the members of a group participate to try to improve their work interactions.[62] For example, group members discuss with a change agent who is a trained group facilitator the quality of the interpersonal relationships between team members and between the members and their supervisor. The goal of team building is to improve the way group members work together—to improve group processes to achieve process gains and reduce process losses that are occurring because of shirking and free-riding. Team building does *not* focus on what the group is trying to achieve.

Team building is important when reengineering reorganizes the way people from different functions work together. When new groups are formed, team building can help group members quickly establish task and role relationships so that they can work together effectively. Team building facilitates the development of functional group norms and values and helps members develop a common approach to solving problems.

The change agent begins the team-building process by watching group members interact and identifying the way the group currently works. Then the change agent talks with some or all of the group members one on one to get a sense of the problems that the group is experiencing or just to identify where the group process could be improved. In a subsequent team-building session that normally takes place at a location away from the normal work context, the change agent discusses with group members the observations he or she has made and asks for their views on the issues brought to their attention. Ideally, through this discussion team members develop a new appreciation about the forces that have been affecting their behavior. Group members may form small task forces to suggest ways of improving group process or to discuss specific ways of handling the problems that have been arising. The goal is to establish a platform from which group members themselves, with no input from the change agent, can make continuous improvements in the way the group functions.

Intergroup training
An OD technique that uses team building to improve the work interactions of different functions or divisions.

Intergroup training takes team building one step further and uses it to improve the ways different functions or divisions work together. Its goal is to improve organizational performance by focusing on a function's or division's joint activities and output. Given that cross-functional coordination is especially important in reengineering and total quality management, intergroup training is an important OD technique that organizations can exploit to implement change.

Organizational mirroring
An OD technique in which a facilitator helps two interdependent groups explore their perceptions and relations in order to improve their work interactions.

A popular form of intergroup training is called **organizational mirroring**, an OD technique designed to improve the effectiveness of interdependent groups.[63] Suppose that two groups are in conflict or simply need to learn more about each other and one of the groups calls in a consultant to improve intergroup cooperation. The consultant begins by interviewing members of both groups to understand how each group views the other and to uncover possible problems the groups are having with each other. The groups are then brought together in a training session, and the consultant tells them that the goal of the session is to explore perceptions and relations in order to improve work relationships. Then, with the consultant leading the discussion, one group describes its perceptions of what is happening and its problems with the other group, while the other group sits and listens. Then the consultant reverses the situation—hence, the term *organizational mirroring*—and the group that was listening takes its turn discussing its perceptions of what is happening and its problems, while the other group listens.

As a result of that initial discussion, each group appreciates the other's perspective. The next step is for members of both groups to form task forces to discuss ways of dealing with the issues or problems that have surfaced. The goal is to develop action plans that can be used to guide future intergroup relations and provide a basis for follow-up. The change agent guiding this training session needs to be skilled in intergroup relations because both groups are discussing sensitive issues. If the process is not managed well, intergroup relations can be further weakened by this OD technique.

Total Organizational Interventions

Organizational confrontation meeting

An OD technique that brings together all of the managers of an organization meet to confront the issue of whether the organization is effectively meeting its goals.

A variety of OD techniques can be used at the organization level to promote organization-wide change. One is the **organizational confrontation meeting**.[64] At this meeting, all of the managers of an organization meet to confront the issue of whether the organization is effectively meeting its goals. At the first stage of the process, again with facilitation by a change agent, top management invites free and open discussion of the organization's situation. Then the consultant divides the managers into groups of seven or eight, ensuring that the groups are as heterogeneous as possible and that no bosses and subordinates are members of the same group (so as to encourage free and frank discussion). The small groups report their findings to the total group, and the sorts of problems confronting the organization are categorized. Top management uses this statement of the issues to set organizational priorities and plan group action. Task forces are formed from the small groups to take responsibility for working on the problems identified, and each group reports back to top management on progress that has been made. The result of this process is likely to be changes in the organization's structure and operating procedures. Restructuring, reengineering, and total quality management often originate in organization-wide OD interventions that reveal the kinds of problems that an organization needs to solve.

SUMMARY

Organizational change is an ongoing process that has important implications for organizational effectiveness. An organization and its members must be constantly on the alert for changes from within the organization and from the outside environment, and they must learn how to adjust to change quickly and effectively. Often, the revolutionary types of change that result from restructuring and reengineering are necessary only because an organization and its managers ignored or were unaware of changes in the environment and did not make incremental changes as needed. The more an organization changes, the easier and more effective the change process becomes. Developing and managing a plan for change are vital to an organization's success. Chapter 10 has made the following major points:

1. Organizational change is the movement of an organization away from its current state and toward some future state to increase its effectiveness. Forces for organizational change include competitive forces; economic, political, and global forces; demographic and social forces; and ethical forces. Organizations are often reluctant to change because resistance to change at the organization, group, and individual levels has given rise to organizational inertia.

2. Sources of organization-level resistance to change include power and conflict, differences in functional orientation, mechanistic structure, and organizational culture. Sources of group-level resistance to change include group norms, group cohesiveness, and groupthink and escalation of commitment. Sources of individual-level resistance to change include uncertainty and insecurity, selective perception and retention, and habit.

3. According to Lewin's force-field theory of change, organizations are balanced between forces pushing for change and forces resistant to change. To get an organization to change, managers must find a way to increase the forces for change, reduce resistance to change, or do both simultaneously.

4. Types of change fall into two broad categories: evolutionary and revolutionary. The main instruments of evolutionary change are sociotechnical systems theory, total quality management, and the development of flexible workers and work teams. The main instruments of revolutionary change are reengineering, restructuring, and innovation.

5. Action research is a strategy that managers can use to plan the change process. The main steps in action research are (a) diagnosis and analysis of the organization, (b) determining the desired future state, (c) implementing action, (d) evaluating the action, and (e) institutionalizing action research.

6. Organizational development (OD) is a series of techniques and methods to increase the adaptability of organizations. OD techniques can be used to overcome resistance to change and to help the organization to change itself.

7. OD techniques for dealing with resistance to change include education and communication,

participation and empowerment, facilitation, bargaining and negotiation, manipulation, and coercion.

8. OD techniques for promoting change include, at the individual level, counseling, sensitivity training, and process consultation; at the group level, team building and intergroup training; and at the organizational level, organizational confrontation meetings.

DISCUSSION QUESTIONS

1. How do evolutionary change and revolutionary change differ?
2. What is a business process, and why is reengineering a popular instrument of change today?
3. Why is restructuring sometimes necessary for reengineering to take place?

4. What are the main steps in action research?
5. What is organizational development, and what is its goal?

ORGANIZATIONAL THEORY IN ACTION

Practicing Organizational Theory: Managing Change

Break up into groups of three to five people and discuss the following scenario:

You are a group of top managers of one of the Big Three carmakers. Your company has been experiencing increased competition from other carmakers whose innovations in car design and manufacturing methods have allowed them to produce cars that are higher in quality and lower in cost than yours. You have been charged with preparing a plan to change the company's structure to allow you to compete more effectively, and you have decided on two main changes. First, you plan to reengineer the company and move from a multidivisional structure (in which each division produces its own range of cars) to one in which cross-functional product teams become responsible for developing new car models that will be sold by all the divisions. Second, you have decided to implement a total quality management program to raise quality and decentralize decision-making authority to the teams and make them responsible for achieving higher quality and lower costs. Thus, the changes will disrupt role relationships at both the divisional and functional levels.

1. Discuss the nature of the obstacles at the divisional, functional, and individual levels that you will encounter in implementing this new structure. Which do you think will be the most important obstacles to overcome?
2. Discuss some ways you can overcome obstacles to change to help your organization move to its desired future state.

Making the Connection #10

Find an example of a company that has recently gone through a major change. What type of change was it? Why did the organization make the change, and what does it hope to achieve from it?

The Ethical Dimension #10

Imagine that you are managers responsible for reengineering an organization into cross-functional teams, which will result in the layoff of over 30% of the employees.

1. Discuss the resistance to change at the organization and individual levels that you will likely encounter.
2. How will you manage the change process to behave ethically to those employees who will be terminated, and to those who will be reassigned to new jobs and face a new organizational culture?

Analyzing the Organization: Design Module #10

This module focuses on the extent to which your organization has been involved in major change efforts recently and on its approach to promoting innovation.

Assignment

1. Does *revolutionary* or *evolutionary* best describe the changes that have been taking place in your organization?
2. In what types of change (such as restructuring) has your organization been most involved? How successful have these change efforts been?
3. With the information that you have at your disposal, discuss (a) the forces for change, (b) obstacles to change, and (c) the strategy for change your organization has adopted.

CASE FOR ANALYSIS

Sears Changes Again and Again

Sears, the well-known department store chain, has experienced huge problems in the 1990s that have caused it to transform itself. In the early 1990s, Sears was losing billions of dollars because sales at its stores were falling and because its acquisitions of financial services businesses such as Allstate Insurance and Dean Witter brokerage had not proved to be profitable. The company was searching desperately for a new strategy to allow it to compete successfully, and for the first time in its history the Sears board of directors selected an outsider, Albert Martinez, a senior executive at upscale Saks Fifth Avenue, to become its new CEO.

Martinez moved quickly to change strategy and structure at Sears and to improve the company's performance. First, he decided to sell all Sears financial services businesses in order to focus the company on its core department store business, and he closed the famous Sears catalogue, which had been losing money for years. Then, he crafted a new look for Sears stores. Martinez decided that Sears should be a moderately price department store chain with a focus on the target customer of the "middle-American mom," and he flooded the stores with women's apparel under the advertising theme "The Softer Side of Sears." At the same time, he restructured operations, cutting 50,000 employees, flattening the company's huge bureaucracy, and even selling its landmark building in Chicago, the 110-story Sears Tower. Martinez's new strategy seemed to work wonders for Sears's bottom line. Within three years, losses of billions a year were changed into profits of hundreds of millions as Sears reinvented itself and female customers returned.[65] However, nothing remains constant in the world of retailing, and this situation didn't last long.

Sears's "softer-side" marketing campaign did not work for long; soon, analysts were describing Sears's adult clothing as a series of "fashion misses"; styles didn't catch on and customers didn't return. Stores like Target and Wal-Mart stole

its customers. Throughout the 1990s, sales grew only at 4%, and in 2000, Martinez stepped down as CEO. Alan Lacy, Sears's chief financial officer became CEO.[66]

As CFO, Lacy had championed Sears's "hard side"—appliances, car batteries, and power tools, even though Martinez had championed clothing—and he had made appliances the most profitable part of Sears's business. As CEO, Lacy decided that clothing was a liability for the company and that only Sears's hard side offered the possibility for a turnaround.[67] He decided that perhaps Sears should be a store that sold only hard-good retail products or, at least, this should be its main emphasis. He also decided that Sears's new store chain, The Great Indoors, should be expanded. The Great Indoors sells every kind and range of appliances and kitchens from the least expensive Frigidaires to the most expensive Kitchen Aid and Viking products. Although there is growing competition from Wal-Mart and The Home Depot, which also began selling appliances in 2000, Sears has one very important advantage: With 12,000 technicians, it has one of the largest repair service fleets in the United States.

In addition to its Great Indoors concept, Lacy also decided that Sears should focus and develop an online business to sell its hard products such as appliances and Craftsman Tools.[68] In 2002, Sears announced that it was buying Land's End, the huge online and catalogue clothes retailer, to expand its online presence.

Finally, a major change happened to Sears in 2005 when a merger between K-mart and Sears was announced. Top managers decided that the only way to complete against Wal-Mart and Target was to combine and streamline their operations to reduce costs. Thus, Sears is once again reinventing itself to become a store than can survive and prosper in the twenty-first century.

DISCUSSION QUESTIONS

1. What were the major changes that Sears made over time?
2. Search for recent articles on Sears that describe the impact of these changes. How effective have its recent change efforts been?

REFERENCES

1. M. Beer, *Organizational Change and Development* (Santa Monica, CA: Goodyear, 1980); J. I. Porras and R. C. Silvers, "Organization Development and Transformation," *Annual Review of Psychology*, 42 (1991), 51–78.
2. C. Argyris, R. Putman, and D. M. Smith, *Action Science* (San Francisco: Jossey-Bass, 1985).
3. R. M. Kanter, *The Change Masters: Innovation for Productivity in the American Corporation* (New York: Simon and Schuster, 1984).
4. C.W.L. Hill and G. R. Jones, *Strategic Management: An Integrated Approach*, 3e (Boston: Houghton Mifflin, 1995).
5. Ibid.
6. G. R. Jones, *Organizational Theory: Text and Cases* (Reading, MA: Addison-Wesley, 1995).
7. C.W.L. Hill, *International Business* (Chicago, IL: Irwin, 1994).
8. C. A. Bartlett and S. Ghoshal, *Managing Across Borders* (Boston: Harvard Business School Press, 1989).
9. C. K. Prahalad and Y. L. Doz, *The Multinational Mission: Balancing Local Demands and Global Vision* (New York: Free Press, 1987).
10. D. Jamieson and J. O'Mara, *Managing Workforce 2000: Gaining a Diversity Advantage* (San Francisco: Jossey-Bass, 1991).
11. S. E. Jackson and Associates, *Diversity in the Workplace: Human Resource Initiatives* (New York: Guilford Press, 1992).
12. W. H. Shaw and V. Barry, *Moral Issues in Business*, 6e (Belmont, CA: Wadsworth, 1995).
13. T. Donaldson, *Corporations and Morality* (Upper Saddle River, NJ, Prentice Hall, 1982).
14. "Nike Battles Backlash from Overseas Sweatshops," *Marketing News*, November 9, 1998, p. 14.
15. J. Laabs, "Mike Gives Indonesian Workers a Raise," *Workforce*, December 1998, pp.15–16.
16. W. Echikson, "It's Europe's Turn to Sweat About Sweatshops," *Business Week*, July 19, 1999, p. 96.
17. www.addidas.com, 2006.
18. www.thegap.com, 2006.
19. M. Hannan and J. Freeman, "Structural Inertia and Organizational Change," *American Sociological Review*, 49 (1989), 149–164.
20. L. E. Greiner, "Evolution and Revolution as Organizations Grow," *Harvard Business Review* (July–August 1972), 37–46.
21. R. M. Kanter, *When Giants Learn to Dance: Mastering the Challenges of Strategy* (New York: Simon and Schuster, 1989).
22. J. P. Kotter and L. A. Schlesinger, "Choosing Strategies for Change," *Harvard Business Review* (March–April 1979), 106–114.
23. T. Burns and G. M. Stalker, *The Management of Innovation* (London: Tavistock, 1961).
24. P. R. Lawrence and J. W. Lorsch, *Organization and Environment* (Boston: Harvard Business School Press, 1972).
25. R. Likert, *The Human Organization* (New York: McGraw-Hill, 1967).
26. C. Argyris, *Personality and Organization* (New York: Harper and Row, 1957).
27. This section draws heavily on K. Lewin, *Field-Theory in Social Science* (New York: Harper and Row, 1951).
28. D. Miller, "Evolution and Revolution: A Quantum View of Structural Change in Organizations," *Journal of Management Studies*, 19 (1982), 11–151; D. Miller, "Momentum and Revolution in Organizational Adaptation," *Academy of Management Journal*, 2 (1980), 591–614.
29. C. E. Lindblom, "The Science of Muddling Through," *Public Administration Review*, 19 (1959), 79–88; P. C. Nystrom and W. H. Starbuck, "To Avoid Organizational Crises, Unlearn," *Organizational Dynamics*, 12 (1984), 53–65.
30. E. L. Trist, G. Higgins, H. Murray, and A. G. Pollock, *Organizational Choice* (London: Tavistock, 1965); J. C. Taylor, "The Human Side of Work: The Socio-Technical Approach to Work Design," *Personnel Review*, 4 (1975), 17–22.
31. E. L. Trist and K. W. Bamforth, "Some Social and Psychological Consequences of the Long Wall Method of Coal Mining," *Human Relations*, 4 (1951), 3–38; F. E. Emery and E. L. Trist, "Socio-Technical Systems" (London: Proceedings of the 6th Annual International Meeting of the Institute of Management Sciences, 1965), pp. 92–93.
32. E. L. Trist, G. Higgins, H. Murray, and A. G. Pollock, *Organizational Choice* (London: Tavistock, 1965); J. C. Taylor, "The Human Side of Work: The Socio-Technical Approach to Work Design," *Personnel Review*, 4 (1975), 17–22.
33. For a review, see D. R. Denison, "What Is the Difference Between Organizational Culture and Organizational Climate? A Native's Point of View on a Decade of Paradigm Wars," *Academy of Management Review*, 21 (1996), 619–654.
34. W. Edwards Deming, Out of the Crisis (Cambridge, MA: MIT Press, 1989); M. Walton, *The Deming Management Method* (New York: Perigee Books, 1990).
35. J. McHugh and B. Dale, "Quality Circles," in R. Wild, ed., *International Handbook of Production and Operations Research* (London: Cassel, 1989).
36. S. M. Young, "A Framework for the Successful Adoption and Performance of Japanese Manufacturing Techniques in the U.S.," *Academy of Management Review*, 17 (1992), 677–700.
37. Young, "A Framework for the Successful Adoption and Performance of Japanese Manufacturing Practices in the U.S."
38. R. Parthasarthy and S. P. Sethi, "The Impact of Flexible Automation on Business Strategy and Organizational Structure," *Academy of Management Review*, 17 (1992), 86–111
39. "Return of the Stopwatch," *The Economist*, January 23, 1993, p. 69.

40. M. Hammer and J. Champy, *Reengineering the Corporation* (New York: HarperCollins, 1993).

41. M. Hammer, "Reengineering Work: Don't Automate, Obliterate," *Harvard Business Review* (July–August 1990), 104–112.

42. www.hallmark.com, "Facts About Hallmark," 2000.

43. S. J. Freeman and K. S. Cameron, "Organizational Downsizing: A Convergence and Reorientation Framework," *Organizational Science*, 4 (1993), 10–29.

44. P. Brent, "3 Molson Executives Ousted in Decentralization Move," *Financial Post–Toronto*, December 20, 1995, p.3.

45. R. L DeWitt, "The Structural Consequences of Downsizing," *Organizational Science*, 4 (1993), 30–40.

46. "The Salaryman Rides Again," *The Economist*, December 4, 1995, p. 64.

47. Jones, Organizational Theory; R. A. Burgelman and M. A. Maidique, *Strategic Management of Technology and Innovation* (Homewood, IL: Irwin, 1988).

48. Lewin, *Field-Theory in Social Science*, pp. 172–174.

49. This section draws heavily on P. A. Clark, *Action Research and Organizational Change* (New York: Harper and Row, 1972); L. Brown, "Research Action: Organizational Feedback, Understanding and Change," *Journal of Applied Behavioral Research*, 8 (1972), 697–711; N. Margulies and A. P. Raia, eds., *Conceptual Foundations of Organizational Development* (New York: McGraw-Hill, 1978).

50. W. L. French and C. H. Bell, *Organizational Development* (Upper Saddle River, NJ: Prentice Hall, 1990).

51. L. Coch and J.R.P. French, "Overcoming Resistance to Change," *Human Relations*, 1 (1948), 512–532.

52. French and Bell, *Organizational Development*.

53. Ibid.

54. W. L. French, "A Checklist for Organizing and Implementing an OD Effort," in W. L. French, C. H. Bell, and R. A. Zawacki, *Organizational Development and Transformation* (Homewood, IL: Irwin, 1994), pp. 484–495.

55. Kotter, Schlesinger, and Sathe, *Organization*, p. 487.

56. W. G. Bennis, *Organizational Development: Its Nature, Origins, and Perspectives* (Reading, MA: Addison-Wesley, 1969).

57. Kotter and Schlesinger, "Choosing Strategies for Change."

58. B. Dumaine, "The New Non-Manager Managers," *Fortune*, February 22, 1993, pp. 80–84.

59. E. H. Schein, *Organizational Psychology* (Upper Saddle River, NJ: Prentice Hall, 1980).

60. R. T. Golembiewski, "The Laboratory Approach to Organization Change: Schema of a Method," in Margulies and Raia, eds., *Conceptual Foundations of Organizational Development*, pp. 198–212; J. Kelley "Organizational Development Through Structured Sensitivity Training," ibid., pp. 213–228.

61. E. H. Schein, *Process Consultation* (Reading, MA: Addison-Wesley, 1969).

62. M. Sashkin and W. Warner Burke, "Organization Development in the 1980s," *Journal of Management*, 13 (1987), 393–417; D. Eden, "Team Development: Quasi-Experimental Confirmation Among Combat Companies," *Group and Organization Studies*, 5 (1986), 133–146; K. P. DeMeuse and S. J. Liebowitz, "An Empirical Analysis of Team Building Research," *Group and Organization Studies*, 6 (1981), 357–378.

63. French and Bell, *Organizational Development*.

64. R. Beckhard, "The Confrontation Meeting," *Harvard Business Review* (March–April 1967), 159–165.

65. P. Sellers, "Sears: The Turnaround Is Ending, the Revolution Has Begun," *Fortune*, April 28, 1997, pp. 106–118.

66. A. Appelbaum, "The Softer Side of Sears," *Money*, November 2000, pp. 44–46.

67. M. Tatge, "The Harder Side of Sears," *Forbes*, November 11, 2000, pp. 24–26.

68. "Sears Chief Lacy Says 3 Initiatives Are Key to Growth of Retailer," *The Wall Street Journal*, November 9, 2000, p. A10.

Organizational Transformations: Birth, Growth, Decline, and Death

Learning Objectives

Organizations that successfully carve out a niche in their environments so that they can attract resources (such as customers) face a series of problems in their struggle for growth and survival. This chapter examines the organizational change and transformation problems that occur over the life cycle of an organization. Managers who understand the factors that lead to organizational birth and growth, that influence maturity, and that cause decline and death will be able to change their organization's strategy and structure to increase its effectiveness and chances of survival.

After studying this chapter you should be able to:

1. Appreciate the problems involved in surviving the perils of organizational birth and what founders can do to help their new organizations to survive.

2. Describe the typical problems that arise as an organization grows and matures, and how an organization must change if it is to survive and prosper.

3. Discuss why organizational decline occurs, identify the stages of decline, and explain how managers can change their organizations to prevent failure and eventual death or dissolution.

THE ORGANIZATIONAL LIFE CYCLE

Organizational life cycle
A sequence of stages of growth and development through which organizations may pass.

Why do some organizations survive and prosper while others fail and die? Why do some organizations have the ability to manage their strategies, structures, and cultures to gain access to environmental resources while others fail at this task? To answer these questions, researchers have suggested that we need to understand the dynamics that affect organizations as they seek a satisfactory fit with their environment.[1] It has been suggested that organizations experience a predictable sequence of stages of growth and change: the **organizational life cycle**.

Figure 11.1
A Model of the
Organizational Life Cycle

Organizations pass through
these four stages at different
rates, and some do not experience every stage.

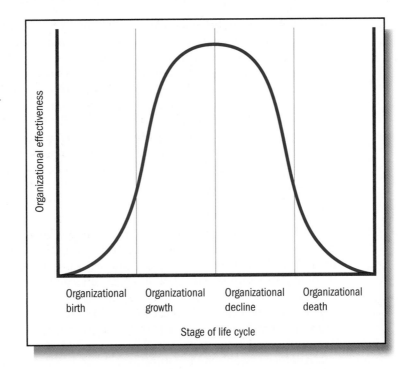

The four principal stages of the organizational life cycle are birth, growth, decline, and death (see Figure 11.1).[2] Organizations pass through these stages at different rates, and some do not experience every stage. Moreover, some companies go directly from birth to death without enjoying any growth if they do not attract customers or resources. Some organizations spend a long time in the growth stage, and many researchers have identified various substages of growth through which an organization must navigate. There are also substages of decline. Some organizations in decline take corrective action, change quickly, and turn themselves around.

The way an organization can change in response to the problems it confronts determines whether and when it will go on to the next stage in the life cycle and survive and prosper or fail and die. This chapter examines each stage in detail.

ORGANIZATIONAL BIRTH

Entrepreneurs
People who recognize and take
advantage of opportunities to
use their skills and competences
to create value.

Organizational birth
The founding of an organization-
a dangerous life cycle stage
associated with the greatest
chance of failure.

Liability of newness
The dangers associated with
being the first in a new
environment.

Organizations are born when individuals, called **entrepreneurs**, recognize and take advantage of opportunities to use their skills and competences to create value.[3] Michael Dell found a new way to market low-priced computers to customers: mail order. Debbi Fields developed a tasty, moist chocolate-chip cookie. Liz Claiborne exploited a niche in the women's clothing market—business attire for women. Dell, Fields, and Claiborne saw an opportunity to create value (for computer users, cookie lovers, and businesswomen), and each of them seized the opportunity by founding an organization to produce goods or services.[4] Dell Computer follows a low-cost business-level strategy: Dell's computers are less expensive than competitors' computers. Mrs. Fields Cookies follows a differentiation business-level strategy: The company produces a cookie for which customers are willing to pay a premium price.

Organizational birth, the founding of an organization, is a dangerous stage of the life cycle and is associated with the greatest chance of failure. The failure rate is high because new organizations experience the **liability of newness**—the dangers associated with being the first in a new environment.[5] This liability is great for several reasons.

Entrepreneurship is an inherently risky process. Because entrepreneurs undertake *new* ventures, there is no way to predict or guarantee success.[6] Entrepreneurs bear this uncertainty because they stand to earn potentially huge returns if their businesses take off. Much of the time, however, entrepreneurs make mistakes in judgment or planning, and the result is organizational death.[7]

A new organization is fragile because it lacks a formal structure to give its value-creation processes and actions stability and certainty. At first everything is done by trial and error. An organizational structure emerges gradually, as decisions about procedures and technology are made. Eventually, for example, it may become clear that one manager should manage money coming in from customers (accounts receivable), another should manage money being paid out to suppliers (accounts payable), and another should obtain new accounts. But at first, in a new organization, the structure is in the mind of the founder; it is not formalized in a chart or a set of rules. The structure is flexible and responsive, allowing the organization to adapt and perfect its routines to meet the needs of its environment.

A flexible structure can be an advantage when it allows the organization to change and take advantage of new opportunities, but it can also be a disadvantage. A formal structure provides stability and certainty by serving as the organization's memory. Structure specifies an organization's activities and the procedures for getting them done. If such procedures are not written down, a new organization can literally forget the skills and procedures that made it successful. A formal structure provides an organization with a firm foundation from which to improve on existing procedures and develop new ones.[8]

Another reason why organizational birth is a dangerous stage is that conditions in the environment may be hostile to a new organization. Resources, for example, may be scarce or difficult to obtain because many established organizations are competing for them.

Developing a Plan for a New Business

One way in which entrepreneurs can address all these issues is through the crafting of a business plan, which outlines how they plan to compete in the environment. The steps in the development of a business plan are listed in Table 11.1.

Planning for a new business begins when an entrepreneur notices an opportunity to develop a new or improved good or service for the whole market or for a specific market niche. For example, an entrepreneur might notice an opportunity in the fast-food market to provide customers with healthful fast food such as rotisserie

Table 11.1
Developing a Business Plan

1. Notice a product opportunity, and develop a basic business idea
Goods/services
Customers/markets
2. Conduct a strategic (SWOT) analysis
Identify opportunities
Identify threats
Identify strengths
Identify weaknesses
3. Decide whether the business opportunity is feasible
4. Prepare a detailed business plan
Statement of mission, goals, and financial objectives
Statement of strategic objectives
List of necessary resources
Organizational timeline of events

chicken served with fresh vegetables. This is what the founders of the Boston Market restaurant chain did.

The next step is to test the feasibility of the new product idea. The entrepreneur conducts as thorough a strategic planning exercise as possible, using SWOT analysis, the analysis of organizational strengths and weaknesses and environmental opportunities and threats. Potential threats might be that KFC will decide to imitate the idea and offer its customers rotisserie chicken (KFC actually did this after Boston Market identified the new market niche). The entrepreneur should conduct a thorough analysis of the external environment (see Chapter 3) to test the potential of a new product idea and must be willing to abandon an idea if it seems likely that the threats and risks may overwhelm the opportunities and returns. Entrepreneurship is always a very risky process, and many entrepreneurs become so committed to their new ideas that they ignore or discount the potential threats and forge ahead—only to lose their shirts.

If the environmental analysis suggests that the product idea is feasible, the next step is to examine the strengths and weaknesses of the idea. At this stage the main strength is the resources possessed by the entrepreneur. Does the entrepreneur have access to an adequate source of funds? Does the entrepreneur have any experience in the fast-food industry, such as managing a restaurant? To identify weaknesses, the entrepreneur needs to assess how many and what kind of resources will be necessary to establish a viable new venture—such as a chain of chicken restaurants. Analysis might reveal that the new product idea will not generate an adequate return on investment. Or it might reveal that the entrepreneur needs to find partners to help provide the resources needed to open a chain on a sufficient scale to generate a high enough return on investment.

After conducting a thorough SWOT analysis, if the entrepreneur decides that the new product idea is feasible, the hard work begins: developing the actual business plan that will be used to attract investors or funds from banks. Included in the business plan should be the same basic elements as in the product development plan: (1) a statement of the organization's mission, goals, and financial objectives; (2) a statement of the organization's strategic objectives, including an analysis of the product's market potential, based on the SWOT analysis that has already been conducted; (3) a list of all the functional and organizational resources that will be required to implement the new product idea successfully, including a list of technological, financial, and human resource requirements; and (4) a timeline that contains specific milestones for the entrepreneur and others to use to measure the progress of the venture, such as target dates for the final design and the opening of the first restaurant.

Many entrepreneurs do not have the luxury of having a team of cross-functional managers to help develop a detailed business plan. This obviously is true for solo ventures. One reason why franchising has become so popular in the United States is that an entrepreneur can purchase and draw on the business plan and experience of an already existing company, thereby reducing the risks associated with opening a new business.

In sum, entrepreneurs have a number of significant challenges to confront and conquer if they are to be successful. It is not uncommon for an entrepreneur to fail repeatedly before he or she finds a venture that proves successful. It also is not uncommon for an entrepreneur who establishes a successful new company to sell it in order to move on to new ventures that promise new risks and returns. An example of just such an entrepreneur is Wayne Huizenga, who bought many small waste disposal companies to create the giant WMX waste disposal company, which he eventually sold. A few years later Huizenga took control of Blockbuster Video and, by opening and buying other video store chains, turned Blockbuster Video into the biggest video chain in the United States, only to sell it in 1994. A historical example of an entrepreneur who transformed the steel industry is profiled in the following organizational insight.

Andrew Carnegie, born in Scotland in 1835, was the son of a master handloom weaver who, at that time, employed four apprentices to weave fine linen tablecloths.[9] His family was well-to-do, yet 10 years later they were living in poverty. Why? Advances in weaving technology had led to the invention of steam-powered weaving looms that could produce large quantities of cotton cloth at a much lower price than was possible through handloom weaving. Handloom weavers could not compete at these low prices, and Carnegie's father was put out of business. In 1848 his family, like hundreds of thousands of other families in Europe at this time, decided to emigrate to the United States to find work and survive.

The Carnegies settled near Pittsburgh, where they had relatives; the father continued to weave tablecloths and sell them door-to-door, making around $6 dollars a week. His mother, who had come from a family of cobblers, took in shoes for repair and made around $4 a week. After finding work as a "bobbin boy" (a worker who replaced spools of thread on power looms in a textile factory), Carnegie took home $1.20 for a 60-hour week.

Once his employer discovered that he could read and write, a rare skill at this time, Carnegie became a bookkeeper for the factory. In his spare time he became a telegraph messenger and learned telegraphy. He began to deliver telegrams to Tom Scott, a top manager at the Pennsylvania Railroad, who came to appreciate Carnegie's drive and talents. Scott made him his personal telegrapher for the astonishing sum of $35 a week. Carnegie was now 17 years old; only seven years later, when he was 24, he was promoted to Scott's job as superintendent of the Western Division of the railroad. At 30, he was offered the top job of superintendent of the whole railroad! Carnegie had other ambitions, however. During his time at the railroad, he had invested cleverly in railroad stock and was now a wealthy man with an income of $48,000 a year, of which only $2,800 came from his railroad salary.

While a manager at the railroad, Carnegie had made his name by continually finding ways to use resources more productively to reduce costs and increase profitability. His company's stock price had shot up—which explains why he was offered the railroad's top job. Carnegie saw an opportunity to apply his cost-cutting skills in the backward steel industry. Carnegie had noticed U.S. railroads' growing demand for steel as they built new U.S. railways rapidly in the 1860s. At that time, steel was made using small-batch production, an expensive labor-intensive process we discussed in Chapter 9, and the steel produced cost $135 a ton.[10]

In searching for ways to reduce steel-making costs, Carnegie was struck by the fact that many different companies performed each of the different operations necessary to convert iron ore into finished steel products. One company smelted iron ore into "pig iron"; another company then transported the pig iron to other companies that rolled the pig iron into bars or slabs. Many other companies then bought these bars and slabs and made them into finished products such as steel rails, nails, wire, and so on. Intermediaries who bought the products of one company and then sold them to another connected the activities of these different companies. The many exchanges or "hand-offs" involved in converting iron ore into finished products greatly increased operating costs. At each stage of the production process, steel had to be shipped to the next company and reheated to make it soft enough to work on. Moreover, these intermediaries were earning large profits for providing this service, something that also raised the cost of the finished products.

The second thing that Carnegie noticed was that the steel produced by British steel mills was of a higher quality that that made in U.S. mills. The British had made major advances in steel-making technology, and U.S. railroads preferred to buy their steel rails. Carnegie made frequent trips to Britain to sell U.S. railroad stock. On one trip he saw a demonstration of Sir Henry Bessemer's new "hot blasting" method for making steel. Bessemer's famous process made it possible to produce great quantities of higher-quality steel continuously, as a process, not in small batches. Carnegie instantly realized the enormous cost-saving potential of the new technology. He rushed to become the first steel maker in the U.S. to adopt it.[11]

Carnegie sold all his stocks and invested his capital to create the Carnegie Steel Company, which was the first low-cost Bessemer steel-making plant in the United States. Determined to retain the profit intermediaries were making in his business, he also decided his company would perform all the steel-making operations necessary to convert iron ore into finished products. For example, he constructed rolling mills to make steel rails next to his blast furnace so that iron ore could be converted into finished steel products in one continuous process.

Carnegie's innovations led to a dramatic fall in steel-making costs and revolutionized the U.S. steel industry. His new production methods reduced the price of U.S. steel from $135 a ton to $12, but his company was enormously profitable with a profit margin that was close to 50%. Most of his competitors could not compete with his low prices and were driven out of business. He ploughed all his profits back into building his steel business and constructed many new low-cost steel plants. By 1900, his company had become the leading U.S. steel maker, and he was one of the richest men in the world.

A POPULATION ECOLOGY MODEL OF ORGANIZATIONAL BIRTH

Population ecology theory
A theory that seeks to explain the factors that affect the rate at which new organizations are born (and die) in a population of existing organizations.

Population of organizations
The organizations that are competing for the same set of resources in the environment.

Environmental niches
Particular sets of resources.

Population density
The number of organizations that can compete for the same resources in a particular environment.

The way in which Carnegie transformed the U.S. steel industry is a story about how and why the number and nature of companies in an industry change over time. **Population ecology theory** seeks to explain the factors that affect the rate at which new organizations are born (and die) in a population of existing organizations.[12] A **population of organizations** comprises the organizations that are competing for the same set of resources in the environment. All the fast-food restaurants in College Station, Texas, constitute a population of restaurants that compete to obtain environmental resources in the form of dollars that students are willing to spend on food. IBM, Compaq, Dell, AST, Gateway, and the other personal computer companies constitute a population of organizations that are seeking to attract environmental resources in the form of dollars that consumers are willing to spend on personal computing. Different organizations within a population may choose to focus on different **environmental niches**, or particular sets of resources or skills. Dell Computer chose to focus on the mail-order niche of the personal computer environment; IBM and HP originally focused on the business niche; and Apple focused on the publishing and higher education niche.

Number of Births

According to population ecology theory, the availability of resources determines the number of organizations in a population. The amount of resources in an environment limits **population density**—the number of organizations that can compete for the same resources in a particular environment.[13] Population ecology theorists assume that growth in the number of organizational births in a new environment is rapid at first as new organizations are founded to take advantage of new environmental resources, such as dollars that people are willing to spend on personal computing (see Figure 11.2).[14]

Two factors account for the rapid birth rate. The first is that as new organizations are founded, there is an increase in the knowledge and skills available to generate similar new organizations. Many new organizations are founded by entrepreneurs who leave existing companies to set up their own companies. Many new computer companies were founded by people who left pioneering organizations such as Xerox, HP, and IBM.

Figure 11.2
Organizational Birth Rates over Time

According to population ecology theory, the rate of birth in a new environment increases rapidly at first and then tapers off as resources become less plentiful and competition increases.

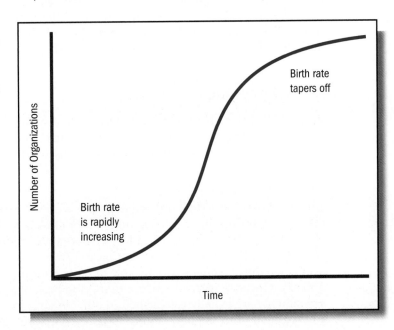

The second factor accounting for the rapid birth rate in a new environment is that when a new kind of organization is founded and survives, it provides a role model. The success of a new organization makes it relatively easy for entrepreneurs to found similar new organizations, because success confers legitimacy, which will attract stakeholders. Fast-food restaurants, for example, were a relatively untested kind of organization until McDonald's proved their ability to attract resources in the form of customers. Entrepreneurs watched McDonald's create and succeed in the U.S. fast-food market and then imitated McDonald's by founding similar companies, such as Burger King and Wendy's. McDonald's became a U.S. institution, gave the population of fast-food organizations legitimacy, and allowed them to attract stakeholders such as customers, employees, and investors. Now fast food is taken for granted in many countries around the world.

Once an environment is populated with a number of successful organizations, the organizational birth rate tapers off (see the S-shaped curve in Figure 11.2).[15] Two factors work to decrease the rate at which organizations are founded. First, births taper off as the availability of resources in the environment for late entrants diminishes.[16] Companies that start first, like McDonald's or Microsoft, have a competitive edge over later entrants because of first-mover advantages. **First-mover advantages** are the benefits an organization derives from being an early entrant into a new environment. They include customer support, a recognized brand name, and the best locations for new businesses like restaurants. Latecomers enter an environment that is partially depleted of the resources that they need to grow. Investors, for example, are reluctant to lend money to new firms because their chances of survival in an established competitive environment are poor unless they can somehow discover and keep control of a new niche, as Dell Computer did. Similarly, the best managers and workers prefer to work in organizations that have established reputations and offer secure employment opportunities.

The second factor that decreases the birth rate is the difficulty of competing with existing organizations for resources.[17] Potential entrepreneurs are discouraged from entering an industry or market because they understand that the larger the number of companies already competing for resources, the more difficult and expensive the resources will be to obtain. To obtain new customers, new companies may need to overspend on advertising or innovation, or they may need to reduce their prices too much. Moreover, existing companies may band together and make it very hard for new companies to enter the market. They may engage in collusion, agreeing (illegally) to set their prices at artificially low levels to drive new rivals out of an industry, or they may erect barriers to entry by investing heavily in advertising so that it is very expensive for new companies to enter the market. Thus, the owners of the Boston Market chain might believe there are already too many fast-food restaurants in College Station to make entry into that market profitable.

Survival Strategies

Population ecologists have identified two sets of strategies that organizations can use to gain access to resources and enhance their chances of survival in the environment: (1) r-strategy versus K-strategy and (2) specialist strategy versus generalist strategy.

r-Strategy Versus K-Strategy

Organizations that follow an **r-strategy** are founded early in a new environment—they are early entrants. Organizations that follow a **K-strategy** are founded late—they are late entrants.[18] The advantage of an r-strategy is that an organization obtains first-mover advantages and has first pick of the resources in the environment. As a result, the organization is usually able to grow rapidly and develop skills and procedures that increase its chance of surviving and prospering. Organizations that follow a K-strategy are usually established in other environments and wait to enter a new environment until the uncertainty in that environment is reduced and the correct

First-mover advantages
The benefits an organization derives from being an early entrant into a new environment.

r-strategy
A strategy of entering a new environment early.

K-strategy
A strategy of entering an environment late, after other organizations have tested the water.

way to compete is apparent. These organizations then take the skills they have established in other environments and use them to develop effective procedures that allow them to compete with and often dominate organizations following the r-strategy.

The difference between r-strategy and K-strategy is evident in the situation that emerged in the personal computer industry. In 1977, Apple Computer founded the personal computer market by developing the Apple I. Other small companies quickly followed Apple's lead. Each of them pursued an r-strategy and developed its own personal computer. Many of these companies were successful in attracting resources, and the population of personal computer companies grew quickly. IBM, the dominant player in the mainframe computer market, realized the potential in the personal computer market. It adopted a K-strategy and moved to develop its own personal computer (based on Microsoft's MS-DOS operating system), which it introduced in 1981. The ability to put its massive resources to work in the new environment and to exploit its brand name gave IBM a competitive advantage. As the MS-DOS operating system became the industry standard, IBM drove many of the smaller r-strategists out of the market. IBM even threatened Apple Computer for awhile, but Apple was able to hang onto its loyal customers and weather the storm of competition.

K-strategists can often outperform r-strategists when they are competing for the same environmental niche. Apple Computer, for example, focused its activities very heavily on the school and university markets for computers. IBM competed heavily in the business market. Thus, IBM primarily hurt competitors that were trying to occupy the business niche.

Specialist Strategy Versus Generalist Strategy

Specialists
Organizations that concentrate their skills to pursue a narrow range of resources in a single niche.

Generalist
Organizations that spread their skills thinly to compete for a broad range of resources in many niches.

The difference between a specialist and a generalist strategy is defined by the breadth of the environmental niche—the set of resources—for which an organization competes. Specialist organizations (or **specialists**) concentrate their skills to pursue a narrow range of resources in a single niche. Generalist organizations (or **generalists**) spread their skills thinly to compete for a broad range of resources in many niches.[19] By focusing their activities in one niche, specialists develop core competences that allow them to outperform generalists in that niche. Specialists are likely to offer customers much better service than the service offered by generalists, or they may be able to develop superior products because they invest all their resources in a narrow range of products. Intel, for example, invests all its resources in producing state-of-the-art microprocessors and does not bother with other kinds of electronic or computer components.

Generalists can often outcompete specialists when there is considerable uncertainty in the environment and when resources are changing so that niches emerge and disappear continually. Generalists can survive in an uncertain environment because they have spread their resources thinly. If one niche disappears, they still have others in which to operate. If a specialist's niche disappears, however, there is a much higher chance of organizational failure and death.

Specialists and generalists often coexist in many environments. The reason for their coexistence is that successful generalists create the conditions that allow specialists to operate successfully.[20] Large department stores, for example, create a demand for different kinds of fashionable clothes. To meet that demand, boutiques set up and specialize in one kind of clothing, such as evening wear or sportswear. This is the opportunity for the entrepreneur.

The Process of Natural Selection

The two sets of strategies—specialist versus generalist and r versus K—give rise to four strategies that organizations can pursue: r-specialist, r-generalist, K-specialist, and K-generalist (see Figure 11.3).[21]

Figure 11.3
Strategies for Competing
in the Resource
Environment

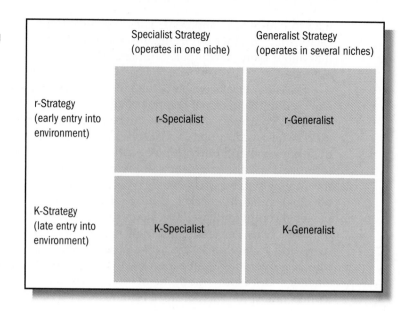

	Specialist Strategy (operates in one niche)	Generalist Strategy (operates in several niches)
r-Strategy (early entry into environment)	r-Specialist	r-Generalist
K-Strategy (late entry into environment)	K-Specialist	K-Generalist

Early in an environment, as a niche develops and new resources become available, new organizations are likely to be r-specialists—organizations that move quickly to focus on serving the needs of particular customer groups. Many new organizations grow and prosper, as did Apple Computer. As they grow, they often become generalists and compete in new niches. While this is happening, however, K-generalists (usually the divisions or subsidiaries of large companies like IBM or General Electric) move into the market and threaten the weakest r-specialist organizations. Eventually, the strongest r-specialists, r-generalists, and K-generalists dominate the environment by serving multiple market segments and by pursuing a low-cost or differentiation strategy. Large companies, having chosen the K-generalist strategy, often create niches for new firms to enter the market, so K-specialists are founded to exploit the new market segments. In this way, generalists and specialists can coexist in an environment because they are competing for different sets of resources.

The early beginnings of the car industry provide a good example of this organizational birth process. The first car companies (such as Packard and Dusenberg) were small crafts operations that produced high-priced cars for small market segments. These companies were the original r-specialists. Then Henry Ford realized the potential for establishing a mass market via mass production, and he decided to pursue a K-generalist strategy by producing a low-priced, standardized car for the mass market. Similarly, at GM, Alfred Sloan was rapidly pursuing a K-generalist strategy based on differentiation. He positioned GM's different car divisions to serve the whole range of market segments, from low-price Chevrolets to high-price Cadillacs. The low price and variety of car models available eventually drove many of the small r-specialists out of business. GM and Ford, together with Chrysler, proceeded to dominate the environment. Many new small companies pursuing K-specialist strategies then emerged to serve specialist segments that these companies had left open. Luxury-car manufacturers like Cord and Packard produced high-priced vehicles and prospered for awhile, and foreign car manufacturers such as Rolls Royce, Mercedes, and Bugatti were popular. In the 1970s, Japanese companies like Toyota and Honda entered the U.S. market with a K-specialist strategy, producing cars much smaller than the vehicles that the Big Three were making. The huge popularity of these new cars gave the Japanese companies access to resources and allowed them to switch to a K-generalist strategy, directly threatening the Big Three. Thus, over time, new generations of organizations are born to take advantage of changes in the distribution of resources and the appearance of new niches.

New organizations are always emerging to take advantage of new opportunities. The driving force behind the population ecology model of organizational birth is **natural selection**, the process that ensures the survival of the organizations that have the skills and abilities that best fit with the environment.[22] Over time, weaker organizations, such as those with old-fashioned or outdated skills and competences or those that cannot adapt their procedures to fit with changes in the environment, are selected out of the environment and die. New kinds of organizations emerge and survive if they can stake a claim to an environmental niche. In the car industry, Ford was a more efficient competitor than the craft shops, which declined and died because they lost their niche to Ford. In turn, Japanese companies, which continued to innovate and develop new skills, entered the U.S. car market. When customers selected Japanese cars because they wanted smaller, better quality vehicles, U.S. carmakers were forced to imitate their Japanese competitors in order to survive.

Natural selection is a competitive process. New organizations survive if they can develop skills that allow them to fit with and exploit their environment. Entrepreneurship is the process of developing new capabilities that allow organizations to exploit new niches or find new ways of serving existing niches more efficiently. Over time, entrepreneurship leads to a continuous cycle of organizational birth as new organizations are founded to exploit new opportunities in the environment. Amazon.com offers a good illustration of this process.

Natural selection
The process that ensures the survival of the organizations that have the skills and abilities that best fit with the environment.

FOCUS ON NEW INFORMATION TECHNOLOGY
Amazon.com, Part 6

Jeff Bezos was the first entrepreneur both to realize that the Internet could be used to effectively sell books and to act on the opportunity by establishing Amazon.com. As such he gave his company a first-mover advantage over rivals, which has been an important component of its strong position in the marketplace. Being early, Amazon.com was able to capture customer attention, and keep their loyalty—45% of its business is repeat business. Moreover, Amazon.com's very success has made it difficult for new competitors to enter the market and the birth rate into the industry has tapered off substantially.

First, new "unknown" competitors face the major hurdle of attracting customers to their Web sites rather than to Amazon.com's. Second, even "known" competitors such as Barnes & Noble and Borders, which have imitated Amazon's strategy and developed their own online bookstores, have faced the problem of luring away Amazon's customer base and securing their position. Being late entrants, these organizations essentially followed a k-strategy, while Amazon.com followed an r-strategy. This delay in going online has cost them dearly in the current highly competitive environment.

Indeed, the process of natural selection has been operating in the book-selling industry. As discussed in earlier chapters, many small, specialized bookstores have closed their doors. Even large bricks-and-mortar bookstores that may carry hundreds of thousands of books have been unable to compete with an online bookstore that can offer customers all 1.5 million books in print at a 10% price discount.

In 2000, a new round of competition took place in the book-selling industry when Amazon.com and its competitors announced a 50% discount off the price of new best-selling books to protect and grow their market share. Amazon.com and its largest competitors, Barnes & Noble and Borders, were locked in a fierce battle to see who would dominate the book-selling industry. Amazon.com is winning the online book-selling war; Borders gave up the struggle and formed an alliance with Amazon.com; and Barnes & Noble continues to run a far second. The book market did not provide Amazon.com with sufficient resources to survive and become profitable, however; it changed its strategy and sought new market niches in which it could compete profitably. As we discussed earlier, Amazon.com started to sell more varieties of products and moved from being a specialist online bookstore to a generalist online retailer.[23] The changes to its strategy and structure not only have allowed it to survive, but its profitability has also been increasing throughout the 2000s; its future looks rosy indeed.

THE INSTITUTIONAL THEORY OF ORGANIZATIONAL GROWTH

Organizational growth
The life cycle stage in which organizations develop value creation skills and competences that allow them to acquire additional resources.

If an organization survives the birth stage of the organizational life cycle, what factors affect its search for a fit with the environment? Organizations seek to change themselves to obtain control over scarce resources and reduce uncertainty. They can increase their control over resources by growing and becoming larger.

Organizational growth is the life cycle stage in which organizations develop value-creation skills and competences that allow them to acquire additional resources. Growth allows an organization to increase its division of labor and specialization and thus develop a competitive advantage. An organization that is able to acquire resources is likely to generate surplus resources that allow it to grow further. Over time, organizations thus transform themselves: They become something very different from what they were when they started. Microsoft took the resources that it obtained from its popular MS-DOS system, for example, and used them to employ more computer programmers, who developed new software applications to bring in additional resources. In this way, Microsoft grew from strength to strength and transformed itself into a software company that competes in almost all segments of the market: It is trying to become the dominant player in the wireless and online entertainment and video-game industry, for example. It is having less success in the Internet software applications market, however, where strong rivals like Google and Yahoo! exist.

Although size can increase an organization's chances of survival and stability, Microsoft and other companies should not pursue growth as an end in itself. Growth should be the by-product of an organization's ability to develop core competences that satisfy the needs of its stakeholders and so provide access to scarce resources.[24] **Institutional theory** studies how organizations can increase their ability to grow and survive in a competitive environment by becoming *legitimate*, that is, accepted, reliable, and accountable, in the eyes of their stakeholders.

Institutional theory
A theory that studies how organizations can increase their ability to grow and survive in a competitive environment by satisfying their stakeholders.

New organizations suffer from the liability of newness, and many die because they do not develop the competences they need to attract customers and obtain scarce resources. To increase their survival chances as they grow, organizations must gain acceptability and legitimacy from their stakeholders by satisfying the latter's needs. Institutional theory argues that it is as important to study how organizations develop skills that increase their legitimacy in stakeholders' eyes as it is to study how they develop skills that increase their technical efficiency. Institutional theory also argues that to increase their chances of survival, new organizations adopt many of the rules and codes of conduct found in the institutional environment surrounding them.[25]

Institutional environment
The set of values and norms in an environment that governs the behavior of a population of organizations.

The **institutional environment** is the set of values and norms that govern the behavior of a population of organizations. For example, the institutional environment of the banking industry comprises strict rules and procedures about what banks can and cannot do and penalties and actions to be taken against banks that break those rules. Banks that follow rules and codes of conduct are considered trustworthy and legitimate by stakeholders, such as customers, employees, and any group that controls the supply of scarce resources.[26] Banks that are considered legitimate are able to attract resources and improve their chances of survival. A new organization can strengthen its legitimacy by imitating the goals, structure, and culture of successful organizations in its population.[27]

Organizational Isomorphism

Organizational isomorphism
The similarity among organizations in a population.

As organizations grow, they may copy one another's strategies, structures, and cultures and try to adopt certain behaviors because they believe doing so will increase their chances of survival. As a result, **organizational isomorphism**—the similarity among organizations in a population—increases. Three processes that explain why organizations become similar have been identified: coercive, mimetic, and normative isomorphism.[28]

Coercive Isomorphism

Isomorphism is said to be *coercive* when an organization adopts certain norms because of pressures exerted by other organizations and by society in general. As the dependence of one organization on another increases, the dependent organization is likely to become increasingly similar to the more powerful organization. For example, we discussed in the last chapter how the general public has put pressure on Wal-Mart and other organizations to boycott goods made by children in third-world countries, and these companies have responded by creating codes of supplier conduct. Coercive isomorphism also results when organizations are forced to adopt nondiscriminatory, equitable hiring practices because they are mandated by law.

Mimetic Isomorphism

Isomorphism is *mimetic* when organizations intentionally imitate and copy one another to increase their legitimacy. A new organization is especially likely to imitate the structure and processes of successful organizations when the environment is very uncertain and the new organization is trying to find the structure, strategy, culture, and technology that will allow it to survive.[29] Because of mimetic isomorphism, the similarity of a population of similar organizations, such as fast-food restaurants, increases along the lines suggested by the S-shaped curve in Figure 11.2.

McDonald's was the first organization to operate a national chain of fast-food restaurants. Ray Kroc, the man who orchestrated its growth, developed rules and procedures that were easy to replicate in every McDonald's restaurant. Standardization allowed the individual restaurants within the McDonald's organization to imitate one another, so that each part could reach the same high standards of performance. Entrepreneurs who later entered the fast-food industry saw how successful McDonald's was and imitated many of the techniques and procedures that McDonald's had developed. Thus, customers expect to see the same kinds of food on the menus of all fast-food restaurants, they expect certain standards of speed and cleanliness, and they expect to clear their own tables. Retail stores also imitated one another in devising their codes of ethical conduct so that no particular retailer could be singled out as being unresponsive. Although imitating the most successful organizations in a population increases efficiency and chances for success, there is a limit to how much a new organization should imitate an existing one. The first organization in the industry gains a first-mover advantage. If late arrivals model themselves too closely on the leader, customers might see no reason to try the newer restaurant. Each new organization needs to develop some unique competences to differentiate itself and define the niche where it has access to most resources. Wendy's principal claim to fame is that it can provide customers with a customized burger, unlike the McDonald's burger, which is totally standardized; Burger King, unlike McDonald's, offers charbroiled instead of fried burgers.

Normative Isomorphism

Isomorphism is *normative* when organizations come to resemble each other because over time they indirectly adopt the norms and values of other organizations in the environment. Organizations acquire norms and values in several ways. Managers and employees often move from one organization to another and bring with them the norms and values of their former employers. Many new telecommunications companies, for example, recruit managers from large companies such as AT&T and Verizon. Similarly, Dell Computer recruits managers who know how to run a growing computer company because they have worked in one. Organizations also indirectly acquire norms and values through industry, trade, and professional associations. Through meetings and publications, these associations promote specific ideas to their members. Because of this indirect influence, organizations within an industry come to develop a similar view of the world.

Disadvantages of Isomorphism

Although organizational isomorphism can help new and growing organizations develop stability and legitimacy, it has some disadvantages.[30] Organizations may learn ways to behave that have become outdated and no longer lead to organizational effectiveness. The pressure to imitate may reduce the level of innovation in the environment. For many years, for example, the Big Three U.S. carmakers were happy to imitate one another and produce big, fuel-inefficient cars. Innovations to reduce the costs of making a car or to significantly improve design, efficiency, and quality were few and slow in coming because no company took the lead. The entry of new companies from abroad was needed to show U.S. automakers that new manufacturing procedures could be developed.

GREINER'S MODEL OF ORGANIZATIONAL GROWTH

Institutional theory is one way to look at how the need to achieve legitimacy leads a growing organization to change its structure, strategy, and culture and imitate those of successful organizations. If organizations do model themselves on one another in this way, it follows that both the imitators and the imitated encounter similar kinds of strategic and structural problems as they grow. Many organizational life cycle theorists believe that organizations encounter a predictable series of problems that must be managed if organizations are to grow and survive in a competitive environment. One of the best known of these life cycle models of organizational growth is Greiner's model (see Figure 11.4), which proposes that an organization passes

Figure 11.4
Greiner's Model of Organizational Growth

Each stage that Greiner identified ends with a crisis that must be resolved before the organization can advance to the next stage. *Source*: Reprinted by permission of *Harvard Business Review*. An excerpt from "Evolution and Revolution as Organizations Grow." by L. E. Greiner, July–August 1972, by the President and Fellows of Harvard College; all rights reserved.

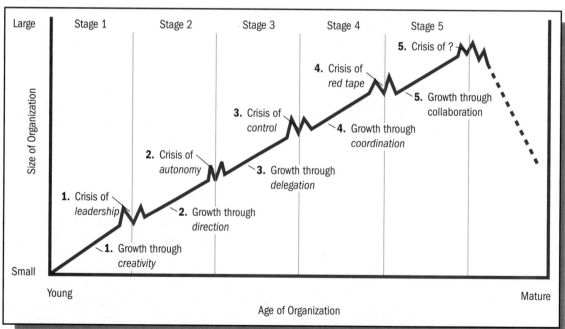

through five sequential growth stages during the course of organizational evolution and that each stage ends in a crisis due to a major problem that the organization encounters.[31] To advance from one stage to the next, an organization must successfully change itself and solve the organizational problem associated with each crisis.

Stage 1: Growth Through Creativity

Greiner calls the first stage in the cycle the *growth through creativity stage*. In this stage (which includes the birth of the organization), entrepreneurs develop the skills and abilities to create and introduce new products for new market niches. As entrepreneurs create completely new procedures and adjust existing procedures, a great deal of organizational learning occurs. The organization learns which products and procedures work and continually adjusts its activities so that it can continue to expand. In this stage, innovation and entrepreneurship go hand in hand, as an organization's founders work long hours to develop and sell their new products with the hope of being rewarded by future profits. Compaq, for example, was started by some former Texas Instruments managers who designed a new computer from scratch and brought the first model to market in 18 months on a shoestring budget. In the creativity stage, the norms and values of the organization's culture, rather than the hierarchy and organizational structure, control people's behavior.

Once a new organization is up and running, a series of internal forces begins to change the entrepreneurial process. As the organization grows, the founding entrepreneurs confront the task of having to manage the organization, and they discover that management is a very different process from entrepreneurship. Management involves utilizing organizational resources to effectively achieve organizational goals. Thus, for example, in its manufacturing operations, management is confronted with the problem of making the production process more efficient. Early in the life of a new company, however, management is not likely to pay much attention to efficiency goals. Entrepreneurs are so involved in getting the organization off the ground that they forget the need to manage organizational resources efficiently. Similarly, they are so involved in providing customers with high-quality products that they ignore the costs involved. Thus, after securing a niche, the founding entrepreneurs are faced with the task of managing their organization, a task to which they are often not really suited and for which they lack the skills.

Crisis of Leadership

Frequently, when an entrepreneur takes control of the management of the organization, significant problems arise that eventually lead to a *crisis of leadership*. CEO and founder Rod Canion, for example, had made Compaq a dominant force in the computer market. But when the price of computers tumbled in 1992, Compaq, a high-priced computer maker, lost its market niche. The firm's stock price plunged, and shareholders realized that the founding entrepreneur was not the best person to manage the company as it searched for a way to turn itself around. The board of directors replaced Canion with a professional manager, Ekhard Pfeiffer, who implemented a low-cost strategy that was very successful. However, in 1999 Pfeiffer was replaced by Michael Capellas, his deputy at Compaq, because of his failure to successfully integrate Digital Equipment into Compaq after Compaq merged with this company.

Stage 2: Growth Through Direction

The crisis of leadership ends with the recruitment of a strong top management team to lead the organization through the next stage of organizational growth: *growth through direction*. The new top management team takes responsibility for directing the company's strategy, and lower-level managers assume key functional responsibilities. In this stage, a new CEO such as Michael Capellas chooses an organizational strategy and designs a structure and culture that allow the organization to meet its effectiveness goals as it grows. As we saw in Chapter 6, a functional or divisional structure is established to allow the organization to regain control of its activities, and decision making becomes more centralized. Then the adoption of formal, standardized rules and procedures allows each organizational function to monitor and control its activities more efficiently. Managers in production, for example, develop procedures to track cost and quality information, and the materials management function develops efficient purchasing and inventory control systems.

Often, growth through direction turns around an organization's fortunes and propels the organization up the growth curve to new levels of effectiveness, as happened at Compaq in the early 1990s. As an organization continues to grow rapidly, however, the move to centralize authority and formalize decision making often leads to a new crisis.

Crisis of Autonomy

With professional managers now running the show, many organizations experience a *crisis of autonomy*, which arises because the organization's creative people in departments such as R&D, product engineering, and marketing become frustrated by their lack of control over new product development and innovation. The structure designed by top managers and imposed on the organization centralizes decision making and limits the freedom to experiment, take risks, and be internal entrepreneurs. Thus the increased level of bureaucracy that comes in the growth-through-direction stage lowers entrepreneurial motivation. For instance, top management approval may be needed to start new projects, and successful performance at low levels of the hierarchy may go unnoticed or at least unrewarded as the organization searches for ways to reduce costs. Entrepreneurs and managers in functional areas such as R&D begin to feel frustrated when their performance goes unrecognized and when top managers fail to act on their recommendations to innovate. Employees and managers feel lost in the growing organizational bureaucracy and become more and more frustrated with their lack of autonomy.

This situation occurred in Compaq toward the end of the 1990s, when its rapid growth but deteriorating performance because of competition from Dell Computer led its top managers to more tightly control costs and expenses. The level of innovation fell and Compaq was slow to respond to the need to move online, both to sell its computers and to obtain low-cost inputs. Things started to go from bad to worse and the company was plunged into crisis.

What happens if the crisis of autonomy is not resolved? Internal entrepreneurs are likely to leave the organization. In high-tech industries, entrepreneurs often cite frustration with bureaucracy as one of the main reasons they leave one company to start their own.[32] In the 1980s, for example, Kodak bought many small entrepreneurial companies to help increase its sales and profitability. Top Kodak managers then intervened in these companies and imposed centralized control over many of them. As a result, many of their managers left because they resented their loss of control and decision making.

The departure of an organization's entrepreneurs not only reduces its ability to innovate but also creates new competitors in the industry. By not resolving the crisis of autonomy, an organization creates a major problem for itself and limits its ability to grow and prosper.[33]

Stage 3: Growth Through Delegation

To solve the crisis of autonomy, organizations must delegate authority to lower-level managers in all functions and divisions and link their increased control over organizational activities to a reward structure that recognizes their contributions. Thus, for example, managers and employees may receive bonuses and stock options that are directly linked to their performance. In essence, *growth through delegation* allows the organization to strike a balance between the need for professional management to improve technical efficiency and the need to provide room for entrepreneurship so that the organization can innovate and find new ways of reducing costs or improving its products. We have already seen how Bill Gates at Microsoft delegates authority to small teams and creates a setting in which members can act entrepreneurially and control their own activities. Gates also rewards team members with stock options, and the most successful team members become highly visible stars of the organization. At the same time, however, Gates and his top management team control the meshing of the activities of different teams to execute the company's long-term strategy. Gates designed Microsoft's structure to avoid the crisis of autonomy, and the organization has profited hugely from his forethought.

Thus, in the growth-through-delegation stage, more autonomy and responsibility are given to managers at all levels and functions. Moving to a product team structure or a multidivisional structure, for example, is one way in which an organization can respond to the need to delegate authority. These structures can reduce the time needed to get new products to market, improve strategic decision making, and motivate product or divisional managers to penetrate markets and respond faster to customer needs. At this stage in organizational growth, top managers intervene in decision making only when necessary. Growth through delegation allows each department or division to expand to meet its own needs and goals, and organizational growth often proceeds at a rapid pace. Once again, however, the organization's very success brings on another crisis: Explosive growth can cause top managers to feel that they have lost control of the company as a whole.

Crisis of Control

When top managers compete with functional managers or corporate-level managers compete with divisional managers for control of organizational resources, the result is a *crisis of control*. The need to resolve the crisis of autonomy by delegating authority to lower-level managers increases their power and control of organizational resources. Lower-level managers like this extra power because it is associated with prestige and access to valued rewards. If managers use this power over resources to pursue their own goals at the expense of organizational goals, the organization becomes less effective. Thus, power struggles over resources can emerge between top- and lower-level managers. Sometimes during this power struggle top management tries to recentralize decision making and take back control over organizational activities. However, this action is doomed to failure because it brings back the crisis of autonomy. How does the organization solve the crisis of control so that it can continue to grow?

Stage 4: Growth Through Coordination

To resolve the crisis of control, as we saw in Chapter 4, an organization must find the right balance between centralized control from the top of the organization and decentralized control at the functional or divisional level. Top management takes on the role of coordinating different divisions and motivating divisional managers to take a company-wide perspective. In many organizations, for example, divisions can cooperate and share resources in order to create new products and processes that benefit the organization as a whole. In Chapter 8, we saw how this kind of coordination is very important for companies pursuing a strategy of related diversification. If companies are growing internationally, coordination is even more important. Top functional managers and corporate headquarters staff must create the "matrix in the mind" that facilitates international cooperation between divisions and countries.

At the same time, corporate management must use its expertise to monitor and oversee divisional activities to ensure that divisions use their resources efficiently, and must initiate company-wide programs to review the performance of the various divisions. To motivate managers and align their goals with those of the organization, organizations often create an internal labor market in which the best divisional managers are rewarded with promotion to the top ranks of the organization, while the most successful functional-level managers gain control over the divisions. If not managed correctly, all this coordination and the complex structures to handle it will bring about yet another crisis.

Crisis of Red Tape

Achieving growth through coordination is a complex process that has to be managed continuously if organizations are to be successful. When organizations fail to manage this process, they are plunged into a *crisis of red tape*. The number of rules and procedures increases, but this increased bureaucracy does little to increase organizational effectiveness and is likely to reduce it by stifling entrepreneurship and other productive activity. The organization becomes overly bureaucratic and relies too much on the formal organization and not enough on the informal organization to coordinate its activities. How can an organization cut itself free of all the confining red tape so that it can once again function effectively?

Stage 5: Growth Through Collaboration

In Greiner's model, *growth through collaboration* becomes the way to solve the crisis of red tape and push the organization up the growth curve. Growth through collaboration emphasizes "greater spontaneity in management action through teams and the skillful confrontation of interpersonal differences. Social control and self-discipline take over from formal control."[34] For organizations at this stage of the growth cycle, Greiner advocates the use of the product team and matrix structures, which, as we discussed in Chapter 6, many large companies use to improve their ability to respond to customer needs and introduce new products quickly. Developing the interpersonal linkages that underlie the "matrix in the mind" for managing global linkages is also a part of the collaborative strategy. Collaboration makes an organization more organic by making greater use of mutual adjustment and less use of standardization.

Changing from a mechanistic to an organic structure as an organization grows is a difficult task fraught with problems. Although both DaimlerChrysler and Xerox moved to a product team structure to streamline their decision making, this change was not made until *after* both companies had experienced huge problems with their structures—problems that increased costs, reduced product quality, and severely reduced their effectiveness. Indeed, both companies came close to bankruptcy.

MANAGERIAL IMPLICATIONS

ORGANIZATIONAL BIRTH AND GROWTH

1. Analyze the resources available in an environment to determine whether a niche to be exploited exists.
2. If a niche is discovered, analyze how the population of organizations currently in the environment will compete with you for the resources in the niche.
3. Develop the competences necessary to pursue a specialist strategy in order to attract resources in the niche.
4. Carefully analyze the institutional environment to learn the values and norms that govern the behavior of organizations in the environment. Imitate the qualities and actions of successful organizations, but be careful to differentiate your product from theirs to increase the returns from your specialist strategy.
5. If your organization survives the birth stage, recognize that it will encounter a series of problems as it grows and differentiates.
6. Recognize the importance of creating an effective top management team and of delegating authority to professional managers in order to build a stable platform for future growth.
7. Then, following principles outlined in earlier chapters, manage the process of organizational design to meet each growth crisis as it emerges. Establish an appropriate balance between centralizing and decentralizing authority, for example, and between standardization and mutual adjustment.

Greiner's growth model shows organizations continuing to grow through collaboration until they encounter some new, unnamed crisis, but it is possible that an organization's growth path leads down, as shown by the direction of the dashed line in Figure 11.4. For many organizations, the next stage in the life cycle is not continued growth but organizational decline.

Greiner's model suggests that organizations at all stages of growth encounter problems—crises that will lead to organizational decline if an organization does not change its strategy or structure. **Organizational decline** is the life cycle stage that an organization enters when it fails to "anticipate, recognize, avoid, neutralize, or adapt to external or internal pressures that threaten [its] long-term survival."[35] The liability of newness, for example, threatens young organizations, and the failure to develop a stable structure can cause early decline and failure. Similarly, in Greiner's model, the failure to adapt strategy and structure to suit changing conditions can result in crisis and failure. Regardless of whether decline sets in at the birth or the growth stage, it results in the decrease of an organization's ability to obtain resources from its stakeholders.[36] A declining company may be unable to attract financial resources from banks, customers, or human resources, because the best managers or employees prefer to work for the most successful organizations.

Decline sometimes occurs because organizations grow too much.[37] The experience of Compaq, IBM, and Chrysler suggests that there is a tendency for organizations to grow past the point that maximizes their effectiveness. Figure 11.5 illustrates the relationship between organizational size and organizational effectiveness. The figure shows that organizational effectiveness is highest at point A, where effectiveness E_1 is associated with organizational size S_1. If an organization grows past this point—for example, to point S_2—effectiveness falls to E_2, and the organization ends up at point B.

Effectiveness and Profitability

An important method that stakeholders such as managers and investors employ to assess organizational effectiveness is to compare how well one company in an

Organizational decline
The life cycle stage that an organization enters when it fails to anticipate, recognize, avoid, neutralize, or adapt to external or internal pressures that threaten its long-term survival.

Figure 11.5
The Relationship Between Organizational Size and Organizational Effectiveness

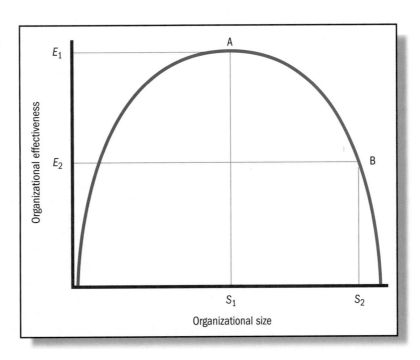

industry is performing relative to others by measuring its profitability relative to theirs. In evaluating organizational effectiveness, it is crucial to understand the difference between a company *making a profit* and *being profitable*, that is, a company's *profitability*.

Profit is simply the total or absolute monetary difference between a company's sales revenues and operating costs; if its sales are $10 million and costs $8 million, it has made a profit of $2 million. **Profitability** measures how well a company is making use of its resources by investing them in ways that create goods and services that it can sell at a price that generates profit.

The important difference between them is that the size of the profit that a company makes in one year says little about how well its managers are making use of resources and its ability to generate future profits. In the car industry, for example, in good economic times, companies like Ford, GM, and Toyota may make billions of dollars of profit each year but this tells us little about their relative profitability—which company is most effective now and will be in the future. Profitability, on the other hand, gives managers and investors much more information to assess how well one company is performing against others in its industry. To see why this is so consider the following example.

Imagine that there are three large companies in an industry and each pursues a different business model. Company A decides to make and sell a no-frills low-priced product; Company B offers customers a state-of-the-art high-priced product; Company C decides to offer a mid-priced product targeted at the average customer. The company that has invested its capital in such a way that (1) it is making the most productive use of its resources (which leads to low operating costs) *and* (2) has created a product that customers are clamoring to buy even at a premium price (which leads to high sales revenues) will have the highest profitability.

Suppose, for example, that Company A makes a profit of $50 million, B makes $25 million, and Company C makes $10 million. Does this mean Company A has outperformed Company B and C and is generating most returns for its stockholders? To answer this question, we need to calculate their relative profitability. Determining profitability is a two-step process. First, it is necessary to compute a company's profit, which is the difference between sales revenues and operating costs. Second, it is necessary to divide that profit by the total amount of capital invested in productive resources—property, plant, equipment, inventories, and other assets—to make and sell the product. Now we know how much capital each company has invested to generate that profit.

Suppose we find out that Company A has made $50 million profit on $500 million of invested capital, Company B has made $25 million on $100 million of invested capital, and Company C has made $10 million on $300 million. Company A's profitability is 10%, Company B's is 25%, and Company C's is 3%. *Company B is generating profit at two and a half times the rate of A, while C is only marginally profitable.* Company B has done the most to build its stockholders' wealth because its higher level of profitability will have increased the demand for and price of its stock. The importance of considering the relative profitability of companies, rather than differences in their total profit, is clear.

As noted earlier, company profitability is usually considered over time because it is seen as an indicator of a company's ability to generate future profit and capital. Figure 11.6 depicts how the profitability of these three companies has changed over time. Company B's profitability has been increasing rapidly over time; Company A's at a much lower rate; and Company C's has hardly increased at all. As an investor, which company's stock would you buy? Because the stock of a company normally rises as its profitability rises and vice versa, Company B would have been the most profitable company to invest in by far. Company A is also making a respectable return for its investors; it is profitable and holding its own in the industry. However, it needs to reorganize to find new ways to compete with Company B, perhaps by copying or imitating Company B. Company C is making a profit, but it is only

Profitability
A measurement of how well a company is making use of resources relative to its competitors.

Figure 11.6
Differences in Profitability

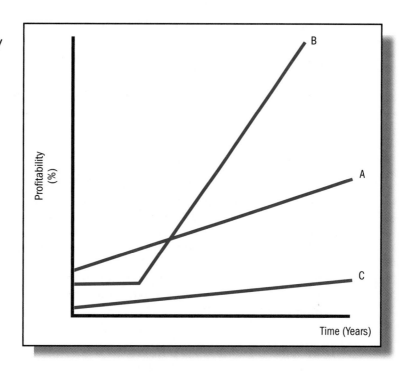

marginally profitable. Its owners have to decide if the benefits of staying in business outweigh the costs—the falling value of its shares and possible future losses. With such low profitability, it may be very hard to find new ways to make better use of its resources and increase its profitability. At such a competitive disadvantage, however, it might become clear to managers and investors that Company C's capital would be better used in some other business. Company C's managers might decide to sell their company's assets and go out of business.

In any industry, companies are in competition (1) to develop new and improved products to attract customers, and (2) to find ways to make more productive use of their resources to reduce their operating costs. In the supermarket industry, for example, competition from Wal-Mart forced Kroger and Albertson's to find better ways to use their resources to maintain and increase profitability. Kroger, for example, invested its capital to build attractive new stores and install new kinds of IT to allow it to lower its operating costs. Albertson's has not done so well and is in decline; in 2005, it was bought by private investors who will seek to turn the company around and make it profitable.

Greiner's model assumes that managers have the ability to identify and solve organizational crises and so can restore company profitability if performance begins to fall. In today's highly-competitive global environment, there are many external and internal forces outside managers' control that may prevent them from using organization resources to increase sales and profitability. Two factors that may prevent an organization from growing profitably, or lead to continuing decline and loss in effectiveness, are organizational inertia and environmental changes.

Organizational Inertia

Organizational inertia
Forces inside an organization that make it resistant to change.

An organization may not easily adapt to meet changes in the environment because of **organizational inertia**—the forces inside an organization that make it resistant to change. Greiner and other adaptation theorists focus on organizations' ability to change and adapt to new conditions in their environments. Population ecology theorists are more pessimistic, believing that organizations do not have the ability to quickly or easily change their strategy or structure to avoid decline. Instead, they believe that organizations are subject to considerable inertia, which prevents them from changing. Some factors that cause inertia were discussed in the last chapter; three more are risk aversion, the desire to maximize rewards, and an overly bureaucratic culture. When these factors operate together, the problems facing managers are greatly compounded.

Risk Aversion

As organizations grow, managers often become risk averse—that is, they become unwilling to bear the uncertainty associated with entrepreneurial activities.[38] As a result, the organization becomes increasingly difficult to change. Risk aversion may set in for several reasons. Managers' overriding concern may be to protect their positions; thus, they undertake relatively safe or inexpensive projects, so that if the projects fail, their burden of blame will be light. Managers might try to maximize the chance of success by pursuing projects that have already brought the organization success. Managers might institute bureaucratic rules and procedures that give close control over new ventures, but also stifle innovation and entrepreneurship.

The Desire to Maximize Rewards

Research suggests that managers' desire for prestige, job security, power, and the strong property rights that bring large rewards is associated more with organizational size than with profitability.[39] Thus, managers may increase the size of the company to maximize their own rewards even when this growth reduces organizational effectiveness. The management teams of many large companies such as Goodyear, Kodak, and Polaroid have been accused of pursuing their own goals at the expense of shareholders, customers, and other stakeholders. Those management teams lacked any incentive to improve organizational effectiveness because they would not gain personally from doing so, and until recently there were no powerful stakeholders to discipline them and force them to streamline operations. The changes made at both DaimlerChrysler and Xerox, for example, came when new management teams took over. Of course in companies such as Tyco, Enron, and Arthur Andersen, the pursuit of personal interest led to many unethical and illegal acts that led to the downfall of these companies.

Overly-Bureaucratic Culture

As discussed in Chapter 7, in large organizations, property rights (such as salaries and stock options) can become so strong that managers spend all their time protecting their specific property rights instead of working to advance the organization's interests. Top managers, for example, resist attempts by subordinate managers to take the initiative and act in an entrepreneurial manner because subordinates who demonstrate superior skills and abilities may threaten the position of their managers and their managers' property rights.[40] Another bureaucracy-related problem is that, as C. Northcote Parkinson pointed out, in a bureaucracy, managers want to multiply subordinates, not rivals. To this end, managers limit the freedom of subordinates to protect their own positions. One way of limiting freedom is to establish a tall organizational hierarchy so that subordinates can be closely controlled and scrutinized. Another way is to develop a bureaucratic culture that emphasizes the status quo and the need for conformity to organizational procedures. Such a culture might be desirable in the armed forces, but it is not beneficial to a large company fighting for survival in an uncertain environment.

Although the behavior of managers is sometimes a major cause of organizational inertia and decline, it is important to realize that managers may not be deliberately trying to hurt the organization. Bureaucratization and risk aversion may creep up on organizations unexpectedly.

Changes in the Environment

Environmental changes that affect an organization's ability to obtain scarce resources may lead to organizational decline. The major sources of uncertainty in the environment are complexity, the number of different forces that an organization has to manage; dynamism, the degree to which the environment is changing; and richness, the amount of resources available in the environment (see Figure 3.2). The greater the uncertainty in the environment, the more likely that some organizations in a population, especially organizations affected by inertia, will go into decline.

Sometimes the niche that an organization occupies erodes, and managers no longer have the incentive or ability to change strategy to improve the organization's access to resources. That is what happened to IBM when the demand for mainframe computers fell.[41] Sometimes the environment becomes poorer, and increased competition for resources threatens existing organizations that have not been managing their growth very effectively. Sometimes an "environmental jolt" changes the forces in the environment and precipitates an immediate crisis.[42] Increasing competition from new low-price airlines and soaring fuel prices, for example, caused serious problems for large U.S. airlines such as Delta and United. Both of them responded with downsizing that involved the layoff of thousands of employees.

The combination of an uncertain, changing environment and organizational inertia makes it difficult for top management to anticipate the need for change and to manage the way organizations change and adapt to the environment. In Chapter 12, we examine how organizations can promote organizational learning, a process that facilitates changes and overcomes inertia. Here we discuss a model that charts the main stages of the decline process, just as Greiner's model charted the main stages of the growth process.

Weitzel and Jonsson's Model of Organizational Decline

Organizational decline occurs by degrees; Weitzel and Jonsson have identified five stages of decline (see Figure 11.7).[43] At each stage except the dissolution stage, management action (shown by the dashed line) can reverse the decline.

Stage 1: Blinded

In the blinded stage, the first decline stage identified by Weitzel and Jonsson, organizations are unable to recognize the internal or external problems that threaten their long-term survival. The most common reason for this blindness is that organizations do not have in place the monitoring and information systems that they need to measure organizational effectiveness and identify sources of organizational inertia. Internal signals that indicate potential problems are excessive numbers of personnel, a slowdown in decision making, a rise in conflict between functions or divisions, and a fall in profits. At this stage, access to good information and an effective top management team can prevent the onset of decline and allow the organization to maintain its pattern of growth. To avoid decline, managers need to monitor internal and external factors continuously so that they have the information to take timely corrective action. Taking action to correct problems at this stage and to reverse the decline process, however, does not necessarily mean that the organization will continue to grow.

Stage 2: Inaction

If an organization does not realize that it is in trouble in the blinded stage, its decline advances to the inaction stage. In this stage, despite clear signs of deteriorating performance such as decreased sales or profits, top management takes little action to correct problems. This inaction may reflect managers' misinterpretation of information and belief that the situation reflects a short-term environmental change that the organization will weather. Inaction may also occur because managers are pursuing

Figure 11.7
Weitzel and Jonsson's Model of Organizational Decline

At each stage, action by management can halt the decline. *Source*: Adapted from "Decline in Organizations: A Literature integration and Extension," by W. Weitzel and E. Jonsson, published in *Administrative Science Quarterly*, (c) Cornell University, 1989, Vol. 34, No. 1. Reprinted by permission.

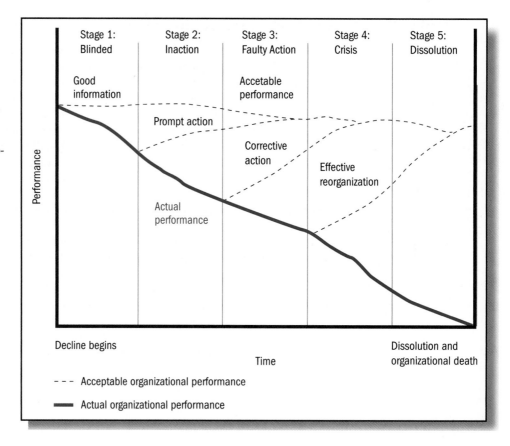

goals that benefit them at the expense of other stakeholders. Organizational inertia, too, may delay managers' response to the situation. Management may follow tried-and-true approaches to solve the organization's problems—approaches that may be inappropriate in the current situation.[44]

As the inaction stage progresses, as Figure 11.7 shows, the gap between acceptable performance and actual performance increases, and prompt action by managers is vital to reverse the decline. Managers may take steps to downsize by reducing the number of personnel, or they may scale back the scope of their operations. They may also change the organization's structure to overcome any organizational inertia that has set in as a result of the organization's large size or complex operations.

Stage 3: Faulty Action
When managers fail to halt decline at the inaction stage, the organization moves into the faulty action stage. Problems continue to multiply despite corrective action. Managers may have made the wrong decisions because of conflict in the top management team, or they may have changed too little too late because they feared that a major reorganization might do more harm than good. Often managers fear that radical change may threaten the way the organization operates and put the organization at risk.[45] For example, Kodak's last five CEOs were either unable or unwilling, because of organizational inertia, to make the radical structural and strategy changes that were needed to turn the company around. Only after Antonio Perez, its new CEO, took over has Kodak committed itself to the competitive reality of digital imaging and slashed its workforce and facilities. By then Kodak was in stage 4, the crisis stage, however. Very often, an organization reaches the faulty-action stage because managers become overly committed to their current strategy and structure and fear changing them even though they are clearly not working to halt the decline. The way a new CEO at Nissan turned around the company is discussed in the following organizational insight.

In 1999, Japanese carmaker Nissan was in big trouble; its performance was rapidly declining. No longer profitable, its debt had soared to more than $19 billion, and its market share both at home and in the vital U.S. market was dropping fast. In decline, it welcomed an offer by Renault, the French carmaker, to buy a controlling interest in its operations for $5.4 billion and to pump in money to turn around its performance. Nissan immediately dispatched Carlos Ghosn, an expert in managing turnarounds, to take control of the company. Ghosn had fixed Michelin's U.S. division by ruthless cost-cutting; he was then recruited as Renault's COO to turn that company around and cut $4 billion in annual expenses. Now, he was poised to do the same at Nissan.

Ghosn was one of the first non-Japanese CEOs of a major Japanese company. His appointment generated considerable resistance from Nissan's Japanese managers, who did not want a foreigner in charge—especially one who seemed likely to shake up the company. Ghosn quickly saw that the problem was that Nissan used 24 different car platforms to produce its cars, and that this required it to operate with too many expensive factories. Ghosn knew that to reduce costs it would be necessary to close five factories and eliminate a dozen car platforms to wipe out $5 billion in operating costs. However, this was Japan, where lifetime employment is still widespread, and such a move would shock the company's employees. So, operating in great secrecy to push his restructuring through, he waited to tell Nissan's board of directors about his plant-closing plans until the night before his public announcement. He also told them that if they did not back his decision he would close down seven factories instead.[46]

The stunned Japanese gave in, but a public outcry took place in Japan as a foreign CEO proposed to break long-held Japanese norms. Ghosn was forced to travel with a bodyguard as he went from one Japanese Nissan facility to another to inspect and share his views on how Nissan must change in the future. He made clear to Nissan's employees that his strategy was not just cost-cutting; he also told Nissan engineers and managers that he was going to change Nissan's culture and thus the way they worked. Japanese companies are notoriously bureaucratic and hierarchical; they operate with conservative, cautious values that make subordinates reluctant to make suggestions to their superiors. Top managers are always jockeying to protect their turf—hence, the 24 different product platforms—and change is always slow and incremental.

Ghosn destroyed these values by creating strict performance targets for managers, based on reducing costs and introducing innovative new vehicles, which could only be reached if managers reengineered the way the company worked. In particular, its engineers, designers, and other functional experts were instructed to be bold in their approach to new vehicle design and production. He created autonomous product teams empowered to make radical changes to vehicle design; he decentralized control, and the top managers who resisted were retired or moved around. Moreover, he insisted that Nissan's engineers and functional experts cooperate with those from Renault to speed innovation, share resources, and to transform Nissan's values and norms. His goal quite simply was to transform the company and change the way it operated. One result is that today Nissan operates with only 10 global platforms.[47]

Ghosn succeeded. Nissan, which also owns Infinity, has introduced a whole stream of futuristic vehicles in the 2000s that have received rave reviews and resulted in soaring sales. Today, Nissan is highly profitable, and in Japan Ghosn has become a famous celebrity, even a national hero. He is revered as one foreigner who could show the Japanese how things could be done better. In 2005, Ghosn's success led to his appointment as the CEO of Renault. Today, he and the Renault–Nissan board meet once a month to make the medium- and long-range decisions presented to them by a score of cross-company teams energized by the company's turnaround and new success.

Stage 4: Crisis

By the time the crisis stage has arrived, only radical changes to an organization's strategy and structure can stop the decline and allow the organization to survive. An organization experiencing a crisis has reached a critical point in its history, and the only chance of recovery is a major reorganization. If managers wait until the organization reaches stage 4 before taking action, change is very difficult to achieve and must be drastic because organizational stakeholders are starting to dissolve or restrict their relationships with the organization.[48] The best managers may already have left because of fighting in the top management team. Investors may be unwilling to risk lending their money to the organization. Suppliers may be reluctant to send the inputs the organization needs because they are worried about getting paid.

Very often by the crisis stage only a new top management team can turn a company around. To overcome inertia, an organization needs new ideas so that it can adapt and change in response to new conditions in the environment.[49] Often the new organization that emerges from an effective reorganization resembles the old organization in name only.

Stage 5: Dissolution

When an organization reaches the dissolution stage, it cannot recover, and decline is irreversible. At this point, the organization has lost the support of its stakeholders, and its access to resources shrivels as its reputation and markets disappear. If new leaders have been selected, they are likely to lack the organizational resources to institute a successful turnaround and develop new routines. The organization probably has no choice but to divest its remaining resources or liquidate its assets and enter bankruptcy proceedings. In either case, it moves into dissolution, and organizational death is the outcome.

As organizational death occurs, people's attachment to the organization changes. They realize that the end is coming and that their attachment to the organization is only temporary.[50] The announcement of organizational death signals to people that efforts to prevent decline have failed and that further actions by participants are futile. As the disbanding process begins, the organization severs its links to its stakeholders and transfers its resources to other organizations. Inside the organization, formal closing or parting ceremonies serve as a way of severing members' ties to the organization and focusing members on their new roles outside the organization.

The need to manage organizational decline is as great as the need to manage organizational growth. In fact, the processes of growth and decline are closely related to one another: The symptoms of decline often signal that a new path must be taken to allow the organization to grow successfully. As many large organizations have found, the solution to their problem may be to shrink and downsize and focus their resources on a narrower range of products and markets. If an organization cannot adapt to a changing environment, it generally faces organizational death.

MANAGERIAL IMPLICATIONS

ORGANIZATIONAL DECLINE

1. To prevent the onset of organizational decline, continually analyze the organization's structure to pinpoint any sources of inertia that may have emerged as your organization has grown and differentiated.
2. Continually analyze the environment, and the niche or niches that your organization occupies, to identify changes in the amount or distribution of resources.
3. Recognize that because you are a part of the organization it may be difficult for you to identify internal or external problems. Call on other managers, members of the board of directors, and outside consultants to analyze the organization's current situation or stage of decline.
4. If you are the founder of the business, always keep in mind that you have a duty to your stakeholders to maximize the chances of your organization's survival and success. Be prepared to step aside and relinquish control if new leadership is required.

SUMMARY

Organizations have a life cycle consisting of four stages: birth, growth, decline, and death. They pass through these stages at different rates, and some do not experience every stage. To survive and prosper, organizations have to change in response to various internal and external forces. An organization must make changes to its structure and culture at critical points in its life cycle. If successfully managed, an organization continues to grow and differentiate. An organization must adapt to an uncertain and changing environment

and overcome the organizational inertia that constantly threatens its ability to adapt to environmental changes. The fate of organizations that fail to meet these challenges is death. Their place is taken by new organizations, and a new cycle of birth and death begins. Chapter 11 has made the following main points:

1. Organizations pass through a series of stages as they grow and evolve. The four stages of the organizational life cycle are birth, growth, decline, and death.

2. Organizations are born when entrepreneurs use their skills and competences to create value. Organizational birth is associated with the liability of newness. Organizational birth is a dangerous stage because entrepreneurship is a risky process, organizational procedures are new and undeveloped, and the environment may be hostile.

3. Population ecology theory states that organizational birth rates in a new environment are very high at first but taper off as the number of successful organizations in a population increases.

4. The number of organizations in a population is determined by the amount of resources available in the environment.

5. Population ecologists have identified two sets of strategies that organizations can use to gain access to resources and to enhance their chances of survival: r-strategy versus K-strategy (r = early entry; K = late entry) and specialist strategy versus generalist strategy.

6. The driving force behind the population ecology model is natural selection, the process that ensures the survival of the organizations that have the skills and abilities that best fit with the environment.

7. As organizations grow, they increase their division of labor and specialization and develop the skills that give them a competitive advantage, which allows them to gain access to scarce resources.

8. Institutional theory argues that organizations adopt many of their routines from the institutional environment surrounding them in order to increase their legitimacy and chances of survival.

Stakeholders tend to favor organizations that they consider trustworthy and legitimate.

9. A new organization can enhance its legitimacy by choosing the goals, structure, and culture that are used by other successful organizations in its populations. Similarity among organizations is the result of coercive, mimetic, and normative isomorphism.

10. According to Greiner's five-stage model of organizational growth, organizations experience growth through (a) creativity, (b) direction, (c) delegation, (d) coordination, and (e) collaboration. Each growth stage ends in a crisis that must be solved by making the appropriate changes if the organization is to advance successfully to the next stage and continue to grow.

11. If organizations fail to manage the growth process effectively, the result is organizational decline, the stage an organization enters when it fails to anticipate, recognize, or adapt to external or internal pressures that threaten its survival.

12. Factors that can precipitate organizational decline include organizational inertia and changes in the environment.

13. Organizational decline occurs by degrees. Weitzel and Jonsson have identified five stages of decline: (a) blinded, (b) inaction, (c) faulty action, (d) crisis, and (e) dissolution. Managers can turn the organization around at every stage except the dissolution stage.

14. Organizational death occurs when an organization divests its remaining resources or liquidates its assets. As the disbanding process begins, the organization severs its links to its stakeholders and transfers its resources to other organizations.

DISCUSSION QUESTIONS

1. What factors influence the number of organizations that are founded in a population? How can pursuing a specialist strategy increase a company's chances of survival?

2. How does r-strategy differ from K-strategy? How does a specialist strategy differ from a generalist strategy? Use companies in the fast-food industry to provide an example of each strategy.

3. Why do organizations grow? What major crisis is an organization likely to encounter as it grows?

4. Why do organizations decline? What steps can top management take to halt decline and restore organizational growth?

5. What is organizational inertia? List some sources of inertia in a company like IBM or GM.

6. Choose an organization or business in your city that has recently closed, and analyze why it failed. Could the organization have been turned around? Why or why not?

ORGANIZATIONAL THEORY IN ACTION

Practicing Organizational Theory: Growing Pains

Form groups of three to five people and discuss the following scenario:

You are the top managers of a rapidly growing company that has been having great success in developing Web sites for large *Fortune* 500 companies. Currently, you employ more than 150 highly skilled and qualified programmers, and to

date you have operated with a loose, organic operating structure that has given them considerable autonomy. Although this has worked, you are now experiencing problems. Performance is dropping because your company is fragmenting into different self-contained teams that are not cooperating and not learning from one another. You have decided that somehow you need to become more bureaucratic or mechanistic, but you recognize and wish to keep all the advantages of your organic operating approach. You are meeting to discuss how to make this transition.

1. What kind of crisis are you experiencing, according to Greiner's model?
2. What kinds of changes will you make to your operating structure to solve this crisis, and what will be the problems associated with implementing these changes?

Making the Connection #11

Find an example of an organization that is experiencing a crisis of growth or an organization that is trying to manage decline. What stage of the life cycle is the organization in? What factors contributed to its growth crisis? What factors led to its decline? What problems is the organization experiencing? How is top management trying to solve the problems?

The Ethical Dimension #11

Managers have many opportunities to pursue their own interests and can use their power to take advantage of their subordinates, limit their freedom, and even steal their ideas. At the same time, managers may have a natural tendency to become risk averse.

1. What kind of ethical code should an organization create to try to prevent the selfish managerial behaviors that can contribute to inertia?
2. How can an organization use ethics to encourage managers to maintain a risk-taking attitude that benefits all stakeholders?

Analyzing the Organization: Design Module #11

This module focuses on the way your organization is managing (a) the dynamics associated with the life cycle stage that it is in and (b) the problems it has experienced as it evolved.

Assignment

Using the information at your disposal, answer the following questions.

1. When was your organization founded? Who founded it? What opportunity was it founded to exploit?
2. How rapid was the growth of your organization, and what problems did it experience as it grew? Describe its passage through the growth stages outlined in Greiner's model. How did managers deal with the crisis that it encountered as it grew?
3. What stage of the organizational life cycle is your organization in now? What internal and external problems is it currently encountering? How are managers trying to solve these problems?
4. Has your organization ever shown any symptoms of decline? How quickly were managers in the organization able to respond to the problem of decline? What changes did they make? Did they turn the organization around?

CASE FOR ANALYSIS

The Body Shop Reaches Middle Age

In 1976, Anita Roddick, a former flower child and the owner of a small hotel in southern England, had an idea. Rising sentiment against the use of animals in testing cosmetics and a wave of environmentalism that focused on "natural" products gave her the idea for a range of skin creams, shampoos, and lotions made from fruit and vegetable oils rather than animal products. Moreover, her products would not be tested on animals. Roddick began to sell her line of new products from a small shop she opened in Brighton, a seaside town, and the results surpassed her wildest expectations. Her line of cosmetics was an instant success; customers were immediately attracted to it. Recognizing that she had discovered an unmet market niche for natural cosmetics, she moved quickly to take advantage of it. To speed the growth of her new organization in Britain and Europe, she began to franchise the right to open stores called "The Body Shop" to sell her products. By 1993, there were over 700 of these stores around the world, with combined sales of over $250 million.

Although Roddick used franchising and alliances with other individuals and companies in Europe to grow her company, in her push to enter the U.S. market in the early 1990s she decided that her company would own (not franchise) its stores. Her rationale was that this would give her more control over U.S. operations and also allow her to retain a greater share of the profits. Forgoing the rapid expansion that franchising would have made possible was a costly mistake.

Large U.S. cosmetic companies like Estée Lauder and entrepreneurs like Leslie Wexner of The Limited were quick to see the opportunities that Roddick had opened up in this rapidly growing market segment. They moved fast to imitate her product lines and operating philosophy, emphasizing the "naturalness" of their products, and began to market their own natural cosmetics. For example, Estée Lauder brought out its Origins line of cosmetics, and Wexner opened the Bath and Body Works to sell his own line of natural cosmetics. Because most U.S. consumers were not familiar with The Body Shop's brand name, both these ventures have been very successful and have gained a large share of the market.

The competitive threat from imitators forced Roddick to quickly begin to franchise The Body Shop in the United States, and by 1995 over 250 stores had been opened. Although they have been successful, Roddick admits that the delay in opening them gave her competitors the opportunity to establish their own brand names and robbed her enterprise of the uniqueness that its products enjoy throughout Europe. The Body Shop has not enjoyed the success that it expected in the United States, and she has come under increasing pressure from investors who are concerned that The Body Shop's flat sales signaled the start of a decline in the company's fortunes. In 1998, a new CEO took control of the company to try to head it back on the right path; the company has recovered and is prospering. However, it is not the same company now, with the same ideals that it was when it was started.

DISCUSSION QUESTIONS

1. What mistakes did Roddick make over time?
2. What strategies could Roddick have adopted to grow her company successfully?

REFERENCES

1. R. E. Quinn and K. Cameron, "Organizational Life Cycles and Shifting Criteria of Effectiveness: Some Preliminary Evidence," *Management Science, 29* (1983), 33–51.

2. I. Adizes, "Organizational Passages: Diagnosing and Treating Life Cycle Problems of Organizations," *Organizational Dynamics, 8* (1979), 3–25; D. Miller and P. Freisen, "Archetypes of Organizational Transitions," *Administrative Science Quarterly, 25* (1980), 268–299.

3. F. H. Knight, *Risk, Uncertainty, and Profit* (Boston: Houghton Mifflin, 1921); I. M. Kirzner, *Competition and Entrepreneurship* (Chicago: University of Chicago Press, 1973).

4. H. G. Manne, *Insider Trading and the Stock Market* (New York: The Free Press, 1966).

5. A. Stinchcombe, "Social Structure and Organizations," in J. G. March, ed., *Handbook of Organizations* (Chicago: Rand McNally, 1965), pp. 142–193.

6. J. A. Schumpeter, *The Theory of Economic Development* (Cambridge, MA: Harvard University Press, 1934).

7. H. Aldrich, *Organizations and Environments* (Upper Saddle River, NJ: Prentice Hall, 1979).

8. R. R. Nelson and S. Winter, *An Evolutionary Theory of Economic Change* (Cambridge, MA: Harvard University Press, 1982).

9. www.u-s-history.com, Andrew Carnegie.

10. andrewcarnegie.tripod.com, "History of Andrew Carnegie."

11. www.ussteel.com, 2005.

12. M. T. Hannan and J. H. Freeman, *Organizational Ecology* (Cambridge, MA: Harvard University Press, 1989).

13. G. R. Carroll, "Organizational Ecology," *Annual Review of Sociology, 10* (1984), 71–93; G. R. Carroll and M. Hannan, "On Using Institutional Theory in Studying Organizational Populations," *American Sociological Review, 54* (1989), 545–548.

14. Aldrich, *Organizations and Environments.*

15. J. Delacroix and G. R. Carroll, "Organizational Foundings: An Ecological Study of the Newspaper Industries of Argentina and Ireland," *Administrative Science Quarterly, 28* (1983), 274–291; Carroll and Hannan, "On Using Institutional Theory in Studying Organizational Populations."

16. Ibid.

17. M. T. Hannan and J. H. Freeman, "The Ecology of Organizational Foundings: American Labor Unions, 1836–1975," *American Journal of Sociology, 92* (1987), 910–943.

18. J. Brittain and J. Freeman, "Organizational Proliferation and Density Dependent Selection," in J. Kimberly and R. Miles, eds., *Organizational Life Cycles* (San Francisco: Jossey-Bass, 1980), pp. 291–338; Hannan and Freeman, *Organizational Ecology.*

19. G. R. Carroll, "The Specialist Strategy," *California Management Review, 3,* (1992) 126–137; G. R. Carroll, "Concentration and Specialization: Dynamics of Niche Width in Populations of Organizations," *American Journal of Sociology, 90* (1985), 1262–1283.

20. Carroll, "Concentration and Specialization."

21. M. Lambkin and G. Day, "Evolutionary Processes in Competitive Markets," *Journal of Marketing, 53* (1989), 4–20; W. Boeker, "Organizational Origins: Entrepreneurial and Environmental Imprinting at the Time of Founding," in G. R. Carroll, *Ecological Models of Organization* (Cambridge, MA: Ballinger, 1987), pp. 33–51.

22. Aldrich, *Organizations and Environments,* p. 27.

23. www.amazon.com, 2006.

24. J. Pfeffer and G. R. Salancik, *The External Control of Organizations* (New York: Harper and Row, 1978).

25. J. Meyer and B. Rowan, "Institutionalized Organizations: Formal Structure as Myth and Ceremony," *American Journal of Sociology, 83* (1977), 340–363; B. E. Ashforth and B. W. Gibbs, "The Double Edge of Organizational Legitimation," *Organization Science, 1* (1990), 177–194.

26. L. G. Zucker, "Institutional Theories of Organization," *Annual Review of Sociology, 13* (1987), 443–464.

27. B. Rowan, "Organizational Structure and the Institutional Environment: The Case of Public Schools," *Administrative Science Quarterly, 27* (1982), 259–279; P. S. Tolbert and L. G. Zucker, "Institutional Sources of Change in the Formal Structure of Organizations: The Diffusion of Civil Service Reform, 1880–1935," *Administrative Science Quarterly, 28* (1983), 22–38.

28. P. DiMaggio and W. Powell, "The Iron Cage Revisited: Institutional Isomorphism and Collective Rationality in Organizational Fields," *American Sociological Review, 48* (1983), pp. 147–160.

29. J. Galaskiewicz and S. Wasserman, "Mimetic Processes Within an Interorganizational Field: An Empirical Test," *American Sociological Review, 48* (1983), 454–479.

30. Ashforth and Gibbs, "The Double Edge of Organizational Legitimation."

31. This section draws heavily on L. E. Greiner, "Evolution and Revolution as Organizations Grow," *Harvard Business Review* (July–August 1972), 37–46.

32. A. C. Cooper, "Entrepreneurship and High Technology," in D. L. Sexton and R. W. Smilor, eds., *The Art and Science of Entrepreneurship* (Cambridge, MA: Ballinger, 1986), pp. 153–168; J. R. Thorne and J. G. Ball, "Entrepreneurs and Their Companies," in K. H. Vesper, ed., *Frontiers of Entrepreneurial Research* (Wellesley, MA: Center for Entrepreneurial Studies, Babson College, 1981), pp. 65–83.

33. G. R. Jones and J. E. Butler, "Managing Internal Corporate Entrepreneurship: An Agency Theory Perspective," *Journal of Management, 18* (1992), 733–749.

34. Greiner, "Evolution and Revolution as Organizations Grow," p. 43.

35. W. Weitzel and E. Jonsson, "Decline in Organizations: A Literature Integration and Extension," *Administrative Science Quarterly, 34* (1989), pp. 91–109.

36. K. S. Cameron, M. U. Kim, and D. A. Whetten, "Organizational Effects of Decline and Turbulence," *Administrative Science Quarterly, 32* (1987), 222–240; K. S. Cameron, D. A. Whetten, and M. U. Kim, "Organizational Dysfunctions of Decline," *Academy of Management Journal, 30* (1987), 126–138.

37. G. R. Jones, R. Kosnik, and J. M. George, "Internationalization and the Firm's Growth Path: On the Psychology of Organizational Contracting," in R. W. Woodman and W. A. Pasemore, *Research in Organizational Change and Development* (Greenwich, CT: JAI Press, 1993).

38. A. D. Chandler, *The Visible Hand* (Cambridge, MA: Belknap Press, 1977); H. Mintzberg and J. A. Waters, "Tracking Strategy in an Entrepreneurial Firm," *Academy of Management Journal, 25* (1982), 465–499; J. Stopford and L. T. Wells, *Managing the Multinational Enterprise* (London: Longman, 1972).

39. A. A. Berle and C. Means, *The Modern Corporation and Private Property* (New York: Macmillan, 1932); K. Williamson, "Profit, Growth, and Sales Maximization," *Economica, 34* (1966), 1–16.

40. R. M. Kanter, *When Giants Learn to Dance: Mastering the Challenges of Strategy* (New York: Simon and Schuster, 1989).

41. L. Greenhalgh, "Organizational Decline," in S. B. Bacharach, ed., *Research in the Sociology of Organizations* (Greenwich, CT: JAI Press, 1983), pp. 231–276.

42. A. Meyer, "Adapting to Environmental Jolts," *Administrative Science Quarterly, 27* (1982), 515–537.

43. Weitzel and Jonsson, "Decline in Organizations."

44. W. H. Starbuck, A. Greve, and B.L.T. Hedberg, "Responding to Crisis," in C. F. Smart and W. T. Stansbury, eds., *Studies in Crisis Management* (Toronto: Butterworth, 1978), pp. 111–136.

45. M. Hannan and J. Freeman, "Structural Inertia and Organizational Change," *American Sociological Review, 49* (1984), 149–164. D. Miller, "Evolution and Revolution: A Quantum View of Structural Change in Organizations," *Journal of Management Studies, 19* (1982), pp. 131–151.

46. www.businessweek.com, "Nissan's New Boss," October 4, 2004.

47. www.nissan.com, 2005.

48. Weitzel and Jonsson, "Decline in Organizations," p. 105.

49. B.L.T. Hedburg, P. C. Nystrom, and W. H. Starbuck, "Camping on Seesaws, Prescriptions for a Self-Designing Organization," *Administrative Science Quarterly, 21* (1976), 31–65; M. L. Tushman, W. H. Newman, and E. Romanelli, "Convergence and Upheaval: Managing the Steady Pace of Organizational Evolution," *California Management Review, 29* (1986), 29–44.

50. R. I. Sutton, "The Process of Organizational Death," *Administrative Science Quarterly, 32* (1987), 542–569.

Decision Making, Learning, Knowledge Management, and Information Technology

Learning Objectives

Decision making results in choices that determine the way an organization operates and how it changes or transforms itself over time. Organizations have to continually improve the way decisions are made so that managers and employees can learn new, more effective ways to act inside the organization and respond to a changing environment.

After studying this chapter you should be able to:

1. Differentiate among several models of decision making that describe how managers make decisions.

2. Describe the nature of organizational learning and the different levels at which learning occurs.

3. Explain how organizations can use knowledge management and information technology to promote organizational learning to improve the quality of their decision making.

4. Identify the factors, such as the operation of cognitive biases, that reduce the level of organizational learning and result in poor decision making.

5. Discuss some techniques that managers can use to overcome these cognitive biases and thus open the organization up to new learning.

ORGANIZATIONAL DECISION MAKING

In previous chapters, we have discussed how an organization and its managers design a structure and a culture that match the organization's environment; choose a technology to convert inputs into outputs; and choose a strategy to guide the use of organizational skills and resources to create value. In making these choices, managers are making decisions. Indeed, everything that goes on in an organization involves a decision of some kind. Clearly, an organization is not only a value-creation machine but a decision-making machine as well. At every level and in every subunit, people continuously make decisions, and how well they make them determines how much value their organization creates.

Organizational decision making is the process of responding to a problem by searching for and selecting a solution or course of action that will create value for organizational stakeholders. Whether the problem is to find the best inputs, to decide on the right way to provide a service to customers, or to figure out how to deal with an aggressive competitor, in each case managers must decide what to do. In general, managers are called upon to make two kinds of decisions: programmed and nonprogrammed.

Programmed decisions are repetitive and routine. Rules, routines, and standard operating procedures can be developed in advance to handle them.[1] Many of the routines and procedures for selecting appropriate solutions are formalized in an organization's rules and standard operating procedures and in the values and norms of its culture.

Nonprogrammed decisions are novel and unstructured. No rules, routines, or standard operating procedures can be developed to handle them. Solutions must be worked out as problems arise.[2] Nonprogrammed decision making requires much more search activity and mutual adjustment by managers to find a solution than does programmed decision making. For example, nonroutine research and development is based on nonprogrammed decision making by researchers who continually experiment to find solutions to problems. Similarly, the creation of an organization's strategy involves nonprogrammed decision making by managers who experiment to find the best way to use an organization's skills and resources to create value and who never know in advance whether they are making the right decision.

Nonprogrammed decision making forces managers to rely on judgment, intuition, and creativity to solve organizational problems; they cannot rely on rules and standard operating procedures to provide nonprogrammed solutions. *Nonprogrammed decisions* lead to the creation of a new set of rules and procedures that would allow organizational members to make appropriate *programmed* decisions.

All organizations have to develop the capacity to make both programmed and nonprogrammed decisions. Programmed decision making allows an organization to increase its efficiency and reduce the costs of making goods and services. Nonprogrammed decision making allows the organization to change and adapt to its environment and to generate new ways of behaving so that it can effectively take advantage of its environment. Programmed decision making provides stability and increases predictability. Nonprogrammed decision making allows the organization to change and adapt itself so that it can deal with unpredictable events. In the next section, we examine several models of organizational decision making.

Organizational decision making
The process of responding to a problem by searching for and selecting a solution or course of action that will create value for organizational stakeholders.

Programmed decisions
Decisions that are repetitive and routine.

Nonprogrammed decisions
Decisions that are novel and unstructured.

MODELS OF ORGANIZATIONAL DECISION MAKING

Early models of decision making portrayed decision making as a rational process in which all-knowing managers made decisions that allowed organizations to adjust perfectly to the environment in which they operated.[3] Newer models recognize that decision making is an inherently uncertain process in which managers grope for solutions that may or may not lead to outcomes favorable to organizational stakeholders.

The Rational Model

According to the *rational model*, decision making is a straightforward, three-stage process (see Figure 12.1).[4] In stage 1, managers identify problems that need to be solved. The managers of an effective organization, for example, spend a great deal of

Figure 12.1
The Rational Model of Decision Making

This model ignores the uncertainty that typically plagues decision making.

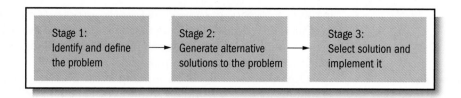

Stage 1:
Identify and define the problem

Stage 2:
Generate alternative solutions to the problem

Stage 3:
Select solution and implement it

time analyzing all aspects of their organization's specific and general environments to identify conditions or problems that call for new action. To achieve a good fit between an organization and its environment, they must analyze the environment and recognize the opportunities or threats it presents. In stage 2, managers individually or collectively seek to design and develop a list of alternative solutions and courses of action to the problems they have identified. They study ways to take advantage of the organization's skills and resources to respond to opportunities and threats. In stage 3, managers compare the likely consequences of each alternative and decide which course of action offers the best solution to the problem they identified in stage 1.

Under what "ideal" circumstances can managers be sure that they have made a decision that will maximize stakeholders' satisfaction? The ideal situation is one in which there is no uncertainty: Managers know all the courses of action open to them. They know the exact effects of all alternatives on stakeholders' interests. They are able to use the same set of objective criteria to evaluate each alternative, and they use the same decision rules to rank each alternative; therefore, they can make the one best or right decision—the decision that will maximize the return to organizational stakeholders.[5] Do such conditions exist? If they did, managers could always make decisions that would perfectly position their organizations in the environment to acquire new resources and make the best use of existing resources.

This ideal state is the situation assumed by the rational model of organizational decision making. The rational model ignores the ambiguity, uncertainty, and chaos that typically plague decision making. Researchers have criticized as unrealistic or simplistic three assumptions underlying the rational model: (1) the assumption that decision makers have all the information they need; (2) the assumption that decision makers are smart; and (3) the assumption that decision makers agree about what needs to be done.

Information and Uncertainty

The assumption that managers are aware of all alternative courses of action and their consequences is unrealistic. In order for this assumption to be valid, managers would need access to all the information necessary to make a decision, would need to collect information about every possible situation the organization might encounter, and would need accurate knowledge about the likelihood of each situation's occurring.[6] Clearly, collecting all this information would be very expensive, and the *information costs*, a form of transaction costs, associated with this model would be exorbitant.[7]

The assumption that it is possible to collect all the information needed to make the best decision is also unrealistic.[8] Because the environment is inherently uncertain, every alternative course of action and its consequences cannot be known. Furthermore, even if it were possible to collect information to eliminate all uncertainty, the costs of doing so would be as great as, or greater than, any potential profit the organization could make from selecting the best alternative. Thus nothing would be gained from the information.

Suppose a fast-food company thinks that some new kind of sandwich has the potential to attract large numbers of new customers. According to the rational model, to identify the right kind of sandwich, the company would do extensive market research, test different kinds of sandwiches with different groups of customers, and evaluate all alternatives. The cost of adequately testing *every* alternative for *all* possible different groups of customers, however, would be so high that it would swallow up any profit the new sandwich might generate from increased sales. The rational model ignores the fact that organizational decision making always takes place in the midst of uncertainty, which poses both an opportunity and a threat for an organization.

Managerial Abilities

The rational model assumes that managers possess the intellectual capability not only to evaluate all the possible alternative choices but to select the best solution as well. In reality, managers have only a limited ability to process the information required to make decisions, and most do not have the time to act as the rational model demands.[9] The intelligence required to make a decision according to the rational model would exceed any one manager's mental abilities and necessitate the employment of an enormous number of managers. The rational model ignores the high level of *managerial costs*.

Preferences and Values

The rational model assumes that different managers have the same preferences and values and that they will use the same rules to decide on the best alternative. The model also assumes that managers agree about what are the most important organizational goals. These "agreement assumptions" are unrealistic.[10] In Chapter 4, we discussed how managers in different functions are likely to have different subunit orientations that lead them to make decisions that favor their own interests over those of other functions, other stakeholders, or the organization as a whole.

To sum up, the rational model of decision making is unrealistic because it rests on assumptions that ignore the information and managerial problems associated with decision making. The Carnegie model and other newer models take these problems into consideration and provide a more accurate picture of how organizational decision making takes place.

The Carnegie Model

In an attempt to describe the realities of the decision-making process more accurately, researchers introduced into decision-making theory a new set of assumptions that have come to be called the *Carnegie model*.[11] Table 12.1 summarizes the differences between the Carnegie and the rational models of decision making. The Carnegie model recognizes the effects of "satisficing," bounded rationality, and organizational coalitions.

Satisficing

Satisficing
Limited information searches to identify problems and alternative solutions.

In an attempt to explain how organizations avoid the costs of obtaining information, the Carnegie model suggests that managers engage in **satisficing**, limited information searches to identify problems and alternative solutions.[12] Instead of searching for all possible solutions to a problem, as the rational model suggests, managers resort to satisficing—that is, they decide on certain criteria that they will use to

Table 12.1 Differences Between the Rational and the Carnegie Models of Decision Making

RATIONAL MODEL	CARNEGIE MODEL
Information is available	Limited information is available
Decision making is costless	Decision making is costly (e.g., managerial costs, information costs)
Decision making is "value free"	Decision making is affected by the preferences and values of decision makers
The full range of possible alternatives is generated	A limited range of alternatives is generated
Solution is chosen by unanimous agreement	Solution is chosen by compromise, bargaining, and accommodation between organizational coalitions
Solution chosen is best for the organization	Solution chosen is satisfactory for the organization

evaluate possible acceptable solutions.[13] The criteria automatically limit the set of possible alternatives. The managers then select one alternative from the range of alternatives that they have generated. Thus, satisficing involves a much less costly information search and puts far less of a burden on managers than does the rational model.

Bounded Rationality

The rational model assumes that managers possess the intellectual capacity to evaluate all possible alternatives. The Carnegie model assumes that managers are limited by **bounded rationality**—a limited capacity to process information. The fact that they have limited information-processing capacity, however, does not mean that managers will take the first acceptable solution they are offered.[14] Managers can improve their decision making by sharpening their analytical skills. Managers can also use technology like computers to improve their decision-making skills.[15] Thus, bounded rationality in no way implies lack of ability or motivation. The Carnegie model recognizes that much of decision making is subjective and relies on managers' prior experience, beliefs, and intuition.

Organizational Coalitions

The rational model ignores the variation in managers' preferences and values and the impossibility of developing decision rules that allow different managers to evaluate different alternatives in the same way. The Carnegie model, in contrast, explicitly recognizes that the preferences and values of managers differ and that conflict between managers and different stakeholder groups is inevitable.[16] However, this does not mean that the organization has to bear the costs of forcing managers to agree to use the same criteria to make decisions.

The Carnegie model views an organization as a coalition of different interests, in which decision making takes place by compromise, bargaining, and negotiation between managers from different functions and areas of the organization. Any solution chosen meets the approval of the dominant coalition, the collection of managers or stakeholders who have the power to select a solution and commit resources to implement it.[17] Over time, as interests change, the makeup of the dominant coalition changes and so does decision making. The Carnegie model recognizes that decision making is not a neutral process with objective decision rules but a process during which managers formulate decision rules as they pursue their goals and interests.

To sum up, the Carnegie model recognizes that decision making takes place in an uncertain environment where information is often incomplete and ambiguous. It also recognizes that decisions are made by people who are limited by bounded rationality, who satisfice, and who form coalitions to pursue their own interests. The Carnegie model offers a more accurate description of how decision making takes place in an organization than does the rational model. Yet Carnegie-style decision making is rational because managers act intentionally to find the best solution to reach their desired goal, despite uncertainty and disagreement over goals. The response of General Electric to the question of whether GE should continue to make its own washing machines or buy machines made by other companies illustrates decision making in accordance with the Carnegie model.

The Incrementalist Model

In the Carnegie model, satisficing and bounded rationality drastically reduce the number and complexity of alternatives that need to be analyzed. According to the *incrementalist model* of organizational decision making, managers select alternative courses of action that are only slightly, or incrementally, different from those used in the past, thus lessening their chances of making a mistake.[21] Often called the science of "muddling through," the incrementalist model implies that managers rarely make major decisions that are radically different from decisions they have made before.[22]

Bounded rationality
A limited capacity to process information.

In the 1990s GE faced a major decision. GE's appliance division, maker of well-known products such as dishwashers, ranges, refrigerators, and washing machines, was fighting declining profitability; Appliance Park, GE's complex of factories near Louisville, Kentucky, which employed 10,000 of the company's 22,000 workers, was losing a substantial amount of money. The washing machine operations, technologically outdated, were contributing significantly to this loss, and GE had to evaluate two alternative courses of action: Should GE spend $70 million and make a major investment in new technology to bring the washing machine operations up to date so that GE could compete into the next century, or should GE close down its washing machine operations and buy from another manufacturer washing machines that it would sell under its own brand name?

To evaluate each alternative, GE's managers tried to decide which one would lead to the best long-term outcome for the organization. They used criteria such as manufacturing costs, quality, profitability, and product development costs to evaluate each alternative. One of the factors that GE was most concerned about was whether the unions in its Appliance Park operations would agree to flexible work arrangements that would reduce labor costs. There had already been significant job losses, and GE managers had been sitting down with the unions to hammer out a new work agreement that would allow the corporation to evaluate its future labor costs. Using information on future labor costs and internal forecasts of future product development and manufacturing costs, managers tried to assess whether the investment would lead to a profit. At the same time, managers talked to companies like Maytag and Whirlpool to determine what it would cost GE to have them make a washing machine according to GE specifications.[18]

If GE could buy another manufacturer's washing machine for less than it would pay to make its own, then it seemed to make sense to choose the less costly alternative. However, GE's managers had to evaluate the effects of other factors. For example, if GE stopped making washing machines, it would lose a core competence in washing machine production that it would be unable to recover.

Suppose the company that GE chose as its supplier failed to live up to its agreement and put only its old technology into the machines it supplied GE, or suppose it produced for GE machines that were much lower in quality than the machines it produced for itself. GE would be at the mercy of its suppliers. On the other hand, suppose the unions reneged on the contract and refused to cooperate after GE had made the investment in modernizing the washing machine plant.

The situation was further complicated by appliance division managers who were lobbying for the investment because it would protect their jobs and the jobs of 15,000 workers. The division managers championed the advantages of the investment for improving the competitive advantage of the division. Corporate managers, however, had to evaluate the potential return of the investment to the entire organization.

GE's managers had a very difficult time evaluating the pros and cons of each alternative. Because of uncertainty, they could not accurately predict the consequences of any decision they made and had to rely on their knowledge of and experience in the appliance market. However, they decided that GE would make the investment and continue to produce its own washing machines. New lines of modern washing machines were introduced throughout the 1990s. In 1999, GE opened a $5 million reliability Growth Test Center, and it tripled the amount it spends on R&D in 1999 to produce appliances that never break down and that "delight" its customers.[19] Nevertheless in the 2000s, GE, like Maytag, has been losing money from its appliance division, while main rival Whirlpool has experiencing record sales and profits, in part because of its TQM program. In 2004, GE decided to reduce overhead costs by combining the functional operations of its appliance division with its lighting division, which makes over 6,000 kinds of lightbulbs, and its industrial division, which makes all kinds of electrical equipment for residential or industrial use.[20] By eliminating the duplication of functional resources between divisions such as accounting, sales, and so on, it hopes to reduce its cost structure and so increase profitability.

Instead, they correct or avoid mistakes through a succession of incremental changes, which eventually may lead to a completely new course of action. During the muddling-through process, organizational goals and the courses of action for achieving them may change, but they change very slowly so that corrective action can be taken if things start to go wrong.

The incrementalist model is very different from the rational model. According to the rational model, an all-knowing decision maker weighs every possible alternative course of action and chooses the best solution. According to the incrementalist model, managers, limited by lack of information and lack of foresight, move cautiously one step at a time to limit their chances of being wrong.

The Unstructured Model

The incrementalist approach works best in a relatively stable environment where managers can accurately predict movements and trends. In an environment that changes suddenly or abruptly, the incrementalist approach might prevent managers from changing quickly enough to meet new conditions, thus causing the organization to go into decline. The *unstructured model* of organizational decision making, developed by Henry Mintzberg and his colleagues, describes how decision making takes place when uncertainty is high.[23]

The unstructured model recognizes the incremental nature of decision making and how decision making takes place in a series of small steps that collectively add up to a major decision over time. Incremental decisions are made within an overall decision-making framework consisting of three stages—identification, development, and selection—that are similar to the stages shown in Figure 12.1. In the *identification* stage, managers develop routines to recognize problems and to understand what is happening to the organization. In the *development* stage, they search for and design alternatives to solve the problems they have defined. Solutions may be new plans or modifications of old plans, as in the muddling-through approach. Finally, in the *selection* stage, managers use an incremental selection process—judgment and intuition, bargaining, and to a lesser extent formal analysis (typical of the rational model)—to reach a final decision.[24]

In the unstructured model (unlike the incrementalist model), whenever organizations encounter roadblocks, they rethink their alternatives and go back to the drawing board. Thus decision making is not a linear, sequential process but a process that may evolve unpredictably in an unstructured way. For example, decision making may be constantly interrupted because uncertainty in the environment alters managers' interpretations of a problem and thus casts doubt on the alternatives they have generated or the solutions they have chosen. The managers must then generate new solutions and find new strategies that help the organization adapt to and modify its environment.

Mintzberg's approach emphasizes the unstructured nature of incremental decision making: Managers make decisions in a haphazard, intuitive way, and uncertainty forces them to constantly adjust to find new ways to behave in the constantly changing situation. The organization tries to make the best decisions it can, but uncertainty forces it to adopt an unstructured way of making decisions. Thus the unstructured model tries to explain how organizations make nonprogrammed decisions, and the incrementalist model tries to explain how organizations improve their programmed decisions over time.

The Garbage Can Model

The view of decision making as an unstructured process is taken to its extreme in the *garbage can model* of organizational decision making.[25] This model turns the decision-making process around and argues that organizations are as likely to start making decisions from the *solution side* as from the *problem side*. In other words, decision makers may propose solutions to problems that do not exist; they create a problem that they can solve with solutions that are already available.

Garbage can decision making arises in the following way: An organization has a set of solutions, or skills, with which it can solve certain problems—for example, how to generate new customers, how to lower production costs, or how to innovate products. Possessing these skills, the organization seeks ways to use them, so managers create problems, or decision-making opportunities, for themselves. Suppose a company has skills in making custom-designed furniture. The head of the marketing department persuades the company president that the organization should take advantage of these skills by expanding internationally. Thus a new problem—how to manage international expansion—is created because of the existence of a solution—the ability to make superior custom-designed furniture.

While an organization is encountering new problems of its own making, it is also trying to find solutions to problems it has identified in its environment or in its internal operations. To further complicate the decision-making process, different coalitions of managers may champion different alternatives and compete for resources to implement their own chosen solutions. Thus decision making becomes like a "garbage can" in which problems, solutions, and the preferences of different individuals and coalitions all mix and contend with one another for organizational attention and action. In this situation, an organization becomes an organized anarchy in which the selection of alternatives depends on which coalition's or manager's definition of the situation holds sway at the moment.[26] Chance, luck, and timing are important determinants of what the organization decides to do, because the problem that is currently the major source of uncertainty facing the organization has the best chance of being dealt with. Outcomes for the organization become more uncertain than usual, and decision making becomes fluid, unpredictable, and even contradictory.

The reality of decision making in organizations is clearly a far cry from the process described by the rational model. Instead of benefiting from the wisdom of all-knowing managers generating all possible solutions and agreeing on the best one so that decisions can be programmed over time, real organizations are forced to make unprogrammed decisions in an unstructured, garbage-can-like way in order to deal with the uncertainty of the environment that surrounds them. The way in which Microsoft dealt with the Netscape challenge is instructive in this respect, as discussed in the following organizational insight.

ORGANIZATIONAL INSIGHT 12.2
Microsoft Is Not All-Seeing After All

The success of Microsoft might lead to a belief that Bill Gates and his managers possess some superhuman ability to predict the future and thus make the choices that will lead it to dominate in most segments of the computer market in which it competes. Although there is no doubt that Microsoft has many talented managers, indeed it employs several "futurists" whose only job is to try to predict how the future of the software industry will evolve, it has nevertheless found itself caught unaware by changes in the environment at several points in its history. The way in which it confronted the challenge from Netscape in the Internet browser market is one of these.

Microsoft, like most other large computer companies, was aware of developments in the Internet and the importance of the growing World Wide Web in the 1990s. Indeed, it began its MSN Internet service to provide consumers access to the Web and to provide information and entertainment content for customers. However, Microsoft's managers had a vision of the Internet as a thing that they could control through the MSN network. They believed the typical customer would be happy to come to Microsoft for service and thus they could actually control the way the Web developed over time. This belief proved totally erroneous because of the speed at which the Web was growing and developing and the many avenues customers could use to gain access to the Web and to its content.

What shocked Microsoft most was the introduction, by Netscape of its first Web browser at the end of 1994, which made it easy for people to surf the Web and to explore its potential. The Netscape browser was hugely popular, and by the summer of 1995 it enjoyed an 80% market share. Microsoft had no such product under development, although it had been warned by two low-level programmers of the threat that Microsoft faced because of its arrogant stance with regard to developing its proprietary MSN service.

In a classic example of garbage can thinking, in the fall of 1994 Bill Gates decided that the fate of Microsoft hung on the development of its own Web browser—this was the solution to its survival. He mobilized over half of the company's software resources to counter this threat. Hundreds of teams of programmers were created and were instructed to take apart the Netscape browser; each was to focus on developing one part of the new browser software. Their task was to produce a Microsoft browser clone that would be compatible with its new Windows 95 operating system, due for release in 1995.

At record-breaking speed, these teams worked to develop the new browser software; cost was no object—survival was the goal. In August 1995, less than one year after the Netscape revolution, Microsoft had its own browser, Internet Explorer, and thereafter Microsoft used its enormous market power to promote its browser and to crush Netscape. Microsoft's decision to give its browser away free, something made possible because of its control of the operating and applications market, effectively made it impossible for Netscape to become profitable. Internet Explorer's market share increased rapidly, and Netscape was bought and integrated into AOL in November 1998.

Nevertheless, the speed at which the uses of the Internet and Internet software applications has been accelerating in

(continued)

In summary: Decision making drives the operation of an organization. At the core of every organization is a set of decision-making rules and routines that bring stability and allow the organization to reproduce its structure, activities, and core competences over time. These routines provide the organization with a memory and provide managers with programmed solutions to problems, which in turn increases organizational effectiveness.[27] However, as we saw in Chapter 11, routines also can give rise to inertia. If an organization gets in a rut and cannot make decisions that allow it to adapt to and modify its environment, it may fail and die. To prevent this from happening, managers need to encourage organizational learning.

THE NATURE OF ORGANIZATIONAL LEARNING

Organizational learning
The process through which managers seek to improve organization members' capacity to understand and manage the organization and its environment so that they can make decisions that continuously raise organizational effectiveness.

Because decision making takes place in an uncertain environment, it is not surprising that many of the decisions that managers and organizations make are mistakes and end in failure. Others, of course, allow the organization to adapt to the environment and to succeed beyond managers' wildest dreams. Organizations survive and prosper because managers make the right decisions—sometimes through skill and sound judgment, sometimes through chance and good luck. For decision making to be successful over time, organizations must improve their ability to learn new behaviors and unlearn inefficient old ones. One of the most important processes that helps managers to make better nonprogrammed decisions—decisions that allow them to adapt to, modify, and change the environment to increase an organization's chances of survival—is organizational learning.[28] **Organizational learning** is the process through which managers seek to improve organization members' desire and ability to understand and manage the organization and its environment so that they make decisions that continuously raise organizational effectiveness.[29]

Today, organizational learning is a vital process for organizations to manage because of the rapid pace of change affecting every organization. As previous chapters have discussed, organizations are racing to develop new and improved core competences that can give them a competitive advantage. They are fighting to respond to the low-cost competitive challenges from foreign organizations. They are searching for every opportunity to use advanced materials technology and information systems to more effectively pursue their strategies and manage their structures. Indeed, the tendency of organizations to experiment with restructuring and reengineering that occurred in the 1990s was motivated by managers' realization that they had to learn new ways to operate more efficiently if they were to survive. Consequently, managers must understand how organizational learning occurs and the factors that can promote and impede it.

Types of Organizational Learning

Exploration
Organizational members' search for and experimentation with new kinds or forms of organizational activities and procedures.

In studying organizational learning, James March has proposed that two principal types of organizational learning strategies can be pursued: exploration and exploitation.[30] **Exploration** involves organizational members searching for and experimenting with new kinds or forms of organizational activities and procedures to increase effectiveness. Learning that involves exploration might involve finding new ways of managing the environment—such as experimenting with the use of strategic alliances and network organizations—or inventing new kinds of organizational structures for managing organizational resources—such as product team structures and cross-functional teams.

Exploitation involves organizational members learning ways to refine and improve existing organizational activities and procedures in order to increase effectiveness. Learning that involves exploitation might involve implementing a total quality management program to promote the continuous refinement of existing operating procedures, or developing an improved set of rules to perform specific kinds of functional activities more effectively. Exploration is therefore a more radical learning process than exploitation, although both are important in increasing organizational effectiveness.[31]

A **learning organization** is an organization that purposefully designs and constructs its structure, culture, and strategy so as to enhance and maximize the potential for organizational learning (explorative and exploitative) to take place.[32] How do managers create a learning organization, one capable of allowing its members to appreciate and respond quickly to changes taking place around it? By increasing the ability of employees, at every level in the organization, to question and analyze the way an organization currently performs its activities and to experiment with new ways to change it to increase effectiveness.

Levels of Organizational Learning

In order to create a learning organization, managers need to encourage learning at four levels: individual, group, organizational, and interorganizational[33] (see Figure 12.2). Some principles for creating a learning organization at each level have been developed by Peter Senge and are discussed in the following sections.[34]

Individual

At the individual level, managers need to do all they can to facilitate the learning of new skills, norms, and values so that individuals can increase their own personal skills and abilities and thereby help build the organization's core competences. Senge has argued that for organizational learning to occur, each person in an organization needs to develop a sense of *personal mastery*, by which he means that organizations should empower individuals and allow them to experiment and create and explore what they want. The goal is to give employees the opportunity to develop an intense appreciation for their work that translates into a distinctive competence for the organization. As part of attaining personal mastery, and to give employees a deeper understanding of what is involved in a particular activity, organizations need to encourage employees to

Exploitation
Organizational members' learning of ways to refine and improve existing organizational procedures.

Learning organization
An organization that purposefully designs and constructs its structure, culture, and strategy so as to enhance and maximize the potential for organizational learning to take place.

Figure 12.2
Levels of Organizational Learning

To create a learning organization, managers must use systems thinking and recognize the effects of one level of learning on another.

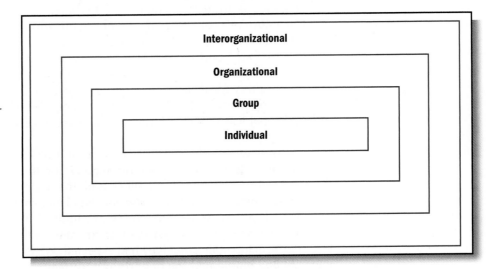

develop and use complex *mental models* that challenge them to find new or better ways of performing a task. To give an analogy, a person might mow the lawn once a week and treat this as a chore that has to be done. However, suppose the person decides to study how the grass grows and to experiment with cutting the grass to different heights and using different fertilizers and watering patterns. Through this study, he or she notices that cutting the grass to a certain height and using specific combinations of fertilizer and water promote thicker growth and fewer weeds, resulting in a better-looking lawn that needs less mowing. What had been a chore may become a hobby and the personal mastery achieved from the new way of looking at the task may become a source of deep personal satisfaction. This is the message behind Senge's first principle for developing a learning organization—namely, organizations must encourage each of their individual members to develop a similar commitment and attachment to their jobs so that they will develop a taste for experimenting and risk taking.[35]

A learning organization can encourage employees to form complex mental models and develop a sense of personal mastery by providing them with the opportunity to assume more responsibility for their decisions. This can be done in a variety of different ways. Employees might be cross-trained so that they can perform many different tasks, and the knowledge that they gain may give them new insight into how to improve work procedures. On the other hand, perhaps a specific task that was performed by several different workers can be redesigned or reengineered so that one worker, aided by an advanced information system, can perform the complete task. Again, the result may be an increase in the level of organizational learning as the worker finds new ways to get the job done. Recall that one of the aims of reengineering is to fundamentally rethink basic business processes. Reengineering is about promoting organizational learning.

Group

At the group level, managers need to encourage learning by promoting the use of various kinds of groups—such as self-managed groups or cross-functional teams—so that individuals can share or pool their skills and abilities to solve problems. Groups allow for the creation of synergism—the idea that the whole is much more than the sum of its parts—which can enhance performance. In terms of Thompson's model of task interdependence discussed in Chapter 9, for example, the move from a pooled, to a sequential, to a reciprocal form of task interdependence will increase the potential for synergism and group-level learning because group members have more opportunity to interact and learn from one another over time. "Group routines" and "shared pools of collective meaning" that enhance group effectiveness may develop from such group interactions.[36] Senge refers to this kind of learning as *team learning*, and he argues that team learning is more important than individual-level learning in promoting organizational learning because most important decisions are made in subunits such as groups, functions, and divisions.

The ability of teams to bring about organizational learning was unmistakable when Toyota revolutionized the work process in the former GM factory discussed in Chapter 10. Large performance gains were achieved in the NUMMI factory when Toyota's managers created work teams and empowered team members to take over the responsibility for measuring, monitoring, and controlling their own behavior to find ways continuously to increase performance. The power of teams to bring about organizational learning is also revealed in another of Toyota's attempts to increase effectiveness.

Experimenting with ways to increase technical efficiency, Toyota decided to produce cars in fully roboticized factories embodying the latest, most advanced manufacturing technology. As a result, when it built a new manufacturing plant in Kyoto, Toyota's engineers focused on perfecting the plant's materials technology, and workers were simply an appendage to the machines. Within a few years, however, it became clear to Toyota's managers that the new technology had not produced the large performance gains that they had expected. Why? According to Toyota, the new factories had eliminated the opportunity for team learning; workers were neither asked nor expected to contribute their ideas for improving efficiency. Computers are only as good as the people who program them, and programmers were not the ones working on the production line. Toyota has since junked its fully roboticized factories, and in its new factories it has made sure that people in teams can contribute their knowledge and skills to increase effectiveness.

Organization

At the organizational level, managers can promote organizational learning through the way they create an organization's structure and culture. An organization's structure can be designed to inhibit or facilitate intergroup communication and problem solving, and this affects team members' approach to learning. Mechanistic and organic structures, for example, encourage different approaches to learning. The design of a mechanistic structure seems likely to facilitate exploitative learning, while the design of an organic structure seems more likely to facilitate explorative learning. Indeed, organizations need to strike a balance between a mechanistic and an organic structure in order to take advantage of both types of learning.

Culture, too, is likely to be an important influence on learning at the organizational level. Another of Senge's principles for designing a learning organization emphasizes the importance of *building shared vision*, by which he means building the ongoing frame of reference or mental model that all organizational members use to frame problems or opportunities and that binds them to an organization. At the heart of this vision is likely to be the set of terminal and instrumental values and norms that guide behavior in a particular setting and that affect the way people interact with individuals and groups outside an organization, that is, organizational culture. Thus, yet another important aspect of organizational culture is its ability to promote or inhibit organizational learning and change.

Indeed, in a study of 207 companies, John Kotter and James Heskett distinguished between adaptive cultures and inert cultures in terms of their ability to facilitate organizational learning.[37] **Adaptive cultures** are those that value innovation and encourage and reward experimenting and risk taking by middle- and lower-level managers. **Inert cultures** are those that are cautious and conservative, do not value middle- and lower-level managers taking such action, and, indeed, may actively discourage such behavior. According to Kotter and Heskett, organizational learning is higher in organizations with adaptive cultures because managers can quickly introduce changes in the way the organization operates that allow the organization to adapt to changes occurring in the environment. This does not occur in organizations with inert cultures. As a result, organizations with adaptive cultures are more likely to survive in a changing environment and, indeed, should have higher performance than organizations with inert cultures—exactly what Kotter and Heskett found.

Interorganizational

Organizational structure and culture not only establish the shared vision or framework of common assumptions that guide learning inside an organization, but they also determine how learning takes place at the interorganizational level. For example, organizations with organic, adaptive cultures are more likely to actively seek out new ways to manage interorganizational linkages with other organizations while mechanistic, inert cultures are slower to recognize or to take advantage of new kinds of linkage mechanisms.

In general, interorganizational learning is important because organizations can improve their effectiveness by copying and imitating each other's distinctive competences. The last chapter discussed how mimetic, coercive, and normative processes encourage organizations to learn from each other in order to increase their legitimacy, but this can also increase their effectiveness. In the automobile industry, for example, Japanese car manufacturers came to the United States after World War II to learn U.S. manufacturing methods and took this knowledge back to Japan where they improved upon it. This process was then reversed in the 1980s when struggling

Adaptive cultures
Cultures that value innovation and encourage and reward experimentation and risk taking by middle and lower-level managers.

Inert cultures
Cultures that are cautious and conservative, and do not encourage risk taking by middle and lower-level managers.

U.S. carmakers went to Japan to learn about the advances that Japanese carmakers had pioneered, took this knowledge back to the U.S., and improved upon it.

Similarly, organizations can encourage explorative and exploitative learning by cooperating with their suppliers and distributors to find new and improved ways of handling inputs and outputs. Enterprise-wide IT systems, business-to-business networks, strategic alliances, and network organizations are important vehicles for increasing the speed at which new learning takes place because they open up the organization to the environment and give organizational members new opportunities to experiment and find new ways to increase effectiveness.

In fact, Senge's fifth principle of organizational learning, *systems thinking*, emphasizes that in order to create a learning organization, managers must recognize the effects of one level of learning on another. Thus, for example, there is little point in creating teams to facilitate team learning if an organization does not also take steps to give its employees the freedom to develop a sense of personal mastery. Similarly, the nature of interorganizational learning is likely to be affected by the kind of learning going on inside an organization.

By encouraging and promoting organizational learning at each of these four levels—that is, by looking at organizational learning as a system—managers can create a learning organization that facilitates an organization's quick response to the changes in the environment that are constantly taking place around it. To enhance an organization's ability to create value, managers need to promote both explorative and exploitative learning and then use this learning in ways that will promote organizational effectiveness. Managers need to recognize, however, that empowering workers, allowing teams to take control of their own activities, and creating an organic, adaptive organization all expose an organization to risk. Risk increases because the explorative learning that takes place may disrupt taken-for-granted routines and assumptions so that managers have to carefully manage the changes taking place (an issue discussed in Chapter 13). On the other hand, very often the problem is not too *much* learning taking place but too *little*. Several factors may impede organizational learning, and when this happens the quality of decision making falls and effectiveness suffers. In the next section an important technique for promoting organizational learning, knowledge management, is discussed. Then the many factors that may impede learning are examined.

KNOWLEDGE MANAGEMENT AND INFORMATION TECHNOLOGY

Knowledge management
A type of IT-enabled organizational relationship that has important implications for both organizational learning and decision making.

As we have seen in previous chapters, new information technologies are having profound effects on the way an organization operates. IT-enabled organizational structure allows for new kinds of tasks and job-reporting relationships among electronically connected people that promote superior communication and coordination. One type of IT-enabled organizational relationship that has important implications for both organizational learning and decision making is **knowledge management**, the sharing and integrating of expertise within and between functions and divisions through real-time, interconnected IT.[38] To understand the importance of knowledge management, consider how Accenture, profiled in the following organizational insight, has developed a knowledge management system to improve the ability of its consultants to acquire the vital new knowledge that allows them to better serve the needs of their clients.

As the example of Accenture suggests, one important benefit from utilizing a knowledge management system is the development of synergies between people and groups, which may result in competitive advantage in the form of product or service differentiation. Unlike more rigid bureaucratic organizing methods, IT-enabled organizations can respond more quickly to changing environmental conditions such as increased global competition.

Accenture, the largest global management consulting company, has been a pioneer in using IT to revolutionize its business practices. As it grew to employ more than 70,000 employees in more than 46 countries in 2001, its CEO, Joe Forehand, and other top managers realized they needed a new way to organize and lead an army of global consultants. Specifically, top managers realized that because only Accenture's consultants in the field could diagnose and solve client problems, the firm needed a managerial hierarchy that facilitated creative, on-the-spot, decentralized decision making. Moreover, they realized that to increase effectiveness Accenture needed to find a way to allow consultants to share each others' firsthand knowledge and expertise, which, after all, is the source of its competitive advantage.

To accomplish both these goals Accenture decided to create a knowledge management system and substitute direct control by managers with control through a sophisticated in-house IT system.[39] First, they restructured the managerial hierarchy, eliminating many levels of managers. Then they went about setting up an organization-wide information management system to allow consultants to make their own decisions while providing them with access to an expert knowledge system that provided advice when they needed to solve client problems.[40]

The change process began by equipping every consultant with a laptop computer. Using sophisticated in-house IT, each consultant was linked to all of the company's other consultants and became a member of a specific group that specialized in the needs of a particular kind of client, such as consumer product firms or brokerage companies. The group therefore possessed collective expert knowledge about a particular kind of client. To find a solution to a problem, the members of a specific group could email others in the group who were working at different client sites to see if they had faced similar client problems.

If group members still couldn't solve the problem, consultants communicated with members of other groups by tapping into Accenture's company-wide knowledge management database containing volumes of potentially relevant information. In this way different groups could share state-of-the-art business practices; it was likely another group had encountered the same problem in a different context and thus a solution did exist. Consultants who found clues using the electronic knowledge management system then communicated directly with consultants in other groups through a combination of phone, voice mail, email, and videoconferencing to gain access to the most current information being gathered and applied at existing client sites.[41] By utilizing these resources, consultants kept abreast of the innovative practices within their own firm and within client firms.[42] Remember that Accenture's consulting contracts with individual clients run into the millions of dollars; the enhancement in learning gained through an electronic knowledge management system is vital.

Accenture has found that its knowledge management system, by flattening its structure, decentralizing authority, and enlarging and enriching roles, has increased its consultants' creativity and performance. By providing employees with more information to make a decision and enabling them to coordinate easily with other people, IT has given consultants much more freedom to make decisions. On the other hand, senior managers can easily manage what their consultants do by monitoring their progress electronically and taking corrective action as necessary. The end result is that Accenture has grown to be one of the most profitable of all global consulting companies.[43]

What kind of knowledge management system should managers design for their organizations? Is the same kind of system suitable for all kinds of organizations? Or would we expect organizations with a more mechanistic or organic orientation to develop and adopt different kinds of systems?

Knowledge Management: Codification Versus Personalization

One solution to this question has been proposed by Hansen, Nohria, and Tierney, who argue that organizations should choose between a codification or personalization approach to creating an IT-based knowledge management system.[44] With a *codification approach*, knowledge is carefully collected, analyzed, and stored in databases where it can be retrieved easily by users who input organization-specific commands and keywords. Essentially, a codification approach results in collection of standardized organization best practices, rules, and SOPs that can be drawn upon by anyone who needs them. It is a form of bureaucratic control than can result in major gains in technical efficiency and allow an organization to better manage its environment. For example, Dell Computer uses an advanced in-house codification approach to manage its transactions with its global suppliers. All suppliers have access to

Dell's knowledge management system, which gives them real-time access to its changing input demands, allows them to forecast demand for their products months in advance, and enables them to redesign their products so they will fit better with Dell's future needs. The cost savings that have resulted from this system have been tremendous and have made Dell and its suppliers the low-cost leaders in the PC industry.

A codification approach, however, is only suitable when the product or the service being provided is itself quite standardized so that best practices can continually be discovered and entered into the knowledge management system. It works best when the different functions in the organization are able to provide standardized information—about changing customer demands or product specifications, for example—that provides vital input to other functions so that the level of mutual adjustment and learning between functions increases, resulting in major gains in effectiveness. In this sense, a knowledge management system allows an organization with a more mechanistic structure to react in a more "organic" fashion, albeit the flexibility is provided by new, sophisticated IT protocols based on the codification of standardized organizational knowledge.

By contrast, a *personalization approach* to knowledge management is pursued when an organization needs to provide customized products or solutions to clients, when technology is changing rapidly, and when employees rely much more on know-how, insight, and judgment to make decisions. In these cases, it is very difficult (often impossible) to write down or even verbalize a course of action that leads to a solution. Often, the solution results from mutual adjustments between people, such as occurs in the intensive technology described in Chapter 9.

In a personalization approach, information systems are designed to show employees who in the organization might possess the knowledge they might need or who might have confronted a similar problem in the past. In a consulting company such as Accenture, for example, individual consultants will write up synopses of the ways they have solved client problems, and the nature of these problems, so that others in the organization can gain a sense of what they are doing. Working in teams, consultants can also spread their knowledge across the organization, often globally, and IT is used to facilitate direct interactions between people and the exchange of know-how by informing employees about upcoming seminars and visiting internal experts, for example.

Over time, as an organization like Accenture confronts more examples of a similar type of problem, consultants can increasingly codify this informal know-how into best practices that can be shared more widely throughout the organization. An organization's information system plays an especially crucial role, for competitive success depends on the speed with which it can provide clients with a state-of-the-art solution to their problems. Given that software is advancing all the time, such solutions change continually. An organization's ability to provide a quick, customized solution, and to translate this rapidly into best practices, will often depend on the degree to which it is *specialized*, for example by industry or product or service, and therefore deals with a narrower and deeper range of problems. That is why so many small, specialized software and consulting computer companies exist.

Knowledge management is therefore an important tool for increasing the level of integration inside an organization, among people, functions, and even divisions. In the 1990s many companies moved to develop electronic knowledge management systems to speed learning and decision making; for many of them, it has resulted in success. It is important to remember, however, that knowledge management is expensive; people must be employed to help codify knowledge and disseminate it throughout the organization. Today, so much information is available to managers through IT systems that an organization can be swamped in it, and the process of discovering the best practices and solutions requires a lot of search and judgment in its own right. Companies like Buckman Laboratories, Chevron, and Texas Instruments have saved hundreds of millions of dollars by implementing knowledge management systems; they also are spending hundreds of millions to maintain these systems. Organizations must always compare the benefits and costs of using IT and knowledge management to facilitate learning, and over time modify them to suit changing conditions.

FACTORS AFFECTING ORGANIZATIONAL LEARNING

Although knowledge management can enhance organizational learning, a model that illustrates several factors that may actually *reduce* the level of learning over time has been developed by Paul C. Nystrom and William H. Starbuck. This model illustrates how problems may arise that prevent an organization from learning and adapting to its environment and that therefore cause an organizational crisis to emerge.[45] Nystrom and Starbuck define a crisis as any situation that seriously threatens an organization's survival.

According to Nystrom and Starbuck, as organizations learn to make decisions, they develop rules and standard operating procedures that facilitate programmed decision making. If an organization achieves success by using its standard procedures, this success may lead to complacency and deter managers from searching for and learning from new experiences.[46] Thus past (successful) learning can inhibit new learning and lead to organizational inertia. If programmed decision making drives out nonprogrammed decision making, the level of organizational learning drops. Blindness and rigidity in organizational decision making may then set in and lead to a full-blown crisis.

Managers often discount warnings that problems are impending and do not perceive that crises are developing. Even if they notice, they may attribute the source of the problems to temporary disturbances in the environment and implement what Nystrom and Starbuck call "weathering-the-storm strategies," such as postponing investments, downsizing the workforce, or centralizing decision making and reducing the autonomy of people at low levels in the organization. Managers adopt this incrementalist approach to decision making because sticking to what they know is much safer than setting off in new directions (explorative learning) where consequences are unknown. Managers continue to rely on the information obtained from their existing operating routines to solve problems—information that does not reveal the real nature of the problems they are experiencing.

Another reason why past learning inhibits new organizational learning is that managers' mind-sets or cognitive structures shape their perception and interpretation of problems and solutions. A **cognitive structure** is the system of interrelated beliefs, preferences, expectations, and values that a person uses to define problems and events.[47] In an organization, cognitive structures reveal themselves in plans, goals, stories, myths, and jargon. Cognitive structures shape the way a CEO or members of the top management team make decisions, and they predetermine what managers perceive as opportunities and threats in the environment. Two managers (or two top management teams), for example, might perceive the same "objective" environment very differently because of differences in their cognitive structures.

A classic example of how cognitive structure influences decision making occurred after World War II, when Sears, Roebuck and Montgomery Ward were planning their postwar strategies. The top management team at Sears believed that there would be a boom in consumer spending after the war and that the environment was very favorable for large-scale investment and expansion. Managers at Sears set out to establish a nationwide store system to take advantage of the anticipated surge in demand. Managers at Montgomery Ward interpreted the environment differently. They believed that consumers would save their money. Consequently, Montgomery Ward's postwar expansion program was much smaller and less ambitious than Sears's. After the war, consumer spending boomed, and the environment became richer and richer. Sears could take advantage of this change in the environment, but Montgomery Ward could not. As a result, Sears grew to become the dominant retailer of the 1960s.

Cognitive structure
The system of interrelated beliefs, preferences, expectations, and values a person uses to define problems and events.

Just as top managers' cognitive structures can produce successful learning, they can also cause a crisis. During the early 1990s, for example, Sears was unable to respond to the challenges posed by the new retailing environment because it relied on past learning to make new business decisions (an incrementalist approach to decision making). Sears's decisions have been shown to be inferior to those made by Wal-Mart, for example, whose top management team has made the best predictions about customer demands for low-cost retailing in the 1980s and 1990s. (Montgomery Ward went out of business in 1999.) Why do top managers often cling to outdated ideas and use inappropriate cognitive structures to interpret events and problems—something that leads to faulty learning? It is useful to look at some factors that distort managers' perceptions and flaw organizational learning and decision making.

Organizational Learning and Cognitive Structures

As noted earlier, cognitive structures are the systems of beliefs, preferences, expectations, and values that develop over time and predetermine a person's responses to and interpretations of situations. When a manager confronts a problem, his or her cognitive structure shapes the interpretation of the information at hand, that is, the manager's view of a situation is shaped by prior experience and customary ways of thinking—by the manager's mind-set.[48] That view, however, might be distorted.

Over many years, for example, the cognitive structures of IBM's top managers reinforced the idea that organizations needed mainframe computers to handle their information-processing needs. IBM, therefore, sought to develop core competences in the design, manufacture, and servicing of mainframe computers. When PCs became increasingly popular in the early 1980s, IBM viewed them as machines suitable only for managers' personal information-processing needs or as a way of linking managers to a mainframe. IBM did not regard personal computers as an alternative to the mainframe because its managers were fixated on the idea that mainframes, and only mainframes, could satisfy organizations' information-processing needs. When major advances in software and microchip technology allowed PCs to handle and store increasing volumes of information, IBM managers discounted these developments. The company searched for better ways to tie PCs into mainframes through networking, and it worked to improve the network capabilities of mainframe computers by developing new operating languages such as UNIX.

The cognitive structures of IBM managers led to a misinterpretation or undervaluing of new information. IBM's managers discounted the threat that PCs posed and continued to operate as if mainframe computers would dominate the market forever. When events proved their view of the environment to be distorted, it was too late to take corrective action. IBM was in crisis. A new CEO, Lou Gerstner, was brought in to change the programmed routines and cognitive structures that were dominating and skewing decision making. His solution was to move IBM into the computer consulting business, and by 2002 IBM was making over 40% of its revenues from this new business. This new approach had changed the mind-sets of its managers and employees.

Types of Cognitive Biases

Researchers have identified several factors that lead managers to develop a cognitive structure that causes them to misperceive and misinterpret information. These factors are called **cognitive biases** because they systematically bias cognitive structures and affect organizational learning and decision making. As Figure 12.3 shows, cognitive biases affect the way managers process information. Cognitive dissonance, illusion of control, and several other cognitive biases that influence organizational learning and decision making are discussed next and are illustrated by an examination of IBM's problems in changing its strategy and structure in the 1990s.[49]

Cognitive biases

Factors that systematically bias cognitive structures and affect organizational learning and decision making.

Figure 12.3
The Distortion of
Organizational Decision
Making by Cognitive
Biases

Cognitive dissonance and
other cognitive biases affect
managers information-
processing abilities and distort
managers' interpretation of a
problem.

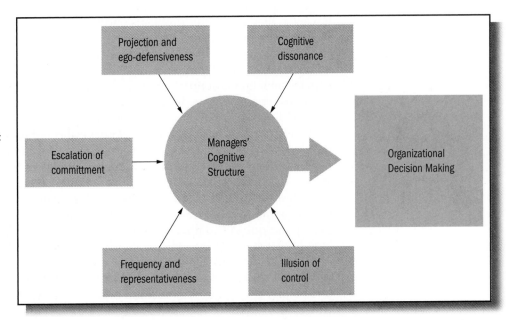

Cognitive Dissonance

Cognitive dissonance
The state of discomfort or anxiety that a person feels when
there is an inconsistency
between his or her beliefs and
actions.

Cognitive dissonance is the state of discomfort or anxiety that a person feels when there is an inconsistency between his or her beliefs and actions. According to cognitive dissonance theory, decision makers try to maintain consistency between their images of themselves, their attitudes, and their decisions.[50] Managers seek or interpret information that confirms and reinforces their beliefs, and they ignore information that does not. Managers also tend to seek information that is only incrementally different from the information they already possess, and that therefore supports their established position.

Cognitive dissonance theory explains why managers tend to misinterpret the real threats facing an organization and attempt to muddle through even when it is clear to many observers that the organization is in crisis. The operation of this cognitive bias might help account for the faulty learning and decisions of IBM's top managers during the 1980s. Whenever they received outside information suggesting that PC research was threatening the viability of mainframes, they discounted it and relied on information that they had generated to support their own view of mainframes. The desire to reduce cognitive dissonance pushes managers to adopt flawed incremental solutions.

Illusion of Control

Some people, like entrepreneurs, seem able to bear high levels of uncertainty; others prefer the security associated with working in established organizations. Regardless of one's tolerance for ambiguity, however, uncertainty is very stressful. When an organization's environment or future is uncertain, managers do not know whether they have made the right choices, and considerable organizational resources are often at stake. Research has shown that managers can reduce their level of stress about uncertainty by strengthening their perception that they are in control of a situation.[51] Belief in one's personal ability to control uncertainty can reduce the level of stress one feels. However, as a manager's perception of control increases, the cognitive bias known as "illusion of control" alters his or her perceptions.

Illusion of control
A cognitive bias that causes
managers to overestimate the
extent to which the outcomes of
an action are under their personal control.

Illusion of control is a cognitive bias that causes managers to overestimate the extent to which the outcomes of an action are under their personal control and the extent to which they possess the skills and abilities needed to manage uncertainty and complexity.[52] In uncertain situations in which their ability and competence are really being tested, managers may develop irrational beliefs about their personal ability to manage uncertainty. They may, for example, overestimate their ability to use their skills in new ventures and embark on a huge acquisition program. Soon, however, they encounter problems and realize that they lack the ability to manage the more complex organization effectively.

Very frequently, when top managers lose control, they try to centralize authority, in the mistaken belief that centralization will increase their control and allow them to turn the situation around. Because their perception of control is an illusion, the organizational crisis deepens. IBM, for example, finally established a PC division to produce and market personal computers. But the division never got the autonomy it needed to devise a strategy that would have allowed it to compete successfully with the clone makers and respond to the frequent price cutting and discounting characteristic of the personal computer industry. Managers in the PC division were constantly overseen by IBM's top managers, who believed that they alone had the ability to control the division's strategy. Because they were blinded by the illusion of control, no organizational learning took place; the PC division's managers were unable to respond quickly to the moves of its competitors and were unable to develop a long-term strategy to give the division a strong competitive advantage.

It is not uncommon for a strong CEO or the members of an entrenched top management team to develop the illusion that only they have the ability to manage the uncertainty facing the organization and to lead the organization to success, even when it is in crisis.

Frequency and Representativeness

Frequency
A cognitive bias that deceives people into assuming that extreme instances of a phenomenon are more prevalent than they really are.

Frequency and representativeness are tendencies that often lead people to misinterpret information.[53] **Frequency** is a cognitive bias that deceives people into assuming that extreme instances of a phenomenon are more prevalent than they really are. Suppose purchasing managers have had a particularly bad experience with a supplier that has been shipping them large quantities of defective goods. Because of severe manufacturing problems caused by the defective parts, the managers decide to sever relations with that supplier. The frequency bias may cause them to become very fearful of relying on other suppliers for their inputs. They may instead decide to vertically integrate their operations so that they control their inputs, even though vertical integration will increase costs. Although there is no rational reason to believe that a new supplier will be as bad as, or worse than, the rejected supplier, the managers jump to an expensive solution to avoid the risk, and faulty learning has occurred.

Representativeness
A cognitive bias that leads managers to form judgments based on small and unrepresentative samples.

Representativeness is a cognitive bias that leads managers to form judgments based on small and unrepresentative samples. Exposure to a couple of unreliable suppliers, for example, prompts managers to generalize and believe that all suppliers are untrustworthy and unreliable, again leading to faulty learning.

Frequency and representative biases can also work in the opposite direction. A company that has great success with a new product may come to believe that this product is the wave of the future and devote all its resources to developing a new product line for which there actually is little demand. FedEx, for example, believed that the demand for international express delivery would increase dramatically as companies became increasingly global. It came to this conclusion because it had been receiving more and more requests for international delivery. Federal Express thus decided to invest a huge amount of resources to buy and operate a fleet of planes and overseas facilities to handle global express delivery. The decision was a disaster. The volume of express packages shipped to Europe turned out to be only half of that shipped in the United States, and the cost of operating the new global structure was enormous. After major losses, Federal Express decided to form strategic alliances with foreign delivery companies to deliver the mail (rather than go it alone), and this new strategy has been successful. As this example shows, a bad decision can be made because a CEO and top management team overgeneralize from a limited range of knowledge and experience. The operation of many of these cognitive biases can be seen in the story of e-grocers (highlighted in the following organizational insight), some of the thousands of dot.com companies that failed because of their managers' mistaken beliefs about the ease of operating virtual companies and developing viable business models.

The potential uses of information technology and the Internet for improving responsiveness to customers became clear to companies in many industries in the late 1990s. One of these industries was the food delivery or supermarket industry. Entrepreneurs decided that developing an ordering system that allowed customers to use the Internet to order their food online and creating a production system to deliver the food to their homes had enormous potential. For example, virtual grocer Webvan raised more than $1 billion to develop both the information system and physical infrastructure of warehouses and hot and cold delivery trucks that it needed to deliver food to customers. Other competitors like GroceryWorks.com and Homegrocer.com made similar kinds of investments. These online stores did attract customers, and by 2000 they had more than $1 billion in sales.

Bricks-and-mortar (B&M) supermarkets like Kroger's, Albertson's, and Safeway watched with some trepidation as their online rivals developed and managed their operations. By 2001, the question of which operating model was going to be the most successful was settled when many of the online grocers like Webvan announced that they were going out of business because of mounting losses. Why?

First, the new e-grocers did not possess the experience and ability to master the complex inventory management, sourcing, transportation, distribution, warehousing, and logistics necessary to operate successfully in this market, unlike their well-established B&M rivals. Second, e-grocers had totally underestimated the problems and costs of operating the production and physical delivery service

necessary to get products to customers. The average cost of home delivery for Webvan and other grocers was around $30, a cost they could not pass on to the customers they were trying to attract.

Managers at the e-grocers had totally overestimated their ability to manage the value-chain activities necessary to get products to customers. In other words, they suffered from the illusion of control bias in believing they had the skills to manage what is a very complex organization. E-grocers had also totally underestimated the complexity of their operating environment because of their misplaced confidence in the power of the Internet. In retrospect it is clear that dot.com entrepreneurs had watched other start-ups and had suffered from the frequency and representativeness biases in overestimating how many of these start-ups were successes and how easy a virtual business model was to operate. It is also interesting that dot.com companies also rarely gave up the battle until their resources were completely exhausted and their stockholders would lend no new money because the value of their stock was plunging. This situation might be explained by the operation of the cognitive biases discussed here.

Today, the only online grocers that still exist are those like Peabody, which operate only in large cities like Chicago and Boston where there are millions of well-heeled customers, living in close proximity, who are willing to pay premium prices for home grocery delivery. The growing success of low-price grocer Wal-Mart against Kroger's and others suggests that this situation will not change in the near future.

Projection and Ego-Defensiveness

Projection
A cognitive bias that allows managers to justify and reinforce their own preferences and values by attributing them to others.

Projection is a cognitive bias that allows managers to justify and reinforce their own preferences and values by attributing them to others.[54] Suppose a top management team is dominated by managers who are threatened by a deteriorating economic situation and doubt their ability to manage it. Feeling threatened and powerless, the team may accuse other lower-level managers of being unable to control the situation or of lacking the ability or desire to do so. Thus, top managers project their own feelings of helplessness onto others and blame them. Obviously, when projection starts to operate, it can become self-reinforcing: Everybody blames everybody else, and the culture of the organization deteriorates.

Ego-defensiveness
A cognitive bias that leads managers to interpret events in such a way that their actions appear in the most favorable light.

Ego-defensiveness also affects the way managers interpret what is happening in the organization. **Ego-defensiveness** is a cognitive bias that leads managers to interpret events in such a way that their actions appear in the most favorable light. If an organization is employing more and more managers but profitability is not increasing, managers may emphasize that they are positioning the organization for future growth by putting in place the infrastructure to support future development, such as happened at Webvan and the other e-grocers. Ego-defensiveness results in little organizational learning, and faulty decision making ultimately leads to a manager's replacement or an organization's failure.

Escalation of Commitment

Escalation of commitment
A cognitive bias that leads managers to remain committed to a losing course of action and refuse to admit that they have made a mistake.

The bias toward escalation of commitment is another powerful cause of flawed learning and faulty decision making.[55] According to the Carnegie model of decision making, managers generate a limited number of alternative courses of action, from which they choose one that they hope will lead to a satisfactory (if not optimum) outcome. But what happens if they choose the wrong course of action and experience a negative outcome, such as when FedEx found itself losing enormous amounts of money as a result of its international express delivery venture? A logical response to a negative outcome would be a reevaluation of the course of action. Research, however, indicates that managers who have made an investment in a mistake tend to persist in the same behavior and increase their commitment to it, even though it is leading to poor returns and organizational ineffectiveness. **Escalation of commitment** is a cognitive bias that leads managers to remain committed to a losing course of action, and to refuse to admit that they have made a mistake, perhaps because of ego-defensiveness or because they are gripped by the illusion of control. In later decision making, they try to correct and improve on their prior (bad) decision rather than acknowledge that they have made a mistake and turn to a different course of action. At FedEx, for example, the CEO realized the error and quickly moved to redeploy resources to make the international express delivery venture viable, and he succeeded.

At IBM, by contrast, managers' commitment to mainframe computers escalated even though the market for mainframes was shrinking. Top managers at IBM refused to redeploy significant organizational resources to develop skills in servers and PCs. They continued to invest resources to improve mainframes and tried to maintain them as the technology of the future. IBM spent billions of dollars to improve the storage and information-processing capacity of mainframe computers instead of finding new ways to take advantage of IBM's skills and resources.

The bias toward escalation of commitment is clearly reinforced by an incrementalist approach to decision making. Managers prefer to modify existing decisions to make them fit better with new conditions rather than to work out new solutions. Although this method of decision making may work in stable environments, it is disastrous when technology or competition is rapidly changing.

The net effect of all of the cognitive biases is that managers lose their ability to see new problems or situations clearly and to devise new responses to new challenges—and the level of learning falls. The flawed decision making that results from these biases hampers an organization's ability to adapt and modify its environment. By hampering organizational learning, biased decision making threatens an organization's ability to grow and survive. What can an organization do to develop a less incremental and more unstructured approach to decision making? How can it make managers receptive to learning new solutions and to challenging the assumptions they use to make decisions? Nystrom and Starbuck argue that when organizational learning and decision making are seriously affected by out-of-date or wrong cognitive structures, only radical actions can correct the situation and bring the organization back on the path to success.[56] Research has suggested several steps that managers and organizations can take to raise the level of organizational learning and promote organizational change.

IMPROVING DECISION MAKING AND LEARNING

Organizational inertia and cognitive biases make it difficult to promote organizational learning and maintain the quality of organizational decision making over time. How can managers avoid using inappropriate routines, beliefs, and values to interpret and solve problems? There are several ways in which an organization can overcome the effect of cognitive biases and promote organizational learning and change. It can implement strategies for organizational learning, increase the breadth and diversity of the top management team, use devil's advocacy and dialectical inquiry to evaluate proposed solutions, utilize game theory, and develop a collateral organizational structure.

Strategies for Organizational Learning

Managers have to continuously unlearn old ideas and constantly test their decision-making skills by confronting errors in their beliefs and perceptions. Three ways in which they can stimulate the unlearning of old ideas (and the learning of new ones) are by listening to dissenters, by converting events into learning opportunities, and by experimenting.[57]

Listening to Dissenters

To improve the quality of decision making, top managers can make it their policy to surround themselves with people who hold different and often opposing points of view. They can try to collect new information to evaluate the new interpretations and alternatives generated by dissenters.

Unfortunately, research has shown that top managers do not listen carefully to their subordinates and tend to surround themselves with yes-men who distort the information they provide, enhancing good news and suppressing bad news.[58] Moreover, because of bounded rationality, managers may be reluctant to encourage dissent because dissent will increase the amount of information they have to process.

Converting Events into Learning Opportunities

Nystrom and Starbuck discuss one unidentified company that appointed a "Vice President for Revolutions," whose job was to step in every four years and shake up the organization by transferring managers and reassigning responsibilities so that old, taken-for-granted routines were reexamined and people could bring new points of view to various situations. It did not make much difference what specific changes were made. The objective was to make them large enough so that people were forced to make new interpretations of situations. After each shake-up, productivity increased for two years and then declined for the next two, until the organization was shaken up again.[59]

More generally, an organization needs to design and manage its structure and culture—in ways that were discussed earlier—so that managers are motivated to find new or improved responses to a situation. Total quality management, for example, is based on the idea of making people responsible for continuously reexamining their jobs to see whether improvements that result in increased quality and productivity can be made. Similarly, as noted earlier, different kinds of organizational structure (for example, mechanistic or organic) can encourage or discourage organizational learning.

An interesting study conducted in California when hospitals were jolted by a doctor's strike shows the influence of organizational culture in decision making. The study found that responses by hospitals to this crisis were strongly influenced by the way in which each hospital typically made decisions in uncertain situations.[60] Hospitals that had organic structures characterized by decentralized decision making and that frequently redesigned their structures were accustomed to both learning and unlearning. As a result, these hospitals dealt with the strike much better than did hospitals with centralized, mechanistic structures and a formalized, programmed approach to decision making.

Experimenting

To encourage explorative learning, organizations must encourage experimenting, the process of generating new alternatives and testing the validity of old ones. Experimenting can be used to improve both incremental and garbage can decision-making processes. To test new ways of behaving, such as new ways to serve customers or to manufacture a product, managers can run experiments that deviate only slightly from what the organization is currently doing. Or, taking a garbage can approach, managers can brainstorm and come up with new solutions that surprise even themselves. Managers who are willing to experiment avoid overcommitment to previously worked-out solutions, reduce the likelihood of misinterpreting a situation, and can learn from their failures.

Utilizing Game Theory

As we have already discussed, organizations are in a constant competitive struggle with rivals in their industry to secure scarce resources. In understanding the dynamics of decision making between competitors in the environment, a useful tool that can help managers improve decision making and enhance learning is *game theory,* in which interactions between organizations are viewed as a competitive game. If companies understand the nature of the competitive game they are playing, they can often make better decisions that increase the likelihood of their obtaining scarce resources.[61]

From a game theory perspective, companies in an industry can be viewed as players that are all simultaneously making choices about which decisions to make to maximize their effectiveness. Managers must examine the potential effectiveness of each decision that they make. The value they get from making a certain choice—the payoff—varies depending on the strategies that rivals select. There are two basic types of game—sequential move games and simultaneous move games. In a *sequential move game,* such as chess, players move in turn, and one player can select a strategy to pursue after considering its rival's choice of strategies. In a *simultaneous move game,* the players act at the same time, in ignorance of their rival's current actions.

In the environment both sequential and simultaneous move games are commonplace, as managers compete for scarce resources. Indeed, game theory is particularly useful in analyzing situations where a company is competing against a limited number of rivals in its domain and they are highly interdependent—something very common in most environments. In such a setting, the value that can be created by making a certain choice—for example, to pursue a low-cost or differentiation strategy—depends critically on the strategies pursued by rivals. The basic principles that underlie game theory can be useful in determining which choices to make and strategies to select to manage the environment.

A fundamental premise of game theory is that, when making decisions, managers need to think in two related ways. First, they need to look forward, think ahead, and anticipate how rivals will respond to competitive moves. Second, managers need to reason backward to determine which moves their company should currently pursue, given their assessment of how rivals will respond to various future moves. If managers do both these things, they should be able to make the decision that will lead to the best choice—to make the move that will lead to the greatest potential returns. This cardinal principle of game theory is known as *look forward and reason back;* to understand its importance, consider this scenario.

UPS and FedEx, which specialize in the next-day delivery of packages, dominate the U.S. air express industry. They have very high costs because they need to invest in a nationwide, capital-intensive network of aircraft, trucks, and package-sorting facilities. For these companies, the key to increasing their effectiveness is to attract more customers, growing volume so that they can reduce the average cost of transporting each package. Suppose a manager at UPS calculates that if UPS cuts prices for their next-day delivery service by 10%, the volume of packages they ship will grow by over 25%, and so will UPS's total revenues and profits. Is this a smart choice? The answer depends upon whether the manager has remembered to look forward and reason back and think through how FedEx would respond to UPS's price cuts.

Because UPS and FedEx are competing directly against each other, their choices are interdependent. If UPS cuts prices, FedEx will lose market share; its volume of shipments will decline; and its profits will suffer. FedEx is unlikely to accept this. Rather, if UPS cuts prices by 10%, FedEx is likely to follow, make the same choice, and cut its prices by 10% to hold onto its customers. The net result is that the average level of prices in the industry will fall by 10%, as will revenues; both players will see their profits decline, and the environment will become poorer. To avoid this situation, and make better decisions, managers need always to look forward and reason back—an important principle of learning.

Decision trees can be used to help in the process of looking forward and reasoning back. Figure 12.4 maps out the decision tree for the simple game analyzed here from the perspective of UPS. (Note that this is a sequential move game.) UPS moves first, and then FedEx must decide how to respond. You will see that UPS has to choose between two strategies: cutting prices by 10% or leaving them unchanged. If it leaves prices unchanged, it will continue to earn its current level of profitability, which is $100 million. If it cuts prices by 10% one of two things can happen—FedEx matches the price cut, or FedEx leaves its prices unchanged. If FedEx matches UPS's price cut (FedEx decides to fight a price war), profits are competed away and UPS's profit will be $0. If FedEx does not respond, however, and leaves its prices unaltered, UPS will gain market share and its profits will rise to $300 million. So the best pricing strategy for UPS to pursue depends upon its assessment of FedEx's likely response.

You will note that Figure 12.4 assigns probabilities to the different responses from FedEx, specifically there is a 75% chance that FedEx will match UPS's price cut and a 25% chance that it will do nothing. These probabilities come from each company's assessment of the other's likely decision, based on their past history of making decisions in the environment—from looking at the history of FedEx's responses to UPS's price moves and vice versa. Although both sets of managers cannot calculate exactly what the profit impact and probabilities would be, they can make an informed decision by collecting information and devoting resources to learning about their rivals and about the environment. This illustrates a second basic principle of game theory: Know thy rivals! To improve learning, managers must put themselves in the position of a rival to answer the question of how that rival is likely to act in a particular situation. If a company's managers are to be effective at looking forward and reasoning back, they must have a good understanding of what their rival is likely to do under different scenarios, and they need to be able to extrapolate their rival's future behavior based on this understanding.

Nature of the Top Management Team

The way the top management team is constructed and the type of people who are on it affect the level of organizational learning.[62] There are various ways to construct a

Figure 12.4
A Decision Tree for UPS's Pricing Strategy

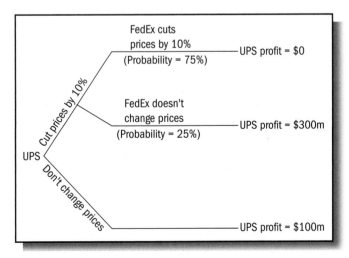

Figure 12.5
Types of Top-Management Teams

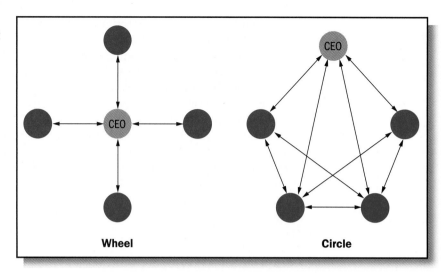

top management team, and each has different implications for the processing of information, organizational learning, and the quality of decision making.[63] Figure 12.5 shows two top management configurations, each of which has different implications for the level of learning taking place. In the wheel configuration, organizational learning is decreased because managers from the different functions report separately to the CEO. Rather than coordinate their own actions as a team, they send all information to the CEO, who processes this information, arrives at a decision, and communicates the decision back to the top managers. Research suggests that the wheel works best when problems are simple and require minimal coordination among top team members.[64] When problems are complex and nonprogrammed decision making is required, the wheel configuration slows organizational learning because all coordination takes place through the CEO.

In the circle configuration, top managers from different functions interact with each other and with the CEO. That is, they function as a team—something that promotes team and organizational learning. Research has suggested that the circle works best for complex problems requiring coordination among group members to arrive at a solution. The circle design solves complex problems much more quickly than the wheel arrangement: Communication around the circle takes less time because there is more opportunity for team and organizational learning between all top managers.[65]

The level and quality of organizational learning and decision making by the top management team is also a function of the personal characteristics and backgrounds of team members.[66] An organization that draws its top management team from many different industries and different functional backgrounds can promote organizational learning and decision making. Diversity in the top management team also exposes managers to the implications and consequences of many alternative courses of action. Such exposure may cause managers to examine their own expectations and assumptions more closely.

At IBM, for example, members of the top management team had been promoted from within the organization. There were no outsiders to propose credible alternative courses of action and thus force IBM's top managers to examine their assumptions. By contrast, Coca-Cola was concerned that its top managers' lack of international experience could hurt the organization's emerging global strategy. To provide new direction, many overseas-born managers were appointed to its top management team; one of them, Roberto Goizueta, was once its CEO.

It has been found that the most learning takes place when there is considerable heterogeneity among team members and when managers from different functions have an opportunity to express their views. When managers bring different information and viewpoints to bear on a problem, the organization can avoid

groupthink, the conformity that emerges when like-minded people reinforce one another's tendencies to interpret events and information in similar ways.[67] It has also been found that top management teams function most effectively when their membership is stable and there is not too much entry into or departure from the team.[68] When team membership is stable, group cohesiveness increases and promotes communication among members and improved decision making.[69]

Designing and managing the top management team to promote organizational learning is a vital task for a CEO.[70] Often, an organization picks as CEO the person who has the functional and managerial background needed to deal with the most pressing issues facing the organization. Caterpillar, GM, and Ford all picked as CEOs managers who had extensive experience in international business because the organizations' major problems all centered on the challenge of meeting global competition.[71]

Sometimes the only way to promote organizational learning is to change the CEO or the top management team. Although an organization might retain the rare top manager who has dissented from prevailing beliefs and perceptions, removing top managers can be the quickest way to erase organizational memory and programmed decision making, so that the organization can develop new routines. Thus, for example, HP's board of directors ousted Carly Fiorino in 2005 and installed Mark Hurd, who had no previous experience in the computer industry, as CEO. The board's rationale seemed to be that HP needed a new person with new views and new solutions to improve profitability.

Persuasive Communication

In organizations, a major means of promoting learning is through employing persuasive communication. **Persuasive communication** is the attempt by one person or group to transmit and share information with another person or group to get the latter to understand, agree with, and work to achieve new and challenging objectives. For persuasive communication to be effective, it is often necessary to frame or "package" information in ways that influence other people to accept or believe in it. Some of the most important situations in which there is a need for persuasive communication arise when one party lacks any authority to influence the other party. For example, managers in one department often need to influence managers from other departments but have *no* authority over them; they have to persuade and convince managers in the other function to follow or adopt their goals or objectives. Similarly, an employee who works in a group may sometimes wish to influence coworkers to follow new ideas but lack authority over them.

There are many issues involved in developing a competency in persuasive communication to promote organizational learning. Five factors determine how persuasive a message will be: the characteristics of the sender, active listening, the content of the message, the medium or channel through which it is sent, and finally the characteristics of the receiver.

Characteristics of the Sender

Messages are always more persuasive when they are sent by people who are *credible*, meaning that the receiver believes that the sender occupies a job position that gives them access to accurate information about work issues or objectives. Leaders are credible because they have formal authority; they may also possess expert and/or referent power and use this power to influence others. Other factors that promote credibility are moral integrity and emotional intelligence. If the receiver believes the sender is an honest, trustworthy person, they are more likely to believe the information they receive is accurate or true.

Often, people able to persuade and influence others possess good speaking and listening skills. When speaking, they don't speak too quickly, and they marshal their arguments logically—they know how to use every word to effect. Often, they will return to the same important points time and time again to ensure the key facts are not only being communicated but also emphasized and made significant. Persuasive speakers invite questions to clarify issues and generate interest and support for their ideas. They use their personal qualities to "emotionally charge" their words to convince their listeners that theirs is the *right* approach to solving a problem, that they *know* what they are doing, and that their plan will *succeed*.

Active Listening

Effective senders and receivers also need to be good listeners, and "active listening" is an important ingredient of persuasive communication. Persuasive senders need to actively listen to see how their arguments are being received, and then they can clarify issues and add information to get their points across. Active listeners also avoid interrupting and maintain their interest in what the other party is saying. They give the other party time to frame their thoughts and get to the punch line. People who interrupt and finish the others person's sentences for them often miss the real intentions behind the other's words and message because they put their own view of the situation first.

Content of the Message

The content of the message, that is, the nature of the information and arguments it contains, will also influence the learning process. The receiver of a message is always evaluating the meaning and implications of the information they are being given; they may be looking for the theme behind the information or looking for ambiguities or inconsistencies in the arguments. A competent sender knows this and is careful not to offer the receiver a one-sided or incomplete account of why some issue is important. The sender needs to present all sides of an argument, even those that seem to go against their position, to increase their credibility. At the same time, they always shift back to their major theme, using a few strong arguments to persuade and win over the receiver and promote learning.

Method of Communication

In general, face-to-face communication and telephone conversations are most appropriate for persuasive communication; formal written letters, memos, and email are best suited for conveying detailed, factual information that requires time and effort to digest and act on. Thus, both kinds are necessary to further the organizational learning process. In practice, written methods are more commonly used at the beginning of the learning process when managers and employees collect the information needed to decide how to respond to some new development, such as a change in the environment. The sender and receiver share this information and use it to persuade the other about the best course of action to pursue. In the hours or days before a final decision is made, however, the sender and receiver resort to a more face-to-face persuasive approach; they begin to exchange fewer emails and they increasingly pick up the telephone. Depending on the complexity of the issue or the level of disagreement between them, face-to-face meetings now become the preferred method of communication: Face-to-face meetings allow for the processing of the most information, both logical and emotional, to make the optimum decision.

People who are competent in persuasive communication have a good understanding of the implications of using these different methods. They know when and when not to send an email; when it is time to make a phone call; and when it is vital to knock on the other person's door. Former President Lyndon Johnson was a master at persuasive communication. To influence senators to vote for his bills, he would first send his aides to persuade them and give them written information. Later, he would call them on the telephone to discuss the issues and further his case. Then, in the days and hours before the final vote on a bill he would charge down to Congress, locate the swing-vote senators, and literally push them against the wall or into a corner. There he would put his hands on their shoulders, squeeze their arms, put his face close to theirs, and either cajole or threaten them until they were persuaded to do what he wanted! This physical approach is very common among powerful people, or people who know how to get their way.

Characteristics of the Receiver

Because in any learning situation a receiver, upon replying, becomes a sender, much of the previous discussion is also applicable to the sender as well. Receivers, for example, can learn to develop their credibility, use their emotional intelligence, and select the best method to transmit a message back to the sender. In addition, however, there are certain characteristics of the receiver that are relevant in persuasive communication.

First, receivers who are themselves highly competent and have high self-esteem are less likely to be taken in or swayed by logical or emotional information and arguments they believe are flawed. They find it easier to "cut through the chaff" and go to the heart of an issue to determine if, for example, the sender is acting to further their own personal interests or in a way that will benefit their department or company. The receiver can then decide on what is the most appropriate way to react to the sender's message. Second, people with high self-esteem are very useful to have around because they are frequently the ones who *will* challenge the ideas or suggestions of others or a leader, when they sense those ideas are flawed. Such people act as devil's advocates.

Devil's Advocacy and Dialectical Inquiry

Devil's advocate
A person who is responsible for critiquing ongoing organizational learning.

A **devil's advocate** is a person who is willing to stand up and question the beliefs of more powerful people, resists influence attempts, and who works to convince others that new ideas or plans may be flawed or wrong and harmful. Devil's advocacy and a related technique, dialectical inquiry, are ways of overcoming cognitive biases and promoting organizational learning.[72] Figure 12.6 shows how these strategies differ from one another and from the rational approach to decision making. The goal of both is to improve decision making.

An organization that uses devil's advocacy institutionalizes dissent by assigning a manager or management team the role of devil's advocate. The devil's advocate is responsible for critiquing ongoing organizational learning and for questioning the assumptions the top management team uses in the decision-making process. 3M

Figure 12.6
How Devil's Advocacy and Dialectical Inquiry Alter the Rational Approach to Decision Making

Devil's advocacy and dialectical inquiry improve decision making by making managers aware of several possible solutions to a problem and by encouraging the analysis of the pros and cons of each proposed solution before a final decision is made.

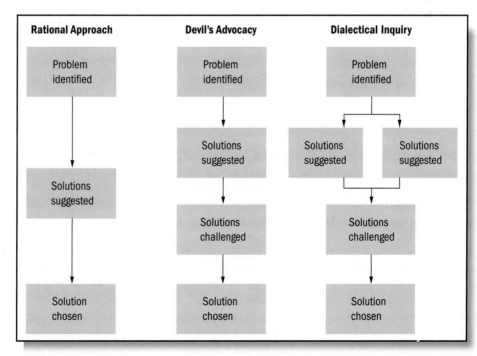

makes excellent use of devil's advocacy. At 3M, product managers submit proposals for a new product to a product development committee composed of top managers. The committee acts as devil's advocate. It critiques the proposal and challenges assumptions (such as the estimated size of the market for the product or its cost of manufacturing) in order to improve the plan and verify its commercial viability. 3M directly attributes its product development successes to the use of devil's advocacy.

An organization that uses dialectical inquiry creates teams of decision makers. Each team is instructed to generate and evaluate alternative scenarios and courses of action and then recommend the best one. After hearing each team's alternatives, all of the teams and the organization's top managers sit down together to cull the best parts of each plan and synthesize a final plan that offers the best chance of success.

Collateral Organizational Structure

Finally, an organization can attempt to improve learning and decision making by establishing a *collateral organizational structure*—that is, an informal organization of managers that is set up parallel to the formal organizational structure to "shadow" the decision making and actions of managers in the formal organization.[73] Managers in the formal structure know that their decisions are being evaluated by others and become used to examining the assumptions that they use to test alternatives and arrive at a solution. An organization establishes a collateral structure to improve the organization's ability to learn and adjust to new situations, and to enhance its ability to make decisions in an unstructured way. A collateral organizational structure allows an organization to maintain its capacity for change at the same time that it maintains its stability.

MANAGERIAL IMPLICATIONS

DECISION MAKING AND LEARNING

1. Try to guard against blindness and rigidity in decision making, be on the lookout for new problems, and be open to new solutions.
2. Develop a questioning attitude, and never discount warnings that problems are impending.
3. Analyze the cognitive structures through which you and your subunit define problems. Question whether these beliefs or values reflect the realities of the situation.
4. Examine your decision making to determine whether cognitive biases are affecting the quality of your decisions.
5. To protect the quality of your decision making, develop strategies to enhance organizational learning. For example, listen to your opponents, experiment with new solutions, encourage diversity, and use dialectical inquiry.

SUMMARY

The problems that many established companies encounter are a warning about the need to encourage organizational learning so that organizations have the ability to continuously adapt to and modify their environments. Strategy and structure are the tools that an organization uses to fashion its future; the decisions about strategy and structure that an organization makes now will determine its fate years from now. Too often, managers view strategy and structure as given and unchangeable and not as things to be experimented with and altered to move the organization forward. When strategy and structure are seen as something to be protected or hidden behind, they become a source of organizational inertia that eventually may bring an organization to its knees. Managers need to understand the way in which an organization's current strategy and structure can constrain organizational learning, and they need to understand how cognitive biases can affect learning and distort the decision-making process. Chapter 12 has made the following main points:

1. Organizational decision making is the process of responding to a problem by searching for and

selecting a solution or course of action that will create value for organizational stakeholders.

2. Managers make two basic types of decisions: programmed and nonprogrammed. Programmed decisions provide an organization with stability and increase efficiency. Nonprogrammed decisions allow an organization to adapt to changes in its environment and find solutions to new problems.

3. The rational model of decision making outlines how decision making takes place when there is no uncertainty. It ignores the effects of information costs and managerial costs.

4. Newer models of decision making recognize the effects of uncertainty, information, bounded rationality, satisficing, and bargaining by coalitions on the decision-making process. The Carnegie, incrementalist, unstructured, and garbage can models provide a more realistic picture of how organizational decision making takes place.

5. Organizational learning is the process through which managers seek to improve organization members' desire and ability to understand and manage the organization and its environment so that they can make decisions that continuously raise organizational effectiveness. There are two main kinds of learning—explorative and exploitative—and both are necessary to raise the quality of decision making.

6. The routines and procedures that an organization uses to make programmed decisions can cause organizational inertia. When programmed decision making drives out nonprogrammed decision making, the level of organizational learning drops. To encourage organizational learning, managers can act at the individual, group, organizational, and interorganizational levels.

7. Information technology and knowledge management systems can be developed to improve decision making and enhance organizational learning. The two main approaches to knowledge management are codification and personalization.

8. Cognitive structures (sets of interrelated beliefs, preferences, expectations, and values) affect the way managers interpret the problems facing an organization and shape the way they make decisions.

9. Cognitive biases may distort the way managers process information and make decisions. Common cognitive biases include cognitive dissonance, the illusion of control, frequency and representativeness, projection and ego-defensiveness, and escalation of commitment.

10. There are several ways in which an organization can counter the effect of cognitive biases and raise the level of learning and decision making. It can implement strategies for organizational learning, use game theory, increase the breadth and diversity of the top management team, use devil's advocacy and dialectical inquiry to evaluate proposed solutions, and develop a collateral organizational structure.

DISCUSSION QUESTIONS

1. What are the critical differences between the rational and the Carnegie approaches to decision making? What are the critical differences between the incrementalist and the garbage can models? Which models best describe how decision making takes place in (a) a fast-food restaurant and (b) the research and development laboratory of a major drug company?

2. What is organizational learning? In what ways can managers promote the development of organizational learning by acting at various levels in the organization? By using knowledge management?

3. How can knowledge management promote organizational learning? What determines which kind of knowledge management system a company should adopt?

4. How do cognitive biases affect organizational learning and the quality of decision making? What can be done to reduce their negative impact?

ORGANIZATIONAL THEORY IN ACTION

Practicing Organizational Theory: Store Learning

Form groups of three to five people and discuss the following scenario:

You are a group of top managers of a major clothing store, and you are facing a crisis. Your establishment has been the leading clothing store in your city for the last 15 years. In the last three years, however, two other major clothing store chains have opened up, and they have steadily been luring away your customers—your sales are down 30%. To find out why, you have been surveying some of your former customers and have learned that they perceive, for whatever reason, that your store is just not keeping up with changing fashion trends and new forms of customer service. In examining how your store operates, you have come to realize that over time the 10 buyers who purchase the clothing and accessories for your store have been buying increasingly from the same set of clothing suppliers; they have become reluctant to try new ones. Moreover, your salespeople rarely, if ever, make suggestions for changing the way your store operates. Your goal is to shake up store employees and improve store performance.

1. Devise a program to increase the level of organizational learning.
2. In what specific ways can you promote the level of learning at all levels?

Making the Connection #12

Find an example of an organization that has been using information technology to change the way it makes decisions or increase its level of learning. Why is the organization making these changes? What is it doing to stimulate new learning?

The Ethical Dimension #12

Managers' desire or willingness to act ethically and make ethical decisions can be affected by any cognitive biases that are operating in a particular context.

1. Discuss how the various cognitive biases can lead managers to behave unethically. Do you see any theme or pattern in how these biases operate on ethics?

2. Which kinds of techniques or tools discussed in this chapter can be best used to combat the problem of cognitive biases?

Analyzing the Organization: Design Module #12

This module focuses on organizational decision making and learning and on the way your company has changed its strategy and structure over time.

Assignment

1. Given the pattern of changes your organization has made to its strategy and structure over time, which of the decision-making models best characterizes the way it makes decisions?
2. At what hierarchical level does responsibility for non-programmed decision making seem to lie in your organization? What problems do you see with the way your company makes decisions?
3. Characterize your organization's ability to learn over time. Evaluate its capacity to adapt itself to and modify the environment.
4. Can you pinpoint any cognitive biases that may have affected the way managers made decisions or influenced their choice of strategy or structure? What was the effect of these cognitive biases?

CASE FOR ANALYSIS

Encouraging Learning at Baxter International

Baxter International is a global health-care products company. In the 1990s, Baxter, like other health-care companies, enjoyed annual growth rates of over 20%. In such a rich environment, top managers had been happy to decentralize decision-making authority to the heads of the various divisions and let managers in these divisions decide how to allocate funds to promote specific research and development projects. Managers in each division were also rewarded on the basis of the performance of their individual divisions. As a result of these factors, they confined their energies to their division and did not take a company-wide view.

The problems with such a division-focused approach to decision making became obvious in the late 1990s when the global health-care environment became very competitive because of a combination of factors such as cheap generic drugs; the emergence of powerful buyers, such as HMOs, who demanded lower prices; and increased competition from new biotechnology companies. All these factors put pressure on health-care companies like Baxter to find ways both to reduce costs and to speed the rate of new product development, but it found it hard to respond.

The problem facing Baxter's CEO, Vernon R. Loucks, Jr., was how to stimulate organizational learning and increase the company managers' desire and ability to understand and manage the organization and its environment so that they could make the decisions that would continually raise organizational performance. Specifically, realizing that Baxter's main problem was that divisional managers only made decisions with their own division in mind, how could he get them to take an organization-wide view to encourage them to experiment with new ways of creating value?

Loucks decided on a radical move. To change the managers' mind-set, he would totally change the way they were rewarded. Instead of rewarding them based on the performance of their divisions, in the future they would be rewarded based upon an increase in the stock price of the whole company. Moreover, top managers would be required to buy seven times their annual salary in company stock, and middle managers would also be rewarded with stock options linked to company performance.[74]

The change in the reward system precipitated a complete change in managers' approach to decision making and learning. They began to experiment with new kinds of strategies and structures, and they started to take an organization-wide approach to decision making. At their regular meetings, divisional heads started to challenge each other's decisions and the assumptions on which the decisions were made. They also began to realize that each of them possessed a stock of knowledge that could be useful to the other divisions, and they now had the incentive (through the new reward system) to cooperate with other divisions to capitalize on that knowledge. Inside each division, and between divisions, employees started to become involved in teams to discuss these new ideas and develop new interdivisional projects. As a result, now when any manager makes a proposal to invest resources for a specific project, managers at all levels engage in a spirited debate and subject it to rigorous evaluations, since they see that their own "money" is at stake.

Baxter's managers' new "systems viewpoint" and their mind-set, which allows them to see the company and not just their individual divisions, have resulted in enormous synergies being reaped at Baxter as the divisions learn to share their skills and resources. The company's share price has increased, rewarding managers for their new approach and reinforcing their desires to further promote and develop the new learning approach.[75]

DISCUSSION QUESTIONS

1. What problems was Baxter International experiencing?
2. How did the company try to solve these problems?
3. How could it have made use of IT and knowledge management?

REFERENCES

1. H. A. Simon, *The New Science of Management Decision* (New York: Harper and Row, 1960), p. 206.
2. Ibid.
3. S. Keiser and L. Sproull, "Managerial Response to Changing Environments: Perspectives on Sensing from Social Cognition," *Administrative Science Quarterly, 27* (1982), 548–570; G. T. Allison, *The Essence of Decision* (Boston: Little, Brown, 1971).
4. Simon, *The New Science of Management Decision.*
5. H. A. Simon, *Administrative Behavior* (New York: Macmillan, 1945).
6. Ibid.; J. G. March and H. A. Simon, *Organizations* (New York: Wiley, 1958).
7. J. G. March, "Bounded Rationality, Ambiguity, and the Engineering of Choice," *Bell Journal of Economics, 9* (1978), 587–608.
8. J. G. March, "Decision Making Perspective," in A. Van De Ven and W. Joyce, eds., *Perspectives on Organizational Design and Behavior* (New York: Wiley, 1981), pp. 205–252.
9. Simon, *Administrative Behavior.*
10. R. M. Cyert and J. G. March, *A Behavioral Theory of the Firm* (Upper Saddle River, NJ: Prentice Hall, 1963).
11. P. D. Larkey and L. S. Sproull, *Advances in Information Processing in Organizations,* vol. 1 (Greenwich, CT: JAI Press, 1984), pp. 1–8.
12. March and Simon, *Organizations.*
13. H. A. Simon, *Models of Man* (New York: Wiley, 1957); A. Grandori, "A Prescriptive Contingency View of Organizational Decision Making," *Administrative Science Quarterly, 29* (1984), 192–209.
14. Simon, *The New Science of Management Decision.*
15. H. A. Simon, "Making Management Decisions: The Role of Intuition and Emotion," *Academy of Management Executives, 1* (1987), 57–64.
16. Cyert and March, *A Behavioral Theory of the Firm.*
17. Ibid.
18. Z. Schiller, "GE's Appliance Park: Rewire, or Pull the Plug?" *Business Week,* February 8, 1993, p. 30.
19. J. Ward, "GE Center Makes Things Fail So It Can Make Them Better," *The Courier Journal,* September 12, 1999, p. 1.
20. www.ge.com, 2005.
21. C. E. Lindblom, "The Science of Muddling Through," *Public Administration Review, 19* (1959), pp. 79–88.
22. Ibid., p. 83.
23. H. Mintzberg, D. Raisinghani, and A. Theoret, "The Structure of Unstructured Decision Making," *Administrative Science Quarterly, 21* (1976), 246–275.
24. Ibid., p. 257.
25. M. D. Cohen, J. G. March, and J. P. Olsen, "A Garbage Can Model of Organizational Choice," *Administrative Science Quarterly, 17* (1972), 1–25.
26. Ibid.
27. G. P. Huber, "Organizational Learning: The Contributing Processes and the Literature," *Organizational Science, 2* (1991), 88–115.
28. B. Hedberg, "How Organizations Learn and Unlearn," in W. H. Starbuck and P. C. Nystrom, eds., *Handbook of Organizational Design,* vol. 1 (New York: Oxford University Press, 1981), pp. 1–27.
29. P. M. Senge, *The Fifth Discipline: The Art and Practice of the Learning Organization* (New York: Doubleday, 1990).
30. J. G. March, "Exploration and Exploitation in Organizational Learning," *Organizational Science, 2* (1991), 71–87.
31. T. K. Lant and S. J. Mezias, "An Organizational Learning Model of Convergence and Reorientation," *Organizational Science, 5* (1992), 47–71.
32. M. Dodgson, "Organizational Learning: A Review of Some Literatures," *Organizational Studies, 14* (1993), 375–394.
33. A. S. Miner and S. J. Mezias, "Ugly Duckling No More: Pasts and Futures of Organizational Learning Research," *Organizational Science, 7* (1990), 88–99.
34. P. Senge, *The Fifth Discipline: The Art and Practice of the Learning Organization* (New York: Doubleday, 1990).
35. P. Senge, "The Leader's New Work: Building Learning Organizations," *Sloan Management Review* (Fall 1990), 7–23.
36. Miner and Mezias, "Ugly Ducking No More."
37. J. P. Kotter and J. L. Heskett, *Corporate Culture and Performance* (New York: The Free Press, 1992).
38. M. Dodgson, "Organizational Learning: A Review of Some Literatures.
39. A. Williams, "Arthur Andersen IT Initiatives Support Shifts in Business Strategy," *Information Week,* September 11, 2000, pp. 14–18.
40. T. Davenport and L. Prusak, *Information Ecology* (New York: Oxford University Press, 1997).
41. www.arthurandersen.com, 2000.
42. Williams, "Arthur Andersen," p. 172.
43. www.arthurandersen.com, 2000.
44. M.T. Hansen, N. Nohria, and T. Tierney, "What's Your Strategy for Managing Knowledge?" *Harvard Business Review* (March–April 1999), 3–19.
45. P. C. Nystrom and W. H. Starbuck, "To Avoid Organizational Crises, Unlearn," *Organizational Dynamics, 12* (1984), 53–65.
46. Y. Dror, "Muddling Through—Science or Inertia?" *Public Administration Review, 24* (1964), 103–117.
47. Nystrom and Starbuck, "To Avoid Organizational Crises, Unlearn."
48. S. T. Fiske and S. E. Taylor, *Social Cognition* (Reading, MA: Addison-Wesley, 1984).
49. See G. R. Jones, R. Kosnik, and J. M. George, "Internalization and the Firm's Growth Path: On the Psychology of Organizational Contracting," in R. W. Woodman and W. A. Pasemore, eds., *Research in Organizational Change and Development,* vol. 7 (Greenwich, CT: JAI Press, 1993), pp. 105–135, for an account of the biases as they operate during organizational growth and decline.
50. L. Festinger, *A Theory of Cognitive Dissonance* (Stanford, CA: Stanford University Press, 1957); E. Aaronson, "The Theory of Cognitive Dissonance: A Current Perspective," in L. Berkowitz, ed., *Advances in Experimental Social Psychology, 4* (1969), 1–34.

51. J. R. Averill, "Personal Control over Aversive Stimuli and Its Relationship to Stress," *Psychological Bulletin, 80* (1973), 286–303.

52. E. J. Langer, "The Illusion of Control," *Journal of Personality and Social Psychology, 32* (1975), 311–328.

53. A. Tversky and D. Kahneman, "Judgment Under Uncertainty: Heuristics and Biases," *Science, 185* (1974), 1124–1131.

54. R. De Board, *The Psychoanalysis of Organizations* (London: Tavistock, 1978).

55. B. M. Staw, "The Escalation of Commitment to a Course of Action," *Academy of Management Review, 6* (1978), 577–587; B. M. Staw and J. Ross, "Commitment to a Policy Decision: A Multi-Theoretical Perspective," *Administrative Science Quarterly, 23* (1978), 40–64.

56. Nystrom and Starbuck, "To Avoid Organizational Crises, Unlearn."

57. Ibid.

58. L. Porter and K. Roberts, "Communication in Organizations," in M. Dunnette, ed., *Handbook of Industrial and Organizational Psychology* (Chicago: Rand McNally, 1976).

59. Nystrom and Starbuck, "To Avoid Organizational Crises, Unlearn."

60. A. D. Meyer, "Adapting to Environmental Jolts," *Administrative Science Quarterly, 27* (1982), 515–537; A. D. Meyer, "How Ideologies Supplant Formal Structures and Shape Responses to Environments," *Journal of Management Studies, 7* (1982), 31–53.

61. For a basic introduction to game theory, see A. K. Dixit and B. J. Nalebuff, *Thinking Strategically* (London: WW Norton, 1991). Also see A. M. Brandenburger and B. J. Nalebuff, "The Right Game: Using Game Theory to Shape Strategy," *Harvard Business Review* (July–August 1995), 59–71; and D. M. Kreps, *Game Theory and Economic Modeling* (Oxford: Oxford University Press, 1990).

62. D. C. Hambrick, *The Executive Effect: Concepts and Methods for Studying Top Managers* (Greenwich, CT: JAI Press, 1988).

63. D. G. Ancona, "Top-Management Teams: Preparing for the Revolution," in J. S. Carroll, ed., *Applied Social Psychology and Organizational Settings* (Hillsdale, NJ: Lawrence Erlbaum Associates, 1990).

64. M. Shaw, "Communications Networks," in L. Berkowitz, ed., *Advances in Experimental Social Psychology*, vol. 1 (New York: Academic Press, 1964).

65. Ibid.

66. S. Finkelstein and D. C. Hambrick, "Top-Management Team Tenure and Organizational Outcomes: The Moderating Role of Managerial Discretion," *Administrative Science Quarterly, 35* (1990), 484–503.

67. I. L. Janis, *Victims of Groupthink*, 2e (Boston: Houghton Mifflin, 1982).

68. K. M. Eisenhardt and C. B. Schoonhoven, "Organizational Growth: Linking Founding Team, Strategy, Environment, and Growth Among U.S. Semiconductor Ventures, 1978–1988," *Administrative Science Quarterly, 35* (1990), 504–529; L. Keck and M. L. Tushman, "Environmental and Organizational Context and Executive Team Structure," *Academy of Management Journal, 36* (1993), 1314–1344.

69. A. J. Lott and B. E. Lott, "Group Cohesiveness and Interpersonal Attraction: A Review of Relationships with Antecedent and Consequent Variables," *Psychological Bulletin, 14* (1965), 259–309.

70. D. L. Helmich and W. B. Brown, "Successor Type and Organizational Change in the Corporate Enterprise," *Administrative Science Quarterly, 17* (1972), 371–381; D. C. Hambrick and P. A. Mason, "Upper Echelons: The Organization as a Reflection of Its Top Managers," *Academy of Management Journal, 9* (1984), 193–206.

71. R. F. Vancil, *Passing the Baton* (Boston: Harvard Business School Press, 1987).

72. C. Schwenk, "Cognitive Simplification Processes in Strategic Decision Making," *Strategic Management Journal, 5* (1984), 111–128.

73. D. Rubenstein and R. W. Woodman, "Spiderman and the Burma Raiders: Collateral Organization Theory in Practice," *Journal of Applied Behavioral Science, 20* (1984), pp. 1–21; G. R. Bushe and A. B. Shani, *Parallel Learning Structures: Increasing Innovations in Bureaucracies* (Reading, MA: Addison-Wesley, 1991).

74. V. R. Loucks, Jr., "Business World: An Equity Cure for Managers," *The Wall Street Journal*, September 26, 1995, p. 19.

75. "Baxter Receives the 'Grand Prix Quebecois de la Qualité,'" *Canada Newswire*, September 30, 1999, p. 1.

Chapter 13

Innovation, Intrapreneurship, and Creativity

Learning Objectives

As discussed in Chapter 10, innovation is one of the most important types of organizational change because it results in a continuing stream of new and improved goods and services that create value for customers and profit for a company. Indeed, one important way of assessing organizational effectiveness is the rate or speed at which a company can bring new products to market; this is a function of the level of intrapreneurship and creativity inside an organization.

After studying this chapter you should be able to:

1. Describe how innovation and technological change affect each other.

2. Discuss the relationship among innovation, intrapreneurship, and creativity.

3. Understand the many steps involved in creating an organizational setting that fosters innovation and creativity.

4. Identify the ways in which information technology can be used to foster creativity and speed innovation and new product development.

INNOVATION AND TECHNOLOGICAL CHANGE

Innovation
The process by which organizations use their skills and resources to develop new goods and services or to develop new production and operating systems so that they can better respond to the needs of their customers.

Innovation is the process by which organizations use their resources and competences to develop new or improved goods and services or to develop new production and operating systems so that they can better respond to the needs of their customers.[1] Innovation can result in spectacular success for an organization. Apple Computer changed the face of the computer industry when it introduced its personal computer; Honda changed the face of the small motorbike market when it introduced small 50cc motorcycles; Mary Kay cosmetics changed the nature of the way cosmetics are sold when it introduced its at-home cosmetics parties and personalized style of selling; Toyota revolutionized the car production system to increase product

366

quality; and Chrysler's adoption of a new operating system, the product team structure, was an innovation that many other companies have copied.

Although innovation brings about change, it is also associated with a high level of risk because the outcomes of research and development activities are often uncertain.[2] It has been estimated that only 12% to 20% of R&D projects result in products that get to market.[3] Thus, although innovation can lead to change of the sort that organizations want—the introduction of profitable new technologies and products—it can also lead to the kind of change that they want to avoid—technologies that are inefficient and products that customers don't want. (The way in which organizations can manage the innovation process to increase the chance of successful learning taking place is discussed in detail later in the chapter.)

In Chapter 9, technology is defined as the skills, knowledge, experience, body of scientific knowledge, tools, machines, and equipment that are used in the design, production, and distribution of goods and services. Technology is central to the operations and products of most organizations. Changes in technology are at the heart of the innovation process, and at present the world is characterized by a rapid rate of technological change.[4]

Generally speaking, there are two types of technological change: quantum change and incremental change. **Quantum technological change** refers to a fundamental shift in technology that revolutionizes products or the way in which they are produced. Recent examples of quantum changes in technology include the development of the first personal computers, which revolutionized the computer industry, and the development of genetic engineering techniques (biotechnology), which are promising to revolutionize the treatment of illness by replacing conventional pharmaceutical compounds with genetically engineered medicines. New products or operating systems that incorporate a quantum technological improvement are referred to as **quantum innovations**. The introduction in 1971 of Intel's 4004 microprocessor, the first "computer on a chip" ever produced, is an example of a quantum product innovation. Quantum innovations are likely to cause major changes in an environment and to increase uncertainty because they force organizations to change the way they operate.

Incremental technological change refers to technological change that represents a refinement of some base technology, and **incremental innovations** refer to products or operating systems that incorporate those refinements. For example, since 1971, Intel has produced a series of improvements in its original 4004 microprocessor. These subsequent improvements include the 8088, 8086, 286, 386, 486, and Pentium chips. Similarly, flexible manufacturing, robots, and TQM are examples of incremental innovations. They improved the quality of cars and forced U.S. carmakers to make major organizational changes in response to conditions in the new competitive environment.[5]

As one might expect, quantum innovations are relatively uncommon. As Philip Anderson and Michael Tushman note, "At rare and irregular intervals in every industry, innovations appear that command a decisive cost or quality advantage and that strike not at the margins of the profits and the outputs of existing firms, but at their foundations and their very lives."[6] Anderson and Tushman call these kinds of quantum innovations "technological discontinuities," and in their model of innovation, a technological discontinuity sets off an era of ferment (see Figure 13.1), where there is intense competition between companies in an industry to develop the design that will become the dominant model for others to copy—just as Intel's chips are the dominant design in the microprocessor industry.

After the dominant design emerges, the next period of the technology cycle involves an era of incremental change and innovation where companies compete to elaborate on the base technology. Most companies spend most of their time engaged in incremental product innovation. For example, every time a car company redesigns a basic model, it is engaged in incremental product innovation, but this is nevertheless a very competitive process. In 2001, for example, five models of hatchback cars were competing in the market. By 2002, all the major carmakers had sensed the

Quantum technological change
A fundamental shift in technology that revolutionizes products or the way they are produced.

Quantum innovations
New products or operating systems that incorporate quantum technological improvements.

Incremental technological change
Technological change that represents a refinement of some base technology.

Incremental innovations
Products or operating systems that incorporate refinements of some base technology.

Figure 13.1
The Technology Cycle

Source: "Technological Discontinuties and Dominant Designs: A Cyclical Model of Technological Change," by P. Anderson and M. L Tushman, published in *Administrative Science Quarterly*, 1990, 35. Reprinted by permission of *Administrative Science Quarterly* ©, 1990, Cornell University.

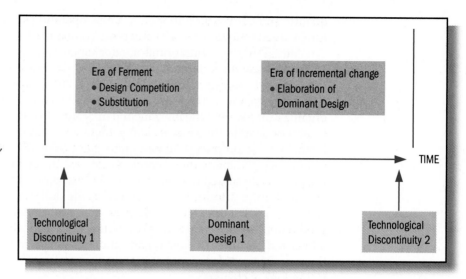

growing popularity of the hatchback car and 25 hatchback models were competing for the same customers.

Sometimes, a second technological discontinuity may occur, which starts the whole process again. For example, in 2002 Toyota announced the introduction of an emission-free new SUV that was powered by fuel-cell technology, which threatened to revolutionize the car industry. The only waste product the car produces is water. In the meantime, its hybrid technology, which also uses batteries to help power the engine, took off as gas prices soared in 2005. Also, in 2005 Honda announced it would begin to mass-produce fuel cells to power not only cars, but homes and businesses as well.

The innovations that result from quantum and incremental technological change are all around us. Microprocessors, wireless phones and personal digital assistants (PDAs), word-processing software, online information services, computer networks, camcorders, compact disc players, videocassette players, and the genetically engineered medicines produced by biotechnology either did not exist a generation ago or were considered to be exotic and expensive products. Now these products are commonplace, and they are being continually improved. Organizations whose managers helped develop and exploit these new technologies have often reaped enormous gains. They include many of the most successful and rapidly growing organizations today: Dell Computer, Microsoft, Intel, AOL, Cisco Systems, Motorola, Sony, Matsushita, and Amgen.

However, although some organizations have benefited from technological change, other have seen their markets threatened. The decline of mainframe and midrange computer companies such as IBM, and the failure of others such as DEC, Unisys, and Wang, is a direct reflection of the rise of the PC. Traditional telephone companies the world over have seen their market dominance threatened by companies offering wireless service, and the decline of once-dominant consumer electronics companies such as RCA can be directly linked to their failure to develop innovative products such as VCRs and compact disc players.

Technological change is thus both an opportunity and a threat—it is both creative and destructive.[7] It helps create new product innovations that managers and their organizations can exploit, but at the same time these new innovations can harm or even destroy demand for older, established products. Thus, for example, the development of the microprocessor by Intel has helped create a host of new product opportunities, including PCs, but at the same time it has destroyed demand for older products. Conventional typewriters, for instance, have been replaced by the combination of PCs and word-processing software—putting typewriter companies out of business in the process.

When a company's managers use its resources in an enterprising way, the result is a stream of innovations that create new and improved products and increase its profitability. Companies invest enormous amounts of money in research and development to develop innovative new products. It also costs a great deal to build new manufacturing facilities to make the products and to pay for the nationwide marketing campaign that will be necessary to attract customers.

It would hardly be fair or equitable if, after a company spends hundreds of millions of dollars on these activities, a competitor could just come along and piggyback on the company's innovations and begin to produce a copycat product. If it were easy to do such a thing, few companies would make the investment necessary to develop new products. Technological progress would fall and the standard of living in a society would advance little over time.

As Chapter 6 discusses, property rights give people and organizations the right to own and control productive resources and to profit from them. To motivate entrepreneurs and companies to take risks and invest in new ventures whose payoff is unknown, laws have been enacted to protect the profits that result from successful efforts to innovate or create new products. People and companies are given the legal property rights to own and protect their creations by the granting of patents, copyrights, and trademarks.

Patents give their owners the property right to use, control, license, and otherwise profit from their creation—a new product such as a door handle, machine, new drug, and so on for a period of 20 years from the date the patent is issued by the U.S. Patent Office. In other words, patents confer a monopoly right on their owner—the individual inventor or company that has conducted and paid for the research that led to the new product. One of the most profitable patents is that received by pharmaceutical companies that develop new drugs that better treat some illness or disease. Merck, the company that developed Prozac and Viagra, made billions from the sale of these drugs, for example. Once a patent has expired, however, any company can manufacture a copy of the original drug—a generic drug—which is sold at a much lower price than the patented drug. The monopoly profits of the company that invented the drug then disappear.

Copyrights, which confer a monopoly right on the owner, are typically granted to people who create intellectual property like written or visual works—books, video games, poems, and songs. The owner of the copyright can sell it to other individuals or companies; movie companies sometimes buy the rights to turn a book into a movie. Copyrights last for much longer periods than patents—often for the lifetime of the work's creator and beyond.

Currently, laws governing the length of copyrights are changing. Many believe that copyrights should be granted for much shorter periods, perhaps for just 20 years or the life of their creator. When a copyright expires, intellectual property enters the public domain and becomes a public good, meaning that anyone can make use of it at no cost.

To increase the benefits from their creations, innovators of new products and services are also given the legal right to the trademarks that they use to identify their products to customers. Trademarks are property rights to the name of a product (such as Nescafe or Ivory Soap), any symbols or logos associated with it, and the company that produces it (such as Nestlé or Procter & Gamble). Trademarks give the owner the sole legal right to use these names or symbols and control the uses to which these products are put, for example, advertising.

Because people and companies have to invest their creativity, time, and money to obtain copyrights and trademarks and develop a "brand name," it is only fair to allow them to benefit from the "identity" of their creations. Thus, J. K. Rowling, the creator of Harry Potter, holds the copyrights to her books, and she and her publishing company own the trademarks associated with the Harry Potter brand name. Nobody can issue Harry Potter toys or clothing without paying a licensing fee to them because they own the trademark—just as no company has the right to use another company's patent unless it pays to use it.

The law protects property and resources. The issue of who holds the rights to written resources in the digital age became a hotly debated topic in 2005, when Google announced its intention to scan millions of books and then make them available over the Web at no cost to users. Google quickly found itself embroiled in lawsuits with publishing companies that claimed Google was violating the copyrights to these works. How long an author, artist, or company should be able to claim copyright over intellectual property is a concern that the courts will have to resolve. The following organizational insight profiles the way the Rolling Stones developed a set of entrepreneurial skills to take advantage of their brand name and copyrights, which has made them the wealthiest rock band in the world.

The Product Life Cycle

When technology is changing, organizational survival requires that managers quickly adopt and apply new technologies to innovate new products. Managers who do not do so soon find that they have no market for their existing products—and

ORGANIZATIONAL INSIGHT 13.1
The Rolling Stones Are Not Gathering Moss

The Rolling Stones have been one of the world's leading rock bands since the early 1960s, when they burst onto the music scene as the "bad boys" of rock and roll. As with most rock groups in those days, they were an unproven product with no track record. Desperate to sign recording contracts, the Stones, like most early rock bands, found themselves in a weak bargaining position when dealing with record companies such as Decca, the company with which they initially signed. As a result, despite their enormous initial success they received a relatively small percentage of the profits that their best-selling records were generating. Later, when these contracts expired, the Rolling Stones were able to renegotiate contracts with record companies on their own terms because the Stones were world famous. They also used their fame to find new avenues for entrepreneurship.

Since 1989, the Stones, under the leadership of Mick Jagger, the CEO of Rolling Stones Inc., have based their business model on finding ways to use their product—their unique music and rock persona—to generate profit. Since 1989 the Stones have earned more than $1.5 billion in revenues; about $500 million has come from royalties earned on the sales of their records and songs. But, the incredible success of their world tours generated the remaining $1 billion from the ticket sales, merchandising, and company sponsorship associated with their tours. The way the Stones "create" their world tours shows how entrepreneurial they are.

It all began with the Steel Wheels tour in 1989 when, for the first time, the Stones, working with a Canadian promoter named Michael Cohl, took total control of all aspects of their tour. Before this, the Stones, like most rock bands, put together a schedule of cities to tour. They would then contact well-known promoters in those cities to take responsibility for staging the concert and selling tickets. The Stones would then receive a percentage of total concert revenues as their payment. With this business model, the promoters were taking away over 60% of total revenues. Cohl proposed a new model whereby he would assume responsibility for all 40 concert venues on the Steel Wheels tour and guarantee to pay the Stones $1 million per concert—a much larger amount than they had received in the past. Cohl felt he could do this because his approach cut out the profits earned by the promoters; he also would be able to negotiate merchandising contracts to promote Stones t-shirts, posters, and so on, and to get corporate sponsorship for the tour.

After they had played the first several venues, it became clear to Cohl that he was losing money on each one. To make the tour a success, they would *all* have to find new ways to cut costs and increase revenues. From this point on, the Stones became directly involved in every decision concerning staging, music, advertising and promotion, and even the price of concert tickets—which has shot up in every tour since Steel Wheels. The Stones, and particularly Jagger, faced a huge task in learning how to improve the concert tour business model, but they persevered and have continued to refine and develop their approach in every subsequent tour. In the end, the Steel Wheels tour made over $260 million, and the Stones made far more than the $40 million they were promised. In later tours from Packing Them In to the huge Voodoo tour in 1995, world revenues from concerts surged. Tickets for the Licks 2003 tour were priced from $50 to $350.

When Mick Jagger and Keith Richard, who are both now in their early 60s, were asked how long they planned to go on touring, their answer was "until we drop." In May 2005 they announced that the Stones would begin yet another tour starting in Boston in the fall. The Stones reinvent themselves on every tour as creative artists, and performing at the level expected of them calls for a new burst of enterprise every time they get on the stage.

destroy their organizations. Sony, for example, long the leader with its Walkman, suddenly lost its leading position in the music player business when Apple came along with its iPod players in 2004. The Rolling Stones release new records and tour often to keep their product current and fashionable.

The rate of technological change in an industry—and particularly the length of the product life cycle—determines how important it is for managers to innovate. This is especially true when copyrights and patents do not stop rivals from introducing their own version of a product, such as Sony's new range of digital music players to compete with the iPod or the emergence of rap bands like the Black Eyed Peas to compete with the music made by the Stones.

Product life cycle
The changes in demand for a product that occur over time.

The **product life cycle** reflects the changes in demand for a product that occur over time.[8] Demand for most successful products passes through four stages: the embryonic stage, growth, maturity, and decline. In the *embryonic stage* a product has yet to gain widespread acceptance; customers are unsure what the product has to offer, and demand for it is minimal. If a product does become accepted by customers (and many do not), demand takes off, and the product enters its growth stage. In the *growth stage* many consumers are entering the market and buying the product for the first time; demand increases rapidly. This is the stage that PDAs, such as iPods and Palm Pilots, are currently in. The growth stage ends and the *mature stage* begins when market demand peaks because most customers have already bought the product (there are relatively few first-time buyers left). At this stage demand is typically replacement demand. In the car market, for example, most cars are bought by people who already have a car and are either trading up or replacing an old model. Products such as wireless telephones, PCs for home use, and online information services are also currently in this stage. The *decline stage* follows the mature stage if and when demand for a product falls. Falling demand often occurs because a product has become technologically obsolescent and superseded by a more advanced product. For example, demand for every generation of VCR, CD, or DVD falls as they are superseded by newer, technically advanced models with more features.

Rate of Technological Change

One of the main determinants of the length of a product's life cycle is the rate of technological change.[9] Figure 13.2 illustrates the relationship between the rate of technological change and the length of product life cycles. In some industries—such as PCs, semiconductors, and disk drives—technological change is rapid and product life

Figure 13.2
Technological Change and Length of the Product Life Cycle

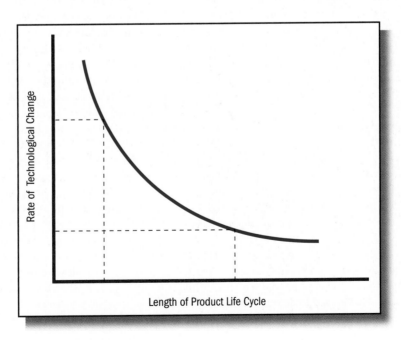

Rate of Technological Change (vertical axis)

Length of Product Life Cycle (horizontal axis)

cycles are very short. For example, technological change is so rapid in the computer disk drive industry that a disk drive model becomes technologically obsolete about 12 months after introduction. The same is true in the PC industry, where product life cycles have shrunk from three years during the late 1980s to a few months today.

In other industries the product life cycle is somewhat longer. In the car industry, for example, the average product life cycle is about five years. The life cycle of a car is so short because fairly rapid technological change is producing a continual stream of incremental innovations in car design, such as the introduction of door airbags, advanced electronic microcontrollers, plastic body parts, and more fuel-efficient engines. In contrast, in many basic industries where the pace of technological change is slower, product life cycles tend to be much longer. In steel or electricity, for example, change in product technology is very limited, and products such as steel girders and electrical cable can remain in the mature stage indefinitely.

Role of Fads and Fashion

Fads and fashion are important determinants of the length of product life cycles.[10] A 5-year-old car design is likely to be technologically outmoded and look out of date and thus lose its attractiveness to customers. Similarly, in the restaurant business, the demand for certain kinds of food changes rapidly. The Cajun or Southwest cuisine popular one year may be history the next as Caribbean fare becomes the food of choice. Fashion considerations are even more important in the high-fashion end of the clothing industry, where last season's clothing line is usually out of date by the next season, and product life cycles may last no more than three months. Thus, fads and fashions are another reason why product life cycles may be short and why operating in such an industry can be risky, as the experience of The Gap suggests.

ORGANIZATIONAL INSIGHT 13.2
Innovation at The Gap

The environment of the clothing industry is highly uncertain, meaning it is very difficult to predict customers' changing tastes and thus stock the clothing that will most appeal to them. The CEO of The Gap, Millard "Mickey" Drexler, brought his chain of stores to prominence in the 1990s because of his uncanny ability to predict customer tastes and design clothing to suit them—the form that innovation takes in the clothing industry. The Gap brand became a fashion statement of the 1990s, and by 2000, sales revenue at Gap Inc., the well-known clothes store chain, rose above $10 billion for the first time. However, its stock price, which had hit a peak in 1999, had declined sharply. Why?

To build sales, Millard's strategy had been to open new kinds of stores that offered a different mix of clothing to customers. So, for example, in its Gap division the company had opened Kids Gap stores and Baby Gap. It also started the Banana Republic store chain, and, very important, the Old Navy store chain, which had grown rapidly and been responsible for much of Gap's increase in sales.[11]

By the late 1990s, however, Drexler found that he could not manage the innovation process, that is, manage the design process for all the clothes sold by each of his three main divisions. He decided to delegate full responsibility for innovating to the presidents of each store chain. Jenny Ming, for example, was the president of Old Navy, and she and her team of managers were charged with finding the best selection of clothing to appeal to customers. One result of their actions was to champion a line of purple clothing for the spring season.

Drexler's decision to decentralize authority over innovation to the store level caused major problems.[12] The presidents of his chains did not have his ability to predict future clothing trends, fads, and fashions and made mistakes in the kinds of clothing they stocked; the decision to carry purple was a disaster, for example, and the clothes were left on the shelves. Chain managers also began to stock similar kinds of clothes so customers became confused about why the chains were different and this also hurt sales and revenues. The Gap was doing a much poorer job of meeting the needs of its customers.

By the summer of 2000, Drexler decided that although he was right to give divisional managers major responsibility to manage the design process, it was also necessary to have centralized control at the top. Such control would provide the coordination necessary between store chains to ensure that they all worked together to stock a unique mix of clothing, and that the mix would be the right one to appeal to customer tastes. He took back more control and

(continued)

installed a new IT system to speed the design process; The Gap's performance improved in the 2000s.[13] However, Drexler could not regain his early momentum and in 2002 he turned the helm over to Paul Dressler, a former Disney manager who once ran the Magic Kingdom.

CEO Dressler has successfully used his skills in brand marketing to turn around The Gap's performance.[14] He has rejuvenated its product line by focusing on designing and stocking products that customers want. In addition, he has sought out new market niches where The Gap can attract new kinds of customers. For example, in 2005 the company announced that it was preparing to test a new specialty retail chain aimed at women over age 35, especially the baby boomers, the nearly 40 million women born between 1946 and 1964.[15] Clearly, innovation is alive and well at The Gap; it is also alive and well at J. Crew, the clothing retailer now managed by its CEO, Mickey Drexler, who has also turned around its performance!

Whether short product life cycles are caused by rapid technological change, changing fads and fashions, or some combination of the two, the message for managers is clear: The shorter the length of your product's life cycle, the more important it is to innovate products quickly and on a continuing basis. In industries where product life cycles are very short, managers must continually develop new products; otherwise, their organizations may go out of business. The PC company that cannot develop a new and improved product line every six months will soon find itself in trouble. The fashion house that fails to develop a new line of clothing for every season cannot succeed, nor can the small restaurant, club, or bar that is not alert to current fads and fashions. Even in the car industry it is vital that managers continually develop new and improved models every five years or so.

Increasingly, there is evidence that in a wide range of industries product life cycles are becoming more compressed as managers focus their organizations' resources on innovation to increase responsiveness to customers. To attract new customers, managers are trying to outdo each other by being the first to market with a product that incorporates a new technology or that plays to a new fashion trend.[16] In the car industry, a typical 5-year product life cycle is being reduced to three years as managers are increasingly competing with one another to attract new customers and encourage existing customers to upgrade and buy the newest product.[17]

Entrepreneurship as "Creative Destruction"

The widespread changes brought about by increasing global competition and advancing technology are often referred to as the process of "creative destruction." This process leads old, inefficient companies to be driven out of business by new, more efficient ones. This is "creative" because the new companies use new global and technological opportunities to make better products or lower the costs of making existing products. Established companies that fail to invest in new technologies find themselves at such a competitive disadvantage they are driven out of business. The new start-ups become the companies that will lead the industries of the future. Similarly, the emergence of new industries—such as digital computing and communication, biotechnology, robotics, fuel cell, and home video games and music players— have created massive disruptions in the business world.

The industrial revolution is another example of how the process of creative destruction works. The old agricultural age, where wealth depended on land and physical labor, gave way to the age of steam-powered machinery and transportation. The new industrialists who used their capital to create new low-cost industries destroyed the old craft guilds. The information technology age represents the latest wave of major technological change that has forced most kinds of businesses to invest in IT to avoid being left behind by those entrepreneurial companies that do make such investments and then forge ahead.

Intrapreneurs
Entrepreneurs inside an organization who are responsible for the success or failure of a project.

Innovation, Intrapreneurship, and Creativity

The leaders of innovation and new product development in established organizations are **intrapreneurs**, employees who notice opportunities for either quantum or incremental product improvements and are responsible for managing the product development process to obtain them. Many managers, scientists, or researchers employed by existing companies engage in intrapreneurial activity. On the other hand, people like Jeff Bezos or Michael Dell or Debby Fields who start new business ventures and found organizations are entrepreneurs. They assume the risk and receive many of the returns associated with the new business venture.[18]

There is an interesting relationship between entrepreneurs and intrapreneurs. Many intrapreneurs become dissatisfied when their superiors decide neither to support their creative new product ideas nor to fund development efforts that the intrapreneurs think will succeed. What do intrapreneurs who feel that they are getting nowhere do? Very often they decide to leave an organization and start their own organization to take advantage of their new product ideas. In other words, intrapreneurs become entrepreneurs and found companies that may compete with the companies they left.

Many of the world's most successful organizations have been started by frustrated intrapreneurs who became entrepreneurs. William Hewlett and David Packard left Fairchild Semiconductor, an early industry leader, when managers of that company would not support their ideas; their company, HP, soon outperformed Fairchild. Compaq Computer was founded by Rod Canion and some of his colleagues, who left Texas Instruments (TI) when managers there would not support Canion's idea that TI should develop its own personal computer. To prevent the departure of talented people, organizations need to take steps to promote internal entrepreneurship. In the next section, we consider issues involved in promoting successful entrepreneurship in both new and existing organizations. First, however, it is useful to discuss the origin of these new product ideas—creativity.

All innovation begins with creative ideas. It is important to realize, however, that creative ideas are not just those that lead to major new inventions or achievements: Creative ideas are any that take existing practices a step farther than the norm. **Creativity** is nothing more than going beyond the current boundaries, whether those boundaries are technology, knowledge, social norms or beliefs.[19] Deciding that PCs don't have to be beige and could be black or blue or even made of clear plastic is a creative idea, just as putting together the first PC was a creative idea. Although the latter may be more memorable, and made Steve Jobs and Stephen Wozniak, the founders of Apple Computer famous, the millions of small creative ideas and actions that have gone into improving PCs are nevertheless highly significant and valuable. Michael Dell's creative idea of selling PCs over the phone, while not in the same league as making the first PC, has nevertheless made him as famous as Jobs and Wozniak, and a good deal richer.

From this perspective, most people have been and will be creative in their normal endeavors. Thus, it is important in an organization that employees grasp the fact that their input, suggestions, and ideas are valuable. An organization should take steps to acknowledge their importance. Organizations can do this through the values and norms of their organizational culture, as discussed later, or they can do so by providing financial rewards for good suggestions, as many organizations do. It is important to realize that creativity is everywhere, not just confined to some far-away research laboratory.

Creativity is not just making new things; it is also combining and synthesizing two or more previously unrelated facts or ideas and making something new or different out of them. It is also modifying something to give it a new use or to make it perform better. Synthesis and modification are much more common than creation, and this is why incremental innovation is more common than radical innovation. As Anderson puts it, "We forget that moving a desk so that work flows smoother is also creativity. It's modification. And creativity also blooms when we redesign a job description so that related tasks are given to the same person. That's synthesis. It's even creativity when we cut our losses on a worthless industrial adhesive by slapping it on the back of our secretary's note pad . . . that bit of creation is the 3M 'Post-it' notes, but nothing is going to make your firm creative unless you first help individuals to unlock their willingness to try."[20]

As Nonaka puts it, the process of innovation and creating new knowledge depends on the ability of managers to tap into the tacit or hidden and highly

Creativity

Ideas going beyond the current boundaries, whether those boundaries are based on technology, knowledge, social norms, or beliefs.

subjective insights, intuitions, and hunches of people everywhere in an organization.[21] The source can be a brilliant researcher's insight, a middle manager's intuition about changing market trends, or a shop-floor worker's tacit knowledge built up by intense involvement in the work process over a number of years. The issue is to transform personal knowledge into organizational knowledge that results in new products. This can be very complicated because such tacit knowledge is very difficult to verbalize; it is know-how accumulated by experience and often hard to articulate in rules, formulas, or principles.

To obtain such tacit knowledge, it is often necessary to learn through observation, imitation, or modeling. Also, over time, through team interactions, team members learn how to share their knowledge and often team routines and "recipes" develop that are specific to a group and to an organization that lead to innovative kinds of behaviors. Some of these can be written down, though many are present only in the interactions between team members—in their knowledge of each other. Note too that from such interactions additional tacit knowledge may be created so that organizational knowledge builds up and spills over.[22]

A **knowledge-creating organization** is one where such innovation is going on at all levels and in all areas. Often, different teams will meet to pool their information. In this way knowledge is shared throughout the organization and new heights can be reached. Team leaders, as middle managers, have to confront the hard task of translating creative new ideas into the stream of products that customers will buy. It is at this point that the question of how to create and design an organizational setting to promote creativity and innovation becomes the crucial issue. Note that the process of creating such a setting is equally a form of innovation as the development of the actual products that can result from it.

MANAGING THE INNOVATION PROCESS

How should managers control the innovation process in high-tech companies, software and dot.com companies like Amazon.com, or in supermarkets and restaurants in order to raise the level of both quantum and incremental innovation? There are several related methods that managers can use. These same methods also serve to overcome the resistances to change discussed in Chapter 10, which will reduce the level of innovation if left unattended. For example, different functions may be differently affected by the kinds of technological change taking place and thus resist change, and managers may fail to recognize new product opportunities because of the existence of cognitive biases.

Project Management

One technique that has proved useful at promoting radical, but especially incremental, innovation is **project management**, the process of leading and controlling a project so that it results in the effective creation of new or improved products. A **project** is a subunit whose goal centers on developing the products or service on time, within budget, and in conformance with predetermined performance specifications—the criteria for assessing effectiveness. In the race to produce advanced technological products quickly, the issues of managing a project both to reduce the time it takes to bring a new product to market and to reduce the costs of innovation are becoming increasingly important. It is useful to examine the role of project managers (PMs) and analyze what they do.

Effective project management begins with a clearly articulated plan that takes a product from its concept phase, to its initial test phase, to the modification phase, and to the final manufacturing or—in the case of services—set-up phase. Of all these phases, the concept phase typically involves the most work and cost, since the task facing the product development team is to take the latest research findings or thinking and to use them to create goods and services that people and organizations will want to use.

How does a project manager's job differ from that of a typical manager in an organization? First, a project manager is managing a higher proportion of highly skilled and educated professionals. Typically, there will be many scientists and engineers of all kinds working on a project. The most immediate issues to face are how to balance the centralization and decentralization of authority and how to hold these professional employees accountable for their actions so that their creative efforts can be harmonized with a project's time frame. However, it is the uncertainty surrounding a project—the fact that unexpected problems, delays, and breakthroughs may be encountered—that creates the sense of urgency, risk, and suspense surrounding its completion. Harmonizing creative effort with cost and time considerations is a very difficult thing to do.

Often, PMs' past experience and intuition will allow them to judge how well or how poorly progress is being made toward a goal. Balancing the conflicting demands of performance, budget, and time schedule, and resolving the conflicts among them, is a difficult process, especially as projects often are ongoing for one to three years or longer. One of the hardest tasks of a PM is to maintain the momentum of the project, as team members such as engineers or designers fail repeatedly to come up with solutions to problems, and the project threatens to flounder. Overcoming inertia, suggesting possible solutions, brainstorming, and providing encouragement and positive feedback are essential parts of the PM's job. On the other hand, scientists and engineers can be perfectionists whose only goal is to increase the product's performance, and it is important that the PM keep the goals of time and cost in mind, convincing engineers that the search for a perfect product will turn out to be a disaster if it results in one that is so expensive customers will not wish to buy it.

It is the ability to think ahead and perform effective advanced planning that is often key to a PM's success. Based on past experience, effective PMs know what typical problems arise, and they know how to organize and control employees to address them. Thus, when a crisis occurs, as it usually does, resources will be ready to confront it.

Another important aspect of PMs' advanced planning involves a plan to deal with top corporate executives, who will be watching anxiously and evaluating the performance of the project, looking for signs of success or failure. Selling their ideas and their project is the never-ending job of PMs. Later, we discuss how PMs must be product champions, the people who have to believe in the project; if they are not committed to its success, others in the organization are likely to have little enthusiasm for it. The ability to present new product ideas effectively and to crystallize the meaning and importance of a project are major determinants of a PM's ability to obtain continuing funding for a slow-moving project—even to ensure the survival of the project, for it is common for many projects to be terminated midcourse.

To help with advanced planning, to uncover bottlenecks and prevent crises where possible, and to help speed progress toward the goal, a tool commonly employed by project managers is *quantitative modeling*. Modeling allows PMs to develop "What if?" scenarios and to experiment with finding new and better ways of performing the sequential, and parallel, steps involved in reaching the final product.

One common modeling approach is to develop a *PERT/CAM network* or *GANTT chart*, which are essentially flowcharts of a project that can be built with many proprietary software packages (such as Microsoft's Project 2000).[23] These software packages focus on (1) modeling the sequences of actions necessary to reach a project's goal and (2) relating these actions to cost and time criteria, such as the per-week cost of the scientists and engineers employed in the project, to (3) sort out and define the optimal path for reaching the goal. Once the PM has chosen a particular path to follow, these programs provide ongoing feedback on project performance that can be used to assess current project performance.

One of the first, and simplest, of these modeling techniques, the *critical path method* (CPM), captures the essence of what these models try to achieve. The goal of CPM is to determine (1) which particular tasks or activities of the many that have to be performed are critical in their effect on project time and cost and thus (2) determine how to sequence or schedule critical tasks so that a project can meet a target date at a minimum cost. Finding the critical path thus provides an optimal solution to the needs of a particular project. The flowchart in Figure 13.3 illustrates the critical tasks involved in building a house.

The optimal sequencing of tasks that have to be performed to reach the completed product is often worked out by a team that experiments with different possible sequences. In this simple example of building a house, the most efficient sequencing of steps can be easily discovered. For many more complex projects, however, the analysis of these steps constitutes an important learning tool; many unforeseen interactions between these steps can be uncovered by a careful analysis. Attention is then paid to how to shorten the path—how to reorganize, combine, or resequence tasks to cut time and cost and improve performance. Frequently, a team will experiment by building prototypes of a new facilities layout or task structure if how to make a product or provide a service is the key issue.

Note the link to reengineering an organization, discussed in Chapter 10, where the move to combine the activities of different specialists or functions and focus on business processes, not activities, is also a way of shortening the critical path. PERT/CRM software packages permit the user to examine and compare many different kinds of configurations to find the best path to job completion. Modern IT systems, such as computer-aided design (CAD) (discussed in Chapter 9), can completely change task sequencing, especially when organizational developments such

Figure 13.3
CPM Project Design

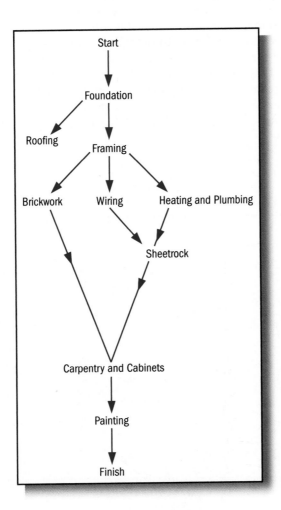

as flexible work teams, product teams, and network structures are factored into the equation.

Indeed, such developments have made the job of the project manager increasingly prominent in many organizations. Successful PMs are often those who rise to more general management positions because of their demonstrated competency in understanding how to design organizational structure and IT systems to facilitate the flow of innovative new goods and services. Project management is often a prerequisite for promotion to top management positions today.

Stage-Gate Development Funnel

One of the mistakes that top managers often make in managing the innovation process is trying to fund too many development projects at any one point in time. The result is that limited financial, functional, and human resources are spread thinly over too many different projects. As a consequence, no single project or PM is given the resources that are required to make a project succeed and the level of successful innovation falls.

Given the nature of this problem, it is necessary for managers to develop a structured process for evaluating different new product development proposals and deciding which to support. A common solution to this problem is to implement a stage-gate development funnel[24] (see Figure 13.4). The purpose of a *stage-gate funnel* is to establish a structured and coherent innovation process that both improves control over the product development effort and forces managers to make choices among competing new product development projects so that resources are not spread thinly over too many projects.

The funnel has a wide mouth (stage 1) in order initially to promote innovation by encouraging as many new product ideas as possible from both new and established project managers. Companies establish a wide mouth by creating incentives for employees to come up with new product ideas. Some organizations run "bright ideas" programs, which reward prospective project managers for submitting new product ideas that eventually make it through the development process. Others allow research scientists to devote a certain amount of work time to their own projects. For example, Hewlett-Packard and 3M have a 15% rule: 15% of a research scientist's workweek can be devoted to working on a project of his or her own choosing.

Figure 13.4
A Stage-Gate Development Funnel

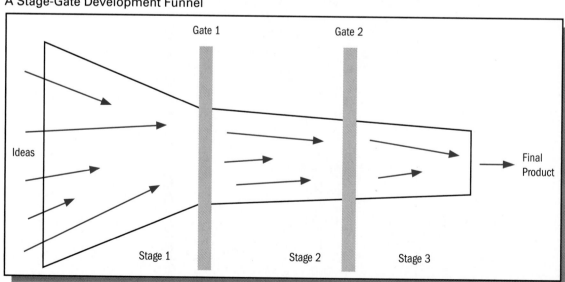

Ideas may be submitted by individuals who may assume the role of project manager if a project is approved.

These new product ideas are then written up in the form of a brief new product development proposal and submitted to a cross-functional team of managers who evaluate the proposal at gate 1. At gate 1, the proposal is reviewed in terms of its fit with the strategy of the organization and its technical feasibility. Proposals that are consistent with the strategy of the organization and judged technically feasible will be passed on to stage 2; the rest will be turned down (although the door is often left open for reconsidering the proposal at a later date).

The primary goal in stage 2 is for the prospective project manager to draft a detailed new product development plan that specifies all of the information required to make a decision about whether to go ahead with a full-blown product development effort. Included in the new product development plan should be factors such as strategic and financial objectives, an analysis of market potential, a list of desired product features, a list of technological requirements, a list of financial and human resource requirements, a detailed development budget, and a timeline that contains specific milestones (for example, dates for prototype completion and final launch). The project manager is often aided in drafting the plan by a cross-functional team that spends considerable time in the field with customers trying to understand how to tailor the product to their needs.

Once completed, the plan is reviewed by a senior management committee (at gate 2). Here the review focuses on a detailed look at the new product development plan and considers whether the proposal is attractive given its market potential, and viable given the technological, financial, and human requirements of actually developing the product. This review is made in light of all other product development efforts being undertaken by the organization. One goal at this point is to ensure that limited technical, financial, and human resources are used to their maximum effect.

At gate 2, projects are either rejected, sent back for revision, or allowed to proceed to the development phase (stage 3). The stage 3 development effort can last anywhere from six months to 10 years, depending upon the industry and product type. For example, some electronics products have development cycles of six months; it takes three to five years to develop a new car; about five years to develop a new jet aircraft; and as much as 10 years to develop a new medical drug.

Using Cross-Functional Teams and a Product Team Structure

As just noted, establishing cross-functional teams is a critical element in any structured new product development effort.[25] Although successful innovation begins in the R&D function, the way the activities of the R&D department are coordinated with the activities of other functions is crucial.[26] Figure 13.5 identifies the many functions necessary for successful innovation. In addition to R&D, they include product engineering, process engineering, materials management, manufacturing, and marketing.

Because those different groups usually have different orientations and attitudes, coordinating their activities is difficult. The link between R&D and the product and process engineering groups, for example, is vital to the conversion of research results into a product that is designed efficiently and can be produced cheaply. R&D scientists, however, may complain that the potential of "their" new product is being sacrificed if the engineers tinker with its design to make production either easy or cheap. In turn, engineering may feel that R&D is too emotionally committed to the product and has lost sight of the market in its pursuit of technical excellence.

Both R&D and engineering also need to coordinate with manufacturing to ensure that the new product can be made cost effectively and reliably. A link with marketing will ensure that the product possesses the features and qualities that customers need and want and that R&D resources are not being spent to create or improve a product that customers do not want. Marketing may discover, for

Figure 13.5
Innovation as a Cross-Functional Activity

Successful innovation depends on the coordination of the activities of the research and development department with the activities of other departments.

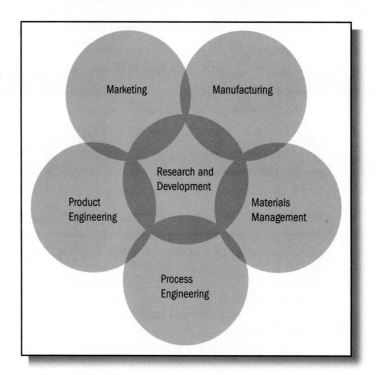

example, that customers are not willing to pay the price that the organization will be forced to charge for the product. This marketing information may conflict with R&D's and engineering's views about producing a high-quality product, even at a high price.

Marketing, engineering, and manufacturing personnel need to be core members of successful new product development teams. The term *core members* refers to a nucleus of three to six people who bear primary responsibility for the product development effort. In addition to core members, others typically work on the project as the need arises, but it is the core members who stay with the project from inception to completion of the development effort. To ensure that core members are not distracted by other development projects, they are usually assigned to only one development project at a time. In addition, for particularly important new product development projects, core members may be taken out of their regular functional role for the duration of the project and assigned to work on the project full-time.

Many organizations have been unable to manage the functional linkages necessary for successful product innovation, and the results have often been disastrous. A list of innovative products for which there was little demand includes the RCA laser disc player, the Kodak photo CD player, and the cost-ineffective supersonic Concorde airliner. In Chapter 6, we discussed various structures that organizations can use to manage activities in conditions of great uncertainty. Two of them, product team structure and matrix structure, are especially suitable for managing innovation in high-tech organizations. Both of these structures focus on creating cross-functional teams to pursue new product development from the concept and design stage, through manufacturing, to the marketing and sales stage. These structures allow each function to develop an understanding of the problems and interests of the other functions, and they reduce communication problems. Decentralizing authority to the team also forces team members to cooperate and develop a shared understanding of the project.

Even though a product team structure facilitates innovation and the new product development process, it is often not sufficient to solve the coordination problem. Many organizations use additional integrating mechanisms to facilitate innovation: team leaders and project champions, "skunk works," new venture divisions, and joint ventures.

Team Leadership

Although establishment of a cross-functional product development team may be a necessary condition for successful innovation, it is not a sufficient condition. If a cross-functional team is to succeed, it must have the right kind of leadership, and it must be managed in an effective manner.[27]

One important consideration is to have a team leader who can rise above his or her functional background and take a cross-functional view. Another issue is how much power and authority should be given to the team leader. Here a distinction can be made between lightweight and heavyweight team leaders.[28] A *lightweight team leader* is a mid-level functional manager who has lower status than the head of a functional department. The lightweight team leader is not given control over human, financial, and functional resources. Not a true project manager, this leader remains under the control of a functional department head. If the lightweight leader wants access to resources, he or she must pursue the heads of functional departments to allocate them for a period of time. This arrangement weakens the power and authority of the team leader, who is subservient to the heads of functional departments. The result can be limited cross-functional coordination. Still, this arrangement might be appropriate in those cases where minor modifications of an existing product are all that is required.

A *heavyweight team leader* is a true project manager who has higher status within the organization. The heavyweight team leader is given primary control over key human, financial, and technical resources for the duration of the project. This allows the heavyweight leader to lay first claim to key resources and, if necessary, to override the wishes of the heads of the functions. For example, the heavyweight leader may be able to insist that a certain marketing and engineering manager be assigned full-time to the project, even if the heads of the engineering and marketing departments are not in favor of this assignment. This power gives the heavyweight team leader a much greater chance of assembling a cross-functional team capable of successfully developing a new product. Researchers who study this issue argue that heavyweight team leaders make most sense in the case of important new product development efforts.[29]

Heavyweight team leaders often function as product champions—the people who take ownership of the project, solve problems as they occur, smooth over disputes between team members, and provide leadership to the team. Sometimes the product champion is not formally appointed and emerges informally during the innovation process. The way in which Don Frey, a product champion at Ford, worked with Lee Iacocca to develop the Ford Mustang in the early 1960s illustrates the importance of the product champion role.

Skunk Works and New Venture Divisions

A *skunk works* is a task force, a temporary team, that is created to expedite new product design and to promote innovation by coordinating the activities of functional groups.[30] The task force consists of members of the engineering and research departments and other support functions such as marketing and is assigned to other facilities, often at a location away from the rest of the organization. This setting provides the opportunity for the intensive face-to-face interactions necessary to generate successful innovation. Together, the members of the task force "own the problem" and become internal entrepreneurs, or *intrapreneurs*, people inside an organization who are responsible for the success or failure of the project. Thus, a skunk works is an island of innovation and provides a large organization with a small-organization-type setting in which team members have the opportunity and motivation to bring a new product to market quickly. Ford created a skunk works to develop the new Mustang that was introduced in 1993.

Hewlett-Packard, 3M, and other organizations have also recognized the advantages of a small-organization atmosphere for fostering entrepreneurship in their employees. Thus, as viable new product developments occur in corporate R&D laboratories, these organizations create a *new venture division*, a new division that is

Don Frey, an R&D engineer, was a product champion at Ford Motor Company. At Ford's R&D laboratories, Frey was assigned to projects that seemed new and interesting, but he never got to talk to customers and never got involved in operational decision making about what to offer the customer and how much new developments would cost. As a result, for many years, he and other R&D engineers worked on products that never got to market. Frustrated by the lack of payoff from his work, Frey began to question the utility of a corporate R&D laboratory that was so far removed from operations and the market. In 1957, he moved from R&D to head the passenger car design department, where he would be closer to market operations. In this new position, Frey was much closer to the customer and directed the energies of his department to producing innovations that customers wanted and were willing to pay for.

Frey soon concluded that in the automobile business the best R&D was incremental: Year by year a car was improved to meet customer demands. He also saw how important it was to use customer complaints as a guide for investing R&D resources to get the most benefit. Equipped with this new perspective on innovation, he was made a member of Ford's top planning committee in 1961, and he became interested in developing a new car for the emerging "sporty car segment."

Frey and his staff saw the possibility of designing a car for this segment and began championing the development of a product. Ford, however, had just lost a fortune on the Edsel and was reluctant to start a new car. Because there was no corporate support for Frey's ideas, all of the early engineering and styling of what became the Mustang were carried out with bootleg funds—funds earmarked for something else. By 1962, Frey and his team had produced the first working prototype of the Mustang and believed they had a winner. Top management in general and Henry Ford II in particular were not impressed and offered no support, still fearing the new car might turn out to be another Edsel.

Luckily for the Mustang team, Lee Iacocca became vice president and general manager of Ford in 1962, and he bought into the Mustang concept. Believing that the Mustang would be a huge success, Iacocca risked his reputation to convince top management to back the idea. In the fall of 1962, after much pressure, funds to produce the car were allocated. With Frey as product champion, the Mustang was completed from approval to market in only 18 months. When the Mustang was introduced in 1964, it was an instant success, and over 400,000 Mustangs were sold.

Frey went on to champion other innovations in Ford vehicles, such as disc brakes and radial tires. Reflecting on his experiences as a product champion, he offered some coaching tips for future product champions: Innovation can start anywhere and from small beginnings, and product champions must be prepared to use all the skill they have to pull people and resources together and to resist top managers and financial experts who use numbers to kill new ideas.[31] As Frey's experience suggests, innovation is a risky business, and product champions have to go out on a limb to take on the disbelievers.

allocated a complete set of value-creating functions to manage a project from beginning to end.[32] Unlike a skunk works, which is dissolved when the product is brought to market, a new venture division assumes full responsibility for the commercialization of the product and is normally an independent division. Project members become the heads of the division's functions and are responsible for managing the functional structure created to bring the new product to market.

Establishing the balance of control between the division and the corporate center can become a problem in a new venture division. As the new division absorbs more and more resources to fulfill its mission, the corporate center may become concerned about the commercial success of the project. If corporate managers begin to intervene in the division's activities, divisional managers begin to lose their autonomy, and the division's entrepreneurial attitude may start to decline. On the other hand, major problems can arise if an organization sets up many independent new venture divisions to spur innovation. The first problem is the expense involved, which can quickly drive up a company's costs. A second problem is that the divisions may pursue their own goals and sometimes these might conflict with the goals of the whole organization. Finally, managing new venture divisions is a difficult process that requires considerable organizational skill. Managers must create the right kind of organizational structure if they are to be successful. Utilizing the right kinds of IT systems is also vital; this important issue is discussed later in the chapter.

Joint Ventures

Joint ventures between two or more organizations, discussed in Chapter 3, are another important means of managing high-tech innovation. A joint venture allows organizations to combine their skills and technologies and pool their resources to embark on risky R&D projects. A joint venture is similar to a new venture division in that a new organization is created in which people can work out new procedures that lead to success. When both companies share revenues, risks, and costs, this often can result in the development of a stream of profitable new products. Joint ventures can also cause problems, however, if the venture partners begin to come into conflict over future development plans. This often happens when, over time, the venture begins to favor one partner over another. Given this possibility, many joint venture agreements have clauses allowing one partner to buy the other out, or giving one partner 51% ownership of the venture, to ensure that the gains from future innovation can be achieved.

Creating a Culture for Innovation

Organizational culture also plays an important role in shaping and promoting innovation. Values and norms can reinforce the entrepreneurial spirit and allow an organization to respond quickly and creatively to a changing environment. As we saw in Chapter 7, three factors that shape organizational culture are organizational structure, people, and property rights (see Figure 7.2).

Organizational Structure

Because organizational structure influences the way people behave, creating the right setting is important to fostering an intrapreneurial culture. Several factors can stunt innovation and reduce the ability of an organization to introduce new products as it grows.

Increasing organizational size may slow innovation. As organizations grow, decision making slows down. Decisions have to be made through established channels in a sizable hierarchy, and a thriving bureaucracy may stifle the entrepreneurial spirit. As an organization becomes more bureaucratic, people may become more conservative and unwilling to take risks, and those most willing and able to innovate may become discouraged and leave the organization.

As organizations age, they tend to become less flexible and less innovative.[33] Relatively old, inflexible organizations may fail to notice new opportunities for new products because of what one writer has described as "the inability of many traditional mature firms to anticipate the need for productive change and their resistance to ideas advanced by creative people."[34] In addition, it is difficult for people to remain entrepreneurial throughout their careers. Thus, as organizations and their personnel age, there may be an inherent tendency for both to become more conservative.

With organizational growth comes complexity, and an increase in vertical and horizontal differentiation may hurt innovation. An increase in hierarchical levels makes it hard for employee entrepreneurs to exercise meaningful authority over projects. They may be under the constant scrutiny of upper-level managers who insist on signing off on projects. Similarly, when the skills and knowledge needed for innovation are spread across many subunits and functions, it is difficult for a product manager or product champion to coordinate the innovation process and secure the resources needed to bring a project to fruition.[35]

To promote innovation, organizations need to adopt a structure that can overcome those problems. Organic structures based on norms and values that emphasize lateral communication and cross-functional cooperation tend to promote innovation. Matrix and product team structures possess these organic characteristics and provide the autonomy for people to make their own decisions. In addition, many organizations use the informal organization to overcome obstacles presented by the formal structure. Such organizations give their employees wide latitude to act outside formal task definitions and to work on projects where they think they can make a contribution. Hewlett-Packard and 3M informally grant employees the right to use organizational resources to work on projects of their own choosing. Sony allows its scientists to move from project to project and to select a team to work on where they feel they can make the best contribution. Apple and Microsoft confer on their top R&D scientists the title "research fellow" and give them the autonomy and resources to decide how to put their skills to best use. When a research fellow's research leads to a promising new product development, a project team is established.

People

The culture of innovation in high-tech organizations is fostered by the characteristics of employees themselves. In many research settings, people cooperate so closely on product development that they become increasingly similar to one another. They buy into the same set of organizational norms and values and thus are able to communicate well with each other. In turn, organizational members select new members who buy into the same set of values, so that over time a recognizable culture that promotes communication and the flow of new ideas emerges. However, an organization needs to guard against too much similarity in its scientists, lest they lose sight of new or emerging trends in the industry. IBM scientists, for example, fixated on improving mainframe computers and ignored signs that customers wanted better personal computers, not more sophisticated mainframes. To maintain a capacity to innovate successfully, a high-tech organization must strive to maintain diversity in its scientists and to allow them to follow divergent paths. The uncertainty associated with innovation makes it important for people to be adaptable and open to new ideas. One way to encourage flexibility and open-mindedness is to recruit people who are committed to innovation but who travel along different pathways to achieve it. This is what 3M seems to do, as described in the following organizational insight.

ORGANIZATIONAL INSIGHT 13.4
Fostering Innovation at 3M

3M is one of the most successful innovators of new products in the world. 3M uses many different technologies to innovate thousands of new and improved products for companies and individual consumers each year. To encourage successful new product development, 3M has set a challenging stretch goal that 30% of its revenues should be earned from new products developed in the last three years. This goal encourages its employees to act as entrepreneurs and to search out new opportunities to create products that customers will value and buy.

Sometimes, the process of developing new products at 3M begins with finding a technology to make a product that will better meet an existing customer need. In 1904, for example, 3M's engineers developed a new technology that allowed them to bond grit to paper and the result was a blockbuster product—the first sandpaper. 3M developed this technology because it knew from watching its customers that there was a large unmet need and thus potential market for an inexpensive, easy to use abrasive.

In many cases, it is more difficult for a company to discover customer needs—or even to discover potential uses for a new product. The way another 3M product, Scotch masking tape, was developed illustrates this. The story of Scotch tape began when Dick Drew, a 3M scientist, visited an auto body shop in St. Paul, Minnesota, to test a new kind of sandpaper he was developing. Two-tone cars were popular then, and Drew watched as paint shop employees improvised a method to keep one color of paint from being oversprayed onto the other. They used a paint shield made of a combination of heavy adhesive tape and butcher paper. Very often, as they pulled their shield off when the paint was dry, it took the other color paint with it. Employees joked with Drew that it would be a good idea if 3M could develop a product that made their job easier.[36]

Drew realized that what was needed was a tape with a *weaker* glue or adhesive that would not pull the paint off. He went back to his lab to develop such a glue and, after many attempts, used it to develop the first masking tape. Paint shop employees now had a way to detach butcher paper from a car and achieve a first-class paint job. Once the success of the new product was proved, Drew began to think about other uses to which masking tape could be put. It soon became clear that the common need for a reliable way to seal, wrap, package, or attach something meant that the uses for masking tape were endless. Drew continued his research; in 1930, he invented clear cellophane tape to meet many of these other kinds of customer needs.

Property Rights

The uncertainty associated with innovation makes it difficult for managers to evaluate the performance of highly skilled R&D scientists. Managers cannot watch scientists to see how well they are performing. Often their performance can be evaluated only over a long time—perhaps years. Moreover, innovation is a complex, intensive process that demands skills and abilities inherent in the scientist, not in the organization. When scientists come up with a new idea, it is relatively easy for them to take it and establish their own organizations to exploit the benefits from it. Indeed, much technological innovation occurs in new organizations founded by scientists who have left large organizations to branch out on their own. Given these issues, strong property rights are needed to align the interests of R&D scientists with the interests of the organization.[37]

An organization can create career paths for its R&D employees and project managers and demonstrate that success is closely linked to future promotion and rewards. Career paths can be established not only inside the R&D function but also among R&D, project management, and general management functions. Inside the R&D function, successful scientists can be groomed to manage future R&D projects. After some years in R&D, however, many scientists move to take control of manufacturing operations or to assume other management responsibilities. Because of the experience they gained in various functions, these managers are in a position to ensure that future R&D activities are aligned with customer needs and to serve as project managers.

Strong property rights can also be created if an organization ties individual and group performance to large monetary premiums. Innovative employees should receive bonuses and stock options that are proportional to the increase in profitability that can be attributed to their efforts. Making employees owners in the organization will discourage them from leaving and will provide them with a strong incentive to perform well. Many successful high-tech organizations, such as Merck and Apple, do this; one in five of Microsoft's employees is a millionaire as a result of the organization's policy of giving stock options to employees. Remember, the last thing that Bill Gates wants is for his best employees to leave and found their own organizations that then compete with Microsoft.

By focusing on property rights, people, and structure, an organization can create a culture in which norms and values foster innovation and the search for excellence in new product development.

MANAGERIAL IMPLICATIONS

INNOVATION

1. Research and development activities must be integrated with the activities of the other functions if the innovation process is to be successful.
2. Employees must be given autonomy and encouraged to use organizational resources to facilitate the continuous development of new products and processes.
3. Project managers, a stage-gate product development funnel, cross-functional teams, appropriate team leadership, a skunk works, and new venture divisions should be created to provide a setting that encourages entrepreneurship.
4. Top management must create a culture that supports innovation and that recognizes and rewards the contributions of organizational members—for example, by linking rewards directly to performance.

INNOVATION AND INFORMATION TECHNOLOGY

Previous chapters have discussed how IT can raise organizational effectiveness, particularly by reducing operating costs. Why? Because of **information efficiencies**, the cost and time savings that occur when IT allows individual employees to perform their current tasks at a higher level, assume additional tasks, and expand their roles in the organization due to advances in the ability to gather and analyze data.[38] The ability of IT to enhance a person's task knowledge and technical skills is also an important input into the innovation process, however. In fact, IT facilitates the innovation process because it promotes creativity in many ways and affects many aspects of the process of bringing new problem-solving ideas into use.

First, IT facilitates creativity by improving the initial base of knowledge to draw from when employees engage in problem solving and decision making. To the degree that IT creates a larger and richer pool of codified knowledge for any given employee to draw from, and allows these employees to work together, innovative potential is increased. Examples of knowledge codification from utilizing knowledge management were discussed in Chapter 12. For example, at large consultancy firms like Accenture and McKinsey & Co., groups of experienced consultants assemble knowledge online from every level of the firm and then use in-house IT to disseminate information to consultants throughout the organization—information that would otherwise not have been available to them.

Knowledge or information availability alone will not lead to innovation; it is the ability to *creatively use* knowledge that is the key to promoting innovation and creating competitive advantage.[39] Prahalad and Hamel, for example, suggest that it is not the level of knowledge a firm possesses that leads to innovation and competitive advantage, but the velocity with which it is circulated in the firm.[40] Organizations must take steps to ensure that they use knowledge to develop distinctive competences at both the individual and functional levels, and particularly between functions.

Similarly, it is very likely that a reshuffling of tasks will occur as new IT systems increase the ability of people or subunits to acquire and process information. This leads to many more opportunities for creatively combining, modifying, and synthesizing information leading to the incremental innovations discussed earlier. For example, what before might have been a task that requires the inputs of three different people or subunits becomes a task that one individual or function can perform more creatively and effectively because IT helps to increase both the amount and quality of information that can be adequately processed. IT also facilitates cross-functional and divisional communication and coordination that can promote the sharing of tacit knowledge between people and groups, leading to increased organizational knowledge.

Innovation and Information Synergies

In fact, one of the most important performance gains that result from IT occurs when two or more individuals or subunits pool their resources and cooperate and collaborate across role or subunit boundaries, creating **information synergies**. Information synergies occur when IT allows individuals or subunits to adjust their actions or behaviors to the needs of the other individuals or subunits on an ongoing basis and achieve gains from team-based cooperation.

IT changes organizational forms and promotes creativity and innovation inside both network and virtual organizational forms. IT-enabled virtual forms composed of electronically connected people or firms facilitate knowledge sharing and innovation. Compared to face-to-face communication, for example, the use of electronic communication has increased the amount of communication within the organization. IT's ability to link and enable employees within and between functions and divisions—whether through database repositories, teleconferencing, or electronic mail—helps lead to information synergies. The application of IT has been shown to promote cross-functional workflows, make critical information more accessible and transparent to employees, and increase the incidence of problem-solving leading to innovation.[41]

The downside to linking employees must be noted as well. It is possible that not only the amount of good advice information seekers receive will increase, but bad advice may increase as well. However, many firms work to ensure the reliability of information received via electronically weak ties by forming online communities where collections of experienced employees within a given area can be located (e.g., a software developers' forum, a sales force intranet, a manufacturing discussion group). Developing a knowledge management system also helps to ensure high-quality information and advice.

Boundary-spanning activity
The interactions of people and groups across the organizational boundary to obtain valuable information and knowledge from the environment to help promote innovation.

IT also allows for an increase in **boundary-spanning activity**—interacting with individuals and groups outside the organization to obtain valuable information and knowledge from the environment—that helps promote innovation. IT allows an employee to search for and absorb new knowledge that is relevant to a problem at hand.[42] For example, in complex organizations employees working on one task or project may wish to obtain useful knowledge residing in other operating units, but the employees may not know whether or not this knowledge exists and where it might reside. IT, through knowledge management systems, allows employees to search their network for information.

IT has many other useful properties that can promote incremental and quantum technological change. IT allows researchers and planners to communicate more easily and less expensively across time and geographic location; to communicate more rapidly and with greater precision to targeted groups; to more selectively control access and participation in a communication event or network; to more rapidly and selectively access information created outside the organization; to more rapidly and accurately combine and reconfigure information; and to more concisely store and quickly use experts' judgments and decision models. All these qualities can enhance creativity and make project management more effective. Amazon.com is a company using IT to make creative decisions and broaden its product line, becoming a consultant itself and selling its own creative ideas.

FOCUS ON NEW INFORMATION TECHNOLOGY:
Amazon.com, Part 7

Jeff Bezos's use of the Internet to sell books can probably be regarded as a quantum innovation in this industry. However, innovation at Amazon.com has not stopped there. Bezos and his top management team have engaged in a series of incremental innovations to grow and expand Amazon.com's core competences as an online retailer.[43]

Although Bezos initially chose to focus on selling books, he soon realized that Amazon.com's information technology could be used to sell other kinds of products. He began to search for products that could be sold profitably over the Internet. First, he realized that CDs were a natural product extension to offer customers, and Amazon.com announced its intention of becoming the "earth's biggest book and music store." Then Amazon opened a holiday gift store to entice customers to send gifts as well as books and CDs as presents; offered a gift-wrapping service; and launched a free electronic greeting card service to announce the arrival of the Amazon gift. Finally, realizing the popularity of online auctions, Bezos moved to enter this market by purchasing Livebid.com, the Internet's only provider of live online auctions; in 1999, Bezos also entered into an agreement with Sotheby's, the famous auction house.

Since 2000, Bezos has moved aggressively to use Amazon.com's developing expertise in the virtual storefront to forge alliances with companies like Toys "Я" Us, Office Depot, Circuit City, Target, and many others to allow their customers to buy at Amazon.com but to pick up purchases from their stores. It has also offered a consulting service to organizations that wish to develop the customer-friendly storefront that Amazon.com is famous for. As discussed in previous chapters, it has also used its IT competences to widen its product line and to keep its line up to date with regard to the ongoing changes in electronics and digital technology that are constantly altering the mix of products it offers in its virtual store.

As a result of these incremental innovations to Amazon.com's business, Bezos has transformed his company from "online bookseller" to "leading Internet product provider." The company's share price has soared in the 2000s after plunging during the dot.com bust, because investors believe that Amazon.com will become a highly profitable online retail business.

IT and Organizational Structure and Culture

IT also affects the innovation process through its many effects on organizational structure. Specialization typically leads to the development of subunit orientations that reduce the ability of employees to understand the wider context within which they are contributing their skills and expertise. IT can mitigate this tendency by providing greater information access to specialists through such technologies as email, corporate intranets, access to the Internet, and so on.

To speed innovation, many organizations have begun to move decision making lower in the organization to take advantage of specialized workers who possess more accurate and timely local information. IT helps this process in two ways. First, IT gives lower-level employees more detailed and current knowledge of consumer and market trends and opportunities. For example, IT in customer support centers directed at solving customer problems via the Internet has become a widespread means of increasing effectiveness.

Second, IT can produce information synergies because it facilitates increased communication and coordination between decentralized decision makers and top managers. Now, as decision-making authority moves lower in the hierarchy, it may become better aligned.[44] The Gap, discussed earlier, would have greatly benefited from a sophisticated online computer-aided design system (CAD) that allowed designers throughout the organization to see what the others were doing.

Third, IT means that fewer levels of managers are needed to handle problem solving and decision making, which results in a flatter organization. In addition, because IT provides lower-level employees with more freedom to coordinate their actions, information synergies may emerge, as employees experiment and find better ways of performing their tasks.

IT can also promote innovation through its effects on organizational culture. IT facilitates the sharing of beliefs, values, and norms because it allows for the quick transmission of rich, detailed information between people and subunits. IT thus can enhance the motivational effects of cultural values supportive of innovation. Using IT, an organization can make available to employees a slew of supportive messages and statements, often contained in an organization's mission statement, corporate goals, operating procedures, and so on. Email, voice mail, and intranets, for example, provide mechanisms for transferring and disseminating information about the organization to employees and can help promote the cultural shared norms, values, and expectations that can facilitate innovation.

SUMMARY

Managing the process of innovation and change to enhance organizational effectiveness is a central challenge facing managers and organizations today. An increasing rate of technological change and an increase in global competition are two forces that are putting enormous pressure on organizations to find new and better ways of organizing their activities to increase their ability to innovate and create value. Chapter 13 has made the following major points:

1. Innovation is the development of new products or new production and operating systems (including new forms of organizational structures).
2. There are two types of innovation: quantum innovations, which are the result of quantum shifts in technology, and incremental innovations, which result from the refinements to an existing technology. Technological change that results in quantum innovations can create opportunities for an organization to introduce new products, but it can also be a threat, since it can increase the level of competition.
3. Innovation, intrapreneurship and creativity are closely related concepts and each is vital to build a knowledge-creating organization.
4. There are a number of techniques that managers can use to help promote innovation. These include project management, using a stage-gate development funnel, using cross-functional teams and a product team structure, establishing strong team leadership, making use of skunk works and new venture divisions, and creating a culture for innovation.
5. IT creates information efficiencies and information synergies and thus is an important tool for promoting creativity and innovation, especially through its effects on organizational design, structure and culture.

DISCUSSION QUESTIONS

1. What is the relationship between quantum and incremental technological change?
2. What is the relationship among creativity, intrapreneurship and innovation?
3. What is project management? How should managers decide which projects to pursue?
4. What steps would you take to create (a) a structure and (b) a culture congenial to innovation in a high-tech organization?
5. What are information synergies and in what ways can they enhance innovation?

ORGANIZATIONAL THEORY IN ACTION

Practicing Organizational Theory: Managing Innovation

Form groups of three to five people and discuss the following scenario:

You are the top managers in charge of a chain of stores selling high-quality, high-priced men's and women's clothing. Store sales are flat, and you are increasingly concerned that the clothing your stores offer to customers is failing to satisfy changing customer needs. You think that the purchasing managers are failing to spot changing fads and fashions in time, and you believe that store management is not doing enough to communicate to purchasing managers what customers are demanding. You want to revitalize your organization's product development process, which, in the case of your stores, means designing, selecting, and stocking the products that customers want.

1. Using the chapter material, outline the way you will create a program to increase creativity and intrapreneurship at the store and corporate level. For example, how will you encourage input from employees and customers, and who will be responsible for managing the program?
2. How will you make use of IT and organizational structure to facilitate the innovation process?

The Ethical Dimension

Some intrapreneurs make discoveries that earn millions or even billions of dollars of product sales for the companies for which they work, but because this was not addressed in their employment contracts, they do not share in these profits. Other intrapreneurs make discoveries in the course of their work but do not share this information with their companies. They leave their organizations and found their own to exploit this knowledge.

1. Think about the ethical issues involved in each of these scenarios. Is it ethical either for the organization or the individual to act in this way?
2. Is there a way of solving the ethical dilemma posed in each of these cases?

Making the Connection #13

Find an example of an organization that has been trying to promote its level of innovation. What kind of innovation is it principally trying to promote? How is it attempting to do so? What has been its success so far?

Analyzing the Organization: Design Module #13

This model focuses on the extent to which your organization has been involved in efforts to promote innovation.

Assignment

1. With the information that you have at your disposal, discuss (a) the forces for change, and (b) the obstacles to change in your company.
2. With what kind of innovation (quantum or incremental) has your organization been most involved?
3. In what ways, if any, has your organization sought to manage the innovation process and alter its structure or culture to increase its capacity to develop new products or services?

CASE FOR ANALYSIS

Too Much Innovation at Lucent

In the early 2000s, increasing competition made it imperative for many high-tech companies to find a way to innovate and differentiate their products to sustain or increase their competitive advantage. Take Lucent Technologies, which makes Internet routers and other communications equipment. Lucent was one of the high-flying high-tech companies of the 1990s. To promote the speedy development of new products, former CEO Richard McGinn had decided that Lucent should be set up as 11 independent business divisions, each of which would focus on a particular product and market.[45] His goal was to drive innovation and develop a steady stream of new products to compete with market leader Sysco Systems.

In creating venture divisions, however, McGinn set in motion a whole set of problems that ultimately led to the company's downfall. First, enormous communications and coordination problems arose because managers in one division did not know what managers in the others were doing. Incompatible kinds of products were being developed, new technology was not being shared across divisions, and it was a nightmare trying to sell Lucent's range of products globally because the 11 business units were each handling their own global sales. For example, because of poor decision making and communication managers had backed the development of the wrong kind of router, one based on capacity rather than speed; speed turned out to be what customers wanted. By contrast, Nortel Networks, one of Lucent's major competitors, had developed fast optical or light-based routers, and its market share was surging. Second, the cost of managing all these new venture divisions was enormous because they each had their own set of functions, including R&D, which is a major expense for a high-tech organization. Thus, not only were revenues falling, but costs were increasing.

The failed new venture strategy forced McGinn to leave the company. His successor, Henry Schacht, decided effectiveness would increase if Lucent reorganized the 11 different units into just five business units. This would make managers more accountable for their actions, and they would be better able to communicate and avoid mistaken innovation and failed product development. Schacht and his managers spent hundreds of millions of dollars to restructure the company and laid off over 15,000 employees.

By 2001, however, it was clear that Lucent could no longer afford the luxury of having even five divisions because of mounting losses and the need to reduce costs. In July and October, Schacht announced that Lucent would reorganize again both to reduce costs and allow it better to focus its resources to speed the new product development process. Another 20,000 employees were to be laid off (nearly one-half of Lucent's total employees were laid off as a result of the restructuring). Lucent announced that it was combining the five units into only two business divisions:[46] an Integrated Network Solutions division would handle all its land-line products such as routers, switching, and data software; and a Mobility Solutions division would handle the company's wireless products.

Managers hoped this new structure would perform more flexibly and organically and allow it to respond faster and more effectively to the rapidly changing information technology environment. They also knew it would save billions of dollars and would be a much more efficient method of organizing. They were right: By focusing its resources on a few key products, Lucent has been able to build a strong customer base and it is prospering in the 2000s—albeit as a much smaller company.

DISCUSSION QUESTIONS

1. What problems did Lucent encounter as it tried to speed product innovation?

2. What approach did its new top managers adopt to solve these problems?

REFERENCES

1. R. A. Burgelman and M. A. Maidique, *Strategic Management of Technology and Innovation* (Homewood, IL: Irwin, 1988).

2. G. R. Jones and J. E. Butler, "Managing Internal Corporate Entrepreneurship: An Agency Theory Perspective," *Journal of Management*, 18 (1992), 733–749.

3. E. Mansfield, J. Rapaport, J. Schnee, S. Wagner, and M. Hamburger, *Research and Innovation in the Modern Corporation* (New York: Norton, 1971).

4. R. D'Aveni, *Hyper-Competition* (New York: The Free Press, 1994).

5. P. Engardio and N. Gross, "Asia's High-Tech Quest: Can the Tigers Compete Worldwide?" *Business Week*, December 7, 1992, pp. 126–130.

6. P. Anderson and Michael L. Tushman, "Technological Discontinuities and Dominant Designs: A Cyclical Model of Technological Change," *Administrative Science Quarterly*, 35 (1990), 604–633; quoting J. Schumpeter, *Capitalism, Socialism, and Democracy* (New York: Harper Brothers, 1942).

7. The concept of creative destruction goes back to the classic work of J. A. Schumpeter, ibid.

8. V. P. Buell, *Marketing Management* (New York: McGraw-Hill, 1985).

9. See M.M.J. Berry and J. H. Taggart, "Managing Technology and Innovation: A Review," *R & D Management* 24 (1994), 341–353; and Clark and Wheelwright, *Managing New Product and Process Development* (New York: The Free Press, 1993).

10. E. Abrahamson, "Managerial Fads and Fashions: The Diffusion and Rejection of Innovations," *Academy of Management Review*, 16 (1991), 586–612.

11. www.gapinc.com, 2000.

12. L. Clifford, "A Gap Mishap–But It Still Deserves a Look," *Fortune*, September 18, 2000, pp. 45–47.

13. www.gap.com, 2002.

14. B. Stone, "Filling in The Gap," *Newsweek*, October 7, 2002, p. 48.

15. www.thegap.com, 2005.

16. See Berry and Taggart, "Managing Technology and Innovation"; M. Gort and J. Klepper, "Time Paths in the Diffusion of Product Innovations," *Economic Journal*, September 1982, pp. 630–653. Looking at the history of 46 products, Gort and Klepper found that the length of time before other companies entered the markets created by a few inventive companies declined from an average of 14 years for products introduced before 1930 to 4.9 years for those introduced after 1949—implying that product life cycles were being compressed. See also A. Griffin, "Metrics for Measuring Product Development Cycle Time," *Journal of Production and Innovation Management*, 10 (1993), 112–125.

17. Clark and Wheelwright, *Managing New Product and Process Development*. See also G. Stalk and T. M. Hout, *Competing Against Time* (New York: The Free Press, 1990).

18. T. Lonier, "Some Insights and Statistics on Working Solo," www.workingsolo.com.

19. J.V. Anderson, "Weirder Than Fiction: The Reality and Myth of Creativity," *Academy of Management Executive*, 6 (1992), pp. 40–42.

20. Ibid, p. 43.

21. I. Nonaka, "The Knowledge Creating Company," *Harvard Business Review* (November–December 1991), 1–9.

22. Ibid.

23. www.microsoft.com/mspress/books/sampchap/4652a.asp?

24. K. B. Clark and S. C. Wheelwright, *Managing New Product and Process Development*.

25. A. Griffin and J. R. Hauser, "Patterns of Communication Among Marketing, Engineering, and Manufacturing," *Management Science*, 38 (1992), 360–373; R. K. Moenaert, W. E. Sounder, A. D. Meyer, and D. Deschoolmeester, "R&D-Marketing Integration Mechanisms, Communication Flows, and Innovation Success," *Journal of Production and Innovation Management*, 11 (1994), 31–45.

26. R. A. Burgelman and M. A. Maidique, *Strategic Management of Technology and Innovation*.

27. G. Barczak and D. Wileman, "Leadership Differences in New Product Development Teams," *Journal of Product Innovation Management*, 6 (1989), 259–267; E. F. McDonough and G. Barczak, "Speeding Up New Product Development: The Effects of Leadership Style and Source of Technology," *Journal of Product Innovation Management*, 8 (1991), 203–211; K. B. Clark and T. Fujimoto, "The Power of Product Integrity," *Harvard Business Review* (November–December 1990), 107–119.

28. K. B. Clark and S. C. Wheelwright, *Managing New Product and Process Development*.

29. Ibid.

30. M. A. Maidique and R. H. Hayes, "The Art of High Technology Management," *Sloan Management Review* (Winter 1984), 18–31.

31. D. Frey, "Learning the Ropes: My Life as a Product Champion," *Harvard Business Review* (September–October 1991), 46–56.

32. R. A. Burgelman, "Designs for Corporate Entrepreneurship in Established Firms," *California Management Review*, 26 (1984), 154–166.

33. H. Mintzberg and J. A. Waters, "Tracking Strategy in an Entrepreneurial Firm," *Academy of Management Journal*, 25 (1982), 465–499; P. Strebel, "Organizing for Innovation over an Industry Life Cycle," *Strategic Management Journal*, 8 (1987), 117–124.

34. R. M. Kanter, *The Change Masters* (New York: Simon and Schuster, 1983).

35. G. R. Jones and J. E. Butler, "Managing Internal Corporate Entrepreneurship: An Agency Theory Perspective," *Journal of Management*, 18 (1992), 733–749.

36. www.3M.com, 2006.

37. Ibid.

38. T. Dewett and G. R. Jones, "The Role of Information Technology in the Organization: A Review, Model, and Assessment," *Journal of Management*, 27 (2001), 313–346.

39. B. Leavy, "The Concept of Learning in the Strategy Field: Review and Outlook," *Management Learning*, 29 (1998), 447–466.

40. C. K. Prahalad and G. Hamel, "The Core Competency of the Corporation," *Harvard Business Review* (May–June 1990), 43–59.

41. J. F. Rockart and D. DeLong, *Executive Support Systems: The Emergence of Top Management Computer Use* (Burr Ridge, IL: Dow-Jones Irwin); J. F. Rockart, and J. E. Short, "IT and the 1990s: Managing Organizational Interdependencies," *Sloan Management Review*, 30 (1989), 17–33.

42. M. T. Hanson, "The Search Transfer Problem: The Role of Weak Ties in Sharing Knowledge Across Organizational Subunits," *Administrative Science Quarterly*, 44 (1999), 82–111.

43. www.amazon.com, 2002.

44. Dewitt and Jones, op. cit.

45. C. Arnst, R. O. Crockett, A. Reinhardt, and J. Shinai, "Lucent: Clean Break, Clean Slate," *Business Week*, November 6, 2000, pp. 172–180.

46. www.lucent.com, 2006.

Managing Conflict, Power, and Politics

Learning Objectives

This chapter focuses on the social and interpersonal processes that affect the way managers make decisions and the way organizations change and adapt to their environments. Specifically, it examines the causes, nature, and consequences of organizational conflict, power, and politics.

After studying this chapter you should be able to:

1. Describe the nature of organizational conflict, its sources, and the way it arises between stakeholders and subunits.

2. Identify the mechanisms by which managers and stakeholders can obtain power and use that power to influence decision making and resolve conflict in their favor.

3. Explain how and why individuals and subunits engage in organizational politics to enhance their control over decision making and obtain the power that allows them to influence the change process in their favor.

4. Appreciate the importance of managing an organization's power structure to overcome organizational inertia, and to bring about the type of change that promotes performance.

WHAT IS ORGANIZATIONAL CONFLICT?

As noted in Chapter 2, an organization consists of different groups of stakeholders, each of which contributes to the organization in return for rewards. Stakeholders cooperate with one another to contribute jointly the resources an organization needs to produce goods and services. At the same time, however, stakeholders compete with one another for the resources the organization generates from these joint activities.[1] To produce goods and services, an organization needs the skills and abilities of managers and employees, the capital provided by shareholders, and the inputs provided by suppliers. Inside and outside stakeholders, such as employees, management, and shareholders, however, compete over their share of the rewards and resources that the organization generates.

393

Figure 14.1
Cooperation and Competition Among Organizational Stakeholders

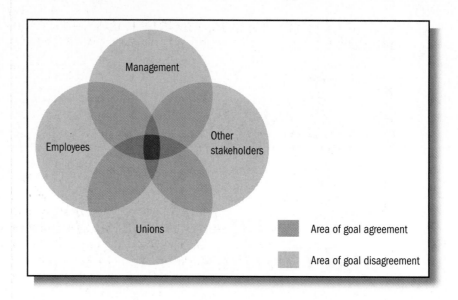

To grow, change, and survive, an organization must manage both cooperation and competition among stakeholders. As Figure 14.1 suggests, each stakeholder group has its own goals and interests, which overlap somewhat with those of other groups because all stakeholders have a common interest in the survival of the organization. But stakeholders' goals and interests are not identical, and conflict arises when one group pursues its own interests at the expense of other groups. **Organizational conflict** is the clash that occurs when the goal-directed behavior of one group blocks or thwarts the goals of another.

Because the goals, preferences, and interests of stakeholder groups differ, conflict is inevitable in organizations.[2] Although conflict is often perceived as something negative, research suggests that some conflict is good for an organization and can improve organizational effectiveness. Beyond some point (point A in Figure 14.2), however, extreme conflict between stakeholders can hurt organizational performance.[3]

Organizational conflict
The clash that occurs when the goal-directed behavior of one group blocks or thwarts the goals of another.

Figure 14.2
The Relationship Between Conflict and Organizational Effectiveness

Research suggests that there is an optimal level of conflict within an organization. Beyond that point (point A), conflict is likely to be harmful.

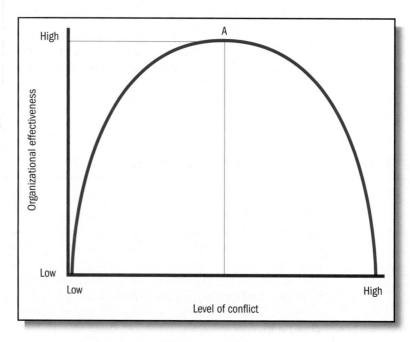

Why is some conflict good for an organization? Conflict can be beneficial because it can overcome organizational inertia and lead to organizational learning and change. When conflict within an organization or conflict between an organization and elements in its environment arises, the organization and its managers must reevaluate their view of the world. As we saw in Chapter 12, conflict between different managers or between different stakeholder groups can improve decision making and organizational learning by revealing new ways of looking at a problem or the false or erroneous assumptions that distort decision making. For example, conflict at AT&T between the board of directors and top managers about the slow pace at which top managers were restructuring the company caused a radical change in managerial attitudes. A new top management team was appointed to increase the pace of change and to overcome AT&T's conservative approach. Similarly, conflict between divisional managers at IBM resulted in a major change in organizational focus, from a purely mainframe focus to a more consulting-oriented focus.

The conflict that arises when different groups perceive the organization's problems in different ways and are willing to act on their beliefs is a built-in defense against the organizational inertia produced by a top management team whose members have the same vision of the world. In short, conflict can improve decision making and allow an organization better to change and adapt to its environment.[4]

Beyond a certain point, however, conflict stops being a force for good and becomes a cause of organizational decline. Suppose, for example, conflict between managers (or between other stakeholders) becomes chronic, so that managers cannot agree about organizational priorities or about how best to allocate resources to meet organizational needs. In this situation, managers spend all their time bargaining and fighting, and the organization gets so bogged down in the process of decision making that organizational change is slow in coming. Innovation is, of course, more or less impossible in such a setting. In a somewhat vicious cycle, the slow and ponderous decision-making characteristic of organizations in decline leads to even greater conflict because the consequences of failure are so great. An organization in trouble spends a lot of time making decisions—time that it cannot afford because it needs to adapt quickly to turn itself around. Thus, although some conflict can jolt an organization out of inertia, too much conflict can cause organizational inertia: As different groups fight for their own positions and interests, they fail to arrive at consensus, and the organization drifts along; failure to change makes the organization go from bad to worse.[5]

Many analysts claim that both AT&T and IBM faced this difficult situation. Top managers knew they had to make radical changes to their organization's strategy and structure, but they could not do so because different groups of managers lobbied for their own interests and for cutbacks to fall on other divisions. Conflict among divisions and the constant fight to protect each division's interests resulted in a slow rate of change and worsened the situation. In both companies, the boards of directors removed the CEO and brought in newcomers—Michael Armstrong and Louis Gerstner—who they hoped would overcome opposition to change and develop a strategy that would promote organizational interests, not just the interests of a particular group.

On balance, then, organizations need to be open to conflict, to recognize its value both in helping to identify problems and in contributing to the generation of alternative solutions that improve decision making. Conflict can promote organizational learning. However, in order to exploit the functional aspects of conflict and avoid the dysfunctional effects, managers must learn how to control it. Louis R. Pondy developed a useful model of organizational conflict. Pondy first identifies the sources of conflict and then examines the stages of a typical conflict episode.[6] His model provides many clues about how to control and manage conflict in an organization.

Pondy views conflict as a process that consists of five sequential episodes or stages, summarized in Figure 14.3. No matter how or why conflict arises, managers can use Pondy's model to interpret and analyze a conflict situation and take action to resolve it—for example, by redesigning the organization's structure.

Stage 1: Latent Conflict

In the first stage of Pondy's model, *latent conflict*, no outright conflict exists; however, the potential for conflict to arise is present, though latent, because of the way an organization operates. According to Pondy, all organizational conflict arises because vertical and horizontal differentiation lead to the establishment of different organizational subunits with different goals and often different perceptions of how best to realize those goals. In business enterprises, for example, managers in different functions or divisions can generally agree about the organization's central goal, which is to maximize the organization's ability to create value in the long run. But they may have different ideas about how to achieve this goal: Should the organization invest resources in manufacturing to lower costs or in research to develop new products? Five potential sources of conflict between subunits have been identified: subunits' interdependence, subunits' differing goals, bureaucratic factors, incompatible performance criteria, and competition for resources.[7]

Interdependence

As organizations differentiate, each subunit develops a desire for autonomy and begins to pursue goals and interests that it values over the goals of other subunits or of the organization as a whole. Because the activities of different subunits are interdependent, subunits' desire for autonomy leads to conflict between groups. Eventually, each subunit's desire for autonomy comes into conflict with the organization's desire for coordination.

Figure 14.3
Pondy's Model of Organizational Conflict

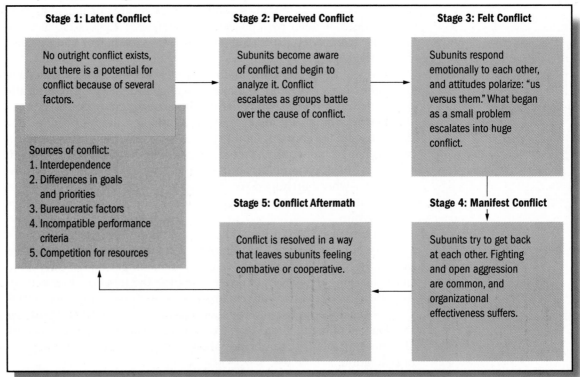

Stage 1: Latent Conflict

No outright conflict exists, but there is a potential for conflict because of several factors.

Sources of conflict:
1. Interdependence
2. Differences in goals and priorities
3. Bureaucratic factors
4. Incompatible performance criteria
5. Competition for resources

Stage 2: Perceived Conflict

Subunits become aware of conflict and begin to analyze it. Conflict escalates as groups battle over the cause of conflict.

Stage 3: Felt Conflict

Subunits respond emotionally to each other, and attitudes polarize: "us versus them." What began as a small problem escalates into huge conflict.

Stage 4: Manifest Conflict

Subunits try to get back at each other. Fighting and open aggression are common, and organizational effectiveness suffers.

Stage 5: Conflict Aftermath

Conflict is resolved in a way that leaves subunits feeling combative or cooperative.

In terms of Thompson's model of technology, discussed in Chapter 9, the move from pooled to sequential to reciprocal task interdependence between people or subunits increases the degree to which the actions of one subunit directly affect the actions of others.[8] When task interdependence is high, conflict is likely to occur at the individual, functional, and divisional levels. If it were not for interdependence, there would be no potential for conflict to occur among organizational subunits or stakeholders.[9]

Differences in Goals and Priorities

Differences in subunit orientation affect the way each function or division views the world and cause each subunit to pursue different goals that are often inconsistent or incompatible. Once goals become incompatible, the potential for conflict arises because the goals of one subunit may thwart the ability of another to achieve its goals. As we discussed in Chapter 12, top managers often have different goals and priorities that may cause conflict in the decision-making process. The way in which the CEO and chief operating officer of Kodak fought over plans for reorganizing the company shows how differences in goals can lead to organizational conflict.

ORGANIZATIONAL INSIGHT 14.1
Conflict Causes Slow Change at Kodak

Eastman Kodak, whose ubiquitous little yellow film boxes have long been a part of the American scene, has been experiencing declining performance for years. As with IBM and General Motors, Kodak was slow to react to the threat of competition in its central business, and a ponderous decision-making style has stifled its attempts to restructure its activities. In the early 1990s, CEO Kay Whitmore, a Kodak veteran, was reluctant to make the drastic changes that Kodak needed to regain its competitiveness. Although Kodak's management had repeatedly tried to turn the company's fortunes around, nothing had really worked, and the company's share price had been declining steadily for years.

Thus, in 1993, investors on Wall Street were delighted to hear about the appointment of Christopher Steffen as Kodak's new chief operating officer. Steffen had a reputation as a "turnaround artist" who had performed miracles at Chrysler and Honeywell, and news of his appointment sent Kodak's stock price up by 17%. Investors thought that an outsider would finally bring a breath of fresh air and fresh ideas to Kodak's inbred top management team. Investors were therefore shocked when Steffen announced his resignation from the company less than a week after his appointment, citing "differences with the company's approach to problem solving."[10]

Apparently he and CEO Whitmore had very different ideas about how to restructure the company and the speed at which restructuring should be done. Steffen reportedly wanted to institute a massive cost-cutting regime, including large layoffs. He proposed a revolutionary change strategy and wanted to implement it right away. Whitmore, pursuing Kodak's traditional consensus approach to decision making, wanted much slower, evolutionary change, even though this approach had failed in the past. In short,

Steffen and Whitmore came into conflict over the company's priorities. As in the past, Kodak's entrenched management team had the power to carry the day and resist attempts by Steffen and stockholders to change the way the company operated. Stockholders reacted to Steffen's departure by sending the company's share price down by over 10%, but within months the price shot back up when Whitmore was ousted by a concerned board of directors and replaced by the chairman of Motorola, George Fisher. Fisher made several changes that Kodak needed, but he was unable to turn its performance around.

In January 2000, Kodak's board decided on a new CEO, Dan Carp, and Fisher was out. Karp, a Kodak veteran, got the job because he had great support from other Kodak executives to expand its push into electronic imaging.[11] They backed his candidacy in some part to protect their own jobs. By 2003 it became clear that Karp was still trying to rescue Kodak's empire and to avoid the radical restructuring necessary to save the troubled company. Carp was not the right person to take on this role, especially as he was obligated to many of Kodak's top managers who had lobbied for his appointment to the top job.

So, in 2003 Kodak's board of directors hired Antonio Perez, a former HP executive, as its new president and COO, to reorganize the company. Perez did make the hard choices—closing divisions and laying many more thousands of managers and employees. In 2005, his success led to his appointment as Kodak's new CEO, and he became responsible for implementing the new downsized, streamlined company's new digital imaging strategy.[12] However, intense competition in the digital photography market, and declining film sales, has not allowed Perez to bring Kodak back to profitability—the best he has been able to do is to stem its losses and its future is still uncertain.

Bureaucratic Factors

The way in which task relationships develop in organizations can also be a potential source of conflict. Over time, conflict can occur because of status inconsistencies between different groups in the organization's bureaucracy. A classic type of bureaucratic conflict occurs between staff and line functions.[13] A *line function* is directly involved in the production of the organization's outputs. In a manufacturing company, manufacturing is the line function; in a hospital, doctors are the line function; and in a university, professors are the line function. *Staff functions* advise and support the line function and include functions such as personnel, accounting, and purchasing. In many organizations, people in line functions come to view themselves as the critical organizational resource and people in staff functions as secondary players. Acting on this belief, the line function constantly uses its supposedly lofty status as the producer of goods and services to justify putting its interests ahead of the other functions' interests. The result is conflict.[14]

Incompatible Performance Criteria

Sometimes conflict arises between subunits not because their goals are incompatible but because the organization's way of monitoring, evaluating, and rewarding different subunits brings them into conflict. Production and sales can come into conflict when, to achieve the goal of increased sales, the sales department asks manufacturing to respond quickly to customer orders—an action that raises manufacturing costs. If the organization's reward system benefits sales personnel (who get higher bonuses because of increased sales) but penalizes manufacturing (which gets no bonus because of higher costs), conflict will arise.

The way an organization designs its structure to coordinate subunits can affect the potential for conflict. The constant conflict between divisions at CS First Boston, a large American investment bank, shows how incompatible reward systems can produce conflict. CS First Boston was formed by the merger of two smaller banks: First Boston (based in New York) and Crédit Suisse (based in London). From the beginning, the two divisions of the new bank were at odds. Although the merger was formed to take advantage of synergies in the growing transatlantic investment banking business, the divisions could never cooperate with one another, and managers in both were fond of openly criticizing the banking practices of their peers to anybody who would listen.

As long as the performance of one unit of the bank did not affect the other, the lack of cooperation between them was tolerated. In the 1990s, however, the performance of the European unit began to affect the American unit, and conflict started to build. First Boston made record profits from issuing and trading debt securities, and its managers were expecting hefty bonuses. However, those bonuses were not paid. Why? The London arm of the organization had incurred huge losses, and although the losses were not the fault of the Boston-based bank, the corporation's top managers decided not to pay bonuses to their U.S. employees because of the losses from Europe.

As you can imagine, this inequitable decision, punishing U.S. employees for an outcome that they could not control, led to considerable conflict within the organization. Relations between the U.S. and European arms of the bank became even more strained; the divisions began fighting with top management. When employees decided that the situation would not change in the near term, they began to leave CS First Boston in droves. Many senior managers left for competitors, such as Merrill Lynch and Goldman Sachs.[15] Clearly, redesigning the reward system so that it does not promote conflict between divisions should be one of management's major priorities.[16]

Competition for Scarce Resources

Conflict would never be a problem if there was always an abundance of resources for subunits to use. When resources are scarce, as they always are, choices about resource allocation have to be made, and subunits have to compete for their share.[17] Divisions fight to increase their share of funding because the more funds they can obtain and invest, the faster they can grow. Similarly, at the functional level there can be conflict over the amount of funds to allocate to sales, or to manufacturing, or to R&D to meet organizational objectives. Thus, to increase access to resources, functions promote their interests and importance often at one another's expense.

Together, these five factors have the potential to cause a significant level of conflict in an organization. At stage 1, however, the conflict is latent. The potential for conflict exists, but conflict has not yet surfaced. In complex organizations with high levels of differentiation and integration, the potential for conflict is especially great. The subunits are highly interdependent and have different goals and complicated reward systems, and the competition among them for organizational resources is intense. Managing organizational conflict to allocate resources to where they can produce the most value in the long run is very difficult.

Stage 2: Perceived Conflict

The second stage of Pondy's model, *perceived conflict*, begins when a subunit or stakeholder group perceives that its goals are being thwarted by the actions of another group. In this stage, each subunit begins to define why the conflict is emerging and to analyze the events that have led up to it. Each group searches for the origin of the conflict and constructs a scenario that accounts for the problems that it is experiencing with other subunits. The manufacturing function, for example, may suddenly realize that the cause of many of its production problems is defective inputs. When production managers investigate, they discover that materials management always buys inputs from the lowest cost sources of supply and makes no attempt to develop the kind of long-term relationships with suppliers that can raise the quality and reliability of inputs. Materials management reduces input costs and improves this function's bottom line, but it raises manufacturing costs and worsens that function's bottom line. Not surprisingly, manufacturing perceives materials management as thwarting its goals and interests.

Normally at this point the conflict escalates as the different subunits or stakeholders start to battle over the cause of the problem. To get materials management to change its purchasing practices, manufacturing complains about materials management to the CEO and whoever else will listen. Materials management is likely to dispute the charge that its purchase of low-cost inputs leads to inferior quality. Instead, it attributes the problem to manufacturing's failure to provide employees with sufficient training to operate new technology and dumps responsibility for the quality problems back in manufacturing's lap. Even though both functions share the goal of superior product quality, they attribute the poor quality to very different causes.

Stage 3: Felt Conflict

At the *felt conflict* stage, subunits in conflict quickly develop an emotional response toward each other. Typically, each subunit closes ranks and develops a polarized us-versus-them mentality that puts the blame for the conflict squarely on the other subunit. As conflict escalates, cooperation between subunits falls, and so does organizational effectiveness. It is difficult to speed new product development, for example, if research and development, materials management, and manufacturing are fighting over quality and final product specifications.

As the different subunits in conflict battle and argue their point of view, the conflict escalates. The original problem may be relatively minor, but if nothing is done to solve it, the small problem will escalate into a huge conflict that becomes increasingly difficult to manage. If the conflict is not resolved now, it quickly reaches the next stage.

Stage 4: Manifest Conflict

In the *manifest conflict* stage of Pondy's model, one subunit gets back at another subunit by attempting to thwart its goals. Manifest conflict can take many forms. Open aggression between people and groups is common. There are many stories and myths in organizations about boardroom fights in which managers actually come to blows as they seek to promote their interests. Infighting in the top management team is very common as managers seek to promote their own careers at the expense of others. When Lee Iacocca was at Ford Motor Company, for example, and Henry Ford II decided to bring in the head of General Motors as the new Ford CEO, Iacocca engineered the downfall of the new CEO within one year in order to promote his own rise to the top. Eventually, Iacocca lost the battle: Henry Ford forced Iacocca out because he feared that Iacocca would usurp his power.

A very effective form of manifest conflict is passive aggression—frustrating the goals of the opposition by doing nothing. Suppose there is a history of conflict between sales and production. One day, sales desperately needs a rush order for an important client. What might the manager of production do? One strategy is to agree informally to the sales department's request but then do nothing. When the head of sales comes banging on the door, the production manager says innocently, "Oh, you meant last Friday. I thought you meant *this* Friday." The situation that existed at Morgan Stanley in 2005 illustrates the damaging effects of manifest conflict.

In general, as the example of Morgan Stanley suggests, once conflict is manifest, organizational effectiveness suffers because coordination and integration between managers and subunits break down. Managers need to do all they can to prevent conflict from reaching the manifest stage, for two reasons: because of the breakdown in communication that is likely to occur and because of the aftermath of conflict.

Stage 5: Conflict Aftermath

Sooner or later, organizational conflict is resolved in some way, often by the decision of some senior manager. Sooner or later, if the sources of the conflict have not been resolved, the disputes and problems that caused the conflict arise again in another

ORGANIZATIONAL INSIGHT 14.2
Conflict at Financial Giant Morgan Stanley

Morgan Stanley is one of Wall Street's most prestigious financial institutions; however, in the 2000s it has been plagued with infighting and conflict among its managers over the best way to realize the value of its assets. A turning point came in 2001, when John Mack, a member of its top management team, announced that he was leaving the company after a bitter ongoing quarrel with its CEO Phil Purcell. Mack had publicly announced that he thought "Purcell was not up to the job" and was leading Morgan Stanley into financial disaster. However, the board of directors took Purcell's side and Mack was forced out.

After his departure, conflict at Morgan Stanley among its financial units only grew worse; some supported Purcell, but when the company's profitability continued to fall others began to follow Mack's path and lobby for him to step down. As Morgan's performance continued to decline, its stock price plunged and many of its talented people began to leave. In June 2005 the board of directors came to realize that Mack has been right; Purcell resigned as CEO.

Who to choose as CEO to heal the rifts between its financial experts and units? Many Morgan executives lobbied in favor of Mack, arguing that he had the vision needed to lead the company. But, the board restated its opposition to Mack—it was hard for directors to admit he had been right and they had been wrong. However, Morgan now faced the prospect of losing hundreds more of its most talented financial experts to competitors because of all the turmoil taking place. So, to try to reduce conflict and keep its managers Morgan's board caved in and, cap in hand, went to Mack to offer him the CEO's job. Mack, who had spent most of his career at Morgan, agreed to return, and his task has been to find ways to resolve conflicts at the bank and restore the morale of its employees in order to return it to its former leading position.

context. What happens when the conflict reappears depends on how it was resolved the first time. Suppose that sales comes to production with a new request. How are sales and production likely to behave? They probably will be combative and suspicious of each other and will find it hard to agree on anything. But suppose that sales and marketing had been able to solve their earlier dispute amicably and were able to agree on the need to respond flexibly to the needs of an important customer. The next time sales comes along with a special request, how is production likely to react? The production manager will probably have a cooperative attitude, and both parties will be able to sit down and work out a joint plan that suits the needs of both functions.

Every episode of conflict leaves a *conflict aftermath* that affects the way both parties perceive and react to future episodes. If a conflict is resolved before it gets to the manifest conflict stage, then the aftermath will promote good future working relationships. If conflict is not resolved until late in the process, or is not resolved at all, the aftermath will sour future working relationships, and the organizational culture will be poisoned by permanently uncooperative relationships. John Mack's task was to prevent this from occurring at Morgan Stanley, to find ways to get its managers to put the past behind them and cooperate to get the company back on track.

MANAGING CONFLICT: CONFLICT RESOLUTION STRATEGIES

Because organizational conflict can rapidly escalate and sour an organization's culture, managing organizational conflict is an important priority.[18] An organization must balance the need to have some "good" conflict (which overcomes inertia and allows new organizational learning) with the need to prevent "good" conflict from escalating into "bad conflict" (which causes a breakdown in coordination and integration between functions and divisions). In this section, we look at a few conflict resolution strategies designed to help organizations manage organizational conflict. Later in the chapter, we look at organizational politics as another way of managing organizational conflict when the stakes are high and when divisions and functions can obtain power to influence organizational outcomes, such as decisions about how to change or restructure an organization, in their favor.

The method an organization chooses to manage conflict depends on the source of the problem. At CS First Boston, the problem was an inequitable reward system that penalized one subunit for the poor performance of another. To solve this problem, CS First Boston's management needs to remove the source of the conflict by changing the way its reward systems operate—that is, by devising an equitable reward system. At Kodak, the source of the conflict was top managers' fight to protect their positions and property rights, and the conflict was resolved only by changing the top management team. These examples suggest the two strategies that managers are likely to use to resolve conflict: changing an organization's structure to reduce or eliminate the cause of the conflict or trying to change the attitudes of individuals or replacing the individuals themselves.[19]

Acting at the Level of Structure

Because task interdependence and differences in goals are two major sources of conflict, altering the level of differentiation and integration to change task relationships is one way to resolve conflict. An organization might change from a functional structure to a product division structure in order to remove a source of conflict between manufacturing managers who are unable to control the overhead costs associated with different kinds of products. Moving to a product structure makes it much easier to assign overhead costs to different product lines. Similarly, if product managers are finding it difficult to convince departments to cooperate to speed product development, the move to a product team structure, in which different functional managers are assigned permanently to a product line, will remove the source of the problem.

If divisions are battling over resources, corporate managers can increase the number of integrating roles in the organization and assign top managers the responsibility for solving conflicts between divisions and for improving the structure of working relationships.[20] In general, increasing the level of integration is one major way in which organizations can manage the problem of differences in subunit goals. To resolve potential conflict situations, organizations can increase their use of liaison roles, task forces, teams, and integrating mechanisms (see Figure 4.5).

Another way to manage conflict is to make sure that the design of an organization's hierarchy of authority is in line with its current needs. As an organization grows and differentiates, the chain of command lengthens, and the organization is likely to lose control of its hierarchy. This loss of control can be a major source of conflict: People are given the responsibility for making decisions but lack the authority to do so because a manager above them must sign off on every move they make. Flattening the hierarchy, so that authority relationships are clearly defined, and decentralizing authority can remove a major source of organizational conflict. One source of such conflict occurs when two or more people, departments, or divisions compete for the same set of resources. This situation is likely to be disastrous because decision making is impossible when different people claim the right to control the same resources. For this reason, the military and some other organizations have established very clear lines of authority; there is no ambiguity about who reports to whom and who has control of what resources.

Good organizational design should result in the creation of an organizational structure that minimizes the potential for organizational conflict. However, because of inertia, many organizations fail to manage their structures and change them to suit the needs of a changing environment. As a result, conflict increases and organizational effectiveness falls.

Acting at the Level of Attitudes and Individuals

Differences in goals and in beliefs about the best way to achieve organizational goals are inevitable because of differences between functions and divisions. One way to harness conflict between subunits and prevent the polarization of attitudes that results during the stage of felt conflict in Pondy's model is to set up a procedural system that allows parties in conflict to air their grievances and hear other groups' points of view. Committees or teams, for example, can provide a forum in which subunits in dispute can meet face to face and negotiate directly with one another. In this way, subunits can clarify the assumptions they are using to frame the problem, and they can develop an understanding of one another's motives. Very often the use of a procedural system reveals that the issue in dispute is much smaller than was previously thought and that the positions of the parties are more similar than anyone had realized.

A procedural system is especially important in managing industrial conflicts between managers and unions. When a union exists, formal procedures govern the resolution of disputes to ensure that the issue receives a fair hearing. Indeed, an important component of bargaining in labor disputes is attitudinal structuring—a process designed to influence the attitudes of the opposing party and to encourage the perception that both parties are on the same side and want to solve a dispute amicably.[21] Thus, strikes become the last resort in a long process of negotiation.

Often, an organization engages a *third-party negotiator* to moderate a dispute between subunits or stakeholders.[22] The third-party negotiator can be a senior manager who occupies an integrating role or an outside consultant employed because of expertise in solving organizational disputes. The negotiator's role is to prevent the polarization of attitudes that occurs during the felt conflict stage and thus prevent the escalation to manifest conflict. Negotiators are skilled in managing organizational conflict so as to allow new learning to take place. Often, the negotiator supports the weaker party in the dispute to make sure that both sides of the argument get heard.

Another way of managing conflict through attitude change is by the exchange and rotation of people between subunits to encourage groups to learn each other's points of view. This practice is widespread in Japan. Japanese organizations continually rotate people from function to function so that they can understand the problems and issues facing the organization as a whole.[23]

When attitudes are difficult to change because they have developed over a long period of time, the only way to resolve a conflict may be to change the people involved. This can be done by permanently transferring employees to other parts of the organization, promoting them, or firing them. We have already seen that top management teams are often replaced to overcome inertia and change organizational attitudes. Analysts attribute a large part of the conflict at CS First Boston to the attitudes of a few key top managers who had to be removed.

An organization's CEO is an important influence on attitudes in a conflict. The CEO personifies the values and culture of the organization, and the way the CEO acts affects the attitudes of other managers directly. As head of the organization, the CEO also has the ultimate power to resolve conflict between subunits. A strong CEO actively manages organizational conflict and opens up a debate, allowing each group to express its views. The strong CEO can then use his or her power to build a consensus for a resolution and decision and can motivate subunits to cooperate to achieve organizational goals. In contrast, a weak CEO can actually increase organizational conflict. When a CEO fails to manage the bargaining and negotiation process between subunits, the strongest subunits (those with the most power) are encouraged or allowed to fight for their goals at the expense of other subunits. A weak CEO produces a power vacuum at the top of the organization, enabling the strongest members of the organization to compete for control. As consensus is lost and infighting becomes the order of the day, conflict becomes destructive.

MANAGERIAL IMPLICATIONS

CONFLICT

1. Analyze the organizational structure to identify potential sources of conflict.
2. Change or redesign the organizational structure to eliminate the potential for conflict whenever possible.
3. If conflict cannot be eliminated, be prepared to intervene quickly and early in the conflict to find a solution.
4. Choose a way of managing the conflict that matches the source of the conflict.
5. Always try to achieve a good conflict aftermath so that cooperative attitudes can be maintained in the organization over time.

WHAT IS ORGANIZATIONAL POWER?

Organizational power
The ability of one person or group to overcome resistance by others to resolve conflict and achieve a desired objective or result.

The presence of a strong CEO is important in managing organizational conflict. Indeed, the relative power of the CEO, the board of directors, and other top managers is important in understanding how and why organizations change and restructure themselves and why this benefits some people and subunits more than others. To understand how and why organizational conflict is resolved in favor of different subunits and stakeholders, we need to look closely at the issue of power.

What is power, and what is its role in organizational conflict? According to most researchers, **organizational power** is the mechanism through which conflict gets resolved. It can be defined as the ability of one person or group to overcome resistance by others to achieve a desired objective or result.[24] More specifically, organizational power is the ability of A to cause B to do something that B would not otherwise have done.[25] Thus, when power is used to resolve conflict, the element of coercion exists. Actors with power can bring about outcomes they desire over the opposition of other actors.

The possession of power is an important determinant of the kind of decisions that resolve a conflict—for example, decisions concerning the allocation of resources or the assignment of responsibility between managers and subunits.[26] When decisions are made through bargaining between organizational coalitions, the relative power of the various coalitions to influence decision making is what determines how conflicts get resolved and which subunits benefit from the decision-making process.

Thus conflict and power are intimately related. Conflict is caused by the existence of different individuals or groups that need to cooperate to achieve organizational objectives but must compete for organizational resources and have different individual or group goals and priorities. When a situation arises that causes these groups to compete for resources, conflict emerges. When the issue is sufficiently important, individuals and groups use their power to influence decision making and obtain outcomes that favor them.

SOURCES OF ORGANIZATIONAL POWER

If people, groups, and divisions engage in activities to gain power within an organization, where do they get the power from? What gives one person or group the power to influence, shape, or control the behavior of others? To answer these questions, we must recognize the sources of power in an organization. Figure 14.4 identifies seven of them.

Authority

Authority, power that is legitimized by the legal and cultural foundations on which an organization is based, is the ultimate source of power in an organization.[27] The power of the President of the United States, for example, is based on the Constitution of the United States, which specifies the rights and obligations of the President and the conditions under which that person can seek or be removed from office. In a similar way, authority in an organization derives from the organization's legal charter, which allows shareholders, through the board of directors, to grant a CEO the formal power, or authority, to use organizational resources to create value for shareholders.

Figure 14.4
Sources of Organizational Power

All functions and divisions gain power from one or more of these sources.

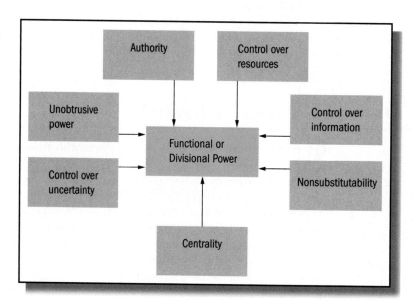

In turn, the CEO has the right to grant authority to other top managers in the organization, and they have the right to confer it on their subordinates.

People who join an organization accept the legal right of the organization to control their behavior. In exercising authority, a manager exercises a legal right to control resources, including human resources. The way in which authority is distributed depends on the organizational setting. As discussed in Chapter 5, in organizations that are centralized, authority is retained by top managers. In organizations that are decentralized, authority is delegated to those lower in the hierarchy, who are then held responsible for the way they use organizational resources. When authority is centralized, there is generally less scope for people to engage in behaviors aimed at gaining power. Because top managers keep power among themselves, it is difficult for coalitions to form. In such centralized organizations, however, a culture often develops in which people become afraid to take responsibility for decisions or to initiate new action for fear they will overstep their authority and be censured by top management. Instead, subordinates ingratiate themselves to top management in the hope of receiving favor, and they compete to curry favor with their superiors. Thus the effectiveness of decision making in a centralized organization can be reduced as managers surround themselves with yes-men and few important decisions get made.

Frequently, managers negotiate the limits of their authority among themselves, and more senior managers give authority to subordinates by making a conscious decision to decentralize. Sometimes, however, a subordinate who is active or competitive can indirectly take away a superior's authority by gradually assuming more and more of the supervisor's duties and responsibilities. The result, over time, is that even though the superior has legitimate authority, the subordinate has the real power. Superiors who are aware that this indirect seizure of authority can happen may take steps to prevent it. They may make a point of exercising their authority to show subordinates that they possess it, or they may insist on the display of certain rituals or symbols of their power—such as a big office and a personal secretary.

One of the classic ways in which superiors hold onto power is by restricting the information they give to subordinates to make a decision. If a manager gives out too much information, the subordinate will know as much as the manager does, and power over the subordinate will be lost. As a result of this fear, managers hoard information and do not share it with subordinates. However, if managers withhold too much and subordinates cannot make decisions, managers are likely to become overburdened, and the quality of decision making in the organization declines.

Managers have to realize that there is a difference between the decentralization of authority and the loss of authority: Decentralizing authority to a subordinate does not necessarily reduce a manager's authority, because the manager continues to bear the responsibility for whatever decisions the subordinate makes. Thus, when subordinates make decisions that have important consequences, the responsibility and authority of the superior also increase. If subordinates fail, however, the manager also bears the consequences. If the failure is big enough, the decision to decentralize can result in the loss of power—that is, the loss of the official position that carries the authority in the organization.

As noted elsewhere, *empowerment* is the deliberate decentralization of authority to encourage subordinates to assume responsibility for organizational activities.[28] The goal of empowerment is to give subordinates wide latitude to make decisions and thus motivate them to make best use of their skills to create value. In an organization that decentralizes authority and empowers employees, all organizational members can gain authority as the organization prospers and attracts more resources. Employees who assume more authority and responsibility often demand more rights from the organization, such as higher salaries, increased job security, or bonuses tied to organizational performance.

Empowerment is also important at the corporate divisional level. As we have seen, in some organizations the corporate center is reluctant to delegate authority to the divisional level and prefers to centralize decision making. The problem with this choice is that divisional managers become afraid to experiment and to initiate new action even though they are close to a problem and have more information and knowledge about it than corporate managers have. Thus divisions become unable to devise strategies that allow them to capitalize on opportunities in the environment, and both divisional and organizational performance suffer. For this reason, Bill Gates, chairman of Microsoft, and many other CEOs deliberately empower divisional managers and make them responsible for their divisions' ultimate success in the marketplace. Gates believes that it is impossible to manage a company as large and diverse as Microsoft unless managers at the divisional level and below have the authority and responsibility to innovate and make decisions. At Microsoft, the corporate center's primary role is to make resource allocation decisions for the whole organization, and to ensure the different divisions produce software that can be seamlessly integrated with the software written by other divisions so that Microsoft can offer its standardized software platform to all kinds of customers.

Control over Resources

Power is not a fixed quantity. Managers who make decisions and perform actions that benefit the organization, such as making changes that raise performance, can increase their power. Just as an organization's power grows as the organization controls more and more resources in its environment, power within an organization comes from the control of resources.[29] To survive, organizations require resources such as capital, human skills, raw materials, and customers. If a resource is particularly critical for an organization, the individual or subunit that has control over that resource has a good deal of power. At a company like Merck, for example, the R&D skills and knowledge necessary to develop new drugs are a critical resource. Given this fact, who has the most power at Merck? The answer is senior scientists, because they possess the knowledge on which the success of the organization depends. Similarly, at companies that rely heavily on the success of their marketing efforts, like Coca-Cola or McDonald's, the marketing department has considerable power because it is the department that can attract customers—the critical scarce resource.

Money or capital is, in a way, the ultimate organizational resource because money buys other resources. This explains the ultimate power of top managers. Legally, they control the allocation of money in the organization and thus control its future. The ability to allocate financial resources, however, is not the only source of a manager's or subunit's power. The ability to generate financial resources is also an important source of power.[30] The power of top managers at Merck rests in their ability to allocate R&D funds to various projects. The scientists, however, are the ones who invent the drugs that generate future revenues for the company, and their ability to generate resources gives them supreme power in the organization. In a multi-divisional company, the divisions that generate revenues from customers have considerable power. In a university setting, the most powerful departments are ones like engineering, chemistry, and agriculture, which generate the most revenues because they attract millions of dollars for sponsored research. At many schools, athletics programs and alumni groups have considerable power because of their ability to generate revenues.

Control over Information

Information can be a very important and scarce organizational resource. Access to strategic information and the control of the information flow to, from, and between subunits are sources of considerable power in the decision-making and change process.[31] It is possible to shape the views of others by carefully tailoring the information they receive. Andrew Pettigrew, in a study of the decision to buy a certain kind of computer system at a department store, showed how Jim Kenny, the head of management services, was able to influence the behavior of other senior managers by controlling the flow of information to them. Kenny was able to act as a "gate-keeper." Pettigrew observed, "By sitting at the junction of the communications channels between his subordinates, the manufacturers, and the board, Kenny was able to exert biases in favor of his own demands and at the same time feed the board negative information about the demands of his opponents."[32] Even in the face of strong opposition by other managers, Kenny was able to bring about change that resolved the conflict in his favor by controlling the information used to evaluate alternatives. In conflicts, senior managers have been known to deliberately manipulate other managers by supplying them with information that causes them to make bad decisions, so that in the contest for power in the organization they lose out to managers with better performance records.[33]

The control of information is the source of the power of many people or subunits in specialized roles.[34] The power of doctors in a hospital or mechanics in a garage stems from their ability to control specific knowledge and information. People who consult an expert have to take that person's word on trust or else get a second opinion. Similarly, functions may have power because they control the information and knowledge that are necessary to solve organizational problems. Researcher Michael Crozier found that maintenance engineers in the French tobacco-processing plants he was investigating enjoyed an inordinate amount of power despite their low status in the organizational hierarchy.[35] The reason for their power was that the principal problem in the company's routine mass production technology was machine breakdown. The maintenance engineers were the only people who knew how to repair the machines, and they had systematically used this knowledge to develop a considerable power base in the organization. Moreover, they jealously guarded their knowledge, refusing to write down repair procedures or share them with others, realizing that if they did so they would undermine their own power.

All subunits possess some expert information and knowledge, but the functions or divisions that control critical information have the most. They are the ones most able to bring about change, especially change that favors their interests, although this is no guarantee that such change will benefit the whole organization. This is the danger that accompanies the use of power in the organizational change process: how to ensure change will increase, rather than reduce organizational performance.

Nonsubstitutability

If no one else can perform the tasks that a person or subunit performs, that person or subunit is nonsubstitutable. Only it can provide resources that another subunit or the organization wants. The maintenance engineers at the French tobacco plant had made themselves nonsubstitutable: Only they could reduce one of the major uncertainties facing the plant—machine breakdown. As a result of their nonsubstitutability, they exerted considerable power.[36]

Centrality

As we saw earlier, Jim Kenny had power because he could control information flows and was central to the decision-making process. In his role as manager of information services, he could provide others with information that reduced the uncertainty they were experiencing about orders or accounts. Similarly, the subunits that are most central to resource flows have the ability to reduce the uncertainty facing other subunits.[37] Often, an organization's strategy is a crucial determinant of which subunit is central in an organization. In a company like Coca-Cola, which is driven by marketing, other subunits—product development, manufacturing, sales—depend on the information collected by the marketing department. The marketing department is central because it supplies a resource that all the other functions need: knowledge about customers and their future needs. R&D is not central at Coca-Cola because it responds to the needs of other functions—for example, to the marketing function's decision that the company should develop "vanilla" Coke. In a biotechnology company like Amgen, whose differentiation strategy depends on R&D, R&D becomes the central function, and marketing shapes its behavior to suit the needs of R&D.

Control over Uncertainty

A subunit that can actually control the principal sources of uncertainty or the contingencies facing the organization has significant power.[38] The R&D function in a biotechnology organization is powerful because the major source of uncertainty is whether the organization can discover safe, new drugs. In a hospital, doctors have power because only they have the ability to diagnose and treat patient problems, the main source of uncertainty for a hospital.

Over time, as the contingencies facing an organization change, some subunits rise in power, while the power of others whose services are no longer so valuable falls.[39] In business organizations after World War II, for example, the main source of uncertainty was the need to manufacture products fast enough to meet the demand for consumer goods that had built up during the war years. Manufacturing became the most important subunit during the postwar period, and many CEOs came from the manufacturing department. Then, during the 1960s, with manufacturers producing at full capacity, companies' main contingency became the need to sell their products, and marketing rose in prominence. With the 1970s came recession. Companies diversified to compete in new industries, and accounting and finance became the powerful organizational function. Thus the power of subunits rises and falls as their ability to cope with organizational uncertainties changes.

Unobtrusive Power: Controlling the Premises of Decision Making

Another important source of power is the power of the dominant coalition—that is, the coalition that has the most power—to control the decision-making process so that the decisions made in a conflict situation favor the interests of the coalition. When different subunits share similar interests, they often join in a coalition to increase their power to pursue their common goals. The enhanced power of the coalition is then brought to bear on the decision-making process against coalitions that are pursuing different goals. The power flowing from the ability to control the premises behind decision making is called *unobtrusive power* because others are generally not aware that the coalition is shaping their perceptions or interpretations of a situation.[40]

The power of a coalition lies in its ability to control the assumptions, goals, norms, or values that managers use to judge alternative solutions to a problem. As a result of unobtrusive power, many alternatives that some parties in a conflict might like to evaluate are ruled out because they do not fit with the ruling coalition's view of the situation. Thus, even before decision making starts, the coalition in power has ensured that the decision that is eventually made will support its interests.

An example will clarify how unobtrusive power can work. Profits can be increased in two basic ways: by expanding sales revenues or by decreasing costs. If sales and marketing form the dominant coalition in an organization, then the option of cutting costs receives little attention, and decision making focuses on how the organization should invest its resources to increase sales. Conversely, when production is in the power seat, the goal of investing resources in new advanced machinery to reduce costs is likely to be an important factor influencing the selection of a course of action.

A specific coalition's ability to resolve conflict in its favor depends on which coalition has the balance of power in the organization. Organizational power is a dynamic concept, and organizational strategy can change quickly as the balance of power shifts from one coalition to another.[41]

USING POWER: ORGANIZATIONAL POLITICS

Organizational politics
Activities taken within organizations to acquire, develop, and use power and other resources to obtain one's preferred outcomes in a situation in which there is uncertainty or disagreement about choices.

Given the size of the benefits that can be gained by managers who use organizational power to bring about change that resolves conflicts in their favor, it is not surprising that managers want to acquire as much power as they can and then use it to get what they want. **Organizational politics** comprises, in the words of Jeffrey Pfeffer, "activities taken within organizations to acquire, develop, and use power and other resources to obtain one's preferred outcomes in a situation in which there is uncertainty or disagreement about choices."[42] To manage the change process to get conflicts resolved in their favor, individuals, subunits, and coalitions often engage in political activity and behavior to enhance the power and influence they have. Even if organizational members or subunits have no personal desire to play politics, they still must understand how politics operates because sooner or later they will come up against a master player of the political game. In such situations, apolitical managers (those who do not engage in politics) get all the tedious assignments or the responsibility for projects that do little to enhance their career prospects. Astute political managers get the visible and important projects that bring them into contact with powerful managers and allow them to build up their own power base, which they can use to enhance their chances of promotion.

Tactics for Playing Politics

To understand the political component of organizational life, we need to examine the political tactics and strategies that individuals and subunits use to increase their chances of winning the political game. The reward for success is change that gives them a greater share of organizational resources—authority, money, status, and so on. Individuals and subunits can use many political tactics to obtain the power to achieve their goals and objectives.

Increasing Indispensability
One prime political tactic that an individual or subunit can use to increase power is to become indispensable to the organization. Indispensability can be achieved by an increase in nonsubstitutability or an increase in centrality.

Increasing Nonsubstitutability
Wily managers deliberately engage in behaviors and actions that make them non-substitutable.[43] They may develop specialized organizational skills, such as knowledge of computers that allow them to solve problems for other managers. They may specialize in an area of increasing concern to the organization—such as international trade regulations, pollution control, or health and safety—so that they eventually are in a position to control a crucial contingency facing the organization. Individuals and subunits that use these tactics are often called in to solve problems as they arise, and the ability to come up with solutions increases their status and prestige.

Increasing Centrality
Managers can increase their indispensability by making themselves more central to an organization. They can deliberately accept responsibilities that bring them into contact with many functions or with many managers so that they can enhance their personal reputation and that of their function. By being central, they may also enhance their ability to obtain information that they can use to make themselves and their functions nonsubstitutable. By being able to reduce the uncertainty experienced

by others—for example, by obtaining and supplying information or by helping out on rush projects—they make others dependent on them. Then, in return for their help, they can request favors (such as access to privileged information) from other people and groups and feed this information to other managers, who in turn become obligated to them and who share even more information. Following this process, politically astute managers cultivate both people and information and are able to build within the organization a personal network of contacts that they can use to pursue personal goals such as promotion, and functional goals such as increasing the supply of scarce resources.

Associating with Powerful Managers

Another way to obtain power is by attaching oneself to powerful managers who are clearly on their way to the top. By supporting a powerful manager and making oneself indispensable to that person, it is possible to rise up the organizational ladder with that person. Top managers often become mentors to aspiring lower-level managers because planning for the managerial succession is an important organizational task of top managers.[44] CEOs typically promote their friends, not their enemies. Managers who have taken the initiative to develop skills that make them stand out from the crowd and who are central and nonsubstitutable have the best chance of being selected as protégés by powerful managers who are seeking people to groom as their successors.

To identify the powerful people in an organization, it is necessary to develop skills in sensing who has power. A politically savvy manager figures out the key people to cultivate and the best ways to get their attention. Indicators of power include an individual's personal reputation and ability to (1) influence organizational decision-making outcomes, (2) control significant organizational resources, and (3) display symbols of prestige and status such as access to the corporate jet or limousine.[45]

A secondary way to form an attachment with powerful people is to take advantage of common ties such as graduation from the same school or university or similarity in socioeconomic background. Recall from Chapter 7 on organizational culture that top managers typically select as associates or successors other managers who are like themselves. They do so because they believe that shared norms and values are evidence of reliability or trustworthiness. Not surprisingly, then, it is not uncommon for managers to go to considerable lengths to look and behave like their superiors and to imitate or copy the habits or preferences of a senior person. Imitation has been called the sincerest form of flattery, and flattery is never wasted on those in power. The more powerful the person, the more he or she is likely to appreciate it. Nowhere is this clearer than in the behavior of top managers and the board of directors at the corrupt telecommunications company, WorldCom.

Building and Managing Coalitions

Forming a coalition of different interests, stakeholders, individuals, and subunits around some common issue is a political tactic that a manager can use to obtain the power to resolve a conflict in her or his favor. Coalitions are often built around a trade-off: A supports B on an issue of interest to B in return for B supporting A on an issue of interest to A. Coalitions can be built through many levels in an organization, between various functions or divisions, and between important external or internal stakeholders. It is very important, for example, for top-level managers to build personal relationships with powerful shareholders or with members of the board of directors. Many of the most intense political contests occur at this level because the stakes are so high. The CEO needs the support of the board in any contest with members of the top management team. Without it, the CEO's days are numbered. At HP Carly Fiorina lost the support of the board once it was clear she would not meet targets for reducing costs that were supposed to follow the merger between HP and Compaq.

In 2002 WorldCom, the giant telecommunications company, entered Chapter 11 bankruptcy after its was revealed that its top executives had deliberately overinflated revenues by $11 billion dollars. Not just top executives (such as former CEO Bernie Ebbers) were implicated—so were eight of WorldCom's 11-member board of directors who were at the helm when the company booked these billions of dollars and provided $408 million in personal loans and lucrative pensions benefits to Ebbers. How could WorldCom's board of directors have failed in their oversight role?

Four of these eight board members had long–term personal and business ties to Ebbers and had been appointed to the board at his urging. Two of these four directors sat on WorldCom's compensation and stock option committee, which granted Ebbers these huge personal loans. At least one of these two directors reportedly also struck a deal with Ebbers whereby Ebbers gave him access to company aircraft for $1 a month plus a $400-an-hour usage fee, when the real cost of using such aircraft is hundreds of thousands of dollars a year. In return, this director agreed to Ebbers' huge severance package, which also ran into the hundreds of millions after he resigned.[46]

Small wonder then that in the fall of 2002, with these directors still collecting large fees and receiving huge perks from WorldCom, critics were calling for their removal from the board. They had not resigned voluntarily and legally the company could not unilaterally replace them until WorldCom's next general meeting. However, WorldCom was able to fill three other vacancies with new directors, such as former U.S. Attorney General Nicholas Katzenbach and Dennis Beresford, a former chairman of the Financial Accounting Standards Board, who could ensure that these unethical directors could do no more harm to a company that has cost its shareholders billions of dollars and whose future is still in doubt.

Facing legal action, most of these directors have paid-millions of dollars back to the company to avoid criminal prosecution. Former WorldCom boss Ebbers was sentenced to 25 years in prison in July 2005 for leading the largest corporate fraud in U.S. history. It was the toughest sentence imposed on an executive since the fall of Enron in 2001 touched off a record-breaking wave of business scandals. Even with possible time off for good behavior, Ebbers, 63, will remain locked up until 2027, when he would be 85 years old. The sentence came four months after Ebbers was convicted of using his power as CEO to oversee the $11 billion WorldCom fraud.

Building alliances with important customers is another valuable tactic, as is developing long-term relationships with the officers of the banks and other financial institutions from which a company obtains its capital. The more external linkages top managers can develop, the more chips they have to put on the table when the political game gets rough. Similarly, the ability to forge inside alliances with the managers of the most important subunits provides aspiring top managers with a power base that they can use to promote their personal agendas. In the game of organizational politics, having a lot of friends greatly enhances one's claim to power in the organization.

Skills in coalition building are important to success in organizational politics because the interests of parties to a coalition change frequently, as the environment changes. To maintain the coalition's consensus, the coalition has to be actively managed. Co-optation is a particularly important tool in coalition management. Recall from Chapter 3 that co-optation is a strategy that allows one subunit to overcome the opposition of a second subunit by involving it in decision making. Giving an opponent a place on an important committee or an important managerial role in solving organizational problems makes the opponent part of the coalition, with rights to share in the rewards from the outcome of the political decision-making process.

Influencing Decision Making

Perhaps the most important political tactic a manager, group, division, or coalition can pursue to acquire, increase, and use power is to influence the politics of decision making. Possessing and using power (as a result of increasing indispensability, associating with powerful people, and knowing how to build and manage coalitions) is not the only skill needed to play politics. Knowing how and when to use power is equally important. As we saw earlier, the use of power to influence decision making is most effective when the power is unobtrusive. If other managers and coalitions become aware that they are being manipulated, they are likely to oppose the interests of the coalition doing the manipulating—or at least to insist that any decisions that are made also favor their interests. This is the thought behind the notion that a person who uses power loses it: Once the opposition realizes that a manager is using power to influence a decision in his or her favor, opponents will start to lobby for their interests and try to protect their claims to the resource at stake.

Two tactics for controlling the decision-making process so that the use of power seems to be legitimate—that is, in the organization's interests and not in the pursuit of self-interest or self-promotion—are controlling the agenda and bringing in an outside expert.[47]

Controlling the Agenda

Managers and coalitions like to be on, and particularly in control of, committees so that they can control the agenda or business of the committee. By controlling the agenda, they are able to control the issues and problems to be considered by important decision makers—such as how and when to change an organization's strategy and structure. Thus a coalition of powerful managers can prevent consideration of any issue that they do not support by not putting it on the agenda. In this way conflict remains either latent or in the felt stage because the opposition does not get the chance to air its view on problems or solutions. The ability to control the agenda is similar to the ability to control the premises of decision making. Both tactics limit the alternatives considered in the decision-making process. The way the U.S. sugar lobby harms many organizations by using its power to protect its interests illustrates this issue.

Bringing in an Outside Expert

When a major conflict exists, such as when top managers are deciding how to change or restructure the organization, all managers and coalitions know that individuals and groups are fighting for their interests and perhaps for their political survival. Every subunit manager wants the axe to fall on other subunits and wants to try to benefit from whatever change takes place. Self-interested managers and coalitions, knowing that the solution they want will be perceived by other subunits as politically motivated, are eager to legitimize their position, and so they often bring in an outside expert who is considered to be neutral. The supposedly objective views of the expert are then used to support the position of the coalition in power.

In some cases, however, the experts are not neutral at all but have been coached by the coalition in power and know exactly what the coalition's view is so that they can develop a favorable scenario. When this scenario is presented to the groups in conflict, the "objectivity" of the expert's plan is used to sway decision making in favor of the coalition in power. The opposition is outgunned and accepts the inevitable.

In sum, there are many tactics that individuals, managers, subunits, and coalitions can use to obtain power and play organizational politics. The success of attempts to influence and control decision making to resolve conflicts in a certain way depends on individuals' ability to learn the political ropes and hone their political skills.

The Costs and Benefits of Organizational Politics

Organizational politics is an integral part of decision making in an organization. Coalitions form to control the premises behind decision making, to lobby for their interests, to control the path of organizational change, and to resolve organizational conflict in their own favor. Because the stakes are high—the control of scarce resources like promotions and budgets—politics is a very active force in most organizations. When we look to see what changes an organization makes to its strategy or structure, we need to recognize the role that politics plays in these choices. It can improve the choices and decisions that an organization makes, but it can also produce problems and promote conflict if it is not managed skillfully. If, for example, different coalitions continually fight about resource allocation decisions, more time is likely to be spent in making decisions than in implementing the decisions that are made. As a result, organizational effectiveness suffers.

To manage organizational politics and gain its benefits, an organization must establish a balance of power in which alternative views and solutions can be offered and considered by all parties and dissenting views can be heard (see Figure 14.5). It is also important for the balance of power to shift over time, toward the party that can best manage the uncertainty and contingencies facing the organization. An organization that confers power on those who can promote the changes that will help it the most can take advantage of the political process to improve the quality of organizational decision making. By allowing managers to use their power to advance their future objectives, and to form coalitions that compete for support for their agendas, an organization can improve the quality of decision making by encouraging useful and productive debate about alternatives. Thus politics can improve organizational effectiveness if it results in change that allocates resources to where they can produce more value.

An organization's ability to obtain the benefits of politics depends on the assumption that power flows to those who can be of most help to the organization. This assumption means that unsuccessful managers lose power to successful managers and that there is a constant movement of power in the organization as an individual's or a group's power ebbs and flows. Suppose, however, that the top management team in power becomes entrenched and is able to defend its power and property rights against its opponents even though the performance of the organization is faltering. Suppose a top management team has institutionalized its power by occupying all important roles on organizational committees and by carefully selecting supporters for top organizational roles. Suppose the CEO occupies the role of board chair so that he or she can dominate the board of directors. In this situation, top management can use its power to fend off shareholders' attempts to restructure the organization to make better use of organizational resources. Similarly, top management, far from encouraging dissent among promising middle managers, might deny them promotion or decision-making power. By doing this, top management encourages the departure of those who threaten top management's dominant position. In this situation, the power that the top management team has obtained as a result of its ability to control the distribution of property rights threatens organizational performance and survival.[48] Power holders are notoriously reluctant to give up the positions that give them the right to allocate resources and enrich themselves. CEOs in particular rarely give up their positions voluntarily.

Figure 14.5
Maintaining a Balance of Power

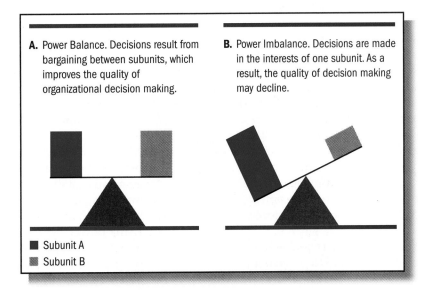

A. Power Balance. Decisions result from bargaining between subunits, which improves the quality of organizational decision making.

B. Power Imbalance. Decisions are made in the interests of one subunit. As a result, the quality of decision making may decline.

■ Subunit A
■ Subunit B

When the balance of power between stakeholders or subunits does not force the allocation of resources to where they can best create value, organizational effectiveness suffers. When powerful managers can suppress the views of those who oppose their interests, debate becomes restricted, checks and balances fade, bad conflict increases, and organizational inertia increases. Today, after the recent scandals in organizations such as Enron, WorldCom, and so on, there is increasing support for measures that would increase the power of stakeholders to remove inefficient top management teams and CEOs who pay themselves exorbitant salaries that often are not tied to organizational performance. Thus, ultimately, whether power and politics benefit or harm an organization is a function of the balance of power among organizational stakeholders.

MANAGERIAL IMPLICATIONS

POWER AND POLITICS

1. Recognize that politics is a fact of organizational life, and develop the skills to understand how politics shapes organizational decision making.
2. Develop a personal power base to influence decision making, and use it to prevent political managers or groups from pursuing their interests at the expense of organizational interests.
3. To obtain power, try to associate with powerful managers and find a powerful mentor, make yourself central and nonsubstitutable, develop personal skills so that you can reduce uncertainty for other subunits or for the organization, seek membership on committees that will give you access to information, and obtain control of organizational resources.
4. Seek to maintain a power balance between individuals or subunits in an organization in order to preserve the quality of organizational decision making.

SUMMARY

Managing conflict, power, and politics is one of an organization's major priorities because these factors determine which decisions the organization makes and therefore, ultimately, its survival. Chapter 14 has made the following main points:

1. Organizational conflict is the clash that arises when the goal-directed behavior of one group blocks or thwarts the goals of another.
2. Conflict can be functional if it overcomes organizational inertia and brings about change. However, too high a level of conflict can reduce the level of coordination and integration between people and subunits and reduce organizational effectiveness.
3. The five stages of Pondy's model of organizational conflict are latent conflict, perceived conflict, felt conflict, manifest conflict, and the conflict aftermath.
4. There are five sources of conflict between subunits: interdependence, differences in goals and priorities, bureaucratic factors, incompatible performance criteria, and competition for scarce resources.
5. Conflict resolution strategies are used to manage organizational conflict and to prevent it from becoming destructive. Two important strategies

are acting at the level of structure to change task relationships and acting at the level of attitudes and individuals to change the attitudes of the parties or the parties themselves.
6. Organizational power is the ability of one actor or stakeholder to overcome resistance by other actors and achieve a desired objective or result.
7. The main sources of power available to managers and subunits are authority, control over resources, control over information, nonsubstitutability, centrality, control over uncertainty or contingencies, and unobtrusive power.
8. Organizational politics comprises activities carried out within organizations to acquire, develop, and use power and other resources to obtain one's preferred outcomes.
9. Tactics that individuals and subunits can use to play politics include increasing indispensability, associating with powerful managers, building and managing coalitions, controlling the agenda, and bringing in an outside expert.
10. Using power to play organizational politics can improve the quality of decision making if the people who have the power are those who can best serve the needs of the organization.

However, if top managers have the ability to control and hoard power and entrench themselves in the organization, the interests of other organizational stakeholders may be jeopardized as decisions are made to serve top management's personal interests. Thus, there needs to be a balance of power between organizational stakeholders.

DISCUSSION QUESTIONS

1. Why and under what conditions can conflict be good or bad for an organization? Would you expect a higher level of conflict in a mechanistic or an organic structure? Why?

2. You have been appointed to manage a large R&D laboratory. You find a high level of conflict among scientists in the unit. Why might this conflict be arising? How will you try to resolve it?

3. Why is it important to maintain a balance of power between different groups of organizational stakeholders?

4. What is unobtrusive power? Why is it so important?

5. How can the design of the organization's structure and culture give some subunits more power than others?

6. Discuss how you, as manager of the R&D function in a cosmetic products company, might try to increase your power and the power of your subunit to control more resources in a battle with marketing and manufacturing.

ORGANIZATIONAL THEORY IN ACTION

Practicing Organizational Theory: Managing Conflict

Form groups of three to five people and discuss the following scenario:

You are a group of top managers of a large, well-established pharmaceutical company that has made its name by pioneering innovative new drugs. Intense competition from other companies in the pharmaceutical industry, plus increasing government pressure to reduce the price of drugs, has put pressure on you to find ways to reduce costs and speed product development. In addition, the emergence of large health maintenance organizations (HMOs) and other large buyers of drugs has made marketing drugs much more difficult, and marketing managers are demanding an increased say in which drugs should be developed and when. To respond to these pressures, you have decided to create cross-functional teams composed of people from R&D, marketing, finance, and top management to evaluate the potential of new drug products and to decide if they should be pursued.

1. How will the change in structure affect the relative power of the different functions?

2. How likely is conflict to occur because of these changes, and what will be the source of the conflict?

3. What can you do to help manage the conflict process to make the new operating system work as you hope it will?

The Ethical Dimension #14

The behavior of WorldCom's top managers and members of its board of directors is said to be quite common in many U.S. companies today. CEOs have considerable power to appoint board members, and the members of a company's compensation and stock option committee have wide latitude to reward the CEO and other top managers as they see fit.

1. Is it ethical for CEOs to be able to appoint the directors who will be evaluating their performance and determining their compensation?

2. What kinds of ethical rules should be developed to ensure that abuses of power and political plays such as those that occurred at WorldCom can be prevented in the future?

Making the Connection #14

Find an example of a conflict occurring between the managers, or between the managers and other stakeholders, of a company. What is the source of the conflict? How are managers using their power to influence the decision-making process?

Analyzing the Organization: Design Module #14

This module focuses on conflict, power, and politics in your organization.

Assignment

1. What do you think are the likely sources of conflict that may arise in your organization? Is there a history of conflict between managers or between stakeholders?

2. Analyze the sources of power of the principal subunits, functions, or divisions in the organization. Which is the most central subunit? Which is the most nonsubstitutable subunit? Which one controls the most resources? Which one handles the main contingencies facing the organization?

3. Which subunit is the most powerful? Identify any ways in which the subunit has been able to influence decision making in its favor.

4. To what degree are the organization's strategic and operational decisions affected by conflict and politics?

CASE FOR ANALYSIS

The Shake-Up in GM's Hierarchy

On April 6, 1992, the normally quiescent board of directors of General Motors, under the leadership of outside director John G. Smale, instituted a revolt against the company's top management team. Horrified by GM's recent $4.5 billion loss and angry at the slow pace of change instituted by GM chairman and chief executive officer Robert Stempel, the board decided to teach GM's top management a lesson.

Stempel lost his leadership of the board's executive committee (GM's top policy-making committee) to Smale, who effectively became his overseer. The board then dismantled Stempel's handpicked team of top managers and replaced them with managers in whom the board had more confidence: John F. ("Jack") Smith, who became president and chief operating officer (COO); and William E. Hoagland, who became the new chief financial officer (CFO). In making these changes, the board effectively told Stempel that if he could not quickly turn around the company's disappointing performance, the board would replace him with Smith and Hoagland. Both men had extensive experience in reducing costs and instituting a turnaround. Jack Smith, for example, had dramatically increased the performance of GM's European operations.

In October 1992, Stempel fell ill, and the board decided to act immediately to finish the changes it had begun in GM's top management. Stempel was forced to retire. Jack Smith became the new CEO. Smale became the new chairman of the board. Hoagland became Smith's right-hand man as GM's new president. With these changes complete, the new top management team moved quickly to change the rest of GM's chain of command.

The problem, in the opinion of car industry analysts, was that GM had become too tall—that is, it had developed too many levels of management. Because the corporate staff was huge, decision making was slow and cumbersome and change difficult to introduce. The task facing GM's new top management team was to flatten the hierarchy, eliminating hierarchical levels and reducing the size of the managerial staff. The team hoped that this move would reduce operating costs, improve communication, and encourage innovation. The task was enormous, however. Some analysts believed that Jack Smith needed to cut GM's bloated management staff by 50%, which would mean terminating 20,000 managers.

The board clearly believed that shareholders' interests would be best served by a new management team that would make tough organizational design decisions. As the new team began a reassessment of operations, the pace of change quickened at GM. In 1993 GM announced its intention to cut 50,000 hourly and 24,000 salaried jobs and to close or consolidate 21 parts and assembly plants by 1995 to save billions of dollars.[49]

In retrospect, the 1992 board revolt proved to be an important milestone in GM's history. From that point on, GM's performance improved every year; in 2002, it announced that it had become as efficient a carmaker as its principal U.S. competitor, Ford. Moreover, it announced that by 2005 it would become as efficient as its Japanese competitors.

DISCUSSION QUESTIONS

1. What kind of power did GM's board use to oust the company's old management team? Why were they able to succeed?

2. How could organizations better achieve a balance of power at the top of the organization to ensure that politics benefits, rather than harms, an organization?

REFERENCES

1. T. Burns, "Micropolitics: Mechanism of Institutional Change," *Administrative Science Quarterly*, 6 (1961), 257–281.
2. J. G. March, "The Business Firm as a Coalition," *Journal of Politics*, 24 (1962), 662–678.
3. L. Coser, *The Functions of Social Conflict* (New York: The Free Press, 1956); S. P. Robbins, *Managing Organizational Conflict: A Non-Traditional Approach* (Upper Saddle River, NJ: Prentice Hall, 1974).
4. J. McCann and J. R. Galbraith, "Interdepartmental Relationships," in P. C. Nystrom and W. H. Starbuck, eds., *Handbook of Organizational Design*, vol. 2 (New York: Oxford University Press, 1981), pp. 60–84.
5. A. C. Amason, "Distinguishing the Effects of Functional and Dysfunctional Conflict and Strategic Decision Making: Resolving a Paradox for Top Management Teams," *Academy of Management Review*, 39 (1996), 12–148.
6. The following discussion draws heavily on these sources: L. R. Pondy, "Organizational Conflict: Concepts and Models," *Administrative Science Quarterly*, 2 (1967), 296–320; R. E. Walton and J. M. Dutton, "The Management of Interdepartmental Conflict: A Model and Review," *Administrative Science Quarterly*, 14 (1969), 62–73.
7. J. D. Thompson, "Organizational Management of Conflict," *Administrative Science Quarterly*, 4 (1960), 389–409; K. Thomas, "Conflict and Conflict Management," in M. D. Dunnette, ed., *The Handbook of Industrial and Organizational Psychology* (Chicago: Rand McNally, 1976).
8. J. D. Thompson, *Organizations in Action* (New York: McGraw-Hill, 1967).
9. J. A. Litterer, "Conflict in Organizations: A Reexamination," *Academy of Management Journal*, 9 (1966), 178–186.
10. A. Miller, S. Nayyar, and S. Sevante, "Picture This Executive Battle," *Newsweek*, May 10, 1993, p. 54.
11. "Kodak Forms 15-Member Senior Management Team," *Business Wire*, October 14, 1999.
12. www.kodak.com, 2005.
13. M. Dalton, "Conflicts Between Staff and Line Managerial Officers," *American Sociological Review*, 15 (1950), 342–351.
14. P. R. Lawrence and J. R. Lorsch, *Organization and Environment* (Homewood, IL: Irwin, 1967).
15. "CS First Boston: All Together Now?" *The Economist*, April 10, 1993, p. 90.
16. M. Siconolfi, "CS First Boston's Hennessy to Relinquish Top Posts," *The Wall Street Journal*, July 3, 1996, p. C1.
17. Coser, *The Functions of Social Conflict*.
18. R. H. Miles, *Macro Organizational Behavior* (Santa Monica, CA: Goodyear, 1980).
19. This discussion draws heavily on E. H. Nielsen, "Understanding and Managing Intergroup Conflict," in P. R. Lawrence, L. B. Barnes, and J. W. Lorsch, *Organizational Behavior and Administration* (Homewood, IL: Irwin, 1976).
20. Lawrence and Lorsch, *Organization and Environment*.
21. R. E. Walton and R. B. McKersie, *A Behavioral Theory of Labor Negotiations: An Analysis of a Social Interaction System* (New York: McGraw-Hill, 1965).
22. R. E. Walton, "Third-Party Roles in Interdepartmental Conflict," *Industrial Relations*, 7 (1967), 29–43.
23. W. G. Ouchi, *Theory Z: How American Business Can Meet the Japanese Challenge* (Reading, MA: Addison-Wesley, 1981).
24. R. M. Emerson, "Power-Dependence Relations," *American Sociological Review*, 27 (1962), 31–41; J. Pfeffer, *Power in Organizations* (Boston: Pitman, 1981).
25. R. A. Dahl, "The Concept of Power," *Behavioral Science*, 2 (1957), 210–215.
26. M. Gargiulo, "Two-Step Leverage: Managing Constraint in Organizational Politics," *Administrative Science Quarterly*, 38 (1993), 1–19.
27. M. Weber, *The Theory of Social and Economic Organization* (New York: The Free Press, 1947).
28. J. A. Conger and R. N. Kanungo, "The Empowerment Process: Integrating Theory and Practice," *Academy of Management Review*, 13 (1988), 471–481.
29. G. R. Salancik and J. Pfeffer, "The Bases and Uses of Power in Organizational Decision Making," *Administrative Science Quarterly*, 19 (1974), 453–473; J. Pfeffer and G. R. Salancik, *The External Control of Organizations: A Resource Dependence View* (New York: Harper and Row, 1978).
30. Salancik and Pfeffer, "The Bases and Uses of Power in Organizational Decision Making."
31. A. M. Pettigrew, "Information Control as a Power Resource," *Sociology*, 6 (1972), 187–204.
32. A. M. Pettigrew, *The Politics of Organizational Decision Making* (London: Tavistock, 1973), p. 191.
33. C. Perrow, *Organizational Analysis: A Sociological View* (Belmont, CA: Wadsworth, 1970).
34. D. Mechanic, "Sources of Power of Lower-Level Participants in Complex Organizations," *Administrative Science Quarterly*, 7 (1962), 349–364.
35. M. Crozier, *The Bureaucratic Phenomenon* (Chicago: University of Chicago Press, 1964).
36. D. J. Hickson, C. R. Hinings, C. A. Lee, R. E. Schneck, and J. M. Pennings, "A Strategic Contingencies Theory of Intraorganizational Power," *Administrative Science Quarterly*, 16 (1971), 216–227.
37. Ibid.
38. Ibid.
39. Pfeffer, *Power in Organizations*, Chapter 3.
40. S. Lukes, *Power: A Radical View* (London: MacMillan, 1974).
41. Pfeffer, *Power in Organizations*, pp. 115–121.
42. Ibid., p. 7.
43. Hickson, Hinings, Lee, Schneck, and Pennings, "A Strategic Contingencies Theory of Intraorganizational Power."
44. E. E. Jennings, *The Mobile Manager* (New York: McGraw-Hill, 1967).
45. J.R.P. French, Jr., and B. Raven, "The Bases of Social Power," in D. Cartwright and A. F. Zander, eds., *Group*

Dynamics (Evanston, IL: Row Peterson, 1960), pp. 607–623.

46. J. Hall, "WorldCom Board Expected to Be Wiped Clean," www.Reuters.com, October 8, 2002.

47. This discussion draws heavily on J. Pfeffer, *Power in Organizations*, Chapter 5.

48. O. E. Williamson and W. G. Ouchi, "The Markets and Hierarchies Program of Research: Origins, Implications, Prospects," in A. E. Van De Ven and W. F. Joyce, eds., *New Perspectives on Organizational Design and Behavior* (New York: Wiley, 1981), pp. 347–406.

49. J. Treece, "The Board Revolt—Business as Usual Won't Cut It Anymore at a Humbled GM," *Business Week*, April 20, 1992, pp. 31–36; "Shakeup at General Motors," *Motor Trend*, July 1992, p. 26.

CASE 1
United Products, Inc.
Jeffrey C. Shuman

Having just returned from lunch, George Brown, president of United Products, Inc., was sitting in his office thinking about his upcoming winter vacation—in a few days, he and his family would be leaving from Boston to spend three weeks skiing on Europe's finest slopes. His daydreaming was interrupted by a telephone call from Hank Stevens, UPI's general manager. Mr. Stevens wanted to know if their two o'clock meeting was still on. The meeting had been scheduled to review actions UPI could take in light of the company's sluggish sales and the currently depressed national economy. In addition, Brown and Stevens were to go over the financial results for the company's recently completed fiscal year—they had just been received from UPI's auditors. Although it had not been a bad year, results were not as good as expected, and this, in conjunction with the economic situation, had prompted Mr. Brown to reappraise the plans he had for the company for the upcoming year.

Company History

United Products, Inc., established in 1941, was engaged in the sales and service of basic supply items for shipping and receiving, production and packaging, research and development, and office and warehouse departments. Mr. Brown's father, the founder of the company, recognized the tax advantages in establishing separate businesses rather than trying to consolidate all of his operations in one large organization. Accordingly, over the years, the elder Mr. Brown had created new companies and either closed down or sold off older companies as business conditions seemed to warrant. As of the mid-1960s, his holdings consisted of a chain of four related sales distribution companies covering the geographic area from Chicago eastward.

In 1967, feeling it was time to step aside and turn over active control of the business to his sons, the elder Mr. Brown recapitalized and restructured his companies, merging some and disposing of others. When the

Jeffrey C. Shuman, Ph.D., Associate Professor of Management, Bentley College, Waltham, MA, Reprinted with permission.

restructuring process was completed, he had set up two major companies. United Products, Inc., was to be run by his youngest son, George Brown, with its headquarters in Massachusetts, while his other son, Richard Brown, was to operate United Products Southeast, Inc., headquartered in Florida.

Although the Brown brothers occasionally worked together and were on each other's board of directors, the two companies operated on their own. As George Brown explained, "Since we are brothers, we often get together and discuss business, but the two are separate companies and each files its own tax return."

During 1972, United Products moved into new facilities in Woburn, Massachusetts. From this location it was thought that the company would be able to serve its entire New England market area effectively. "Our abilities and our desires to expand and improve our overall operation will be enhanced in the new specially designed structure containing our offices, repair facilities, and warehouse," is how George Brown viewed the role of the new facilities. Concurrent with the move, the company segmented the more than 3,500 different items it carried into eight major product categories:

1. Stapling machines. Manual and powered wire stitchers, carton stitchers, nailers, hammers, and tackers
2. Staples. All sizes and types (steel, bronze, monel, stainless steel, aluminum, brass, etc.) to fit almost all makes of equipment
3. Stenciling equipment and supplies. Featuring Marsh hand and electric machines, stencil brushes, boards, and inks
4. Gummed tape machines. Hand and electric, featuring Marsh, Derby, and Counterboy equipment
5. Industrial tapes. Specializing in strapping, masking, cellophane, electrical, cloth, nylon, and waterproof tapes made by 3M, Mystik, Behr Manning, and Dymo
6. Gluing machines. Hand and electric
7. Work gloves. All sizes and types (cotton, leather, neoprene, nylon, rubber, asbestos, and so on)
8. Marking and labeling equipment

In a flyer mailed to United Products' 6,000 accounts announcing the move to its new facilities, the company talked about its growth in this fashion:

Here we grow again–thanks to you–our many long-time valued customers. . . .

Time and circumstances have decreed another United Products transPLANT—this time, to an unpolluted garden-type industrial area, ideally located for an ever-increasing list of our customers. Now, in the new 28,000-square-foot plant with enlarged offices and warehouse, we at UNITED PRODUCTS reach the peak of efficiency in offering our customers the combined benefits of maximum inventories, accelerated deliveries, and better repair services.

By 1974, the company had grown to a point where sales were $3.5 million (double that of four years earlier) and 34 people were employed. Results for 1973 compared to 1972 showed a sales increase of 22 percent and a 40 percent gain in profits. Exhibit 1 contains selected financial figures for 1971, 1972, and 1973, in addition to the fiscal 1973 balance sheet.

Competition

George Brown indicated that UPI does not have clearly defined rivals against whom it competes head on with respect to all of its 3,500-plus items:

It is hard to get figures on competition, since we compete with no one company directly. Different distributors carry lines that compete with various of our product lines, but there is no one company that competes against us across our full range of products.

On a regular basis, Mr. Brown receives Dun & Bradstreet's Business Information Reports on specific firms with which he competes. Mr. Brown feels that since the rival firms are, like his own firm, privately held, the financial figures reported are easily manipulated and therefore are not a sound basis on which to devise strategies and plans. Exhibit 2 contains comparative financial figures for two competing companies, and Exhibit 3 contains D&B's description of their operations, along with D&B's comments about two other firms operating in UPI's New England market area.

Management Philosophy

When Mr. Brown took over UPI in 1967 at the age of 24, he set a personal goal of becoming financially secure and developing a highly profitable business. With the rapid growth of the company, he soon realized his goal of financial independence and in so doing began to lose interest in the company. "I became a rich person at age 28 and had few friends with equal wealth who were my age. The business no longer

Exhibit 1 Selected Financial Information, United Products, Inc.

	11/30/71	11/30/72	11/30/73
Current assets	$ 862,783	$ 689,024	$ 937,793
Other assets	204,566	774,571	750,646
Current liabilities	381,465	223,004	342,939
Net worth	685,884	750,446	873,954
Sales	n.a.*	2,830,000	3,450,000

Statement of financial condition, November 30, 1973:

Cash on hand	$ 46,961	Accounts payable	$ 321,885
Accounts receivable	535,714	Notes payable	20,993
Merchandise in inventory	352,136		
Prepaid insurance, interest, taxes	2,980		
Current assets	$ 937,791	Current liabilities	$ 342,878
Fixtures and equipment	$ 42,891	Retained earnings	$ 471,655
Motor vehicles	49,037	Capital stock	519,800
Land and buildings	658,768	Surplus	354,154
Total assets	$ 1,688,487	Total liabilities	$ 1,688,487

*n.a.: Not available.

Exhibit 2 Financial Information on Rival Firms

East Coast Supply Co., Inc.—Sales $1 Million			
	Fiscal December 31, 1971	Fiscal December 31, 1972	Fiscal December 31, 1973
Current assets	$ 88,555	$ 132,354	$ 163,953
Other assets	16,082	18,045	27,422
Current liabilities	41,472	47,606	74,582
Net worth	63,165	102,793	116,793

Statement of financial condition, December 31, 1973:

Cash	$ 42,948	Accounts payable	$ 39,195
Accounts receivable	86,123	Notes payable	27,588
Merchandise in inventory	34,882	Taxes	7,799
Current assets	$ 163,953	Current liabilities	$ 74,582
Fixtures and equipment	$ 15,211	Capital stock	$ 10,000
Deposits	12,211	Retained earnings	106,793
Total assets	$ 191,375	Total liabilities and net worth	191,375

Atlantic Paper Products, Inc.—Sales $6 Million			
	June 30, 1970	June 30, 1971	June 30, 1972
Current assets	$ 884,746	$1,243,259	$1,484,450
Other assets	93,755	101,974	107,001
Current liabilities	574,855	520,572	1,120,036
Net worth	403,646	439,677	471,415
Long-term debt	0	384,984	

presented a challenge and I was unhappy with the way things were going."

After taking a 10-month "mental vacation" from the business, George Brown felt he was ready to return to work. He had concluded that one way of proving himself to himself and satisfying his ego would be to make the company as profitable as possible. However, according to Mr. Brown, "The company can only grow at approximately 20 percent per year, since this is the amount of energy I am willing to commit to the business."

In 1974, at age 31, Mr. Brown described his philosophical outlook as "very conservative" and surmised that he ran UPI in much the same way as his 65-year-old father would have. In describing his managerial philosophy and some of the operating policies he had established, he said:

I am very concerned about making UPI a nice place to work. I have to enjoy what I'm doing and have fun at it at the same time. I cannot make any more money, since I'm putting away as much money as I can. The government won't allow me to make more money, since I already take the maximum amount.

I like to feel comfortable, and if we grow too quickly, it could get out of hand. I realize that the business won't grow to its potential, but why should I put more into it? . . . The company could grow, but why grow? Why is progress good? You have to pay for everything in life, and I'm not willing to work harder. . . .

Another thing . . . I am a scrupulously honest businessman, and it is very hard to grow large if you're honest. There are many deals that I could get into that would make UPI a lot of money, but I'm too moral a person to get involved. . . .

To me, happiness is being satisfied with what you have. I've got my wife, children, and health. Why risk these for something I don't need? I don't have the desire to make money, because I didn't come from a poor family; I'm not hungry.

Exhibit 3 Descriptions of Major Competitors

East Coast Supply Co., Inc.

Manufacturers and distributes pressure-sensitive tapes to industrial users throughout New England area on 1/10 net 30-day terms. Thirty-four employed including the officers, 33 here. Location: Rents 15,000 square feet on first floor of two-story building in good repair. Premises are orderly. Nonseasonal business. Branches are located at 80 Olife Street, New Haven, Connecticut, and 86 Weybosset Street, Providence, Rhode Island.

Atlantic Paper Products, Inc.

Wholesales paper products, pressure-sensitive tapes, paper specialties, twines, and other merchandise of this type. Sales to industrial accounts and commercial users on 1/10 net 30-day terms. There are about 1,000 accounts in eastern Massachusetts, and sales are fairly steady throughout the year. Employs 60, including officers. Location: Rents 130,000 square feet of floor space in a six-story brick, mill-type building in a commercial area on a principal street. Premises orderly.

The Johnson Sales Co.

Wholesales shipping room supplies, including staplings and packing devices, marking and stencil equipment. Sells to industrial and commercial accounts throughout the New England area. Seasons are steady. Terms are 1/10 net 30 days. Number of accounts not learned; 15 are employed including the owner. Location: Rents the first floor of a two-story yellow brick building in good condition. Housekeeping is good.

Big City Staple Corp.

Wholesales industrial staples, with sales to 2,000 industrial and commercial firms, on 1/10 net 30-day terms. Territory mainly New Jersey. Employs ten including the officers. Seasons steady and competition active. Location: Rents 5,000 square feet in one-story cinder block and brick structure in good condition; premises in neat order. Located on well-traveled street in a commercial area.

I have never liked the feeling of owing anything to anyone. If you can't afford to buy something, then don't. I don't like to borrow any money and I don't like the company to borrow any. All of our bills are paid within 15 days. I suppose I've constrained the business as a result of this feeling, but it's my business. The company can only afford to pay for a 20 percent growth rate, so that's all we'll grow.

Organizational Structure

Upon returning to the company from his "mental vacation" in 1971, George Brown realigned UPI's organizational structure as shown in Exhibit 4 (the company does not have a formal organizational chart; this one is drawn from the case researcher's notes). With respect to the way his company was organized, he remarked:

We have to have it on a functional basis now. We are also trying something new for us by moving to the general manager concept. In the past when I was away, there was no one with complete authority; now my general manager is in change in my absence.

In discussing the new structuring of the organization, Mr. Brown was quick to point out that the company had not established formalized job descriptions. "Job descriptions are not worth anything. My people wear too many hats, and besides, we're too small to put it in writing." At present the company employs 34 people, including Mr. Brown.

Mr. Brown is quick to point out that he has never had a personnel problem. "All my people enjoy working here." He believes that "nobody should work for nothing" and has therefore established a personal goal of seeing to it that no one employed by UPI makes less than $10,000 per year. Mr. Brown commented on his attitude toward his employees:

The men might complain about the amount of responsibility placed on them, but I think it's good for them. It helps them develop to their potential. I'm a nice guy who is interested in all of my people. I feel a strong social obligation to my employees and have developed very close relationships with all of them. My door is always open to them no matter what the problem may be.

I make it a policy never to yell at anyone in public; it's not good for morale. Maybe it's part of my conservative philosophy, but I want everyone to call me Mr. Brown, not George. I think it's good for people to have a Mr. Brown. Although I want to run a nice friendly business, I have learned that it's hard to be real friends

Exhibit 4 UPI Organization Chart, December 1974

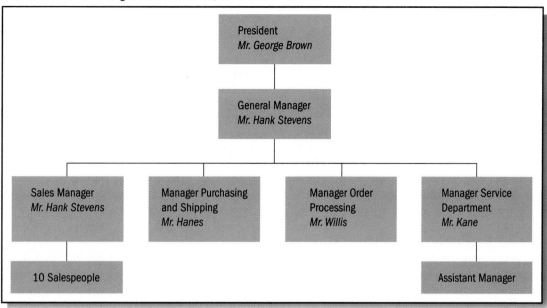

with an employee. You can only go so far. Employers and employees cannot mix socially; it just doesn't work out over the long run.

This is not your normal business. I am very approachable; I don't demand much and I allow an easy, open dialogue with my employees. Seldom do I take any punitive action. I'm just not a hard-driving tough guy. . . . I'm an easygoing guy.

It would take much of the enjoyment out of the business for me to come in here and run this place like a machine.[1]

I find it hard to motivate the company's salespeople. Since we have so much trouble finding good, capable people, I'm not likely to fire any that I have. This situation makes it hard for me to put pressure on them to produce.

The bonus system, if you want to call it that, is, I guess, what you'd call very arbitrary. I have not set up specific sales quotas, or targeted goals for my inside people, so, as a result, I base my bonus decisions on my assessment of how well I feel an employee performed during the past year.

Recently, I've given some thought to selling the company. I could probably get around $3–$4 million for it. If I did that, I'm not sure what I would do with my time. Besides my family and UPI, there is not much that I am interested in. A couple of years ago, when I took my extended vacation, I got bored and couldn't wait to get back to the company.

UPI's Planning Process

George Brown claims to be a firm believer in planning. "I find myself spending more and more time planning for the company. Currently, I'm averaging about 50 percent of my time and I see this increasing." As he described it, the planning process at United Products is really a very loose system:

We have no set way as to how we do the planning. Basically, the process is directed at ways of increasing the profitability of the company. I look at the salespeople's performance on a weekly and monthly basis and use this information in the development of the plans. Since we have a very informal planning process, we only forecast out one year at most. The company's plans are reevaluated each month and, if necessary, new plans are set. Only on rare occasions have we ever planned beyond one year. However, I think the current economic and political situation may force us to develop plans that cover a two-year period.

I am familiar with commonly accepted theory about planning systems, but I do not feel it is necessary for UPI to institute, in a formal manner, any of those I've read about. We perform many of the activities advocated in the planning models, but we do them in a relaxed, casual fashion. For example, I am a member of many organizations connected with my business and receive industry newsletters on a regular basis. In addition, I receive input from friends and business associates both inside and outside my line of business. Since we do not have a formal process, planning tends to be a continuous process at UPI.

Although goals are not formally developed and written down, Mr. Brown said he established targets

---

[1]When the case researcher arrived at the plant one afternoon, he observed Mr. Brown running around the office deeply involved in a water fight with one of his office girls. By the way, he lost.

for the company to achieve in the areas of sales, profits, and organizational climate:

1. Increase sales volume by 20 percent per year.
2. Increase gross profit margin 0.5 to 1 percent per year.
3. Make UPI a friendly place to work.

Mr. Brown feels that the company has been able to grow at about 20 percent a year in the past and should be able to realize that level in the future. In addition, he believes that sales growth is a necessary evil: "Those companies that don't grow are swallowed up by the competition, and besides, given the amount of energy I'm willing to exert, I think 20 percent is a reasonable level of growth."

In the area of profits, the company actually sets no specific targeted figures other than simply an increase in the gross profit margin (as already stated). Mr. Brown observed:

We do not set a goal because we would not have a way of measuring it. I have no way of knowing how much money I am making until the end of the year, without spending considerable time and effort.

When asked about UPI's strengths and weaknesses, Mr. Brown indicated that the company had four areas of strength:

1. The number of different products carried.
2. The quality of its employees, particularly salespeople.
3. The absence of any debt.
4. Purchasing capabilities.

The major weakness he viewed was an inability to get and train new personnel—primarily in the area of sales.

Sales Force

UPI's salespeople are not assigned a sales quota for the year, but rather are evaluated based on Mr. Brown's assessment of the particular salesperson's territory and initiative. He feels his salespeople make more than those of his competitors. Several of UPI's 10 salespeople have earned as much as $40,000 in a single year. All salespeople are compensated on a straight, sliding-scale, commission basis calculated as follows:

8 percent for the first $180,000 in sales

7 percent for the next $60,000

6 percent for the next $60,000

5 percent for all sales over $300,000

Mr. Brown is pleased with the sales success of his company and feels that United Products' greatest strength is its ability to "sell anything to anybody." Still, he perceives UPI's main problem as finding good salespeople. "There just aren't good salespeople around and this is a problem because salespeople are the lifeblood of our business."

UPI's Management Team

At the time of the company's reorganization. Hank Stevens was brought in as general manager and assistant to the president. Over the past several years, Mr. Stevens's areas of responsibility have grown to an extent where they now comprise approximately 80 percent of the activities that were formerly done by Mr. Brown. As a result, George Brown sometimes finds himself with little to do and often works only five hours per day. As he described it:

Hank's discretionary power has increased steadily since he arrived here—partly as a result of the extent of responsibility I've placed on him and partly due to his aggressiveness. As it now stands, he makes almost all of the daily operating decisions for the company, leaving me with only the top-management decisions. Let's be realistic . . . there just aren't that many top-management decisions that have to be made here in the course of a day. A lot of the time, I walk around the plant checking on what other people are doing and, I guess, acting as a morale booster.

When asked about the management capabilities of Hank Stevens, Mr. Brown responded by saying, "Hank probably feels that he is working at a very fast pace, but when you evaluate the effectiveness of his actions, he is actually moving forward at what I would consider to be a very slow pace. However, everything else considered, Hank is the best of what is around. I guess if I could find a really good sales manager, I would add him to the company and relieve Hank of that area of responsibility."

Hank Stevens

Hank Stevens, 32, joined UPI at the time of the reorganization in 1970 after having graduated from a local university with a B.S. in economics. As general manager, Mr. Stevens's responsibilities include planning, purchasing, and sales management, as well as involvement in other decisions that affect UPI's policies. Mr. Stevens feels that he has been fortunate in that "ever since I came to UPI, I've reported to the president and in essence have had everyone else reporting to me."

When asked about the goals of UPI, Mr. Stevens responded, "As I see it, we have goals in three major areas: profitability, sales level, and personal relationships." In discussing his own personal goals, Hank explained that he hoped the organization would grow and that, as a result, he would be able to grow along with it. Since Mr. Stevens works so closely with Mr. Brown, he has given considerable thought to his boss's business philosophy:

I feel that George's business philosophy is unique. I guess the best way to describe it is to say that above all he is a businessman. Also, he has very high moral values and as a result of that he is extremely honest and would never cheat anybody. Actually, the company would probably look better financially if it was run by someone who didn't operate with the same values as George.

When asked about the sales force at UPI, Mr. Stevens commented, "When a new salesman starts with the company, he does so with full salary. After a period of about two years, we change him over to a commission basis." As has always been the case, UPI concentrated its sales efforts on large customers. Mr. Stevens noted that "on the average the company processes approximately 105 orders per day, with an average dollar value per order of roughly $132. It's not that we won't write small orders, we just don't solicit business from small accounts. It just makes more sense to concentrate on the larger accounts."

Jim Hanes

Jim Hanes, 24, has been with UPI for over six years and during that time has worked his way up from assistant service manager to his current position as the number three man in the company—manager of purchasing and shipping. Jim is responsible for the front office, repair work, and the warehouse. He feels that his reporting responsibility is approximately 60 percent to Mr. Stevens and 40 percent to Mr. Brown. "Since I have responsibility for all merchandise entering and leaving the company, I get involved with both Hank and George, and therefore I guess I report to both of them."

In talking about where he would go from his present position, he explained:

I guess the next step is for me to become a salesman so that I can broaden my background and move up in the company. However I am a little worried; I don't think the salespeople in our company are given the right sales training. As the system works now, a new salesman is assigned to work with an experienced salesperson for about six weeks—after which time he is given his own territory. Perhaps if our sales manager had had more experience as a salesman, he would handle the training differently.

In commenting on his understanding of Mr. Brown's philosophy, Jim summed up his position: "George is a very open person. I think he is too honest for a businessman. He certainly gives his people responsibility. He gives you the ball and lets you run with it. I don't think enough planning is done at UPI.

At most, it appears that we look ahead one year, and even then what plans are developed are kept very flexible."

UPI's Corporate Strategy

When asked about UPI's current strategy, Mr. Brown responded that "the company is presently a distributor in the industrial packaging equipment, shipping supplies, and heavy-duty stapling equipment business. In the past when we've wanted to grow, we have either added new lines of merchandise or added more salespeople, or both. For example, this past year I got the idea to create what I call a contract sales department. It is a simple concept. I took one man, put him in an office with a telephone and a listing of the Fortune top 1,000 companies, and told him to call and get new business. You would be surprised at how easy it was to pick up new accounts."

Mr. Stevens looks at UPI as being in the distribution and shipping of packaging supplies business. "In order for UPI to reach the goals that have been set, we have to sell more products. That is, we can grow by adding new salespeople, adding more product lines, purchasing more effectively, and undertaking more aggressive sales promotion."

Mr. Brown believes that UPI should try to maximize the profit on every item sold. To do this the company tries to set its prices at a level that is approximately 10 percent above the competition. Mr. Brown explained his pricing philosophy:

I don't understand why people are afraid to raise prices. If you increase the price, you will pick up more business and make more money. That allows you to keep the volume low and still make more money. In addition, although the customer may pay more, he gets more. The higher price allows me to provide top-notch service to all my customers.

In his view, UPI is an innovative company. "Until very recently we were always innovating with new products and new applications. Now I think it's again time that we started to look for additional new and exciting products."

Brown was aware that UPI's strategic emphasis on service, together with his business philosophy, had resulted in UPI's organization being larger than it had to be, given the level of business. Mr. Brown explained the reasoning behind this condition. "I know the organization is bigger than it has to be. We could probably handle three times the present volume of business with our present staff and facility. I think it's because of my conservative attitude: I've always wanted the organization to stay a step ahead of what is really needed. I feel comfortable with a built-in backup system and therefore I am willing to pay for it."

In December 1974, Mr. Brown talked optimistically about the future. He felt that sales should reach the $6–$7 million range by 1978. "Looked at in another way, we should be able to grow at 20–25 percent per year without any particular effort." He went on to say:

I want to grow and therefore I am making a concerted effort. I am constantly looking for possible merger avenues or expansion possibilities. I do not want to expand geographically. I would rather control that market area we are now in.

I recently sent a letter to all competitors in New England offering to buy them out. Believe it or not, no one responded.

I do not see any problems in the future. The history has been good; therefore, why won't it continue to be?

Growth is easy. All I have to do is pick up a new line and I've automatically increased sales and profits. Basically we are distributors, and we operate as middlemen between the manufacturers and users. In light of what has been happening in the market, I feel that supply and demand will continue to be a problem. Therefore, I am giving serious thought to integrating vertically and becoming a manufacturer. This will guarantee our supply.[2]

Actually, I don't want to do the manufacturing. I think it would be better if I bought the manufacturing equipment and then had someone else use it to make my products.

The Future

Nevertheless, after reviewing with his accountant the results for the just-completed fiscal year, Mr. Brown was concerned about UPI's future course. "I know changes have to be made for next year as a result of this year, but I'm not sure what they should be." Mr. Brown continued:

I think this next year is going to be a real bad year. Prices will probably fall like a rock from the levels they reached during 1974 and as a result those items that would have been profitable for the company aren't going to be, and we have much too large an inventory as it is. It isn't easy to take away customers from the competition. As a result of this, I feel we have to step up our efforts to get new lines and new accounts. Recently, I've given some thought to laying off one or two people for economic reasons, but I'm not sure. I will probably give raises to all employees even though it's not a good business decision, but it's an ingrained part of my business philosophy.

When asked if he had informed his employees of his concern about the future, Mr. Brown referred to the minutes of a sales meeting that had been held in November 1974:

. . . Mr. Brown then presided at the meeting, and announced that Al King had won the coveted "Salesman of the Month" award. This was a "first" for our Al, and well deserved for his outstanding sales results in October. Congratulations and applause were extended to him by all present. The balance of the meeting was then spent in a lengthy, detailed discussion, led by Mr. George Brown, of the general, overall picture of what the future portends in the sales area as a result of the current inflationary, recessionary, and complex competitive conditions prevailing in the economy.

The gist of the entire discussion can be best summarized as follows:

1. Everyone present must recognize the very real difficulties that lie ahead in these precarious economic times.
2. The only steps available to the salespeople and to the company for survival during the rough period ahead are as follows:
   a. Minimize contacts with existing accounts.
   b. Spend the majority of time developing new accounts on the less competitive products, and selling new products to established accounts.
3. Concentrate on and promote our new items.
4. Mr. Brown and inside management are making and will continue to make every concerted effort to find new products and new lines for the coming year.

In preparation for his meeting with Hank Stevens, Mr. Brown had drawn up a list of activities to which Hank should address himself while running UPI during George's upcoming vacation. Mr. Brown believed that upon his return from Europe his activities at UPI would be increasing as a result of the problems caused by the uncertain economic conditions. The first item on the list was a possible redefinition of UPI's marketing strategy. Mr. Brown now believed that UPI would have to be much more liberal with respect to new products considered for sale. "I'm not saying we are going to get into the consumer goods business, but I think we need to give consideration to handling consumer products that require no service and that carry a high-profit-margin factor for the company."

As he sat at his desk thinking about possible changes he could make in UPI's planning process, Mr. Brown was convinced that if he hadn't done some planning in the past, the situation would be more drastic than it was. Yet at the same time, he wasn't sure that a more structured and formalized planning process would put UPI in any better position to face the more difficult times that he saw ahead.

---

[2]Refer to Exhibit 5 which contains minutes of a United Products sales meeting held at the end of 1973.

Exhibit 5   Minutes of UPI's Sales Meeting, December 5, 1973

Mr. Brown presided at the meeting. His opening remarks highlighted the extraordinary times our country and our company are going through as far as the general economy and the energy crisis are concerned, and the extraordinary effects of these unusual crises on people and businesses, including our company and our sources of supply.

He thanked all present for the many thoughtful, considered, and excellent suggestions that they had offered in writing as to how the salespeople and their company might best handle the gasoline crisis without incurring an undue loss of sales and profits, and still maintain the high standards of service to which UNITED PRODUCTS' thousands of satisfied customers are accustomed.

The whole situation, according to Mr. Brown, boils down to a question of supply and prices. Mr. Brown reported that on his recent trip to the Orient, there were very few companies that wanted to sell their merchandise to us—rather, THEY WANTED TO BUY FROM US MANY OF THE ITEMS WE NORMALLY BUY FROM FOREIGN COMPANIES, i.e., carton-closing staples, tape, gloves, et cetera . . . and at inflated prices!!! The Tokyo, Japan, market is so great that they are using up everything they can produce—and the steel companies would rather make flat steel than the steel rods that are used for making staples. A very serious problem exists, as a result, in the carton-closing staple field not only in Japan, but also in Europe and America.

Mr. Brown advised that every year the company's costs of operating increase just as each individual's cost of living goes up and up yearly. Additional personnel, increased group and auto insurance premiums, increased Social Security payments, new office equipment and supplies, new catalogues, "Beeper system" for more salespeople—all of these costs accumulate and result in large expenditures of money. Manufacturers cover their increased operating costs by pricing their products higher—but to date, UNITED PRODUCTS has never put into their prices the increased costs resulting from increased operating expenses. Last year, the 3 percent increase that the company needed then was put into effect by many of you. HOWEVER, in order for the company to realize that additional profit, this 3 percent price increase had to be put into effect ACROSS THE BOARD . . . all customers . . . all items!

That Did Not Happen!!!

Mr. Brown advised that UNITED PRODUCTS got LAMBASTED when all of the sources of supply started to increase their prices. When SPOTNAILS, for example, went up 10 percent, the salespeople only increased their prices 7 percent. We did *not get the 3 percent price increase above the manufacturers' price increase*—and we needed it then and need it even more NOW.

Eliminating the possibility of cutting commissions, there are three possible solutions for the problem and how to get this much needed and ABSOLUTELY IMPERATIVE additional 3 percent PRICE INCREASE ACROSS THE BOARD to cover the constantly growing operating costs for running a successful, progressive-minded and growing business whose high standards of service and performance are highly regarded by customers and sources of supply alike, namely:

a. A 3 percent increase on all items to all customers across the board

b. A surcharge on all invoices or decrease in discounts allowed off LIST

c. A GCI charge (government cost increase) on all invoices

Considerable discussion regarding these three possibilities resulted in the following conclusions concerning the best method for obtaining this special 3 percent ACROSS THE BOARD PRICE INCREASE, as follows:

a. A new PRICE BOOK should be issued with all new prices to reflect not only the manufacturers' new increased prices, but in addition the 3 percent UNITED PRODUCTS PRICE INCREASE. All of the salespeople agreed that it would be easier to effect the additional 3 percent price increase if the 3 percent was "built in" on their price book sheets.

b. This new PRICE BOOK will be set up in such a way that prices will be stipulated according to quantity of item purchased . . . with no variances allowed. WITH NO EXCEPTIONS, the price of any item will depend on the quantity a customer buys.

c. Some items will continue to be handled on a discount basis—but lower discounts in order to ascertain that UNITED PRODUCTS is getting its 3 percent price increase.

d. Until these new PRICE BOOKS are issued, all salespeople were instructed to proceed IMMEDIATELY to effect these 3 percent price increases.

Ten New Accounts Contest

Seven of our ten salespeople won a calculator as a result of opening up 10 new accounts each . . . a total of 70 NEW ACCOUNTS for our company!!! However, both Mr. Brown and Mr. Stevens confessed that the dollar volume amount stipulated in the contest had been set ridiculously low, as a "feeler" to determine the success and effectiveness of such a contest. All the salespeople voiced their approval of all of the contests offered to them—and agreed that they had enjoyed many excellent opportunities of increasing their personal exchequers.

(continued)

Mr. Brown again reminded all present that we have an excellent printed letter, which is available for sending to every new customer—and urged all to take advantage of this service by the office personnel by clearly indicating on their sales and order slips "NEW CUSTOMER." The procedure is but another step towards our goal of becoming more and more professional in our approach with our customers.

New Catalogs

Mr. Brown advised that by the first of the new year, hopefully, all our hard-cover catalogues with their new divider breakdowns will be ready for hand-delivering to large accounts. These catalogues cost the company over $5 and should only be distributed by hand to those customers who can and will make intelligent and effective use of them.

Excessive Issuance of Credits

As a result of a detailed study made by Mr. Brown of the nature and reasons for the ever-increasing number of credits being issued, he instructed all of the salespeople to follow these procedures when requesting the issuing of CREDITS:

a. Issue the CREDIT at the right time.

b. Do not sell an item where it is not needed.

c. NEVER PUT "NO COMMENT" for the reason why merchandise is being returned. EVERY CREDIT MUST HAVE A REASON FOR ITS ISSUANCE.

The ever-increasing number of CREDITS being issued is extremely costly to the company: (1) new merchandise comes back 90-plus days after it has been billed, and frequently, if not always, is returned by the customer FREIGHT COLLECT: (2) CREDIT 9-part forms, postage for mailing, and extra work for both the Bookkeeping and Billing and Order Processing Departments mean higher expenses for the Company. More intelligent, considered and selective selling, plus greater care on the part of the Order Processing personnel, according to Mr. Brown, could easily eliminate a large percentage of these CREDITS.

C A S E   2
The Paradoxical Twins: Acme and Omega Electronics
John F. Veiga

Part I

In 1955, Technological Products of Erie, Pennsylvania was bought out by a Cleveland manufacturer. The Cleveland firm had no interest in the electronics division of Technological Products and subsequently sold to different investors two plants that manufactured printed circuit boards. One of the plants, located in nearby Waterford, Pennsylvania, was renamed Acme Electronics, and the other plant, within the city limits of Erie, was renamed Omega Electronics, Inc. Acme retained its original management and upgraded its general manager to president. Omega hired a new president, who had been a director of a large electronics research laboratory, and upgraded several of the existing personnel within the plant.

Acme and Omega often competed for the same contracts. As subcontractors, both firms benefited from the electronics

This case was developed from material gathered from the two firms by Dr. John F. Veiga. All names and places have been disguised.

boom of the early 1960s and both looked forward to future growth and expansion. Acme had annual sales of $10 million and employed 550 people. Omega had annual sales of $8 million and employed 480 people. Acme was consistently more effective than Omega and regularly achieved greater net profits, much to the chagrin of Omega's management.

Inside Acme

The president of Acme, John Tyler, credited his firm's greater effectiveness to his managers' abilities to run a "tight ship." He explained that he had retained the basic structure developed by Technological Products because it was most efficient for high-volume manufacture of printed circuits and their subsequent assembly. Tyler was confident that had the demand not been so great, its competitor would not have survived. "In fact," he said, "we have been able to beat Omega regularly for the most profitable contracts, thereby increasing our profits." Acme's basic organization structure is

Exhibit 1 Acme Electronics Organization Chart

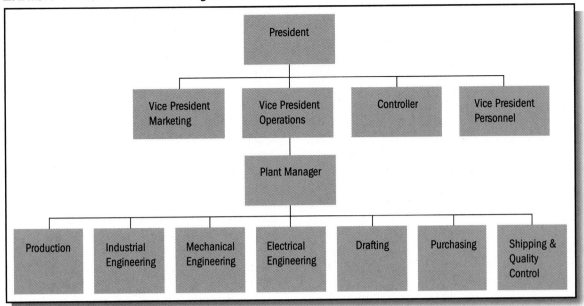

shown in Exhibit 1. People were generally satisfied with their work at Acme; however, some of the managers voiced the desire to have a little more latitude in their jobs. One manager characterized the president as a "one-man band." He said, "While I respect John's ability, there are times when I wish I had a little more information about what is going on."

Inside Omega

Omega's president, Jim Rawls, did not believe in organization charts. He felt that his organization had departments similar to Acme's, but he thought the plant was small enough that things such as organization charts just put artificial barriers between specialists who should be working together. Written memos were not allowed, since, as Jim expressed it, "the plant is small enough that if people want to communicate, they can just drop by and talk things over." Other members of Omega complained that too much time was wasted "filling in" people who could not contribute to the problem solving. As the head of the mechanical engineering department expressed it, "Jim spends too much of his time and mine making sure everyone understands what we're doing and listening to suggestions." A newer member of the industrial engineering department said, "When I first got here, I wasn't sure what I was supposed to do. One day I worked with some mechanical engineers and the next day I helped the shipping department design some packing cartons. The first months on the job were hectic, but at least I got a real feel for what makes Omega tick." Most decisions of any significance were made by the management team at Omega.

Part II

In 1966, the integrated circuits began to cut deeply into the demand for printed circuit boards. The integrated circuits (ICs), or "chips," were the first step into micro-miniaturization in the electronics industry. Because the manufacturing process for ICs was a closely guarded secret, both Acme and Omega realized the potential threat to their futures and both began to seek new customers aggressively. In July 1966, one of the major photocopy manufacturers was looking for a subcontractor to assemble the memory unit for its new experimental copier. The projected contract for the job was estimated to be $5–$7 million in annual sales. Both Acme and Omega were geographically close to this manufacturer and both had submitted highly competitive bids for the production of 100 prototypes. Acme's bid was slightly lower than Omega's; however, both firms were asked to produce 100 units. The photocopy manufacturer told both firms that speed was critical because their president had boasted to other manufacturers that they would have a finished copier available by Christmas. This boast, much to the designer's dismay, required pressure on all subcontractors to begin prototype production before final design of the copier was complete. This meant that Acme and Omega would have at most two weeks to produce the prototypes or delay the final copier production.

Part III

Inside Acme

As soon as John Tyler was given the blueprints (Monday, July 11, 1966), he sent a memo to the purchasing department requesting them to move forward on the purchase of all necessary materials. At the same time, he sent the blueprints to the drafting department and asked that they prepare manufacturing prints. The industrial engineering department was told to begin methods design work for use by the production department foremen. Tyler also sent a memo to all department heads and executives indicating the critical time constraints of this job and how he expected everyone to perform as efficiently as they had in the past. On Wednesday, July 13, purchasing discovered that a particular component used in the memory unit could not be purchased or shipped for two weeks because the manufacturer had shut down for summer vacations. The head of purchasing was not overly concerned by this obstacle, because he knew that Omega would face the same problem. He advised Tyler of this predicament, who in turn decided that Acme would build the memory unit except for the one component and then add that component in two weeks. Industrial engineering was told to build this constraint into their assembly methods. On Friday, July 15, industrial engineering notified Tyler that the missing component would substantially increase the assembly time if it was not available from the start of assembly. Mr. Tyler, anxious to get started, said that he would live with that problem and gave the signal to go forward on the assembly plans. Mechanical engineering received manufacturing prints on Tuesday, July 12, and evaluated their capabilities for making the chassis required for the memory unit. Because their procedure for prototypes was to get estimates from outside vendors on all sheet metal work before they authorized in-house personnel to do the job, the head of mechanical engineering sent a memo to the head of drafting requesting that vendor prints be drawn up on the chassis and that these prints then be forwarded to purchasing, which would obtain vendor bids. On Friday, July 15, Mr. Tyler called the head of mechanical engineering and asked for a progress report on the chassis. He was advised that mechanical engineering was waiting for vendor estimates before they moved forward.

Mr. Tyler was shocked by the lack of progress and demanded that mechanical engineering begin building those "damn chassis." On Monday, July 18, Mr. Tyler received word from the shipping department that most of the components had arrived. The first chassis were sent to the head of production, who began immediately to set up an assembly area. On Tuesday, July 19, two methods engineers from industrial engineering went out to the production floor to set up the methods to be used in assembly. In his haste to get things going, the production foreman ignored the normal procedure of contacting the methods engineers and set up what he thought would be an efficient assembly process. The methods engineers were very

upset to see assembly begin before they had a chance to do a proper layout. They told the foreman they had spent the entire weekend analyzing the motions needed and that his process was very inefficient and not well balanced. The methods engineers ordered that work be stopped until they could rearrange the assembly process. The production foreman refused to stop work. He said, "I have to have these units produced by Friday and already I'm behind schedule."

The methods engineers reported back to the head of industrial engineering, who immediately complained to the plant manager. The plant manager sided with the production foreman and said, "John Tyler wants these units by Friday. Don't bother me with methods details now. Once we get the prototypes out and go into full production, then your boys can do their thing." As the head of industrial engineering got off the phone with the plant manager, he turned to his subordinates and said, "If my boss doesn't think our output is needed, to hell with him! You fellows must have other jobs to worry about, forget this one." As the two methods engineers left the head industrial engineer's office, one of them said to the other, "Just wait until they try to install those missing components. Without our methods, they'll have to tear down the units almost completely."

On Thursday, July 21, the final units were being assembled, although the process was delayed several times as production waited for chassis from mechanical engineering to be completed. On Friday, July 22, the last units were finished while John Tyler paced around the plant. Late that afternoon, Tyler received a phone call from the head designer of the photocopier manufacturer, who told Tyler that he had received a call on Wednesday from Jim Rawls of Omega. He explained that Rawls's boys had found an error in the design of the connector cable and had taken corrective action on their prototypes. He told Tyler that he checked out the design error and that Omega was right. Tyler, a bit overwhelmed by this information, told the designer that he had all of the memory units ready for shipment and that as soon as they received the missing component, on Monday or Tuesday, they would be able to deliver the final units. The designer explained that the design error would be rectified in a new blueprint he was sending over by messenger and that he would hold Acme to the delivery date on Tuesday.

When the blueprint arrived, Tyler called the production foreman in to assess the damages. The alterations in the design would call for total disassembly and the unsoldering of several connections. Tyler told the foreman to put extra people on the alterations first thing on Monday morning and to try to finish the job by Tuesday. Late Tuesday afternoon the alterations were finished and the missing components were delivered. Wednesday morning, the production foreman discovered that the units would have to be torn apart again to install the missing components. When John Tyler was told this, he "hit the roof." He called industrial engineering and asked if they could help out. The head of industrial engineering told Tyler that his people would study the situation and get back to him first thing in the morning. Tyler decided to wait for their study because he was concerned that tearing apart the units again could weaken several of the soldered contacts and increase their potential rejection. Thursday, after several heated debates between the production foreman and the methods engineers, John Tyler settled the argument by ordering that all units be taken apart again and the missing component installed. He told shipping to prepare cartons for delivery on Friday afternoon. On Friday, July 29, 50 prototypes were shipped from Acme without final inspection. John Tyler was concerned about his firm's reputation, so he waived the final inspection after he personally tested one unit and found it operational. On Tuesday, August 2, Acme shipped the last 50 units.

Inside Omega

Jim Rawls called a meeting on Friday, July 8, that included department heads to tell them about the potential contract they were to receive. He told them that as soon as he received the blueprints, work could begin. On Monday, July 11, the prints arrived and again the department heads met to discuss the project. At the end of the meeting, drafting had agreed to prepare manufacturing prints while industrial engineering and production would begin methods design. On Wednesday, July 13, at a progress report session, purchasing indicated a particular component would not be available for two weeks, when the manufacturer reopened from summer vacation shutdown. The head of electrical engineering suggested using a possible substitute component, which was made in Japan, containing all of the necessary characteristics. The head of industrial engineering promised to have the methods engineers study the assembly methods to see if the unit could be produced in such a way that the missing component could be installed last.

The head of mechanical engineering raised the concern that the chassis would be an obstacle if they waited for vendor estimates and he advised the group

that his people would begin production even though it might cost more. On Friday, July 15, at a progress report session, industrial engineering reported that the missing component would increase the assembly time substantially. The head of electrical engineering offered to have one of his engineers examine the missing component specifications and said he was confident that the Japanese component would work. At the end of the meeting, purchasing was told to order the Japanese components.

On Monday, July 18, a methods engineer and the production foreman formulated the assembly plans, and production was set to begin on Tuesday morning. On Monday afternoon, people from mechanical engineering, electrical engineering, production, and industrial engineering got together to produce a prototype just to ensure that there would be no snags in production. While they were building the unit, they discovered an error in the connector cable design. All of the engineers agreed, after checking and rechecking the blueprints, that the cable was erroneously designed. People from mechanical engineering and electrical engineering spent Monday night redesigning the cable and on Tuesday morning, the drafting department finalized the changes in the manufacturing prints. On Tuesday morning, Jim Rawls was a bit apprehensive about the design changes and decided to get formal approval. Rawls received word on Wednesday from the head designer of the photocopier firm that he could proceed with the design changes as discussed on the phone. On Friday, July 22, the final units were inspected by quality control and were then shipped.

Part IV: Retrospect

Ten of Acme's final memory units were ultimately defective, while all of Omega's units passed the photocopier firm's tests. The photocopier firm was disappointed with Acme's delivery delay and incurred further delays in repairing the defective Acme units. However, rather than give the entire contract to one firm, the final contract was split between Acme and Omega, with two directives added: (1) Maintain zero defects and (2) reduce final cost. In 1967, through extensive cost-cutting efforts, Acme reduced its unit cost by 20 percent and was ultimately awarded the total contract.

CASE 3
Continental Can Company of Canada, Ltd.
Paul R. Lawrence
revised by John P. Kotter

By the fall of 1963, Continental Can Company of Canada had developed a sophisticated control system for use in its plants. This control system, begun in the years following World War II, stressed competition within the company as well as against other companies in the industry. Within its division at Continental, the can manufacturing plant at St. Laurent, Quebec, had become a preferred site for production management trainees as a result of its successful use of control systems. According to a division training executive:

> The St. Laurent people look at the controls as tools. They show trainees that they really work. The French-Canadian atmosphere is good too. In a French-Canadian family everything is open and aboveboard. There are no secrets. Trainees can ask anyone anything and the friendliness and company parties give them a feel for good employee relations.

Products, Technology, and Markets

Continental Can Company of Canada in 1963 operated a number of plants in Canada. The principal products of the St. Laurent plant were Open Top food cans, bottle caps and crowns, steel pails, and general line containers. Of these, Open Top cans constituted the largest group. They were manufactured for the major packers of vegetable products—peas, beans, corn, and tomatoes—and for the soup manufacturers. Beer and soft drink cans were a growing commodity, and large quantities of general line containers of many different configurations were produced to hold solvents, paints, lighter fluids, waxes, antifreeze, and so on. Several styles of steel pails of up to five-gallon capacity were also produced to hold many specialized products.

Most of the thousands of different products, varying in size, shape, color, and decoration, were produced to order. Typical lead times between the customer's order and shipment from the plant were two to three weeks in 1963, having been reduced from five and one-half weeks in the early 1950s, according to St. Laurent plant executives.

"Continental Can Co." by Paul R. Lawrence. Copyright © 1977 by the President and Fellows of Harvard College. Harvard Business School case 478-017. This case, prepared by C. Bourke under the direction of John P. Kotter, is based on a case originally written by Paul R. Lawrence. This case was prepared as the basis for class discussion rather than to illustrate either effective or ineffective handling of an administrative situation. Reprinted by permission of the Harvard Business School.

Quality inspection in the can manufacturing operation was critical, as the can maker usually supplied the closing equipment and assisted in or recommended the process to be used in the final packing procedure. In producing Open Top food cans, for example, the can body was formed, soldered, and flanged at speeds exceeding 400 cans per minute. After the bottom, or end unit, was assembled to the body, each can was air tested to reject poor double seams or poor soldering or plate inclusions that could cause pinholes. Both side seams and double seams underwent periodic destruction testing to ensure that assembly specifications were met. Although a number of measuring devices were used in the process, much of the inspection was still visual, involving human inspection and monitoring. The quality of the can also affected the filling and processing procedure: It had to withstand internal pressures from expansion of the product as it was heated, and then it had to sustain a vacuum without collapsing when it was cooled. Costly claims could result if the container failed in the field and the product had to be withdrawn from store shelves.

Almost all of the containers required protective coatings inside and out, and the majority were decorated. The coating and decorating equipment was sophisticated and required sizable investment. This part of the operation was unionized, and the lithographers, or pressmen, were among the highest paid of the various craftsmen in the plant.

Most of the key equipment was designed and developed by the parent organization over many years. The St. Laurent plant spends substantial sums each year to modernize and renovate its equipment. Modernization and the implementation of new techniques to increase speed, reduce material costs, and improve quality were a necessity as volume increased. Over the years, many of the small-run, handmade boxes and pails were discontinued and the equipment scrapped. Other lines were automated and personnel were retrained to handle the higher mechanical skills and changeovers required. In spite of these changes, however, according to a general foreman, a production worker of the 1940s could return in 1963 and not feel entirely out of place. Many of the less skilled machine operators were required to handle several tasks on the higher speed equipment. In general, most of the jobs in the plant were relatively unskilled and highly repetitive and gave the worker little control over method or pace. The die makers, who made and repaired the dies, the machine repairmen, and those who made equipment setup changes between different products were considered the most highly skilled.

All production workers below the rank of assistant foreman were unionized; however, there had never been a strike at the plant. Wages were high compared to other similar industries in the Montreal area. The union was not part of the Master Agreement that governed all other plants in Canada and most of the plants in the United States, but management made every effort to apply equality to this plant. Output standards were established for all jobs, but no bonus was paid for exceeding standards.

The metal can industry was relatively stable with little product differentiation. The St. Laurent plant to some extent shipped its products throughout Canada, although transportation costs limited its market primarily to eastern Canada. While some of the customers were large and bought in huge quantities (between 300 and 500 million cans), many were relatively small and purchased a more specialized product.

The Plant Organization

Plant Management

Andrew Fox, the plant manager at St. Laurent since 1961, had risen from an hourly worker through foreman up to plant manufacturing engineer in the maintenance end of the business. He had developed an intimate first-hand knowledge of operations and was frequently seen around the plant, a cigar clenched between his teeth.

As plant manager, Fox had no responsibility for sales or research and development activities. In fact, both Fox and the district sales manager in his area had separate executives to whom they reported in the division headquarters, and it was in the superior of these executives that responsibility for both sales and production first came together.

Fox commented about the working relationships at the St. Laurent plant:

You will see that frequently two managers with different job titles are assigned responsibility for the same task. [He implied that it was up to them to work out their own pattern of mutual support and cooperation.] However I don't have to adhere strictly to the description. I may end up asking a lot more of the man at certain times and under certain conditions than is ever put down on paper. In effect, the staff[1] runs the plant. We delegate to the various staff department heads the authority to implement decisions within the framework of our budget planning. This method of handling responsibility means that staff

[1]The personnel reporting directly to Fox. The organization chart (see Exhibit 1) was prominently displayed on the wall of the lobby. See Exhibit 2 for other information on personnel.

members have to be prepared to substantiate their decisions. At the same time, it gives them a greater sense of participation in and responsibility for plant income. We endeavor to carry this principle into the operating and service departments. The foreman is given responsibility and encouraged to act as though he were operating a business of his own. He is held responsible for all results generated in his department and is fully aware of how any decisions of his affect plant income.

Our division personnel counsel and assist the plant staff, and the plant staff counsel and assist the department foreman. Regular visits are made to the plant by our division manager and members of his staff. The principal contact is through the division manager of manufacturing and his staff, the manager of industrial engineering, the manager of production engineering, and the manager of quality control. [There was no division staff officer in production control.]

However, the onus is on the plant to request help or assistance of any kind. We can contact the many resources of Continental Can Company, usually on an informal basis. That is, we deal with other plant managers directly for information when manufacturing problems exist, without going through the division office.

Each member of the staff understands that we, as a plant, have committed ourselves through the budget to provide a stated amount of income, and regardless of conditions that develop, this income figure must be maintained. If sales are off and a continuing trend is anticipated, we will reduce expenses wherever possible to retain income. Conversely, if we have a gain in sales volume, we look for the complete conversion of the extra sales at the profit margin rate. However, this is not always possible, especially if the increase in sales comes at a peak time when facilities are already strained.

Fox was assisted by Robert Andrews, the assistant plant manager. Andrews, promoted from quality control manager in 1961, was responsible for all manufacturing operations within the plant. Andrews appeared more reserved than Fox, talked intently, and smiled easily while working with the persons who reported to him. Fifteen salaried supervisors reported to Andrews and helped him control the three-shift operation of the plant and its 500 hourly workers. (During peak periods in the summer, the plant employed as many as 800 people; most of the additional workers were the sons and daughters of plant employees.)

ANDREWS Our foreman have full responsibility for running their departments: quality conditions of equipment, employee relations, production according to schedule, control of inventory through accurate reporting of spoilage and production, and cost control. He is just as accountable for those in his department as the plant manager is for the entire plant.

Exhibit 1 St. Laurent Plant (March 1, 1963)

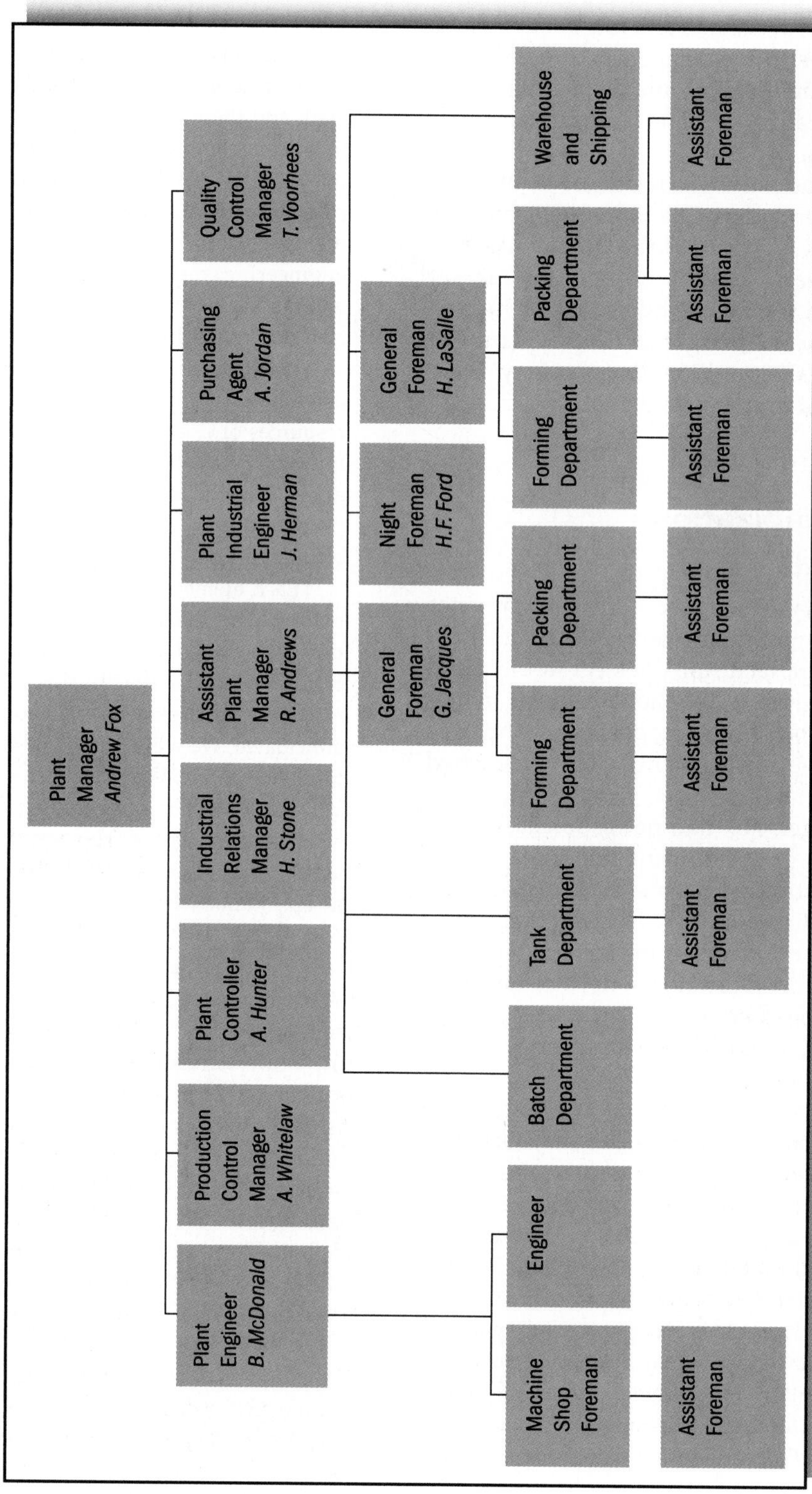

Exhibit 2 Information About Certain Personnel

Name, Position	Approximate Age	Approximate Length of Service		College Education
		St. Laurent	CCC	
Andrew Fox, Plant Manager	40–45	8	18	None
Robert Andrews, Assistant Plant Manager	35	3	8	Agricultural engineering
A. Hunter, Plant Controller	50	15	23	None
A. Whitelaw, Production Control Manager	45	18	18	None
Harold Stone, Industrial Relations Manager	45–50	5	29	None
Joe Herman, Plant Industrial Engineer	30–35	1	10	Engineering
Tom Voorhees, Quality Control Manager	30	5	5	Engineering in Netherlands
G. E. Jacques, General Foreman	45–50	25	25	None
Henri LaSalle, General Foreman	50	18	18	None
L. G. Adams, District Sales Manager	45–50	18	18	None

Andrews added that supervisory positions carried a good deal of status. Each supervisor had a personal parking spot and office and was expected to wear white shirts.[2] Andrews spoke of these symbols as an important aspect of the supervisor's position of authority. "He is no longer the best man with the wrench—he is the man with the best overall supervisory qualification."

Production Control

Al Whitelaw, the production control manager, had worked all of his 18 years with Continental Can at the St. Laurent plant. He was responsible for planning and controlling plant inventories and production schedules to meet sales requirements consistent with efficient utilization of facilities, materials, and manpower. Whitelaw spoke quickly and chain-smoked cigarettes. According to him the main task of his job was ". . . to try to achieve the maximum length of run without affecting service or exceeding inventory budgets."

Whitelaw was assisted by a scheduler for each major operating department and by clerks to service the schedulers. The schedulers worked closely with the department foremen in the plant and were in fre-

quent telephone contact with the sales offices. Whitelaw commented: "We in production control are the buffer between sales and operating people."

To facilitate their work, Whitelaw and Andrews headed biweekly production control meetings, each lasting about one hour. Fox, the plant manager, was a frequent observer. These meetings were attended by the two general foremen. Each production foreman and the production control scheduler working for his department came to the meeting at a prearranged time, and when their turn came, they reported on operations in their department and on problems they were encountering. Most of the questions, as well as instructions given in the meeting, came from Andrews. It was also he who usually dismissed one foreman/scheduler pair and called on the next. Questions from Andrews or Whitelaw were seldom clearly addressed to either the foreman or the scheduler. They were answered more frequently by the scheduler than the foreman, and often a scheduler would supplement comments made by the foreman. Generally, the schedulers were younger but spoke with more self-assurance than the foremen.

In these meetings, there were frequent references to specific customers, their needs, complaints, and present attitudes toward Continental Can. Both Whitelaw and Andrews tended to put instructions and decisions in terms of what was required to satisfy some particular customer or group of customers.

---

[2]The plant manager, management staff, foremen, and clerks in the office all wore white shirts and ties but no coats. The union president (a production worker) wore a white shirt but no tie. All other personnel wore colored sports shirts.

A recent meeting involving a foreman, Maurice Pelletier, and the scheduler for his department, Dan Brown, is illustrative of the process. It was observed that while Dan presented the status report Maurice shook his head in disagreement without saying anything. Dan was discussing his plan to discontinue an order being processed on a certain line on Friday to shift to another order and then to return to the original order on Tuesday.

ANDREWS   I don't think your plan makes much sense. You go off on Friday and then on again Tuesday.

MAURICE   [to Dan] Is this all required before the end of the year? [This was asked with obvious negative emotional feeling and then followed by comments by both Andrews and Whitelaw.]

DAN   Mind you—I could call sales again.

WHITELAW   I can see the point, Dan. It is sort of nonsensical to change back after so short a run.

MAURICE   This would mean our production would be reduced all week to around 300 instead of 350. You know it takes four hours to make the changeover.

DAN   But the order has been backed up.

ANDREWS   It is backed up only because their [sales] demands are unreasonable.

DAN   They only asked us to do the best we can.

ANDREWS   They always do this. We should never have put this order on in the first place.

MAURICE   If you want to we could . . . [Makes a suggestion about how to handle the problem.]

ANDREWS   Production-wise, this is the best deal [Agreeing with Maurice's plan.]

DAN   Let me look at it again.

ANDREWS   Production-wise, this is best; make the changeover on the weekend.

WHITELAW   [Summarizes; then to Dan] The whole argument is the lost production you would have.

MAURICE   It'll mean backing up the order only one day.

ANDREWS   [After another matter in Maurice's department has been discussed and there is apparently nothing further, Andrews turns to Dan and smiles.] It's been a pleasure, Dan.

[Dan then returned the smile weakly and got up to leave, somewhat nervously.]

As Whitelaw left the conference room after the meeting he was heard to comment:

Danny got clobbered as you could see. I used to stand up for him, but he just doesn't come up here prepared. He should have the plans worked out with his foreman before they come up.

When discussing his job, Whitelaw frequently commented on how he thought a decision or problem would affect someone else in the plant:

If all you had to do was manage the nuts and bolts of production scheduling and not worry about the customer or how people were going to react, this would be the easiest job in the whole plant. You could just sit down with a paper and pencil and lay it out the best way. But because the customer is so important and because you've got to look ahead to how people are going to react to a given kind of schedule, it makes the whole job tremendously complicated. It isn't easy!

Other Personnel and Functions

Hunter, the plant accountant, reported directly to the plant manager, although he was functionally responsible to the division controller. The major tasks for Hunter's department were the development and application of many thousands of individual product costs and the coordination of the annual sales and income budget, developed by the responsible operating and staff groups. Explaining another of his duties, Hunter noted:

We are the auditors who see that every other department is obeying rules and procedures. It is our responsibility to know all that is in the instruction manuals. There are twelve volumes of general instructions and lots of special manuals.

Joe Herman, the plant industrial engineer, explained the responsibilities of his department:

We're active in the fields of time study, budgetary control, job evaluation, and methods improvement. Our company is on a standard cost system—that is, all our product costs are based on engineered standards, accurately measuring all labor, direct and indirect, and material that is expended in the manufacture of each and every item we make in our plants. All the jobs in the St. Laurent plant, up to and including the foremen, have been measured and standards set. However, all our standards are forwarded to division, which checks them against standards in use at other plants. There are companywide benchmarks for most standards, since most of the machinery is the same in other Continental Can plants.

Herman noted that the budgeted savings from methods improvement was approximately $600,000 for the year, and he expected to exceed that by a substantial amount.

Harold Stone, the industrial relations manager, was proud that the St. Laurent plant had never experienced a strike and that formal written grievances were almost unheard of. Stone ran training programs and monitored safety, absenteeism, and turnover data. The St. Laurent plant had an outstanding record in these areas. Stone attributed this to the high wages and fringe benefits of the plant. He also maintained campaigns on housekeeping and posted slogans and comments, in both French and English, on job security and industrial competition. Also, he was responsible for the display of a five-foot chart on an easel near the main entrance that showed the manufacturing efficiency rating (actual production cost versus standard cost) of the previous month for each of the Continental Can Company plants and their standing within the division.

Regarding Continental Can's personnel policy, Stone stated:

We believe that it is important that the supervisor and the employee understand each other, that they know what the other person thinks about business, profit, the importance of satisfying the customer, and any other aspect of business. We also believe that rapport between the supervisor and the employee can be improved in the social contacts that exist or that can be organized. For this reason, we sponsor dances, bowling leagues, golf days, fishing derbies, picnics, baseball leagues, supervision parties, management weekends, and many unofficial get-togethers. Over many years we have been convinced that these activities really improve management-labor relations. They also provide a means for union and management to work closely together in organizing and planning these events. These opportunities help provide a mutual respect for the other fellow's point of view.

It was Stone's responsibility to maintain the confidential file in connection with Continental's performance appraisal program for salaried employees. Procedures for handling the program were spelled out in one of the corporate manuals. Two forms were completed annually. One called for a rating of the employee by his supervisor, first on his performance of each of his responsibilities outlined in the Position Analysis Manual and then on each of 12 general characteristics such as cooperation, initiative, job knowledge, and delegation. In another section, the supervisor and the appraised employee were jointly required to indicate what experience, training, or self-development would improve the performance or prepare for the advancement of the employee prior to the next appraisal. The appraisal was to be discussed between the supervisor and the employee; the latter

was required to sign the form, and space was given for any comments he or she might want to make. The second form was not shown to the employee. It called for a rating on overall performance, an indication of promotability, and a listing of potential replacements. It was used for manpower planning, and after comments by the supervisor of the appraiser, it was forwarded to the division office.

Managerial Practices

Managing with Budgets

Management at the St. Laurent plant coordinated their activities through a number of informal, as well as scheduled, meetings. Impromptu meetings of two or more members of management were frequent, facilitated by the close proximity of their offices. Among the formal meetings, the most important was the monthly discussion of performance against the budget. This meeting was attended by all of the management staff as well as production supervisors. Other regularly scheduled meetings included the production control meeting (twice weekly) and the plant cost reduction committee meetings.

In discussing the budget, Fox explained that the manufacturing plant was organized as a profit center. Plant income was determined by actual sales, not a transfer price. Therefore, income was adversely affected when sales failed to come up to the forecast on which the budget was based and when sales prices were reduced to meet competition. Fox also explained that sales managers also have their incentives based on making or exceeding the budget and that their forecasts had tended to be quite accurate. Overoptimism regarding one group of products had usually been offset by underestimation of sales of other products. However, because no adjustment was permitted in budgeted profit when sales income was below forecast, the fact that sales were running 3 percent below the level budgeted for 1963 was forcing the plant to reduce expenses substantially in order to equal or exceed the profit budgeted for the year.

When asked whether the budget was a straitjacket or if there were some accounts that left slack for reducing expenses in case sales fell below forecast, Fox replied:

We never put anything in the budget that is unknown or guessed at. We have to be able to back up every single figure in the budget. We have to budget our costs at standard, assuming that we can operate at standard. We know we won't all the time. There will be errors and failures, but we are never allowed to budget for them.

Hunter agreed with Fox, stating. "In this company there is very little opportunity to play footsy with the figures."

Fox conceded that there were some discretionary accounts like overtime and outside storage that involved arguments with the division. For example, "I might ask for $140,000 for overtime. The division manager will say $130,000, so we compromise at $135,000." As far as cost-reduction projects are concerned, Fox added that ". . . we budget for more than the expected savings. We might have $100,000 in specific projects and budget for $150,000."

Fox went on to note that equipment repairs and overhauls could be delayed to reduce expenses. But even the overhaul schedule was included as part of the budget, and any changes had to be approved at the division level.

Robert Andrews complained that the budget system didn't leave much room for imagination. He felt that overly optimistic sales estimates were caused by the sales-people being fearful of sending a pessimistic estimate up to the division. These estimates, according to Andrews, were a major source of manufacturing inefficiency.

Andrews was asked whether he was concerned about increasing production volume, and he replied:

> We have standards. So long as we are meeting the standards, we are meeting our costs and we do not worry about increasing production. We don't tell the foreman that he needs to get more goods out the door. We tell him to get rid of the red in his budget. I'm content with a 100 percent performance. I'd like 105 percent, but if we want more production it is up to industrial engineering to develop methods changes.

Andrews talked about the necessary skills for a foreman:

> The foreman should be good at communications and the use of available control procedures. The foreman is expected to communicate effectively with all plant personnel, including staff heads. Our control procedures are easy to apply. In each department there is an engineered standard for each operation covering labor, materials, and spoilage. Without waiting for a formal statement from accounting, a foreman can analyze his performance in any area and take corrective action if necessary. Then he receives reports from accounting to assist him in maintaining tight cost control. One is a daily report that records labor and spoilage performance against standard. The monthly report provides a more detailed breakdown of labor costs, materials and supplies used, and spoilage. It also establishes the efficiency figure for the month. This report is discussed at a monthly meeting of all my supervisors. Generally, the plant industrial engineer and a member of the accounting staff are present. Each foreman explains his variances from standard and submits a forecast for his next month's performance.

The Bonus Plan

Andrew Fox indicated that the budget was also used in rewarding employees of Continental Can. The incentive for managers was based on performance of the plant compared to budget. According to Fox:

> The bonus is paid on the year's results. It is paid as a percentage of salary to all who are eligible—the ones on the organization chart (see Exhibit 1). There are three parts to it—one part is based on plant income, one on standards improvement or cost cutting, and the third on operating performance. We can make up to 20 percent by beating our plant income target and 25 percent on cost reduction and operating efficiency together. But we have to make 90 percent of our budgeted income figure to participate in any bonus at all. I think we have the 25 percent on efficiency and cost reduction pretty well sewn up this year If we go over our budgeted income, we can get almost 35 percent bonus.

In years past, St. Laurent managers had made about 10 percent of their salaries from the bonus. The improved performance was the result of a change in the design of the bonus plan. Hunter explained the effect of the change:

> At one time the bonus plan was based on departmental results and efficiency. Under this there was a tendency for the departments to work at cross-purposes, to compete rather than cooperate with each other. For the last seven or eight years, the emphasis has been on the plant, not the department. The latest plan is geared not only to the attainment of budgeted cost goals, but also to the attainment of budgeted income. This is consistent with the attention we are placing on sales. I think the company was disturbed by what they sensed was a belief that those at the plant level can't do much about sales. Now we are trying to get the idea across that if we make better cans and give better service, we will sell more.

Foremen and Production Workers

General Foremen

Guillaume Jacques and Henri LaSalle were the general foremen on two of the three shifts. They described their jobs as working closely with both the assistant plant manager and the production control manager, but more with the latter. Jacques and LaSalle were asked how they balanced employee satisfaction with the requirements of the budget. Jacques commented:

> Management not only asks me to meet the budget, but to do better. So you've got to make the worker understand the importance of keeping under budget. I get them in the office and explain that if we don't meet the budget, we'll have to cut down somewhere else. It is mathematical. I explain all this to them; management has given me a budget to meet, I need them for this, they need me to

give them work. We work like a team. I try to understand them. All supervisors work under tension. Myself, I ask the men to go out to have a beer with me, to go to a party. It relaxes them from our preoccupations. Right now, for example, there is this party with the foremen coming up. At these gatherings it is strictly against the rules to talk about work. These things are necessary.

LaSalle explained that while foremen have a copy of the budget for their department, the workers see only a machine operating standard. The standard was set so that if he works the machine at full capacity, he achieves 110 percent of standard. LaSalle told of his way of handling workers:

Well, there is usually some needling when a man is down below standard. He's told, "Why don't you get to be part of the crew?" It doesn't hurt anything . . . you only get a good day's work out of people if they are happy. We strive to keep our people happy so they'll produce the standard and make the budget. We try to familiarize them with what is expected of them. We have targets set for us. The budget is reasonable, but it is not simple to attain. By explaining our problems to the workers, we find it easier to meet the budget.

Foremen

Most of the foremen were aware of, and accepted, the necessity of keying their activities to the work standards and budgets. One young, and purportedly ambitious, foreman commented about this job:

What I like about this department is that I am in charge. I can do anything I like as long as I meet the budget. I can have that machine moved—send it over there—as long as I have a good reason to justify it. The department, that's me. I do all the planning and I'm responsible for results. I'm perfectly free in the use of my time [gives examples of his different arrival times during the past week and the fact that he came in twice on Saturday and once on Sunday for short periods].

While other foremen expressed dislike for some of the pressures inherent in their jobs, there was general satisfaction. One notable exception was a foreman with many years' service, who said:

We have a meeting once a month upstairs. They talk to us about budgets, quality, etc. That's all on the surface; that's b—s—. It looks good. It has to look good but it is all bull. For example, the other day a foreman had a meeting with the workers to talk about quality. After that an employee brought to his attention a defect in some products. He answered, "Send it out anyway," and they had just finished talking to us about quality.

Foremen tended to view the production worker as irresponsible and uninterested, insofar as his job is concerned, only in his paycheck and quitting time.

One foreman said, "We do all the work; they do nothing." Even an officer of the union, speaking about the workers, commented:

They don't give a damn about the standards. They work nonchalantly, and they are very happy when their work slows up. If the foreman is obliged to stop the line for two minutes, everyone goes to the toilet. There are some workers who do their work conscientiously, but this is not the case with the majority.

Workers

Several of the production workers expressed feelings of pressure, although others declared that they were accustomed to their work and that it did not bother them. One said:

Everyone is obsessed with meeting the standards—the machine adjuster, the foreman, the assistant foreman. They all get on my nerves.

One old-timer clearly differentiated the company, which he considered benevolent, from his foreman:

I can understand that these men are under tension just as we are. They have meetings every week. I don't know what they talk about up there. The foremen have their standards to live up to. They're nervous. They don't even have a union like us. So if things go bad, well, that's all. They make us nervous with all this. But there's a way with people. We don't say to a man, "Do this, do that." If we said, "Would you do this?" it is not the same thing. You know a guy like myself who has been here for 35 years knows a few tricks. If I am mad at the foreman, I could do a few little things to the machine to prevent it from keeping up with standards and no one would know.

While some workers stated they would work for less money if some of the tension were relieved, the majority were quite content with their jobs.[3]

Enforcing The Budget

By November 1963, sales for the year had fallen below expectations and the management bonus was in jeopardy as a result.

One day in early November there was an unusual amount of activity in the accounting section. Fox came into the area frequently, and he and Hunter from time to time would huddle with one of the accountants over some figures. Hunter explained that the extra activity was in response to a report on the October results that had been issued about a week before.

Fox decided to schedule a joint meeting of the management staff and the line organization to go over

---

[3]In a Harvard Business School research study of 12 plants in the United States and Canada, the St. Laurent plant workers ranked highest of the 12 plants in job satisfaction.

the October results. This was a departure from the usual practice of having the groups in separate meetings. Prior to the meeting Fox outlined what he hoped to accomplish in the meeting:

Those figures we got last week showed that some of the accounts did what they were expected to do, some did more, and some did a good deal less. The thing we have to do now is to kick those accounts in the pants that are not making the savings they planned to make. What we've been doing is raising the expected savings as the time gets shorter. It may be easy to save 10 percent on your budget when you've got six months; but with only six weeks, it is an entirely different matter. The thing to do now is to get everybody together and excited about the possibility of doing it. We know how it can be done. Those decisions have already been made. It's not unattainable even though I realize we are asking an awful lot from these men. You see, we are in a position now where just a few thousand dollars one way or the other can make as much as 10 percent difference in the amount of bonus the men get. There is some real money on the line. It can come either from a sales increase or an expense decrease, but the big chunk has to come out of an expense decrease.

Fox did not feel there would be a conflict in the meeting about who is right and who is wrong:

We never fight about the budget. It is simply a tool. All we want to know is what is going on. There are never any disagreements about the budget itself. Our purpose this afternoon is to pinpoint those areas where savings can be made, where there is a little bit of slack, and then get to work and pick up the slack.

Fox talked about his style of handling cost and people problems:

When budgeted sales expenses get out of line, management automatically takes in other accounts to make up the losses. We'll give the department that has been losing money a certain period of time to make it up. Also, anytime anybody has a gain, I tell them I expect them to maintain that gain.

The manager must make the final decisions and has to consider the overall relationships. But there are some things I can't delegate—relations with sales, for example. The manager and not production control, must make the final decisions.

Larry Adams, the sales manager in our district, feels that the budget gets in the way of the customer's needs. He thinks the budget dominates the thinking and actions around here. Maybe he's right. But I have to deal with the people and problems here.

The manager must be close to his people. I take a daily tour of the plant and talk to the people by name. My practice as a manager is to follow a head-on approach. I don't write many memos. When I have something to say I go tell the person or persons right away. That's why I'm holding a meeting this afternoon.

Bob Andrews commented on the methods used to pick up the projected savings:

When you have lost money in one sector you have to look around for something else that you can "milk" to make up the difference. But we don't ask for volunteers; we do the "milking." Those guys just have to do what we say. How much we can save pretty much depends on how hard the man in the corner office wants to push on the thing. I mean, if we really wanted to save money, we probably could do it, but it would take a tremendous effort on everybody's part and Fox would really have to crack the whip.

Because of Fox's comments on relationships with sales, Larry Adams, the district sales manager, was asked about his feelings on working with the production people at the St. Laurent plant:

The budget comes to dominate people's thinking and influence all their actions. I'm afraid even my salesmen have swallowed the production line whole. They can understand the budget so well they can't understand their customers. And the St. Laurent plant boys are getting more and more local in their thinking with this budget. They're not thinking about what the customer needs today or may need tomorrow; they just think about their goddamned budget.

If the customer will not take account of your shortcomings, and if you can't take account of the customer's shortcomings, the two of you will eventually end up at each other's throats. That's what this budget system has built into it. Suppose, for example, you want to give a customer a break. Say he has originally planned for a two-week delivery date, but he phones you and says he really has problems and if you possibly could he would like about four days knocked off that delivery date. So I go trotting over to the plant, and I say, "Can we get it four days sooner?" Those guys go out of their minds, and they start hollering about the budget and how everything is planned just right and how I'm stirring them up. They get so steamed up I can't go running to them all the time, but only when I really need something in the worst way. You can't let those plant guys see your strategy, you know. It is taking an awful lot out of a guy's life around here when he has to do everything by the numbers.

Special Budget Meeting

The meeting was held in the conference room at 4:00 P.M. Fox and Hunter sat at the far end of the table, facing the door, with an easel bearing a flip chart near them. The chart listed the projected savings in budgeted expenses for November and December, account by account. The group of about 30 arranged themselves at the table so that, with only a couple of exceptions, the management staff personnel and general foremen sat closest to Fox and Hunter and the foremen and assistant foremen sat toward the foot of the table.

Fox opened the meeting and declared that performance against the budget for October would first be reviewed, followed by discussion of the November and December projections. He stated rather emphatically that he was "disappointed" in the October performance. Although money had been saved, it represented good performance in some areas but rather poor performance in others. Fox declared that the gains made in the areas where performance had been good must be maintained and the weak areas brought up.

He then turned the meeting over to Hunter, who reviewed the October results, reading from the report, which everyone had in front of him. Where performance was not good, he called on the individual responsible for that area to explain. The typical explanation was that the original budgeted figure was unrealistic and that the actual amount expended was as low as it could possibly be under the circumstances. Fox frequently broke into the explanation with a comment like, "Well, that is not good enough" or, "Can you possibly do better for the rest of the year?" or, "I hope we have that straightened out now." When he sat down, the person giving the explanation was invariably thanked by Hunter.

Next, Hunter, followed by Whitelaw, commented on the sales outlook for the remainder of the year. They indicated that for two months as a whole sales were expected to be about on budget. After asking for questions and getting one from a foreman, Fox said:

Well now, are there any more questions? Ask them now if you have them, Everybody sees where we stand on the bonus, I assume. Right?

Fox then referred to the chart on plant expense savings and began to discuss it, saying:

The problem now is time. We keep compressing the time and raising the gain [the projected savings for the year had been raised $32,000 above what had been projected in October]. You can only do that so long. Time is running out, fellows. We've got to get on the stick.

Several times Fox demanded better upward communication on problems as they came up. Referring to a specific example, he said:

This sort of thing is absolutely inexcusable. We've got to know ahead of time when these mix-ups are going to occur so that we can allow for and correct them.

As Hunter was covering manufacturing efficiency projections for November, he addressed Andrews:

Now we have come to you, Bob. I see you're getting a little bit more optimistic on what you think you can do.

Andrews replied:

Yes, the boss keeps telling me I'm just an old pessimist and I don't have any faith in my people. I'm still a pessimist, but we are doing tremendously. I think it's terrific, fellows [pointing to a line graph]. I don't know whether we can get off the top of this chart or not, but at the rate this actual performance line is climbing, we might make it. All I can say is, keep up the good work. . . . I guess I'm an optimistic pessimist.

During the discussion of projected savings for December in the equipment maintenance account, Hunter commented:

Where in the world are you fellows going to save $8000 more than you originally said you would save?

Jones responded:

I'd just like to say at this point to the group that it would be a big help if you guys would take it easy on your machines. That's where we are going to save an extra $8,000–simply by only coming down to fix the stuff that won't run. You're really going to have to make it go as best you can. That's the only way we can possibly save the kind of money we have to save. You have been going along pretty well, but all I've got to say is I hope you can keep it up and not push those machines too hard.

Although Jones spoke with sincerity, a number of foremen sitting near the door exchanged sly smiles and pokes in the ribs.

Fox concluded the meeting at about 5:30, still chewing on his cigar:

There are just a couple of things I want to say before we break up. First, we've got to stop making stupid errors in shipping. Joe [foreman of shipping], you've absolutely got to get after those people to straighten them out. Second, I think it should be clear, fellows, that we can't break any more promises. Sales is our bread and butter. If we don't get those orders out in time, we'll have no one but ourselves to blame for missing our budget. So I just hope it is clear that production control is running the show for the rest of the year. Third, the big push is on now! We sit around here expecting these problems to solve themselves, but they don't! It ought to be clear to all of you that no problem gets solved until it's spotted. Damn it, I just don't want any more dewy-eyed estimates about performance for the rest of the year. If something is going sour, we want to hear about it. And there's no reason for not hearing about it! [Pounds the table, then voice falls and a smile begins to form.] It can mean a nice penny in your pocket if you can keep up the good work. That's all I've got to say. Thank you very much.

The room cleared immediately, but Whitelaw lingered on. He reflected aloud on the just-ended meeting:

I'm afraid that little bit of advice there at the end won't make a great deal of difference in the way things work out. You have to play off sales against production. It's built into the job. When I attend a meeting like that one and I see all those production people with their assistants and see the other staff managers with their assistants, and I hear fellows refer to corporate policy that dictates and supports their action at the plant level, I suddenly realize that I'm all alone up there. I can't sit down and fire off a letter to my boss at the division level like the rest of those guys can do. I haven't got any authority at all. It is all based strictly on my own guts and strength. Now Bob is a wonderful guy—I like him and I have a lot of respect for him—but it just so happens that 80 percent of the time he and I disagree. He knows it and I know it; I mean it's nothing we run away from; we just find ourselves on opposite sides of the question, and I'm dependent upon his tact and good judgment to keep us from starting a war.

Boy, it can get you down—it really can after a while, and I've been at it for—God—20 years. But in production control you've got to accept it—you're an outcast. They tell you you're cold, that you're inhuman, that you're a bastard, that you don't care about anything except your schedule. And what are you going to say? You're just going to have to swallow it because basically you haven't got the authority to back up the things you know need to be done. Four nights out of five I am like

this at the end of the day—just completely drained—and it comes from having to fight my way through to try to get the plant running as smoothly as I can.

And Andrews up there in that meeting. He stands up with his chart and he compliments everybody about how well they are doing on efficiency. You know, he says, "Keep up the good work," and all that sort of stuff. I just sat there—shaking my head. I was so dazed you know; I mean I just keep saying to myself, "What's he doing? What's he saying? What's so great about this?" You know if I could have, I'd have stood up and said, "Somebody go down to my files in production control and pick out any five customer orders at random—and letters—and bring them back up here and read them—at random, pick any five." You know what they would show? Broken promises and missed delivery dates and slightly off-standard items we've been pushing out the door here. I mean, what is an efficient operation? Why the stress on operating efficiency? That's why I just couldn't figure out why in the world Andrews was getting as much mileage out of his efficiency performance as he was. Look at all the things we sacrifice to get that efficiency. But what could I do?

In early 1964, the report being sent by Fox to the division would show that profits for 1963 had exceeded the amount budgeted and that operating efficiency and cost reduction had both exceeded the budget by a comfortable margin, despite the fact that sales had fallen about 3 percent below budget. This enabled the mangers and supervisors at the St. Laurent plant to attain the salary bonuses for which they had been striving.

C A S E   4
TRW Systems Group (A and B Condensed)
Paul H. Thompson
revised by Joseph Seher and John P. Kotter

TRW Inc. was formed in 1957 by the merger of Thompson Products, Inc., and the Ramo-Wooldridge Corporation. Thompson Products, a Cleveland-based manufacturer of auto and aircraft parts, had provided $500,000 to help Simon Ramo and Dean Wooldridge get started in 1953.

Copyright © 1976 by the President and Fellows of Harvard College. Harvard Business School case 476-117. This case was prepared by Joseph A. Seher under the direction of John P. Kotter. It is a condensation of the A and B cases originally written by Paul H. Thompson under the direction of Gene W. Dalton. This case was prepared as the basis for class discussion rather than to illustrate either effective or ineffective handling of an administrative situation. Reprinted by permission of the Harvard Business School.

History of TRW Inc. and TRW Systems Group*

Ramo-Wooldridge Corporation grew quickly by linking itself with the accelerating ICBM program sponsored by the Air Force. After winning the contract for the technical supervision of the ICBM program, R-W gradually expanded its capabilities to include advance

---

*In its brief history, this part of TRW, Inc. had had several names: The Guided Missiles Division of Ramo-Wooldridge, Ramo-Wooldridge Corporation, Space Technology Laboratories (S.T.L.), and most recently, TRW Systems Group. Frequently used abbreviations of TRW Systems Group are TRW Systems and Systems Group.

planning for future ballistic weapons systems and space technology and by providing technical advice to the Air Force.

R-W was considered by some industry specialists to be a quasi-government agency. In fact, some of its competitors in the aerospace industry resented R-W's opportunities for auditing and examining their operations.

Because of this close relationship with the Air Force, RW was prohibited from bidding on hardware contracts. This prevented the company from competing for work on mainframes or on assemblies. In 1959, after the merger with Thompson, TRW decided that the hardware ban was too great a liability and moved to free the Systems Group from its limiting relationship with the Air Force.

The Air Force was reluctant to lose the valued services of the Systems Group. But it agreed to a solution that called for the creation by the Air Force of a non-profit organization, the Aerospace Corporation, to take over the advance planning and broad technical assistance formerly given by the Systems Group. TRW agreed to recruit, from its own personnel, a staff of top technicians to man Aerospace, and in 1960, about 20 percent of Systems' professional people went over to Aerospace.

The Systems Group had to undergo a difficult transition from serving a single customer to a competitive organization. The change involved worrying about marketing and manufacturing and dealing with different types of contracts. Previously, Systems had worked on a cost-plus-fixed-fee basis, but now worked on incentive contracts rewarding performance and specified delivery dates, while penalizing failures.

Systems thrived in the new competitive arena (see Exhibit 1), winning a number of important contracts. Nestled in the sunny southern California region at Redondo Beach, the Systems Group worked in a free and open atmosphere. According to an article in *Fortune*, Systems' competitive advantage was its professional personnel:

S.T.L. is headed by 38-year-old Rube Mettler, who holds the title of president of the subsidiary. A Ph.D. from Caltech, he served with Hughes Aircraft, and was a consultant at the Pentagon before coming to Ramo-

Wooldridge in 1955, where he made his mark directing the Thor program to completion in record time. Of his technical staff of 2,100, more than 35 percent hold advanced degrees, and despite their youth they average 11 years of experience per man; in other words, most of them have been in the space industry virtually since the space industry began. They are housed mostly in a group of four long, low buildings for research, engineering, and development in the campus-like Space Center at Redondo Beach. Some of them are occupied in the various labs for research in quantum physics, programming, and applied mathematics, intertial guidance and control, etc.; others simply sit in solitude in their offices and think, or mess around with formulas on the inevitable blackboard. But typically, the materialization of all this brainpower is accomplished in one medium-sized manufacturing building called FIT (Fabrication, Integration, and Testing), which has but 800 employees all told. FIT has a high bay area to accommodate its huge chamber for simulating space environment and other exotic testing equipment.[1]

The Aerospace Industry

Observers have described the industry in which Systems competed as a large job shop subject to frequent changes. T. C. Miller and L. P. Kane, experts on the aerospace industry, described it as follows:

Because of rapid changes in technology, in customer requirements, and in competitive practices, product lines in the aerospace industry tend to be transitory. The customers' needs are finite and discrete. . . . Although the aerospace industry as a whole has grown steadily during the last decade, the fluctuations of individual companies underscore the job-shop nature of the defense work. Aerospace industry planners must be constantly aware of the possibility of cancellation or prolongation of large programs.[2]

The rapid changes and temporary nature of the programs had several effects on companies within the industry. Sales and profits fluctuated with the number and size of contracts the company had; the level of activity in the company fluctuated, which meant hiring and later laying off large numbers of employees; and each plant went from full utilization of physical facilities to idle capacity.

The fluctuations resulted in a highly mobile work force that tended to follow the contracts, moving from a company that had finished a contract to one that was beginning a new contract. But the employees were

Exhibit 1 Comparative Profile of TRW Systems Group

	June 1960	February 1963
Customers	8	42
Contracts	16	108
Total personnel	3,860	6,000
Technical staff	1,400	2,100
Annual sales rate	$63 million	$108 million

[1]*Fortune*, February 1963, p. 95.
[2]T. C. Miller, Jr., and L. P. Kane, "Strategies for Survival in the Aerospace Industry," *Industrial Management Review*, Fall 1965, pp. 22–23.

highly trained and could find other jobs without difficulty. Miller and Kane pointed out:

> The industry's ratios of technical employment to total employment and of technical employment to dollar volume of sales are higher than those in any other industry. Moreover, 30 percent of all persons privately employed in research and development are in the aerospace industry.[3]

TRW Systems tried to minimize these fluctuations and their effects by limiting the size of a contract for which they might compete. They would rather have had ten $10 million contracts than one $100 million contract; also they had a policy of leasing a certain portion of their facilities in order to maintain flexibility in their physical plant.

In pursuing a conscious policy of growth, they competed for many contracts. By winning a reasonable number of these contracts, the company grew; and when one contract ran out, there were others always starting up. As a result, between 1953 and 1963 Systems did not have a single major layoff.

Another characteristic of the industry was the complexity of the products being produced. There were thousands of parts in a space rocket and they had to interrelate in numerous subtle ways. If one part didn't come up to specifications, it might harm hundreds of others. Since the parts and systems were so interdependent, the people in the various groups, divisions, and companies who made and assembled the parts were also highly interdependent. These interdependencies created some organizational problems for the companies in the industry, which forced them to develop a new type of organization called the matrix organization.

TRW Systems' Organization

Exhibit 2 shows an organization chart for TRW in 1963 with the various functional divisions and the offices for program management (the word *project* is often used interchangeably for *program*). These different systems interrelated in what was called a matrix organization. The relationship between program offices and the functional divisions was a complex one, but can best be explained in a simple fashion by noting that instead of setting up, for example, a systems engineering group for the Atlas missile and another separate systems group for the Titan missile program, all the systems engineers were assigned organizationally to the Systems Division. This Systems Division was one of five technical divisions, each staffed with MTS (Members Technical Staff) working in a particular functional area. The various program offices coordi-

nated the work of all the functional groups working on their particular programs and, in addition, handled all relationships with the contracting customer. It will be noted that the program offices were, formally, on the same organizational level as the functional divisions.

The engineers in these functional divisions were formally responsible to the director of their division, but they might also have a "dotted line" responsibility to a program office. For example, an electrical engineer would be responsible to his manager in the Electronics Division even though he might spend all of his time working for the Atlas program office. While working on the program he would report to the Atlas program director through one of his assistants.

Functional Organization

Each functional division served as a technology center and focused on the disciplines and skills appropriate to its technology. Generally, a number of operations managers reported to the division manager, each of whom was in charge of a group of laboratories dealing with similar technologies. The laboratory directors who reported to the operation managers were each responsible for a number of functional departments that were organized around technical specialties. The engineers in these laboratory departments were the people who performed the actual work on program office projects.

Program Office Organization

A program manager maintained overall management responsibility for pulling together the various phases of a particular customer project. His office was the central location for all project-wide activities such as the project schedule, cost and performance control, system planning, system engineering, system integration, and contract and major subcontract management. Assistant project managers were appointed for these activities as warranted by the size of the project.

The total project effort was divided into subprojects, each project being assigned to a specific functional organization according to the technical specialty involved. The manager of the functional organization appointed a subproject manager with the concurrence of the project manager. The subproject manager was assigned responsibility for the total subproject activity and was delegated management authority by the functional division management and by the assistant project manager to whom he reported operationally for the project. The subproject manager was a full-time member of the project organization, but he was not considered a member of the project office; he remained a member of his functional organization. He was accountable for performance in his functional specialty to the manager of his functional area, usually a laboratory manager. The functional manager was

---

[3] Ibid., p. 20.

Exhibit 2 Organization Chart, 1963

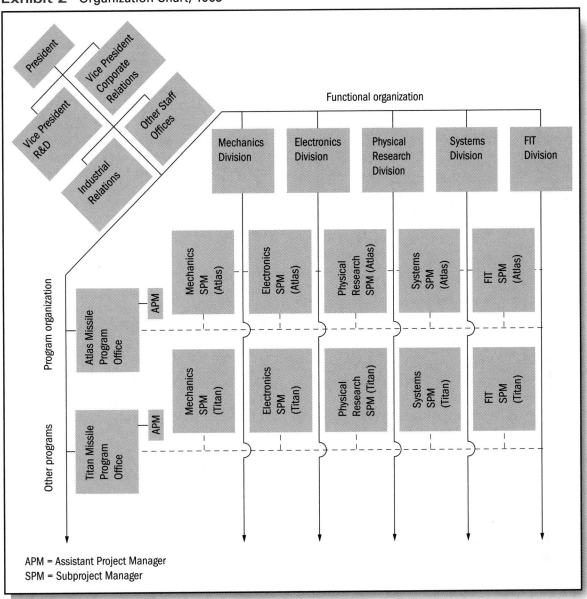

APM = Assistant Project Manager
SPM = Subproject Manager

responsible for the performance evaluation of the subproject manager. The subproject manager thus represented both the program office and his functional area and was responsible for coordinating the work of his subproject with the engineers within the functional area. Normally each functional area was involved in work on several projects simultaneously. One manager defined the subproject manager's responsibility this way:

> The subproject manager is a prime mover in this organization, and his job is a tough one. He is the person who brings the program office's requirements and the lab's resources together to produce a subsystem. He has to deal with the pressures and needs of both sides of the matrix and is responsible for bringing a subsystem together. He has to go to the functional department

managers to get engineers to work on his project, but about all he can say is, "Thanks for the work you've done on my subproject." But he does have program office money as a source of power, which the functional managers need to fund their operations. The technical managers are strong people. They are not "yes" men; they have their own ideas about how things ought to be done. You do not want them to be "yes" men either. Otherwise, you've lost the balance you need to make sure that technical performance is not sacrificed for cost and schedule expediencies, which are of great importance to the program office. The functional managers are also interested in long-range applications of the work they are doing on a particular project.

This often puts the subproject manager in a real bind; he gets caught between conflicting desires. It is especially difficult because it is hard for him not to identify with the program office because that's the focus of his interest. But he is paid by the lab and that is also where he must go to get his work done. If he is smart he will identify with his subsystem and not with either the program office or the lab. He must represent the best course for his subproject, which sometimes means fighting with the program office and the departments at different times during the life of the subproject. If he reacts too much to pressures from either side, it hurts his ability to be objective about his subproject, and people will immediately sense this.

The casewriter asked Jim Dunlap, Director of Industrial Relations, what happened when an engineer's top bosses disagreed on how he should spend his time. He replied:

The decisions of priority on where a man should spend his time are made by Rube Mettler because he is the only common boss. But, of course, you try to get them to resolve it at a lower level. You just have to learn to live with ambiguity. It's not a structured situation. It just can't be.

You have to understand the needs of Systems Group to understand why we need the matrix organization. There are some good reasons why we use a matrix. Because R&D-type programs are finite programs—you create them, they live, and then they die—they have to die or overhead is out of line. Also, there are several stages in any project. You don't necessarily need the same people on the project all the time. In fact, you waste the creative people if they work until the end finishing it up. The matrix is flexible. We can shift creative people around and bring in the people who are needed at various stages in the project. The creative people in the functions are professionals and are leaders in their technical disciplines. So the functional relationship helps them to continue to improve their professional expertise. Also, there is a responsiveness to all kinds of crises that come up. You sometimes have 30 days to answer a proposal—so you can put together a team of guys from everywhere. We're used to temporary systems; that's the way we live.

Often an engineer will work on two or three projects at a time and he just emphasizes one more than others. He's part of two systems at the same time.

The key word in the matrix organization is interdependency. Matrix means multiple interdependencies. We're continually setting up temporary systems. For example, we set up a project manager for the Saturn project with twenty people under him. Then he would call on people in systems engineering to get things started on the project. Next he might call in people from the Electronics Division, and after they finish their work the project would go to FIT (Fabrication, Integration, and Testing) where it would be manufactured. So what's involved is a lot of people coming in and then leaving the project.

There is a large gap between authority and responsibility and we plan it that way. We give a man more responsibility than he has authority and the only way he can do this job is to collaborate with other people. The effect is that the system is flexible and adaptive, but it's hard to live with. An example of this is that the project manager has no authority over people working on the project from the functional areas. He can't decide on their pay, promotion, or even how much time they'll spend on his project as opposed to some other project. He has to work with the functional heads on these problems. We purposely set up this imbalance between authority and responsibility. We design a situation so that it's ambiguous. That way people have to collaborate and be flexible. You just can't rely on bureaucracy or power to solve your problems.

The casewriter talked to a number of people in various positions at TRW Systems Group, and their comments about the matrix could be summarized as follows:

It is difficult to work with because it's flexible and always changing, but it does work; and it's probably the only organization that could work here.

Nearly everyone the casewriter talked with indicated that Systems Group was a "good place to work" and that they enjoyed the freedom they had. However, one critic of the system, a member of the administrative staff, presented his complaints about the system as follows:

People think this is a country club. It's a college campus atmosphere. Top management thinks everyone is mature and so they let them work as if they were on a college campus. They don't have rules to make people come to work on time or things like that. Do you know that 60–70 percent of the assigned parking spaces are empty at 8:30 A.M.? Personnel did a study of that—people are late. It's a good place to work for people who want complete freedom. But people abuse it. They don't come to work on time; they just do what they want around here. Its very democratic here. Nobody is telling you what to do and making all the decisions, but it can border on anarchy.

The management philosophy is that everybody will work harmoniously and you don't need a leader. But I think there has to be leadership, some one person who's responsible.

The casewriter than asked the question, "Isn't the project engineer responsible?" and the reply was:

The project engineer is a figurehead—in many cases he doesn't lead. I know one project engineer who provides no leadership at all. Besides, the matrix is constantly agitating. It's changing all the time, so it's just a bucket of worms. You never know where you stand. It's like ants on a log in a river and each one thinks he's steering—when none of them are. It's true that the top-level managers can make this philosophy work on their level. But we can't on our level. Let me give you an example. Mettler says he wants everything microfilmed, but he doesn't tell others to let me do it. I have responsibility but no authority in the form of a piece of paper or statement that I can do it. I just can't walk into some guy's empire and say I'm here to microfilm all of your papers. It's like an amoeba, always changing so you never know where your limits are or what you can or can't do.

As a contrasting view, one of the laboratory heads felt that the lack of formal rules and procedures was one of the strengths of the organization. He commented:

This is not a company characterized by a lot of crisp orders and formal procedures. Quite honestly, we operate pretty loosely as far as procedures, etc., are concerned. In fact, I came from a university environment, but I believe there's more freedom and looseness of atmosphere around here than there was as a faculty member. I think if you have pretty average people, you can have a very strict line type of organization and make it work, and maybe that's why we insist on being different. You see, I think you can also have a working organization with no strict lines of authority if you have broader-gauged people in it. I like to think that the individuals in the company are extremely high caliber and I think there is some evidence to support that.

Another manager supported the matrix organization with the following comments:

The people around here are really committed to the job. They'll work 24 hours a day when it is necessary, and sometimes it's necessary. I was on a team working on a project proposal a few months ago and during the last week of the proposal there were people working here around the clock. We had the secretaries come in on different shifts and we just stayed here and worked. I think that Mettler makes this matrix organization work. It's a difficult job but people have faith that Mettler knows what he's doing so they work hard and it comes out all right.

Evolution of Career Development

In 1962, TRW Systems Group began a management development program called Career Development. Jim Dunlap, the Director of Industrial Relations, had responsibility for this program along with his other duties in Industrial Relations (see Exhibit 3).

Early History of Career Development (1957–1965)

"What are we doing about management development?" Simon Ramo was asked in 1957. Ramo replied: "We don't believe in management development. We hire bright, intelligent people and we don't plan to insult their intelligence by giving them courses in courage."

In 1961, as Systems was trying to expand its customer base and cope with its new competitive environment, Rube Mettler became President. Mettler asked a consulting firm for advice on how best to make the transition to a competitive firm. "Systems needs men with experience in business management," the consultants said. "You will have to hire experienced top-level administrators from outside the firm. There aren't any here." Mettler agreed with them about needing top-level administrators. "But we'll develop our own people," Mettler added. Mettler confided in others that he feared that a manager with experience in another organization would have to unlearn a lot of bad habits before he could be successful at TRW.

Mettler put Dunlap in charge of the development program at TRW. Mettler made it clear to Dunlap that he wanted a task-oriented, dynamic development program to fit the special needs of the Systems Group.

Dunlap felt he needed assistance to implement the kind of program Mettler wanted. "The one thing I did was to entice Shel Davis to come into Industrial Relations," commented Dunlap. "He impressed me as a restless, dynamic, creative sort of guy." Davis had worked in a line position in one of TRW's other divisions.

With the help of an outside consultant, Dunlap and Davis began to design a development program. Early in 1962, forty top managers were interviewed about what they felt was needed. One manager characterized the feelings of the entire group: "We need skills in management. Every time a new project starts around here, it takes half of the project schedule just bringing people on board. If we could have a quicker start-up, we'd finish these projects on time."

Dunlap, Davis, and the consultant went to work on a plan to fit these specific needs. Dunlap set up a two-day offsite meeting to discuss their plans and recommendations with some of the top managers. At the meeting, Dunlap and Davis talked about two, relatively new, applied behavioral science techniques (called team development and T-groups) as ways of meeting the needs of managers.[4] Dave Patterson was there and was impressed by this approach. Patterson had recently been appointed head of a new project and asked for their assistance: "I have a new team and I'm ready to hold a team-building meeting next week. Can you arrange it?"

Shel Davis, along with a consultant, held an offsite team development session for Patterson. After the

---

[4]Team development (or team building) refers to a development process designed to improve the performance and effectiveness of people who work together. Laboratory T-groups (training groups) is a form of experiential learning away from the normal environment. Using unstructured groups, participants attempt to increase their sensitivity to their own and others' behavior as well as factors that hinder group interaction and effectiveness.

Exhibit 3 Industrial Relations

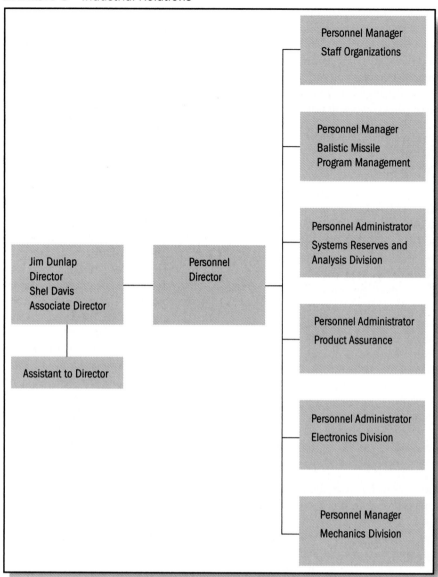

meeting, Patterson's project group improved its working relationships with manufacturing. The success of this experiment became well known throughout the company. Mettler asked Patterson what effect the meeting had had. "It saved us six weeks on the program. About a million bucks," Patterson replied. This impressed people.

Late in 1962 Davis and Dunlap prepared a "white paper" on possible approaches in career development and sent it to the top 70 people. Most of the managers responded that TRW should improve its skills in three areas: communications and interpersonal skills, business management skills, and technical skills. Davis described the conversation he and Dunlap had with Mettler.

Jim and I talked with Mettler about the kind of program we wanted in the company and what we did and didn't

want to do. As it turned out, we were in agreement with Mettler on almost every issue. For example, we decided not to make it a crash effort but to work at it and to take a lot of time making sure people understood what we wanted to do and that they supported it. We also decided to start at the top of the organization rather than at the bottom. During these discussions, they decided to call the training effort Career Development rather than organizational development or management development because Mettler didn't want to give the impression that they were going to concentrate on administrative training and neglect technical training.

Shortly after the white paper came out, Shel Davis and Jim Dunlap began to invite people to T-groups run by professionals outside of TRW. About 12 people took advantage of this opportunity between January and May of 1963. Ten of the 12 later reported that it was a "great experience." As a result, Mettler continued to support Dunlap and Davis, telling them, "Try things—if they work, continue them; if they don't, modify them, improve them, or drop them."

In April 1963, Davis and Dunlap decided to hold a team development meeting for the key people in Industrial Relations. The two men felt that once employees at the Systems Group started going to T-groups there would be a growing demand for "Career Development" activities, which the IR group would be asked to meet. The team development session, they felt, would help train the IR staff to meet this demand.

Dunlap and Davis next decided to run some T-groups themselves within TRW. Dunlap argued for limiting this effort to twenty people. Davis wanted forty, saying, "Hell, let's go with it. Let's do too much too fast and then it will really have an effect on the organization. Otherwise, it might not be noticed." Dunlap and Davis eventually decided to run four T-groups of 10 people each.

The chain of events following that activity was later described by Frank Jasinski, who became Director of Career Development in 1964:

After that things really started to move. There was a strong demand for T-group experience. But we didn't just want to send people through labs like we were turning out so many sausages. We wanted to free up the organization, to seed it with people who had been to T-groups. The T-groups were to be just the beginning of a continuing process.

This continuing process was in several stages and developed over the three-year period. Maybe I can describe it in terms of one manager and his work group. First, the manager volunteered to go to a T-group (we have kept the program on a voluntary basis). Before he went to the T-group, there was a pre-T-group session where the participants asked questions and got prepared for the T-group experience. Then they went through the T-group.

After the T-group, there were three or four sessions where the T-group participants got together to discuss the problems of applying the T-group values back home. After the manager had been through the T-group, some of the members of his work group could decide to go to a T-group. The next stage was when the manager and his group decided they wanted to undertake a team development process where they could work on improving intragroup relations, that is, how they could be more effective as a team.

Following a team development effort could be an interface meeting. This is the kind Alan East had. It seems Alan's department, Product Assurance, was having trouble getting along with a number of different departments in the organization. Alan felt if they were going to do their job well they had to be able to work

effectively with these other groups. So he got three or four of his people together with the key people from five or six other departments and they worked on the interdepartmental relationship. Still another type of meeting that is similar is the intergroup meeting. If two groups just can't get along and are having difficulties, they may decide to hold an off-site meeting and try to work on the problems between them.

We also started doing some technical training and business management training. As with all of our training, we try to make it organic: to meet the needs of the people and the organization. We tend to ask, "What is the problem?" Specific skills training may not be the answer. For example, a manager calls us and says he wants his secretary to have a review course in shorthand because she is slipping in her ability to use it. We might say, "Let's talk about it; maybe her shorthand is slipping because she doesn't use it enough and maybe she wants more challenging work. Why don't we get together with you and your secretary and discuss it?" We have held several meetings with bosses and their secretaries to improve boss-secretary relationships. When they understand each other better, the secretary is more willing to help her boss and she is also in a better position to do so.

Such a large increase in Career Development activities required a rapid build-up of uniquely trained personnel. This problem was met in part by the use of outside consultants. Systems Group was able to interest a number of the national leaders in T-group-type activities to act as consultants, to serve as T-group trainers, and to work with the divisions on team-building activities. By December 1964, they had built up a staff of nine outside consultants.[5]

For the program to work on a day-to-day basis, they felt a need to build a comparable internal staff. It was decided that the personnel manager in each division not only would be responsible for traditional personnel activities but would also be an internal consultant on Career Development activities. Lynn Stewart, one of the outside consultants working with the Systems Group, described how TRW obtained a group of trained personnel managers:

Systems Group needed to build some internal change agents, which meant expanding the Industrial Relations effort. It required the development of the skills of people in Industrial Relations, especially the personnel managers. They were able to retool some of the people in Industrial Relations by sending them to T-groups. Some were not able to make the transition. They were transferred or fired. All of this was done to provide a staff that could service the needs created when people returned from T-groups.

---

[5]This group consisted of senior professors at some of the largest business schools in the country and nationally recognized private consultants.

Exhibit 4

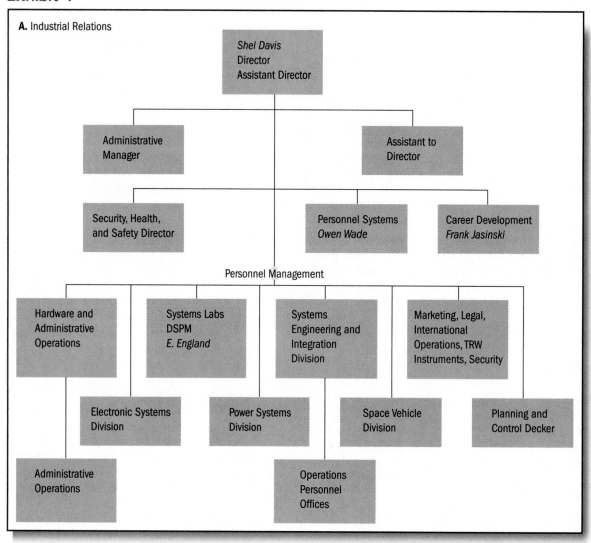

A. Industrial Relations

Shel Davis
Director
Assistant Director

Administrative Manager

Assistant to Director

Security, Health, and Safety Director

Personnel Systems
Owen Wade

Career Development
Frank Jasinski

Personnel Management

Hardware and Administrative Operations

Systems Labs DSPM
E. England

Systems Engineering and Integration Division

Marketing, Legal, International Operations, TRW Instruments, Security

Electronic Systems Division

Power Systems Division

Space Vehicle Division

Planning and Control Decker

Administrative Operations

Operations Personnel Offices

In December 1964, Jim Dunlap announced that he had been promoted to Vice President of Human Relations for TRW Inc. and would be moving to Cleveland. He also announced that Shel Davis would succeed him as Director of Industrial Relations. (Exhibit 4 presents an organization chart of Industrial Relations as of January 1965).

A number of the personnel managers became concerned about the future of Industrial Relations. They knew Shel Davis had openly referred to the day-to-day personnel activities as "personnel crap," and they wondered what changes he would make. One personnel manager expressed this feeling when he said, "There were some undertones of a threat in Jim's leaving which might break the balance of prudence and loose Shel upon the group, forcing us to work exclusively on Career Development and to neglect our day-to-day personnel responsibilities."

By summer, 1966, however, most of the people in Industrial Relations felt that Shel Davis had adjusted to his role as Director of Industrial Relations and was doing a good job of balancing the demands of Career Development and the day-to-day personnel activities.

Career Development in 1966

By 1966, Career Development activities had greatly increased since their initiation in 1963 (see Exhibit 5). While T-groups continued to be used, the major effort of the department was in facilitating team building and intergroup labs.

Team Development

There was a number of different types of team development activities. One was an effort to get a new team started faster. TRW repeatedly created temporary teams to accomplish recurring tasks. The tasks were quite similar, but the team membership changed considerably. One example was a team established to prepare a proposal to bid on a particular contract. More

Exhibit 4 (continued)

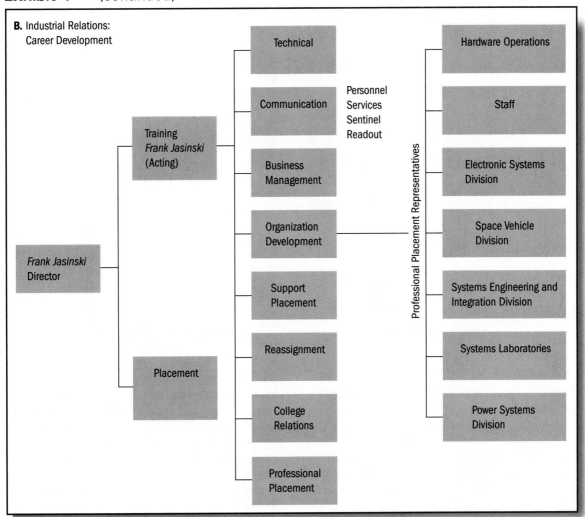

B. Industrial Relations: Career Development

than a dozen organizations would contribute to the final product: the written proposal. On major proposals, the representatives from the administrative and nontechnical areas remained fairly constant. The technical staff, however, varied with the task and usually was entirely new from proposal to proposal. This changing team membership required constant "bringing up to speed" of new members and repeated creation of a smoothly working unit. As the new team came together, a team development session, usually off-site, helped to get the team working together sooner and would save time in the long run. A session would last one or two days and the participants would try to identify potential problems in working together and then begin to develop solutions for such problems. Lynn Stewart, an outside consultant, described a team development session for a launch team:

TRW has a matrix organization so that any one man is a member of many systems simultaneously. He has interfaces with many different groups. In addition, he is continually moving from one team to another, so they need

team development to get the teams off to a fast start. On a launch team, for example, you have all kinds of people who come together for a short time. There are project directors, manufacturing people, the scientists who designed the experiments, and the men who launch the bird. You have to put all of those men together into a cohesive group in a short time. At launch time they can't be worrying about an organizational chart and how their respective roles change as preparation for the launch progresses. Their relationships do change over time, but they should work that through and discuss it beforehand, not when the bird is on the pad. The concept of the organization is that you have a lot of resources and you need to regroup them in different ways as customers and contracts change. You can speed up the regrouping process by holding team development sessions.

Another type of team development activity was one with an ongoing group. Typically, the manager would come to the personnel manager in his division and express an interest in team development for his

Exhibit 4 (continued)

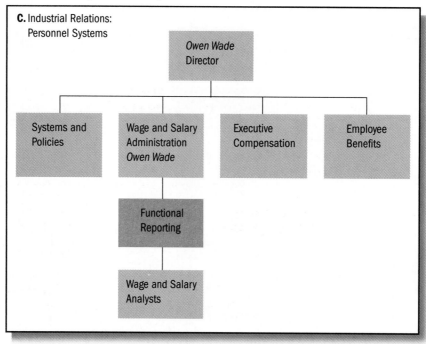

C. Industrial Relations:
   Personnel Systems

```
                    Owen Wade
                    Director
                        │
    ┌───────────┬───────┴──────┬──────────────┐
Systems and   Wage and Salary  Executive      Employee
Policies      Administration   Compensation   Benefits
              Owen Wade
                   │
              Functional
              Reporting
                   │
              Wage and Salary
              Analysts
```

group. If both agreed it would be beneficial, they would begin to plan such a session. First, an effort would be made to identify an agenda for the one- or two-day off-site meetings. This would be developed in one of two ways. The personnel manager or the consultant could interview, on an individual basis, all the people who would be attending the session to identify problem areas on which they needed to work. He would then summarize the problems identified in his interviews and distribute this summary to the participants a day or two before the session was held. Another method sometimes used to develop an agenda was to get all of the participants together on site for two or three hours several days before the off-site meeting. The participants would then be divided into subgroups and would identify problem areas to work on. At the extended off-site staff meeting, the intention was that the group would be task oriented, addressing itself to the question, "How can we improve the way our groups work together?" They would look at how the group's process got in the way of the group's performance. The manager of the group would conduct the meeting, but the personnel manager and an outside consultant would be there to help the group by observing and raising issues that the group should look at. There had been a number of similar team development sessions at TRW, and the people involved felt that they had been worthwhile in that they had improved the group's effectiveness.

Another type of team development activity that was carried out on a continuous basis was the critiquing of the many meetings held in the organization. The casewriter sat in on a staff meeting of the

Industrial Relations Department that was attended by the personnel managers and key people in the staff groups of Personnel Systems and Career Development. The purpose of the meeting was to plan the projects to be undertaken by Personnel Systems and Career Development throughout the remainder of the year. This included a discussion of what projects the personnel managers would like undertaken and a priority listing as to which were most important. Owen Wade, Director of Personnel Systems, led the discussion during the first hour and a half of the meeting while the group discussed projects for Personnel Systems. Frank Jasinski, Director of Career Development, led the discussion in the last hour of the meeting, in which projects for Career Development were discussed. Near the end of the meeting the following discussion took place:

SHEL DAVIS We only have ten minutes left so we had better spend some time on a critique of the meeting. Does anyone have any comments?

ED (Personnel Manager) We bit off more than we could chew here. We shouldn't have planned to do so much.

DON (Personnel Manager) I felt we just floated from 10:30 to 10:45. We got through with Frank and his subject and then nothing was done until the break.

BOB (Personnel Manager) Why didn't you make that observation at 10:30, Don, so

Exhibit 4 (continued)

D. Industrial Relations:
  Security, Health, and Safety

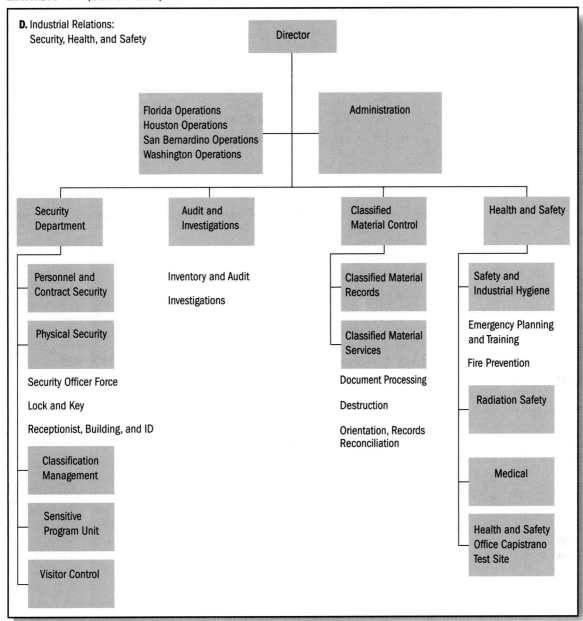

we could do something about it? Do you feel intimidated about making a process observation?

DON No. I felt like I was in the corner earlier. But not after making this observation. Besides, I did say earlier that we weren't doing anything and should move on, but I guess didn't say it loud enough for people to hear me.

ED Don, that is the first time you've made a process observation in six months. I wish you'd make more of them.

SHEL I think Owen's presentation was very good because he had estimated the

number of man-weeks of work required for each of the projects. Frank's presentation was less effective because his didn't have that.

JASINSKI I have a question on the manpower requirements. I spent seven or eight hours preparing for this meeting in setting priorities on all the projects we had listed and then it wasn't followed up in this meeting. [Two or three people echoed support for this statement.]

BOB I thought we were asked to do too much in preparing for this meeting. It

Exhibit 5   Career Development Activities, 1963–1965

Activities	1963		1964		1965	
	Courses	Attendees	Courses	Attendees	Courses	Attendees
Orientation	49	627	32	369	32	1,146
Colloquia	51	3,060	31	5,580	7	1,525
Invited lectures	2	800	4	1,600	—	—
Evening courses	12	261	17	438	16	651
Staff education	—	767	—	1,066	—	1,166
Technical courses	—	—	3	97	6	377
Internal leadership laboratories (T-groups)	1	45	4	104	4	151
External leadership laboratories (T-groups)	—	20	—	17	—	27
Team development meetings	—	—	4	76	44	671

was just too detailed and too much work, so I rebelled and refused to do it.

WADE   (Director of Personnel Systems) Well, from my point of view on the staff side of the fence, I feel pressured and as if I'm asked to do too much. The personnel managers have a very different set of rules. You don't plan as much as we have to and I think you should plan more.

One of the participants commented that a large number of the meetings at TRW were critiqued in a similar manner.

Intergroup and Interface Labs

As a result of the nature of the work at TRW and of the matrix organization, there was a great deal of interaction between the various groups in the organization. Sometimes this interaction was characterized by conflict; the Career Development staff began to work on ways to help groups deal with this conflict. One such effort, the first interface lab, developed out of an experience of Alan East, Director of Product Assurance, Mr. East commented on his experience:

I came to Product Assurance from a technical organization, so I knew very little of what Product Assurance was about. First, I tried to find out what our objectives were. I talked to our supervisors, and I found there was a lack of morale. They thought they were second-class citizens. They were cowed by the domineering engineers and they felt inferior. I decided one of the problems was that people outside Product Assurance didn't understand us and the importance of our job. I concluded that that was easy to solve: We'd educate them. So, we set out to educate the company. We decided to call a meeting, and we drew up an agenda. Then, as an afterthought, I went to

see Shel Davis to see if he had some ideas on how to train people. But he just turned it around. He got me to see that rather than educating them, maybe we could find out how they really saw us and why. Well, we held an off-site meeting and we identified a lot of problems between Product Assurance and the other departments. After the meeting, we came back and started to work to correct those problems.

After East's successful interface meeting, the idea caught hold and similar meetings were held by other groups. Harold Nelson, the Director of Finance, held an interface meeting between four members of his department and a number of departments that had frequent contact with Finance. The purpose of the meeting was to get feedback on how Finance was seen by others in the organization. Commenting on the effectiveness of the meeting, Nelson added, "They were impressed that we were able to have a meeting, listen to their gripes about us, and not be defensive. The impact of such meetings on individuals is tremendous. It causes people to change so these meetings are very productive."

Del Thomas, a participant in the interface meeting with Finance, represented another department. Thomas observed that, prior to the meeting, his group felt Finance was too slow in evaluating requests and that Nelson and his subordinates ". . . were too meticulous, too much like accountants." Thomas felt the meeting improved the performance of Finance:

I think Harold [Nelson] got what he was looking for, but he may have been surprised there were so many negative comments. I think there are indications that the meeting has improved things. First, Harold is easier to get ahold of now. Second, since the meeting, Harold brought in a new man to evaluate capital expenditures, and he's doing a top job. He's helpful, and he has speeded up the process. I think the atmosphere of the whole Finance group is changing. They are starting to think more of "we the company" and less of "us and them."

Evaluation of the Career Development Effort

Jim Dunlap, the Vice President for Human Relations, was asked to evaluate the effect of Career Development on TRW Systems. Dunlap pulled two studies from his desk drawer. The first, a report by a government official titled "Impulse for Openness," noted in its summary:

It is not our intention, nor certainly that of TRW Systems, to imply that either the company reorganization or the physical progress is solely the result of the Career Development program, but it does appear that the program had a substantial impact on the success of the company. The data shown completes the picture of changes in the company during the period under discussion. Employment at 6,000 in 1962 and over 11,000 in March 1966 will most likely double by the end of this year. Sales more than tripled between 1962 and 1965. Professional turnover decreased from 17.1 percent in 1962 to 6.9 percent in March 1966. The average for the aerospace industry in this area of California is approximately 20 percent.

Also, Dunlap revealed the results of a study by a professional organization to which many of Systems. Group employees belong. It took a survey of all of its members, asking them to rank 54 firms in the aerospace industry on six different factors. The respondents ranked TRW Systems first in "desirability as an employer," seventh for "contribution to aerospace," and second in "salary."

Dunlap also added his personal comments on the efforts of the Career Development program:

It's very hard to make an evaluation of the program and say it has saved us "X" million dollars. But there are several indications that it has been effective. Turnover is down significantly and I've heard a lot of people say, "I stayed at TRW because of the Career Development activities." Some people make more definite claims for the program. Dave Patterson says our Team Development Process saved us $500,000. Rube Mettler is convinced the program has improved our skills so that we've won some contracts we wouldn't have gotten otherwise. I believe it has improved our team performance. All of our proposal teams spend two days of team building before they start on the proposal. Every program starts with an off-site team development lab. They help build a team esprit de corps, and it creates an openness so they are better able to solve problems.

A number of employees were willing to discuss their attitudes toward the Career Development program.

Denis Brown, a member of the administrative staff, and a participant in the activities of Career Development, felt the program was valuable. Denis noted:

They took the OGO launch crew off-site and improved their effectiveness. Well, a launch is very tense, and if one guy is hostile toward another, it may mean a failure that costs $20 million. I don't know how much they spent on Career Development, but say it's a quarter of a million dollars. If one man improves his relationship with another and it saves a launch and $20 million, you've made it back many times over. The company feels it is a good thing, and it has worked well, so they'll continue it.

Jim Whitman, a subproject manager, had high praise for Career Development. Whitman credited the program for making groups more effective in communicating and working with one another. Recounting his own experiences, Whitman added that the program led to better collaboration and working conditions between the design engineer and the fabrication engineer.

But other employees were less enthusiastic. John Ward, a member of a program office, discussed his participation in Career Development activities. Ward felt that some of the off-site sessions were "rather grueling affairs, particularly when you are the center of attention." But Ward added that the session he attended was valuable:

In my opinion, the reason it was worthwhile is that under the pressure of work people cannot—I use the word cannot when I should say will not—take the time to sit down and discuss some very basic issues to get the air cleared. Even in a small group people tend to wear blinders. You think about your own problems because you have so many of them, so you tend to build up a fence to keep some of the other fellow's problems from getting through. He talks about them but you don't hear them; you don't get the significance of what he's trying to tell you. But if you go away with instructions that people are not to bother you unless it is really important, you create an environment where there is time to work out some of these things.

One member of the administrative staff, Dan Jackson, had very different views on Career Development. Jackson noted:

Idealistically, it's a good thing. If in the real world people lived that way, were open and sincere and could tell each other their feelings without getting hurt, it would be excellent. But people just aren't that way in the real world. The people who are enthusiastic about this—Mettler, Hesse, Davis, etc.—are at a level in the company where they can practice this. They're just dealing with other vice presidents and top-level people. But down on my level it won't work. We've got to produce things down here and people just aren't responsible and we can't just be nice to people all the time. We have to get some work done.

I think that the trainers at the lab live that way and that's all right, but they tend to be frustrated headshrinkers. They want to be psychiatrists, but they don't have the training—so they do sensitivity training. Its kind of like running a therapy group. I think the techniques they use are pretty good, like having one group inside talking and one group on the outside observing, but the people running it aren't well enough trained. They may be the best that are available, but they are not good enough. Frankly, I think these trainers are really just trying to find out their own problems, but they do it by getting mixed up in other people's problems.

Jackson continued, observing that participation in these activities was not completely voluntary:

Oh, it's voluntary, but you are kind of told you had better go. You aren't fired if you don't, but there's pressure put on you to go. One of our Ph.D.'s walked out after two days at a T-group. I don't think it has hurt his career but people know he took a walk. He just felt it was a sin, morally wrong, what was going on up there.

While Jackson seemed to express the most negative attitudes toward Career Development, there was a widely circulated story about a man who had suffered a nervous breakdown after attending a T-group. Jim Dunlap was asked to comment on the incident:

Yes, one group had a traumatic experience, or as they say, "cracked up." Very early in the program we decided that the people in personnel should go to a T-group so they'd understand what we were going to do. I asked this fellow if he'd like to go. He took it as an order and he went. But I was only asking him to go. If I'd known more about him, I wouldn't have asked him if he wanted to go. But I just saw him at work and he seemed to be getting along all right, although I knew that he didn't enjoy his job. He wanted to get into education. But I didn't know he was having troubles at home and that things weren't going very well for him in general. He was just kind of holding himself together as best he could. He went to the T-group and it caused him to start thinking about his situation and he fell apart; he had a nervous breakdown. After the T-group was over he went home, but he didn't go to work. He stayed home for a week or two. Finally, he decided he needed help and began to see a psychiatrist. Apparently that was just what he needed because he then decided to get that job in education, which he liked very much. He seems to have solved his problems, so everything has turned out for the best. But it scared the hell out of us at the time.

CASE 5
Texana Petroleum Corporation
Jay W. Lorsch, Paul R. Lawrence, and James A. Garrison

During the summer of 1966, George Prentice, the newly designated Executive Vice President for domestic operations of the Texana Petroleum Corporation, was devoting much of his time to thinking about improving the combined performance of the five product divisions reporting to him (see Exhibit 1). His principal concern was that corporate profits were not reflecting the full potential contribution that could result from the close technological interdependence of the raw materials utilized and produced by these divisions. The principal difficulty, as Prentice saw it, was that the division general managers reporting to him were not working well together.

As far as I can see, the issue is, Where do we make the money for the corporation? Not, How do we beat the other guy? Nobody is communicating with anybody else at the general manager level. In fact, they are telling a bunch of secrets around here.

Recent Corporate History

The Texana Petroleum Corporation was one of the early major producers and marketers of petroleum products in southwestern United States. Until the early 1950s, Texana had been almost exclusively in the business of processing and refining crude oil and selling petroleum products through a chain of company-operated service stations in southwestern United States and in Central and South America. By 1950, company sales had risen to approximately $500 million, with accompanying growth in profits. About 1950, however, Texana faced increasingly stiff

Exhibit 1 Texana Petroleum Company—Partial Organization Chart, 1966

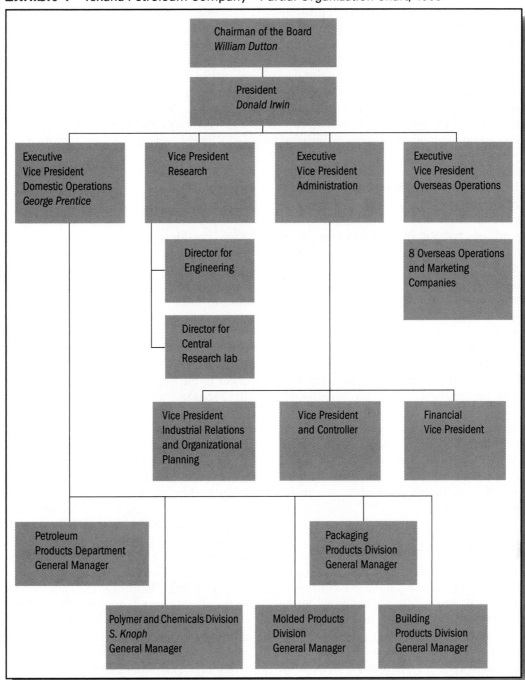

competition at the retail service station level from several larger national petroleum companies. As a result, sales volume declined sharply during the early 1950s, and by 1955 sales had fallen to only $300 million and the company was operating at just above the break-even point.

At this time, because of his age, Roger Holmes, who had been a dominant force in the company since its founding, retired as President and Chief Executive Officer. He was replaced by Donald Irwin, 49, who had been a senior executive with a major chemical com-

pany. William Dutton, 55, was appointed Chairman of the Board to replace the retiring Board Chairman. Dutton had spent his entire career with Texana. Prior to his appointment as Chairman, he had been Senior Vice President for Petroleum Products, reporting to Holmes.

Irwin and Dutton, along with other senior executives, moved quickly to solve the problems facing Texana. They gradually divested the company's retail outlets and abandoned the domestic consumer petroleum markets. Through both internal development and acquisition they expanded and rapidly increased the company's involvement in the business of processing petroleum for chemical and plastics products. In moving in this direction, they were rapidly expanding on initial moves made by Texana in 1949, when the company built its first chemical processing plant and began marketing these products. To speed the company's growth in these areas, Irwin and Dutton selected aggressive general managers for each division and gave them a large degree of freedom in decision making. Top management's major requirement was that each division general manager create a growing division with a satisfactory return on investment capital. By 1966, top management had reshaped the company so that in both the domestic and foreign markets it was an integrated producer of chemicals and plastic materials. In foreign operations the company continued to operate service stations in Latin America and in Europe. This change in direction was successful, and by 1966 company sales had risen to $750 million, with a healthy rise in profit.

In spite of this success, management believed that there was a need for an increase in return on invested capital. The financial and trade press, which had been generous in its praise of the company's recovery, was still critical of the present return on investment, and top management shared this concern. Dutton, Irwin, and Prentice were in agreement that one important method of increasing profits was to take further advantage of the potential cost savings that could come from increased coordination between the domestic operating divisions, as they developed new products, processes, and markets.

Domestic Organization, 1966

The product divisions' reports to Mr. Prentice represented a continuum of producing and marketing activities from production and refining of crude oil to the marketing of several types of plastics products to industrial consumers. Each division was headed by a general manager. While there was some variation in the internal organizational structure of the several divisions, they were generally set up along functional lines (manufacturing, sales, research and development). Each division also had its own controller and engineering activities, although these were supported and augmented by the corporate staff. While divisions had their own research effort, there was also a Central Research Laboratory at the corporate level, which carried on longer range research of a more fundamental nature that was outside the scope of the activities of any of the product divisions.

The *Petroleum Products Division* was the remaining nucleus of the company's original producing and refining activities. It supplied raw materials to the Polymer and Chemicals Division and also sold refining products under long-term contracts to other petroleum companies. In the early and mid-1950s, this division's management had generated much of the company's revenue and profits through its skill in negotiating these agreements. In 1966, top corporate management felt that this division's management had accepted its role as a supplier to the rest of the corporation and that there were harmonious relations between it and its sister divisions.

The *Polymer and Chemicals Division* was developed internally during the late 1940s and early 1950s as management saw its share of the consumer petroleum market declining. Under the leadership of Seymour Knoph (who had been General Manager for several years) and his predecessor (who in 1966 was Executive Vice President-Administration), the division had rapidly developed a line of chemical and polymer compounds derived from petroleum raw materials. Most of the products of this division were manufactured under licensing agreement or were materials with formulations that were well understood. Nevertheless, technical personnel in the division had developed an industrywide reputation for their ability to develop new and improved processes. Top management of the division took particular pride in this ability. From the beginning, the decisions of what products to manufacture were based to a large extent upon the requirements of the Molded and Packaging Products Divisions. However, Polymer and Chemicals Division executives had always attempted to market these same products to external customers and had been highly successful. These external sales were extremely important to Texana, since they assured a large enough volume of operation to process a broad product line of polymer chemicals profitably. As the other divisions had grown, they had required a larger proportion of the division's capacity, which meant that Polymer and Chemicals Division managers had to reduce their commitment to external customers.

The *Molded Products Division* was also an internally developed division, formed in 1951. Its products were a variety of molded plastic products ranging from toys and household items to automotive and electronic parts. This division's major strengths were its knowledge of molding technology and particularly its marketing ability. While it depended upon the Polymer and Chemicals Division for its raw materials, its operations were largely independent of those of the Packaging Products and Building Products Divisions.

The *Packaging Products Division* was acquired in 1952. Its products were plastic packaging materials, including films, cartons, bottles, etc. All of these products were marketed to industrial customers. Like the Molded Products Division, the Packaging Division depended on the Polymer and Chemicals Division as a source of raw materials but was largely independent of other end-product divisions.

The *Building Products Division* was acquired in 1963 to give Texana a position in the construction materials market. The division produced a variety of insulation roofing materials and similar products and marketed them to the building trade. It was a particularly attractive acquisition for Texana because, prior to the acquisition, it had achieved some success with plastic products for insulation and roofing materials. Although the plastic products accounted for less than 20 percent of the total division sales in 1965, plans called for these products to account for over 50 percent of division sales in the next five years. Its affiliation with Texana gave this division a stronger position in plastic raw materials through the Polymer and Chemicals Division.

Selection and Recruitment of Management Personnel

The rapid expansion of the corporation into these new areas had created the need for much additional management talent, and top management had not hesitated to bring new men in from outside the corporation, as well as to advance promising younger men inside Texana. Most managers, in both the internally developed and acquired divisions, had spent their careers inside the division, although some top division managers were moved between divisions or into corporate positions.

In speaking about the type of people he had sought for management positions, Donald Irwin described his criteria in a financial publication:

We don't want people around who are afraid to move. The attraction of Texana is that it gives the individual responsibilities that aren't diluted. It attracts the fellow who wants a challenge.

Another corporate executive described Texana managers:

It's a group of very tough-minded, but considerate, gentlemen with an enormous drive to get things done.

Another manager, who had been with Texana for his entire career, and who considered himself to be different from most Texana managers, described the typical Texana manager as follows:

Texana attracts a particular type of person. Most of these characteristics are personal characteristics rather than professional ones. I would use terms such as cold, unfeeling, aggressive, and extremely competitive, but not particularly loyal to the organization. He is loyal to dollars, his own personal dollars. I think this is part of the communication problem. I think this is done on purpose. The selection process leads in this direction. I think this is so because of contrast with the way the company

operated 10 years ago. Of course, I was at the plant level at that time. But today the attitude I have described is also in the plants. Ten years ago, the organization was composed of people who worked together for the good of the organization because they wanted to. I don't think this is so today.

Location of Division Facilities

The Petroleum Products, Polymer and Chemicals, and Packaging Products Divisions had their executive offices located on separate floors of the Texana headquarters building in the Chicago "Loop." The plants and research and development facilities of these divisions were spread out across Oklahoma, Texas, and Louisiana. The Molded Products Division had its headquarters, research and development facilities, and a major plant in an industrial suburb of Chicago. This division's other plants were at several locations in the Middle West and on the East Coast. The Building Products Division's headquarters and major production and technical facilities were located in Fort Worth, Texas. All four divisions shared sales offices in major cities from coast to coast.

Evaluation and Control of Division Performance

The principal method of controlling and evaluating the operations of these divisions was the semiannual review of division plans and the approval of major capital expenditures by the executive committee.[1] In reviewing performance against plans, members of the executive committee placed almost sole emphasis on the division's actual return on investment against budget. Corporate executives felt that this practice, together with the technological interdependence of the divisions, created many disputes about transfer pricing.

In addition to these regular reviews, corporate executives had frequent discussions with division executives about their strategies, plans, and operations. It had been difficult for corporate management to strike the proper balance in guiding the operations for the divisions. This problem was particularly acute with regard to the Polymer and Chemicals Division because of its central place in the corporation's product line. One corporate staff member explained his view of the problem:

This whole matter of communications between the corporate staff and the Polymer and Chemicals Division has been a fairly difficult problem. Corporate management used to contribute immensely to this by trying to get into the nuts and bolts area within the Polymer and Chemicals

---

[1]The executive committee consisted of Messrs. Dutton, Irwin, and Prentice, as well as the vice president of research, the executive vice president of administration, and the executive vice president of foreign operations.

organization, and this created serious criticisms; however I think they have backed off in this matter

A second corporate executive, in discussing this matter for a trade publication report, put the problem this way:

We're trying to find the middle ground. We don't want to be a holding company, and with our diversity we can't be a highly centralized corporation.

Executive Vice President—Domestic Operations

In an effort to find this middle ground, the position of Executive Vice President—Domestic Operations was created in early 1966, and George Prentice was the first to hold the position. Prior to this change, there had been two Senior Domestic Vice Presidents—one in charge of the Petroleum and Polymer and Chemicals Divisions and the other in charge of the end-use divisions. Mr. Prentice had been Senior Vice President in charge of the end-use divisions before the new position was created. He had held that position for only two years, having come to it from a highly successful marketing career with a competitor.

At the time of his appointment, one press account described Mr. Prentice as "hard-driving, aggressive, and ambitious—an archetype of the self-actuated dynamo Irwin has sought out."

Shortly after taking his new position, Prentice described the task before him:

I think the corporation wants to integrate its parts better and I am here because I reflect this feeling. We can't be a bunch of entrepreneurs around here. We have got to balance discipline with entrepreneurial motivation. This is what we were in the past, just a bunch of entrepreneurs and if they came in with ideas we would get the money, but now our dollars are limited, and especially the Polymer and Chemical boys haven't been able to discipline themselves to select from within ten good projects. They just don't seem to be able to do this, and so they come running in here with all ten good projects, which they say we have to buy, and they get upset when we can't buy them all.

This was the tone of my predecessors [Senior Vice Presidents]. All of them were very strong on being entrepreneurs, I am going to run it different[ly]. I am going to take a marketing and capital orientation. As far as I can see, there is a time to compete and a time to collaborate, and I think right now there has been a lack of recognition in the Polymer and Chemicals executive suite that this thing has changed.

Other Views of Domestic Interdivisional Relations

Executives within the Polymer and Chemicals Division, in the end-use divisions, and at the corporate level shared Prentice's view that the major breakdown in interdivisional relations was between the Polymer and Chemicals Division and the end-use divisions. Executives in the end-use divisions made these typical comments about the problem:

I think the thing we have got to realize is that we are wedded to the Polymer and Chemicals Division whether we like it or not. We are really tied up with them. And just as we would with any outside supplier or with any of our customers, we will do things to maintain their business. But because they feel they have our business wrapped up they do not reciprocate in turn. Now let me emphasize that they have not arbitrarily refused to do the things that we are requiring, but there is a pressure on them for investment projects and we are low man on the pole. And I think this could heavily jeopardize our chances for growth.

I would say our relationships are sticky, and I think this is primarily because we think our reason for being is to make money, so we try to keep Polymer and Chemicals as an arm's length supplier. For example, I cannot see, just because it is a Polymer and Chemicals product, accepting millions of pounds of very questionable material. It takes dollars out of our pocket, and we are very profit-centered.

The big frustration, I guess, and one of our major problems, is that you can't get help from them [Polymer and Chemicals]. You feel they are not interested in what you are doing, particularly if it doesn't have a large return for them. But as far as I am concerned this has to become a joint-venture relationship, and this is getting to be real sweat with us. We are the guys down below yelling for help. And they have got to give us some relief.

My experience with the Polymer and Chemicals Division is that you cannot trust what they say at all, and even when they put it in writing you can't be absolutely sure that they are going to live up to it.

Managers within the Polymer and Chemicals Division expressed similar sentiments:

Personally, right now I have the feeling that the divisions' interests are growing further apart. It seems that the divisions are going their own ways. For example, we are a polymer producer but the molding division wants to be in a special area, so that means they are going to be less of a customer to us, and there is a whole family of plastics being left out that nobody's touching, and this is bearing on our program. . . . We don't mess with the Building Products Division at all, either. They deal in small volumes. Those that we are already making we sell to them; those that we don't make we can't justify making because of the kinds of things we are working with. What I am saying is that I don't think the corporation is integrating, but I think we ought to be, and this is one of the problems of delegated divisions. What happens is that an executive heads this up and goes for the place that makes the most money for the division, but this is not necessarily the best place from a corporate standpoint.

We don't have as much contact with sister divisions as I think we should. I have been trying to get a liaison with guys in my function but it has been a complete flop. One of the problems is that I don't know who to call on in these other divisions. There is no table of organization, nor is there any encouragement to try and get anything going. My experience has been that all of these operating divisions are very closed organizations. I know guys up the line will say that I am nuts about this. They say to just call over and I will get an answer. But this always has to be a big deal, and it doesn't happen automatically, and it hurts us.

The comments of corporate staff members describe these relationships and the factors they saw contributing to the problem:

Right now I would say there is an iron curtain between the Polymer and Chemicals Division and the rest of the corporation. You know, we tell our divisions they are responsible, autonomous groups, and the Polymer and Chemicals Division took it very seriously. However, when you are a three-quarter-billion-dollar company, you've got to be coordinated or the whole thing is going to fall apart—it can be no other way. The Domestic Executive Vice President thing has been a big step forward to improve this, but I would say it hasn't worked out yet.

The big thing that is really bothering [the Polymer and Chemicals Division] is that they think they have to go develop all new markets on their own. They are going to do it alone independently, and this is the problem they are faced with. They have got this big thing, that they want to prove that they are a company all by themselves and not rely upon packaging or anybody else.

Polymer and Chemicals Division executives talked about the effect of this drive for independence of the divisional operating heads on their own planning efforts:

The Polymer and Chemicals Division doesn't like to communicate with the corporate staff. This seems hard for us, and I think the [recent major proposal] was a classic example of this. That plan, as it was whipped up by the Polymer and Chemicals Division, has massive implications for the corporation both in expertise and in capital. In fact, I think we did this to be a competitive one-up on the rest of our sister divisions. We wanted to be the best-looking division in the system, but we carried it to an extreme. In this effort, we wanted to show that we had developed this concept completely on our own. . . . Now I think a lot of our problems with it stemmed from this intense desire we have to be the best in this organization.

Boy, a big doldrum around here was shortly after Christmas (1965) when they dropped out a new plant,

right out of our central plan, without any appreciation of the importance of this plant to the whole Polymer and Chemicals Division's growth. . . . Now we have a windfall and we are back in business on this new plant. But for a while things were very black and everything we had planned and everything we had built our patterns on were out. In fact, when we put this plan together it never really occurred to us that we were going to get it turned down, and I'll bet we didn't even put the plans together in such a way as to really reflect the importance of this plant to the rest of the corporation.

A number of executives in the end-use divisions attributed the interdivisional problems to different management practices and assumptions within the Polymer and Chemicals Division. An executive in the packaging division made this point:

We make decisions quickly and at the lowest possible level, and this is tremendously different from the rest of Texana. I don't know another division like this in the rest of the corporation.

Look at what Sy Knoph has superfluous to his operation compared to ours. These are the reasons for our success. You've got to turn your guys loose and not breathe down their necks all the time. We don't slow our people down with staff. Sure, you may work with a staff, the wheels may grind, but they sure grind slow.

Also, we don't work on detail like the other divisions do. Our management doesn't feel they need the detail stuff. Therefore, they're [Polymer and Chemical] always asking us for detail which we can't supply. Our process doesn't generate it and their process requires it, and this always creates problems with the Polymer and Chemicals Division. But I'll be damned if I am going to have a group of people running between me and the plant, and I'll be goddamned if I am going to clutter up my organization with all the people that Knoph has got working for him. I don't want this staff, but they are sure pushing it on me.

This comment from a Molding Division manager is typical of many about the technical concerns of the Polymer and Chemicals Division management:

Historically, even up to the not-too-distant past, the Polymer and Chemicals Division was considered a snake pit as far as the corporate people were concerned. This was because the corporate people were market-oriented and Polymer and Chemicals Division was technically run and very much a manufacturing effort. These two factors created a communication barrier, because to really understand the Polymer and Chemicals Division problems, they felt that you had to have a basic appreciation of the technology and all the interrelationships.

Building on this strong belief, the Polymer and Chemicals Division executives in the past have tried to communicate in technical terms, and this just further hurt the relationship, and it just did not work. Now they are coming up with a little bit more business or commercial orientation, and they are beginning to appreciate that they have got to justify the things they want to do in a business or commercial orientation, and they are beginning to appreciate that they have got to justify the things they want to do in a business sense rather than just a technical sense. This also helps the problem of maintaining their relationships with the corporation as most of the staff is nontechnical; however, this has changed a little bit in that more and more technical people have been coming on and this has helped from the other side.

They work on the assumption in the Polymer and Chemicals Division that you have to know the territory before you can be an effective manager. You have got to be an operating guy to contribute meaningfully to their problems. However, their biggest problem is this concentration on technical solutions to their problems. This is a thing that has boxed them in the most trouble with the corporation and the other sister divisions.

These and other executives also pointed to another source of conflict between the Polymer and Chemicals Division and other divisions. This was the question of whether the Polymer and Chemicals Division should develop into a more independent marketer, or whether it should rely more heavily on the end-use divisions to "push" its products to the market.

Typical views of this conflict are the following comments by end-use division executives:

The big question I have about Polymer and Chemicals is, What is their strategy going to be? I can understand them completely from a technical standpoint—this is no problem. I wonder what is the role of this company? How is it going to fit into what we and others are doing? Right now, judging from the behavior I've seen, Polymer and Chemicals could care less about what we are doing in terms of integration of our markets or a joint approach to them.

I think it is debatable whether the Polymer and Chemicals Division should be a new product company or not. Right now we have an almost inexhaustible appetite for what they do and do well. As I see it, the present charter is fine. However, that group is very impatient, aggressive, and they want to grow, but you have got to grow within guidelines. Possibly the Polymer and Chemicals Division is just going to have to learn to hang on the coattails of the other divisions, and do just what they are doing now, only better. I think the future role of the Polymer and Chemicals Division is going to be, at any one point in time for the corporation, that if it looks like a product is needed, they will make it. . . . They are going to be suppliers because I will guarantee you that if the moment comes and we can't buy it elsewhere, for example, then I darn well know

they are going to make it for us regardless of what their other commitments are. They are just going to have to supply us. If you were to put the Polymer and Chemicals Division off from the corporation, I don't think they would last a year. Without their huge captive requirements, they would not be able to compete economically in the commercial areas they are in.

A number of other executives indicated that the primary emphasis within the corporation on return on investment by divisions tended to induce, among other things, a narrow, competitive concern on the part of the various divisional managements. The comment of this division executive was typical:

As far as I can see, we [his division and Polymer and Chemicals] are 180 degrees off on our respective charters. Therefore, when Sy Knoph talks about this big project, we listen nicely and then we say, "God bless you, lots of luck," but I am sure we are not going to get involved in it. I don't see any money in it for us. It may be a gold mine for Sy, but it is not for our company; and as long as we are held to the high profit standards we are, we just cannot afford to get involved. I can certainly see it might make good corporate sense for us to get it, but it doesn't make any sense in terms of our particular company. We have got to be able to show the returns in order to get continuing capital, and I just can't on that kind of project. I guess what I am saying is that under the right conditions we could certainly go in but not under the present framework; we would just be dead in terms of dealing with the corporate financial structure. We just cannot get the kinds of returns on our capital that the corporation has set to get new capital. In terms of the long run, I'd like very much to see what the corporation has envisioned in terms of a hookup between us, but right now I don't see any sense in going on. You know my career is at stake here, too.

Another divisional executive made this point more succinctly:

Personally, I think a lot more could be done from a corporate point of view and this is frustrating. Right now, all these various divisions seem to be viewed strictly as an investment by the corporate people. They only look at us as a banker might look at us. This hurts us in terms of evolving some of these programs because we have relationships that are beyond financial relationships.

The remarks of a corporate executive seemed to support this concern:

One of the things I worry about is, Where is the end of the rope on this interdivisional thing? I'm wondering if action really has to come from just the division. You know, in this organization, when they decide to do something new it has always been a divisional proposal—they were coming to us for review and approval. The executive committee ends up being a review board; not us, working downward. With this kind of pattern, the talent of the corporate people is pretty well seduced into asking questions and determining whether a thing needs guidelines. But I think we

ought to be the idea people as well, thinking about where we are going in the future, and if we think we ought to be getting into some new area, then we tell the divisions to do it. The stream has got to work both ways. Now it is not.

CASE 6
W. L. Gore & Associates, Inc.
Frank Shipper and Charles C. Manz

On July 26, 1976, Jack Dougherty, a newly minted M.B.A. from the College of William and Mary bursting with resolve, dressed in a dark blue suit, reported for his first day at W.L. Gore & Associates. He presented himself to Bill Gore, shook hands firmly, looked him in the eye, and said he was ready for anything.

What happened next was one thing for which Jack was not ready. Gore replied, "That's fine, Jack, fine. Why don't you look around and find something you'd like to do." Three frustrating weeks later he found that something, dressed in jeans, loading fabric into the mouth of a machine that laminated the company's patented Gore-Tex membrane to fabric. By 1982, Jack had become responsible for all advertising and marketing in the fabrics group. This story was part of the folklore that was heard over and over about W. L. Gore. By 1991, the process was slightly more structured. New associates took a journey through the business before settling into their own positions, regardless of the position for which they were hired. A new sales associate in the Fabric Division might spend six weeks rotating through different areas before concentrating on sales and marketing. Among other things, he or she might learn how Gore-Tex fabric was made, what it could and could not do, how Gore handled customer complaints, and how it made investment decisions.

Anita McBride related her early experience at W. L. Gore & Associates this way:

Before I came to Gore, I had worked for a structured organization. I came here, and for the first month it was fairly structured because I was going through training and this is what we do and this is how Gore is and all of that, and I went to Flagstaff for that training. After a month I came down to Phoenix, and my sponsor said. "Well, here's your office, and here's your desk," and walked away. And I thought, "Now what do I do," you

know? I was waiting for a memo or something, or a job description. Finally, after another month, I was so frustrated I felt, "What have I gotten myself into?"

And so I went to my sponsor and I said, "What the heck do you want from me? I need something from you." And he said, "if you don't know what you're supposed to do, examine your commitment, and opportunities."

Background

W. L. Gore & Associates evolved from the late Wilbert L. Gore's experiences personally, organizationally, and technically. He was born in Meridian, Idaho, near Boise, in 1912. By age six, he claimed he had become an avid hiker in the Wasatch Mountain Range in Utah. In those mountains, at a church camp, he met Genevieve (called Vieve by everyone), his future wife. In 1935, they got married, which was, in their eyes, a partnership—a partnership that lasted a lifetime.

He received both a bachelor of science degree in chemical engineering in 1933 and a master of science degree in physical chemistry in 1935 from the University of Utah. He began his professional career at American Smelting and Refining in 1936; moved to Remington Arms Company in 1941; and moved once again to E.I. Du Pont de Nemours in 1945, where he held positions of research supervisor and head of operations research. While at Du Pont, he worked on a team to develop applications for polytetrafluoroethylene, frequently referred to as PTFE in the scientific community and known as Teflon by consumers. On this team, Wilbert Gore, called Bill by everyone, felt a sense of excited commitment, personal fulfillment, and self-direction. He followed the development of computers and transistors and believed that PTFE had the ideal insulating characteristics for use with such equipment.

He tried a number of ways to make a PTFE-coated ribbon cable, without success. A breakthrough came in his home basement laboratory. He was explaining the problem to his son, Bob. Bob saw some PTFE sealant

Frank Shipper. Franklin P. Perdue School of Business. Salisbury State University and Charles C. Manz. College of Business. Arizona State University. Reprinted with permission.

tape made by 3M and asked his father, "Why don't you try this tape?" His father then explained to his son, "Everyone knows you cannot bond PTFE to itself." So, Bob went on to bed.

Bill Gore remained in his basement lab and proceeded to try what everyone knew would not work. About 4:00 A.M., he woke his son, waving a small piece of cable around and saying excitedly, "It works, it works." The following night, father and son returned to the basement lab to make ribbon cable coated with PTFE.

For the next four months, Bill Gore tried to persuade Du Pont to make a new product—PTFE-coated ribbon cable. By this time in his career, Bill Gore knew some of the decision makers at Du Pont. After he had talked to a number of them, it became clear that Du Pont wanted to remain a supplier of raw materials and not a fabricator.

Bill began to discuss with his wife the possibility of starting their own insulated wire and cable business. On January 1, 1958, their wedding anniversary, they founded W. L. Gore & Associates, which they viewed as another partnership. The basement of their home served as their first facility. After finishing dinner on their anniversary, Vieve turned to her husband of 23 years and said, "Well, let's clear up the dishes, go downstairs, and get to work."

Bill Gore was 45 years old with five children to support when he left Du Pont. He left behind a career of 17 years and a good and secure salary. To finance the first two years of the business, they mortgaged their house and took $4000 from savings. All of their friends cautioned them against taking the risk.

The first few years were rough. In lieu of salary, some of their employees accepted room and board in the Gore home. At one point, 11 employees were living and working under one roof. Then came the order from the city of Denver's water department that put the company on a profitable footing. One afternoon, Vieve answered a phone call while sifting PTFE powder. The caller indicated that he was interested in the ribbon cable, but wanted to ask some technical questions and so asked for the product manager. Vieve explained that Bill was out running some errands at the moment. Next, the caller asked for the sales manager and, finally, the president. Vieve explained that they were also out. The caller became outraged and hollered, "What kind of company is this anyway?" With a little diplomacy, the Gores eventually secured an order for $100,000. This order put the company over the hump and it began to take off.

W. L. Gore & Associates continued to grow and develop new products primarily derived from PTFE, including its best-known product, Gore-Tex. In 1986, Bill Gore died while backpacking in the Wind River Mountains of Wyoming. Before he died, however, he had become chairman and his son, Bob, president. Vieve remained as the only other officer, secretary-treasurer.

The Operating Company

W. L. Gore & Associates was a company without titles, hierarchy, or any of the conventional structures associated with enterprises of its size. The titles of president and secretary-treasurer were used only because they were required by the laws of incorporation. In addition, Gore did not have a corporate-wide mission or code of ethics statement; nor did it require or prohibit business units from developing such statements for themselves. Thus, the associates of some business units who felt a need for such statements had developed them. The majority of business units within Gore did not have such statements. When questioned about this issue, one associate stated. "The company belief is that (1) its four basic operating principles cover ethical practices required of people in business and (2) it will not tolerate illegal practices." Gore's management style was often referred to as "unmanagement." The organization had been guided by Bill's experiences on teams at Du Pont and had evolved as needed.

For example, in 1965, W. L. Gore & Associates was a thriving and growing company with a facility on Paper Mill Road in Newark, Delaware, with about 200 employees. One warm Monday morning in the summer, Bill Gore was taking his usual walk through the plant. All of a sudden he realized he did not know everyone in the plant. The team had become too big. As a result, the company established a policy that no facility would have over 150 to 200 employees. Thus was born the expansion policy of "Get big by staying small." The purpose of maintaining small plants was to accentuate a close-knit and interpersonal atmosphere.

By 1991, W. L. Gore & Associates consisted of forty-four plants worldwide with over 5,300 associates. In some cases, the plants were clustered together on the same site, as in Flagstaff, Arizona, with four plants on the same site. Twenty-seven of those plants were in the United States and 17 were overseas. Gore's overseas plants were located in Scotland, Germany, France, Japan, and India.

Products

The products that W. L. Gore made were organized into eight divisions—electronic, medical, waterproofing fabrics, fibers, industrial filtration, industrial seals, coatings, and microfiltration.

The electronic products division produced wire and cable for various demanding applications in aerospace, defense, computers, and telecommunications. The wire and cable products had a reputation for unequaled reliability. Most of the wire and cable was used where conventional cables could not operate. For example, Gore wire and cable assemblies were used in the space shuttle Columbia because they would stand the heat of ignition and the cold of space. Gore wire was used in the moon vehicle shuttle that scooped up samples of moon rocks, and Gore's microwave coaxial assemblies opened new horizons in microwave technology. On Earth, the electrical wire products helped make the world's fastest computers possible because electrical signals could travel through them at up to 90 percent of the speed of light. Because of the physical properties of the Gore-Tex material used in their construction, the electronic products were used extensively in defense systems, electronic switching for telephone systems, scientific and industrial instrumentation, microwave communications, and industrial robotics. Reliability was a watchword for all Gore products.

In medical products, reliability was literally a matter of life and death. Gore-Tex-expanded PTFE was an ideal material used to combat cardiovascular disease. When human arteries were seriously damaged or plugged with deposits that interrupt the flow of blood, the diseased portions could often be replaced with Gore-Tex artificial arteries. Gore-Tex arteries and patches were not rejected by the body, because the patient's own tissues grew into the grafts' open porous spaces. Gore-Tex vascular grafts came in many sizes to restore circulation to all areas of the body. They had saved limbs from amputation and saved lives. Some of the tiniest grafts relieved pulmonary problems in newborns. Gore-Tex was also used to help people with kidney disease. Associates were developing a variety of surgical reinforcing membranes, known as Gore-Tex cardiovascular patches, which could literally mend broken hearts, by patching holes and repairing aneurysms.

Through the waterproof fabrics division, Gore technology had traveled to the top of the world on the backs of renowned mountaineers. Gore-Tex fabric was waterproof and windproof, yet breathable. Those features had qualified Gore-Tex fabric as essential gear for mountaineers and adventurers facing extremely harsh environments. The PTFE membrane blocked wind and water but allowed sweat to escape. That made Gore-Tex fabric ideal for anyone who worked or played hard in foul weather. Backpackers had discovered that a single lightweight Gore-Tex fabric shell would replace a poplin jacket and a rain suit and dramatically outperform both. Skiers, sailors, runners, bicyclists, hunters, fishermen, and other outdoor enthusiasts had also become big customers of garments made of Gore-Tex fabric. General sportswear and women's fashion footwear and handwear of Gore-Tex fabric were as functional as they were beautiful. Boots and gloves, both for work and recreation, were waterproof, thanks to Gore-Tex liners. Gore-Tex was even becoming government issue for many military personnel. Wet suits, parkas, pants, headgear, gloves, and boots kept the troops warm and dry on foul-weather missions. Other demanding jobs also required the protection of Gore-Tex fabric because of its unique combination of chemical and physical properties.

The Gore-Tex fiber products, like the fabrics, ended up in some tough places. The outer protective layer of NASA's spacesuit was woven from Gore-Tex fibers. Gore-Tex fibers were in many ways the ultimate in synthetic fibers. They were impervious to sunlight, chemicals, heat, and cold. They were strong and uniquely resistant to abrasion.

Industrial filtration products, such as Gore-Tex filter bags, reduced air pollution and recovered valuable solids from gases and liquids more completely than alternatives; they also did it more economically. They could make coalburning plants smoke-free, contributing to a cleaner environment.

The industrial seals division produced joint sealant, a fixable cord of porous PTFE that could be applied as a gasket to the most complex shapes, scaling them to prevent leakage of corrosive chemicals, even at extreme temperature and pressure. Steam valves packed with Gore-Tex valve stempacking never leaked and never needed to be repacked.

The coatings division applied layers of PTFE to steel castings and other metal articles by a patented process. Called Fluoroshield protective coatings, this fluorocarbon polymer protected processing vessels in the production of corrosive chemicals.

Gore-Tex microfiltration products were used in medical devices, pharmaceutical manufacturing, and chemical processing. These membranes removed bacteria and other microorganisms from air or liquids, making them sterile.

Financial Information

W. L. Gore was a closely held private corporation. Financial information was as closely guarded as proprietary information on products and processes. Eighty percent of the stock was held by the Gore family and veteran associates, 10 percent by current associates, and 10 percent by others.

According to Shanti Mehta, an associate, Gore's return on assets and equity ranked it among the top 5 percent of major companies. According to another source, W. L. Gore & Associates was working just fine by any financial measure. It had had 27 straight years of profitability and positive return on equity. The compounded growth rate for revenues at W. L. Gore over the past 20 years had been over 18 percent, discounted for inflation.[1] In 1969, total sales were $6 million; in 1982, $125 million; in 1983, $160 million; in 1985, $250 million; in 1987, $400 million; in 1988, $426 million; and in 1989, $600 million. This growth had largely been financed without debt.

---

[1]By comparison, only 11 of the 200 largest companies in the Fortune 500 have had positive ROE each year from 1970–1988, and only two other companies missed only one year. The revenue growth rate for these 13 companies was 5.4 percent compared to 2.5 percent for the entire Fortune 500.

Organizational Structure

Bill Gore wanted to avoid smothering the company in thick layers of formal "management." He believed they stifled individual creativity. As the company grew, he knew a way had to be devised to help new people get started and to follow their progress. This was seen as particularly important when it came to compensation. W. L. Gore & Associates developed what it called the "sponsor" program to meet those needs. When people applied to W. L. Gore, they were initially screened by personnel specialists, as in most companies. For those who met the basic criteria, there were interviews with other associates. Before a person was hired, an associate must have agreed to be that person's sponsor. The sponsor was to take a personal interest in the new associate's contributions, problems, and goals. The sponsor was both a coach and an advocate. The sponsor tracked the new associate's progress, helping and encouraging, dealing with weaknesses, and concentrating on strengths. Sponsoring was not a short-term commitment. All associates had sponsors and many had more than one. When individuals were hired, they had a sponsor in their immediate work area. If they moved to another area, they also had a sponsor in that work area. As associates' responsibilities grew, they could acquire additional sponsors.

Because the sponsoring program looked beyond conventional views of what made a good associate, some anomalies occurred in the hiring practices. Bill Gore proudly told the story of "a very young man" of 84 who walked in, applied, and spent five very good years with the company. The individual had 30 years of experience in the industry before joining Gore. His other associates had no problems accepting him, but the personnel computer did. It insisted his age was 48.

An internal memo by Bill Gore described three kinds of sponsorship and how they might work:

1. The sponsor who helps a new associate get started on the job. Also, the sponsor who helps a present associate get started on a new job (starting sponsor).
2. The sponsor who sees to it that the associate being sponsored gets credit and recognition for contributions and accomplishments (advocate sponsor).
3. The sponsor who sees to it that the associate being sponsored is fairly paid for contributions to the success of the enterprise (compensation sponsor).

A single sponsor could perform any one or all three kinds of sponsorship. A sponsor was a friend and an associate. All the supportive aspects of the friendship were also present. Often (perhaps usually) two associates sponsored each other as advocates.

W L. Gore & Associates had been described not only as unmanaged, but also as unstructured. Bill Gore referred to the structure as a lattice organization. A lattice structure is portrayed in Exhibit 1. The characteristics of this structure were:

1. Direct lines of communication—person-to-person—with no intermediary.

Exhibit 1 The Lattice Structure

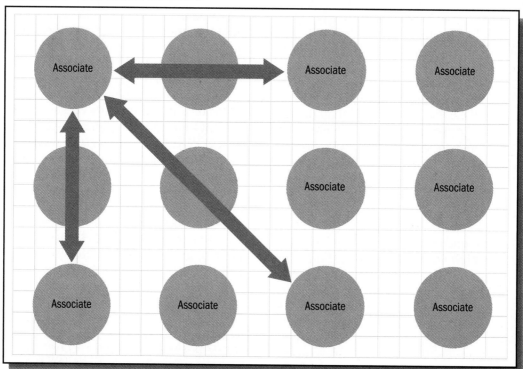

2. No fixed or assigned authority.
3. Sponsors, not bosses.
4. Natural leadership defined by followership.
5. Objectives set by those who must "make them happen."
6. Tasks and functions organized through commitments.

The structure within the lattice was described by the people at Gore as complex and had evolved from interpersonal interactions, self-commitment to group-known responsibilities, natural leadership, and group-imposed discipline.

Bill Gore once explained this structure by saying, "Every successful organization has an underground lattice. It's where the news spreads like lightning, where people can go around the organization to get things done." Another description of what was occurring within the lattice structure was constant cross-area teams—the equivalent of quality circles going on all the time. When a puzzled interviewer told Bill he was having trouble understanding how planning and accountability worked, Bill replied with a grin, "So am I. You ask me how it works—it works every which way."

The lattice structure did have some similarities to traditional management structures. For instance, a group of 30 to 40 associates who made up an advisory group met every six months to review marketing, sales, and production plans. As Bill Gore has conceded, "The abdication of titles and rankings can never be 100 percent."

The lattice structure was not without its critics. As Bill Gore stated, "I'm told from time to time that a lattice organization can't meet a crisis well because it takes too long to reach a consensus when there are no bosses. But this isn't true. Actually, a lattice, by its very nature, works particularly well in a crisis. A lot of useless effort is avoided because there is no rigid management hierarchy to conquer before you can attack a problem."

The lattice had been put to the test on a number of occasions. For example, in 1975, Dr. Charles Campbell, the University of Pittsburgh's senior resident, reported that a Gore-Tex arterial graft had developed an aneurysm. An aneurysm is a bubble-like protrusion that is life-threatening. If it continued to expand, it would explode. Obviously, this kind of problem had to be solved quickly and permanently.

Within only a few days of Dr. Campbell's first report, he flew to Newark to present his findings to Bill and Bob Gore and a few other associates. The meeting lasted two hours. Bill Hubis, a former policeman who had joined Gore to develop new production methods, had an idea before the meeting was over. He returned to his work area to try some different production techniques. After only three hours and 12 tries, he had developed a permanent solution. In other words, in three hours, a potentially damaging problem to both patients and the company was resolved. Furthermore,

Hubis's redesigned graft went on to win widespread acceptance in the medical community. By 1991, it dominated the market with a 70 percent share.

One critic, Eric Reynolds, founder of Marmot Mountain Works Ltd. of Grand Junction, Colorado, and a major Gore customer, said, "I think the lattice has its problems with the day-to-day nitty-gritty of getting things done on time and out the door. I don't think Bill realizes how the lattice system affects customers. I mean, after you've established a relationship with someone about product quality, you can call up one day and suddenly find that someone new to you is handling your problem. It's frustrating to find a lack of continuity." He went on to say. "But I have to admit that I've personally seen at Gore remarkable examples of people coming out of nowhere and excelling."

Bill Gore was asked a number of times if the lattice structure could be used by other companies. His answer was, "No. For example, established companies would find it very difficult to use the lattice. Too many hierarchies would be destroyed. When you remove titles and positions and allow people to follow whomever they want, it may very well be someone other than the person who has been in charge. The lattice works for us, but it's always evolving. You have to expect problems." He maintained that the lattice system worked best when put in place in start-up companies by dynamic entrepreneurs.

Organizational Culture

In addition to the sponsor program, Gore associates were asked to follow four guiding principles:

1. Try to be fair.
2. Use your freedom to grow.
3. Make your own commitments, and keep them.
4. Consult with other associates before taking any action that may hurt the reputation or financial stability of the company.

The four principles were often referred to as fairness, freedom, commitment, and discretion. The last principle was also often referred to as the waterline principle. The terminology was drawn from an analogy to ships. If someone poked a hole in a boat above the waterline, the boat would be in relatively little real danger. But if someone poked a hole below the waterline, the boat would be in immediate danger of sinking.

In practice, the fourth principle provided associates with a great deal of discretion. For example, W. L. Gore had no travel policy, no request for travel forms, no prohibition against first-class travel, and no expense reports. The associate called an internal travel consultant and gave the individual his or her requirements. All tickets issued to Gore travelers were accompanied by a note that stated, "The normal coach fare is

X, you've saved Y." Upon return, the associate could file a travel investment report and be reimbursed for his or her savings investment.

According to Debbie Sharp, "Very few people take advantage of this. It's only the infrequent travelers who sometimes get carried away. If we see expenses that stand out, we'll call the traveler and ask him to be more careful next time. But no one ever pays money back on an investment report."

The travel consultant also had a high amount of discretion. For example, W. L. Gore had been doing business with three different rental car companies when one became more expensive. The travel consultant dropped that firm and picked up another without checking with anyone else.

The operating principles were put to a test in 1978. By this time, word about the qualities of Gore-Tex was being spread throughout the recreational and outdoor markets. Production and shipment had begun in volume. At first, a few complaints were heard. Next, some of the clothing started coming back. Finally, a great deal of the clothing was being returned. The trouble was that the Gore-Tex was leaking. Waterproof fabric was one of the two major properties responsible for Gore-Tex's success. The company's reputation and credibility were on the line.

Peter W. Gilson, who led Gore's fabric division, said, "It was an incredible crisis for us at that point. We were really starting to attract attention, we were taking off—and then this." In the next few months, Peter and some of his associates made a number of those below-the-waterline decisions. First, the researchers determined that certain oils in human sweat were clogging the pores in Gore-Tex and altering the surface tension of the membrane, allowing water to pass through. They also discovered that a good washing could restore the waterproof property. At first, this solution, known as the "Ivory Snow Solution," was accepted.

A single letter from "Butch," a mountain guide in the Sierras, changed the company's position. Butch wrote how he had been leading a group and, "My parka leaked and my life was in danger." As Gilson said, "That scared the hell out of us. Clearly, our solution was no solution at all to someone on a mountaintop." All of the products were recalled. As Gilson said, "We bought back, at our own expense, a fortune in pipeline material. Anything that was in the stores, at the manufacturers, or anywhere else in the pipeline."

In the meantime, Bob Gore and other associates set out to develop a permanent fix. One month later, a second generation Gore-Tex had been developed. Gilson told dealers that if at any time a customer returned a leaky parka, they should replace it and bill the company. The replacement program cost Gore roughly $4 million.

One thing that might strike an outsider was the informality and amount of humor in the Gore organization. One of the most common words heard in meetings was "bullshit!" In contrast, other commonly heard words were "responsibilities" and "commitments." This was an organization that seemed to take what it did very seriously, but its members did not take themselves too seriously.

Gore, for a company of its size, had a very short organizational pyramid. The pyramid consisted of Bob Gore, the late Bill Gore's son, as president, and Vieve, Bill Gore's widow, as secretary-treasurer. All the other members of the Gore organization were referred to as associates. Words such as *employees*, *subordinates*, and *managers* were taboo in the Gore culture.

Gore did not have any managers, but it did have many leaders. Bill Gore described in an internal memo the kinds of leadership and the role of leadership:

1. The associate who is recognized by a team as having a special knowledge or experience (for example, this could be a chemist, computer expert, machine operator, salesman, engineer, lawyer). This kind of leader gives the team guidance in a special area.

2. The associate the team looks to for coordination of individual activities to achieve the agreed-on objectives of the team. The role of this leader is to persuade team members to make the commitments necessary for success (commitment seeker).

3. The associate who proposes necessary objectives and activities and seeks agreement and team consensus on objectives. This leader is perceived by the team membership as having a good grasp of how the objectives of the team fit in with the broad objective of the enterprise. This kind of leader is often also the "commitment-seeking" leader.

4. The leader who evaluates relative contributions of team members (in consultation with other sponsors) and reports these contribution evaluations to a compensation committee. This leader may also participate in the compensation committee on relative contribution and pay and reports changes in compensation to individual associates. This leader is then also a compensation sponsor.

5. The leader who coordinates the research, manufacturing, and marketing of one product type within a business, interacting with team leaders and individual associates who have commitments regarding the product type. These leaders are usually called product specialists. They are respected for their knowledge and dedication to their products.

6. Plant leaders who help coordinate activities of people within a plant.

7. Business leaders who help coordinate activities of people in a business.

8. Functional leaders who help coordinate activities of people in a "functional" area.

9. Corporate leaders who help coordinate activities of people in different businesses and functions and who try to promote communication and cooperation among all associates.

10. Intrapreneuring associates organize new teams for new businesses, new products, new processes, new devices, new marketing efforts, and new or better methods of all kinds. These leaders invite other associates to "sign to" for their project. It is clear that leadership is widespread in our lattice organization and that it is continually changing and evolving. The situation that leaders are frequently also sponsors should not [blur the fact] that these are different activities and responsibilities. Leaders are not authoritarians, managers of people, or supervisors who tell us what to do or forbid us doing things; nor are they "parents" to whom we transfer our own self-responsibility. However, they do often advise us of the consequences of actions we have done or propose to do. Our actions result in contributions, or lack of contribution, to the success of our enterprise. Our pay depends on the magnitude of our contributions. This is the basic discipline of our lattice organization.

Many other aspects were arranged along egalitarian lines. The parking lot did not have any reserved parking spaces except for customers and the handicapped. There was only one area in each plant in which to eat. The lunchroom in each new plant was designed to be a focal point for employee interaction. As Dave McCarter of Phoenix explained, "The design is no accident. The lunchroom in Flagstaff has a fireplace in the middle. We want people to like to be here." The location of the plant was also no accident. Sites were selected based on transportation access, a nearby university, beautiful surroundings, and climate appeal. Land cost was never a primary consideration. McCarter justified the selection by stating, "Expanding is not costly in the long run. The loss of money is what you make happen by stymieing people into a box."

Not all people functioned well under such a system, especially initially. For those accustomed to a more structured work environment, there were adjustment problems. As Bill Gore said, "All our lives most of us have been told what to do, and some people don't know how to respond when asked to do something—and have the very real option of saying no—on their job. It's the new associate's responsibility to find out what he or she can do for the good of the operation." The vast majority of the new associates, after some initial floundering, adapted quickly.

For those who required more structured working conditions and could not adapt, Gore's flexible workplace was not for them. According to Bill, for those few, "It's an unhappy situation, both for the associate and the sponsor. If there is no contribution, there is no paycheck."

As Anita McBride, an associate in Phoenix, said, "It's not for everybody. People ask me, Do we have turnover? And, yes, we do have turnover. What you're seeing looks like utopia, but it also looks extreme. If you finally figure the system, it can be real exciting. If you can't handle it, you've got to go—probably by your own choice, because you're going to be so frustrated."

Associates had also encountered criticism from outsiders who had problems with the idea of no titles. Sarah Clifton, an associate at the Flagstaff facility, was being pressed by some outsiders as to what her title was. She made one up and had it printed on some business cards—SUPREME COMMANDER. When Bill Gore learned what she did, he loved it and recounted the story to others.

In rare cases, an associate "is trying to be unfair," in Bill's own words. In one case, the problem was chronic absenteeism and in the other the individual was caught stealing. "When that happens, all hell breaks loose," said Bill Gore. "We can get damned authoritarian when we have to."

Over the years, Gore & Associates faced a number of unionization drives. The company neither tried to dissuade an associate from attending an organizational meeting nor retaliated when fliers were passed out. Each attempt was unsuccessful. None of the plants had been organized to date. Bill believed no need existed for third-party representation under the lattice structure. He asked the question, "Why would associates join a union when they own the company? It seems rather absurd."

Overall, the associates appeared to have responded positively to the Gore system of unmanagement and unstructure. Bill estimated the year before he died that "the profit per associate is double" that of Du Pont.

Associate Development

Ron Hill, an associate in Newark, said W. L. Gore "will work with associates who want to advance themselves." Associates were offered many in-house training opportunities. Most were technical and engineering-focused because of the type of organization W. L. Gore was, but the company also offered in-house programs in leadership development. In addition, the company had cooperative programs with associates to obtain training through universities and other outside providers in which Gore picked up most of the educational costs for the associates. The emphasis in employee development, as in many parts of W. L. Gore, was that the associate must take the initiative.

Compensation

Compensation at W. L. Gore & Associates took three forms—salary, bonus, and an Associates' Stock Option Program (ASOP).[2] Entry-level salary was in the

---

[2]Gore's ASOP is similar legally to an ESOP (Employee Stock Option Plan). Gore simply does not use the word employee in any of its documentation.

middle of the range for comparable jobs. According to Sally Gore, daughter-in-law of the founder, "We do not feel we need to be the highest paid. We never try to steal people away from other companies with salary. We want them to come here because of the opportunities for growth and the unique work environment." Associates' salaries were reviewed at least once a year and more commonly twice a year. The reviews were conducted by a compensation team for most workers in the facility in which they worked. The sponsors for all associates acted as their advocates during this review process. Before meeting with the compensation committee, the sponsor checked with customers or whomever used the results of the person's work to find out what contributions had been made. In addition, the evaluation team considered the associate's leadership ability and willingness to help others develop to their fullest.

Besides salaries, W. L. Gore had a bonus and ASOP profit-sharing plan for all associates. The bonus consisted of 15 percent of the company's profits distributed among all associates twice a year. In addition, the firm bought company stock equivalent to 15 percent of the associates' annual income and placed it in an (ASOP) retirement fund. Thus, an associate became a stockholder after being at Gore for one year. Bill wanted all associates to feel they were the owners.

The principle of commitment was seen as a two-way street. W. L. Gore & Associates tried to avoid layoffs. Instead of cutting pay, which was seen at Gore as disastrous to morale, the company used a system of temporary transfers within a plant or cluster of plants and voluntary layoffs.

Research and Development

Research and development, like everything else at Gore, were unstructured. There was no formal research and development department. Yet the company held over 150 patents, although most inventions were held as proprietary or trade secrets. Any associate could ask for a piece of raw PTFE, known as a silly worm, with which to experiment. Bill Gore believed all people had it within themselves to be creative.

The best way to understand how research and development worked was to see how inventiveness had previously occurred at Gore. By 1969, the wire and cable division was facing increased competition. Bill Gore began to look for a way to straighten out the PTFE molecules. As he said, "I figured out that if we ever could unfold those molecules, get them to stretch out straight, we'd have a tremendous new kind of material." He thought that if PTFE could be stretched, air could be introduced into its molecular structure. The result would be greater volume per pound of raw material without affecting performance. Thus, fabricating costs would be reduced and the profit margins

would be increased. Going about this search in a scientific manner, Bill Gore and his son, Bob, heated rods of PTFE to various temperatures and then slowly stretched them. Regardless of the temperature or how carefully they stretched them, the rods broke.

Working alone late one night in 1969 after countless failures, Bob, in frustration, yanked at one of the rods violently. To his surprise, it did not break. He tried it again and again with the same results.

The next morning, Bob demonstrated his breakthrough to his father, but not without some drama. As Bill Gore recalled, "Bob wanted to surprise me so he took a rod and stretched it slowly. Naturally, it broke. Then he pretended to get mad. He grabbed another rod and said, 'Oh the hell with this,' and gave it a pull. It didn't break—he'd done it." The new arrangement of molecules changed not only the wire and cable division, but also led to the development of Gore-Tex and what is now the largest division at Gore plus a host of other products.

Initial field-testing of Gore-Tex was conducted by Bill and Vieve in the summer of 1970. Vieve made a hand-sewn tent out of patches of Gore-Tex. They took it on their annual camping trip to the Wind River Mountains in Wyoming. The very first night in the wilderness, they encountered a hail storm. The hail tore holes in the top of the tent, but the bottom filled up like a bathtub from the rain. As Bill Gore stated. "At least we knew from all the water that the tent was waterproof. We just needed to make it stronger, so it could withstand hail."

The second largest division began on the ski slopes of Colorado. Bill was skiing with his friend Dr. Ben Eiseman of the Denver General Hospital. As Bill Gore told the story, "We were just about to start a run when I absentmindedly pulled a small tubular section of Gore-Tex out of my pocket and looked at it. 'What is that stuff?' Ben asked. So I told him about its properties. 'Feels great,' he said,' What do you use it for?' 'Got no idea,' I said. 'Well give it to me,' he said, 'and I'll try it in a vascular graft on a pig.' Two weeks later, he called me up. Ben was pretty excited. 'Bill,' he said 'I put it in a pig and it works. What do I do now?' I told him to get together with Pete Cooper in our Flagstaff plant, and let them figure it out." Now hundreds of thousands of people throughout the world walk around with Gore-Tex vascular grafts.

Every associate was encouraged to think, experiment, and follow a potentially profitable idea to its conclusion. For example, at a plant in Newark, Delaware, a machine that wrapped thousands of yards of wire a day was designed by Fred L. Eldreth, an associate with a third-grade education. The design was done over a weekend. Many other associates had contributed their ideas through both product and process breakthroughs.

Even without a research and development department, innovations and creativity worked very well at

Gore & Associates. The year before he died, Bill Gore claimed. "The creativity—the number of patent applications and innovative products—is triple" that of Du Pont.

Marketing Strategy

Gore's marketing strategy was based on making the determination that it could offer the best valued products to a marketplace, that people in that marketplace appreciated what it manufactured, and that Gore could become a leader in that area of expertise. The operating procedures used to implement the strategy followed the same principles as other functions at Gore.

First, the marketing of a product revolved around a leader who was referred to as a product champion. According to Dave McCarter, "You marry your technology with the interests of your champions, as you've got to have champions for all these things no matter what. And that's the key element within our company. Without a product champion you can't do much anyway, so it is individually driven. If you get a person interested in a particular market or a particular product for the marketplace, then there is no stopping them."

Second, a product champion was responsible for marketing the product through commitments with sales representatives. Again according to McCarter, "We have no quota system. Our marketing and our salespeople make their own commitments as to what their forecasts are. There is no person sitting around telling them that that is not high enough, you have to increase it by 10 percent, or whatever somebody feels is necessary. You are expected to meet your commitment, which is your forecast, but nobody is going to tell you to change it. . . . There is no order of command, no chain involved. These are groups of independent people who come together to make unified commitments to do something, and sometimes when they can't make those agreements . . . you may pass up a marketplace, . . . but that's OK because there's much more advantage when the team decides to do something."

Third, the sales representatives were on salary. They were not on commission. They participated in the profit sharing and ASOP plans in which all other associates participated.

As in other areas of Gore, the individual success stories came from diverse backgrounds. McCarter related one of these success stories as follows:

> I interviewed Sam one day. I didn't even know why I was interviewing him actually. Sam was retired from AT&T. After 25 years, he took the golden parachute and went down to Sun Lakes to play golf. He played golf a few months and got tired of that. He was selling life insurance.
>
> I sat reading the application; his technical background interested me. . . . He had managed an engineer-

ing department with 600 people. He'd managed manufacturing plants for AT&T and had a great wealth of experience at AT&T. He said, "I'm retired. I like to play golf, but I just can't do it every day so I want to do something else. Do you have something around here I can do?" I was thinking to myself, this is one of these guys I would sure like to hire, but I don't know what I would do with him.

> The thing that triggered me was the fact that he said he sold insurance and here is a guy with a high degree of technical background selling insurance. He had marketing experience, international marketing experience. So the bell went off in my head that we were trying to introduce a new product into the marketplace that was a hydrocarbon leak protection cable. You can bury it in the ground and in a matter of seconds it could detect a hydrocarbon (gasoline, etc.). I had a couple of other guys working on it who hadn't been very successful with marketing it. We were having a hard time finding a customer.

> Well, I thought that kind of a product would be like selling insurance. If you think about it, why should you protect your tanks? It's an insurance policy that things are not leaking into the environment. That has implications, big-time monetary. So, actually, I said, "Why don't you come back Monday? I have just the thing for you." So he did. We hired him; he went to work, a very energetic guy. Certainly a champion of the product, he picked right up on it, ran with it single-handed. . . . Now it's a growing business. It certainly is a valuable one, too, for the environment.

In the implementation of its marketing strategy, Gore relied on cooperative and word-of-mouth advertising. Cooperative advertising was especially used to promote Gore-Tex fabric products, which were sold through a number of clothing manufacturers and distributors, including Apparel Technologies, Lands' End, Austin Reed, Timberland, Woolrich, North Face, Grandoe, and Michelle Jaffe. Gore engaged in cooperative advertising because the associates believed positive experiences with any one product would carry over to purchases of other and more Gore-Tex fabric products. Apparently, this strategy was paying off. Richard Zuckerwar, president of the Grandoe Corporation, said about his company's introduction of Gore-Tex gloves. "Sports activists have had the benefit of Gore-Tex gloves to protect their hands from the elements. . . . With this handsome collection of gloves . . . you can have warm, dry hands without sacrificing style."

The power of informal marketing techniques extended beyond consumer products. According to McCarter, "In the technical end of the business, company reputation probably is most important. You have to have a good reputation with your company." He went on to say that without a good reputation, a company's products would not be considered seriously by many industrial customers. In other words, the sale was often made before the representative called. Gore had been very successful using its marketing strategies to secure a market leadership position in a number of areas ranging from waterproof outdoor clothing to vascular grafts.

Acknowledgments

A number of sources were especially helpful in providing background material for this case. The most important sources were the W. L. Gore associates who generously shared their time and viewpoints about the company. We especially appreciate the input received from Anita McBride, who spent hours with us sharing her personal experiences as well as providing many resources, including internal documents and videotapes. In addition, Trish Hearn and Dave McCarter added much to this case by sharing their personal experiences and ensuring that the case accurately reflected the Gore company and culture.

REFERENCES

Aburdene, Patricia, and John Nasbitt. *Reinventing the Corporation.* New York: Warner Books, 1985.

Angrist, S. W. "Classless Capitalists," *Forbes,* May 9, 1983, pp. 123–24.

Franlesca, L. "Dry and Cool," *Forbes,* August 27, 1984, p. 126. "The Future Workplace," *Management Review,* July 1986, pp. 22–23.

Hoerr, J. "A Company Where Everybody Is the Boss," *Business Week,* April 15, 1985, p. 98.

Levering, Robert. *The 100 Best Companies to Work for in America.*

McKendrick, Joseph. "The Employees as Entrepreneur," *Management World,* January 1985, pp. 12–13.

Milne, M. J. "The Gorey Details," *Management Review,* March 1985, pp. 16–17.

Posner, B. G. "The First Day on the Job," *Inc.,* June 1986, pp. 73–75.

Price, Kathy. "Firm Thrives Without Boss," *AZ Republic,* February 2, 1986.

Rhodes, Lucien. "The Un-Manager," *Inc.,* August 1982, p. 34.

Simmons, J. "People Managing Themselves: Un-Management at W. L. Gore Inc.," *Journal for Quality and Participation,* December 1987, pp. 14–19.

Trachtenberg, J. A. "Give Them Stormy Weather," *Forbes,* March 24, 1986, pp. 172–74.

Ward, Alex. "An All-Weather Idea," *The New York Times Magazine,* November 10, 1985, sec. 6.

Weber, Joseph. "No Bosses. And Even 'Leaders' Can't Give Orders," *Business Week,* December 10, 1990, pp. 196–97.

"Wilbert L. Gore," *Industry Week,* October 17, 1983, pp. 48–49.

C A S E   7
Three Roads to Innovation
Ronald A. Mitsch

Innovation is important to most companies, but it is our lifeblood at 3M. We like to keep innovation coming from all directions: by developing new technologies and new applications for them, by assessing customer needs, and by anticipating market trends in all areas in which we operate.

That presents a considerable management challenge. How do you develop all those channels for innovation and keep them open? How do you turn innovation into product successes? How do you ensure that those processes are going on, day in and day out, year in and year out?

One thing 3M discovered is that innovation does not just happen unless you make sure people know it is a top priority—and then provide them with enough freedom and resources to make it work. It certainly is not going to happen without top management's commitment to innovation as a key ingredient in the company's overall business strategy and planning.

Journal of Business Strategy. Sept/Oct 1990, pp. 18–21. Reprinted with permission of Faulkner & Gray. Inc., II Penn Plaza. New York, NY 10001. 800-535-8403.

Finally, it will not happen without a continuing reassessment of the barriers to innovation that tend to develop over time, despite management's best efforts. To keep abreast of the pace of technological change in the global marketplace, this company needs to continually enhance the prospects for successful innovation. Ultimately, the goal of innovation must be continued quality growth.

One of 3M's best-known examples of quality growth is also a classic case of how the company nurtures one channel of innovation: the development of new technologies and new applications for existing technologies.

3M scientist Arthur Fry had the freedom and found the resources in the company to develop Post-it brand Notes. At the time, he was working on a bookshelf-arranger tape. While doing research for this project, he came up with the idea for a removable, sticky-backed bookmarker as he was singing in a church choir.

Fry began devoting more of his time to the sticky-backed pieces of paper and less and less time to the bookshelf tape, especially when he realized that the former promised to open up a whole new channel of communication. No one complained, because 3M has a company policy that encourages researchers to use 15 percent of their time on projects of their own choosing.

The adhesive Fry used was developed by another scientist, Spencer Silver, in 3M's corporate research laboratories. It was a technology available to Fry and to any other researcher in the company.

At one point, Post-it Notes faced the possibility of an early demise when an initial market test failed. But management sponsors gave it a second life. They personally took the product into the field to see how customers responded.

Freedom, sharing of technologies, and management sponsorship are all essential ingredients of the lab-to-market channel of innovation. These elements have been institutionalized in the 3M culture.

In the company's formative years, 3M's president, William L. McKnight, established policies and philosophies that have withstood the test of more than six decades. He was convinced that new product development and diversification were important to the company's continued growth. McKnight established a practice of promotion from within, encouraged individual initiative, and gave people room to grow on the job.

He also believed that failure is not fatal. Freedom to make honest mistakes is a good general policy, but it is particularly applicable to innovation. No person likes to fail, but it does happen occasionally when a company wants to grow by sponsoring new products and taking risks. The important thing is, one mistake is not a ticket to oblivion.

Out of McKnight's philosophies have developed policies like the 15 percent option, management sponsorship, and a dual-ladder system of promotion. Laboratory employees can advance up a technical ladder, as well as a management ladder, and continue with their first love—research and development.

McKnight's philosophies have been passed on from one management level to another, from one generation to another. But more recent managements have also set strategies to reinforce the innovation philosophy.

Nurturing New Products

To ensure that the company's early pattern of growth through innovative new products continues, a quantifiable new products target has become part of 3M's financial goals. *The company aims to achieve at least 25 percent of its growth each year through new products developed within the last five years.* Every operating unit and its people are evaluated on their ability to reach this goal. To encourage innovation, 3M, in the past decade, has increased the ratio of spending on R&D from 4.6 percent of sales to 6.5 percent.

3M continues to expand and build on two dozen core technologies, which provide a rich source of new products. From the company's nonwoven technology have come oil sorbents; from adhesives, a new class of foam-backed tapes that can replace mechanical fasteners; from fluorochemicals, a new line of carpet stain release treatments; and from the company's oldest technology, abrasives, a line of microabrasives for finishing and polishing high-tech components.

3M does research and development on three levels. Division laboratories develop products and technologies for specific markets, doing shorter-term research for the most part. Sector laboratories work on technologies and applications the divisions will need three to ten years from now. Corporate laboratories conduct basic research that may not lead to products for ten to twenty years.

Sharing technologies and these laboratory resources across the company is of prime importance. Whereas products belong to individual operating units, technologies belong to anyone in the company who needs them. Both formal and informal forums allow technical people from all of the company's divisions and corporate and sector laboratories to share information.

Innovation is recognized in many ways. Two examples: The Golden Step program honors cross-functional teams that introduce successful new products. The Carleton Society, a hall of fame for 3M scientists, honors those who have made long-range contributions to 3M's product and technological leadership. All of these steps nurture the lab-to-market channel.

Yet, the lab-to-market channel is only one route to innovation from which the company derives its growth. Equally important are assessing customer needs and anticipating market trends. All three are increasingly intertwined and essential to innovation.

From 3M's standpoint, one of the critical issues facing the company is to continually focus activities throughout the corporation to produce quality growth. Each of our operating units is encouraged to spend more time in planning and setting priorities for product development based on customer needs and expectations.

The question is, How do we balance priority setting with a climate of freedom? Prioritizing and providing freedom to innovate cannot be trade-offs; both are needed.

Contrary to what one might think, we have found that prioritizing not only enhances productivity and the flow of the products but also affords individual researchers more time for projects of their own choosing.

Once the priorities are in place, the second critical challenge is to develop the products and bring them to market as quickly as possible. The idea is to overcome time-consuming delays and roadblocks built into traditional new product development schedules. Product development often has moved from laboratory to market in sequential order. Process development, marketing, manufacturing, packaging, and other functions become involved step-by-step. But by having all functions involved from the start, development time can be compressed dramatically.

After priorities are established, cross-functional teams are empowered by management to design and develop a product that will meet customer expectations. Several 3M divisions have set up cross-functional action teams to address their most important new product challenges.

The Occupational Health and Environmental Safety Division cut its product development time in half through this process. It substantially increased the number of major new products introduced through action teams consisting of laboratory, marketing, manufacturing, engineering, quality, packaging, and financial people.

Each team is led by a product champion, someone who believes strongly in the value of the project and is committed to making it successful. Each team also has a management sponsor who serves as a cheerleader, helps get access to needed resources, and helps teams stay on track.

A third critical issue for the 1990s is the need to satisfy customer expectations. Staying close to customers is a 3M tradition that dates back to McKnight. He believed in going into the back shops of factories to see how the company's products were being used and to get ideas for new products. The vertical organizational structure he set up has made it easy to keep 3M operating units small enough so that people, from top management on down, get to know their customers.

In the 1990s, 3M is adding some new twists to this practice. The company's divisions are doing more involved market research to pinpoint present and future customer needs. The goal is to reemphasize a longstanding tradition of regularly sending lab people into the field to help keep research focused on high-priority projects that meet customer expectations.

Cross-functional teams work closely with customers. For example, many of 3M's carpet treatments and many of its tape closures for disposable diapers were developed either in joint efforts or in close consultation with carpet-fiber makers and diaper makers.

A recent addition to 3M's line of data cartridges for off-line storage of computer data illustrates how innovation occurs in response to changing customer needs and expectations.

The company's Data Storage Products Division found that with equipment and usage changing, one computer maker needed a cartridge that operated in environmental temperature extremes, another wanted to reduce friction in tape handling, and a third needed better acoustic noise properties.

A multifunctional team developed a new line of cartridges that not only met those challenges but also operated at higher speeds. Other data cartridge users, as well as the three customers seeking special features, are benefiting from this new product line.

Another major channel of innovation—anticipating market trends—also requires the organization to stay close to the customer.

Studying industry trends and talking to customers of our X-ray films made it clear that electronic diagnostic equipment was the wave of the future. That knowledge prompted the development of one of the company's most recent new products—the 3M Laser Imager for electronic medical imaging.

The Laser Imager "writes" digital signals from CAT scanners and other electronic diagnostic equipment onto a proprietary 3M film. It gives doctors a high-quality, hard-copy image of the scanner information that they had never had before.

Development of the Laser Imager drew on existing 3M imaging, materials, and hardware technologies. The high-priority effort eventually brought together a team from five different laboratories from the United States and abroad, as well as outside optical suppliers.

The project was initiated by management, but it was the persistence and diligence of the team that proved to be the driving force once the project began.

Failure is Not Fatal

If we gain a lot from each successful program at 3M, we also learn as much or more from every failure. For example, we tried to market a line of suntan lotions that adhered to the skin without being sticky; it protected the skin even after a 30 minute swim. There was nothing wrong with the product's performance: however, we were not successful in the marketplace. The suntan lotions were competing against the products of well-established competitors who offered broad lines of well-known skin care products.

CASE 8
The Scaffold Plank Incident
Stewart C. Malone and Brad Brown

What had started as a typically slow February day in the lumber business had turned into a moral dilemma. With 12 inches of snow covering the ground, construction (and lumber shipments) had ground to a halt and on the 26th of the month, the company was still $5,000 below break-even point. In the three years since he had been in the business, Bob Hopkins knew that a losing February was nothing unusual, but the country seemed to be headed for a recession, and as usual, housing starts were leading the way into the abyss.

Bob had gone to work for a commercial bank immediately after college but soon found the bureaucracy to be overwhelming and his career progress appeared to be written in stone. At the same time he was considering changing jobs, one of his customers, John White, offered him a job at White Lumber Company. The job was as a "trader," a position that involved both buying and selling lumber. The compensation was incentive-based and there was no cap on how much a trader could earn. White Lumber, although small in size, was one of the bank's best accounts. John White was not only a director of the bank but one of the community's leading citizens.

It was a little after 8:00 A.M. when Bob received a call from Stan Parrish, the lumber buyer at Quality Lumber. Quality was one of White Lumber's best retail dealer accounts, and Bob and Stan had established a good relationship.

"Bob, I need a price and availability on 600 pieces of 3 × 12 Doug fir-rough-sawn—2 & better grade—16-feet long," said Stan, after exchanging the usual pleasantries.

"No problem, Stan. We could have those ready for pickup tomorrow and the price would be $470 per thousand board feet."

"The price sounds good, Bob. I'll probably be getting back to you this afternoon with a firm order," Stan replied.

Bob poured a third cup of coffee and mentally congratulated himself. Not bad, he thought—a two-truck order and a price that guaranteed full margin. It was only a half-hour later that Mike Fayerweather, his partner, asked Bob if he had gotten any inquiries on a truck of 16-foot scaffold plank. As Bob said he hadn't, alarm bells began to go off in his brain. While Stan had not said anything about scaffold plank, the simi-

This case was prepared by Stewart C. Malone and Brad Brown, University of Virginia. This case was prepared as a basis for class discussion rather than to illustrate either effective or ineffective handling of administrative situations.

larities between the inquiries seemed to be more than coincidence.

While almost all lumber undergoes some sort of grading, the grading rules on scaffold plank were unusually restrictive. Scaffold planks are the wooden planks that are suspended between metal supports, often many stories above the ground. When you see painters and window-washers six stories in the air, they generally are standing on scaffold plank. The lumber had to be free of most of the natural defects found in ordinary construction lumber and had to have unusually high strength in flexing. Most people would not be able to tell certified scaffold plank from ordinary lumber, but it was covered by its own rules in the grading book, and if you were working 10 stories above the ground, you definitely wanted to have certified scaffold plank underneath you. White Lumber did not carry scaffold plank, but its rough 3 × 12s certainly would fool all but the expertly trained eye.

At lunch, Bob discussed his concerns about the inquiry with Mike.

"Look, Bob, I just don't see where we have a problem. Stan didn't specify scaffold plank, and you didn't quote him on scaffold plank," observed Mike. "We aren't even certain that the order is for the same material."

"I know all that, Mike," said Bob, "but we both know that four inquiries with the same tally is just too big a coincidence, and three of those inquiries were for Paragraph 171 scaffold plank. It seems reasonable to assume that Stan's quotation is for the same stuff."

"Well, it's obvious that our construction lumber is a good deal cheaper than the certified plank. If Stan is quoting based on our 2 & better grade and the rest of his competition is quoting on scaffold plank, then he will certainly win the job," Mike said.

"Maybe I should call Stan back and get more information on the specifitions of the job. It may turn out that this isn't scaffold plank job, and all of these problems will just disappear."

The waitress slipped the check between the two lumbermen. "Well, that might not be such a great idea, Bob. First, Stan may be a little ticked off if you were suggesting he might be doing something unethical. It could blow the relations between our companies. Second, suppose he does say that the material is going to be used for scaffolding. We would no longer be able to say we didn't know what it was going to be used for, and our best legal defense is out the window. I'd advise against calling him."

Bob thought about discussing the situation with John White, but White was out of town. Also, White prided himself on giving his traders a great deal of autonomy. Going to White too often for answers to questions was perceived as showing a lack of initiative and responsibility.

Against Mike's earlier warnings, Bob called Stan after lunch and discovered to his dismay that the material was going to be used as scaffold plank.

"Listen, Bob, I've been trying to sell this account for three months and this is the first inquiry that I've had a chance on. This is really important to me personally and to my superiors here at Quality. With this sale, we could land this account."

"But, Stan, we both know that our material doesn't meet the specs for scaffold plank."

"I know, I know," said Stan, "but I'm not selling it to the customer as scaffold plank. It's just regular construction lumber as far as we are both concerned. That's how I've sold it, and that's what will show on the invoices. We're completely protected. Now just between you and me, the foreman on the job winked at me and told me it was going to be scaffolding, but they're interested in keeping their costs down too. Also, they need this lumber by Friday, and there just isn't any scaffold plank in the local market."

"It just doesn't seem right to me," replied Bob.

"Look, I don't particularly like it, either. The actual specifications call for 2-inch thick material, but since it isn't actually scaffold plank, I'm going to order 3-inch planks. That is an extra inch of strength, and we both know that the load factors given in the engineering tables are too conservative to begin with. There's no chance that the material could fail in use. I happen to know that Haney Lumber is quoting a non-scaffold grade in a 2-inch material. If we don't grab this, someone else will and the material will be a lot worse than what we are going to supply."

When Bob continued to express hesitation, Stan said "I won't hear about the status of the order until tomorrow, but we both know that your material will do this job OK—scaffold plank or not. The next year or two in this business are going to be lean for everyone, and our job—yours and mine—is putting lumber on job sites, not debating how many angels can dance on the head of a pin. Now if Quality can't count on you doing your job as a supplier, there are plenty of other wholesalers calling here every day who want our business. You better decide if you are going to be one of the survivors or not! I'll talk to you in the morning, Bob."

The next morning, Bob found a note on his desk telling him to see John White ASAP. Bob entered John's oak-paneled office and described the conversation with Stan yesterday. John slid a company sales order across the desk, and Bob saw it was a sales order for the 3 × 12s to Quality Lumber. In the space for the salesman's name, Bob saw that John had filled in "Bob Hopkins." Barely able to control his anger, Bob said, "I

don't want anything to do with this order. I thought White Lumber was an ethical company, and here we are doing the same thing that all the fly-by-nighters do," sputtered Bob in concluding his argument.

John White looked at Bob and calmly puffed on his pipe. "The first thing you better do, Bob, is to calm down and put away your righteous superiority for a moment. You can't make or understand a good decision when you are as lathered up as you are. You are beginning to sound like a religious nut. What makes you think that you have the monopoly on ethical behavior? You've been out of college for four or five years, while I've been making these decisions for 40 years. If you go into the industry or the community and compare your reputation with mine, you'll find out that you aren't even in the same league."

Bob knew John White was right. He had, perhaps, overstated his case, and in doing so, sounded like a zealot. When he relaxed and felt as though he was once again capable of rational thought, he said, "We both know that this lumber is going to be used for a purpose for which it is probably not suitable. Granted, there is only a very small chance that it will fail, but I don't see how we can take that chance."

"Look, Bob, I've been in this business for a long time, and I've seen practices that would curl your hair. Undershipping (shipping 290 pieces when the order calls for 300), shipping material a grade below what was ordered, bribing building inspectors and receiving clerks, and so on. We don't do those things at my company."

"Don't we have a responsibility to our customers, though?" asked Bob.

"Of course we do, Bob, but we aren't policemen, either. Our job is to sell lumber that is up to specification. I can't and won't be responsible for how the lumber is used after it leaves our yard. Between the forest and the final user, lumber may pass through a dozen transactions before it reaches the ultimate user. If we are to assume responsibility for every one of those transactions, we would probably have time to sell about four boards a year. We have to assume, just like every other business, that our suppliers and our customers are knowledgeable and will also act ethically. But whether they do or don't, it is not possible for us to be their keepers."

Bob interjected, "But we have reason to believe that this material will be used as scaffolding. I think we have an obligation to follow up on that information."

"Hold on, just a second, Bob. I told you once we are not the police. We don't even know who the final user is, so how are we going to follow up on this? If Stan is jerking us around, he certainly won't tell us. And even if we did know, what would we do? If we are going to do this consistently, that means we would have to ask every customer who the final end user is.

Most of our customers would interpret that as us trying to bypass them in the distribution channel. They won't tell us, and I can't blame them. If we carry your argument to its final conclusion, we'll have to start taking depositions on every invoice we sell.

"In the Quality Lumber instance, we are selling material to the customer as specified by the customer, Stan at Quality Lumber. The invoice will be marked. 'This material is not suitable for use as scaffold plank.' Although I'm not a lawyer, I believe that we have fulfilled our legal obligation. We have a signed purchase order and are supplying lumber that meets the specifications. I know we have followed the practices that are customary in the industry. Finally, I believe that our material will be better than anything else that could conceivably go on the job. Right now, there is no 2-inch dense 171 scaffold plank in this market, so it is not as though a better grade could be supplied in the time allotted. I would argue that we are ethically obligated to supply this lumber. If anyone is ethically at fault, it is probably the purchasing agent who specified a material that is not available."

When Bob still appeared to be unconvinced, John White asked him, "What about the other people here at the company? You're acting as though you are the only person who has a stake in this. It may be easy for you to turn this order down—you've got a college degree and a lot of career options. But I have to worry about all of the people at this company. Steve out there on the forklift never finished high school. He's worked here thirty years and if he loses this job, he'll probably never find another one. Janet over in bookkeeping has a disabled husband. While I can't afford to pay her very much, our health insurance plan keeps their family together. With the bills her husband accumulates in a year, she could never get him on another group insurance plan if she lost this job.

"Bob, I'm not saying that we should do anything and then try to justify it, but business ethics in the real world is not the same thing you studied in the classroom. There it is easy to say, 'Oh, there is an ethical problem here. We better not do that.' In the classroom, you have nothing to lose by taking the morally superior ground. Out here, companies close, people lose their jobs, lives can be destroyed. To always say, 'No, we won't do that' is no better than having no ethics at all. Ethics involves making tough choices, weighing costs and benefits. There are no hard-and-fast answers in these cases. We just have to approach each situation individually."

As Bob left John's office, he was more confused than ever. When he first entered his office, he had every intention of quitting in moral indignation, but John's arguments had made a lot of sense to him, and he both trusted and respected John. After all, John White had a great deal more experience than he did and was highly respected in both the community and the lumber industry. Yet he was still uncomfortable with the decision. Was selling lumber to Quality merely a necessary adjustment of his ivory tower ethics to the real world of business? Or was it the first fork in the road to a destination he did not want to reach?

C A S E   9
Beer and Wine Industries: Bartles & Jaymes
Per V. Jenster

At the end of 1986, Bartles & Jaymes conquered the number one position in the wine cooler industry after coming in second to California Coolers since this product hit the consumer goods market. Going into 1987, Bartles & Jaymes and its corporate parent, Ernest & Julio Gallo Winery, were faced with the task of maintaining this market position and increasing sales of its newest product—the wine cooler.

Professor Per V. Jenster. IMD, Lausanne. Switzerland. Reprinted with permission. The author gratefully acknowledges the assistance of students Morlon Bell. Michele Goggins, and Mary Kay, as well as the support provided by the McIntire Foundation. Copyright © 1987.

History of the Firm

Ernest and Julio Gallo Winery, the world's largest, began in 1938 at a tragic point in the brothers' lives. They had just inherited their father Joseph's vineyard after he shot his wife, reportedly chased Ernest and Julio with a shotgun, and committed suicide. Suddenly they were faced with operating the vineyard where they grew up and had gone to work upon completing their education (high school for Julio and junior college for Ernest). The business of growing grapes was all they knew. Joseph Gallo, an immigrant from Italy, came to Modesto, California, and began his small grape-producing company. The fledgling company survived Prohibition due to the fact that the government allowed wine production for medicinal and religious use. The Depression dealt the small company a somewhat more devastating blow. It was at this company low point that Joseph decided on such a dramatic solution to his problems. Though he may have solved his problems, Joseph left his relatively young sons a burden of responsibility and decision making. Shortly after their parents' deaths, Prohibition was repealed and the brothers decided to move from grape growing to wine producing. With two pamphlets on wine making from the local public library and less that $6,000 in hand, the ambitious Gallos began their empire.

Gallo's climb to its dominant position in the wine industry (see Exhibit 1) began slowly. In the 1930s and 1940s, Ernest developed his acute marketing sense and Julio cultivated and refined his wine-making expertise. Initially they sold their product in bulk to bottlers on the East Coast, but in 1938 they decided it would be more profitable to bottle the wine under a Gallo label. In the 1950s, Gallo greatly increased its success with a high-alcohol, low-price product called Thunderbird. This product became exceptionally popular on skid rows and increased Gallo's profitability, but it may have done irreparable damage by saddling Gallo with a "gutter" image. In the 1960s and early 1970s, Gallo's image, not sales, was further tarnished by the "pop-wine" craze of which it was a leader with such products as Boone's Farm and Spanada wines. In the mid-1970s, Ernest Gallo became conscious of and concerned about the fact that even though it had formidable sales, it also had a "brownbag," jug-wine image. At that time, the company decided to attempt to upgrade its image and at the same time maintain its market share and sales. As part of this attempt, it began to produce premium table wines such as Zinfandel, Sauvignon Blanc, Ruby Cabernet, and French Colombard. This push to improve its image continued to be a dominating theme for Gallo.

As Gallo grew, it not only developed its wine sales but became extensively vertically integrated. It had divisions in virtually every step of the wine-producing process. The brothers owned one of the largest intrastate trucking companies in California, which was used to haul wine, grapes, raw materials, sand, lime, etc. Gallo was the only wine producer that made its own bottles, and its Midcal Aluminum Company supplied it with screw tops. Unlike most other wine producers, Gallo took an active role in the marketing of its products. Typical wineries would turn their products over to independent distributors who represented several producers and expected the distributor to get the product to the consumer. These distributors, on the other hand, felt their job consisted of taking orders and making deliveries. Gallo owned many of its distributors, and the independent distributors it used had to be willing to submit to Gallo's regimentation. Gallo was known to "encourage" its independent distributors to exclusively distribute Gallo products. Ten years ago, the Federal Trade Commission took offense at this, charging Gallo with unfair competition and forcing Gallo to sign a consent order. In 1984, the FTC removed the order due to the fact that the wine industry had become more competitive.

In its 50-year history, Gallo developed an extensive product line. It had products geared toward the low-priced, jug-wine market (Carlo Rossi, Chablis Blanc, etc.). It also had a replete category of premium wines, selling more than any competitor, but growth in this market was limited due to the fact that Gallo did not have snob appeal. In 1984, Gallo entered the wine cooler category (a carbonated drink with half white wine and half citrus juice) with its Bartles & Jaymes wine cooler. Gallo followed the lead of such industry innovators as California Cooler, Sun Country Coolers, etc., which fit well with its strategy of building market share through skillful marketing and sales, but not introducing inventive new products. Bartles & Jaymes was marketed in 12-ounce green bottles similar to those used for Michelob beer and aimed at a more sophisticated consumer than its competitors. To help promote this upgraded image, Gallo tried to distance itself from Bartles & Jaymes, and many consumers did not know that Gallo wine was used to make the coolers. In the summer of 1986, Bartles & Jaymes took over the number one position in the wine cooler market with a share of 22.1 percent.

With that initial $6,000, some ingenuity, a little luck, and a lot of spunk, the Gallo brothers built the world's preeminent wine dynasty. Because Gallo was a private, tightly held company, there was no public financial data, but it was estimated that it had annual sales of $1 billion and yearly earnings of $50 million. In comparison, Joe E. Seagram and Sons, the second largest winery, had revenues of $350 million and lost money on its best-selling table wines in 1985.

Exhibit 1   1985 Share of U.S. Wine Market

E. & J. Gallo Winery	26.1%
Seagram & Sons	8.3
Canandaigua Wine	5.4
Brown-Forman	5.1
National Distillers	4.0
Heublein	3.7
Imports	23.4
All others	24.0

Source: From *Advertising Age.* March 24, 1986. Reprinted with permission of Crain Communications Inc.

Background on Key Executives

E. & J. Gallo was a private company owned and operated by the Gallo brothers, Ernest and Julio. Julio, the 77-year-old president of the firm, and Ernest, chairman of the board at 78, ran their company in a very dichotomous manner. Julio was in charge of producing the wine and Ernest marketed and distributed it. They operated in their separate worlds and often did not have daily contact. It seemed to be a game—Julio trying to produce more than Ernest could sell and Ernest trying to sell more than Julio could produce. But the game apparently worked and provided the company with good returns.

Julio, the more easygoing of the two, described himself as a "farmer at heart." He spent much of his time in the fields and overseeing the wine making. Though definitely not a pushover, Julio was not the hard-core, intense businessman that his brother Ernest was. Ernest ruled over the company and usually made the final decisions. He was characterized as being polite, but blunt. He could not bear to relinquish power and control, and it was at his insistence that everything about the operations of the firm was kept secret. He could be a very demanding, driving boss, and when asked about the secret to Gallo's success, he remarked it was a "constant striving for perfection in every aspect of our business."

A looming concern, though not openly addressed or dealt with at Gallo, was the brothers' advancing age. Julio seemed to be training and grooming his son, Robert, and his son-in-law, James Coleman, in his area of expertise. Ernest, on the other hand, had no heir apparent. Two of his sons, David and Joseph, worked with him, but neither was viewed as having the ability to take over their father's job. Joseph was felt to give uneven decisions, and David was described as "occasionally bizarre," The firm had many intelligent, able, top-level executives, but they had no power to make decisions and predominantly strove to please Ernest. The deaths of Ernest and Julio, which were inevitable, could prove to be devastating for the firm.

Internal Operations

Because Gallo was so tightly held and secretive, it was hard to determine how and why things were done the way they were—maybe only Ernest knew. A few loyal senior managers ran the divisions of the vertically integrated firm and reported to Ernest. He had a hand in all major decisions and procedures and went so far as to help write a 300-page, very detailed training manual for sales representatives. Gallo was so secretive that at times even its own employees did not know what was happening. According to Diana Kelleher, former marketing manager at Gallo. "I never saw a profit-and-loss statement; Ernest wouldn't tell anyone the cost of raw materials, overhead, or packaging."

Industry History, and Analysis

It would be difficult to pinpoint exactly when the wine cooler industry emerged. Three separate events were cited to mark the beginning of this prosperous industry. In 1977, Joseph Bianchi, owner of Bianchi Vineyards, observed people at a summer party mixing Seven-Up with wine. In 1981, Thomas Steid, owner of Canada Dry/Graf's Bottling Company, formulated his own wine cooler recipe. The event that was commonly viewed as the beginning of this industry stemmed from the concoction of Michael M. Crete and R. Stuart Bewley produced by California Cooler.

Crete and Bewley's drink was initially served in 1972, to their friends. Little did they know that this new refresher would be a huge success a decade later. Batches of white wine and fruit juice were mixed in a beer barrel and served from a plastic hose. Labels were stuck on by hand and an average workday consisted of bottling 100 to 150 cases. As this product was marketed in the early 1980s, sales began to increase steadily. This campaign spurred national attention toward the new market.

At the point of the cooler's entry, other sectors of the beverage industry were experiencing declining sales. The wine industry had experienced declining table wine sales for two years in a row at the beginning of the 1980s. Likewise, the beer industry was faced with declining sales. It was costing both industries more in advertising to keep their regular customers. Several factors caused such a response in the consumer market. First, drunken driving laws and the crackdown on drinking that they spurred led to more awareness about the negative effects of alcohol. Public interest groups such as MADD (Mothers Against Drunk Driving) played a key role in changing the consumer's perceptions of drinking. Second, there was growing concern for fitness. As the health-conscious consumers grew in number, the tendency to indulge in alcoholic beverages declined. Third, the raising of the legal drinking age presented obstacles to increasing sales. Since younger adults consumed a significant percentage of the alcohol sold, the change in age cut out some sales originally anticipated by beer and wine producers. Fourth, the lobbying to remove liquor advertising from television showed wineries and breweries as the villains in society.

In view of societal factors, a method was needed to help the alcohol industries survive. Thus, an alternative to beer and wine appeared to be the solution in the eyes of Crete and Bewley. They saw the potential and seized the opportunity to capitalize on the venture. To achieve a successful outcome, however, the product had to be positioned properly. The wine cooler was a fruity-tasting, slightly cloudy beverage made from chablis, blended citrus-pineapple juice, fructose, and a slight amount of carbonation. Its targeted consumers were young adults from legal drinking age to 34 years old, both male and female. The cooler was marketed in the same manner as beer, particularly its "coldbox," refrigerator bottling. It was to be less of an elitist drink than wine. It contained more alcohol than beer but less alcohol than wine.

For the wine cooler industry to succeed, several characteristics had to be present. Taste was an important factor to provide a basis for differentiation between products. Points of difference were sought to make individual brands stand out, by varying fruit flavors, packaging, or advertising techniques. Another major characteristic was merchandising, which was relevant to the success of any consumer market. In the wine industry particularly, price was the key to merchandising. It could be extremely difficult for competitors to come up with original ideas to differentiate their product, so most relied on price to help them capture a reasonable percentage of the market.

Several viewpoints have been given about wine coolers. The single-service focus was the major thrust of the cooler's marketing plan. It could be carried easily (exactly like beer) and did not concentrate heavily on the jug mentality of wineries. Coolers also cut across beverage boundaries by "touting the fizz of soft drinks, the popularity of white wine, the freshness of citrus juice, plus a bit of fructose to satisfy the sweet tooth." The cooler fit the desires of the current pluralistic consumer society. It was viewed as "wine for the common man" because it appealed to the beer drinker who wanted a little more alcohol, the wine drinker who wanted a little less, the calorie- and taste-conscious, and the first-time wine drinkers put off by the snobbery of the wine elite. The marketing module appeared to contain all the elements of success—"a firm product identity; a well-defined package and price image; a powerful distribution channel that stressed cold-box merchandising to capitalize on its 'cool' perception and enhance its full price and profit positioning; and advertising that communicated a refreshing message to the public." This segment showed second-generation development. Three trends were cited in the existing industry. One trend focused on the low alcohol content of approximately 6 percent. This aspect was probably influenced by the anti–drunk driving campaigns. Sales of coolers were said to have been spurred by this concern. Another trend was geared toward its thirst-quenching characteristic. Its refreshing health perspective was the focus of the last trend. Coolers were professed to be healthful since they contained half citrus juice.

The wine cooler industry appeared particularly attractive because the product offered high margins and a low base with no capital requirements. It generated better gross dollar margins than beer or wine. The expected annual growth rate was projected to be 13 percent until 1993. The expected growth rate in 1986 was 69 percent. Cooler sales were estimated to account for 17 percent to 20 percent of total wine sales in 1986 as compared to only 1 percent in 1984.

In 1986, the cooler industry was faced with various trends in the beverage world. First, it was reported that Americans were drinking more soft drinks (April 1986). The alcohol industry was still faced with overall declines, but the wine industry was better situated than the beer industry due to the success of the wine cooler. It was predicted that the wine cooler industry would soon be viewed separately from the wine industry. The second area of concern involved the steadily increasing cost of competing. The fight for wholesale and retail distribution was intensifying. This led marketers to cut prices to acquire more shelf space and visibility. Also, coupons were used to increase distribution. As of August 1986, the dollar level was low and the investment spending was high.

The wine cooler industry consisted of approximately forty producers and 154 individual labels during the summer of 1986. Because of the high barriers to entry competition from other segments, particularly the breweries and wineries, did not appear to be substantial. Since the beer and wine markets were mature, the success achieved in the wine cooler industry caused them to take a second look at this area for potential profits. Even though breweries and wineries experienced decreasing sales, only a small portion was attributed to the boom in the wine cooler industry. The soft-drink industry, on the other hand, proved to be a minor problem for coolers due to increased consumption by consumers. The effect of the competition was not significantly shown in the sales figures for coolers, but the potential loomed in the background. Experts raised questions concerning cooler sales. Declines were predicted based on a speculated consumer interest in a variety of flavored drinks. Were coolers a fad or a new and growing industry?

Competition

When California Cooler began peddling its wine cooler, the competition was sparse and far from formidable. Initially, the cost of entry into the new market was relatively low. But by the first quarter of 1986, the world's largest winery, brewery, and distillery were all vying for the top spot and all three were holding fat bankrolls. The cost of entry into the market had risen to $10 million just for advertising. Cooler marketers and industry observers were confident this category would continue to grow steadily for the next few years. It was estimated that 60 to 65 million cases of coolers—including malt-based coolers—would have been sold by the end of 1987, up from 41 million cases in 1985. In 1987, more than 150 kinds of wine coolers were competing with the top seven coolers, which controlled about 90 percent of the market—E. & J. Gallo Winery's Bartles & Jaymes, Brown-Forman

Exhibit 2 Top 10 Cooler Brands' Share of the Market

	1986*	1985
1. Bartles & Jaymes	22.1%	17.5%
2. California Cooler	18.0	26.8
3. Sun Country	13.1	11.7
4. White Mountain	12.4	7.5
5. Calvin Cooler	8.3	6.5
6. Seagram's Golden	6.9	—
7. Seagram's Premium	5.5	9.3
8. Dewey Stevens	2.8	—
9. 20/20	2.5	3.7
10. La Croix	1.5	1.9

Source: From Impact Databank, 1986. Reprinted by permission of M. Shanken Communications, Inc.

*Estimate.

Exhibit 3 1986 Advertising Budgets

Bartles & Jaymes	$30,000,000
Seagram's	30,000,000
California Cooler	25,000,000
Dewey Stevens	20,000,000
Sun Country	20,000,000
White Mountain	12,000,000
Calvin Cooler	10,000,000

Source: From *Advertising Age,* March 24, 1986. Reprinted with permission of Crain Communications, Inc.

Corporation's California Cooler, Canandaigua Wine Company's Sun Country, Joseph Victori Wines' Calvin Cooler, Stroh Brewery Company's malt-based White Mountain cooler, and Joe E. Seagram and Sons' Premium and Golden coolers. (See Exhibit 2.)

Bartles & Jaymes

By October 1986, Gallo's Bartles & Jaymes wine cooler was the largest-selling cooler in the nation, with a 22.1 percent market share. Its standing was quite remarkable in light of Bartles & Jaymes' relatively narrow product line. Gallo produced only one flavor of wine cooler (6 percent alcohol). This clear, less sweet cooler came in sleek 12-ounce green bottles like those of imported beers and was available in the standard four-pack.

Two key factors, advertising and distribution, differentiated the industry leader from its competitors. In 1986, Gallo budgeted $30 million for advertising expenditures for Bartles & Jaymes (see Exhibit 3). The majority of this money was spent on an ad campaign in which Gallo chose to distance its cooler from the parent corporation by creating fictional proprietors named Frank Bartles and Ed Jaymes, who sat on their front porch while Frank delivered low-key, comical monologues about the product. An advertiser with the Bartles & Jaymes campaign said, "Most of the competition was using youthful music and showing young people doing all the predictable things. We thought that if we got into all those clichés, we'd get lost." This was all part of a cold, hard-edged effort on Gallo's part to maintain a sense of warm, down-home, folksy legitimacy around the TV spots that obviously had many Americans believing there really were a Frank Bartles and an Ed Jaymes.

Some observers, including a few of Gallo's competitors, were not as amused by Gallo's marketing strategy as most of America seemed to be. Tom Gibbs,

director of marketing for California Coolers, saw the ads as down-right deceptive. "Yuppies are not Gallo drinkers, so they (Gallo) have tried to disassociate their names from this market." Mr. Gibbs said the public did not know Frank and Ed were not on the level and believed consumers would turn away from the product if they knew the truth. He claimed his company had done interviews after which people quit drinking Bartles & Jaymes once they learned it was a Gallo product—a name, he says, "people equate with jug wines."

Jon Fredrikson, an industry analyst with San Francisco-based wine industry consultants Gomberg. Fredrikson & Associates, said the public might react negatively if the truth got out on a widespread basis, but added that wasn't likely.

Aileen Fredrikson, also with Gomberg, said the campaign had the dual effect of helping beer drinkers relate to the wine cooler market. "Young people can always be convinced to try something once," she said, "but this may be a way to get hard-core beer drinkers to try it, since it's two good ole boys selling it."

The channel of distribution chosen by Gallo was the second key factor in differentiating Bartles & Jaymes from its competitors. Unlike other wine cooler producers who distributed their products through beer distributors, Bartles & Jaymes used Gallo's extensive wine distributorship. Ernest Gallo handpicked each of these distributors and then planned strategies with them down to the last detail, analyzing traffic patterns in every store in the district and the number of Gallo cases each should stock. Ernest Gallo encouraged distributors to hire a separate sales force to sell his products alone. He also tried to persuade distributors to sell his wine exclusively.

California Cooler

Stuart Bewley and Michael Crete were partners who founded California Cooler Company, Stockton, California, just five years ago. The two childhood friends created the product when they started filling washtubs at beach parties with their special mixture—half white wine and half citrus juice. In September 1985, Brown-Forman, a Louisville-based distiller, bought out the segment leader California Cooler for $63 million in cash plus millions more in incentive payments based on future sales.

California Coolers contained 6 percent alcohol and came in a variety of flavors including tropical, Orange, and the original citrus flavor. Crucial to California Cooler's initial success was that it was marketed more as a beer than as a wine. From the beginning, Crete and Bewley wanted a quality package, and from their beer-drinking days, they felt nothing beat a Heineken bottle. So they packaged California Cooler in a green-tinged, twist-top, short-neck bottle, added a gold foil top, and sold it in four-packs for under $4. This, they figured, might draw some beer drinkers. Subsequently, to counter competition, California Cooler introduced several new packages, including 2-liter bottles, 198-milliliter bottles, and, in some areas, quarter and half barrels.

In another important step, they left the natural fruit pulp in the bottle and stressed it on the label. California Cooler was thus further removed from the clear, sipping wine category. California Cooler hoped to get the younger, natural-thinking consumers. The product was positioned as an informal, mainstream American drink, targeted toward males and females from 18 to 35 years of age.

Once the company broke even in early 1983, the co-founders began looking for an advertising agency to help broaden sales from its northern California base. Its only advertising up until that point was a spot radio jingle sung to the tune of the Beach Boys' hit "California Girls." The new advertising campaign positioned California Cooler not as a beer, not as a wine, but "beyond ordinary refreshment." These ads were funny put downs by outsiders who were slightly envious of the hot tubs, health food fetishes, and all-around casual lifestyles of Californians—including their namesake drink, California Cooler. Other ads featured young people and 1960s rock 'n roll. Brown-Forman Corporation spent over $20 million on this ad campaign in 1986, yet still lost its top standing to Bartles & Jaymes. In 1986, California Cooler had an 18.0 percent market share, down from 26.8 percent in 1985 (see Exhibit 2).

Unlike Bartles & Jaymes, California Coolers were distributed by beer distributors, not wine wholesalers. The founders of California Cooler wanted their cooler to be in the "cold box" or refrigerator of a sales account. They felt the movement in beverages was out of the cold box, not the racks. Beer distributors were chosen because they typically had more accounts than their wine counterparts; beer distributors carried fewer products compared to the huge portfolios of wine wholesalers; and as "good ole boys," beer distributors represented their informal product better. More recently, though, to counter Gallo's tremendous distribution strength, California Cooler tried to take advantage of Brown-Forman's distribution muscle—it handled the popular Jack Daniels whiskey—and worked at broadening the overall market for coolers.

Sun Country

Sun Country coolers, produced by Canandaigua Wine, were the third-largest-selling wine coolers, with a 13.1 percent market share. Sun Country coolers were very similar to California Coolers: Both contained 6 percent alcohol; both retained the fruit pulp, which gave them a cloudy appearance; both were available in citrus, tropical, and orange flavors; and both were packaged in green bottles and sold in convenient four-packs or 2-liter bottles.

To help differentiate their product, Canandaigua expanded Sun Country's product line to include two new flavors, cherry and peach. They also pumped up advertising with a $25 million budget and celebrity spokespeople, including Charo, Cathy Lee Crosby, and The Four Tops. The ads targeted both men and women between the ages of 21 and 34.

Canandaigua also hoped to capitalize on exports of Sun Country, already available in Canada, Japan, South Africa, and the United Kingdom. As of 1986, about 600,000 of 10 million cases were exported.

White Mountain

Recognizing the appeal of wine coolers, several brewers entered the market with malt-based products. As of 1986, only Stroh's White Mountain cooler showed any real success and significant sales. White Mountain cooler had a market share of 12.4 percent, up from 7.5 percent in 1985. The majority of its sales came from states where it had a tax and distribution advantage over wine coolers. Several states like Pennsylvania, White Mountain's leading market, barred the sale of wine-based products in supermarkets and other food stores.

White Mountain cooler bore a closer resemblance to beer than to wine. It was derived from malt, but unless the consumers looked closely at the label or the advertising they wouldn't know it, and that was how the brewer wanted it. Rather than attempt to create a market for a subcategory of malt-based coolers, which could be misconstrued as a flavored beer, the brewers simply sold their products as "coolers," taking advantage of the imagery of the winebased products. White Mountain's label said it was an "alcohol beverage with natural fruit juices" and 5 percent alcohol content by weight.

White Mountain cooler was packaged in 12-ounce bottles and sold in six-packs like beer. Stroh's had over a $12 million ad budget behind White Mountain, targeting mainly 21- to 40-year-olds. Stroh's also distributed its cooler through its existing beer distributors.

Seagram

Joe E. Seagram & Sons produced both Seagram's Premium and Seagram's Golden wine coolers. Combined, these two coolers made up 12.4 percent of the market. Seagram's coolers were a clear liquid, not cloudy like those of Sun Country and California Cooler. They came in 12-ounce glass bottles and were available in fourpacks. Unlike the industry leaders, Bartles & Jaymes and California Cooler, which contained 6 percent alcohol, Seagram's coolers had just 4 percent alcohol. The Premium cooler came in a variety of flavors, including citrus, peach, wild berry, and apple cranberry.

Seagram's original ads for the Premium cooler were fast-paced scenes of young people playing outdoor sports, with energetic background music. The cooler ad was intentionally like a beer commercial because Seagram's was aiming its product at beer drinkers and encouraging them to switch. Though men consumed 80 percent of the beer sold, they tended to be skeptical of coolers. But since women consumed almost four times as much beer as wine, Seagram's hoped that women who switched would encourage men to join them.

The citrus-based Premium wine cooler did not receive the market leverage observers had expected. As a result, the company then backed Golden wine coolers, a new line, with a $25 million ad campaign. The campaign starred "Moonlighting" star Bruce Willis, who played the same roguish character he portrayed on the hit ABC-TV series. These ads were once again targeted toward women between the ages of 21 and 35.

Seagram's also introduced a new product into the market—Seagram's Golden Spirits. It was the first line of spirit-based drinks modeled after the wine cooler. It was sold in four-packs of 375-milliliter bottles that closely resembled the Golden wine cooler. The line's four flavors—Mandarin Vodka, Peach Melba Rum, Spiced Canadian (whiskey) and Sunfruit Gin—each contained 5.1 percent alcohol. These flavors were proprietary; consumers could not replicate them in their homes.

The spirit coolers were expected to appeal more to men and to an older audience than wine coolers did. "They're positioned somewhat more serious," said Thomas McInerney, executive VP-marketing, Seagram Distillers. "They are not being given the beach-party image of wine coolers."

Calvin

Calvin Cooler, produced by New York based Joseph Victori Wines, was the fifth-largest-selling cooler. The company broke into early dominance in New York City, thanks to a state law that allowed only New York state liquor products to be sold in grocery stores, when its cooler hit the market in 1984. As of 1986, Calvin Cooler had an 8.3 percent market share and distributed nearly 6 million cases to every state but South Dakota.

However, the cooler still sat behind competitors with stronger distribution channels and two or three times Calvin's $10 million ad budget.

Calvin coolers came in a full line of flavors, including raspberry, one of its most popular flavors. The product was available in both four-packs and 2-liter bottles.

Dewey Stevens

Dewey Stevens Premium Light, produced by Anheuser-Busch, was the first product of its kind. The wine cooler was sold in four-packs of 12-ounce bottles, each containing 4 percent alcohol and only 135 calories. Most wine coolers contained 5 percent to 6 percent alcohol and more than 200 calories. Dewey Stevens contained no artificial sweeteners; Anheuser-Busch cut the calories by cutting its wine content and adding water.

The ad campaign for the cooler made an appeal to active, young women and placed emphasis on the product's lower calorie content.

SELECTED REFERENCES

William Dunn, "Coolers Add Fizz to Flat Wine Market," *American Demographics* (March 1986), pp. 19–20.

Scott Hume, "Drop in Consumption a Sour Note for Industries," *Advertising Age*, April 7, 1986, p. 23.

J. D. Stacy, "The Wine Cooler Phenomenon," *Beverage World* (December 1984), pp. 49–50.

Patricia Winters, "Predict Big Chill for Wine Coolers," *Advertising Age*, August 11, 1986, p. 23.

CASE 10
Bennett's Machine Shop, Inc.

Arthur Sharplin

"This won't even be a one-page month," said Pat Bennett. "Worst month we've ever had." Pat was the owner of Bennett's Machine Shop, an automotive engine rebuilder in Lake Charles, Louisiana. He went on to explain what he meant by a "one-page month": "We write each engine job order on one line of a 32-line yellow legal pad. Last year, we figured out that a breakeven point was about 60 engines a month. If we have three pages in a month, we have really made some money. A single page? We should have gone fishing."

Bennett's engine sales for July 1987 were $57,000, down from $80,000 to $90,000 a year earlier. Pat said, "We install about 40 percent of the engines we rebuild, at about $1,250 a shot. The carryouts average about $750. So I don't expect sales in August to even reach $30,000."

Pat saw his problem as "too little sales to support the overhead cost." He said, "Because of this, we have a day-to-day cash flow problem." After receiving his July financial statement from the accountant, Pat had laid off all the office help (a secretary/bookkeeper and a clerk/parts runner). Pat had released four mechanics and a helper earlier in the year.

Pat himself had been spending most of his time on a tool modification and sharpening contract with Boeing of Louisiana, Inc. (BLI). Bennett's had begun doing this work in February 1987, shortly after Boeing opened its new Louisiana facility, where Air Force KC-135 tankers (a variation of the Boeing 707) were reworked. In July, Boeing had begun returning Bennett's invoices, with a rubber-stamped note that they exceeded the $75,000 contract amount. By mid-August, unpaid billings to Boeing totaled over $60,000. Pat said, "I've cut about everything I can cut and sold about as much as I can sell. I even took out a second mortgage on my condo. If Boeing doesn't pay pretty soon, or a miracle doesn't happen in the machine shop, we're going to be history." The appendix contains excerpts from an interview with Pat Bennett conducted in mid-September 1987.

Company Background

In 1972, Pat Bennett earned a bachelor of science degree in mechanical engineering at McNeese University in Lake Charles. Recalling his senior year, Pat said, "I knew then I would not stick with my engineering career. Besides going through just a real burnout, I already had this machine shop idea. There

were just three automotive machine shops in Lake Charles. And all the operators were in their late 50s. I knew there would be an excellent opportunity for a new shop in just a few years."

After graduation, Pat took a job with a chemical plant contractor as a designer/draftsman. The contract was completed in six months and Pat's employer offered him a chance to move to St. Louis. Instead, he quit and hired on at a local Cities Service plant as a "field engineer." Since all he actually did at the plant was drafting, Pat felt he had been misled. He stuck out his one-year contract—all except the last four hours. Pat said, "On the 365th day when the boss went to lunch, I said 'good-bye' to the man sitting beside me, took just the drafting equipment I could hold in my hand, and walked out the back door." Pat's impetuosity cost him the one week of vacation pay he had accumulated.

For the next year (1974–75), Pat commuted sixty miles to Beaumont, Texas, where he worked for Stubbs-Overbeck, Inc., a petroleum refinery engineering firm. According to Pat, this was "my first real engineering job." He explained:

My first day on the job, they fired the civil engineer. I was sitting there feeling inadequate, worrying what my assignment would be and if I would remember how to do it. I heard the office manager ask two other guys, "Who are we going to get to run the theodolite (a sophisticated surveying instrument) so the design crew can get going?" I got their attention and timidly said, "I know how to run a theodolite." They questioned why a mechanical engineer would know how to do that. I told them I had worked for a civil engineer while in college.

At about the same time, Pat bought a boring bar (a tool used to recondition cylinders in engine blocks) from a farmer for $50. He also sold his wife's washer and dryer for $100 to get the down payment on a valve grinding machine, the other piece of equipment required for the most rudimentary engine rebuilder. At night and on weekends, Pat rebuilt engines in a six-by-eight-foot shack next to the trailer house where he lived with his wife, Cheryl. Customers gave Pat money to buy parts, and he charged them only for his labor.

Pat told of his big entrepreneurial decision:

I worked 10 hours in Beaumont and drove an hour each way in addition to the time I spent doing engines. The drive just got too dangerous. I was sleepy most of the time and kept dozing at the wheel. Finally, one morning on the way to work I almost ran off the road. I had to pull over and sleep and didn't get to work until 9:30. When I got home that evening, Cheryl and I talked it over and decided I should quit my job and try the machine shop business full-time.

Pat rented a small Quonset hut as his first shop, paying the owner $75 for the month he used it. Then he moved to a stall in a service station about a block from the trailer park. There, his rent was one-third of all labor charges. The service station owner made additional profit on engine parts. Pat said, "I could not get any discount on parts. I had no business license. We did not even have a name. But the fellow who ran the service station bought parts at jobber prices."

Near the end of 1975, a local garage owner asked Pat if he would split the rent on a larger building the garage owner was considering. Pat would pay $150 of the $400 monthly rent. Pat agreed, and the arrangement lasted about two years. During that time Pat hired a helper (a pre-med student) and bought a cylinder head grinder and two other specialized machines (all on credit).

In 1977, Pat incorporated his business as Bennett's Machine Shop, Inc. and moved it to a rented building on Prien Lake Road, a busy commercial street. Sales and profits continued to expand through 1979, when his landlady, whom Pat had nicknamed "The Iron Maiden," ordered him to move because of the growing pile of used engines and parts next to the shop building. The shop flooded frequently anyway, and the fire department had complained about the oily rinse water Bennett's discharged into the city storm drains. Pat said, "I told the Iron Maiden that this was about as clean as it was going to get and made plans to move."

"I arranged to borrow $80,000 from Gulf National Bank," said Pat, adding, "I found a two-acre lot on the old Chennault air base for $57,000. I built a 4,000-square-foot building with the other $23,000 plus $3,000 I had saved." Bennett's Machine Shop moved to the new location in December 1979.

Pat said, "The first year we really had any extra money was 1981. We bought 11 pieces of property. We put 20 percent down on all of it and borrowed the rest, about $80,000." That year and the next, Pat added 6000 square feet to the machine shop and built another shop building, all without borrowing. In 1981, Bennett's began to do "over-the-fender" work for the first time, installing engines and some minor general repair work. At about this time, Pat and Cheryl bought a "real house" in nearby Westlake and moved from their mobile home. By 1985, Pat had bought a new condominium in Lake Charles and a 38-foot cabin cruiser. Cheryl was using the Westlake home as a cat sanctuary, and the 60 cats she had taken in required much of her time. Pat had collected 22 "muscle cars" and his personal car was a 1984 Jaguar XJS coupe.

"Then we made our big blunder," said Pat. "I thought it was time to open a new location, not to rebuild engines, but to install them. We bought the back half of an old Dodge dealership on Ryan Street [about three miles from Bennett's Machine Shop]. A Firestone tire store was in the front. Cheryl often reminds me how stupid it was to think I could run the business long-distance."

Pat opened the new shop as Lake Charles Motor Exchange, Inc. He assigned four of his people there. He said, "For 14 months, I pumped money into the new operation." Pat closed the Ryan Street location and sold the facility—he said at a $25,000 profit—in March 1986. "I never realized how personalized the business was," said Pat. He added, "By the way, we proved it again this summer, while I was fooling with Boeing. Things really got out of hand."

Operations

In late 1987, Bennett's Machine Shop was involved in three types of work: engine rebuilding, "over-the-fender" work, and tool sharpening and modification (the Boeing contract). Exhibit 1 shows the layout of Bennett's facilities.

Engine Rebuilding

Rebuilding engines is highly technical work. "The heart of it," said Pat, "is don't let the customer talk you into skipping the machine work. You've got to start with an empty, bare block." An actual case will illustrate the steps involved.

On August 9, 1987, Thomas Winkles, maintenance manager for a local dry cleaning firm and a personal friend of Pat's, ordered a "1974 250 Chevy short block." (A "short block" is a basic engine core, without the cylinder head, oil pan, oil pump, and several other parts that can be reused. These accounted for about 20 percent of the engines Bennett sold.) Pat felt Winkles was qualified to install the engine. "Otherwise," Pat said, "I would have questioned the customer to make sure the job could be done right. Replacing an engine is major surgery. It must not be done by amateurs."

Pat recorded the order on the yellow legal pad mentioned earlier and checked the Four-Star Engine Catalog (published by a national engine rebuilder) for casting numbers of 250-cubic-inch 1974 Chevrolet engines. He found there were two. Notes Pat had made in the catalog revealed that one used a straight and the other an offset starter motor. After having Winkles look to see which he had, Pat wrote the distinguishing feature, "straight starter," above the record on the legal pad.

Pat told the "teardown man," Lac Xuan Huyn, that he had added an order to the list. That day, Lac checked the order record and located the appropriate used engine among the several thousand piled here and there around the shop. (To augment the supply of

Exhibit 1 Layout of Bennett's Facilities

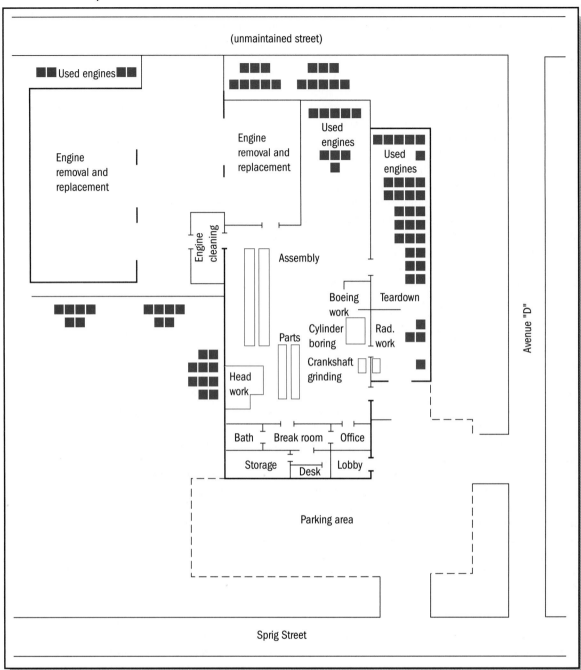

exchange engines from previous jobs, Bennett bought some from a traveling used-engine dealer and from individuals who called or came by from time to time.) Lac disassembled the engine, distributing parts to the crankshaft grinding area (crankshaft, pistons, and connecting rods) and the headwork area (cylinder heads). Lac placed the block near the two cleaning machines—which work like large dishwashers but use caustic soda (lye) instead of regular detergent. He put the camshaft in a wood box. The contents of the box were shipped periodically to Cam-Recon, a shop in

Houston, Texas, for regrinding. Bolts and valve pushrods were placed in appropriate bins. The oil pan and timing cover were set aside for reuse on this or another engine. And certain parts, mostly sheet metal items such as rocker-arm covers, were discarded.

Bennett's machinists were responsible for checking the legal pad record of orders and making sure parts were available for jobs listed there. There were no written procedures, about this or anything else, and the machinists often failed to verify parts availability. Still, the system worked about as intended for the

Winkles engine. Dale LeBlanc, who operated the cylinder boring machines, checked to see that the correct pistons and rings were on hand. He found that the ring set was not in stock. Curtis Manuel, who ground crankshafts and sized connecting rods, located a crankshaft for the engine—as usual, not the one Lac had just delivered. Curtis checked the crankshaft with a micrometer to see how far he would have to grind it and then confirmed that he had all main and connecting rod bearings, in the correct undersizes. Byron Woods, the assembler, checked the parts bins for the following items: gasket set, oil pump, matched camshaft and crankshaft gears, camshaft, camshaft bearings, and valve lifters. No gasket set was in stock. Dale and Byron, separately, called a Bennett's supplier in Houston and ordered needed parts, confirming that parts would arrive by bus or UPS the next day.

Dale washed the engine block in one of the cleaning machines. He then took the block to the cylinder boring area and "magnafluxed" it. This involves sprinkling iron filings over unmachined surfaces and placing a large electromagnet at strategic points. Any crack would have been indicated by a string of concentrated iron filings. None existed. Dale selected a box of six 0.030-inch oversize 250 Chevrolet pistons. After measuring one of the pistons with a micrometer, he proceeded to bore the cylinders, to 0.001 inch larger than the piston size, manually checking cylinder diameters with a hand-held "bore gauge" after each cut. He visually inspected each cylinder for cracks. Then the block was placed in a "honing tank," where, in a bath of number 2 jet fuel, the cylinders were honed to 0.002–0.003 inch beyond the piston size. Dale cleaned the engine again, this time finishing with a steam cleaner. Finally, he sprayed the cylinder walls with light oil and delivered the block to the assembly area.

Still on August 9, Curtis Manuel cleaned the crankshaft he had checked for Winkles's engine. He then positioned it on the crankshaft grinder set up to grind main bearing journals (the shiny surfaces that turn in the main bearings). During grinding, Curtis carefully observed the "Arnold gauge," which he had positioned to indicate the undersize dimension, in ten-thousandths of an inch. After grinding the main journals to 0.010 inch undersize, Curtis moved the shaft to the other grinding machine in an adjacent room and left it set up to do connecting rod journals (Pat said the two machines were located across a wall from each other "to keep from having to rig another electric box"). There, he machined the connecting rod journals to 0.020 inch undersize. The whole operation took about one hour. Curtis then cleaned and oiled the crankshaft, as Dale had done for the block, and placed the shaft in a plastic tube. It, too, was taken to the assembly area.

Not through yet, Curtis searched the waist-high pile of connecting rods and pistons at his work station for six Chevrolet 250 connecting rods. Unsure of his

selection, he called Byron, the assembler, to help verify he had the right ones. Byron confirmed Curtis's choice. Curtis then pressed out each piston pin (the short shaft that joins the piston to the connecting rod). Then he placed each rod in a rod vise and, using a torque wrench (a wrench that indicates the amount of twisting force being applied), tightened the nuts that secure the rod cap. Next, Curtis measured the inside dimension at the crankshaft end of each rod. Finding all measurements to be within specifications (plus or minus 0.0005 inch), he cleaned the rods. He got the box of pistons Dale had used in sizing the cylinders and installed them on the rods. The pistons with rods attached were taken to the assembly area.

If Winkles had ordered a complete engine, instead of just a short block, Scott McConathy or Martin Simmons, the machinists who recondition cylinder heads, would have been involved. Reconditioning a cylinder head mainly consists of resizing the valve guides, grinding valves and valve seats, and regrinding the cylinder head surface. After these operations, the cylinder head is cleaned, reassembled, and painted.

At about 3:00 P.M., Byron finished his previous job and began assembling the Winkles engine. He visually checked each cylinder for cracks. Then he painted the surfaces of the block that would be exposed to oil with "Cast Blast," a grey paint that seals cast iron surfaces and minimizes sludge buildup. Byron also painted the exterior surfaces of the block the appropriate original color. Next, he installed the plugs in the block, which seal holes required for certain casting and machining operations. After that, he manually installed the piston rings on the pistons. Byron then installed the major parts in the block—bearings, camshaft, crankshaft, and pistons—tightening all bolts to specified tightness and checking each part for free movement. Finally, he performed a careful inspection of the entire engine, recording the results on a specially designed form—kiddingly referred to as "the birth certificate."

The finished short block was placed in a bag and banded to a small pallet. The next day, Thomas Winkles picked up his new engine. A few days later, he dropped his old one by Bennett's.

Over-the-Fender Work

Over-the-fender work at Bennett's mainly involved removing and replacing engines. Of course, this often required replacing water hoses, V-belts, and other items that were worn or damaged at the time of the engine job. The engine warranty (12,000 miles or six months) was conditioned upon an exhaust gas analysis, which often revealed the need for carburetor work. Radiator disassembly and cleaning were also required as a condition of warranty, even for carryout engines. In addition to work related to engine replacement, Bennett's accepted general automobile repair work, such as carburetor rebuilding and air-conditioning component replacement.

Unlike the machinists already discussed, the mechanics furnished their own hand tools. Bennett's provided testing equipment, hoists, a pressurized air system, floor jacks and stands, hydraulic lifts, and cleaning equipment. Each mechanic had a separate work stall.

"We had a terrible, terrible parts situation." said Pat. "The situation was so out of control, I was actually looking at parts purchases as overhead and not as a profit producer. Items were either not getting on the tickets, or not getting on the cars." To solve this, Pat assigned one mechanic, his best, as checker, to make sure every part put on each car was on the respective invoice. He also closed all charge accounts with parts suppliers, requiring mechanics to come to Pat or his shop coordinator, Jack Beard, to get a check for any parts purchase. "Now we've got some control over it," said Pat.

Bennett's kept an inventory of common engine filters, ignition components, vacuum hoses and fittings, and nuts and bolts. Mechanics were required to order and pick up other required parts. Pat said, "We don't stock any radiator hoses, belts, or water pumps because there are just too many different ones."

Richard Hardesty, one of the mechanics Pat had laid off in July, leased one of the company's three buildings and the equipment in it to do general automotive repair, engine installations, and exhaust system repairs. Pat explained, "Our whole objective was to get the payroll down. Payroll taxes are a burden. And the $675 lease payment will come in handy. I was able to rent the building to Richard so cheaply because we don't owe anything on it."

Tool Sharpening and Modification

Boeing's operations in Lake Charles involved a great deal of drilling and reaming, especially of rivet holes in the skins of the KC-135s. Many screwed fasteners required countersunk holes to preserve a flush exterior surface. The thousands of drill bits, reamers, and countersinks used by Boeing required frequent modifications and/or sharpening. There were also numerous occasions when specialized tools such as reamer extensions had to be made, modified, or repaired. When Boeing had trouble locating a local supplier for these services, Pat Bennett volunteered to do the work and negotiated a single-source supply contract with Boeing procurement.

Gearing up to do this highly technical work consumed most of Pat's energy and time from February to August 1987. A 1,000-square-foot area of the machine shop building was enclosed and modified to house the tool work. A large horizontal lathe, a cylindrical grinder, two form-relief grinders, two tool and cutter grinders, and a drill bit sharpening machine were pur-

chased and installed in the temperature-controlled enclosure. To find these machines, Pat traveled to Wichita, Cincinnati, Dallas, and Houston.

Boeing was on an extremely tight schedule on its own contract with the air force and there were frequent emergencies, often involving innovative solutions to unique problems. For example, Pat stayed up all one night sharpening and resharpening a special cobalt drill bit then being used to drill through a titanium alloy engine mount. Much experimentation was required on this and other jobs, and Pat worked many nights and weekends to solve problems.

Generally, Pat Bennett picked up the tools to be modified at the Boeing plant, a few hundred yards from the machine shop, and returned them there. Because of a Boeing procedure, the tools only needing sharpening were picked up at a Boeing warehouse at the Lake Charles Port, four miles away. Each batch of tools to be serviced was accompanied by a work order providing instructions for the work to be done. For nonstandard modifications, Pat frequently had to call or visit the supervisor who wrote the order and get clarification of the instructions.

Five machinists, three on days and two on evenings, were hired to do the Boeing work. Two only sharpened drill bits, while the others did the work on countersinks, reamers, and special tools. James Smith, the machinist Pat charged with quality control for the Boeing contract, did most of the particularly innovative operations. For example, James designed and made a number of torque wrench extensions that allowed tightening nuts that were not directly accessible.

Pat personally trained the machinists to do the repetitive operations. "The most difficult operation to perfect," said Pat, "was grinding the flutes of a piloted reamer so that they would cut. We were finally able to do it on a German form-relief grinder. Everything on it was written in German. We couldn't read any of the buttons except the one which said 'halt.'" The machine came to be used solely for grinding the cutting edges on piloted reamers. A large magnifying glass was installed so the machinist could see the tiny flutes. With his left hand, the machinist would orientate one of the six flutes on a reamer. Then, with his right hand, he would move the grinding head into the reamer flute and back, grinding the tiny cutting edge at precisely ten degrees. This was repeated on each of the six flutes. Because of the exactness required, the grinding wheel had to be reshaped daily with a diamond "dresser."

Drill bit sharpening is a fairly standard operation, although the Boeing specification added some complexity. Bennett's drill bit sharpening machine was hardly state-of-the-art, requiring several manual manipulations of each bit sharpened. Still, sharpening each bit took only about 45 seconds.

The two-way form-relief grinder used to sharpen countersinks was almost completely automatic. Once the machinist orientated a countersink to be ground, the machine did the rest. This took about four minutes per countersink.

A great deal of skill was required to set up each of the operations described and especially to do the custom tool making. But, according to Pat, a person of average dexterity could learn any of the repetitive jobs in a day or two.

Personnel

In late 1987, Bennett's employed 16 people in addition to Pat and Jack Beard, the shop coordinator. There were five machinists and a radiator repairman in the automotive machine shop, five mechanics in the service department, and five machinists in the tool grinding shop.

Jack Beard had been with Bennett's four years. He was about 29 years old. A hard worker, Jack often spent 10 hours a day at the shop, including every Saturday—except during hunting season, when Jack and Byron, an assembler, alternated Saturdays. On a weekend in August, Jack rebuilt the engine in a Chevrolet Citation he had just bought. The following Monday, he told Pat, "I can see how they have such a hard time getting any motors built. There is only one air hose, tools are scattered everywhere, and the place is filthy dirty."

Pat observed that Jack was right. He had tried several ways to get the workers to keep the shop clean, at one point assigning each person "just one little area" to clean. "Nothing worked," said Pat, "so that morning I just pulled the main breaker. When everything shut down and the men came to see why, I told them I would restore the power when the shop was clean." Pat said two of the "main culprits" came in to punch in on the time clock—they were on piece rates—so they would be paid for doing the cleaning. Pat objected to paying them "for cleaning up a mess they had a big part in creating," and they both quit. Asked how he replaced the men, Pat replied, "They weren't worth replacing."

The automotive machinists, Lac, Dale, Curtis, Scott, Martin, and Byron, were mentioned earlier. None had been automotive machinists when Bennett hired them, although Curtis had taken a regular machinist course at a local trade school. Lance Hammack, the radiator repairman, also learned his trade at Bennett's. He had been a welder. "It is much easier to teach a person a new trade than to get a person who already knows a trade to change bad work habits," said Pat.

Lac, a Vietnamese, was hired in 1985. Pat said, "He had to bring an interpreter to apply for the job, he could speak so little English. But his attitude—he just seemed so eager. He learned very rapidly. Meticulous. Pays attention to detail. Terribly dependable. I don't know that he ever missed a day—never even asks for time off."

Dale, Curtis, Martin, and Lance had all been with Bennett's less than six months. Dale had been a construction worker before Pat hired him. "Couldn't even read a micrometer," said Pat. "He had some kind of hangup about reading the dial. I got him a micrometer with a digital readout and three days later he was operating the cylinder boring machine." Curtis knew how to run a lathe when he was hired. "So we put him on our crankshaft grinder," said Pat. (The two machines have similarities but are far from identical.) Martin had been a paint and body technician before Pat hired him. "He turns out the prettiest paint jobs on cylinder heads you ever saw," Pat kidded. Martin worked most Saturdays, in addition to full days during the week. Radiator work was not a full-time job at Bennett's, so Lance helped out in the office, drove the delivery truck, and did other tasks.

Scott and Byron had been hired about four years earlier, Scott right out of high school, Byron off the unemployment line. According to Pat, Scott had a strong interest in cars. "He was easy to train, always thinking," said Pat. "I could just give him a few pointers and he would go with it. He is very thorough. I don't have to check anything he tells me. He doesn't mind staying late during the week, but he likes his Saturdays off." Pat said that Scott did almost all the "really difficult head jobs—the overhead cams, heads that need new valve seats." Byron, young and unskilled, had started doing engine "teardowns." "Most machinists are too proud to do that," said Pat. "They think that is the low-class job in the shop. Byron was so easygoing. There was nothing he wouldn't try to learn if you needed him to do it."

Next Byron had mastered the cylinder-boring machine. Pat told how Byron got his next job: "I was grinding the crankshafts at that time. You should have seen me—an Extendaphone on my belt and a Sony Walkman under by shirt. People thought the Walkman was part of the machine. But I was grooving, listening to ''50s' music while I watched the cranks go round and round." Pat's wife, Cheryl, was "acting secretary" (the regular secretary had left due to illness) at the time. She quit after Pat threw a can of blue engine paint at her, so he had to take over the office. Another man, later fired for suspected theft, took over the boring machine, and Byron moved to the crankshaft grinder, relieving Pat. "That was a major accomplishment for Byron," Pat said. "He had never even run a lathe." Byron stayed with that job until March 1987, when he started assembling engines.

The five mechanics were Ronnie Smith, Tim "Tamale" Authemont, Kenneth Thornton, Clyde Brown, and Kevin "Goat" Gauthreaux. Ronnie, in his fourth year at Bennett's, was responsible for inspecting and test driving every vehicle repaired, regardless of who did the work. He also did mechanic work himself—all the carburetor work, certain diesel-to-gasoline conversions, and most of the computer checks. But Ronnie refused to do engine replacements in front-wheel-drive cars. Tim was a helper, supervised and paid by Ronnie. Tim had been with Bennett's over two years, but had worked as Ronnie's helper only about six months.

Kenneth Thornton was the longest-tenured employee Pat had, having hired on eight years earlier, when the shop was on Prien Lake Road. He did most of the engine replacements on front-wheel-drive cars, certain diesel-to-gasoline conversions, and regular repair work.

Clyde and Kevin had worked at Bennett's only a couple of months. Both did all kinds of engine replacements as well as a wide range of other mechanic work. Both were in their early thirties, married, with children. Pat said, "I am really impressed with their attitudes. Unlike many mechanics, they are not afraid of this new generation of cars—mostly transverse-engined, fuel-injected, and computer-controlled."

The machinists who did the tool work were James Smith (Ronnie's brother), James McManus, Craig McMichael, John Shearer, and Billy Lambert. James Smith had worked on and off for Bennett's for about five years, doing various construction jobs. He had hired on full-time in March 1987. Pat said, "In the early weeks of the Boeing job, I was running that German form-relief grinder while James was building the room around me." As the Boeing work had begun to increase, Pat taught James to run the grinder. Pat said, "I would run it on the weekends, he'd do it during the week." James had paid his own way to go with Pat and locate other machines to buy.

James McManus and Billy worked evenings. Craig and John worked days. James and Craig did reamers and countersinks. Billy and John sharpened drill bits. All four were in their early 20s. Pat recruited James and Craig through Sowela Tech, a local vo-tech school, and James continued as a co-op student there. John's father, who worked at the Boeing port warehouse, had recommended his unemployed son to Pat one day as Pat picked up an order, John had later recommended Billy.

The automotive machinists, except for Curtis (who operated the crankshaft grinder), were paid on a piecerate basis, so much for each type of operation and each model of engine. Each had an established hourly rate as well, which was applied to other than normally assigned work. Curtis was paid on an hourly basis.

The mechanics were paid a combination of piece rates, commissions, and hourly rates. Piece rates applied to engine replacements. Most other automotive work was done on a commission basis—each

mechanic got one-half of all labor charges that mechanic generated. Hourly rates were paid for warranty work that was not the mechanic's fault. Pat said, "We don't do like the dealerships and guarantee the mechanics a weekly minimum."

The machinists who did the tool grinding were all paid by the hour. At first, Pat set the machinists' wages according to the Boeing pay scale. But when Boeing tried to hire some of his people, he hiked the rate by about 40 percent. "I pay James Smith more than the rest," said Pat, "but he and I have an agreement that he doesn't get any overtime pay when he works over 40 hours."

Jack Beard, the shop coordinator, and Lance Hammack, the radiator repairman, were also paid by the hour.

Bennett's provided limited fringe benefits. There was a group health plan, paid entirely by the employees. Several chose not to participate. Each employee received six paid holidays each year (after a 90-day waiting period) and a one-week paid vacation each year after the first. Bennett's paid all uniform costs per employee over one dollar a day, although workers were not required to wear them. "I also let the men work on their personal and family cars in the shop after hours and on weekends," said Pat.

Marketing

Exhibit 2 provides demographic and economic data for Bennett's market area.

Sprig Street, where Bennett's was located, was "off the beaten path and far from the business district," according to Pat. He said, "The best thing about the location is it's one block outside the city limits. No one bothers us out here, no matter how messy it gets." It was messy. Except for concrete areas, grass and weeds were everywhere. Piles of greasy used engines were here and there—even next to the street behind the facility. Inside the machine shop building, half the space was occupied by stacks—no, piles—of engines and useless remnants of others long deceased. Individual blocks, heads, and other parts, as well as several derelict cars, littered the property, especially around the edges of driveways and other concrete areas. Everywhere there was grease and oil. Two large pitch-coated septic tanks and a stack of rusting metal shelves added confusion. A dingy, although lighted, 3-by-4-foot sign near the lobby and office area announced "Bennett's Machine Shop—Engine Rebuilding."

Thirty-second television spots featuring Pat Bennett ran throughout the year at a cost of about $350 per month. A feature article written by Pat appeared in the American Press, the local paper, once a month, at a cost of $114 per month. Once a year, when business was slow, a Bennett's supplement would be distributed

Exhibit 2 Geographic and Demographic Data

	Lake Charles	Calcasieu Parish (County)	Southwest Louisiana*	State of Louisiana	United States
Population, 7/80	77,400	167,223	259,809	4,206,000	226,546,000
Per capita income, 1985	$10,183	$10,224	$8,806	$10,741	$12,772
Change in *real* per capita income, 1980–85 (percent change for period)	1.2	1.3	1.6	2.3	2.8
Work force employed in manufacturing, 3/87 (percent)	7.4	17.3	16.2	11.2	18.8
Work force employed in construction, 3/87 (percent)	8.7	9.4	9.0	6.2	3.0
Land area (square miles)	27	1,082	5,083	44,521	3,539,289

*Southeast Louisiana Parishes–Allen, Beauregard, Calcasieu, Cameron, and Jefferson Davis.

with the 48,000-circulation newspaper. The cost was $1,600 for each distribution. The supplement offered discounts, good for two months with presentation of the flyer, on reconditioned engines—$50 on carryouts, $100 on installations. "The first time we did this, two years ago," said Pat, "we had to shut down and just answer the phones and take orders for two days. We sold 28 engines, almost a whole page, that time."

A form letter was sent to engine customers, thanking them for the business and asking for referrals to other prospective customers. Once a year, during the local festival called "Contraband Days," Bennett's subscribed to a radio advertising special. A 30-second spot was run 60 times during a 10-day period at a cost of $450. Pat said, "I've never seen a sale directly related to radio advertising. We did it one time, and they hounded us the next year till I agreed to do it."

Bennett's major competitors for engine sales were Dimick Supply Company, 100,000 Auto Parts, and Hi-Lo Auto Parts. None of these did installations and all bought their engines from large remanufacturers. No local automobile service shop other than Bennett's specialized in rebuilt engines, although most bought and installed them from time to time. Periodically, Pat Bennett checked the prices competitors charged for engines, often by simply calling and asking. He also kept current catalogs and price sheets for the engine remanufacturers who supplied Bennett's competitors. "We get their catalogs because we're a jobber," Pat said, "and sometimes we sell truck engines we buy from others—because the risk is so high if a truck engine fails."

Asked where he set his prices relative to the competition, Pat replied, "We make sure we're a little under everybody except Hi-Lo. They sell almost nothing but short blocks remanufactured in Texas. They are ridiculously low."

Pat said the quality of all the engines was about the same. "But if you have a problem with a Four-Star or a Roadrunner (the brands sold by Bennett's competitors) you bought from, say, Dimick," Pat said, "you have to take it out and wait for them to send it back to Texas. And they normally don't help you with labor." In contrast, he said, a Bennett's customer who has problems "can just bring the car to my front gate, and it's taken care of—if it's within warranty and hasn't been overheated or run out of oil." Pat complained, "Carryout customers will go to somebody else if there is just a $20 difference. It bothers me that customers will bring us their car if anything goes wrong, expecting us to fix it free. They wouldn't think of doing this at Hi-Lo or Dimick." He explained that parts-and-labor warranties, in general, only apply to situations where the labor is supplied by the vendor. "Sometimes." said Pat, "a customer will even call me for advice about some trouble with an engine he bought from a parts house. I tell him to call the parts house."

Mechanic labor at Bennett's was based on the time estimates in the Chilton Flat-Rate Manual (a book that gives estimated times to do all kinds of repair operations for most automobiles and light trucks), priced at $30 per hour. Most good mechanics can beat the flat-rate times significantly, more so on some types of work than on others. Bennett's priced most parts, other than engines, at locally competitive retail. The local parts houses gave Bennett's a 20 percent discount off retail. "List" prices, usually about 40 percent above retail, are shown on parts house invoices. Pat said, "If we think the list price is fair and the customer is unlikely to check with a parts house, we often use list instead of retail."

For the Boeing work, prices were set according to contract. Drill bit sharpening was at so much per item. The other operations were done by the hour. At first,

Boeing allowed Bennett's to charge very profitable prices. After the work had totaled about $137,000, Boeing audited Bennett's costs and revised the prices downward, by more than 50 percent. The audit was conducted by Boeing's vendor cost analysis (VCA) group and involved many lengthy meetings with four different teams of auditors. In fact, Bennett's initial contract was apparently so remunerative that Boeing assigned a "security investigator" who asked many questions implying possible collusion between Pat and various Boeing officials.

Boeing held up payment on past invoices while pressure was exerted on Bennett's to reprice previously submitted invoices at the VCA-determined rates. Pat refused to do that and successfully insisted that the invoices be paid as submitted. Pat did decide to accept the VCA prices during month-to-month renewals of the contract, while Boeing made plans to let the work out for bids. Meanwhile, Pat was trying to decide how to bid the work. He was making money at the new rates. Profits on the earlier contract had more than paid for all his machines. So he was tempted to bid even a little below the VCA numbers. But he knew Boeing was having trouble finding other vendors with even minimal competence to do the work. And he had served Boeing faithfully, and at great cost to his other business, for several difficult months.

Finance

Exhibits 3 and 4 give financial summaries for Bennett's Machine Shop, Inc. For 10 years. Pat Bennett had employed a local accounting firm, Management Services, Inc., to keep financial records, prepare financial statements and sales and income tax returns, submit business license applications, and so forth. During the 1987 tax season, Bennett's was not able to get Management Services to prepare the usual monthly profit and loss statements. Pat explained, "They said they couldn't get to it. So I changed to a real CPA firm in the Lakeside Plaza Building—and that was worse. This guy had less time than Management Services did for us. When he finally, after 60 days, got the first month done, he asked me to come in at nine o'clock one day. I got there at 9:15, and nobody except the secretary was at work. I passed him on the sidewalk with his briefcase and his three-piece suit. That's the last time I saw him."

After firing his new accountant. Pat talked with Dorothy McConathy, who had been assigned his work at Management Services, and asked whom he could get to do his bookkeeping. Pat said, "Dorothy had already told her boss she was going to quit when she got one more account on the side. She already had two, so she agreed to keep my books and gave Management Services notice."

After buying the boring bar when he first started rebuilding engines in 1972, Pat never directly contributed any more equity funds to the business. Equipment vendors furnished financing for most of the machines Pat bought. When Pat started to buy a used crankshaft grinder, which he found at a shop in Plaquemines Parish, he approached the bank that handled his checking account. Pat had taken out a few small personal loans at the bank, but the loan officer who had approved them was gone at the time. The bank president refused to loan Pat the $6,400 he needed to buy the machine.

"I got my little file from him and went over to the new American Bank of Commerce," said Pat. "There, I was a total stranger, but I got the loan." Three years later, Pat needed the $80,000 loan to buy the Chennault property. "American Bank of Commerce wouldn't make a decision," said Pat, "so I went back to Gulf National. My friend Lloyd Rion, the loan officer who was gone that day three years earlier, was there. He gave me the money, and I moved our checking account back." The loan was a 10-year, fixed-rate loan at 10 percent interest.

From 1980 to 1985, Pat took out several 90-day loans to make additions to the shop facilities. The bank allowed him to roll the loans over once. "Those were super productive years. We never had any money problems." said Pat.

When Pat bought the Ryan Street shop in 1985, which he sold 14 months later, the seller financed the whole $180,000, for 10 years at 10–14 percent variable rate. "That's when our trouble started," said Pat. "We loaded up the company with operating loans—a $25,000 three-year loan, a $24,000 five-year loan, and another three-year loan for $12,000, all from Calcasieu Marine Bank. I also let the work force run up to 22 people. It was a real runaway situation."

Pat described 1986 as "one helluva bad year." "That's when we could have used some input from the bookkeeper," said Pat. "I didn't realize that payroll and the taxes related to it were having such a devastating effect. We had almost the same sales as in 1984. Just the increase in payroll-based taxes was $70,000. What really ticked me off was that I had to figure this out and show him (the bookkeeper)." Pat had to refinance the 10-year loan on the Chennault property. "I put off laying off the extra people from January to August," said Pat. "That cost me another $40,000 and made me have to redo the loan." Bennett's showed a $12,000 profit in November that year. Pat said, "It was our first three-page month in a long time. I was scared to death. If we had not made a profit with that kind of sales, I didn't know what else to do." On the way to a New Year's Eve party. Pat made himself a promise: "I will not go through another year like that." A friend asked, "What are you going to do to prevent that—as if you

Exhibit 3 Bennett's Machine Shop, Inc., Income Statements

	Fiscal Year 1985*	Fiscal Year 1986*	Fiscal Year 1987*	4 Mos. 1988**
Revenue				
Automotive	926,243	1,091,890	971,950	140,131
Aircraft Tool	0	0	13,318	140,679
Total revenue	926,243	1,091,890	985,268	280,810
Expenses				
Direct costs				
Materials	456,828	570,372	504,811	64,939
Labor	248,833	316,164	271,858	53,693
Freight	0	0	0	1,031
Total direct costs	705,661	886,536	776,669	119,663
Gross profit	220,582	205,354	208,599	161,147
G & A expenses				
Advertising	10,697	15,831	17,828	1,193
Depreciation	33,550	42,240	29,220	7,359
Equipment leasing	5,680	950	1,657	0
Insurance	23,100	39,298	35,528	11,359
Interest	22,060	24,044	26,504	8,841
Miscellaneous	4,867	7,205	7,020	4,438
Office labor	6,815	11,420	13,300	3,961
Office supplies	5,883	7,015	6,458	2,129
Professional fees	3,696	8,373	6,622	1,175
Taxes	5,623	4,852	5,926	245
Utilities and telephone	15,871	30,767	27,933	8,830
Total G & A expenses	137,842	191,995	177,996	49,530
Net Income	82,740	13,359	30,603	111,617
Withdrawals***	(61,500)	(53,389)	(70,755)	(17,109)
Earnings reinvested	21,240	(40,030)	(40,152)	94,508

*Fiscal years end April 30 of years shown.
**May–August 1988.
***Includes funds to pay income taxes. The corporation is taxed as a partnership/proprietorship under Subchapter 5 of the Internal Revenue Code.

have some control over it?" "I'm going to work my tail off," Pat replied.

The machinery to do the Boeing work was all financed with $37,000 in 90 day notes at Calcasieu Marine. There were no other financial crises until August, when Boeing was holding up payment and engine sales collapsed. Pat was able to sell enough assets to meet the payroll and pay operating expenses, but he was unable to pay maturing loans. So Pat mort-gaged his condominium and consolidated the three term loans into one $45,000 five-year mortgage. Boeing paid its account up to date in early September, and Pat paid off the $37,000 in 90-day notes.

Until 1987, all the loans mentioned above were in Pat's and Cheryl's personal names, although entered on the company books and sometimes secured by company assets. The $45,000 mortgage loan from Calcasieu Marine was put in the company name, "So

Exhibit 4   Bennett's Machine Shop, Inc., Balance Sheets, April 30

	1985	1986	1987	1988*
Assets				
Current assets				
Cash	11,698	1,206	3,475	5,385
A/R, trade	0	1,255	16,662	65,436
N/R, stkhdr.	0	22,568	22,568	22,569
Inventory	37,548	45,436	45,436	45,436
Total c/a	49,246	70,465	88,141	138,826
Fixed assets				
Furniture & equip.	205,292	165,886	193,432	212,209
Buildings	305,657	155,657	155,657	155,657
Total depr.	510,949	321,543	349,089	367,866
Less accu. depr.	(133,559)	(134,067)	(143,834)	(155,081)
Net depr. assets	377,390	187,476	205,255	212,785
Land	126,418	90,000	90,000	90,000
Total fixed assets	503,808	277,476	295,255	302,785
Other assets				
Deposits	492	342	342	342
Total assets	553,546	348,283	383,738	441,953
Liabilities and Capital				
Current liabilities				
A/P, trade & other	12,727	25,062	29,407	31,242
N/P, current	103,160	16,385	60,299	57,775
Accrued payroll, taxes, interest	0	0	3,223	1,571
Total c/l	115,887	41,447	92,929	90,588
Long-term liabilities				
Notes payable	266,720	175,897	200,052	166,099
Stockholders' equity				
Common stock	10,000	10,000	10,000	10,000
Retained earnings	160,939	120,909	80,757	175,265
Total capital	170,939	130,909	90,757	185,265
Total liabilities and capital	553,546	348,253	383,738	441,952

*August 31, 1988.

we could deduct the interest under the new tax law," according to Pat. But Pat and Cheryl had to personally endorse the note and sign continuing guaranty agreements with the bank.

Appendix: Excerpts From Interview With Pat Bennett

Q: What is your main objective for this year?

A: I guess the goal we're all in business for is to make it profitable, and it hasn't been for the past two years.

We've had a real bad downward trend. We might not make a real big profit this year, but I hope we can stop the downward trend and turn it around. That would be a major accomplishment.

Q: What about the longer term?

A: I would like the business to be successful to the point that I would have some freedom to do some of the things I want to do. Travel some, sports in the winter— before I get decrepit. Until recently. I dreamed of having a nicer shop near the downtown area, but that seems out the window now.

Q: Can you be a little more specific about what the business would have to do to satisfy you?

A: If we got back to where net profit, including my total compensation, was $70.000–$100.000 a year—and we've been there—I would think that was okay.

Q: Do you mean in 10 years? Twenty years?

A: I'm not really that patient a person. I mean in the next two to three years. That is very obtainable.

Q: Do you think about 25 years from now, when you will be almost 65?

A: No.

Q: Do you feel responsible to make the business support anyone else but you and Cheryl, in the long or short term?

A: Sure, I probably have more loyalty to some of those guys than I should.

Q: Which ones? Or do you mean all of the workers?

A: I mean as a whole. My dad was a union man his entire life. We grew up with the idea that the company had to provide benefits—medical care, retirement, vacations, days off. Retirement is a big thing Dad always talked about. He always talked about the days before Roosevelt, when there wasn't any Social Security, not much to look forward to.

Q: Do the workers look out for your interests?

A: Sometimes I think they do. But on days like today I wonder.

Q: What happened today?

A: Everybody screwed up. Lack has trouble ordering anybody to do anything. Someday he's got to learn he isn't "one of the gang" anymore. Dale loaded the wrong engine on a customer truck. Lance spent the whole day chasing his tail, pretending to go get parts. One of my good customers asked for his car at 1:00—and it wasn't out until 4:00.

Know what I'm going to do? I'm moving my desk right out to the middle of the shop, right by the boring bars. They'll be nervous with me watching every move. But I'm going to get this mess under control. [Within three weeks. Pat had built a six-by-eight-foot office in the center of the shop near the assembly area. It had one-way windows so that Pat could observe the machinists but could not be seen by them.]

Q: What major changes in the business do you foresee?

A: More diversity. Wait! I mean more diversification. We've had all the diversity we can stand.

Q: What do you mean by diversification?

A: There still are several areas of the engine business that are untouched in Lake Charles. I just did a catalog so we'll be ready to do the parts house business. The closest production shops are in Baton Rouge and Houston, both over two hours away. We've got the whole west side of the state. And the crack repair business, cylinder head cracks mainly, is just untapped. I visited a big diesel shop in Houston that does this. The whole system, really nothing more than a big fire-bricked oven, would cost only a couple of thousand dollars. This is an especially good business with today's thin-wall castings on engines. There are tremendous numbers of heads thrown away. A plain old six-cylinder Chevrolet head is $400 new, bare. I also think we have a good opportunity in the aircraft industry—the tool work, a heat-treating facility. And Boeing is about to certify us for "level II" work, allowing us to make parts which stay on the plane. No more gravy train—we'll have to bid everything. Level II will also let us bid on the work for the big Strategic Petroleum Reserve. They have to send their work 80 miles to New Iberia.

CASE 11
Southwest Airlines

For more than three years, seemingly endless rounds of litigation had thwarted the plan to launch a new Texas airline, to be known as Southwest Airlines. The Texas Aeronautics Commission approved the application in 1968, but legal challenges by incumbent airlines facing new competition for the first time in decades stretched the proceedings all the way to the Texas Supreme Court, which unanimously ruled in Southwest's favor on May 13, 1970.

When the U.S. Supreme Court upheld the Texas court ruling in December, Southwest's founders

Southwest Airlines. Spirit, June, 1996. Reprinted courtesy of Southwest Airlines Spirit.

believed the courtroom battles lay behind them. However, the delays and litigation nearly wrecked Southwest's finances. The company had long since exhausted its original $543,000 in capital, but was able to continue the litigation only because its attorney, determined not to lose, agreed to absorb the legal costs himself.

The lawyer was Herb Kelleher, a transplanted New Jersey native who came to San Antonio to practice law. Kelleher had first been introduced to the idea of creating a new airline by his client. Rollin King, who had an idea that a commercial airline serving Texas's three largest markets might be able to make money. To illustrate his idea, King drew a triangle on a cocktail napkin, with the corners representing the Texas cities of Dallas. Houston, and San Antonio. Initially, Kelleher was skeptical, but as the discussion progressed, so did his interest. By one account, Kelleher's ultimate resolve was cemented with the words, "Rollin, you're crazy. Let's do it." Kelleher agreed to do the initial legal work for a 25 percent discount, but he wound up doing much of the work for free.

In exploring the feasibility of the project, Kelleher's research turned up some intriguing aspects of King's seemingly outlandish idea. Kelleher knew that the Civil Aeronautics Board, the federal regulatory body that had jurisdiction over the airlines, had not authorized the creation of a new major airline since before World War II. Indeed, the major function of the CAB was to prevent competition. But the CAB's jurisdiction extended only to interstate airlines—those with routes extending across state lines. By flying only within the state of Texas. Southwest might be able to avoid CAB jurisdiction.

In fact, a precedent existed. In California, Pacific Southwest Airlines (PSA) had flown for years as an intrastate airline. By avoiding the suffocating regulation of the CAB, PSA was able to offer low fares and frequent flights and had achieved great popularity with its customers. With the stimulus of competition, the California airline market had become the most highly developed in the world. Why couldn't Texas support the same kind of service?

On the competitive front, King and Kelleher were familiar with the sorry state of air service in Texas. Fares were high, flights were often late, and schedules frequently were dictated by the availability of aircraft after flying more lucrative, longer-haul flights where the CAB-regulated airlines made their real money. Short-haul, intrastate service was merely an afterthought, existing primarily as a tail-end segment of a longer flight coming in from New York or Minneapolis, for example.

Kelleher concluded that Texas was ripe for an airline that would focus on the intrastate passenger, offering good, reliable service at a reduced fare and on a schedule designed to meet the needs of local travelers rather than passengers coming in from far-off points.

After three years of litigation, Southwest still had no airplanes, no management team, no employees, and no money. But when the U.S. Supreme Court ruled in its favor, the founders quickly went to work and hired M. Lamar Muse as Southwest's president in January 1971. Muse was a wily veteran of the airline business, trained as an accountant, but possessed the brash and daring temperament of an entrepreneur.

With the certificate from the Texas Aeronautics Commission as Southwest's only valuable asset and its bank account down to $142, Muse somehow managed to raise $1.25 million through the sale of promissory notes. For his management team, Muse put together a group of industry veterans, most of whom had either retired from or been cut loose by old-line airlines. Muse is reported to have claimed that all the top people he hired had been fired by other airlines. "I figured the other airlines were doing such a lousy job that anybody they fired had to be pretty good."

As luck would have it, a slow market caused Boeing to have three new 737–200 aircraft sitting on the tarmac. Southwest recognized the 737 as the perfect aircraft for the mission it had in mind. The 737's modern, fuel-efficient, twin engine configuration would allow highly reliable, efficient, and economical operation in Texas' short-haul intrastate markets. Boeing executives accommodated the cash-strapped Texans by agreeing to finance 90 percent of the cost of the new planes—unheard-of terms for such desirable aircraft.

With airplanes secured and crews hired, Southwest's long-awaited inaugural flight finally seemed at hand. But the entrenched airlines hadn't quit. First, they asked the CAB to exercise its jurisdiction to block the new competition in Texas. The CAB declined to interfere, throwing out the complaints by Braniff and Texas International on June 16, 1971—just two days before Southwest's first scheduled flight. Within hours, lawyers for Braniff and Texas International won a restraining order from a friendly district judge in Austin, banning Southwest from beginning service.

Southwest's leaders were simultaneously outraged and crestfallen. For more than three years, they had fought and won the legal battles. Now, on the eve of seeing their dream come to fruition, they faced the prospect of starting all over.

Kelleher, having left his San Antonio law office without a toothbrush or change of clothes, was in Dallas when he heard of the Austin judge's restraining order. An already rumpled-looking Kelleher headed to Austin, hitching a ride on a proving flight of one of Southwest's new and brightly painted red, orange, and desert-gold 737s. In Austin, Kelleher located Texas Supreme Court Justice Tom Reavely, the man who had written the court's unanimous 1970 opinion authorizing Southwest to fly. Kelleher persuaded Reavely to convene an extraordinary session of the Supreme Court the next day.

Kelleher worked through the night to prepare his papers and arguments for the court. The next day, June 17, 1971, sleepless and wearing the same well-worn suit, he appeared before the full Supreme Court, asking again that Southwest be allowed to take flight.

Finally, the phone in Muse's office rang. It was Kelleher. The Supreme Court not only had heard the arguments, it already had ruled. The district court's restraining order was thrown out. Southwest was free to start service the next day.

"What do I do if the sheriff shows up tomorrow with another restraining order?" Muse asked.

"Leave tire tracks on his back," Kelleher replied.

As 1973 began, Southwest had operated for a year and a half without approaching profitability. Start-up capital, including proceeds of a 1971 stock offering, was almost depleted. A fourth aircraft had been acquired, but it had to be sold to raise cash. Almost miraculously, the schedule had been maintained when Southwest employees, under the leadership of vice president Bill Franklin, invented the "10-minute turnaround," enabling a plane to be fully unloaded and reloaded in 10-minutes at the gate. With the increased productivity from the 10-minute turnaround, Southwest's management found that three planes could do the work of four. Thus was borne one of the precepts of Southwest's success—a plane doesn't make money sitting on the ground.

Still, cash was dwindling, and profitability remained a mere dream. The Dallas-Houston run was doing okay, but loads on the Dallas-San Antonio route were poor, draining the airline of its remaining cash. Muse decided to try a bold move. On January 22, 1973, he cut fares in half, to $13, on the Dallas-San Antonio route—every seat, every flight, no restrictions. What followed was one of the most widely reported and publicly watched conflicts in the history of the airline industry.

Braniff struck back, running full-page ads announcing a "Get Acquainted" fare of $13 between Dallas and Houston. Braniff's plan meant that Southwest would surely go broke if it matched the $13 fare between Dallas and Houston, Southwest's only profitable route.

Southwest's leaders frantically searched for a response. Even if they had known at the time that Braniff and Texas International ultimately would be convicted of federal criminal antitrust violations for their tactics, it would have provided little solace. The judicial system's ultimate judgment was years away. Insolvency was only days away.

The spark of inspiration that saved Southwest from certain liquidation finally came. The airline would give anybody who paid the full $26 fare a bottle of premium liquor—Chivas Regal, Crown Royal, or Smirnoff. But passengers could pay the $13 fare if they preferred.

Southwest vice president Franklin was dispatched to get a truckload of liquor delivered to the airport. To accommodate nondrinkers, Southwest vice president Jess Coker located a stash of leather ice buckets that hadn't sold well at Christmas and bought thousands of them. Somebody asked if it would be legal. Muse said to let Kelleher take care of that.

Muse then decided to write his company's reply to Braniff, which would be carried in Southwest's own full-page ads. After Kelleher removed the profanities and polished up Muse's initial draft, the ad ran under the headline "Nobody's going to shoot Southwest out of the sky for a lousy $13."

Suddenly, public attention was riveted on the air war over Texas. It became front-page news, the lead story on television and radio. For two months, Southwest was the largest liquor distributor in Texas. It was a defining moment, one in which people decided their allegiances for a lifetime.

The overwhelming response to Southwest's underdog crusade produced the first quarterly profit in the company's history and made 1973 Southwest's first profitable year.

"Tell the mayor that Southwest Airlines will be the best partner the city of Chicago ever had," Kelleher is saying into the telephone. It is November 1991, and Kelleher's face betrays a hint of tension and excitement as he makes his pitch to one of the mayor's closest advisers. For years, Southwest's efforts to expand in Chicago were stymied because of the unavailability of gate facilities at Midway Airport.

Southwest had grown beyond its Texas roots. With the passage of the federal Airline Deregulation Act of 1978, the end of the CAB's stranglehold on competition in interstate markets was assured. Southwest promptly became an interstate airline, flying first from Houston to New Orleans in January 1979. Although expansion out of Dallas's Love Field was limited by a 1979 congressional enactment known as the Wright Amendment, named for then-Congressman Jim Wright, who represented Fort Worth and sought to protect the growth of Dallas-Fort Worth International Airport, Southwest nonetheless found abundant opportunities for expansion outside Texas.

Kelleher had moved from the role of lawyer to executive, first becoming acting president in 1978 when Muse resigned after a disagreement with the board of directors, and then becoming full-time president and chief executive officer in September 1981 when Howard Putman resigned to become president of Braniff. Expansion in the West had proved highly successful, although not free of competitive challenges. Using Phoenix as the major base for its westward push, Southwest penetrated most of the major markets in California and the southwestern United States during the eighties and early nineties.

But Chicago had been a particularly frustrating situation. Although Southwest offered 43 flights out of its four overcrowded gates, the demand existed for many more flights, to more destinations. Southwest could not expand to meet the demand because all remaining gates were leased—mostly to hometown favorite Midway Airlines. However, rumors now were swirling that Midway Airlines was about to shut down. Southwest had attempted to obtain leases on some of the gates in return for a cash payment and/or loan that might allow Midway Airlines to remain open. But Midway had transferred leases on all the gates to Northwest Airlines, in anticipation of an acquisition of the entire airline by Northwest. When Northwest announced on November 13, 1991, that it was abandoning plans to acquire the airline, Midway barely had enough cash to finish out the day.

Kelleher desperately wanted access to the Midway gates, which would now sit empty if Midway Airlines shut down. Although the lease belonged to Northwest. Jim Parker, Southwest's creative General Counsel, knew of a loophole—the city retained the right to permit another airline to use the gates any time they were not being used by the primary tenant. If Midway shut down that night, as seemed likely, Parker reasoned there was no way Northwest could occupy all of Midway's gates by the next day. Kelleher arranged a 9 o'clock meeting the next morning in Chicago between Southwest's representatives and top advisers to Mayor Richard M. Daley.

When Southwest's delegation arrived at their Chicago hotel at 1:00 A.M., live TV reports from Midway Airport were confirming the shutdown of Midway Airlines. While Southwest's lawyers planned their strategy that night, the airline's Facilities and Technical Services departments swung into action, diverting deliveries and pulling computer equipment, backwall signage, podium inserts, and hold-room chairs from other cities throughout the system, and shipped them to Chicago. Everyone knew that time was of the essence.

The entire city of Chicago was concerned about the shutdown of Midway Airlines. Not only were 4,300 employees thrown out of work, but serious concern existed about the future of Midway Airport itself, a longtime economic engine of the south side of Chicago. When Southwest's representatives met with the city's leaders at 9:00 A.M., they told the mayor's aides that Southwest Airlines was prepared to spend at least $20 million for the development and promotion of the airport and commit to a program of substantial expansion at Midway Airport if the city would exercise its authority to assure Southwest access to the facilities necessary to effect its growth plan. Negotiations continued throughout the day, as Southwest lawyers pointed to the airline's financial stability, record of developing underutilized airports, outstanding record of customer satisfaction, excellent employee relations, and commitment to community involvement as reasons why the city should choose Southwest over any competitor as its partner for the redevelopment of Midway Airport.

The people of Chicago didn't know much about Southwest Airlines, but apparently they were impressed. At mid-afternoon, the mayor's press aide entered the negotiating room and asked, "You guys have a deal yet? The mayor is having a press conference at 3:30." A letter of agreement and press

release were quickly hammered out, and the deal was done.

Taking a side trip on his way into the press conference, Parker called Calvin Phillips, his contact from the Facilities Department, who had arrived in Chicago along with a dedicated band of volunteers from the Technical Services Department.

"Where's the equipment?" Parker hurriedly inquired.

"It's in Chicago, in a warehouse near the airport."

"We have a letter of agreement. Let's go."

"What if somebody from the department of aviation or Northwest tries to stop us?"

"Tell them to talk to the mayor," Parker replied.

When Mayor Daley announced Southwest Airlines as Chicago's new partner for the redevelopment of Midway Airport, a reporter inquired when he could expect to see some sign of Southwest's growth at the airport. A Southwest spokesman stepped forward, "If you go to the airport, you can see it right now." Daley beamed as reporters scurried for the door to head to the airport. News reports that night were filled with pictures of Midway Airport in transition, with Southwest workers toiling through the night to install Southwest signage and equipment at gate after gate.

A meeting was arranged the next day between representatives of Southwest and Northwest, the titular leaseholder.

"How far have your troops advanced?" the Northwest representative asked.

"I think they stopped at the edge of the A Concourse," Parker replied.

A deal ultimately was negotiated, whereby Northwest relinquished its claim to the former Midway Airlines gates and the city of Chicago entered into a direct lease with Southwest, assuring Southwest's ability to expand in Chicago and the Midwest.

Kelleher sits in his windowless office, contemplating his company's upcoming expansion into Florida. It is January 1996, and Southwest Airlines is approaching the twenty-fifth anniversary of that day in 1971 when Kelleher told Muse to leave tire tracks on the sheriff's back, if necessary.

Southwest's fleet has grown from three 737–200s to more than 220 modern Boeing 737 aircraft. So strong is Southwest's loyalty to the 737 that it is the only major U.S. airline with an all-Boeing fleet. The little airline that had to ask for 90 percent financing from Boeing in 1971 has served as the launch customer for three new models of the 737: the 737–300, now the workhorse of the fleet, the 737–500, and the upcoming 737–700, which will be delivered in 1997.

Since recording its first profit in 1973, Southwest is about to report its 23 consecutive year of profitability. The halls and walls of Southwest's headquarters are filled with mementos of employee celebrations and accomplishments. The "Triple Crown" trophy sits proudly in the lobby, commemorating Southwest's unparalleled record of having the best on-time performance record, fewest mishandled bags, and fewest customer complaints, according to U.S. Department of Transportation consumer reports for four consecutive years. Southwest has become so successful that a 1993 U.S. Department of Transportation study described Southwest Airlines as "the principal driving force behind dramatic fundamental changes" in the U.S. airline industry.

The walls also include mementos of other innumerable achievements—the 1993 book by Robert Levering and Milton Moskowitz naming Southwest Airlines one of the 10 best companies to work for in America; the Air Transport World designation of Southwest as "Airline of the Year" for 1991; the *Condé Nast Traveler* magazine recognition of Southwest as the safest airline in the world for its accident-free history; the 1994 Fortune magazine cover with a zany picture of Kelleher and the caption, "Is Herb Kelleher America's Best CEO?"

But Kelleher is intense, uncharacteristically humorless, as he contemplates his company's upcoming expansion into Florida, a market he has coveted for more than a decade. He knows the competition will be intense, and his mind flashes back to past battles. Florida in 1996 bears striking similarities to California in 1989. Air fares are high, intrastate service poor, and the geography of the state lends itself to a need for high-frequency, low-fare, reliable air service between major metropolitan areas. In California, Southwest's one-time role model, PSA, and its in-state competitor. Air Cal, long ago lost their way and were swallowed up by megacarriers who cared little for short-haul intrastate markets, leaving a vacuum that Southwest gladly filled. Southwest's friendly low-fare service was quickly embraced by Californians with such enthusiasm that Southwest soon carried a majority of California's intrastate passengers.

The West Coast had become intensely competitive, however, United, the largest airline in the world, targeted Southwest as an unwanted intruder, and articulated a goal of eliminating, or at least slowing, Southwest's expansion. To this end, United created its own "airline within an airline," designed to offer low fares and fly largely in markets served by Southwest. In anticipation of the massive resources that could be thrown into the battle by United, an airline many times Southwest's size, Southwest had acquired Salt Lake City–based Morris Air, and launched a major expansion of its own into the Northwest.

After 15 months of competition, though, Southwest seemed to be at least holding its own. Despite a huge influx of new competitive service, Southwest's California traffic was actually up. United officials were no longer maintaining even a pretense that the effort to erode Southwest's base of loyal customers had been successful. To the contrary, Southwest was about to report its most profitable year ever.

Suddenly, a Southwest executive interrupts Kelleher's concentration. "Herb, you're not going to believe what one of our customers just told us."

"What?"

"Guess what happens if you pick up your phone and call 1-800-SOUTHWEST?"

"You mean 1-800-1 FLY SWA. That's our reservations number."

"I know, But guess what happens if you call 1-800-SOUTHWEST?"

Kelleher walks over to his telephone and dutifully dials the number. The answer comes after four rings.

"Shuttle by United reservations. This is Todd."

"What?" Kelleher exclaims in dismay.

"May I help you?"

"Uh. No, thanks."

After a moment of stunned silence, Kelleher explodes in laughter. The world's largest airline has been reduced to impersonating Southwest in an attempt to hold onto its West Coast passengers. An exquisite look of satisfaction settles over Kelleher's face as the laughter subsides.

A moment later, the look of intensity is back.

"Let's talk about Florida."

C A S E   1 2
Pharmacia and Upjohn
Gareth R. Jones

In September 1995, the Upjohn Company, one of the largest pharmaceutical companies in the United States, announced that it was merging with Pharmacia, the largest Swedish

Gareth R. Jones, Texas A & M University.

pharmaceutical company. With Upjohn's annual sales of $3.3 billion and Pharmacia's of $3.6 billion, the merger created the ninth largest pharmaceutical company in the world, Pharmacia & Upjohn. What prompted Upjohn's management to seek a merger that would change the future of the company forever? To answer this question, it is necessary to *study Upjohn's history and its performance in the turbulent pharmaceutical industry of the last decade.*

History

For the first 73 years of its existence, the Upjohn Company was a family-owned and -operated, domestic pharmaceutical company. In 1885, W. E. Upjohn was granted a patent on a manufacturing process that produced a "friable" pill. The new pill disintegrated rapidly in the body to speed the release of medication. This friability contrasted with the hardness of many of the mass-produced pills of the day, which often passed through the body without releasing their contents. This manufacturing process and the secrecy that surrounded it fueled the early growth of the company and made it difficult for other companies to imitate the popular product. The founder speeded the company's growth with a policy of selling his pills at about half the price of the old-style, mass-produced pills, generating considerable hostility from competitors in doing so. The company expanded its product line quickly, offering 500 products by 1892 and 2,000 by 1900.

By 1900, the new technology of compressed tablets superseded the friable pill, and Upjohn had to imitate the innovations of other companies and produce the new tablets. Tablets that disintegrated rapidly in the body were much easier to mass produce. The company began featuring tablets and created a tablet department to speed product development.

From its beginnings, Upjohn was strongly aware of the need to develop marketing strengths to complement the company's research and development and manufacturing skills. Realizing early that the profit potential from mass-produced tablets would be low, Upjohn emphasized the need to develop and market quality-based, high-priced drug products that would give higher profit margins. Perceiving the company as operating in a luxury market, he had the insight to switch its focus from pills to tablets and to emphasize product characteristics. For example, he pioneered the development of pleasantly flavored drugs to suit consumers' tastes. One result was an important innovation called Phenolax, a sweetly flavored laxative. It proved to be a big seller for more than 40 years.

In the next two decades, Upjohn added a number of promising research areas. In 1912, bacterial vaccines became part of the company's product line. Research was begun in endocrinology and digitalis extracts for heart failure in 1914. A pleasant-tasting alkalizer called Citrocarbonate was introduced in 1921 and reached $1 million in annual sales by 1926, the first Upjohn product to do so. This product and the intensive sales effort that accompanied it marked the emergence of the company as a first-class pharmaceutical house. A succession of other introductions followed, including new flavored versions of cough syrup, cod liver oil, and

Kaopectate, still a best-selling antidiarrhea product. Each of these research efforts was stimulated by a perceived need to respond to the demands of the medical community for improved drug products.

Upjohn was always sensitive to the needs of its main "distributors," the doctors who prescribed its products. An aggressive sales push directed toward pharmacists and doctors helped the company to grow through the tough 1930s and into the years of World War II. The medical department was created in 1937 by a member of the founding family, Gifford Upjohn, to upgrade the company's contacts with physicians. This focus became a hallmark of sales efforts at Upjohn. Through the decades that followed, the company continued to differentiate its products and match its sales strategy to the changing composition of the medical profession.

Much of the company's growth through the 1930s and 1940s was tied to vitamins. In 1929, Upjohn was the first to produce a standardized combination of vitamins A and D in the United States. Vitamins accounted for half of the $40 million in sales in 1945 and marked the company as a leader in nutritional supplements. Other products critical to Upjohn's growth included Kaopectate, estrogenic hormone products introduced in the 1930s, antibiotics, and an antidiabetic drug brought out in the 1940s and 1950s.

By 1952, the research department had 421 employees, who viewed their research output as second in quality only to that of Merck & Co. among domestic pharmaceutical companies. The department began to establish broad research areas, which are still important to the company today: antibiotics, steroids, antidiabetes agents, nonsteroidal anti-inflammatory drugs, and central nervous system agents.

The progress of the company's research efforts led to increasing demand for specialty chemicals to manufacture new drug introductions. The company had purchased standardized chemicals in the past, but the growing need for unique materials led to the establishment of the fine chemicals manufacturing division in 1949 to supply the company with its own products. The division expanded into external sales, and by 1984, 40 percent of its production was for other companies.

After World War II, the Upjohn Company continued a modest export program, sending most of its foreign sales representatives to Central and South America. The creation of the export division in 1952 was the first strong corporate signal that management was committed to competing globally. The division was formed in reaction to the globalization strategies of the leading domestic drug companies, which recognized the potential in developing a worldwide market for their products.

In 1958, the 20-member board of directors, 11 of whom were related directly or by marriage to the founder, voted to recommend public ownership. The following year, the Upjohn Company was formally accepted for listing and trading on the New York Stock Exchange. The decision to go public did not end the involvement of the extended family of the founder, W. E. Upjohn, but it did give the company the additional financial resources it needed to become a stronger force in the global pharmaceutical market.

The company continued to expand its international scope quickly to include sales subsidiaries in Canada, England, and Australia. Through the 1960s and 1970s, it added more subsidiaries and sales offices and built two major production facilities outside the continental United States: one in Belgium in 1963 and the other in Puerto Rico in 1974. By the mid-1980s these plants, in combination with the principal facility in Kalamazoo, Michigan, produced pharmaceuticals for sale in more than 150 countries.

Upjohn's first large venture out of pharmaceuticals came via its entry into animal health products in the late 1940s, when it repackaged several human products, such as antibiotics, for animal use. New products specifically for animals began flowing in 1952, and a sales force targeting veterinarians was established, growing from one person in 1956 to 20 in 1957. The sales force gradually increased to 130 by the mid-1980s.

Other agricultural products were added over time. After deciding against entry into fertilizers, the company acquired its core seed company, Asgrow Seed Company, in 1968 to develop new, improved strains of seeds. It added another top-10 domestic seed company, O's Gold, in 1983. The latter was chosen because its sales force and products complemented Asgrow's. In 1974, Upjohn acquired Cobb Breeding Corporation, a producer of chicken broiler breeders, to continue its expansion into animal drugs. In 1986, the company formed a joint venture with Tyson Foods, Inc., to further expand its broiler operations.

Nonagricultural diversification began in the 1960s. The company started manufacturing polymer chemical products in 1962, with the purchase of the Carwin Company, which was combined with the fine chemicals manufacturing operations. The company entered cosmetics in 1964, when several other pharmaceutical companies were doing the same. In 1969, it entered home nursing services when it purchased Homemakers, Inc.

The chemicals business was profitable for many years. After profits peaked in 1979, however, rapid decline set in because of a down cycle in the principal markets for chemicals. The polymer chemicals operation was sold in 1985, but the fine chemicals manufacturing division was retained. The cosmetics business never proved very profitable and was liquidated in 1974. The home nursing service business was renamed Upjohn Healthcare Services. It quickly added new locations and became the market leader in 1974.

By the mid-1980s, Upjohn had become a global, research-based manufacturer and marketer of pharmaceuticals, chemicals, agricultural seeds and specialties, and health services. In 1987, it had research, manufacturing, sales, and distribution facilities in more than 200 locations worldwide. The company generated almost $2.3 billion in sales in 1986, its centennial year, from two broad industrial segments. First, Upjohn's World-Wide Human Health Care Businesses, which concentrates on the development, manufacture, and marketing of drug products globally, accounted for almost 82 percent of total sales in 1986. Second, the agricultural division, which develops and supplies seeds and drugs for use in agriculture and animal production, accounted for slightly more than 18 percent of the company's sales.

Globally, in 1986, 67 percent of Upjohn's sales revenues were generated in the United States, 15 percent in Europe, and 18 percent were scattered elsewhere across the world. By 1986, Upjohn's share of the worldwide pharmaceutical market was 1.5 percent, and top management's ambition was to achieve a minimum of 2 percent of the market by 1990. The realization of this goal would move Upjohn from among the top 15 to among the top 10 drug companies globally.

The middle to late 1980s proved to be a turning point in Upjohn's history, however, as a result of changes both in the domestic and global pharmaceutical industry and because of a series of internal problems that became evident in the company at this time. These problems were to plague Upjohn for the next decade, and it was the attempt to resolve them that led Upjohn's management to seek the merger with Pharmacia in 1995.

The Pharmaceutical Industry Environment

By the late 1970s and early 1980s, important changes were reshaping competition in the domestic and global pharmaceutical markets. First, more countries were imposing greater regulation on the drug approval process. In the United States, the Kefauver-Harris amendment of 1962 placed major new constraints on pharmaceutical manufacturers. They required that companies set forth substantial proof that a drug was safe and effective before the FDA could allow it on the market. As a result of this legislation, the new introduction process became considerably longer and more expensive, which was viewed by many as the single most important nonscientific event to affect the industry since World War II.

The Kefauver-Harris amendment marked the beginning of substantially increased regulation of the domestic pharmaceutical industry. As drug approval time lengthened, valuable years of patent protection were being eroded. The Waxman-Hatch Act of 1984 reflected the tremendous growth in domestic political influence of the Generic Pharmaceutical Industry Association (GPIA).

Another major thrust of the bill was to speed the introduction of generic drugs after patent expiration in order to reduce their price. This put increasing pressure on the profits of the company that developed a new drug. Development costs were estimated to approach $100 million for each new drug introduced in 1986, and they are $150 million today. To placate the large drug companies, the bill guaranteed several drug companies, including Upjohn, the exclusive rights for five years beyond normal patent length to market four major drugs each. These patent extensions were to compensate for the FDA's slow handling of drug registrations over the previous few years.

However, by 1990, approvals for generic copies of patent-expired drugs were being issued at a very rapid pace, and the large drug companies were experiencing price competition on many fronts. Large pharmaceutical companies, including Upjohn, came under intense pressure during the 1990s. In the early 1990s, for example, Upjohn faced the prospect of a loss of patent protection on four of its major revenue-generating drugs: Xanax, an antidepressant; Halcion, a sleeping pill; Micronase, a treatment for diabetes; and Ansaid, an anti-inflammatory agent. Upjohn lost more than $400 million in annual revenues as generic drug companies began producing their own versions of these drugs. In fact, Upjohn avoided losing more money only because it began to produce a generic version of its own drug, Xanax, allowing it to keep 80 percent of prescriptions of the drug. This marked a major move for Upjohn into the production of low-priced generic drugs and over-the-counter drugs sold under its own brand name.

Similar legislative pressures to reduce drug prices were mounting in many other countries. Between 1981 and 1984, the Japanese government ordered price reductions on drugs averaging 40.1 percent. Such legislation marked an industry trend toward, as Upjohn's president and chief operating officer, Lawrence C. Hoff, put it, a "two-tier industry with innovators in one group and a large number of generic manufacturers in the other segment, competing fiercely on the sole basis of price." In the 1990s, many drug companies such as Upjohn have been fighting to gain a foothold in both markets to increase their revenues in a more competitive marketplace. Many countries also had begun protectionist campaigns, restricting drug marketing to products manufactured by the domestic industry. Furthermore, many foreign companies benefited from development support from their respective governments, allowing them to avoid the full cost of their research efforts. Since regulatory procedures, processes, and time orientations differ considerably from one country to another, domestic companies often experienced difficulty in obtaining information on how drugs move through foreign regulatory agencies. Although an attempt to achieve standardization of clinical procedures and disseminate intelligence on postmarketing response of users through an international information network was under way in the 1980s, it never came to fruition.

With increasing competition in research and increasing difficulty and costs in achieving regulatory approval, drug companies began concentrating their research in specific fields of medicine in order to reduce the cost of developing new drugs. To maintain their profitability, companies began specializing in the world's three most lucrative markets for new drugs: heart disease, anti-inflammatory agents and analgesics, and antibiotics. This concentration of resources by major companies in a few specific areas was suggested by an Upjohn spokesperson to be the cause of the scarcity of new drugs classified as breakthrough developments by the FDA in recent years. However, the slowdown in drug innovation seems to be on the verge of reversal. The advent of biotechnology has fueled a surge in new global pharmaceutical products as cures and medications for major diseases begin to appear, albeit at a slower pace than expected.

Another major environmental threat to Upjohn arose from the changing U.S. pharmaceutical environment in the 1990s. In the early 1990s, the new Clinton administration championed the introduction of a national health care system and also proposed that in the future drug companies should be strictly regulated in the amount they could charge for new and existing drugs. Because this would obviously eat into the profits of the large drug companies, their stock price declined.

Although these proposals eventually came to nothing, another major trend was developing in the 1990s: the emergence of managed health care by health maintenance organizations (HMOs). HMOs are national chains of medical and health centers that employ doctors and buy drugs in huge quantities from major pharmaceutical companies. Because they buy in such bulk, HMOs can bargain with pharmaceutical companies for lower prices. This occurred during the 1990s, and squeezed the profit margins of these companies. Moreover, besides pressures from HMOs, mail-order drug companies, such as Medco, sprang up. By virtue of their national customer base and huge buying power, they were also able to bargain with the large drug companies for lower prices by threatening to switch suppliers.

Finally, global competition became intense in the 1990s as the increasing costs of developing drugs, combined with reduced patent protection and competition from generic drug makers, put pressure on pharmaceutical makers to recoup their investments on a global level. In the 1990s, drug companies could only hope to be as profitable as they have been in the past if they could successfully market a drug on a global level.

Thus, pharmaceutical companies have experienced significant environmental challenges in the last decade, challenges that are still becoming stronger. First, there has been increasing price competition in the health care industry from the rapid growth of generic drug companies. Second, there has been an increase in legislative pressures on new drug development, both at home and abroad. Third, there has been an increase in global competition as drug companies vie with each other on a worldwide basis.

In response to all these pressures, a wave of merger activity occurred in the pharmaceutical industry in the 1990s. Merck bought Medco, the national mail-order drug supply company mentioned earlier, for $6.6 billion in 1993; American Home Products bought American Cyanamid for $9.6 billion in 1994; Eli Lilly bought PCS Health Systems, another mail-order drug company, for $4 billion; and Wellcome bought Glaxo Holdings in 1995 for $14.2 billion. The increasing consolidation of the global pharmaceutical industry is still continuing, as companies fight to position themselves for the events in the next century. Clearly, the problem facing Upjohn's management was how to maintain its growth in the domestic and international markets in the face of this increasing industry competition and regulatory pressure. Upjohn, with its very small share of the global market, realized it had to find a global partner if it was to stay in the big league.

Upjohn's New Corporate Strategy

In 1990, Upjohn stated that its pharmaceutical business strategy to the year 2000 was to ensure that it delivered the greatest volume of quality pharmaceuticals to the greatest number of people globally and, at the same time, maintained an appropriate return on investment to ensure its continued growth. Three goals were particularly stressed: (1) sales growth (with concurrent market share growth); (2) a continuing growth in return on investment; and (3) competition based on high quality rather than low price.

The aggressive nature of this approach was indicated by Upjohn's quest to become one of the top 10 drug companies by the mid-1990s. During the early 1990s, however, it became clear that achieving these goals would be difficult because of a number of internal problems that had arisen at this time.

One of its first problems was that the number of new promising drugs waiting in its product-development pipeline for FDA approval dropped off precipitously in the 1990s. Its previous block-buster drugs, such as Xanax and Halcion, were losing their patent protection, and these drugs had not been followed by new blockbusters. As a result, during the early 1990s,

Upjohn faced the prospect of flat revenues, which would not help it to achieve its ambitious goals.

The lack of new drugs in the pipeline was not the result of a lack of investment in research and development. Upjohn continued to invest heavily in R&D. For example, Upjohn invested heavily in biotechnology as a way of promoting new product development. Dr. Ralph E. Christofferson, a longtime consultant, was hired by the company, assigned a budget, given a custom-constructed facility, and instructed to hire the best people in the field. The 150-person staff began working with research professionals in Upjohn's other businesses to show them how the new technology could help applied-research efforts in both human health services and agriculture. However, the pace of new product development was disappointing, and costs were rising. Under any circumstances, the development of new drugs is a very uncertain and risky process, and it has been estimated that only one out of 10 to 15 drugs that start the development process come to the market—hence, the high prices that drug companies are forced to charge.

Besides the lack of new products in the pipeline, Upjohn's previous strategies of vertical integration and diversification were causing problems. Vertical integration had been a part of Upjohn's strategy since its inception. Upjohn pursued backward integration into the production of fine chemicals so that it could maintain quality control from initial chemical manufacture to the final packaging of its products in order to protect the quality of its drugs. Upjohn's production unit purchased most of its bulk chemicals from Upjohn's chemicals unit. In the 1990s, however, vertical integration was proving an expensive strategy that raised costs and did little to increase the bottom line. It had become clear that in many cases it was now cheaper to buy rather than make many of the chemicals that the company needed, so that the costs of vertical integration were now outweighing the benefits.

Similarly, Upjohn's diversification efforts had not produced the gains that had been expected. Its Asgrow seeds division, while profitable, was far removed from its core pharmaceutical business, and few synergies had been obtained. Its home health care business was similarly far removed from the company's core activities. The costs associated with managing all these different businesses were rising, sucking up a lot of top management's time, and did not seem to promise much of a return.

In the early 1990s, Upjohn's top management began to realize that its diversification efforts were not helping the company and were unlikely to help it achieve its central mission of becoming a top-10 global pharmaceutical company. So it sold off various of its chemicals businesses and its home health care business. The turning point for Upjohn came in 1994, when Theodore Cooper, Upjohn's long-time CEO, died and was replaced by John L. Zabriskie, one of Merck's former top managers. Zabriskie took a long, hard look at Upjohn's current strategy and he immediately decided that Upjohn's strategy of using acquisitions to achieve its objectives of diversification and expansion in health and agriculture was not working. Zabriskie decided that he needed to restructure Upjohn, and he moved quickly to do so.

In early 1994, Zabriskie sold off what were now regarded as noncore assets, such as Asgrow Seeds and the chicken-breeding venture with Tyson Foods, among others, getting the company out of the agricultural business. He also eliminated 1,400 managerial jobs by restructuring and consolidating Upjohn's manufacturing and sales and marketing operations. For example, he decreased the number of Upjohn's global manufacturing sites to reduce excess capacity and operating costs in the years ahead. Then, he restructured its U.S. pharmaceutical sales and marketing efforts to focus solely on large customers such as health care systems, HMOs, and insurance providers. Because of Upjohn's new strategy, sales for 1994 reached $3.3 billion, slightly below 1993 sales, but net earnings jumped by 25 percent as costs fell.

Zabriskie then turned his attention to the company's research and development operations. He realized that it was here, in the development of important new pharmaceutical products, that the company's future lay. He decided to refocus the company's R&D efforts on developing 30 major products aimed at product markets that seemed to offer the greatest prospects for future new-product development. Many other R&D programs were terminated to save money. Then Zabriskie pumped more money into R&D to promote these 30 new products. The company spent more than $600 million in 1994, which represented more than 18 percent of sales and was above the industry average, to speed the development of new products to the marketplace.

In the process of refocusing Upjohn's efforts, however, Zabriskie realized that, at best, all that these remedies offered was a short-term fix for the company's problems. It had became clear to him that, especially in view of the wave of mergers taking place within the industry, Upjohn was increasingly becoming a prospective takeover target for another pharmaceutical company seeking a quick way to become a major player. Zabriskie had to find a means of raising Upjohn's global presence and speeding the new-product development process. So even before he had finished with these major restructuring efforts, he convened a meeting of the company's top 20 executives in the summer of 1994 to develop a plan to take Upjohn into the next century as one of the top 10 global pharmaceutical companies.

It became clear from this meeting that none of these executives thought that Upjohn could become a major global player on its own and that the company could not wait for its next generation of drugs to be approved for sale over the next 5 to 10 years if it was to avoid being taken over. Zabriskie and his managers decided that Upjohn must seek a merger partner, one that could remedy Upjohn's weaknesses with its strengths. Accordingly, Zabriskie began to analyze the global pharmaceutical companies that had not yet been taken over to find a potential partner.

Enter Pharmacia

Jan Ekberg, chief executive of Pharmacia, was also very aware of the merger movement proceeding in the pharmaceutical industry. Since 1992, when the previously state-owned company had been privatized, he had been approached by several other European pharmaceutical companies about a possible merger. These companies had realized the potential of Pharmacia, because it had a very strong product-development process, with several promising new drugs in the pipeline. Ekberg was not tempted by these merger opportunities because he saw that Pharmacia's major weakness was its lack of developed sales and marketing channels in the United States, the world's biggest drug market. He realized that to become a global player, Pharmacia would need a strong presence in the U.S. market and that the way to do this was to search for a U.S. partner.

When Zabriskie took over at Upjohn, Ekberg saw an opportunity for a distribution deal between the two companies. He saw that Pharmacia's well developed sales and marketing operations in Europe could efficiently handle the sales of Upjohn's products in Europe, and he saw that Upjohn's U.S. sales and marketing network would provide an avenue to distribute Pharmacia's new drugs in the United States. Ekberg called Zabriskie to discuss the distribution agreement, but Zabriskie, on the lookout for a merger partner, was thinking along different lines.

Like Ekberg, he saw that a combined distribution operation between Pharmacia and Upjohn would allow both companies to offer a much wider product line to HMOs and national drug-supply companies throughout the United States and Europe. Combined distribution operations and a larger presence would give them a better bargaining position and an opportunity to increase global sales volume. However, Zabriskie also saw that, in the short run, the many new drugs in Pharmacia's drug pipeline would compensate for the lack of new drugs in Upjohn's, and remedy Upjohn's major weakness in this area. Given his recent cost-cutting efforts, he also saw that there might be many other areas in which a combined Pharmacia and Upjohn could reduce costs. Pharmacia began to look like the ideal merger partner.

Zabriskie proposed a meeting in Washington, D.C., which quickly led to a whole string of meetings across Europe as a surprised Ekberg began to warm up to the idea of a formal merger rather than just a strategic alliance through a distribution agreement. After some negotiations, both men bought into the idea and began the process of convincing their major stockholders to agree to the merger. They pointed out that after a merger, a combined Pharmacia and Upjohn would allow major cost savings in marketing and sales, manufacturing, and research and development. Each of these activities could be sourced on a global level to the country where factor skills or costs were most favorable, for example, and they announced that they expected to be able to reduce staff by 4,000 people, or 12 percent of the workforce. Alongside this, of course, they expected sales revenues to increase because of the combined company's ability to serve the global marketplace better, so that they saw big profits ahead.

Moreover, the two CEOs also pointed out that the continuing wave of merger activity implied that if they did not agree to a merger now, both companies might be the object of unfriendly takeover attempts. A combined Pharmacia and Upjohn, and a new place as the ninth largest pharmaceutical company in the world, would better position the company and make it a global player by the year 2000.

In August 1995, the two companies announced a tax-free stock swap that would result in a merger of equals. The new company would have its headquarters in London. Zabriskie would be the new CEO, and Ekberg would be the nonexecutive chairman. The company would have an R&D budget of more than $1 billion a year, equal to any major global pharmaceutical company.

In 1996, it was not clear what the future would hold for Pharmacia & Upjohn. Would the new company be able to combine the strengths of both companies, eliminate their weaknesses, and develop a sustainable pipeline of important new drugs so that the company would become a truly global player? Alternatively, would Upjohn's new research and development efforts come to nothing so that the short-term boost to revenues brought about by Pharmacia's new drug pipeline would fizzle out? If this happens, the combined company may itself become a takeover target in the next few years, as the global pharmaceutical industry continues to consolidate. Zabriskie clearly does not believe in this latter scenario. In a public announcement, he claimed that:

> This is a merger that truly constitutes far more than the sum of the parts. The new company will be able to take full advantage of uniquely complementary geographic reach, product portfolio, pipeline, and R&D strengths. As a result of the merger, Pharmacia and Upjohn will have extensive financial and operating resources, market scope, and earnings potential. Consequently, we fully expect the new company to achieve additional growth in expected 1996 earnings per share (EPS), as well as acceleration of future earnings growth.

C A S E   1 3
Philips NV
Charles W. L. Hill

Established in 1891, the Dutch company Philips NV is one of the world's largest electronics enterprises. Its businesses are grouped into four main divisions: lighting, consumer electronics, professional products (computers, telecommunications, and medical equipment), and components (including chips). In each of these areas it ranks alongside the likes of Matsushila, General Electric, Sony, and Siemens as a global competitor. In the late 1980s, the company had several hundred subsidiaries in 60 countries, it operated manufacturing plants in more than 40 countries, it employed approximately 300,000 people, and it manufactured thousands of different products. However, despite its global reach by 1990, Philips was a company in deep trouble. After a decade of deteriorating performance, in 1990 Philips lost $2.2 billion on revenues of $28 billion. A major reason seems to have been the inability of Philips to adapt to the changing

Charles W. L. Hill, University of Washington. Reprinted with permission.

competitive conditions in the global electronics industry during the 1970s and 1980s.

Philips' Traditional Organization

To trace the roots of Philips' current troubles, one has to go back to World War II. Until then, the foreign activities of Philips had been run out of its head office in Eindhoven. However, during World War II the Netherlands was occupied by Germany. Cut off from their home base, Philips' various national organizations began to operate independently. In essence, each major national organization developed into a self-contained company with its own manufacturing, marketing, and R&D functions.

Following the war, top management felt that the company could be most successfully rebuilt through its national organizations. There were several reasons for this belief. First, high trade barriers made it logical that self-contained national organizations be established in each major national market. Second, it was felt that strong national organizations would allow Philips to be responsive to local demands in each country in which it competed. And third, given the substantial autonomy that the various national organizations had gained during the war, top management felt that reestablishing centralized control might prove difficult and yield few benefits.

At the same time, top management felt the need for some centralized control over product policy and R&D in order to achieve some coordination between national organizations. Its response was to create a number of worldwide product divisions (of which there were fourteen by the mid-1980s). In theory, basic R&D and product development policy were the responsibilities of the product divisions, whereas the national organizations were responsible for day-to-day operations in a particular country. Product strategy in a given country was meant to be determined jointly by consultation between the responsible national organization and the product divisions. It was the national organizations that implemented strategy.

Another major feature of Philips' organization was the duumvirate form of management. In most national organizations, top-management responsibilities and authority were shared by two managers—one responsible for "commercial affairs" and another responsible for "technical activities." This form of management had its origins in the company's founders—Anton and Gerard Philips. Anton was a salesman and Gerard an engineer. Throughout the company there seemed to be a vigorous, informal competition between technical and sales managers, with each attempting to outperform the other. Anton once noted:

> The technical management and the sales management competed to outperform each other. Production tried to produce so much that sales would not be able to get rid of it; sales tried to sell so much that the factory would not be able to keep up. [Aguilar and Yoshino, 1987]

The top decision-making and policy-making body in the company was a 10-person board of management. While board members all shared general management responsibility, they typically maintained a special interest in one of the functional areas of the company (for example, R&D, manufacturing, marketing). Traditionally, most of the members of the management board were Dutch and had come up through the Eindhoven bureaucracy, although most had extensive foreign postings, often as a top manager in one of the company's national organizations.

Environmental Change

From the 1960s onward, a number of significant changes took place in Philips' competitive environment

that were to profoundly affect the company. First, due to the efforts of the General Agreement on Tariffs and Trade (GATT), trade barriers fell worldwide. In addition in Philips' home base, Europe, the emergence of the European Economic Community, of which the Netherlands was an early member, led to a further reduction in trade barriers between the countries of Western Europe.

Second, during the 1960s and 1970s a number of new competitors emerged in Japan. Taking advantage of the success of GATT in lowering trade barriers, the Japanese companies produced most of their output at home and then exported to the rest of the world. The resulting economies of scale allowed them to drive down unit costs below those achieved by Western competitors such as Philips that manufactured in multiple locations. This significantly increased competitive pressures in most of the business areas where Philips competed.

Third, due to technological changes, the cost of R&D and manufacturing increased rapidly. The introduction of transistors and then integrated circuits called for significant capital expenditures in production facilities—often running into hundreds of millions of dollars. To realize scale economies, substantial levels of output had to be achieved. Moreover, the pace of technological change was declining and product life cycles were shortening. This gave companies in the electronics industry less time to recoup their capital investments before new-generation products came along.

Finally, as the world moved from a series of fragmented national markets toward a single global market, uniform global standards for electronic equipment were beginning to emerge. This standardization showed itself most clearly in the videocassette recorder business, where three standards initially battled for dominance—the Betamax standard produced by Sony, the VHS standard produced by Matsushita, and the V2000 standard produced by Philips. The VHS standard was the one most widely accepted by consumers, and the others were eventually abandoned. For Philips and Sony, both of which had invested substantially in their own standard, this was a significant defeat. Philips's attempt to establish its V2000 format as an industry standard was effectively killed off by the decision of its own North American national organization, over the objections of Eindhoven, to manufacture according to the VHS standard.

Organizational and Strategic Change

By the early 1980s Philips realized that, if it was to survive, it would have to restructure its business radically. Its cost structure was high due to the amount of duplication across national organizations, particularly in the area of manufacturing. Moreover, as the V2000 incident demonstrated, the company's attempts to compete effectively were being hindered by the strength and autonomy of its national organizations.

The first attempt at change came in 1982 when Wisse Dekker was appointed CEO. Dekker quickly pushed for manufacturing rationalization, creating international production centers that served a number of national organizations and closing many small inefficient plants. He also pushed Philips to enter into more collaborative arrangements with other electronics firms in order to share the costs and risks of developing new products. In addition, Dekker accelerated a trend that had already begun within the company to move away from the dual leadership arrangement within national organizations (commercial and technical), replacing this arrangement with a single general manager. Furthermore, Dekker tried to "tilt" Philips' matrix away from national organizations by creating a corporate council where the heads of product divisions would join the heads of the national organizations to discuss issues of importance to both. At the same time, he gave the product divisions more responsibility to determine companywide research and manufacturing activities.

In 1986, Dekker was succeeded by Cor van de Klugt. One of van de Klugt's first actions was to specify that profitability was to be the central criterion for evaluating performance within Philips. The product divisions were given primary responsibility for achieving profits. This was followed in late 1986 by his termination of the U.S. Philips trust, which had been given control of Philips's North American operations during World War II and which still maintained control as of 1986. By terminating the trust, van de Klugt in theory reestablished Eindhoven's control over the North American subsidiary. Then, in May 1987, van de Klugt announced a major restructuring of Philips. He designated four product divisions—lighting, consumer electronics, components, and telecommunications and data systems—as "core divisions," the implication being that other activities would be sold off. At the same time he reduced the size of the management board. Its policy-making responsibility was devolved to a new group management committee, comprising the remaining board members plus the heads of the core product divisions. No heads of national organizations were appointed to this body, thereby further tilting power within Philips away from the national organizations toward the product divisions.

Despite these changes, Philips' competitive position continued to deteriorate. Many outside observers attributed this slide to the dead hand of the huge head office bureaucracy at Eindhoven (which comprised more than 3,000 people in 1989). They argued that while van de Klugt had changed the organizational chart, much of this change was superficial. Real power, they argued, still lay with the Eindhoven bureaucracy and their allies in the national organizations. In support of this view, they pointed out that since 1986 Philips' work force had declined by less than 10 percent, instead of the 30 percent reduction that many analysts were calling for.

Alarmed by a 1989 loss of $1.06 billion, the board forced van de Klugt to resign in May 1990. He was replaced by Jan Timmer. Timmer quickly announced that he would cut Philips's worldwide work force by 10,000, to 283,000, and launch a $1.4 billion restructuring. Investors were unimpressed—most of them thought that the company needed to lose 40,000–50,000 jobs—and reacted by knocking the share price down by 7 percent. Since then, however, Timmer had made some progress. In mid-1991, he sold off Philips's minicomputer division—which at the time was losing $1 million per day—to Digital Equipment. He also announced plans to reduce costs by $1.2 billion by cutting the work force by 55,000. In addition, he entered into a strategic alliance with Matsushita, the Japanese electronic giant, to manufacture and market the Digital Compact Cassette (DCC). Developed by Philips and due to be introduced in late 1992, the DCC reproduces the sound of a compact disc on a tape. The DCC's great selling point is that buyers will be able to play their old analog tape cassettes on the new system. The DCC's chief rival is a portable compact disc system from Sony called Mini-Disk. Many observers see a replay of the classic battle between the VHS and Betamax video recorder standards in the coming battle between the DCC and the Mini-Disk. If the DCC wins it could be the remaking of Philips.

REFERENCES

Aguilar, F. J., and M. Y. Yoshino. "The Philips Group: 1987." Harvard Business School, Case #388–050.

Anonymous. "Philips Fights the Flab." *The Economist*, April 7, 1992, pp. 73–74.

Bartlett, C. A., and S. Ghoshal. *Managing Across Borders: The Transnational Solution*. Boston, Mass.: Harvard Business School Press, 1989.

Kapstein, J., and J. Levine. "A Would-Be World Beater Takes a Beating." *Business Week*, July 16, 1990, pp. 41–42.

Levine, J. "Philips's Big Gamble." *Business Week*, August 5, 1991, pp. 34–36.

CASE 14
"Ramrod" Stockwell
Charles Perrow

The Benson Metal Company employs about 1,500 people, is listed on the stock exchange, and has been in existence for many decades. It makes a variety of metals that are purchased by manufacturers or specialized metal firms. It is one of the five or six leading firms in the specialty steel industry. This industry produces steels in fairly small quantities with a variety of characteristics. Orders tend to be in terms of pounds rather than tons, although a 1,000-pound order is not unusual. For some of the steels, 100 pounds is an average order.

The technology for producing specialty steels in the firm is fairly well established, but there is still a good deal of guesswork, skill, and even some "black magic" involved. Small changes are made in the ingredients going into the melting process, often amounting to the addition of a tiny bit of expensive alloying material in order to produce varieties of specialty steels. Competitors can analyze one another's products and generally produce the same product without too much difficulty, although there are some secrets. There are also important variations stemming from the type of equipment used to melt, cog, roll, and finish the steel.

In the period that we are considering, the Benson Company and some of its competitors were steadily moving into more sophisticated and technically more difficult steels, largely for the aerospace industry. The aerospace products were far more difficult to make, required more research skills and metallurgical analysis, and required more "delicate" handling in all stages of production, even though the same basic equipment was involved. Furthermore, they were marketed in a different fashion. They were produced to the specifications of government subcontractors, and government inspectors were often in the plant to watch all stages of production. One firm might be able to produce a particular kind of steel that another firm could not produce even though it had tried. These steels were considerably more expensive than the specialty steels, and failures to meet specifications resulted in more substantial losses for the company. At the time of the study about 20 percent of the cash value output was in aerospace metals.

The chairman, Fred Benson, had been president (managing director) of the company for two decades before moving up to this position. He is an elderly man but has a strong will and is much revered in the company for having built it up to its present size and influence. The president, Tom Hollis, has been in office for about four years; he was formerly the sales director

Charles Perrow, Yale University. Reprinted with permission.

and has worked closely with Fred Benson over many years. Hollis has three or four years to go before expected retirement. His assistant, Joe Craig, had been a sales manager in one of the smaller offices. It is the custom of this firm to pick promising people from middle-management and put them in the "assistant-to" position for perhaps a year to groom them for higher offices in their division. For some time these people had come from sales, and they generally went back as managers of large districts, from whence they might be promoted to a sales manager position in the main office.

Dick Benson, the executive vice president (roughly, general manager), is the son of Fred Benson. He is generally regarded as being willing, fairly competent, and decent, but weak and still much under his father's thumb. Traditionally, the executive vice president became president. Dick is not thought to be up to that job, but it is believed that he will get it anyway.

Ramsey Stockwell, vice president of production, had come into the organization as an experienced engineer about six years before. He rose rather rapidly to his present position. Rob Bronson, vice president of sales, succeeded Dick Benson after Benson had a rather short term as vice president of sales. Alan Carswell, the vice president of research, has a doctorate in metallurgy and some patents in his name, but he is not considered an aggressive researcher or an aggressive in-fighter in the company.

The Problem

When the research team studied Benson Metal, there were the usual problems of competition and price-cutting, the difficulties with the new aerospace metals, and inadequate plant facilities for a growing industry and company. However, the problem that particularly interests us here concerned the vice president of production, Ramsey Stockwell. He was regarded as a very competent production man. His loyalty to the company was unquestioned. He managed to keep outdated facilities operating and still had been able to push through the construction of quite modern facilities in the finishing phases of the production process. But he was in trouble with his own staff and with other divisions of the company, principally sales.

It was widely noted that Stockwell failed to delegate authority to his subordinates. A steady stream of people came into his office asking for permission for this and that or bringing questions to him. People who took some action on their own could be bawled out unmercifully at times. At other times they were left on their own because of the heavy demands on Stockwell's time, given his frequent attention to details in some matters, particularly those concerning schedules and priorities. He "contracted" the lines of authority by giving orders directly to a manager or even to a head foreman rather than by working through the intermediate levels. This violated the chain of command, left managers uninformed, and reduced their authority. It was sometimes noted that he had good men under him but did not always let them do their jobs.

The key group of production men rarely met in a group unless it was to be bawled out by Stockwell. Coordinating committees and the like existed mainly on paper.

More serious perhaps than this was the relationship to sales. Rob Bronson was widely regarded as an extremely bright, capable, likable, and up-and-coming manager. The sales division performed like a well-oiled machine but also had the enthusiasm and flashes of brilliance that indicated considerable adaptability. Morale was high, and identification with the company was complete. However, sales personnel found it quite difficult to get reliable information from production as to delivery dates or even what stage in the process a product was in.

Through long tradition, they were able to get special orders thrust into the work flow when they wanted to, but they often could not find out what this was going to do to normal orders, or even how disruptive this might be. The reason was that Stockwell would not allow production people to give any but the most routine information to sales personnel. In fact, because of the high centralization of authority and information in production, production personnel often did not know themselves. "Ramrod" Stockwell knew, and the only way to get information out of him was to go up the sales line to Rob Bronson. The vice president of sales could get the information from the vice president of production.

But Bronson had more troubles than just not wanting to waste his time by calling Stockwell about status reports. At the weekly top-management meeting, which involved all personnel from the vice presidential level and above, and frequently a few from below that level, Bronson would continually ask Stockwell whether something or other could be done. Stockwell always said that he thought it could be. He could not be pressed for any better estimations, and he rarely admitted that a job was, in fact, not possible. Even queries from President Tom Hollis could not evoke accurate forecasts from Stockwell. Consequently, planning on the part of sales and other divisions was difficult, and failures on the part of production were many because it always vaguely promised so much. Stockwell was willing to try anything, and worked his head off at it, but the rest of the group knew that many of these attempts would fail.

While the men under Stockwell resented the way he took over their jobs at times and the lack of information available to them about other aspects of production, they were loyal to him. They admired his ability and they knew that he fought off the continual pressure of sales to slip in special orders, change schedules, or blame production for rejects. "Sales gets all the glory here" said one. "At the semiannual company meeting last week, the chairman of the board and the managing director of the company couldn't compliment sales enough for their good work, but there was only the stock 'well done' for production; 'well done given the trying circumstances.' Hell, Sales is what is trying us." The annual reports over the years credited sales for the good years and referred to equipment failures, crowded or poor production facilities, and the like in bad years. But it was also true that problems still remained even after Stockwell finally managed to pry some new production facilities out of the board of directors.

Stockwell was also isolated socially from the right group of top personnel: He tended to work later than most, had rougher manners, was less concerned with cultural activities, and rarely played golf. He occasionally relaxed with the manager of aerospace sales, who, incidentally, was the only high-level sales person who tended to defend Stockwell. "Ramrod's a rough diamond; I don't know that we ought to try to polish him," he sometimes said.

But polishing was in the minds of many. "Great production man—amazing when he gets out of that mill. But he doesn't know how to handle people. He won't delegate; he won't tell us when he is in trouble with something; he builds a fence around his men, preventing easy exchange," said the president. "Bullheaded as hell—he was good a few years ago, but I would never give him the job again," said the chairman of the board. He disagreed with the president that Stockwell could change. "You can't change people's personalities, least of all production men." "He's in a tough position," said the vice president of sales, "and he has to be able to get his men to work with him, not against him, and we all have to work together in today's market. I just wish he would not be so uptight."

A year or so before, the president had approached Stockwell about taking a couple of weeks off and joining a leadership training session. Stockwell would have nothing to do with it and was offended. The president waited a few months, then announced that he had arranged for the personnel manager and each of the directors to attend successive four-day T-group sessions run by a well-known organization. This had been agreed on at one of the directors' meetings, though no one had taken it very seriously. One by one, the directors came back with marked enthusiasm for the program. "It's almost as if they had our company in mind when they designed it," said one. Some started having evening and weekend sessions with their staff, occasionally using the personnel manager, who had had more experience with this than the others. Stockwell was scheduled to be the last one to attend the four-day session, but he canceled at the last minute—there were too many crises in the plant, he said, to go off that time. In fact, several had developed over the previous few weeks.

That did it, as far as the other vice presidents were concerned. They got together themselves, then with the president and executive vice president, and said that they had to get to the bottom of the problem. A top-level group session should be held to discuss the tensions that were accumulating. The friction between production and sales was spilling over into other areas as well, and the morale of management in general was suffering. They acknowledged that they put a lot of pressure on production, and were probably at fault in this or that matter, and thus a session would do all the directors good, not just Stockwell. The president hesitated. Stockwell, he felt, would just ride it out. Besides, he added, the "Old Man" (chairman of the board) was skeptical of such techniques. The executive vice president was quite unenthusiastic. It was remarked later that Stockwell had never recognized his official authority, and thus young Dick feared any open confrontation.

But events overtook the plan of the vice president. A first-class crisis had developed involving a major order for their oldest and best customer, and an emergency top-management meeting was called, which included several of their subordinates. Three in particular were involved: Joe Craig, assistant to the president, who knows well the problems at the plant in his role as troubleshooter for the managing director; Sandy Falk, vice president of personnel, who is sophisticated about leadership training programs and in a position to watch a good bit of the bickering at the middle and lower levels between sales and production; Bill Bletchford, manager of finishing, who is loyal to Stockwell and who has the most modern-equipped phase of the production process and the most to do with sales. It was in his department that the jam had occurred, due to some massive scheduling changes at the rolling phase and to the failure of key equipment.

In the meeting, the ground is gone over thoroughly. With their backs to the wall, the two production men, behaving somewhat uncharacteristically in an open meeting, charge sales with devious tactics for introducing special orders and for acting on partial and misinterpreted information from a foreman. Joe

Craig knows, and admits, that the specialty A sales manager made promises to the customer without checking with the vice president of sales, who could have checked with Stockwell. "He was right," say Vice president Bronson, "I can't spend all my time calling Ramsey about status reports; if Harrison can't find out from production on an official basis, he has to do the best he can." Ramsey Stockwell, after his forceful outburst about misleading information through devious tactics, falls into a hardened silence, answering only direct questions, and then briefly. The manager of finishing and the specialty A sales manager start working on each other. Sandy Falk, of personnel, knows they have been enemies for years, so he intervenes as best he can. The vice president of research, Carswell, a reflective man, often worried about elusive dimensions of company problems, then calls a halt with the following speech:

> You're all wrong and you're all right. I have heard bits and pieces of this fracas a hundred times over the last two or three years, and it gets worse each year. The facts of this damn case don't matter unless all you want is to score points with your opponents. What is wrong is something with the whole team here. I don't know what it is, but I know that we have to radically rethink our relations with one another. Three years ago this kind of thing rarely happened; now it is starting to happen all the time. And it is a time when we can't afford it. There is no more growth in our bread-and-butter line, specialty steels. The money, and the growth, is in aerospace; we all know that. Without aerospace we will just stand still. Maybe that's part of it. But maybe Ramsey's part of it too; this crisis is over specialty steel, and more of them seem to concern that than aerospace, so it can't be the product shift or that only. Some part of it has to be people, and you're on the hot seat, Ramsey.

Carswell let that sink in, then went on.

> Or maybe it's something more than even these. . . . It is not being pulled together at the top, or maybe, the old way of pulling it together won't work anymore. I'm talking about you, Tom [Hollis], as well as Fred [Benson, the chairman of the board, who did not attend these meetings] and Dick [the executive vice president, and heir apparent]. I don't know what it is, here are Ramsey and Rob at loggerheads; neither of them are fools, and both of them are working their heads off. Maybe the problem is above their level.

There is a long silence. Assume you break the silence with your own analysis. What would that be?

CASE 15
Rondell Data Corporation
John A. Seeger

"God damn it, he's done it again?" Frank Forbus threw the stack of prints and specifications down on his desk in disgust. *The Model 802 wide-band modulator, released for production the previous Thursday, had just come back to Frank's Engineering Services Department with a caustic note that began, "This one can't be produced either. . . ." It was the fourth time production had kicked the design back.*

Frank Forbus, director of engineering for Rondell Data Corporation, was normally a quiet man. But the Model 802 was stretching his patience; it was beginning to look just like other new products that had hit delays and problems in the transition from design to production during the eight months Frank had worked for Rondell. These problems were nothing new at the sprawling old Rondell factory; Frank's predecessor in the engineering job had run afoul of them, too, and had finally been fired for protesting too vehemently about the other departments. But the Model 802 should have been different. Frank had met two months before (July 3, 1978) with the firm's president, Bill Hunt, and with factory superintendent Dave Schwab to smooth the way for the new modulator design. He thought back to the meeting. . . .

"Now we all know there's a tight deadline on the 802," Bill Hunt Said, "and Frank's done well to ask us to talk about its introduction. I'm counting on both of you to find any snags in the system and to work together to get that first production run out by October 2nd. Can you do it?"

"We can do it in production if we get a clean design two weeks from now, as scheduled," answered Dave Schwab, the grizzled factory superintendent. "Frank and I have already talked about that, of course. I'm setting aside time in the card room and the machine shop, and we'll be ready. If the design goes over schedule, though, I'll have to fill in with other runs, and it will cost us a bundle to break in for the 802. How does it look in engineering, Frank?"

"I've just reviewed the design for the second time," Frank replied. "If Ron Porter can keep the salesmen out of our hair and avoid any more last-minute changes, we've got a shot. I've pulled the draftsmen off three other overdue jobs to get this one out. But, Dave, that means we can't spring engineers loose to confer with your production people on manufacturing problems."

"Well, Frank, most of those problems are caused by the engineers, and we need them to resolve the dif-

John A. Seeger, Professor of Management, Bentley College. Reprinted with permission.

ficulties. We've all agreed that production bugs come from both of us bowing to sales pressure, and putting equipment into production before the designs are really ready. That's just what we're trying to avoid on the 802. But I can't have 500 people sitting on their hands waiting for an answer from your people. We'll have to have some engineering support."

Bill Hunt broke in. "So long as you two can talk calmly about the problem I'm confident you can resolve it. What a relief it is, Frank, to hear the way you're approaching this. With Kilmann (the previous director of engineering) this conversation would have been a shouting match. Right, Dave?" Dave nodded and smiled.

"Now there's one other thing you should both be aware of," Hunt continued. "Doc Reeves and I talked last night about a new filtering technique, one that might improve the signal-to-noise ratio of the 802 by a factor of two. There's a chance Doc can come up with it before the 802 reaches production, and if it's possible, I'd like to use the new filters. That would give us a real jump on the competition."

Four days after that meeting, Frank found that two of his key people on the 802 design had been called to production for emergency consultation on a bug found in final assembly: two halves of a new data transmission interface wouldn't fit together because recent changes in the front end required a different chassis design for the back end.

Another week later, Doc Reeves walked into Frank's office, proud as a new parent, with the new filter design. "This won't affect the other modules of the 802 much," Doc had said. "Look, it takes three new cards, a few connectors, some changes in the wiring harness, and some new shielding, and that's all."

Frank had tried to resist the last-minute design changes, but Bill Hunt had stood firm. With a lot of overtime by the engineers and draftsmen, engineering services should still be able to finish the prints in time.

Two engineers and three draftsmen went onto 12-hour days to get the 802 ready, but the prints were still five days late reaching Dave Schwab. Two days later, the prints came back to Frank, heavily annotated in red. Schwab had worked all day Saturday to review the job and had found more than a dozen discrepancies in the prints—most of them caused by the new filter design and insufficient checking time before release. Correction of those design faults had brought on a new generation of discrepancies; Schwab's cover note on the second return of the prints indicated he'd had to release the machine capacity he'd been holding for the 802. On the third iteration, Schwab committed his photo and plating capacity to another rush job. The 802 would be at least one month late getting into production. Ron Porter, vice president for sales, was furious. His customer needed 100 units NOW, he said. Rondell was the customer's only late supplier.

"Here we go again," thought Frank Forbus.

Company History

Rondell Data Corporation traced its lineage through several generations of electronics technology. Its original founder, Bob Rondell, had set the firm up in 1920 as "Rondell Equipment Company" to manufacture several electrical testing devices he had invented as an engineering faculty member at a large university. The firm branched into radio broadcasting equipment in 1947 and into data transmission equipment in the early 1960s. A well-established corps of direct salespeople, mostly engineers, called on industrial, scientific, and government accounts, but concentrated heavily on original equipment manufacturers. In this market, Rondell had a long-standing reputation as a source of high-quality, innovative designs. The firm's salespeople fed a continual stream of challenging problems into the Engineering Department, where the creative genius of Ed "Doc" Reeves and several dozen other engineers "converted problems to solutions" (as the sales brochure bragged). Product design formed the spearhead of Rondell's growth.

By 1978, Rondell offered a wide range of products in its two major lines. Broadcast equipment sales had benefitted from the growth of UHFTV and FM radio; it now accounted for 35 percent of company sales. Data transmission had blossomed, and in this field an increasing number of orders called for unique specifications, ranging from specialized display panels to entirely untried designs.

The company had grown from 100 employees in 1947 to over 800 in 1978. (Exhibit 1 shows the 1978 organization chart of key employees.) Bill Hunt, who had been a student of the company's founder, had presided over most of that growth and took great pride in preserving the "family spirit" of the old organization. Informal relationships between Rondell's veteran employees formed the backbone of the firm's day-to-day operations; all the managers relied on personal contact, and Hunt often insisted that the absence of bureaucratic red tape was a key factor in recruiting outstanding engineering talent. The personal management approach extended throughout the factory. All exempt employees were paid on a straight salary plus a share of the profits. Rondell boasted an extremely loyal group of senior employees and very low turnover in nearly all areas of the company.

The highest turnover job in the firm was Frank Forbus's. Frank had joined Rondell in January 1978, replacing Jim Kilmann, who had been director of engineering for only 10 months. Kilmann, in turn, had replaced Tom MacLeod, a talented engineer who had made a promising start but had taken to drink after a year in the job. MacLeod's predecessor had been a genial old-timer who retired at 70 after 30 years in charge of engineering. (Doc Reeves had refused the directorship in each of the recent changes, saying, "Hell, that's no promotion for a bench man like me. I'm no administrator.")

For several years, the firm had experienced a steadily increasing number of disputes between research, engineering, sales, and production people—disputes generally centered on the problem of new product introduction. Quarrels between departments became more numerous under MacLeod, Kilmann, and Forbus. Some managers associated those disputes with the company's recent decline in profitability—a decline that, in spite of higher sales and gross revenues, was beginning to bother people in 1977. President Bill Hunt commented:

> Better cooperation, I'm sure, could increase our output by 5–10 percent. I'd hoped Kilmann could solve the problems, but pretty obviously he was too young, too arrogant. People like him—conflict type of personality—bother me. I don't like strife, and with him it seemed I spent all my time smoothing out arguments. Kilmann tried to tell everyone else how to run their departments, without having his own house in order. That approach just wouldn't work here at Rondell. Frank Forbus, now, seems much more in tune with our style of organization. I'm really hopeful now.
>
> Still, we have just as many problems now as we did last year. Maybe even more. I hope Frank can get a handle on engineering services soon. . . .

The Engineering Department: Research

According to the organization chart (see Exhibit 1), Frank Forbus was in charge of both research (really the product development function) and engineering services (which provided engineering support). To Forbus, however, the relationship with research was not so clear-cut:

> Doc Reeves is one of the world's unique people, and none of us would have it any other way. He's a creative genius. Sure, the chart says he works for me, but we all know Doc does his own thing. He's not the least bit interested in management routines, and I can't count on him to take any responsibility in scheduling projects, or checking budgets, or what-have-you. But as long as Doc is director of research, you can bet this company will

Exhibit 1 Rondell Data Corporation 1978 Organization Chart

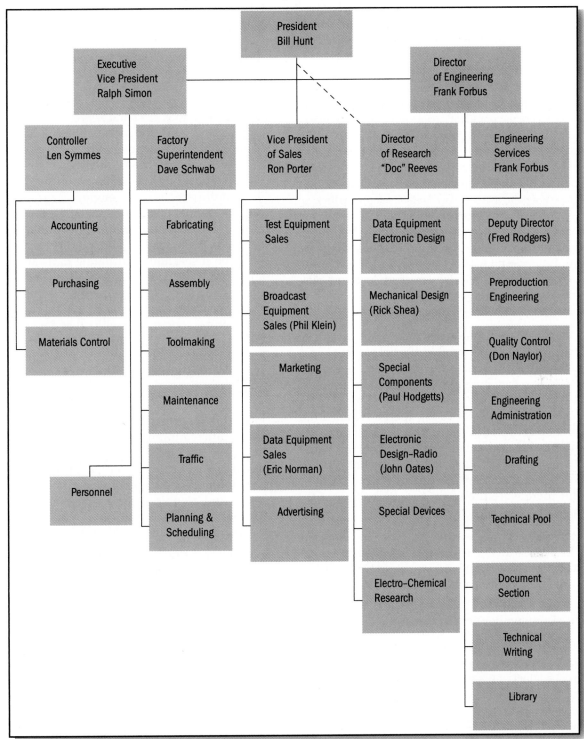

keep on leading the field. He has more ideas per hour than most people have per year, and he keeps the whole engineering staff fired up. Everybody loves Doc—and you can count me in on that, too. In a way, he works for me, sure. But that's not what's important.

"Doc" Reeves—unhurried, contemplative, casual, and candid—tipped his stool back against the wall

of his research cubicle and talked about what was important:

Development engineering. That's where the company's future rests. Either we have it there, or we don't have it.

There's no kidding ourselves that we're anything but a bunch of Rube Goldbergs here. But that's where the biggest kicks come from—from solving development problems, and dreaming up new ways of doing things. That's why I so look forward to the special contracts we get involved in. We accept them not for the revenue they represent, but because they subsidize the basic development work which goes into all our basic products.

This is a fantastic place to work. I have a great crew and they can really deliver when the chips are down. Why, Bill Hunt and I (he gestured toward the neighboring cubicle, where the president's name hung over the door) are likely to find as many people here at work at 10:00 P.M. as at 3:00 in the afternoon. The important thing here is the relationships between people; they're based on mutual respect, not on policies and procedures. Administrative red tape is a pain. It takes away from development time.

Problems? Sure, there are problems now and then. There are power interests in production, where they sometimes resist change. But I'm not a fighting man, you know. I suppose if I were, I might go in there and push my weight around a little. But I'm an engineer and can do more for Rondell sitting right here or working with my own people. That's what brings results.

Other members of the Research Department echoed Doc's views and added some additional sources of satisfaction with their work. They were proud of the personal contacts they built up with customers' technical staffs—contacts that increasingly involved travel to the customers' factories to serve as expert advisers in the preparation of overall system design specifications. The engineers were also delighted with the department's encouragement of their personal development, continuing education, and independence on the job.

But there were problems, too. Rick Shea, of the mechanical design section, noted:

> In the old days I really enjoyed the work—and the people I worked with. But now there's a lot of irritation. I don't like someone breathing down my neck. You can be hurried into jeopardizing the design.

John Oates, head of the radio electronic design section, was another designer with definite views:

> Production engineering is almost nonexistent in this company. Very little is done by the preproduction section in engineering services. Frank Forbus has been trying to get preproduction into the picture, but he won't succeed because you can't start from such an ambiguous position. There have been three directors of engineering in three years. Frank can't hold his own against the others in the company, Kilmann was too aggressive. Perhaps no amount of tact would have succeeded.

Paul Hodgetts was head of special components in the R & D department. Like the rest of the department, he valued bench work. But he complained of engineering services:

> The services don't do things we want them to do. Instead, they tell us what they're going to do. I should

probably go to Frank, but I don't get any decisions there. I know I should go through Frank, but this holds things up, so I often go direct.

The Engineering Department: Engineering Services

The Engineering Services Department provided ancillary services to R & D and served as liaison between engineering and the other Rondell departments. Among its main functions were drafting; management of the central technicians' pool; scheduling and expediting engineering products; documentation and publication of parts lists and engineering orders; preproduction engineering (consisting of the final integration of individual design components into mechanically compatible packages); and quality control (which included inspection of incoming parts and materials, and final inspection of subassemblies and finished equipment). Top management's description of the department included the line, "ESD is responsible for maintaining cooperation with other departments, providing services to the development engineers, and freeing more valuable people in R & D from essential activities that are diversions from and beneath their main competence."

Many of Frank Forbus's 75 employees were located in other departments. Quality control people were scattered through the manufacturing and receiving areas, and technicians worked primarily in the research area or the prototype fabrication room. The remaining ESD personnel were assigned to leftover nooks and crannies near production or engineering sections.

Frank Forbus described his position:

> My biggest problem is getting acceptance from the people I work with. I've moved slowly rather than risk antagonism. I saw what happened to Kilmann, and I want to avoid that. But although his precipitate action had won over a few of the younger R & D people, he certainly didn't have the department's backing. Of course, it was the resentment of other departments that eventually caused his discharge. People have been slow accepting me here. There's nothing really overt, but I get a negative reaction to my ideas.
>
> My role in the company has never been well defined really. It's complicated by Doc's unique position, of course, and also by the fact that ESD sort of grew by itself over the years, as the design engineers concentrated more and more on the creative parts of product development. I wish I could be more involved in the technical side. That's been my training, and it's a lot of fun. But in our setup, the technical side is the least necessary for me to be involved in.
>
> Schwab (production head) is hard to get along with. Before I came and after Kilmann left, there were six months intervening when no one was really doing any

scheduling. No work loads were figured, and unrealistic promises were made about releases. This puts us in an awkward position. We've been scheduling way beyond our capacity to manufacture or engineer.

Certain people within R & D—for instance. John Oates, head of the radio electronic design section—understand scheduling well and meet project deadlines, but this is not generally true of the rest of the R & D department, especially the mechanical engineers who won't commit themselves. Most of the complaints come from sales and production department heads because items—like the 802—are going to production before they are fully developed, under pressure from sales to get out the unit, and this snags the whole process. Somehow, engineering services should be able to intervene and resolve these complaints, but I haven't made much headway so far. I should be able to go to Hunt for help, but he's too busy most of the time, and his major interest is the design side of engineering, where he got his own start. Sometimes he talks as though he's the engineering director as well as president. I have to put my foot down; there are problems here that the front office just doesn't understand.

Salespeople were often observed taking their problems directly to designers, while production frequently threw designs back at R & D, claiming they could not be produced and demanding the prompt attention of particular design engineers. The latter were frequently observed in conference with production supervisors on the assembly floor. Frank went on:

The designers seem to feel they're losing something when one of us tries to help. They feel it's a reflection on them to have someone take over what they've been doing. They seem to want to carry a project right through to the final stages, particularly the mechanical people. Consequently, engineering services people are used below their capacity to contribute and our department is denied functions it should be performing. There's not as much use made of engineering services as there should be.

Frank Forbus's technician supervisor added his comments:

Production picks out the engineer who'll be the "bum of the month." They pick on every little detail instead of using their heads and making the minor changes that have to be made. The 15-to-20-year people shouldn't have to prove their ability any more, but they spend four hours defending themselves and four hours getting the job done. I have no one to go to when I need help. Frank Forbus is afraid. I'm trying to help him but he can't help me at this time. I'm responsible for fifty people and I've got to support them.

Fred Rodgers, whom Frank had brought with him to the company as an assistant, gave another view of the situation:

I try to get our people in preproduction to take responsibility, but they're not used to it and people in other departments don't usually see them as best qualified to solve the problem. There's a real barrier for a newcomer here. Gaining people's confidence is hard. More and more, I'm wondering whether there really is a job for me here.

(Rodgers left Rondell a month later.) Another of Forbus's subordinates gave his view:

If Doc gets a new product idea, you can't argue. But he's too optimistic. He judges that others can do what he does—but there's only one Doc Reeves. We've had 900 production change orders this year—they changed 2,500 drawings. If I were in Frank's shoes I'd put my foot down on all this new development. I'd look at the reworking we're doing and get production set up the way I wanted it. Kilmann was fired when he was doing a good job. He was getting some system in the company's operations. Of course, it hurt some people. There is no denying that Doc is the most important person in the company. What gets overlooked is that Hunt is a close second, not just politically but in terms of what he contributes technically and in customer relations.

This subordinate explained that he sometimes went out into the production department but that Schwab, the production head, resented this. Personnel in production said that Kilmann had failed to show respect for old-timers and was always meddling in other departments' business. This was why he had been fired, they contended.

Don Taylor was in charge of quality control. He commented:

I am now much more concerned with administration and less with work. It is one of the evils you get into. There is tremendous detail in this job. I listen to everyone's opinion. Everybody is important. There shouldn't be distinctions—distinctions between people. I'm not sure whether Frank has to be a fireball like Kilmann. I think the real question is whether Frank is getting the job done. I know my job is essential. I want to supply service to the more talented people and give them information so they can do their jobs better.

The Sales Department

Ron Porter was angry. His job was supposed to be selling, he said, but instead it had turned into settling disputes inside the plant and making excuses to waiting customers. He jabbed a finger toward his desk:

You see that telephone? I'm actually afraid nowadays to hear it ring. Three times out of five, it will be a customer who's hurting because we've failed to deliver on schedule. The other two calls will be from production or ESD, telling me some schedule has slipped again.

The Model 802 is typical. Absolutely typical. We padded the delivery date by six weeks, to allow for contingencies. Within two months, the slack had evaporated. Now it looks like we'll be lucky to ship it before Christmas. (It was now November 28.) We're ruining our reputation in the market. Why, just last week one of our best customers—people we've worked with for 15 years—tried to hang a penalty clause on their latest order.

We shouldn't have to be after the engineers all the time. They should be able to see what problems they create without our telling them.

Phil Klein, head of broadcast sales under Porter, noted that many sales decisions were made by top management. Sales was understaffed, he thought, and had never really been able to get on top of the job.

We have grown further and further away from engineering. The director of engineering does not pass on the information that we give him. We need better relationships there. It is very difficult for us to talk to customers about development problems without technical help. We need each other. The whole of engineering is now too isolated from the outside world. The morale of ESD is very low. They're in a bad spot—they're not well organized.

People don't take much to outsiders here. Much of this is because the expectation is built up by top management that jobs will be filled from the bottom. So it's really tough when an outsider like Frank comes in.

Eric Norman, order and pricing coordinator for data equipment, talked about his own relationships with the Production Department:

Actually, I get along with them fairly well. Oh, things could be better of course, if they were more cooperative generally. They always seem to say, "It's my bat and ball, and we're playing by my rules." People are afraid to make production mad; there's a lot of power in there. But you've got to understand that production has its own set of problems. And nobody in Rondell is working any harder than Dave Schwab to try to straighten things out.

The Production Department

Dave Schwab had joined Rondell just after the Korean War, in which he had seen combat duty (at the Yalu River) and intelligence duty at Pyong Yang. Both experiences had been useful in his first year of civilian employment at Rondell: The wartime factory superintendent and several middle managers had been, apparently, indulging in highly questionable side deals with Rondell's suppliers. Dave Schwab had gathered evidence, revealed the situation to Bill Hunt, and stood by the president in the ensuing unsavory situation. Seven months after joining the company, Dave was named factory superintendent.

His first move had been to replace the fallen managers with a new team from outside. This group did not share the traditional Rondell emphasis on informality and friendly personal relationships and had worked long and hard to install systematic manufacturing methods and procedures. Before the reorganization, production had controlled purchasing, stock control, and final quality control (where final assembly of products in cabinets was accomplished). Because of the wartime events, management decided on a checks-and-balance system of organization and removed these three departments from production jurisdiction. The new production managers felt they had been unjustly penalized by this organization, particularly since they had uncovered the behavior that was detrimental to the company in the first place.

By 1978, the production department had grown to 500 employees, 60 percent of whom worked in the assembly area—an unusually pleasant environment that had been commended by *Factory* magazine for its colorful decoration, cleanliness, and low noise level. An additional 30 percent of the work force, mostly skilled machinists, staffed the finishing and fabrication department. About 60 others performed scheduling, supervisory, and maintenance duties. Production workers were nonunion, hourly-paid, and participated in both the liberal profit-sharing program and the stock purchase plan. Morale in production was traditionally high, and turnover was extremely low.

Dave Schwab commented:

To be efficient, production has to be a self-contained department. We have to control what comes into the department and what goes out. That's why purchasing, inventory control, and quality ought to run out of this office. We'd eliminate a lot of problems with better control there. Why, even Don Taylor in QC would rather work for me than for ESD; he's said so himself. We understand his problems better.

The other departments should be self-contained too. That's why I always avoid the underlings and go straight to the department heads with any questions. I always go down the line.

I have to protect my people from outside disturbances. Look what would happen if I let unfinished, half-baked designs in here—there'd be chaos. The bugs have to be found before the drawings go into the shop, and it seems I'm the one who has to find them. Look at the 802, for example. (Dave had spent most of Thanksgiving Day [it was now November 28] red-penciling the latest set of prints.) ESD should have found every one of those discrepancies. They just don't check drawings properly. They change most of the things I flag, but then they fail to trace through the impact of those changes on the rest of the design. I shouldn't have to do that. And those engineers are tolerance crazy. They want everything to a millionth of an inch. I'm the only one in the company who's had any experience with actually machining things to a millionth of an inch. We make sure that the things that engineers say on their drawings actually have to be that way and whether they're obtainable from the kind of raw material we buy.

That shouldn't be production's responsibility, but I have to do it. Accepting bad prints wouldn't let us ship the order any quicker. We'd only make a lot of junk that had to be reworked. And that would take even longer.

This way, I get to be known as the bad guy, but I guess that's just part of the job. (He paused with a wry smile.) Of course, what really gets them is that I don't even have a degree.

Dave had fewer bones to pick with the Sales Department because, he said, they trusted him.

When we give Ron Porter a shipping date, he knows the equipment will be shipped then.

You've got to recognize, though, that all of our new-product problems stem from sales making absurd commitments on equipment that hasn't been fully developed. That always means trouble. Unfortunately, Hunt always backs sales up, even when they're wrong. He always favors them over us.

Ralph Simon, age 65, executive vice president of the company, had direct responsibility for Rondell's production department. He said:

There shouldn't really be a dividing of departments among top management in the company. The president should be czar over all. The production people ask me to do something for them, and I really can't do it. It creates bad feelings between engineering and production, this special attention that they [R & D] get from Bill. But then Hunt likes to dabble in design. Schwab feels that production is treated like a poor relation.

The Executive Committee

At the executive committee meeting on December 6, it was duly recorded that Dave Schwab had accepted the prints and specifications for the Model 802 modulator, and had set Friday, December 29, as the shipping date for the first 10 pieces. Bill Hunt, in the chairperson's role, shook his head and changed the subject quickly when Frank tried to open the agenda to a discussion of interdepartmental coordination.

The executive committee itself was a brainchild of Rondell's controller, Len Symmes, who was well aware of the disputes that plagued the company. Symmes had convinced Bill Hunt and Ralph Simon to meet every two weeks with their department heads, and the meetings were formalized with Hunt, Simon, Ron Porter, Dave Schwab, Frank Forbus, Doc Reeves, Symmes, and the personnel director attending. Symmes explained his intent and the results:

Doing things collectively and informally just doesn't work as well as it used to. Things have been gradually getting worse for at least two years now. We had to start thinking in terms of formal organization relationships. I did the first organization chart, and the executive committee was my idea too—but neither idea is contributing much help, I'm afraid. It takes top management to make an organization click. The rest of us can't act much differently until the top people see the need for us to change.

I had hoped the committee especially would help get the department managers into a constructive planning process. It hasn't worked out that way because Mr. Hunt really doesn't see the need for it. He uses the meetings as a place to pass on routine information.

Merry Christmas

"Frank, I didn't know whether to tell you now, or after the holiday." It was Friday, December 22, and Frank Forbus was standing awkwardly in front of Bill Hunt's desk.

"But, I figured you'd work right through Christmas Day if we didn't have this talk, and that just wouldn't have been fair to you. I can't understand why we have such poor luck in the engineering director's job lately. And I don't think it's entirely your fault. But..."

Frank only heard half of Hunt's words, and said nothing in response. He'd be paid through February 28.... He should use the time for searching.... Hunt would help all he could.... Jim Kilmann was supposed to be doing well at his own new job, and might need more help....

Frank cleaned out his desk and numbly started home. The electronic carillon near his house was playing a Christmas carol. Frank thought again of Hunt's rationale: Conflict still plagued Rondell—and Frank had not made it go away. Maybe somebody else could do it.

"And what did Santa Claus bring you, Frankie?" he asked himself.

"The sack. Only the empty sack."

COMPANY INDEX

NAME INDEX

SUBJECT INDEX

internal change agents, 290
internalized norms, 104
internal systems approach, 17, 240
international strategy, 228, 230
Internet, 12
  browsers, 339–340
  e-engineering and, 286
interorganizational-level learning, 343–344
interorganizational strategies, 67
intrapreneurs, 373–374, 381
investiture, 183
isomorphism, 312–314

J

Japan
  conflict resolution in, 403
  keiretsu, 70–72
  production and structure in, 213
  third-party linkage mechanisms in, 74
joint ventures, 72, 380, 383
justice model of ethics, 44
just-in-time (JIT) inventory systems, 211, 261–262

K

kanban system, 261
keiretsu, 70–72, 85
  transaction costs and, 79–80
knowledge-creating organizations, 375
knowledge management, 344–347
  codification vs. personalization, 345–347
knowledge technology, 259
K-strategy, 308–310

L

labor markets, multidivisional structure and, 157
language, organizational, 186
large-batch and mass production technology, 242–243
latent conflict, 396–399
laws, ethics and, 42–43
layoffs, 191–192
leadership
  crisis of, 315
  team, 380–381
lean production, 208, 259
learning
  cognitive structures and, 348
  collateral organizational structure and, 360
  converting events into opportunities for, 353
  defined, 340
  dialectical inquiry and, 360
  factors affecting, 347–352
  global, enhancing core competences with, 208
  group-level, 342–343
  illusion of control and, 349–350
  improving, 352–360
  individual-level, 341–342
  interorganizational-level, 343–344
  levels of, 341–344
  by listening to dissenters, 353
  look forward and reason back principle of, 355
  organization-level, 343
  top management teams and, 355–357
  types of, 340–341

learning organizations, 341
liability of newness, 30
liaison roles, 98
line functions, 398
line role, 37–38
linkage mechanisms, 77–78
listening, active, 358
local communities, as stakeholders, 31
location, functional structure and, 148
logos, 369
long-linked technology, 253–255
  tasks and, 254
long-term contracts, 69–70
long wall method, 278
look forward and reason back principle of learning, 355
low-cost business-level strategy, 216

M

maintenance functions, 92
management
  of competitive resource interdependencies, 73–75
  of diversity, 12–13
  ethics and, 42–50
  of external environment, 6
  of integration, 105
  measuring effectiveness, 14–22
  of resource dependencies, 67
  span of control and, 124–126
  of symbiotic resource interdependencies, 67–72
management by objectives (MBO), 135–136
managerial functions, 92–93
managers
  abilities of, in decision making, 335
  associating with power, 410
  authority and, 102
  corporate, 38
  divisional, 38
  functional, 38
  line roles of, 37–38
  staff roles of, 38
  as stakeholders, 29
  in tall hierarchies, 121–123
manifest conflict, 400
manipulation, 294
marketing
  core competence in, 211
  differentiation and, 211
  market structure and, 163–164
market structure, 151, 163–164
masking tape, 384
mass production, 239
  advanced manufacturing technology and, 257–259
  technology, 242–243
mass production technology, 245
  sequential task interdependence and, 253–255
materials management, 211
  computer-aided, 259–261
materials technology, 259
  computer-aided materials management (CAMM), 259–261
  just-in-time inventory systems, 291–292
matrix structure, 164–169
  advantages of, 166
  disadvantages of, 166–167
  global, 231–232
  growth through collaboration and, 318
  hybrid, 168–169

innovation and, 383
  multidivisional, 167–168
measurement, functional structure and, 147
mechanistic structures, 106–107, 193–194, 245
  environment and, 110–112
  resistance to change and, 275
mediating technology, 251–253
mental models, 342
mergers, 72
  for competitive interdependencies, 75
  values/norms and, 178–182
messages, content of, persuasive communication and, 358
mimetic isomorphism, 313
minimum chain of command, principle of, 123
mining industry, 278
mission, 18
modeling, quantitative, 376
modification, 374
moral hazard problem, 39
moral rights model of ethics, 44
motivation, in tall hierarchies, 122
multidivisional structure, 151, 152–158
  advantages of, 156–157
  disadvantages of, 157–158
  matrix, 167–168
multidomestic strategy, 228–230
mutual adjustment
  defined, 103
  intensive technology and, 255–256
  in matrix structure, 166
  nonroutine technology and, 251
  vs. standardization, 104–105

N

natural selection, 309–311
negotiation, 294
networks, 70
network structure, 169–171
  advantages of, 170
  disadvantages of, 170–171
new venture divisions, 380, 381–382
nonprogrammed decisions, 333
nonroutine research, 249–250
nonroutine technology, 251
  organizational structure and, 251
nonsubstitutability, power and, 407, 409
normative isomorphism, 313–314
norms, 103–104
  bureaucracies and, 132–133
  defined, 178
  organic structures and, 107
  resistance to change and, 275
North American Free Trade Agreement (NAFTA), 272

O

objectives, management by, 135–136
obstructionist approach, to social responsibility, 196–197
official goals, 18
operative goals, 18
opportunism, 77
organic structures, 107–108, 193–194, 195
  environments and, 110–112
  for innovation, 383–384
organizational birth, 303–311
  business plan development in, 304–305
  defined, 303
  population ecology model of, 307–311

organizational structure and, 213
value creation with, 211–212
resistance
to change, 274–277
to restructuring, 287
resource dependence theory, 65–66, 75
management strategies and, 67
resources. *See also* environment
accessing global, 208
competition for scarce, conflict and, 398–399
control over, power and, 406
environmental richness in, 63–65
functional, 205–206
organizational, 206
organizational birth rate and, 307–308
responsibility. *See* authority
restructuring, 122, 286–287
revolutionary, 277
revolutionary change, 283–286
rewards
desire to maximize, 322
to stakeholders, 33–34
stock-based compensation schemes, 40
richness, environmental, 63–65
risk
aversion to, 322
in entrepreneurship, 303–304
transaction costs and, 77
rites of enhancement, 185
rites of integration, 185
rites of passage, 185
role ambiguity, 132
role conflict, 132
role orientation, 182
routine manufacturing, 248–249
r-strategy, 308–310
rules
bureaucracies and, 132–133
defined, 103
formalization of, 103
mutual adjustment and, 102–103
socialization in, 103–104

S

sales, differentiation and, 211
sandpaper, 384
Sarbanes-Oxley Act (2002), 40–41
satisficing, 335
Scotch tape, 384
self-contained divisions, 93, 154
product team structure as, 159–160
self-interest, 47–48, 49
self-managed teams, 138–139
senders of communications, characteristics of, 357–358
sensitivity training, 295
sequential move games, 354–355
sequential tactics, 183
outputs and, 254
sequential task interdependence, 253–255, 263
serial tactics, 183
service organizations
hospitals, 255
value creation in, 4
shared vision, building, 343
shareholders, as stakeholders, 28
simultaneous move games, 354–355
skunk works, 380, 381–382
slack resources, 254
small batch and unit technology, 241–242

social forces, 61
for change, 272–273
socialization, 103–104
defined, 182
institutionalized, 184–185
tactics, 182–183
social responsibility, 196–198
accommodative approach to, 197
defensive approach to, 197
defined, 196
obstructionist approach to, 196–197
proactive approach to, 197
reasons for, 197–198
societal ethics, 45–46
span of control, 124–126
specialism, 256
specialist strategy, 309
specialization, 4–6
knowledge management and, 346
specific assets, 77
specific environment, 58–60
speed, 13
sports, 255
stability, 7
staff functions, 398
staff role, 38
stage-gate development funnel, 378–379
stakeholders
conflict and, 393–394
defined, 28
ethics and, 43–45, 51–52
goals of, 32–33
inside, 28–30
outside, 30–32
property rights and, 191–192
rewards to, 33–34
standardization
balancing mutual adjustment with, 103
control and, 129–130
defined, 103
vs. mutual adjustment, 104–105
standard operating procedures (SOPs), 102–103
bureaucracies and, 132–133
steel industry, 306
stock-based compensation schemes, 40
stories, communicating cultural values through, 185–186
strategic alliances
for competitive interdependencies, 74
joint ventures, 72
long-term contracts, 69–70
minority ownership, 70–72
networks, 70
strategy
business-level, 209
corporate-level, 209–210
defined, 12, 205
environment and, 205–210
functional-level, 209, 210–215
functional structure and, 148
global, 228, 231
global expansion, 210
implementing, across countries, 228–232
international, 228, 230
interorganizational, 67
multidomestic, 228–230
transaction costs theory and, 78–82
transnational, 228, 231–232
subunit orientation, 95
subunits
differentiation and, 92–93
integration, 95–100
suppliers

relationships with, 58–59
as stakeholders, 30–31
support functions, 92
survival strategies, 308–309
sweatshops, 273
SWOT analysis, 305
symbiotic interdependencies, 67
symbols, organizational, 187, 369
synergies, information, 386–387
synthesis, 374
systems thinking, 344

T

takeovers, 72
for competitive interdependencies, 75
tall organizations, 118. *See also* hierarchy
communications in, 121
problems with, 121–123
task analyzability, 248
task forces, 98–99
task interdependence, 251
CAMM and, 260
JIT and, 261
pooled, 251–253
reciprocal, 255–256
sequential, 253–254, 263
tasks, long-linked technology and, 254
task variability, 247–248
teams
building, 296
cross-functional, 139
culture and, 8–9
flexible work, 280–283
heavyweight leaders of, 381
integration with, 99
leadership for, 380–381
in matrix structure, 164–166
product, 158–160
self-managed, 138–139
technical approach, 17–18, 240
technical complexity, 241
organizational structure and, 244–246
technological capabilities, targeting for change, 270
technological change
incremental, 367
quantum, 367
rate of, 371–372
technological discontinuities, 367–368
technological forces, 60
technological imperative, 246–247
technology
advanced manufacturing, 257–259
continuous process technology, 243–244
craftswork, 249
defined, 237–239
economies of scale/scope and, 6
engineering production, 249
in general environment, 60
innovation and, 367–375
intensive, 255–256
levels of, 239
long-linked, 253–255
mass production, 245, 257–259
mediating, 251–253
nonroutine, 251
nonroutine research, 249–250
organizational effectiveness and, 239–240
Perrow's types of, 248–250
routine, 250–251
routine manufacturing, 248–249